ECOLOGY OF THE CHILD · *School*

"Portrait of Inclusion"

When anyone asks Lora about her son Mark's developmental problems, she usually looks the person straight in the eye and asks, "Why don't you ask my son? He's right here." Mark's response is, "My body has earthquakes."

Mark is an attractive 4-year-old boy with long, blond hair pulled back into a braided ponytail. He wears a helmet for protection in case of a seizure. In his Head Start classroom, Mark has frequent tantrums and shows a lack of compliance with classroom routines. He speaks rarely, but on occasion surprises everyone by issuing full, clear sentences. Mark uses sign language about half the time and verbal language the other half. Lora says that "when he needs to tell me something important, and when he's really serious, he'll sign." Mark also has delayed fine motor skills, and he is unable to zip or button his clothes. Yet his cognitive skills are two years advanced.

Mark and Lora have both learned that early childhood teachers are not necessarily prepared for inclusive programs. Lora removed Mark from a previous school program when she learned that Mark's teacher, after nine months with Mark in her classroom, did not know that Mark could talk. Lora reports that Mark was rarely involved in social activities in his previous classroom because his teachers "didn't know what to do with him and didn't want to upset him."

Recently in Mark's classroom, a boy took a truck Mark was playing with. Mark emphatically signed "stop" to the little boy. When the boy refused to return the truck, Mark resorted to wrestling with the boy. The teacher intervened, gave the truck back to Mark, removed the other boy, and seated him alone at a table. Lora would never tolerate that sort of behavior from Mark, whom she wants "to be treated the same as everyone else." Instead, a little boy was punished without understanding why, and without learning what Mark was trying to say. Mark's attempts to communicate were futile, and he missed an opportunity to learn the important art of negotiation. And the teacher remained lacking in competence.

When Lora is asked whether Mark has difficulty following directions, listening, and working in groups, Mark himself responds that he "doesn't really get that at school." Some things Mark would change about the program would be to have longer days and a summer program. Lora's ideal schedule would be a totally inclusive one, with therapy and behavior management available for all children in the classroom. Acknowledging that not all schools accept the responsibility to educate children like Mark, Lora says, "Well, they'd better become responsible because the world is inclusive."

Source: S. Janko and A. Porter (1997). *Portraits of Inclusion.* Bloomington, Ind.: Early Childhood Research Institute on Inclusion, Indiana University, School of Education. Reprinted by permission.

What Is the Context?

Mark is part of a Head Start classroom in which early childhood teachers include him just as they include all the other students in the classroom. Mark's mother took responsibility for finding a program where the teachers were prepared for an inclusive program. Ideally, Mark would receive all his services—including therapy and behavior management—in one classroom.

Pivotal Issues for Teachers

What kind of preparation do teachers need to successfully work in an inclusive setting? As a new teacher, what skills would you want to have to be able to work with students with disabilities in your general education classroom? What kind of support would you need from other professionals?

Each chapter's *Ecology of the Child* feature offers a narrative on a child's experience in various ecological contexts.

Educating Exceptional Children

Ninth Edition

Samuel A. Kirk
Late of University of Arizona

James J. Gallagher
University of North Carolina at Chapel Hill

Nicholas J. Anastasiow
Emeritus, Hunter College, City University of New York

Houghton Mifflin Company   Boston • New York

Senior Sponsoring Editor: Loretta Wolozin
Associate Editor: Lisa Mafrici
Senior Project Editor: Kathryn Dinovo
Manufacturing Manager: Florence Cadran
Associate Marketing Manager: Jean Zielinski DeMayo

Cover design: Catherine Hawkes, Cat & Mouse
Cover image: *The Eclipse*, Alma Woodsey Thomas, 1970. National Museum of American Art, Washington, DC/Art Resource, NY.

Contents

Preface   xvi

Chapter 1: Educating the Exceptional Child   1

The Exceptional Child   2
Who Is an Exceptional Child?   2
Categories of Exceptional Children   3
    Prevalence   *4*
    Attention-Deficit Hyperactivity Disorder (ADHD)   *5*

The Context of the Exceptional Child   6
Family, School, Peer Culture, and Community   6
The Ecological Approach   8
The Interaction of Heredity and Environment   8
Intra-Individual Differences   9
Developmental Profiles   9

The Unique Influence of the Family   10
Child-Family Interaction   12
    Parental Response   *12*
    Family Responsibilities   *13*
Changing Family Roles   15
    Working Mothers   *15*
    Parent Empowerment   *15*

ECOLOGY OF THE CHILD: FAMILY   17
    Parents as Collaborators   *19*
    Parents as Advocates   *19*
    Siblings   *20*

The Influence of School, Peer Culture, and the Community   22
    The Influence of Culture   23
    Families from Diverse Cultures   24
    Culture and Assessment   26
    Parents of Children Who Are Gifted and Talented   27

Chapter 2: Exceptional Children and Their Environment   32

A Historical Perspective   34
Residential Schools   34
Public Schools   34

The Exceptional Child and the School   35

ECOLOGY OF THE CHILD: FAMILY, SCHOOL, AND COMMUNITY   36

    Lifespan Perspective   39
       Transition   39
    Referral and Assessment   40

Educational Adaptations for Exceptional Children   42

    Prereferral: Teacher-Assistance Teams   48
    Peer Collaboration for Teachers   48
    Assessment   49

Individual Differences   49

    Individual Differences and the Classroom   50
    The Role of Assessment   50
    Inter-Individual Differences   50
    Culture-Bound Assessment Measures   54
    Developmental Profile   56
    The Individualized Education Program   56
    Case Study: Frank   57
    Educational Restructuring in Special Education   58
    The Inclusion Movement   58
    Inclusion and the General Education Teacher   60

ECOLOGY OF THE CHILD: SCHOOL   62

    Social Relationships in the General Education Classroom   63
    How Much Inclusion Is "Included"?   63
    Restructuring in General Education: America 2000   66

Some Results of Restructuring General Education   66

    Middle Schools   66
    Cooperative Learning   66
    Site-Based Management   67
    The Academic Standards Movement versus the
      Inclusion Movement   68
    Effective Assessment Tools   69
    Accountability   70
    State and Federal Legislation   70
    An Overview   71
    Public Law 88-164   71
    Public Law 94-142   71
    Public Law 99-457 and IDEA (Public Law 105-17)   73
    Federal Actions for Students Who Are Gifted   74
    The Role of the Courts   74
    Conclusion   77

Chapter 3: Early Intervention: Priorities and Programs   82

Overview of Early Intervention   84

    Definitions and Goals   84
    Origins of Early Intervention   84
    Legislative Support for Early Intervention   85

Why Early Intervention?   **87**

   Avoiding Developmental Delays   87

   Preventing Additional Deficits   87

   Are Early Childhood Intervention Programs Effective?   88

What Puts Children at Risk?   **89**

   Genetic Disorders   89

   Events During Pregnancy and Birth   89

   Environmental Risks   90

     Child Abuse   *90*

     Lower Socioeconomic Conditions (Poverty)   *90*

     Substance Abuse   *91*

Prevention Before Birth   **91**

   Genetic Counseling   91

   Prenatal Care   92

     Alpha-Fetoprotein Test   *92*

     Sonography (Ultrasound)   *93*

     Amniocentesis   *93*

     Chorionic Villus Biopsy   *93*

Detecting Disabilities After Birth   **93**

   Screening at Birth   94

   Medical Intervention   94

   Developmental Screening   94

Early Intervention Programs   **95**

   The Individualized Family Services Plan (IFSP)   96

     IDEA, Part C: Legal Requirements of the IFSP   *96*

     The Multidisciplinary Team   *97*

   Settings and Strategies   100

     In a Hospital   *100*

     Home and Family   *101*

   Education Programs   102

     Early Childhood Intervention Center   *102*

     Developmentally Appropriate Practice (DAP)   *103*

     Regular Day-Care and Early Childhood Centers   *104*

     Assessment and Curriculum   *104*

ECOLOGY OF THE CHILD: SCHOOL   106

Family and Lifespan Issues   **108**

   Culture   109

   Coping with Stress   109

   Transition   110

Chapter 4: Children Who Are Gifted and Talented   115

Definitions   **117**

Components of Intellectual Competence   **118**

One Gift or Many?   119

Factors That Contribute to Giftedness and Talent   121
Heredity and Environment   121

Studies of Students Who Are Gifted   122

The Challenges Associated with Giftedness   125

Developmental Profiles   127

ECOLOGY OF THE CHILD: SCHOOL   128

Identification   131

Special Groups of Children Who Are Gifted   133
Girls Who Are Gifted   133
Children of Extraordinary Ability   135
Underachievers Who Are Gifted   136
Culturally Diverse Children Who Are Gifted   138
Children with Disabilities Who Are Gifted   140

Education Reform and Its Effects   141

Educational Adaptations for Children Who Are Gifted and Talented   143
Adapting the Learning Environment   143
Flexible Pacing   143
Grouping   145
Special Courses   146
Inclusion   147
Adapting Curriculum   147
Effective Education Programs   147
Curriculum Compacting   147
Content Acceleration and Enrichment   148
Content Sophistication   149
Content Novelty   150
Adapting Cognitive Strategies   150
Enrichment Triad Experiences   151
Problem Finding and Problem Solving   151
Problem-Based Learning   153
Creativity   154
Instructional Technology   158
Time   158
Student Acceleration   159

Family and Lifespan Issues   160

Chapter 5: Children with Mental Retardation and Developmental Disabilities   165

Definition   166
Intellectual Subnormality   166
Adaptive Behavior   167

Levels of Mental Retardation   169

Biological Factors That Contribute to Mental Retardation   171

Chromosomal Abnormalities   171
Down Syndrome   172
Phenylketonuria   173
Fragile X Syndrome   174
Toxic Agents   174
Fetal Alcohol Syndrome   174
Heavy Metals   175
Infections   176

Environmental Factors That Affect Mental Retardation   176

Characteristics of Children with Mental Retardation or Developmental Disabilities   177

Ability to Process Information   177
Ability to Acquire and Use Language   179
Emotional Problems and Social Acceptance   179

Developmental Profiles   180

Prevention of Mental Retardation   181

ECOLOGY OF THE CHILD: FAMILY   182

Educational Adaptations for Children with Mental Retardation or Developmental Disabilities   185

Adapting the Learning Environment   185
Identifying Students with MR/DD   185
Issues of Inclusion   187
Individualized Education Programs (IEPs)   188
General Education Classroom   188
Teacher Consultants or Facilitators   190
How to Use the Resource Room   190
Special Classes   192
Adapting Curriculum   192
What Are the Goals?   192
Educational Reform and Students with MR/DD   193
Differential Instruction   194
Basic Academic Skills   194
Language and Communication   195
Socialization   196
Prevocations and Work-Study Skills   198
Adapting Teaching Strategies   200
Behavior Modification   200
Fading and Self-Instruction   202
Intrinsic Motivation   203
Cooperative Learning   203
Skills Mastery   204
Technology   205
Can Special Education Make a Difference?   205

Transition   206
     From School to Work   *206*
     Adulthood   *208*

Family and Lifespan Issues   **209**
Family Support   209
Interaction with the Community: The Special Olympics   212

Chapter 6: Children with Learning Disabilities   *218*

A Historical Overview   **219**

Definitions   **220**

Prevalence   **222**

Is There a Single Cause?   **223**

Characteristics of Children with Learning Disabilities   **224**

Classification of Learning Disabilities   **225**
Neuropsychological/Developmental Learning Disabilities   225
     Biological and Genetic Explanations   *226*
     Perceptual-Motor Problems   *227*
     Visual Processing Deficits   *227*
     Auditory Processing Deficits   *227*
     Memory Disorders   *228*
     Attentional Deficits and Hyperactivity   *228*
Academic Achievement Learning Disabilities   229
     Language and Reading Disorders   *229*
     Dyslexia   *229*
     Writing Disorders   *230*
     Spelling Disorders   *230*
     Mathematics Disorders   *230*

ECOLOGY OF THE CHILD: SCHOOL   231
     Deficits in Executive Function or Cognitive Strategies   *233*
Social Disabilities   233

Developmental Profile   **233**

Identification and Assessment   **234**
Diagnosis   235
Early Intervention   236
     Language Disabilities   *237*
     Perceptual-Motor Disabilities   *237*
     Attentional and Other Disabilities   *238*

Educational Adaptations for Children with Learning Disabilities   **239**
Adapting the Learning Environment   239
     Issues of Achievement   *239*
     Collaboration and Inclusion   *240*
Adapting Curriculum   240
     Supportive Inclusion   *241*

Adapting Teaching Strategies 243
Applied Behavioral Analysis 243
Diagnostic Prescriptive Model 245
Mnemonic Devices 247
Cooperative Learning 247
Mastery Learning 247
Cognitive Instruction 247
Approaches to Content Instruction 248
Instructional Technology 251
Transition 252

Family and Lifespan Issues 253

Chapter 7: Children with Emotional and Behavior Disorders 259

Definition 260

Factors Related to Behavior Problems 263
Biological Risk Factors 263
The Influence of Genes 264
Interaction Between Genes and Environment 264
The Influence of Drugs 265
The Interaction of Factors 265
Family Risk Factors 265
School Risk Factors 266
Social Risk Factors 266
Violence in the Schools 266
Family and Culture 267
The Challenge of Substance Abuse 268

Classifications and Characteristics 268
Conduct Disorders 269
Attention-Deficit Hyperactivity Disorder 270
Anxiety-Withdrawal 271

Developmental Profiles 273

Identification and Placement 275

ECOLOGY OF THE CHILD: FAMILY AND COMMUNITY 277

Intervention Strategies 278
Positive Reinforcement 278
Functional Assessment 279
Ecological Strategies 280
Project Re-Ed 281
Time-Out 281
Drug Treatment 283
Treatment Combinations 283

**Educational Adaptations for Children with Emotional and
Behavior Disorders 284**

Adapting the Learning Environment   284
    Understanding Emotional and Behavior Disorders   *284*
    Collaboration: The Role of the Multidisciplinary Team   *284*
    The Helping Teacher   *286*
    The Wraparound Approach   *286*
    Inclusion   *286*
Adapting Curriculum   289
Adapting Teaching Strategies   290
    Skills Mastery Techniques   *290*
Technology   298
    Computers: Aiding Content Mastery and Avoiding
    Negative Response   *298*

Family and Lifespan Issues   298
Transition from School to Work   299
Adulthood   299

Chapter 8: Children with Communication Disorders in Speech and Language   306

Definitions   307

Differences Between Speech Disorders and Language Disorders   308

The Elements of Verbal Language   309

Prevalence of Communication Disorders   310

Language Development: A Brief Overview   313
Characteristics of Language Development   314
The Sequence of Language Development   314

Classification of Communication Disorders   316
Disorders of Articulation-Phonology   316
    The Nature of Articulation-Phonology Disorders   *317*
    Disabilities Associated with Articulation-Phonology Disorders   *317*
Disorders of Fluency and Speech Timing   317
Disorders of Voice   318
Disorders of Language   318

Developmental Delay in Communication   319

Developmental Profile   319

Identification and Assessment   321
Preschool Children and Early Intervention   321
School-Age Children   323
    Screening   *323*
    Evaluation and Diagnosis   *323*
    Developing the IEP   *324*
Linguistic Diversity   324
    Assessment of Non-English-Speaking Children   *324*

Education Adaptations for Children with Communication Disorders in Speech and Language   326

Adapting the Learning Environment   326
  Inclusion   326
  Consultative Service   326
  Itinerant Service   326
  Intensive-Cycle Scheduling   326
  Educational Setting   327
Adapting Teaching Strategies   327
  Speech and Language Therapy   327
  Interactive Approaches   331
  Intervention for Fluency Disorders   331
  Focused Stimulation   332
  Phonological Training   332
  Slow Anditory Processing   333
  Augmented and Alternative Communication   333
Adapting Curriculum   334
  Intervention Priorities   334
  Dialects   334
Technology   335
  Instructional Technology   335
Transition   337

ECOLOGY OF THE CHILD: COMMUNITY   338

Family and Lifespan Issues   339

Chapter 9: Children Who Are Deaf or Hard of Hearing   344

Definitions   345
  Degree of Hearing Loss   346
  Age of Onset of Loss   346
  The Structure of the Ear and Types of Hearing Loss   346

Prevalence of Hearing Loss   349

Causes of Hearing Loss   349
  Genetic Causes   350
  Environmental Causes   351

Characteristics of Children with Hearing Loss   354
  Cognitive Development   354
  Language Development   355
  Social and Personal Adjustment   357
    Interpreters   359
    The Deaf Community   360
    Some Special Services   360

Developmental Profiles   361

The School's Role in Identification   362

The General Education Teacher   363
The Audiologist   364

Means of Testing Hearing Loss   364

Audiometry   364
  Pure-Tone Audiometry   364
  Behavioral Observation Audiometry   364
  Play Audiometry   365
Auditory Brainstem Response   365
Bone-Conductor Test   365
Cochlear Implants   365

ECOLOGY OF THE CHILD: COMMUNITY   366

Educational Adaptations for Children Who Are Deaf or Hard of Hearing   368

Adapting the Learning Environment   368
  Parent Involvement and Early Intervention   368
  Inclusion in Elementary School   370
  Inclusion in Secondary School   370
  The Education Team   371
Adapting Curriculum   371
  Academic Achievement   371
  Components of Successful Programs   372
  Encouraging Academic Achievement at Home   372
Adapting Teaching Strategies   373
  Communication Skills   373
  Communication Methods   375
  Approaches to Teaching Communication   377
  Teacher Strategies   379
Technology   379
  Assistive Technology   379
  Instructional Technology   381
Transition
  Postsecondary Programs   381
  National Information Center on Deafness   382

Family and Lifespan Issues   382

Chapter 10: Children with Visual Impairments   389

Definitions   390

Visual Interpretation of the Human Eye   390

The Human Eye   391
Causes of Visual Impairments   392

Characteristics of Children with Visual Impairments   393

Intellectual Development   393
Language Development   394
Sensory Compensation and Perception   394
Personal and Social Adjustment   395

Developmental Profiles 398

Early Intervention 400

Identification 402

ECOLOGY OF THE CHILD: SCHOOL 404

Educational Adaptations for Children with Visual Impairments 405

Adapting the Learning Environment 408
Inclusion 408
Individualized Education Program 413
Special Schools 413

Adapting Curriculum 415
Literacy 415
Mathematics 416

Adapting Teaching Strategies 416
Communication Skills 417
Environment Skills 421
Skills in the Learning Environment 425
Additional Skills Training 426

Technology 426
Assistive Technology 426

Transition 430
From School to Work 430

Program Evaluation 431

A National Agenda 432

Family and Lifespan Issues 433

A Final Word 433

Chapter 11: Children with Multiple and Severe Disabilities 439

A Note About Terminology 441

Definition 441

Prevalence of Multiple and Severe Disabilities 443

Causes of Multiple and Severe Disabilities 443

Characteristics of Children with Multiple and Severe Disabilities 444

Autism, Pervasive Developmental Disorders (PDD), and Pervasive
Developmental Disorders Not Otherwise Specified (PDDNOS) 444
Autism 445
Rhett Disorder 446
Childhood Disintegrative Disorder 446
Asperger's Disorder 446
Autism and PDDNOS 446

Treatment Programs 446
Lovaas's Young Autism Program 446
TEECH 447
Other Programs 448

Deafblind Impairment　　448
　　The Education Program　　448
　　Early Intervention　　449
Behavior Disturbance and Hearing Impairment　　450
Mental Retardation with Another Disability　　451
Mental Retardation and Cerebral Palsy　　452

Early Intervention　　453

Identification of Children with Multiple and Severe Disabilities　　456

**Educational Adaptations for Children with Multiple and
Severe Disabilities　　457**
Adapting the Learning Environment　　457
　　Inclusion: Integrated Settings　　459
Adapting Curriculum　　461
　　Data Collecting　　461
　　Functional Age-Appropriate Skills　　462
Adapting Teaching Strategies　　464
　　Teaching and Assessing　　464
　　Preschool　　466
　　Primary and Secondary School　　467
　　Teaching Strategies for Nonvocal Students　　469
　　Technology for Nonvocal Students　　469
Technology　　470
　　Instructional Technology　　470
　　Assistive Technology　　470
Transition　　470
　　From Home and School to Community and Work　　470

Family and Lifespan Issues　　473
Living Arrangements　　473
Vocational Opportunities　　474
　　Day Treatment Programs　　474
　　Day Habilitation Programs　　474
　　Sheltered Workshops　　474

ECOLOGY OF THE CHILD: FAMILY　　476
　　Supportive Competitive Employment　　478

*Chapter 12: Children with Physical Disabilities and
Health Impairments　　484*

Definitions　　485

Prevalence of Physical Disabilities and Health Impairments　　486

Causes of Physical Disabilities and Health Impairments　　487
Congenital Disabilities　　487
Acquired Disabilities　　488

Classification and Characteristics　　488

Children with Physical Disabilities   488
   Neurological Conditions   489

ECOLOGY OF THE CHILD: SCHOOL   **492**
   Musculoskeletal Conditions   494

Children with Health Impairments   496
   Metabolic Disorders   496
   Cardiopulmonary Conditions   496
   Acquired Immunodeficiency Syndrome   497
   Cooley's Anemia and Sickle Cell Anemia   499
   Substance Abuse   499
   Other Health-Related Conditions   500

Technology-Dependent Health Conditions   501
   A Home-Care Success Story   501
   Tube Feeding   502
   Intravenous Feeding   503
   Catheterization and Colostomy   503
   Oxygen-Dependent Children   503

Child Abuse   503

Traumatic Brain Injury and Accidents   504

Developmental Profiles   **505**
   Early Intervention   507

Identification of Children with Physical Disabilities and Health Impairments   **507**

Educational Adaptations for Children with Physical Disabilities and Health Impairments   **508**

Adapting the Learning Environment   508
   Inclusion   508
   Instructional Materials and Classroom Equipment   512
   Accessibility of Facilities   512

Adapting Curriculum   513
   Skill Development   513

Adapting Teaching Strategies   516
   Increasing the Understanding of the Disabling Condition   516
   Emphasizing the Quality of Life   516
   Increasing the Sense of Control   517
   Physical Education   517

Technology   517
   Assistive Communication   517

Transition   520

Family and Lifespan Issues   **521**
   Length of Life   521
   Discrimination   521

Afterword: New Millennium, New Opportunities   527
Glossary   532
References   539
Author/Source Index   563
Subject Index   571

Preface

Special education is a dynamic field with abundant new research, alternative curricula, and major technological innovations. Special education is not the exclusive domain of special educators. At some time or other, practically all schoolteachers will have exceptional children in their classrooms, particularly with the current emphasis on the philosophy of inclusion. Increasingly, there is also a strong movement in law and practice to work directly with families and have them be an integral member of the educational team.

Audience and Purpose

Meeting the special needs of children with exceptionalities is the shared responsibility of regular classroom teachers, special education teachers, therapists, psychologists, and other members of the education team, which also includes the parents and families of exceptional children. Our objective in writing this textbook is to assist in the preparation of those individuals for their roles in meeting the educational needs of people with exceptionalities.

Themes

In the ninth edition of *Educating Exceptional Children,* we emphasize an ecological approach to special education. Central among the emphases in the field is increasing awareness of the exceptional child first and foremost as an individual who is influenced by and must cope with the broad contexts or environments of family, peers, school, and society. We call this the ecology of the child. *Educating Exceptional Children* perceives the family's role as central to the education of the child and shows why resolving family needs is critical to successfully educating children with exceptionalities.

We address the ecological theme in several ways. Chapter 3, on early childhood intervention, illustrates the importance of environment early in life. We provide an extensive discussion of risk factors, risk prevention, and the personnel involved in early intervention, as well as detailed examples of model programs. The chapter is oriented to the needs of both teachers and parents.

The ecological theme is reinforced in the "Ecology of the Child" feature in each chapter. It allows us to highlight an exceptional individual's interactions with his or her family, school, or community, and address issues that go beyond the classroom. The commentary that accompanies each feature invites discussion in the classroom.

In this ninth edition we continue our mission of presenting research and information on the best practices from multiple theoretical orientations, to encourage readers to do likewise as a method for formulating their own substantiated view. Acknowledging that education is part of change at large in society, we invite readers to embark on critical thinking and decision making, using as a springboard the text's afterword, "New Millennium, New Opportunities."

Organization of the Text

The first three chapters focus on broader issues affecting all exceptional learners. Chapter 1, *Educating the Exceptional Child,* introduces the reader to exceptional children and discusses why they present an educational challenge. Because approximately one out of every ten or twelve children in the school system is a child with an exceptionality, we are talking about a very large aggregate (although the number of exceptional individuals in any one category can be quite small). A complex interactive set of factors affects the exceptional child—family, peers, school, and community. These factors have to be taken into consideration. We look at the family and the impact of having a child with special needs on the family unit and vice versa. In addition, we explore the general education classroom and adaptations that can be made to support exceptional children in this environment.

Chapter 2, *Exceptional Children and Their Environment,* focuses on the impact of the ecology or environment in interaction with the child with special needs. This includes the history of attempts to educate exceptional children, which follows a trend over time from separation to integration. The chapter focuses on inclusion and the least restrictive environment and its potential impact, as well as the effect of general educational reform issues such as standards and site-based management of exceptional children. Finally, the role of the courts in establishing the rights of exceptional children to a free and appropriate education is presented.

Chapter 3, *Early Intervention: Priorities and Programs,* addresses the impact of recent legislation on services for exceptional children from birth through age five. The concepts of risk, early identification, and the range of programs and personnel involved in early childhood special education are discussed.

The ninth edition of *Educating Exceptional Children* continues to provide basic information about the characteristics and distinctive problems of learners with exceptionalities, using the appropriate categorical terminology. Chapters 4–12 focus on the categories of children with exceptionalities. For children in each category, the chapters cover definitions, prevalence, causes, characteristics, classification, intervention, identification and assessment, special educational adaptations, transition, assistive and educational technology, and lifespan and family issues.

Revisions in This Edition

We have thoroughly updated the coverage in each chapter. Highlights include: Chapter 1, *Educating the Exceptional Child,* expands its section on diversity and has increased coverage of attention disorders. Chapter 2, *Exceptional Children and Their Environment,* has an updated section on educational reform and a new educational adaptation section. Chapter 3, *Early Intervention: Priorities and Programs,* includes a discussion on developmentally appropriate practices, infant programs, and play assessment. Chapter 4, *Children Who Are Gifted and Talented,* includes a new technology section and has many significant updates. Chapter 5, *Children with Mental Retardation and Developmental Disabilities,* introduces a new term applied to this group, "developmental disabilities," and an expanded section on support for families. Chapter 6, *Children with Learning Disabilities,* presents several strategy learning curriculums as well as an expanded section on writing. Chapter 7, *Children with Emotional and Behavior Disorders,* includes a discussion of violence, drugs, and gangs in school. Chapter 8, *Children with Communication Disorders in Speech and Language,* includes a new section on otitis media and specific language impairment (SLI). Chapter 9, *Children Who Are Deaf or Hard of Hearing,* discusses the increasing use of interpreters in classrooms as well as newer assistive technology. Chapter 10, *Children with Visual Impairments,* increases its discussion of personal and social adjustment issues. Chapter 11, *Children with Multiple and Severe Disabilities,* expands its section on pervasive developmental disorders and its five subtypes, and includes a new section on independence training. Chapter 12, *Children with Physical Disabilities and Health Impairments,* updates technological advances in life supports and teaching aids. The afterword, *New Millennium, New Opportunities,* has been updated to discuss potential further trends and issues that will impact on the education of children with disabilities and their families.

This edition expands its Resources for Further Study at the end of each chapter to include listings of relevant journals and professional organizations with their addresses and Web sites.

Features in the Ninth Edition

- **Focusing Questions** help readers set goals and establish purposes for their reading of each important topic.

- **Introductions** offer an overview of the chapter's content and give students a framework into which they can fit new ideas.

- **Educational Adaptations** sections offer extensive suggestions for teaching to the strengths of the exceptional child by varying the learning environment, the content, or the teaching approach. These sections are tabbed for easy reference. The information has been reorganized and is presented in a more easy-to-use format. Each Educational Adaptations section is organized under several consistent headings: Adapting the Learning Environment, Adapting Curriculum, Adapting Teaching Strategies, Technology, and Transition. Chapter 2 now includes an Educational Adaptations section, and they appear in every categorical chapter.

- **Ecology of the Child** (formerly Child in Context) features in each chapter focus on the family, school, or community in relation to the exceptional child. Half of these features are new in this ninth edition.

- **Lifespan and Family Issues** sections appear as the final heading in every chapter. This section allows students to view the individual throughout the lifespan and focus on issues such as the role of the family, work and higher education opportunities, social adjustments in adulthood, and integration into the community.

- **Margin notes** highlight important points and updated material. Over seventy-five margin notes are new in this edition, many of them geared to the general education teacher.

- **Summary of Major Ideas** sections conclude each chapter and highlight in a clear, point-by-point format the major concepts presented in the chapter.

- **Unresolved Issues** sections encourage students to discuss and propose solutions for problems that are still being debated in the field of special education.
- **Key Terms** listed at the end of each chapter are cross-referenced to where in the text the terms are boldfaced and discussed.
- **Questions for Thought** ask students to gather, analyze, and apply information about a range of issues in special education.
- **Resources for Further Study** is a new section that ties together three types of resources:

  –**References of Special Interest** provide annotated lists of high-interest texts.

  –**Journals** section includes the major journals in the category of exceptional children addressed in that chapter.

  –**Professional Organizations** section provides addresses and Web sites for professional special education organizations.
- A **Glossary** at the end of the book defines all key terms.

Ancillaries

The *Instructor's Resource Manual* (IRM) prepared by Krista Swensson of Eastern Mennonite University, combines into a single tool the Study Guide, Instructor's Manual, and Test Bank. The IRM complements the students' and instructors' use of the text and class experiences by emphasizing the skills of organizing, reinforcing, evaluating, and expanding knowledge. Contents include a transition and planning guide; model syllabi; extensive learning and teaching resources for each chapter, including study handouts for students and instructors' support; an assessment section containing multiple-choice items, divergent essay questions, and an answer key for each chapter; and professional resources.

The test items contained in the *Instructor's Resource Manual* are also available in computerized form in a *Test Generator.*

A set of *transparencies,* both two- and one-color, is available to each instructor upon adoption of the text.

Acknowledgments

We are grateful to many of our colleagues and specialists in various exceptionalities for their criticisms and suggestions during the revision of the text. Their critical comments and ideas helped shape and improve our presentation: Shirley Cohen, Hunter College; Christina Curran, Central Washington University; Laurie deBettencourt, University of Virginia; Donald Deshler, University of Kansas; Elizabeth Epanchin, University of South Florida; Kay Alicyn Ferrell, University of Northern Colorado; Sr. Rosemary Gaffney, Hunter College; Katherine Garnett, Hunter College; Carole R. Gothelf, Jewish Guild for the Blind, New York; Jeanne Gullo, Mequon-Theinsville School District, Mequon, Wisconsin; Tim Lackaye, College of New Rochelle; Samuel Odom, Indiana University; Edward Polloway, Lynchburg College; Sandra Rosen, San Francisco State University; Judith Smitheran, St. Vincent Hospital, Sante Fe; Janet Stack, University of Virginia; and Carol Ann Tomlinson, University of Virginia.

We also wish to acknowledge the help provided by Ann Greenberger, developmental editor; Don Braswell, Roberta Parry, Ray McKenzie, Pat McConnell, Kim Summerville; the staff of Houghton Mifflin, including Loretta Wolozin and Lisa Mafrici; and Nancy Benjamin at Books By Design. Their assistance was instrumental in bring this volume to its present condition.

Our families deserve thanks for their tolerance of the necessary time and energy that this text required.

Nick Anastasiow and I were saddened by the death of the senior author of this volume, Sam Kirk, in July 1996. Sam was a true giant in the field of education—scholar, teacher, writer, mentor, policy maker, colleague, and friend. Thousands of children and families who never knew his name have benefited from his insightful work.

James J. Gallagher
Nicholas J. Anastasiow

I
Educating the Exceptional Child

FOCUSING
questions

Who are the children with exceptionalities?

How have approaches to treating individuals with special needs changed over time?

What is the ecological approach?

How do parents respond to the presence of a child with disabilities in the family?

Children with disabilities may come from diverse cultural backgrounds. How does cultural diversity affect the future of such children?

It's not easy to be different. We've all felt the sting of not belonging, of not feeling a part of the group. We've all felt overwhelmed when asked to do things beyond our skills and capabilities, or bored when asked to do simple things that do not challenge us. Of course, being different is not always negative: It is what makes us interesting. But it also forces us to adapt to meet social expectations. When being different means that a child is not able to receive information through the normal senses, is not able to express himself or herself, or processes information too slowly or too quickly, special adaptations in the education program are necessary.

Despite the philosophical commitment to individualization in our education system, classrooms all too often are filled with grade-level textbooks, grade-level lessons, and grade-level expectations that assume that students deviate very little from their age norm—that is, they are "normal." What happens when students are different, when they cannot adapt to the standard education program because of their exceptionalities? The consequences are serious and have lifelong implications.

Adapting to educational programs is precisely the problem that exceptional children face, and some form of special education is necessary for these children to reach their potential. In this book we focus on the specific educational needs resulting from exceptionalities among different groups of children and the range of educational programs developed especially for them.

The Exceptional Child

Our focus is the individual exceptional child and his or her development, including how the forces around that child (family, school, peer culture, and community) adapt to meet his or her needs. We discuss in some detail the family and its adaptations, the school and special education, and other external forces, always with the goal of understanding and helping the special child to cope effectively with the outside world.

WHO IS AN EXCEPTIONAL CHILD?

 We consider a child to be exceptional when his or her differences or disabilities occur to such a degree that school practices must be modified to serve the child's needs.

Many have attempted to define the term *exceptional child*. Some use it when referring to the bright child or the child with unusual talent. Others use it when describing any atypical child. The term is generally accepted, however, to include both the child with developmental disabilities and the child who is exceptionally able. Here we define an **exceptional child** as a child who differs from the average or normal child in (1) mental characteristics, (2) sensory abilities, (3) communication abilities, (4) behavior and emotional development, or (5) physical characteristics. These differences must occur to such an extent that the child requires either a modification of school practices or special educational services to develop his or her unique capabilities.

Of course, this definition is general and raises several questions. What is *average* or *normal*? How extensive must the difference be for the child to require special education? What is special education? What role does the child's environment play in the definition? We ask these questions in different forms throughout this text as we discuss each group or category of exceptional children.

One of the fascinating aspects of children with exceptionalities is that they remind us of the possible variations in child development, for example, the idiot savant child who has mental retardation as well as a specific extraordinary skill, such as being able to tell the correct day of the week of any past or future date. There are many examples of individual differences: the woman with mental retardation who shows areas of normal language development despite serious cognitive deficits (Rondal, 1995), or the child who has endured unimaginable deprivation and abuse and still appears to be developing as a capable learner and socially normal individual (Werner, 1992). One cannot say that such things are impossible. The child or the individual in front of you shows that they are possible and forces you to try to explain them.

Exceptional individuals tell us something important about human development. By studying and teaching children who are remarkably different from the norm, we learn about the many ways children develop and learn, inform ourselves more thoroughly about the developmental processes of all children, and develop our teaching skills and strategies for all children.

CATEGORIES OF EXCEPTIONAL CHILDREN

If we define an exceptional child as one who differs in some way from a group norm, then many children are exceptional. A child with red hair is "exceptional" if all the other children in the class have brown or blond hair. But that difference, though interesting to a pediatrician or geneticist, is of little concern to the teacher. Educationally speaking, a child with red hair is not an exceptional child, because the educational program does not have to be modified to serve the child's needs. Children are considered educationally exceptional only when it is necessary to alter the educational program—for example, if their exceptionality leaves them unable to read or to master learning in the traditional way or places them so far ahead that they are bored by what is being taught.

The term *exceptional child* may mean very different things in education, in psychology, or in other disciplines. In education, we group children of like characteristics for instructional purposes. For example, we put 6-year-olds in the first grade. In the same way and for the same reasons, we create subgroups of exceptional children inside and outside the general classroom. The following groupings are typical:

There are many types of exceptionalities. Some of the categories of exceptionality include mental retardation, giftedness, communication disorders, learning disabilities, visual and hearing impairments, emotional and behavior disorders, and physical and health disabilities.

- Intellectual differences, including children who are intellectually superior and children who are slow to learn (such as giftedness and mental retardation)
- Communication differences, including children with learning disabilities or speech and language disabilities
- Sensory differences, including children with auditory or visual disabilities
- Behavioral differences, including children who are emotionally disturbed or socially maladjusted
- Multiple and severe handicapping conditions, including children with combinations of impairments (such as cerebral palsy and mental retardation, or deafness and blindness)
- Physical differences, including children with nonsensory disabilities that impede mobility and physical vitality

Prevalence

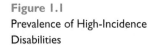 *There is a trend toward identifying increased numbers of students as learning disabled.*

Educational policy makers, those who make the decisions about how we should spend societal resources on education, want to know just how many exceptional children there are. Those numbers will tell us how big an issue this is and how much we, as a society, will have to spend on it. Over 2.5 million school children have been identified as learning disabled, and we currently are spending over 30 billion dollars for special services (Hendrickson, 1996).

Figure 1.1 compares the 1988–1989 school year with the 1995–1996 school year in terms of youngsters in the high-incidence disability categories. (High-incidence disabilities are those categories of disabilities that are more prevalent, that occur more frequently.) This high-incidence group of categories comprise 90 percent of exceptional children. As Figure 1.1 indicates, the "learning disabilities" category not only is the most frequently used classification but has increased by a phenomenal 40 to 50 percent over just a seven-year period.

Is there an epidemic of learning disabilities in this country affecting schoolchildren, or is something else happening? Obviously, there has been some important change in our perceptions of these students (Macmillan & Forness, 1998). (Chapter 6 discusses this trend and its implications.) The other categories of high-incidence disabilities seem to have been relatively stable over the same time period.

Figure 1.2 reflects the prevalence of low-incidence disabilities. While there has been a major jump in the "other health impaired" category over the same seven-year period, the remainder of the categories seem to have remained relatively stable. The numbers of children with visual impairment (slightly over 20 thousand) are surely underestimated—many of the children in the "multiple disabilities" category would have visual impairment as one of their disabilities.

Figure 1.1
Prevalence of High-Incidence Disabilities

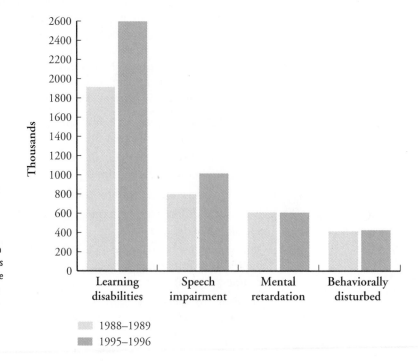

Source: U.S. Department of Education (1991), *Twelfth Annual Report to Congress on Implementation of the Education of the Handicapped Act* and (1997), *Nineteenth Annual Report to Congress on Implementation of the Individuals with Disabilities Education Act.* Washington, DC: U.S. Department of Education.

The generally upward trend in the "multiple disabilities" and "other health impaired" categories may be the result of improvements in medical science. Children born with severe health problems have better chances to survive but often with serious developmental problems.

The increase in the "other health impaired" category is perhaps due to inclusion of autistic children under this label. Few of the subcategories under "other health impaired" reach the 100,000 level, which means public schools have to plan for those children on an individual basis. It is unlikely that a system will have sufficient numbers of students in subcategories of "other health impaired" to justify grouping youngsters with similar classifications and ages together.

Overall, exceptional children total well over 4 million schoolchildren, representing 8 to 10 percent of all children in school. The category of children with special needs represents almost 1 in every 10 children in school. That is one reason for the extensive attention given to exceptional children and to their special education.

Attention-Deficit Hyperactivity Disorder (ADHD)

One of the recent additions to the categories of exceptional children is children with attention-deficit hyperactivity disorder (ADHD). The American Psychiatric Association estimates that 3 percent of American children may suffer from some form of this disorder, although not all of them require special education services.

Three major characteristics have been noted in children with ADHD. They have difficulty (1) maintaining attention, (2) regulating their activity levels, and (3) controlling impulsive behavior (McKinney, Montague, & Hocutt, 1994). All children at one time or another manifest those characteristics. The differences between children who need special help and children who represent the norm are the *severity* of the symptoms (more frequent and severe than in children of similar developmental

Students with attention-deficit hyperactivity disorder (ADHD) have difficulty maintaining attention, which can affect their academic success.

Figure 1.2
Prevalence of Low-Incidence Disabilities

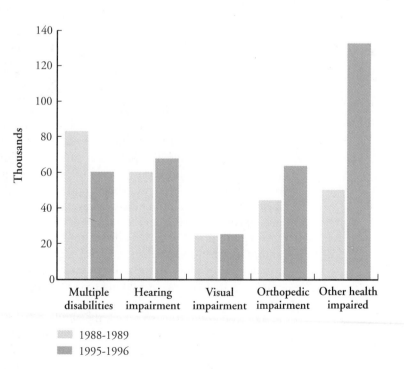

Source: U.S. Department of Education (1991), *Twelfth Annual Report to Congress on Implementation of the Education of the Handicapped Act* and (1997), *Nineteenth Annual Report to Congress on Implementation of the Individuals with Disabilities Education Act.* Washington, DC: U.S. Department of Education.

levels), *early onset* (symptoms began before the age of 7), and *duration* (symptoms persisted for at least six months prior to diagnosis).

Children with attention-deficit hyperactivity disorder (ADHD) have many similarities with other groups of exceptional children, notably children with learning disabilities or behavior disorders, and so appear in a number of chapters in this text.

The Context of the Exceptional Child

When discussing the child as learner, it's important to paint a complete portrait of the child, including the social and family context in which he or she lives. Even as the lead actor on the stage captures our attention, we are aware of the importance of the supporting players and the sets to the play itself. Once we recognize the individuality of each child and the complex and unique forces and circumstances that act on and surround him or her, it is easier to choose or create the most appropriate instructional strategies and the most suitable learning environment.

Figure 1.3 portrays the child at the center of successive layers of influence. The family is the first and often the most influential, but there are other influences: School, peer culture, and community also play roles, often interacting with the family. This is what we refer to as the *context,* or *ecology,* of the exceptional child. These life circles fold into one another and collectively are the child's ecology, which we must understand if we are to make wise decisions about the child's education. Both the family and the community in which exceptional children live are essential to their growth and development. And it is in the public schools that we find the full expression of the community's understanding and commitment: the knowledge, hopes, fears, and myths that are passed on to the next generation.

FAMILY, SCHOOL, PEER CULTURE, AND COMMUNITY

Family, school, peer culture, and community make up the child's context, or ecology.

In the past few years, a major shift has taken place in how educators perceive children with exceptionalities. For many years, we have known that the environment surrounding an exceptional child can influence how well that child will adapt to his or her life situation. We now realize that the environment, or ecology, can play a significant role in the initial development of an exceptionality.

Environment, or ecology, plays a major role in the initial development of an exceptional child.

In the 1950s, it was a well-accepted proposition that the exceptionality was embedded within the child. A child was deaf or blind because of injuries to his or her sensory systems. Cerebral palsy was caused by injury to the central nervous system. As educators expanded the concept of exceptionality to include mild manifestations of exceptionality, students who would have been referred to as having borderline mental retardation, mild behavior problems, or a less severe but still manifest learning disability were found where their "exceptionality" was partially created by their environment as well as their personal characteristics. It became clear that the ability of a child to adapt successfully depended on the nature of the child's environment, as well as on the child's own special characteristics. Increasingly, the approach that educators are taking to cope with the milder forms of exceptionality is to try to aid the child's adjustment by modifying the life circles around the child, in addition to attempting to attack the child's developmental delay problem.

For example, George, age 7, was identified in kindergarten and first grade as being developmentally delayed and not performing as well as his classmates. The school psychologist suggested that George might be mentally retarded. A more thor-

Figure 1.3
The Context/Ecology of the
Exceptional Child

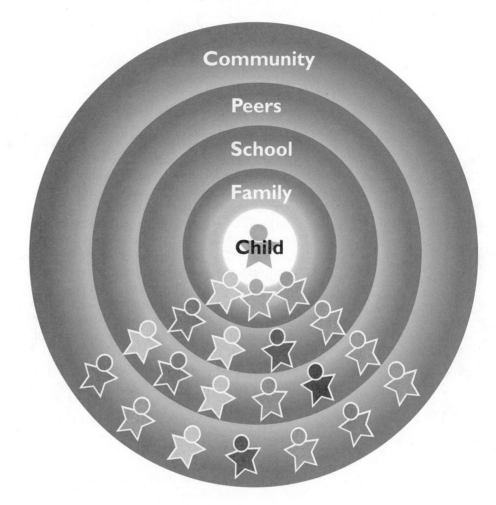

ough evaluation of the life circles around George revealed a barren environment for learning. George's family had many adjustment problems of its own, including the drug problems of the parents. There was also a suggestion of child abuse. George had few friends or few opportunities to learn outside the school setting.

Instead of focusing entirely on the remediation of George's reading problems in school, George's individualized education program (IEP), a plan for the student's education devised by teachers and the parents, suggested that changes be made in George's environment. The school social worker arranged for George to be moved at least temporarily to the home of his uncle. The uncle and his wife were diligent providers, exposing George to a consistent and warm family life and accepting him as a member of their family. George's response to the change was a much improved attitude toward school and increased attention to his lessons. The psychologist, observing these changes, modified his judgment that George was mentally retarded.

This is not to say that the exceptionality of every child can be removed through improvement of the environment. But in cases where ecology appears to play a significant part in the original identification of the exceptionality, making significant changes in the environment can improve the functioning of the child and may cause the exceptionality itself to be reduced or to disappear.

THE ECOLOGICAL APPROACH

Perhaps the most dramatic change in educators' view of how to teach young children has resulted from the adoption of the ecological approach to child development (Bronfenbrenner, 1989). With this recognition of the role of the environment, the field moved from a **medical model of exceptionality,** which assumes that the physical condition or disease exists within the patient, to an **ecological model,** in which we see the exceptional child in complex interaction with many environmental forces.

The ecological approach tries not only to modify the exceptional child's learning and behavior through direct contact with the child but also to improve the environment surrounding the child, including the family and the neighborhood—the entire context of the child. This ecological approach became the strategy of Head Start and other programs targeted at children from economically disadvantaged families. Head Start pays much attention to the family in addition to the child (Zigler, 1995). The ecological model also helps us understand what we can realistically expect to accomplish through intervention programs.

Most educational programs, by themselves, cannot change enough of the ecology or the larger environment to make a substantial difference in the lives of children. To be of greatest effect, the educator has to join hands with those who specialize in the family and the larger environment. As Zigler points out, "no amount of counseling, early childhood curricula, or home visits will take the place of jobs that provide decent incomes, affordable housing, health care, good schools, or safe neighborhoods where children encounter positive role models" (1995, p. 31). One can repeat that statement for exceptional children as well.

The ecological approach seeks to modify the child's behavior directly by improving the context in which the child lives, learns, and plays.

THE INTERACTION OF HEREDITY AND ENVIRONMENT

Few topics stimulate more fascination than the question of how we become what we are. What forces shape our development and sequentially create a confident and complex adult from an apparently helpless infant? For many decades, we have been aware of the effects that both heredity and environment have on the developing child. Because it is the educators' role to change the environment of the child through instruction, it has been tempting to ignore the role of heredity. It is as though we have concluded that we, as educators, don't know much about heredity, so it can't be very important to us.

But the recent dramatic progress in the fields of genetics makes heredity impossible to ignore. Actually we have been through three major stages in our belief systems about the relative influence of heredity and environment, and each stage has had a profound effect on how we behaved as educators. Up until about 1960, it was strongly believed that heredity drove and determined various conditions related to intelligence, such as familial mental retardation (retardation without obvious neurological insult), giftedness, or mental illness. Those beliefs led us to consider it more or less impossible to change such conditions, and the role of educators was to help individuals adapt as well as possible to their hereditary roll of the dice (Plomin & Petrill, 1997).

Starting around 1960, there was a major movement to discover the important role played by environment and to suggest that many exceptionalities can be created by various environmental conditions. It was reasoned that mild mental retardation could be caused by lack of early stimulation or that giftedness emerged only because the environment for some children was incredibly favorable. Educators were encouraged to try to find ways to reverse unfavorable effects through education.

Around 1990, a similar shift in the view of the relative roles of heredity and environment took place. Now the emphasis is on the progressive interaction of heredity and environment and the resulting effects of those interactions. Gottlieb (1997) proposes that by changing the environmental conditions of early childhood we can activate different patterns of genes, which then can result in behavioral changes.

> The present viewpoint takes advantage of the well-accepted fact that only a very small proportion of an individual's genotype participates in the developmental process. . . . In our view, a change in developmental conditions activates heretofore quiescent genes thus changing the usual developmental process and resulting in an altered behavioral or morphological phenotype. (pp. 158–159)

What is important is that the complex interaction between heredity and environment urges the educator to seek out the most stimulating environmental conditions to apply, but always with an eye toward the contributions of heredity.

INTRA-INDIVIDUAL DIFFERENCES

By definition, exceptional children are different from children of the same life age. The differences present educators with many challenges. What sometimes goes unnoticed is that some students differ substantially from others not only along key dimensions of development (inter-individual differences) but also within their own abilities (intra-individual differences). A child may have the intelligence of an 11-year-old but the social behavior of a 6-year-old. Both inter-individual and intra-individual differences are the concern of special educators.

Understanding a child's **intra-individual differences**—the differences in abilities *within* the same child—can help us develop individualized programs of instruction. These programs are tailored to the strengths and weaknesses of the individual child. They do not necessarily consider how that child compares with other children.

Intra-individual differences can show up in any area: intellectual, psychological, physical, or social. A child may be very bright but unable to see or hear. Or a child may be developing normally physically but be unable to relate socially to his or her agemates. It is just as important for teachers to know the child's unique pattern of strengths and weaknesses as it is to know how the child compares with other children.

DEVELOPMENTAL PROFILES

How can educators monitor and explore inter-individual and intra-individual differences? Developmental profiles provide one way to track the range of an individual's differences. Figure 1.4 shows the developmental profiles of two children. Joan is an intellectually gifted 10-year-old. Her mental ability tests at age 14; her achievement in reading and arithmetic tests at from one to four grades beyond her fifth-grade classmates. These are the inter-individual differences between Joan and her classmates. But notice that Joan's performance shows many intra-individual differences. Although mentally she has the ability of a 14-year-old, her physical development is about average for a girl her age, and her social maturity is only

Figure 1.4

Profiles of a Child with Intellectual Gifts and a Child with Mental Retardation

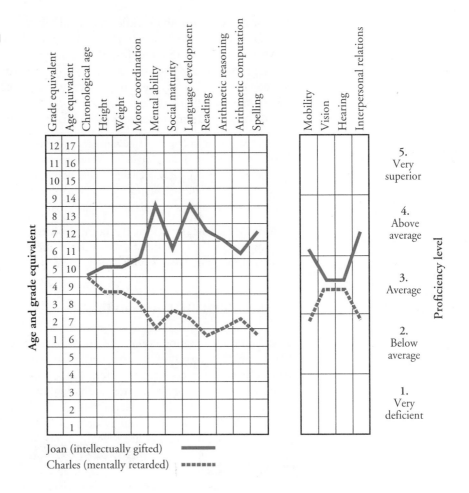

Joan (intellectually gifted) ——————

Charles (mentally retarded) ┅┅┅┅┅

slightly higher. If her parents or teachers expect her to behave like a 14-year-old in every dimension of development because her mental development is at that level, they are going to be disappointed.

The second profile in the figure is of Charles, a child with mental retardation. His profile shows him to be behind in development and performance in almost every dimension. Although he is 10 years old, his mental ability and academic performance are at first- and second-grade levels. These inter-individual differences distinguish Charles from his classmates. In addition, Charles shows substantial intra-individual differences, ranging from the 6- and 7-year-old level in academic achievement to the 9- and 10-year-old levels in physical development and life age.

Joan and Charles have very different exceptionalities. Yet both present similar problems for their teachers and schools: Their inter- and intra-individual differences set them apart from their classmates and require special educational attention.

 Teachers should be alert to procedures for assessing students as exceptional. Note whether any one gender or ethnic or racial group is overidentified as needing special education.

The Unique Influence of the Family

One of the major forces that influence the exceptional child, or any child, is the family. If we expect to be effective in special education, we have to work with the

Families of exceptional children play an important role in early intervention. Parents can teach their children some of the skills and learning tools that will later be reinforced in a school setting. (© Lora E. Askinazi/The Picture Cube)

family system in which the child lives, not just with the child. The trend toward early intervention (before the age of 5) increases the importance of the family. Much of the intervention with young children is directed toward changing the family environment and preparing the parent or parents to care for and teach their child. At the very least, intervention tries to generate more constructive parent-child interactions. (Chapter 3 focuses specifically on early childhood intervention from a variety of perspectives.)

The increasing interest in the family can be attributed to a series of basic assumptions about the exceptional child and his or her family (Bailey, Buysee, Edmondson, & Smith, 1994):

1. Children and families are inextricably intertwined. Intentional or not, intervention with children almost invariably influences families; likewise, intervention and support with families almost invariably influence children.

2. Involving and supporting families is likely to be a more powerful intervention than one that focuses exclusively on the child.

3. Family members should be able to choose their level of involvement in program planning, decision making, and service delivery.

4. Professionals should attend to family priorities for goals and services, even when those priorities differ substantially from professional priorities.

The purpose of this **family-focused approach** is to help parents become more autonomous and less dependent on professionals, to be able to form their own support networks as appropriate instead of being told by "experts" how to raise their children (Zigler & Black, 1989).

Whenever the helping professions (such as medicine, education, and social work) make a major shift from an almost exclusive emphasis on the child to an emphasis on the family, a lot of professionals find themselves in unfamiliar territory. These are the teachers, psychologists, occupational therapists, and others who have been trained under the old "treat the child" model. They now have to change their accustomed practices if the family-focused approach is to become a reality. Many professionals do not feel adequately prepared for this shift (Bailey, Palsha, & Simeonsson, 1993).

CHILD-FAMILY INTERACTION

We stress the importance of viewing the child in the *context* of family and societal forces. Although less easily measured than inter-individual and intra-individual characteristics, these contextual forces nevertheless have a powerful impact on a child's development.

Let us think of two youngsters, Dan and Pablo, each of whom has been born with a moderate case of cerebral palsy, a disorder caused by damage to the parts of the central nervous system that control motor movements. This condition is certain to cause mobility and communications problems for both children. Each will surely find his way into some form of special services that exist in practically all school systems in the United States.

Dan's family viewed his arrival as a true disaster. Dan's mother sees his disability as a serious hindrance to her pursuing her own career goals. Despite her efforts to put such feelings aside, the resentment of what Dan's presence means to her and her interests is hard to submerge entirely. Similarly, Dan's father, struggling in his own career, sees Dan as a heavy and continuing burden of special expenses and needed therapies and, in the end, perhaps continued dependence on the family far into the future. These feelings, too, are hard to contain.

In Pablo's family, however, after the initial disappointment of the diagnosis of cerebral palsy, his arrival was accepted as a special challenge. His mother and father told Pablo's siblings that he will have some problems developing and that it is the responsibility of everyone in the family to help him develop as best he can. Both his mother and his father have felt the sting of social rejection in the past, and they are determined to do whatever they can to make sure that Pablo is accepted as a normal child.

Now think about Dan and Pablo at age 6: Which child do you think is more likely to be responsive to peers and teachers, and which child will become more quickly discouraged by failure and need more external support?

Differences in family attitudes, actions, and support result in variations in how children with special developmental problems such as cerebral palsy adjust to education or cope with their special condition. Thus, it is essential to consider familial and societal variables, in addition to assessing children's developmental profiles, to better understand what has happened to them in their family life before they entered school or even what is happening in their life now beyond the school environment. Interviews can provide important information about the context of the child.

Parental Response

As the example of Dan and Pablo shows, parents nearly always react strongly (positively or negatively) to the birth of an exceptional child. And it is important

It is important to consider the values of the family and the community as a major factor in how the exceptional child will adjust to education.

The relationship between an exceptional child and his or her family is lifelong and complex. Basic family responsibilities include economics, domestic and health care, recreation, self-identity, affection, socialization, and educational and vocational choices. (© Robert Crandall/Medical Images)

⭐ *Parents of a child with serious disabilities must face two crises: the symbolic death at birth of the child-who-could-have-been and the difficulty of providing daily care for the child-who-is.*

to consider those responses, because they happen to every parent, regardless of his or her educational background or socioeconomic level.

Most parents who must cope with a child with serious disabilities face two major crises. The first is the "symbolic death" of the child who was to be. When their child is first diagnosed as having a serious disability, most parents feel shock and then denial, guilt, anger, and sadness before they finally adjust (Peterson, 1987). Some parents react with severe depression (Bristol, Gallagher, & Schopler, 1988). Many move through a type of grieving process, as though their child had died (Farber, 1986), and they may wish to share their experience with others. This common sharing of problems is the basis for forming relationships with other parents experiencing similar situations. Members of groups composed of parents of children with similar disabilities are quite effective in helping new parents by sharing how they have coped with these problems.

The second, quite different crisis that many parents of exceptional children face is the problem of providing daily care for the child. The child who has cerebral palsy or is emotionally disturbed is often difficult to feed, dress, and put to bed. It is the continual, day-by-day responsibilities for care that often weigh families down and require sympathetic professional attention. The realization that their child will not go through the normal developmental process or may never become an independent adult often weighs heavily on the parents.

Family Responsibilities

The relationship between an exceptional child and his or her family is lifelong and complex, beginning with the disclosure of the exceptionality. When a child with disabilities is added to the family, the daily responsibilities grow larger. There is the additional expense, the time, and the energy needed to care for the child; the extra concern for the child's safety; the difficulty of helping the child develop a good self-image and social skills; and the problems of seeing that the child receives an appropriate education. Many ordinary tasks become more difficult and more stressful. Consider Pablo's care:

The responsibilities of two-parent working families are awesome enough without adding the special condition of a child with disabilities. Pablo's father and mother are awakened at 6:30 in the morning by the cries of Pablo's sister. Pablo has to be washed and dressed, a task of considerable difficulty because of his cerebral palsy. Meanwhile Pablo's mother is setting out breakfast while beginning to think about her own workday as a teacher at a local school.

Pablo's father gets Pablo washed and dressed and down to the breakfast table and then begins to think about a shower and shave before going to the construction company where he works. Before work, he must deliver Pablo to the developmental day-care program, where he is in an integrated program with his age peers. The family is fortunate in that Pablo's sister goes to school where the mother teaches, so one transportation problem is solved.

Breakfast is a wild round robin with no one sitting down at the same time. Pablo needs extra help from one of the adults because of his inability to totally control the tools needed to bring cereal and milk to the proper resting place. Mother puts the breakfast dishes in the dishwasher, and father is off with Pablo while mother makes the beds before going off to school.

In the late afternoon and evening, the same procedure is reversed. This time mother has to pick up Pablo because father is at a construction site on the other side of town. She is delayed further by the teacher describing an incident at the day-care center that involved Pablo's conflict with another child over possession of some toy. There is still dinner to prepare and baths to give and stories to read before the children are tucked in. Is it any wonder that the parents are weary at the end of the day and are not looking forward to tomorrow when Pablo is to receive a medical checkup on top of the normal daily activities? Which parent is going to take Pablo to the doctor's office?

Imagine, first of all, this type of routine with only one parent present to do all the tasks required. How much more harried and tired such a mother (most of the time the "one parent") is at the end of the day. Imagine further what would happen if there was not some tacit agreement between the parents about who was supposed to do what, or if there were interpersonal tensions between mother and father because they cannot agree about the proper way to discipline Pablo or just because their own personal needs continually take second place to the requirements of the children. It is not hard to see that this family is key to positive experiences for the exceptional child or why all family members need understanding and support from time to time.

When considering basic family responsibilities, it is important to realize the enormous diversity of families. There has been a substantial increase in single-parent families. Because many single mothers live in poverty, their children are less likely to receive good prenatal and postnatal care, which increases the chances of the children having physical, academic, and emotional problems.

Even in two-parent families that have a child with disabilities, fathers generally do not come to the aid of mothers by increasing their presence, helping around the house, or taking care of the child (Gallagher & Bristol, 1988). The father may get a second job to help pay for the additional expenses and, as a consequence, not be in the home much at all. A mother who thinks that this is an appropriate and loving thing to do accepts it. A mother who sees such actions by the father as a device for avoiding the problem and dodging responsibility may be quite unhappy in that situation.

The perception that each partner is taking responsibility for the family in an acceptable way determines **family harmony** (Bristol, Gallagher, & Schopler, 1988). The important factor for family harmony is whether the mother and father come to an understanding about the roles and responsibilities that each will hold in the family. The specific actions of one or the other parent are less important than the understanding that those behaviors have been agreed upon as appropriate at a particular stage in the family life cycle.

There are many stresses in the lives of families who have children with disabilities, but their lives are also filled with joy, laughter, and fun. These children can light up your heart with a smile just as any child can, and parents of children with disabilities, just like other parents, have their favorite stories of their young child's adventures in development. The child is always a child first and a child with problems second. The task of the professional is to allow that child to bloom and grow to the limit of his or her capabilities.

CHANGING FAMILY ROLES

Traditional family roles have undergone substantive changes. We now shift our focus to some of the causes of those changes—the external forces influencing the family of an exceptional child.

Working Mothers

Perhaps the greatest change in family roles has been in the movement of women into the work force. In 1948, fewer than 11 percent of mothers with children younger than age 6 worked. In the 1990 census, the median figure for the fifty states was 62 percent of mothers with children younger than 6 years of age (Zill & Nord, 1993).

When we spoke in the past of family-professional relationships, we were really speaking mainly of *mother*-professional relationships. Traditionally, fathers have not played a large role in continuous relationships with professionals. Only recently have fathers become a source of study in the families of children with disabilities (Lamb, 1986). This increase in working mothers reflects the way in which families must adapt to the necessity and reality of dual careers.

Parent Empowerment

Parent empowerment refers to the parents as no longer passively and unthinkingly taking advice from a professional or team of professionals about the treatment of their child with special needs. Parents of exceptional children are now expected to play a major and determining role in their child's care, and the professionals are to provide needed counsel and specialized advice.

The expected change in the relationship between the professional (physician, social worker, psychologist, teacher, and so on) and the family of a child with disabilities is often subtle but meaningful. Table 1.1 provides the contrasting approaches of past and present. According to the traditional view, the professional plays the role of the kindly but firm holder of knowledge who tries to provide needed information and skills to the parents. Parents are expected to receive this

Only when both parents understand and accept what each person's role and responsibilities will be in caring for a child with disabilities will there be family harmony.

To help empower parents, teachers might refer parents to any one of the many parent support groups for children with disabilities.

▬ ◗ **TABLE 1.1 Changing Views of Family Participation**	
Traditional Approach	**Current Approach**
Parents' greatest need is to accept the burden of raising their child and to become realistic about his or her limitations.	Families need to be encouraged to dream about what they want for themselves and their child with a disability, and they need assistance in making those dreams come true.
Parents' difficulties in coping with the child are largely psychological or psychiatric in nature, and the proper intervention is psychiatric or psychological counseling.	Families can benefit from each other. One benefit that almost all families need is the emotional resiliency and information that other families have acquired about life with disabilities.
Mothers need respite to alleviate the stress and burden of caring for their child.	Families need for the child with disabilities to have friends and integrated recreational options.
Mothers need the professional to provide clinical information about disability.	Families need information about and inspiration from people with a disability who are successfully integrated into community life.
Mothers need training related to skill development and behavior management so they can be follow-through teachers for their child.	Families need encouragement and ways to ensure that the child has a functional education taught in natural environments by natural helpers in those environments (e.g., family, friends, store clerks, bus drivers, scout leaders).
Many families are financially unable to meet their child's needs and should seek out-of-home placement.	Many families need new policies (e.g., direct subsidies and new tax credits) to help meet the financial demands associated with disability.

Source: From "Changing Views of Family Participation," in *Supporting Families with a Child with a Disability*, by A. Gartner, D. K. Lipsky, and A. P. Turnbull (1991). Baltimore: Paul H. Brookes, pp. 2–3. Reprinted by permission.

advice and counsel and carry out that advice in the best interests of their child. This traditional doctor-patient relationship puts family members in a passive and expectant attitude, waiting for the wisdom of the professional to be delivered before they feel free to act.

The current approach has the family actively seeking and collecting information from many different sources, particularly other parents of children with disabilities who have had experiences similar to their own. In this approach, the parents draw on the expertise of the professional community but make many of their own

"Acting Civil"

Deidre Davis attributes her current success to her parents, Bernice and Hilton, and her unique experience in growing up as a child with a disability.

"My parents gave me confidence and the ability to get to know different people. They instilled in me their appreciation for differences. They also gave me the knowledge that I could set any goal I wanted and that I would have their support. Because of them, I never had any sense of fear or failure," Davis confides.

Davis is the deputy assistant secretary of state for equal employment opportunity and civil rights for the U.S. Department of State. Davis who has T-3 paraplegia (a thoracic-level spinal cord injury), was appointed to her current position by President Clinton in November 1994. . . .

Growing Up

When Davis was 6 years old, she woke up one morning and found she could not walk. Davis says of the event, "I remember thinking, 'Hmm, maybe I'm still asleep. Let me try that again.'" Only Davis was not asleep; a tumor on her spinal cord had temporarily paralyzed her. The tumor was removed, but doctors emphasized she would not walk again.

However, after nine months of intensive rehabilitation, Davis was able to walk with braces. Mrs. Davis remembers, "Deidre never seemed to be afraid, she never cried, and I think we took our strength from her. When she was very young, I remember she said, 'This is my life, and I'm going to make the best of it.' I think she really has."

During Davis's rehabilitation, she had been home-schooled. Davis remembers, "When I was ready to go back to school, my parents decided that it was not conducive for me to go back to the neighborhood school because it was four stories high, with many steps." In other words, accessibility would be a problem. Davis's parents approached the school board and petitioned them to reassign their daughter to a different school. Davis remembers, "They told my parents that they 'shipped all of their handicapped kids' to another city. It didn't matter what your disability was, or your academic prowess, that was where they went." Davis's parents were against this educational homogenization and instead set out to find an accessible full-inclusion school. . . .

School Days

Davis notes that the first few months at her new school were far from easy. She was relentlessly teased and her classmates had plenty of ammunition. Not only was she a minority as a black child at the school, but having a disability set her apart as well. Davis points out some of these children definitely came from racist families, but for others, it was simply a lack of exposure. Davis emphasizes, "My parents and I knew that this school was the best for me academically and physically, so I wasn't going to go home and plead my case, saying, 'Let me out of this' because I knew what the alternative was."

Davis notes that eventually these same children who had been giving her a tough time grew to respect her because she proved herself as a good student and a regular kid. She showed them that she also enjoyed jokes, conversation, and playing. . . .

Davis declares, "My parents taught me to fight for myself. They never went the 'overprotective route' saying things like, 'Don't do that' or 'You're going to hurt yourself.' Their attitude was, 'Whatever you want to do, go ahead and try.'" And she did. . . . Davis excelled at tennis, gaining national ranking as a wheelchair tennis player. Her grandmother had been a professional tennis player in the Black American Tennis league, and her father had taught her how to play the net. Davis remembers, "I couldn't walk well, so I used the tennis racket as a cane, and I'd hit the ball, fall down, get up again, and do the same thing."

Aside from the constant encouragement and determination they had instilled in their daughter, Hilton and Bernice Davis also made a point not to protect or hide Deidre from other children who had special needs. "My parents sent me to a camp where there were other children like myself, and I think that this was a very proactive thing to do," Davis explains. . . . "Although I am not a parent, my own parents have taught me that you have to give a child self-esteem, an opportunity to be his or her own individual, and not to be overprotective. My parents did this for me, and I am truly grateful."

Source: "Acting Civil" by Jennifer C. Stolting from *Exceptional Parent*, September 1998, p. 74. Reprinted with the expressed consent and approval of *Exceptional Parent*, a monthly magazine for parents and families of children with disabilities and special health care needs. Subscription cost is $36 per year for 12 issues; Call 1-877-372-7368. Offices at 555 Kinderkamach Rd., Oradell, NJ 07649.

What Is the Context?

The proactive approach taken by Deidre and her parents provided Deidre with the confidence she needed to achieve her goals. Now an adult, Deidre has a professional position in the U.S. Department of State. At the time Deidre went to school, her parents had to work hard to find her a full-inclusion school that was also wheelchair accessible. But they were determined to provide Deidre with a good education.

Pivotal Issues for Teachers

What characteristics made Deidre an exceptional child? What are Deidre's strengths? How did Deidre's parents respond to their child's disability? How did Deidre's parents act as advocates for her? How did Deidre's peers influence her? How did she influence them? What was it like for Deidre to fit in at a new school?

Parents are active members of the multidisciplinary intervention team for children with disabilities. They can make valuable observations of the child, teach specific skills, and reinforce learning. *(© Jerry Howard/Positive Images)*

decisions about what is best for their child. These and other differences between the traditional and active approaches are described in Table 1.1.

Parents as Collaborators

Many intervention programs for children with disabilities are developed and monitored by a multidisciplinary team. The team may include the child's teacher, special educators, doctors, therapists, and parents. Parents serve three primary functions as collaborators in the child's education program. First, their observations of the child are a valuable source of information to the professionals. This information becomes part of the basis for the child's educational program and the evaluation of that program. Second, parents—especially the parents of preschoolers—often take an active part in the teaching process. They may be trained by team members to teach specific skills (such as living skills, preacademic skills, mobility skills, and communication skills) to their child. Third, with training, parents are able to reinforce learning. They are able to see that the functional skills the child learns in school are applied in the home. The shift over time has been to move the parent closer to the decision-maker role in each of these areas, or at least to encourage the parents to share their child's interests and capabilities with other parents.

Teachers can find support from parents by viewing them as collaborators in the child's education and by paying attention to the information parents provide about their exceptional child.

Parents as Advocates

The recognition that society and schools have a responsibility for exceptional children stemmed in large measure from the activities of some of those children's parents. Parents who were unable to get help for their children from local governments created their own programs in church basements, vacant stores, and any place that would house them. These informal groups, loosely formed around the common needs of the children, often provided important information to new parents struggling to find help for their children with disabilities. They were also a source of emotional support for parents, a means of sharing and solving the problems of accepting and living with exceptional children.

These groups quickly realized that fundamental changes were needed in the allocation of educational resources at local, state, and federal levels. A casual, haphazard approach was not going to provide the kind of help that parents or their exceptional children needed. Accordingly, large parents' groups, such as the National Association of Retarded Citizens and the United Cerebral Palsy Association in the 1940s and 1950s and the Association for Children with Learning Disabilities in the 1960s, began to form. Parents of children with Down syndrome, autism, and other specific conditions have also formed groups to ensure attention to their children's special needs. These parent organizations have successfully stimulated legislation at the state and federal levels providing for additional trained personnel, research, and other programs that have brought children with disabilities to the attention of the general public and have attracted more qualified people into the field.

Organized parents' groups for children who are gifted have only recently been formed and have not yet had the same political influence as the national organizations for children with disabilities. Still, these groups are helping the parents of children who are gifted cope with the problems of precocious development (Gallagher & Gallagher, 1994).

Siblings

We now know enough about the family environment to dismiss the proposition that two children experience the *same* environment when they are growing up merely because they live in the same household. Obviously the home environment is not the same for a child with disabilities as it is for his or her nondisabled sibling or for an older daughter as it is for a younger daughter. We should study the home environment through the eyes of the particular child with whom we are concerned. It is less important to know how much income the family has or how many siblings than it is to know how each family member perceives other family members (McCall, 1987).

Assumptions often made about families with a child with a disability are that the nondisabled sibling is inevitably neglected because the parents must pay so much attention to the child with disabilities, and that as a result the sibling becomes resentful of the child with disabilities. It is now clear that although this set of events may happen, it certainly doesn't have to happen, particularly when the parents are sensitive to sibling rivalry and the needs for attention for the siblings as well as for the child with disabilities (McHale & Gamble, 1989).

As McHale and Harris (1992) point out, siblings of the child with a disability spend at least the same amount of time with their mothers and receive the same type of discipline as their brother or sister with disabilities receives, although they do perform a greater amount of household tasks. The sibling who appears most vulnerable for special adjustment problems seems to be the older sibling to whom the parents have given special child-care responsibilities. As in other family situations, it is not so much the actions of the parents that count as how the sibling interprets those actions. If the sibling is sure of being loved and cared for by the parent, then being given additional responsibilities for the child with disabilities does not seem to matter (Powell & Gallagher, 1993).

Answering the siblings' questions is an important part of the parents' responsibilities. For example, consider the following questions, which are examples of what lies just below the surface in the concerns of siblings (Powell & Gallagher, 1993):

- Why does he behave so strangely?
- Can she grow out of this?
- Will other brothers and sisters also have disabilities?
- Will he ever be able to live on his own?
- Will I be expected to take care of her as an adult?
- Am I loved as much as my brother?
- How can I tell my best friends about my sister?
- What am I supposed to do when other children tease my brother?
- Will my own children be more likely to have a disability?

Just because a sibling doesn't verbalize such questions doesn't mean that he or she is not thinking about them. It is the parents' responsibility to try to answer even unverbalized questions that the brother or sister may have about the child with disabilities and how that special child is affecting, and will affect, the family system.

The number of questions that the sibling has does not diminish over time, and the content of and the concerns evident in the questions reflect developmental changes. For example, an illness or death of one of the parents may heighten the sibling's concern about his or her own responsibilities. If the parents are gone or no longer able to care for the special child, will the sibling be expected to share in the care of the child with disabilities throughout his or her lifetime? Each family has to answer those questions in its own way, but the answers must be clear and unambiguous for all family members. What kind of questions would you have if your brother or sister was a child with disabilities?

What happens when a younger sibling begins to surpass an older brother or sister with disabilities or begins to be ashamed of his or her deviant behavior? One sister described the guilt and love like this:

> I have a short story to tell. It is one of many stories of happiness and sorrow. It is a story of which I am not very proud, and one I have never told my parents. I will tell it now because it is time, and I have learned from my mistakes, as all people can.
>
> George is 21 years old today. He is a frequently happy, often troubled young man who has grown up in a society reluctant to accept and care for him even though he cannot fare for himself.
>
> I am very lucky. My crime was easily forgiven by someone who loved me very much, without reservation. George and I were very young. I was his frequent babysitter. As an older sister more interested in ponies and playing outdoors, I felt a great deal of resentment toward George and, of course, toward my persecutors, my mother and father. It was a day like any other day when I had been told to take care of George. They always seemed the same, those days, because I had no choice in the matter, and if I had one, I would have refused. It was that simple for me. I had better things to do.
>
> We were waiting in the car for our mother to come with the groceries. The recurring memory breaks my heart every time I think of it. He was antagonizing me again. Those unbearable, unreal sounds that haunted and humiliated me. They were the nonsense noises that made the neighborhood children speculate he was from

Mars. I could hear their taunts, and rage welled up in me. How could I have a brother like this? He was not right at all. He was a curse. I screamed at him to "shut up." He kept on. He wouldn't stop. My suppressed anger exploded. I raised my hand and slapped him again and again across his soft, round baby face. George began to cry, low, mournful whimpers. He never once raised a hand to protect himself. Shaking with fear and anger, [unable to think clearly,] I just looked at him. In that swift instance I felt more shame and revulsion for myself than I have ever felt toward anyone. The rude ugliness of it will never leave me. I hugged him to me, begging for forgiveness. And he gave it to me unconditionally. I shall never forget his sweet, sad face as he accepted my hugs.

In that instance I learned something of human nature and the nature of those who would reject people like George. I had been one of them: sullen, uncaring, unwilling to care for someone who came into the world with fewer advantages than I myself had. Today, I am a better person for having lived through both the good times and the bad times that our family experienced as a result of my brother's autism. I have a sense of understanding and compassion that I learned from growing up with George. Best of all, I have my brother, who loves me with all the goodness in his heart.

My message is simple. Look into your hearts and into the hearts of all people to see what is real, what makes them real people. For we are all the same. Accept people for what they are and work to make the world a receptive place—not just for those who are perceived as normal. (Warren, 1985, p. 227)

The Influence of School, Peer Culture, and the Community

The child's social context includes environmental forces beyond the family that interact with the child: the school, peers (neighborhood), and the larger community/society. Culture plays an important role as well, especially when the values of the home come into conflict with those of school and community. Children from diverse cultural backgrounds often encounter conflicting expectations and values in the home and in the school. Teachers can help these children by being acutely aware of the wide range of norms represented in their classrooms. When values honored by the school, such as competitiveness and willingness to work at a desk with a minimum of talking, conflict with a minority subculture's preference for cooperation and for lively discussion about problems, then tensions arise between families and school. Such tensions are often increased by the presence of an exceptional child.

The strength of environmental forces varies as the child grows: Initially the family is predominant in caring for the child and acts as a link between the child and the larger environment. Children from diverse cultural backgrounds may be confused by differences between family values and school or societal values, an issue that the child often confronts for the first time when entering school. The support of the family continues to be important but is joined by other factors as the child grows.

As the child grows older, the peer group becomes a major force. Adolescence, with its focus on social development and career orientation, is a special challenge for the exceptional child. Potential rejection by the peer group can have a power-

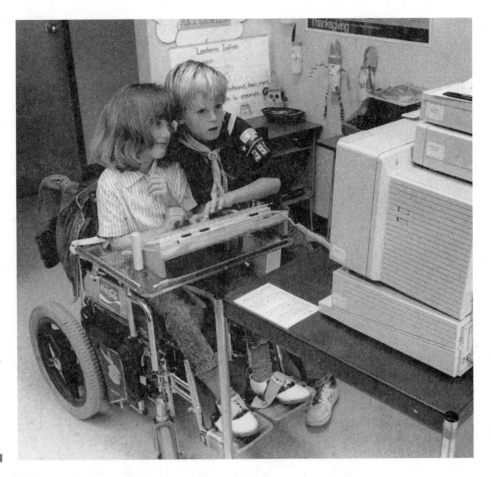

The support of the family in caring for the child continues to be important as the child grows, but it is joined by other factors, especially the school, peers, and the community. *(© Richard S. Orton/The Picture Cube)*

ful influence on the adaptation of the child with disabilities or the child with special talents, as it can on any vulnerable and self-conscious adolescent.

Finally, society, which includes the community and work environment, influences the adult who is trying to make the transition to a relatively independent lifestyle. Throughout their lives, many exceptional adults will be in contact with a support system that includes advocates, educators, friends, and service providers. In addition, representatives of the larger society (such as government leaders) often make rules that determine whether the exceptional child gets needed resources or is given an opportunity to succeed at some level of independence. (We discuss these environments further in Chapter 2.) All these forces contribute to the full picture of the exceptional individual.

THE INFLUENCE OF CULTURE

Culture refers to the attitudes, values, customs, and language that family and friends transmit to children. These attitudes, values, customs, and language have been passed down from generations of ancestors and have formed an identifiable pattern or heritage. The child is embedded in the family, its habits, and its traditions; this is as true for the child with special needs as for one who does not show special needs. Although the child may be only dimly aware of these cultural influences, it makes a world of difference to the child's experiences if his or her family is fourth-generation American or first-generation Italian, Nigerian, or Taiwanese.

Respect for the breadwinner, attitudes toward religion, child-rearing practices, and even political choices or tendencies may reflect the attitudes of the cultural group to which the family belongs. So it is important to consider cultural factors as one more dimension needing study and understanding if we as teachers are to be effective in helping these children fulfill their capabilities.

Here are some examples of how cultural values affect the child with special needs: If a family comes from a culture that emphasizes a dominant masculine role, how will the father of a child with disabilities respond to a female professional? Will he reject her advice and suggestions just to maintain his own masculine self-image? And what does he feel about his son who has disabilities that are so serious that the father despairs of the boy ever being able to play that masculine role? Such issues are not talked about easily but can rest at the heart of parental concerns for many years.

FAMILIES FROM DIVERSE CULTURES

The United States has long been proud of its role of accepting people from cultures around the world. Over the years, immigrants and their children have adapted but not without some pain and difficulty.

One of the first challenges that children from diverse cultures present to educators is whether they can be correctly identified as exceptional children in the first place. Obviously, giving a child who doesn't speak English an IQ test in English is a bad idea. But the problem is more complicated than that.

It appears that children who have had essentially little or no schooling do not even think in the same way as is assumed by intelligence tests (Rogoff & Chavajay, 1995). It apparently takes some schooling to teach them to categorize objects or use logical reasoning and inference. Nonschooled individuals seem to prefer to come to conclusions on the basis of experience rather than relying on the information in the problem alone.

How, then, can we determine if immigrant children are learning disabled, mentally retarded, or merely developing in a typical way for their cultural background? All too often, immigrant or minority children are inappropriately referred to special education services when, in fact, they need a very different set of experiences and grounding in the cognitive nature of the school program (Harry, 1992).

The term *minority* in our society traditionally has been reserved for persons who are "not white." The federal government recognizes five classifications based on race and ethnicity: Native American or Alaskan Native, Asian or Pacific Islander, Hispanic, African American, and Caucasian. But even with those categories there are major differences. Under Hispanic is included Mexican, Puerto Rican, Cuban, Central American, and South American, cultures that are obviously very different from one another. Thus, the term *minority* means little beyond the possibility of adjustment problems for the families and for the child in fitting into a dominant white, European culture, on top of the problem of adapting as an exceptional child.

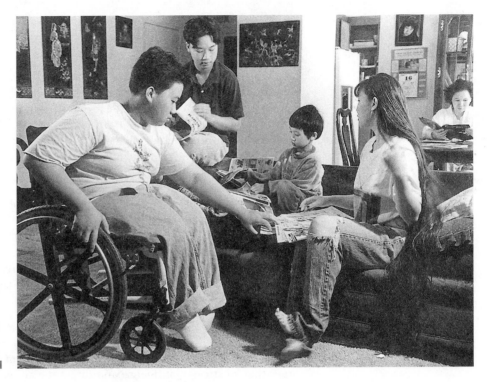

Correctly identifying children from diverse cultures as exceptional is an ongoing challenge. (© *Lydia Gans*)

The following quotations from Harry (1992) give a flavor of some of the family adjustments that have to be made.

> In our countries, when children get spanked, they do not think their parents don't love them. I knew my parents did it because they loved me. They taught me manners and to be obedient. That's the way they see it. But here it's a whole different ballgame and the parents feel like they're in a system that is very fearful because if you behave like a parent should behave, you might lose your children. And the kids use the system. I know kids who have turned their parents in. The kid learns the system right away. So the parents feel helpless. . . . It's not that they hit all the time—it's a last alternative, but you use it and there is a case worker at your door. So the parents are frightened, they feel they're losing control of their children. Child Protective Services—Children's Division! That's the most feared word on the whole West Side!

> When I moved down here I was tired of Jose staying down in the special class. He was always in kindergarten, they never let him pass to the first grade because they say he doesn't know the work. But how can Jose know something if you don't tell him how to do it? All they did was painting and some little stuff—every day the same thing. So when I came here I told them I lost the school papers and I put him in regular first grade. He failed one year but the next year he passed, and he never failed since then, and he gets A's and B's in the regular class because he is very intelligent.

> It is only their opinions that matter. If I do not want the child in a special class, or if I want her in a different school they will still do what they want. Because that is what I tried to do, and Vera [an agency social worker] helped me and we tried, but they did not listen to us. Our opinions are not valued.

Many parents do not want their child in a special class or in a school so far away, but they keep quiet. It is very hard to struggle with these Americans. . . . Here in America, the schools are for Americans.

One of the responsibilities of teachers and teachers-to-be trying to be culturally aware is self-awareness (Turnbull & Turnbull, 1997). It is important that teachers are aware what factors shape their own cultural views, in particular, to know that their cultural beliefs and traditions may work well for them but not necessarily for others. Cultural differences change and modify the special education for individual exceptional children, and adjustments have to be made in each instance.

It is easy—sometimes tempting—to focus on the differences between yourself as a teacher and the families. A useful task is to identify the strengths of the culture of the family. Whatever the immediate problems the family and the exceptional child may come with, it is a rarity that they do not also come with strengths, such as making the child feel loved and accepted, a willingness to seek support from friends and counselors, a strong religious faith, and a caring extended family (Turnbull & Turnbull, 1997). Such strengths are to be respected and used as a foundation on which to build an educational strategy for the child.

It is important for teachers to identify the strengths of students and their families who are from diverse cultures.

CULTURE AND ASSESSMENT

When cultural values and attitudes differ substantially from the middle-class values that so strongly influence and direct the activities of the public schools, then predictable adaptation problems arise for children from culturally diverse circumstances and for their educators (Good, 1987).

Consider Jorge, a 10-year-old Hispanic child with learning disabilities that prevent him from grasping the reading process. Jorge comes from a rich tradition of a close-knit family with common interests and loyalty. The family is wary about the Anglo schools that Jorge is attending. When teachers and psychologists who are of a culture different from that of the family tell the family that something is wrong with Jorge's approach to school, are they reflecting a prejudice against Jorge because of his Hispanic background and his bilingual family? Are they going to help Jorge, or is this a way to prevent Jorge from getting a proper education? Will Jorge's father, misunderstanding the school's message, put even *more* pressure on Jorge to do well in school, assuming that his son is not giving proper effort to his school lessons? The opportunities for misunderstanding from one culture to another are great and can substantially complicate the original learning problems faced by the exceptional child.

One of the observations that can be quickly made is that students in special education programs often are disproportionately of one gender or ethnic or racial background (or a combination). This observation applies whether we are viewing programs for children with mental retardation, with intellectual giftedness, or with emotional disturbance. Such a result has raised many questions in the minds of educators and the general public. Why should there be an excess of African-American students in programs for the mentally retarded (Heller, Holtzman, & Messick, 1982), an excess of Hispanic students in programs for learning disabilities (Cummins, 1986), and an excess of Asian students in programs for the intellectually gifted (Gallagher, 1991)? Some answers to these questions can be found in the nature of the assessment itself, the environmental conditions in which the child was raised, and differing family and school values.

PARENTS OF CHILDREN WHO ARE GIFTED AND TALENTED

Parents with children who are gifted (children who are developing intellectually far in advance of their agemates) have a set of concerns different from those of parents of children with disabilities. Although these concerns do not involve a child's survival or a child's ability to become an independent adult, they can cause worry and conflicts in family life.

Among the concerns common to parents of a child who is gifted and talented is whether they are doing enough to nurture and cultivate their child's talents. Are they, through inaction or the wrong actions, causing their child's obvious talents to wither and diffuse into mediocrity? Once parents realize that they have a child who is gifted, they often become extremely concerned about their parenting. Is their child's ability like a crystal vase that will shatter if they make a false move? These parents often seek counsel and advice to make sure they are doing the right thing. Parents in a cohesive family unit who emphasize optimum achievement for the child as well as high self-esteem do seem to produce more children who are high achievers (Olszewski, Kulieke, & Buescher, 1987). Parents are justified in believing that they are an important influence on their child's development and performance.

Parents who emphasize optimum achievement and high self-esteem seem to produce more children who are high achievers.

Many parents are aware of the importance of education in nurturing the talents of a child with special gifts. How can they be sure that their child is getting a "good education"? They are often concerned about whether the public schools can provide good educational experiences for a gifted child. Such concerns are reinforced when parents are informed that their child cannot enter elementary school until he or she reaches a certain age even though the child can perform at the second- or third-grade level in academic subjects, or that the local school has no special program for children who are gifted but are not yet 9 or 10 years old (Gallagher & Gallagher, 1994).

Another concern is whether their child's obvious differences will lead to rejection by the child's agemates. Many parents remember the fate of other gifted individuals at the hands of their peers (Socrates and Galileo, for example) and, as a consequence, do not want any special attention directed to their child. They may turn down special programs designed to enhance their child's education because such programs would cause the child's special talents to be revealed to the larger (and perhaps unfriendly) peer society.

Undoubtedly, many parents of children with disabilities would willingly exchange places with the parents of a child who is gifted, but we should not assume that the presence of such a child in the family is a source of uncomplicated joy and pleasure to conscientious parents.

In the next chapter, we explore institutional outside forces (such as school, legislation, and the courts) and their effects on the exceptional child.

Summary of Major Ideas

1. The exceptional child differs from the average child to the extent that he or she needs special educational services to reach full potential.

2. The major categories of exceptionality within the field of special education include children with intellectual differences (unusually fast or slow); communication differences; learning disabilities; sensory differences, including auditory and visual impairments; behavioral differences, including problems with emotional and social adaptation; multiple and severe disabilities; and physical differences.

3. A relatively new category, attention-deficit hyperactivity disorder (ADHD), has been added to the exceptional children roster.

4. Special educators have moved from a medical model, which stresses that the physical condition exists within the patient, to an ecological model, which focuses on the individual's interaction with the environment.

5. The success of the family-focused approach depends on its acceptance by professionals.

6. We now know that heredity influences (but does not finally determine) intelligence, temperament, personality, and behavior.

7. Families from diverse cultures may have differing values and child-rearing practices, which compounds the problems of adaptation for the child with special needs in their family.

8. Exceptional children show both inter-individual (among children) and intra-individual (within a child) differences. Both kinds of differences require special adaptation by the teacher and the school.

9. Our new knowledge of genetics suggests that environmental changes can activate previously inactive genes, creating new heredity-environment interactions and affecting behavior.

10. The adjustment of siblings of children with disabilities depends on parental sensitivities to their needs.

11. The new movement toward parent empowerment gives parents more influence on the special or remedial programs established for their child. It also is causing a rethinking of the traditional roles played by professionals.

12. Parents of a child with intellectual gifts do not have the same problems as parents of a child with disabilities, but they do have concerns about how to maximize their child's potential, how to protect against social isolation, whether the school is providing appropriate services for their child, and so on.

Unresolved Issues

Every generation leaves, as its legacy to the next generation, certain problems for which solutions have not been found. There are many issues in the field of special education that today's professionals have been either unable or unwilling to resolve. The end-of-chapter sections entitled "Unresolved Issues" briefly describe widely debated topics as a beginning agenda for the current generation of students, who will face these problems in their professional or private lives.

1. *The identification of exceptional children.* The boundary line separating exceptional children from nonexceptional children has become blurred where children with mild disabilities are concerned. Yet legislation and the courts call for eligibility standards to clearly separate those who should receive spe-

cial help from those who should not. How do we distinguish, for example, between the child who is emotionally disturbed and the child who is suffering a temporary behavior problem?

2. *The family system.* For many years, special educators focused only on the exceptional child and excluded the child's environment. Increasingly we have become aware that the child is only one component in a complex family system and that many elements within that system can have a positive or negative impact on the child. Interacting constructively with the family system is a new objective of special education that has yet to be incorporated fully in our personnel preparation or educational programs.

3. *Lifespan development and transition.* Most special educators see exceptional children only for a limited period of time: the school years. They miss two significant stages of development: early childhood, in which important patterns of behavior are set, and adulthood, the period for which special programs supposedly prepare exceptional children. We are seeing a new awareness of the importance of transitions in the psychosocial life of the individual at whatever point in the developmental sequence it occurs.

4. *Uncertain funding.* A chronic problem facing those who provide services for children with exceptionalities is obtaining the financial support necessary to conduct such programs. There is often disagreement about which level of government (federal, state, local) should pay for these special services. Taxpayers are often reluctant, and sometimes court action or legislative mandates are needed to provide necessary support. Uncertain funding makes it difficult to develop long-range, multiyear plans.

Key Terms

culture p. 23
ecological model of exceptionality p. 8
exceptional child p. 2
family-focused approach p. 11

family harmony p. 15
intra-individual differences p. 9
medical model of exceptionality p. 8
parent empowerment p. 15

Questions for Thought

1. When is a child considered to be educationally exceptional? pp. 2–3

2. What caused the movement from a medical model of exceptionality to an ecological model? p. 8

3. Why is the trend toward early intervention increasing the importance of the family in intervention programs? pp. 10–12

4. What are the special burdens of families with children who are disabled? pp. 13–15

5. What role have parents played in the expansion of services for exceptional children? pp. 19–20

6. What special role do educators play in supporting families with disabled children? p. 22

7. What are the special concerns of children who are gifted? p. 27

Resources for Further Study

REFERENCES OF SPECIAL INTEREST

Dunst, C., Trivette, C., Starnes, A., Hamby, D., & Gordon, N. (1993). *Building and evaluating family support initiatives.* Baltimore: Paul H. Brookes Publishing Co.
This book is a report on a nationwide study of the application and effectiveness of family support programs whose purpose is to enable and empower people by enhancing and promoting individual and family capabilities that support and strengthen family functioning. The authors point out many political, bureaucratic, and economic factors that affect the family support initiative and argue that the belief systems of the families and of the service providers are also key to the implementation of family support policies.

Gottlieb, G. (1997). *Synthesizing nature-nurture: Prenatal roots of instinctive behavior.* Mahwah, NJ: Lawrence Erlbaum Associates.
A fascinating look into the rapidly developing field of genetics and its possible influence on education. In this volume, the author proposes that one can change the behavior of animals and humans through changes in the environment, triggering different sets of genes and changing the developmental process without the long wait for evolution to take place.

Harry, B. (1992). *Cultural diversity, families, and the special education system.* New York: Teachers College Press.
This volume focuses attention on the special conditions of an increasing number of minority families who have children referred for special education services. Harry emphasizes the issues of power and responsibility in the relationship of school systems and the families who are often poor and uninformed about special education and its implications for their children.

Lesar, S., Trivette, C., & Dunst, C. (Eds.). (1996). Families of children and adolescents with special needs [Special issue]. *Exceptional Children, 62*(3), 182–197.
This special issue contains a series of articles that focuses on the families of children and youth with disabilities. The emphasis of most of the articles is on the ecological role played by forces within and outside the family. Issues such as additional stress on the family unit, various strategies for helping families cope with the special needs of their children, and a desirable social policy for families are covered.

Powell, T., & Gallagher, P. (1993). *Brothers and sisters* (2nd ed.). Baltimore: Paul H. Brookes Publishing Co.
This volume provides an excellent synthesis of what is known about an important but often neglected aspect of the families of children with disabilities: the siblings. The authors address the special problems of brothers and sisters adapting to the presence of a child with disabilities. Among their important conclusions is that the quality of family relationships depends more on how the parents treat the various members of the family than on the particular presence of an exceptional child.

Rutter, M., & Rutter, M. (1993). *Developing minds.* New York: Basic Books.
This remarkably clear, readable, and concise portrait of what we know about the development of children and adults provides a fine basis for the consideration of what exceptionality, as a departure from normality, means.

Simeonsson, R. (1994). *Risk, resilience and prevention.* Baltimore: Paul H. Brookes Publishing Co.
Most efforts to improve the conditions of children focus on coping with crises that have become too serious to ignore. This book addresses the issue of preventing problems

from occurring in the first place. Problems such as adolescent pregnancy, child abuse, drug use, dropping out of school, and behavior disorders are discussed by experts.

Turnbull, A., & Turnbull, H. (1997). *Families, professionals, and exceptionality: A special partnership* (3rd ed.). Upper Saddle River, NJ: Merrill.
A popular book focusing on families who have an exceptional child and their needs. It explores the interaction of parents and schools and suggests many ways for both sides to collaborate effectively to the benefit of the exceptional child. The authors are both professionals and parents of an exceptional child, and their understanding of both roles helps to make this a valuable book.

JOURNALS

Exceptional Children
Council for Exceptional
Children (CEC)
1920 Association Dr.
Reston, VA 20191-1589
Voice phone: 703-620-3660
TTY: 703-264-9446
FAX: 703-264-9494
E-mail: cecpubs@cec.sped.org
http://www.cec.sped.org

Journal of Special Education
PRO-ED Journals
5341 Industrial Oaks Blvd.
Austin, TX 78735-8809
http://www.proedinc.com/store/16.html

Journal of Special Education Technology
Peabody College, Box 328
Vanderbilt University
Nashville, TN 37203
615-322-8407
http://peabody.vanderbilt.edu/peabody

Teacher Education and Special Education
Boyd Printing Company, Inc.
49 Sheridan Ave.
Albany, NY 12201

Teaching Exceptional Children
Council for Exceptional Children (CEC)
1920 Association Dr.
Reston, VA 20191-1589
Voice phone: 703-620-3660
TTY: 703-264-9446
FAX: 703-264-9494
E-mail: cecpubs@cec.sped.org
http://www.cec.sped.org

PROFESSIONAL ORGANIZATIONS

Council for Exceptional Children (CEC)
1920 Association Dr.
Reston, VA 20191-1589
Voice phone: 703-620-3660
TTY: 703-264-9446
FAX: 703-264-9494
E-mail: cecpubs@cec.sped.org
http://www.cec.sped.org

2

Exceptional Children and Their Environment

FOCUSING
questions

How has the educational reform movement affected exceptional children?

In what ways can cultural differences affect special education students and programs?

What are some of the learning environments being used today for exceptional children?

How are special educators using technology to teach exceptional students?

How have the courts influenced the development of educational services for exceptional children?

How a society feels about its diverse membership, particularly about citizens who are different, is expressed through the institutions of that society. A close look at the major institutions of our society—the schools, the legislatures, and the courts—should tell us a lot about the place of exceptional children in our society.

- The *schools* design programs to prepare these students for a productive and satisfying adult life.
- The *legislatures* provide the money and authority for the special arrangements necessary to meet the special needs of these students.
- The *courts* rule on what is fair, just, and equitable with regard to these students.

Each of these social institutions has its own rules and traditions that influence how decisions are made and conclusions reached in its domain. This chapter touches briefly on how each of them affects the child who is exceptional in our society. Take, for example, Dan.

Dan is a 5-year-old with Down syndrome, a genetic condition that will affect his entire life. He has mental retardation and other problems caused by this genetic accident. Yet how Dan will fare in life will depend to a large degree on the environmental circumstances around him.

Will Dan do better in a loving, rather than a rejecting, family? Will he do better in a neighborhood with some comfort and resources than he would do in an urban ghetto? Will Dan do better in a school program that recognizes his problems and adapts the program to his needs instead of unfairly expecting him to meet some kind of "normal" standard? Of course!

No matter what the degree of exceptionality, how the child will eventually adapt to life is determined in large measure by how the environmental forces outside the child facilitate or inhibit his or her development. That is why we spend so much time studying these outside forces, which we refer to as the ecology of the child, or the *context* of the child.

In Chapter 1, we stressed the importance of understanding the context of the exceptional child as well as his or her individual characteristics. The family ranks first among influences on the growing and developing child, and the subculture in which the family lives contributes much to his or her development as well. Many other external influences help shape the child's development, particularly later in life. Neither Dan nor his family, though, will likely know the degree to which the actions of legislatures and courts have played a role in his education.

How the exceptional child adjusts to adulthood is determined in large measure by his or her interactions with these forces and the way in which they are mediated by family and by the child's unique characteristics. It is difficult, if not impossible, to predict the outcome of special education services for a specific individual because of the range of each child's response and potential.

We begin with an overview of society's attitudes toward the education of exceptional individuals. By looking at how society has viewed exceptional students and directed its resources to them, we can better understand how schools treat these youngsters and what is expected from them.

◖▬▬ *A Historical Perspective*

During the last century, there have been enormous changes in the way society treats exceptional children, moving from rejection and the charitable isolation of children with disabilities to acceptance of them as contributing members of society. The current level of acceptance has few precedents, representing a much more enlightened view than was evident even in the immediate past.

As we look back in time, we find that the notion of educating *every* child to achieve his or her greatest potential is a relatively new idea. The current use of the term *exceptional* is itself a reflection of radical change in society's view of people who differ from the norm. The world has come a long way from the Spartans' practice of killing infants who didn't meet their standard of normalcy, but the journey has been slow, moving from neglect and mistreatment, to pity and overprotection, and finally to acceptance and integration into society to the fullest extent possible.

In the United States, attitudes toward individuals with disabilities have followed a similar pattern of development. Before 1850 there were few public provisions for children or adults with special needs. They were "stored away" in poorhouses and other charitable centers or left at home and given no educational opportunities. It was estimated that, as late as 1850, 60 percent of the inmates of this country's poorhouses were people who were deaf, blind, "insane," or "idiots."

RESIDENTIAL SCHOOLS

Nineteenth-century reformers such as Horace Mann, Samuel Gridley Howe, and Dorothea Dix gave impetus to the establishment of residential schools for children with disabilities. From 1817 to the beginning of the Civil War, a span of more than forty years, many states established residential schools for children who were deaf, blind, mentally retarded, or orphaned, patterning them after similar schools in Europe. In 1817, the American Asylum for the Education and Instruction of the Deaf, a residential institution, was opened in Hartford, Connecticut. Today it is called the American School for the Deaf. In 1829, the New England Asylum for the Blind— later renamed the Perkins School—was founded in Watertown, Massachusetts. Thirty years later, a residential school for the mentally retarded, the Massachusetts School for Idiotic and Feebleminded Youth, was established in South Boston. This school is now called the Fernald State School for the Mentally Retarded. These schools offered training, but equally important they provided an environment that often protected the individual throughout life (Smith, 1998).

PUBLIC SCHOOLS

The first special class for deaf children in a public school was held in Boston in 1869. Not until 1896 was the first special class for children who were mentally retarded organized, in Providence, Rhode Island. It was followed in 1899 by a class for children with physical impairments and, in 1900, by a class in Chicago for children who were blind. Since 1900, special programs and services for exceptional children have been organized in the majority of public schools throughout the nation.

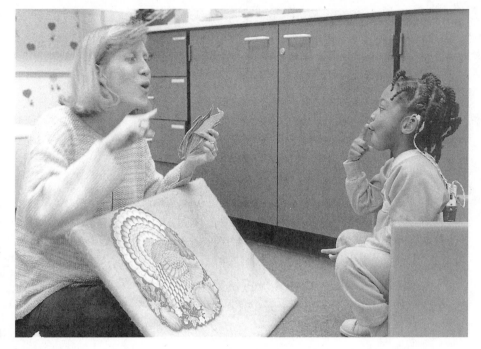

The exceptional child's adjustment to adulthood is determined in large measure by his or her interactions with the school, the culture, and the society and by the way in which these interactions are mediated by the family and the child's unique characteristics. *(© Elizabeth Crews)*

The Exceptional Child and the School

Certainly one of the most significant of all our social institutions is the schools. Schools in large measure are a mirror of our society as a whole. Most of the values taught there reflect the values of the dominant sectors of society. Many of the problems encountered in the schools, such as lack of motivation, drug use, and violence, are part of the larger societal fabric.

The thrust toward greater social and educational integration has brought many exceptional children and adults into the regular educational system and community from segregated settings and focused efforts on extending services to include early childhood and adulthood. In previous decades, the major thrust was to release children with disabilities from large state schools and institutions. Terms such as *de-institutionalization* and *normalization* were used to mark this movement.

The changing social environment of exceptional children has spawned a new and different vocabulary. Two terms that are in common use today are *inclusion* and *continuum of services*. These terms reflect the interest of society in trying to integrate exceptional children and adults more effectively into the community at large.

- **Inclusion** is the process of bringing all, or nearly all, exceptional children into the general classroom for their education.
- **Continuum of services** refers to the range of placements that may constitute the least restrictive environment.

In recent years, special educators have taken a lifespan perspective toward the provision of special education services. This involves the extension of special education services from the traditional school years back to early childhood and forward to adulthood.

"One Child Is Included"

Within the process of systems change there are always individual children who are, by virtue of opportunity, catalysts for change. Our daughter Kate is a "pioneer" in New Jersey, as a second-grader fully participating in Mrs. Johnson's class at McKinley School in Westfield. Since she has been participating in regular classes, it is very difficult to capture the changes in Kate without a "before" and "after" video, but I will try to paint a picture of the differences.

Kate has been receiving intensive special education services since she was 8 months old, when our family began participation in an early intervention program. Joining a program which had at its heart the belief that parents are the experts regarding their children was tremendously empowering and got us off to a good start. It was in this first three years that we created a vision for our family which included the determination that one day Kate would grow up in a world of close friends, that she would have meaningful employment, and that she would contribute to her community.

Even then, we adopted the philosophy of "integrate early and often," though at the time we were not aware of the concept of "inclusion." We just went ahead and enrolled Kate in Baby Dance (an exercise program) and in family day care with typical children two mornings a week. Saying "we just enrolled Kate" grossly minimizes the real level of concern we had about whether we and Kate would survive the experiences, but we made the decision anyway in spite of our fears that we would not find acceptance. In fact, people always reached out to Kate.

After graduating from early intervention, Kate entered a preschool which again focused on creating a "normalized" experience for her. Despite the objections of very caring professionals—"Two programs will be too much for her!"—we registered Kate in a dual program. In the morning she attended our neighborhood Montessori School, and in the afternoon she was bused across the city to a public school program for children with blindness and multiple disabilities. The need for the two programs occurred because it was not possible for her to receive the related services of speech, occupational, and physical therapies and orientation and mobility training within the private school.

One Flash of Insight!

Family members have what I would call "lightning rod" experiences, when they are struck with insight in a flash. The dual program provided us with just this sort of experience. The Montessori school teachers were concerned with educating the "whole child," and sought to develop in children skills of communication, concern for others, and an eagerness to accept new experiences.

Geri Kennedy, Kate's Montessori teacher, wrote of her that "the emergence of spring and warm weather led to the blossoming of friendships between Kate and her classmates. During our daily trips to the playground, we discovered that although she did not yet walk independently, Kate loved to be physically active. The children naturally and enthusiastically included her in their turns on the swing, on the slide, and in the sandbox. Through this increased involvement with the other kids, Kate's language ability expanded much more quickly than it had through contact with her more doting teachers. The children expected Kate to let them know what she wanted, and Kate constantly surprised us with her improving ability to tell them."

Andrea Lo, the newly appointed integration facilitator, realized very soon that we would need to meet regularly to fine-tune the program. She brought Kate's schedule to an early meeting and we problem solved—literally moment by moment—how Kate could be included and actively participate in all aspects of classroom life.

We tried to build in supports by the typical children whenever possible instead of always relying on adults to assist Kate. The integration strategies were prepared by Mrs. Lo and included in Kate's Individualized Education Program. It is important to stress that Kate is working on her own goals and objectives within the regular classroom.

Flexible, Capable Teachers

Mrs. Johnson is Kate's regular teacher. She watched Kate grow from across the hall and "volunteered" to have Kate join her second-grade class. She is challenged by our daughter and has risen to the task. She attended computer classes and a program offered by the Commission for the Blind for teachers in the community. She is a seasoned teacher and approaches her work with a good sense of humor.

What makes Mrs. Johnson just right for Kate is that she "owns" Kate's education. She views herself as the person primarily responsible for our daughter's education and draws upon the consultants who visit her room to guide her. Administrative support from the school principal, Mr. Braynock, has enabled Mrs. Johnson to set aside time to learn new skills.

Special Education: A Service, Not a Place

Currently, Kate attends a regular second-grade class. She is greeted each morning by a friend who serves as a "sighted guide," helping Kate get from the playground to her class, acting as Kate's partner for the week, and sitting next to Kate. Because there was too much daily discussion among all the children about who would be chosen to be Kate's guide, a schedule had to be devised to designate who could be her buddy.

The New Jersey Commission for the Blind provides a braille teacher and an orientation and mobility specialist who are consultants to the regular education teacher and work directly with Kate. Kate has been able to learn most of the alphabet. Now when we go shopping and find a can of peaches, Kate takes a braille stick-on label with the letter "p" and attaches it to the can. When we get home and she puts it away, she remembers that the can with the "p" is for "peaches." It is not necessary for Kate to learn to read "Plato" in school (though who knows what her interests will be!) but we want our daughter to have some functional reading skills.

Kate gave her class a braille lesson, completing a spelling assignment on her braille machine. The children were impressed because Kate knows this special code, and they wanted to learn how to write their names. Her braille teacher showed them how this was done. This past spring, Kate sent each child a valentine that she had signed herself.

The orientation and mobility specialist is very important to Kate. She is teaching Kate how to find her way around her school and the neighborhood by using her cane and good reasoning skills. It's not that easy to learn how to "map" a community in your mind and travel safely.

For forty minutes each day, Kate receives resource room services to work on "survival skills" (activities of daily living), as well as language and math instruction. Recently, after learning about coins during her math lesson, Kate accompanied her resource room teacher, Mrs. Mankowski, across the street to the little convenience store, where she bought her own oatmeal cookies. This "functional" instruction is very important because it helps Kate understand how what she is learning has direct and practical application in the real world.

Whenever possible, related services (those that help Kate benefit from her educational program) have been provided by including other typical kids within her class. For example, the occupational therapist visits Kate's classroom during recess just after lunch. She works with Kate on a game that involves other children. Kate is learning how to play and take turns, which is a very big challenge for children with blindness.

Kate's speech therapist spent a summer researching software for the classroom computer. She was responsible for the installation of an ECHO, which helps Kate recognize what appears on the computer screen. The ECHO is equipped with a voice output so that when Kate types an "a," for example, the machine says "a." The speech therapist has been teaching keyboard skills and invites another child to work with Kate. This has proved beneficial for everyone: The other children learn keyboarding and Kate has good language models around her.

The person with the most demanding job in support of Kate is the teaching assistant, Mrs. Vincenti. She has been Kate's aide over the past four years. Initially, her role was to remain with Kate and guide her throughout the day in the segregated program. Kate views Mrs. Vincenti as her "grandmother" and they have grown very close. At this point, however, we are asking Mrs. Vincenti to step back a bit so that the regular education classroom teacher is primarily responsible for interacting with Kate.

Because changing roles and expectations is very difficult, teaching assistants need support in learning about different ways to assist students. Now Mrs. Vincenti can be more available to help other children in the class while identifying situations where Kate might need a small modification in instruction—a science lesson, for example, during which Mrs. Vincenti hands Kate a live plant when talking about the parts of a plant.

Social Growth . . . For Everyone

In a planning session last week, Ted Kozlik, our director of special education, was reminiscing about a day four years ago when Kate was in a segregated class outside our district. He recalled Kate walking down the hall with her physical therapist, screaming at the top of her lungs. This was not an unusual sight in those days. He remarked that Kate has made tremendous progress in the way she manages her feelings.

"The children in turn had the too rare opportunity to ask questions openly about Kate's blindness and special needs. They began to understand when and where she would need help, and when she would not. They had a chance to explore and ask questions about adaptive aids, such as braille story books, and a 'beeper ball' that became a favorite toy for everyone." There was an overall sense of joy and great expectations.

Kate gradually learned all twenty of the children's names and could recognize many of them by voice cues alone. By contrast, in the afternoon she was treated as if she were severely disabled. She was in a classroom (which had previously served as a storage closet) that included four other children with total blindness and little verbal communication. A series of therapists would interact with Kate in order to provide services. While I know that her teacher loved her and did offer Kate some new experiences designed for a tactile learner, it was very difficult to find a sense of joy in the class.

It was that perception of the absence of joy that really disturbed me, combined with a very uneasy feeling that Kate was, in fact, "learning helplessness." In the morning Montessori program, Kate learned how to negotiate the complex environment of a large Victorian-era school building and became independent in the bathroom to such an extent that she learned where to put her paper towel after she washed her hands. In the afternoon program, she was always guided by an adult and "assisted with toileting." We heard little from Kate about her classmates in the afternoon.

The contrasts in the expectations of Kate were so profound that we were struck—literally clobbered—with the insight that maybe Kate belonged in the real world of regular education. However, it was not until three years later, when Kate taught us another lesson, that we fully acted on this insight.

Opening the Doors

Hank and I wrote a letter to our director of special education and our superintendent of schools requesting an opportunity for Kate to be included in a regular grammar school in our town. We emphasized our wish to work collaboratively with the administration, child evaluation team, and Kate's educators. We reviewed our reasons for wanting an integrated program for Kate. Our reasons then were the same as they are now:

First, we want Kate to have friends. Just being with others creates opportunities for friendship. Sometimes the process of building friendships needs a little support from helping adults and, even better, from peers. Think of the most important moments in your life. Your friends very likely were part of those moments.

Second, we want Kate to contribute to our community. People in our society have many misconceptions about persons with disabilities; being with typical kids gives people a chance to see the strengths in Kate and get beyond some of her challenges. Kate sings in church choir and takes regular swimming lessons at our YMCA. Last year she was invited to join the Brownie troop and learned and taught others about being a good citizen.

Third, we want Kate to learn more in general. Kate participates in an environment which stresses social and academic growth through a wide range of activities. She is exposed to the entire second-grade curriculum with modifications as needed. She is not stuck "getting ready" for the mainstream. She is getting ready for adult life by being included in ordinary places with ordinary people just like anyone else.

Source: Diana Cuthbertson, "One Child Is Included," *Children Today*, 20 (March–April 1991), p. 6. Reprinted by permission.

What Is the Context?

School is a powerful link between the contexts of family and the community. In this article, the three contexts are interrelated: Kate's parents argued for her right to be included; her parents supported her by creating a "vision" of success for the family; the integrated school environment and caring teachers encouraged Kate to make friends and learn more. The social and academic preparation she has received may allow her to avoid a life of sheltered workshops and dependence and instead become a contributing member of the community.

Pivotal Issues for Teachers

Discuss the roles of each teacher-specialist. What are some criteria for successful integration experiences that you can infer from this article?

LIFESPAN PERSPECTIVE

At one time, most children with special needs did not receive special services before the third or fourth grade, after they had failed in the regular school program or had demonstrated that the regular school program was not appropriate for their level of development and learning. Fewer services were available in secondary school, and most ended in the eighth grade. Special educators found themselves looking through a narrow window (from ages 8 to 17) at the development of exceptional children, knowing little about their formative years or families and even less about what happened to them after high school. Today, our view has expanded. We have legislation, such as the Individuals with Disabilities Education Act (IDEA) (PL 105-17), that allows states to mandate that children with identifiable needs and their families receive special services from the child's birth or earliest time of identification.

Transition

Another clear trend is the development of **transition services,** or programs that help exceptional students move from school to work, to the community, or to college.

About 300,000 students who have received special education services leave the school system each year. Until recently, few attempts have been made to follow up on what has happened to those students and see whether the long-range goal of special education services—adjustment to the community—was met. With the new interest in the lifespan of exceptional individuals has come new interest in transition services.

Adjustment to the community seems to consist of three major components: (1) the ability to seek and hold gainful employment, (2) the ability to live independently, and (3) the ability to move around the community without help (Schill, 1988). Even those with severe disabilities can approach these goals. If they cannot work independently, they might find employment in a subsidized industry. If they cannot live independently, they might live in a group home under supervision.

Today there is widespread agreement that transition services are necessary, that many exceptional children cannot adapt to adult life without some help beyond the school years (Blackorby & Wagner, 1996). The new emphasis on transition services is encouraging special educators to work with professionals in other fields, such as vocational educators, members of the business community, psychologists, and counselors. In addition, cooperation between special educators in the secondary schools and those who provide adult services can improve the outcomes of special education programs (Edgar, 1987).

Malian and Love (1998) interviewed 1,285 exceptional students and their parents and teachers to determine what they saw ahead after the secondary school program. Ninety-eight percent of the parents and 93 percent of the students expected further training, most likely a vocational or trade school. Malian and Love felt that educators in postsecondary education could provide the following:

- Teaching students specific relationship-building skills, as well as a working knowledge of how to access rehabilitation training and counseling agencies that can help students make the transition to work and other responsibilities in adult life, even if they do decide to drop out of school

- Setting up a case manager/advocate system to provide effective coordination for accessing services, thus expanding students' sources of support from friends and family to an array of community services like counseling, social work, and occupational therapy (p. 9).

REFERRAL AND ASSESSMENT

Special educators have spent a great deal of time and energy on the development of effective assessment tools. Used properly, these tools can help the school match the individual needs of exceptional students to the appropriate special services available in the school.

The traditional first step toward the development of an effective instructional program for each exceptional child has been to determine the child's individual needs, strengths, and weaknesses. The determination is made through the process of assessment. Test data, interviews, past records, and so on are assembled to draw a portrait of special children once they have been referred to special education services. In recent years an additional step has been taken: the prereferral system by which student problems are confronted *before* a formal referral is made. Children often are referred to special education services because of their persistent inability

Before an effective instructional program can be developed, the child's needs, strengths, and weaknesses must be carefully assessed.

With the new interest in the life-span of exceptional individuals has come new interest in transition services that help exceptional students move from school to the world of work, to the community, or to college. (© Bob Daemmrich/The Image Works)

to respond to the general education program. Sometimes the reason for that inability lies in a student's exceptionality (a serious behavior problem or developmental delay), but sometimes the reason is the limited and inflexible nature of the educational program itself.

Paul, age 8, has been referred to special education because his third-grade teacher, Mrs. Parker, claims he is insolent, talks back to her, isn't mastering his reading and math skills, and is constantly disturbing the other children. Maybe Paul acts that way because he has a serious learning or behavioral disability, but maybe he and the teacher have gotten off on the wrong foot. He may be reacting in a predictable way to his inability to do the schoolwork (which may seem uninteresting to him anyway), and Mrs. Parker doesn't know how to cope with Paul's frustrations. How can a special education teacher sort out the correct answer? Can it even be done?

Educational Adaptations

Exceptional Children

Special education provides to exceptional children necessary services that are not available in the regular school program.

The nature of special education is to provide exceptional children with services not available to them in the regular education program. Special education programs are different from regular programs because they try to take into account the child's inter-individual and intra-individual differences. It's important to realize that special education does *not* exist because regular education has failed. Classroom teachers and typical educational programs simply cannot respond fully to the special needs of exceptional children without a substantial change in the structure, program, and staffing of the typical classroom. Some measure of the scope of special education comes from the Center for Special Education Finance, which estimates that the 1995–1996 expenditures for special education services were $32.6 billion (Chambers, Parrish, Lieberman, & Wolman, 1998).

Instruction can be adapted to the inter-individual and intra-individual differences found in exceptional children in several ways: We can adapt the learning environment to create an appropriate setting in which to learn, change the actual content of lessons or the specific knowledge being taught, adapt teaching strategies, and introduce technology that meets the special needs of exceptional students (Table 2.1).

EDUCATIONAL ADAPTATIONS

The school environment is where all of the many forces acting on exceptional children interact and influence each other. Laws regulate who receives services; courts interpret those laws and apply them to specific circumstances; and families support (or sometimes fail to support) the child's efforts and provide goals, values, and expectations that generally reflect the family's cultural background. The school is particularly important for exceptional children who may need very special kinds of help to become productive adults.

In this chapter, we provide an overview of how the schools have tried to organize themselves and their resources to meet the challenges of accepting and educating exceptional children. Chapter 3 focuses on early childhood issues. In Chapters 4 through 12, we describe specific adaptations for children with specific exceptionalities.

Adapting the Learning Environment

Often, a special learning environment is necessary to help exceptional children master particular content and skills. Making changes in the learning environment, however, has repercussions throughout the entire educational system. That may be one reason why environmental modifications are the subject of greater controversy than are changes in either content or skills.

When we decide to move youngsters from the regular classroom to a resource room for an hour a day, we generate a series of activities. First, we have to allocate space in the school for the **resource room**. Then the classroom teacher must modify instruction to accommodate the students who are out of the class for part of the day. And, of course, a whole battery of special personnel must be brought into the system to identify eligible children and to deliver special services.

The concept of **least restrictive environment** means that teachers attempt to educate a child in the environmental setting that maximizes the chances that the child

TABLE 2.1   Educational Adaptation

Adapting the Learning Environment

One can change the physical setting in which special services are delivered to make the instruction more likely to be effective.

Changing the Curriculum Content

It is often necessary to modify the curriculum content of the lessons to meet the needs of exceptional children who are performing markedly below or above the rest of the class.

Skills Mastery

Special attention is given to exceptional students to ensure that they have the necessary basic skills of reading and arithmetic and of processing information that are crucial to further learning.

Introducing Technology

Special assistive-technology devices help students with exceptionalities to communicate and receive information; instructional-technology devices aid them in mastering necessary knowledge and skills.

with exceptionalities will respond well to the educational goals and objectives set for him or her. Thus, the resource room is preferred to the part-time special class, and the teacher consultant is preferred to the resource room. This concept may mean that the program or setting in the regular classroom must be changed to lessen the likelihood of students being referred to special education in the first place (Chalfant, 1985; Will, 1986).

Recent legislation such as IDEA requires that a continuum of placement options be available to meet the needs of students with disabilities. The law also requires that

> To the maximum extent appropriate, children with disabilities . . . are educated with children who are not disabled, and that special classes, separate schooling, or other removal of children with disabilities from the regular environment occurs only when the nature of severity of the disability is such that education in regular classes with the use of supplementary aids and services cannot be attained satisfactorily. (IDEA Sec. 612[5][B])

The clear intent is to bring the exceptional child as close to the normal classroom setting as is feasible. But the educator must be aware that a special environment may be the most appropriate for a particular child at a particular point in his or her development.

The decision of where the child will receive the best education is aided immeasurably by the availability of options. Sometimes a school system will have only

Instruction can be adapted to the differences found in exceptional children in several ways—by varying the learning environment, the content of lessons, and the skills being taught and by introducing technology that can meet special needs. (© Bob Daemmrich/The Image Works)

★ *A continuum of services has been designed to meet the needs of individual children with disabilities.*

one option (for example, a resource room); in such a case, special education means exercising that option or receiving no special services at all. The term *comprehensive services* usually refers to a variety of options (but rarely to the full range of possibilities) that can be applied to meet the individual needs of each child.

The recent emphasis on *mainstreaming* and *inclusion* often leaves the impression that practically all exceptional children are now back in the regular classroom. Such is far from the case. Figure 2.1 indicates the changes that have taken place in the type of settings used for educational service delivery to children with disabilities during a seven-year period (1988–1995). One can see some real differences during that time, with the percentage of children with disabilities receiving services in the regular classroom increasing from 32 percent to 45 percent, thus supporting the inclusion philosophy. Most of that change appears to be due to a reduction of children in resource rooms. There is also a drop in children with disabilities in separate facilities.

At the same time, it is hard to make major shifts in space assignments despite the real pressure for inclusion as a type of educational reform. These results might surprise those who believe that inclusion is the dominant strategy in special education. But actually the number of children in resource rooms, separate classes, and separate facilities is over 50 percent of the total number of children with disabilities. Any attempt to put all children with disabilities back into the regular classroom, even if that were a good idea, obviously will take a long time.

The data indicate that the schools are using a wide range of placements to try to find the proper setting for maximizing the education of exceptional students. The important question is not "Where are they?" which is merely a question about student geography. The true education question is "What special services are being provided?"

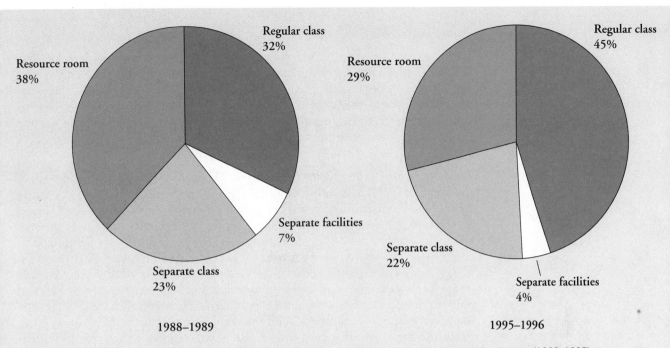

Figure 2.1 Percentage of Students (ages 6–21) in Settings for Service Delivery to Children with Disabilities (1988, 1995)

Source: Adapted from *Twelfth Annual Report to Congress* (1990), Office of Special Education Programs, Washington, DC; and *Nineteenth Annual Report to Congress* (1997), Office of Special Education Programs, Washington, DC.

Adapting Curriculum

Some exceptional children require modifications in the content of the curriculum. For children who are gifted, we can accelerate content or provide different kinds of learning experiences. We can adapt to the limited conceptual abilities of students with mental retardation by relating lessons through direct, concrete experiences to their homes, families, and neighborhoods. Instead of teaching about civilizations of the past or countries in Asia or South America, we can create lessons about students' own towns and cities. We can make linguistic changes in the curriculum for children with hearing problems. We can limit the presentation of visual-channel information for children with visual problems.

Mastery of Skills

One educational objective is the mastery of reading, arithmetic, and writing skills. Most students spend their first three years in school mastering these basic skills, which are often taught in ways that encourage students to practice other skills, like punctuality, attentiveness, and persistence, that can lead to better social adaptation. Exceptional children often need to be taught the skills that average students master without special instruction. In addition, they sometimes must learn special skills to cope with their disability. A blind student may learn braille; a deaf student, American Sign Language. These are critical communication skills. Even gifted children can learn additional techniques for finding and solving problems. All exceptional children require some kind of skill training appropriate to their special needs.

Using Technology

Special education has often led the way in the acceptance and use of technology in education. That achievement may well be due to the unique problems special educators face. Because they are educating children with special needs, they have been willing to try new devices that promise help: modified typewriters, hearing aids, print magnifiers, and machines that trace eye movements as the student reads. Perhaps the most important of these technological devices is the modern computer.

Technology for Children with Disabilities.   There are two quite different uses of technology for children with disabilities: assistive and instructional uses. **Assistive technology** consists of tools that enhance the functioning of people with special disabilities. For the person who is blind, it provides braille readers and typewriters; for the person who is deaf, hearing aids; for the person who cannot speak, communication boards for pointing to and composing messages. Assistive technology can be as sophisticated as a device that translates print into oral language or as simple as a headband and a pointer that allow students who have cerebral palsy to point to text or communication boards. Such devices have dramatically improved individual children's ability to receive and transmit information effectively and are most often used with children with moderate to severe disabilities that create major barriers to communication.

New technologies in the classroom can both assist and instruct the student who is disabled.

Instructional technology involves the computer and related tools that support and expand the computer's usefulness. Instructional technology is developed primarily as a means to deliver content and instruction in an appropriate manner to exceptional children. Table 2.2 provides a list of assistive- and instructional-technology devices.

Major attempts are being made to go beyond the traditional transmission of knowledge and to use technology as a means to aid exceptional children in thinking and problem solving. This is particularly important in view of the difficulty many such students have in transferring knowledge and information from one situation to another. Students both with and without disabilities have major problems with **inert knowledge** (Whitehead, 1928), which is knowledge stored in memory but not linked to other knowledge or applied to problems. Hasselbring (1994) points out that a student may understand how the special characteristics of a camel may help the animal survive desert sandstorms yet fail to understand that this survival illustrates the phenomenon of *adaptation*. When asked about the concept of adaptation, the student may not realize that his or her knowledge of camels is relevant or is a good illustration of adaptation.

There is good reason to believe that problem-oriented instruction is much more likely than fact-oriented instruction to produce transferrable knowledge (Perkins & Salomon, 1989). That is why major efforts are being made to use technology not just to master specific information but as a tool to help in problem solving. It becomes especially important for teachers who work with children with exceptionalities to receive instruction in how to apply technology to their instruction. Currently, few expenditures of funds have been made to prepare teachers to fully utilize available equipment. For the most part, teachers have been left on their own to learn as best they can, or they have been given short-term training introducing them to the technology but rarely allowing them sufficient time to explore the full potential of these new tools.

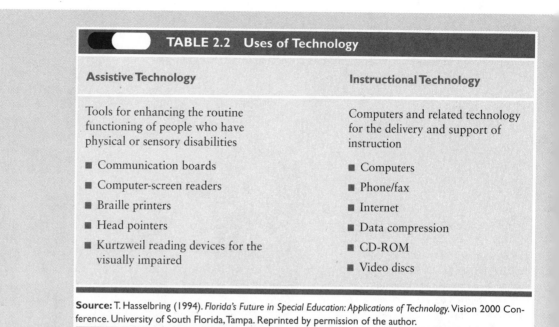

TABLE 2.2 Uses of Technology

Assistive Technology	Instructional Technology
Tools for enhancing the routine functioning of people who have physical or sensory disabilities	Computers and related technology for the delivery and support of instruction
■ Communication boards	■ Computers
■ Computer-screen readers	■ Phone/fax
■ Braille printers	■ Internet
■ Head pointers	■ Data compression
■ Kurtzweil reading devices for the visually impaired	■ CD-ROM
	■ Video discs

Source: T. Hasselbring (1994). *Florida's Future in Special Education: Applications of Technology.* Vision 2000 Conference. University of South Florida, Tampa. Reprinted by permission of the author.

Computers. The computer has the ability to create files for storing information; to organize and present text, video, and numerical data; and to provide access to data and programs. It allows children to learn at their own rate and provides immediate feedback and reinforcement. It makes the process of learning more active and self-directed. The computer has become particularly important in special education because it offers specific advantages to exceptional children:

- Computer programs are available to teach basic reading and arithmetic skills, two important problem areas for many exceptional children.

- Many computer activities use a gamelike format that special educators have found effective for teaching visual motor skills and specific academic skills.

- Youngsters who learn to operate the equipment have the satisfaction of being independent and controlling their own environment, not an everyday experience for most exceptional children.

- The computer can create conditionally branched or nonlinear interactions. The branching capability means that a slow-learning student can be given more items that provide additional practice on the concept to be mastered while the student who demonstrates understanding of the concept can be taken forward in the program without additional unnecessary examples (Barr, 1991).

- The computer makes record keeping much easier. Its tracking system allows the school to keep updated records on tests that students have taken, their progress in individualized programs, and a host of evaluative reports.

The computer is a constantly evolving tool, and we are finding new uses for it on a regular basis.

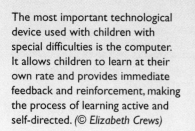

The most important technological device used with children with special difficulties is the computer. It allows children to learn at their own rate and provides immediate feedback and reinforcement, making the process of learning active and self-directed. (© *Elizabeth Crews*)

Prereferral: Teacher-Assistance Teams

Chalfant and his colleagues (Chalfant & Pysh, 1989) have devised a prereferral system, called *teacher-assistance teams*, which is designed to cope with situations like Paul's prior to a child's referral to special education. The team consists of the classroom teacher, the special education teacher, the school psychologist, the principal, and other school staff as appropriate. Team members thoroughly discuss the situation and suggest several alternative instructional strategies to the teacher (in our example, Mrs. Parker). A trial period is determined in which the teacher will apply those approaches in the classroom.

If the child continues to show no improvement, then a referral to special education may be made. Many times, however, the prereferral meeting and prescriptions seem to be all that is necessary to put the child and the teacher on the right track (Chalfant, 1989). The team meeting prevents many unnecessary referrals to special education and strengthens the general program of education as well.

Peer Collaboration for Teachers

One strategy for reducing the number of referrals to special education is the teaming of teachers, a process called *peer collaboration*. Teachers in teams of two or three learn how to discuss a student's problem among themselves and seek an answer prior to referral for special help (Pugash & Johnson, 1995). The teachers learn how to present a problem and pose clarifying questions to explore the dimensions of a problem, such as a student throwing tantrums or failing miserably on tests. On the basis of the problem explorations, they redefine the problem and design three or more possible interventions to address it. Finally, they establish an evaluation plan to determine if the intervention succeeded.

Pugash and Johnson (1995) compared 95 teachers who had received the special peer collaboration training with 96 teachers who had not. The number of referrals for special help had been reduced by half in the group receiving the training but remained the same for the teachers who did not receive such training. This outcome demonstrates again the untapped potential existing in the regular school staff, who can, with preparation, learn to cope with classroom problems without referring them to someone else.

Assessment

In special education, **assessment** "is the systematic process of gathering educationally relevant information to make legal and instructional decisions about the provision of special services" (McLoughlin & Lewis, 1991, p. 3).

An assessment starts with the general issue of whether a school performance problem exists and then moves on to the child's strengths and weaknesses, the content areas affected, and the relationship of any academic problems to the child's learning environment. We finish with a prescription of educational goals and objectives and with strategies to help us meet them. Ongoing evaluation (for example, asking, How effective is the educational program?) gives us the necessary information to revise the educational program.

Assessment specialists use extensive tests, interviews, observations, and ratings to determine the child's inter-individual and intra-individual differences. The analysis of those differences allows them to make better educational decisions about the child. The assessment process involves five steps:

1. *Screening:* quickly and economically finding those children who need more thorough (and costly) examination

2. *Diagnosis, classification, and placement:* collecting additional information to determine which special program the child needs or for which the child is eligible

3. *Instructional planning:* using diagnostic information to design an individualized education program based on the child's needs

4. *Pupil evaluation:* administering tests and other procedures to determine whether a particular student is making expected progress and meeting the objectives that were originally established

5. *Program evaluation:* determining the effectiveness of a special program through tests and observation (Ysseldyke & Shinn, 1981)

Individual Differences

Terminology is important because it is the means by which we acknowledge the exceptionality itself. But it is often only a springboard for learning about the individuality of the exceptional child. We are all aware of how children of the same age vary physically. Some are tall and thin, others are short and chubby, and there is much variation in between. We find this same variation in other areas: intelligence, educational attainment, emotional maturity, and social development. Individual differences are the rule rather than the exception. Children with the same exceptionality will show impressive differences from one another on these characteristics.

INDIVIDUAL DIFFERENCES AND THE CLASSROOM

Individual differences can create a serious problem for the classroom teacher. If a third-grade lesson is directed at average 8-year-olds, what happens to the child in the class whose intellectual development is at age 5? Or to the child with the social maturity and cognitive abilities of an 11-year-old? Or to the youngster with the emotional maturity of a 4-year-old? The teacher has a problem: The lesson is going to be too difficult for one child and too easy for the other, and the third child is creating a behavioral control problem.

When youngsters in the same classroom are markedly different from one another, it is difficult for the teachers to help them reach their academic potential without some kind of assistance. The differentiated program and services that the schools devise for children who differ significantly from the norm is called **special education.** The responsibility for providing an appropriate education to exceptional children, however, is shared by all educational staff of the school. Cooperation and joint planning between regular and special education personnel are important to reach the goal of appropriate educational strategies for all children.

THE ROLE OF ASSESSMENT

It is important to realize that a child develops on many different physical and psychological dimensions at once. To understand a child's problems, we must keep track of individual differences in each of those dimensions.

The task of determining how an individual child is different and along which dimensions has become a major step in identifying and educating exceptional children. Such assessment serves two purposes. First, it identifies which children are eligible for special services. Second, it may provide information by which an individualized plan to meet the child's particular needs can be formulated.

Teachers can use five general approaches to provide an assessment of a child: norm-referenced tests, diagnostic achievement tests, interviews, observations, and informal assessments. We summarize these approaches in Table 2.3. Generally, a combination of tests and procedures is used to detect and thoroughly evaluate a child's inter-individual and intra-individual differences. Each method has advantages and disadvantages.

Inter-Individual Differences

Areas of inter-individual differences include academic aptitude, academic performance, language development, and psychosocial development.

Inter-individual differences are substantial differences among people along key dimensions of development. Special educators and school psychologists assess inter-individual differences along key dimensions such as academic aptitude, academic performance, language development, psychomotor skills, and psychosocial development.

Academic Aptitude.   One area in which inter-individual differences show up is **academic aptitude.** The measure of children's aptitudes can tell teachers and schools a great deal about their student population and how students are performing in relationship to their potential.

TABLE 2.3 Assessment Strategies: Strengths and Weaknesses		
Strategy	**Advantages**	**Disadvantages**
Norm-referenced test	It provides a comparison of a particular child's performance against the performance of a reference group of children, as in intelligence and achievement tests.	It does not provide reasons for the results; for culturally different children, the reference groups used for comparison may be inappropriate.
Diagnostic achievement test	It is designed to provide a profile of strengths and weaknesses, analyses of errors, etc., in arithmetic or reading to pinpoint specific academic problems of the student for remediation.	The scores generated by such instruments often have limited or suspect reliability; consequently, the profiles may not be very valuable.
Interview	Information from the child, parent, teacher, or others can provide perspective and insight into the reasons for the child's current performance.	All interviewees see the child through personal perspectives that may be limited by scope of experience, personal bias, or, in particular, reference to themselves.
Observation	It can provide information based on the child's spontaneous behavior in natural settings and a basis for intervention planning.	The child may not reveal significant behaviors during the observation; the meaning of the child's behavior may be unclear.
Informal assessment	Information from teacher-made tests, particular language samples, portfolios, or descriptions of significant events in the life of the child may yield valuable insights leading to effective educational planning.	It is rarely possible to match a particular child's performance with the performance of others on these measures or observations. Such measures should be used with caution.

For decades, the standard measure of academic aptitude has been the intelligence test. These tests measure the development of memory, association, reasoning, evaluation, and classification—the mental operations so important to school performance. In fact, intelligence tests are accurate predictors of academic performance:

Those who score high on intelligence tests generally do well in school; those who score low generally do poorly.

Any serious problem with or developmental delay in the mental operations that these tests evaluate can create major difficulties in school. Intelligence tests assume a common experience base for most children (and the desire of the child to do well). The results of such tests for youngsters for whom English is a second language or youngsters who have had atypical early childhood experiences need to be used with caution. An example of the areas measured by an intelligence test is seen in Table 2.4, which describes the often-used Wechsler Intelligence Scale for Children–III.

Intelligence tests have come under severe attack in recent years. One reason is that there is strong disagreement over the use and meaning of intelligence quotient (IQ) scores. In the past, those scores have been used (1) to indicate innate intellectual potential, (2) to predict future academic performance, and (3) to indicate a child's present rate of mental development compared with that of same-age children. The sharpest criticism has been raised over the use of IQ scores to indicate intellectual potential. Intelligence tests are not pure measures of intellectual potential and never should be used to try to demonstrate the innate superiority of one sex or ethnic or racial group over another. But they are valuable predictors of academic performance and indicators of current academic aptitude. They are useful when employed for those purposes.

One other criticism has been that standard IQ tests yield a single IQ score, when in fact many people believe that intelligence is multidimensional. Gardner's theory of multiple intelligences (1993) is the most well-known proposal of a multifaceted view of intelligence. Gardner has proposed seven major dimensions of intelligence: *linguistic, musical, logical-mathematical, spatial, bodily-kinesthetic, social awareness,* and *self-awareness.* These dimensions provide some basis for differentiating curriculum, and there are continuing efforts to design programming based on Gardner's model of intelligence.

Academic Performance.   Two well-accepted approaches to describing interindividual differences in academic performance are standard (norm-referenced) achievement tests and diagnostic achievement tests. **Standard (norm-referenced) achievement tests** measure a student's level of achievement compared with that of students of similar age or grade. These tests tell whether the student is achieving at expected levels of performance, but usually they do not tell *why* the student is not performing as well as he or she might. **Diagnostic achievement tests** help determine the process a student is using to solve a problem or decode a reading passage so we can understand why a particular student is not mastering some aspect of the school curriculum, that is, why he or she is not performing at the level of other students. Figure 2.2 shows an analysis of errors as a prelude to education planning.

Language Development.   Language, one of the most complex of human functions, is particularly vulnerable to problems that affect the development of children. Because using language effectively is one of the keys to academic success, it is one dimension to be carefully analyzed, particularly when a student is not performing well.

Receptive language (listening) and expressive language (speaking) often need separate assessment. The Test of Adolescent Language–2 (Hammill, Brown, Larsen, & Weiderholt, 1987) is used to examine the dimensions of listening/vocabulary, listening/grammar, speaking/vocabulary, speaking/grammar, reading/vocabulary, reading/grammar, writing/vocabulary, and writing/grammar. It is a comprehensive measure that allows the special educator to find areas of relative

Intelligence tests are not pure measures of intellectual potential; rather, they are valuable predictors and indicators of academic ability and performance.

Listening and speaking need to be addressed separately from each other.

TABLE 2.4 Wechsler Intelligence Scale for Children–III

Verbal Scale

Information	Questions that ask about common knowledge about events, objects, places, and people are presented orally by the examiner (e.g., "When is Independence Day?").
Similarities	The examinee explains the correspondence between pairs of words (e.g., "How are giraffes and cows alike?").
Arithmetic	The student solves mathematical problems mentally and responds to them verbally (e.g., "If I buy a book for $4.50, how much change will I get from $10?").
Vocabulary	Words are presented orally and the examinee defines them orally (e.g., "What does *crystal* mean?").
Comprehension	Questions that assess understanding of familiar problems and social concepts are presented orally by the examiner (e.g., "Why should I not cross the road against a red light?").
Digit span	The individual repeats a series of numbers forward in the Digits Forward section and a series of numbers in reverse order in the Digits Backward section (e.g., "4-7-2-9-8").

Performance Scale

Picture completion	A picture with a missing part is shown to the examinee, who must identify the missing piece.
Picture arrangement	The individual must correctly sequence a series of pictures.
Block design	The examinee reproduces a pattern using blocks.
Object assembly	The individual assembles five jigsaw puzzles.
Coding	The examinee copies geometric symbols that are paired with either numbers or shapes.
Mazes	The individual completes a series of mazes using a pencil.
Symbol search	The individual searches two groups of paired shapes to locate the target shape.

Source: L. Cohen and L. Spenciner (1998). *Assessment of Children and Youth.* Copyright 1998 by Addison-Wesley Educational Publishers, Inc. Reprinted by permission.

strength and weakness in the child's linguistic processes and to develop specific plans for an individualized program of instruction.

Psychomotor Development. Many children with special needs have associated problems in coordination or mobility, which adds to their basic exceptionality. Obviously, children with cerebral palsy and other conditions that clearly impair the ability to physically move around and that interfere with fine motor control need exercises and practice in motor skills. However, they are not the only candidates for special psychomotor exercise. Some children with learning disabilities, autism, or mental retardation also have problems in the psychomotor areas that need attention. For many children, the individual education program should have improved motor performance as one of the objectives and should detail how such improvements will be brought about.

Psychosocial Development. Another area of inter-individual difference is the individual child's ability to respond to the social environment, or how well the child is able to adapt. Does the child show aggressive tendencies when frustrated? Is he or she able to work cooperatively with others? How does the child react when things don't go right? How well the child is able to do these things when faced with increasingly complex social interactions (for example, with teachers or peers) strongly influences how well he or she will adapt as an adult.

Figure 2.2

Examples of Error Analysis in Diagnosis of Academic Problems

a.	48	b.	91	c.	35	d.	43	e.	45
	+8		×4		−25		×6		+23
	416		157		60		308		67

a. *Grouping:* Student correctly added but did not carry.
b. *Random:* No apparent pattern.
c. *Wrong operation:* Student added instead of subtracted.
d. *Defective algorithm:* Student correctly multiplied but added 1 to 4 before multiplying.
e. *Computational error:* Student added 5 + 3 incorrectly.

Social adaptation also greatly influences how the exceptional child responds to remediation. Many children who fail to respond to special programs have behavioral and social problems, not academic ones. It is difficult to remediate a reading disability if a child has a severe attention problem or becomes aggressive when frustrated. For that reason, special educators often focus on behavioral and social problems at the same time they tackle academic difficulties.

To assess psychosocial development, we often rely on the observations of others—parents, teachers, and caregivers—for information on how the child behaves in different settings. Ratings scales can be used to bring some order to those judgments.

Another strategy is to systematically observe the child at home or school so that we can catalog the child's typical patterns of behavior. When children are able to articulate, we can ask them about their feelings or perceptions of themselves. These self-reports can be very revealing. They might show that a gifted child has a low self-concept even though people around him say he is well adjusted. Or they might show that a child with retardation has an unrealistic view of her own abilities.

Tests of adaptive behavior such as the American Association on Mental Deficiency (AAMD) Adaptive Behavior Scale and the Vineland Social Maturity Scale measure a child's social development. Table 2.5 shows sample items from the Vineland Adaptive Behavior Scales that measure degree-of-coping ability and socialization. Such tests, together with interviews, can also explore histories of violent or antisocial behavior and of eccentric or unacceptable habits and measure both self-direction and responsibility. From the results of the tests and interviews, educators are able to tell how a child is adapting in terms of social and cooperative behaviors, which helps them create an individualized program to meet the child's needs. The accumulated information may sometimes be placed in a developmental profile to provide a quick portrait of the child's development.

Culture-Bound Assessment Measures

A matter of serious concern to special educators is the high number of minority students referred for special education services. There is concern that the measuring instruments that may serve well for many children from the mainstream culture do not communicate accurate information on students who come from different cultural backgrounds and consequently may result in inappropriate placements.

The standard intelligence test, for example, is based on assumptions of a common past experience base for the students. It is expected that the 9- or 10-year-old

TABLE 2.5 Sample Items from the Vineland Adaptive Behavior Scales

Domain	Sample Items
Communication	Turns eyes and head toward sound (ages <1 to 2 years) Uses sentences of four or more words (age 2 years)
Daily living skills	Uses sharp knife to cut food (ages 12 to 15 years) Washes own clothes (ages 16 to 18+ years)
Socialization	Makes own friends (ages 7 to 10 years) Has a hobby (ages 13 to 14 years)
Motor skills	Runs with some falling (age 2 years) Throws ball (age 5+ years)
Maladaptive behavior	Has temper tantrums Displays behaviors that are self-injurious

Source: J. Sattler (1988). Sample items from the Vineland Adaptive Behavior scales. *Assessment of Children* (3rd ed.) (San Diego, CA: Author). Copyright © 1988. Used by permission of the author.

student has come into reasonably frequent contact with such words as *letter, diamond,* and *iron.* If, however, personal experience has not brought the child into contact with such linguistic symbols, the child's ability to learn (the measure of which is one of the key goals of intelligence tests) is possibly underestimated, and the student may be inappropriately referred to special education.

An incorrect diagnosis also can be made if a teacher misinterprets a culturally different child's behavior as disturbing or resistant. Our expectations for students' behavior are shaped by the norms of the majority culture, and those expectations influence our evaluation of students' performance. Gage and Berliner (1988) used punctuality as an example:

> If we have grown up believing that punctuality demonstrates interest and concern, we are offended when someone is late. In cultures where time is a resource to be conserved, punctuality is important. In cultures where time is just a convenient reference for organizing activities, punctuality is far less important and being late is not a sign of disrespect. We may think that children who consistently arrive at school late are unmotivated or uninterested. But we should ask whether time simply has a different meaning for them. Although lateness may be disruptive in school and we may want to correct the problem, we have to be careful about our attributions. Our response to the children should vary according to the causes to which we attribute their behavior. (p. 196)

For all youngsters, special care needs to be taken to see that the procedures or tests used to assess them are fair and valid and to be sure that child and family cultural differences are considered in the design of an individualized education program.

DEVELOPMENTAL PROFILE

We can see how the assessment process works in the case of Diane, a 7-year-old. Diane was a slim child, somewhat small for her age. She was promoted to second grade mainly because of the hopes of her first-grade teacher; her actual performance was not good. In the second grade, Diane was having trouble with basic reading and arithmetic skills. She was an unhappy child who did not talk a lot and who did not have many friends in the classroom.

In some school systems, screening before kindergarten or at the beginning or end of first grade might have picked up Diane's problems. In this kind of screening, every child is examined quickly for major problems in vision, hearing, and learning ability. If a difficulty shows up, the child is referred for an intensive evaluation. In Diane's school system, academic performance takes the place of the screening process. In fact, most students find their way into special education through academic failure or through the perceptive observation of school personnel.

Diane's second-grade teacher recognized a problem and referred the child for diagnostic evaluation. Diane was given a series of tests and interviews to determine whether she did have a problem and to identify that problem. In the process, the diagnostic team eliminated a number of factors that might have caused Diane's difficulty. They looked for signs of physical disabilities, of serious emotional disturbance, of mental retardation, of environmental disadvantage. The goal of the assessment and referral was to identify the support Diane needed to maximize her potential. This is done through the **individualized education program (IEP)**.

In Diane's case, after the initial diagnosis and classification, a more thorough analysis of specific learning problems or difficulties was carried out. Earlier examinations had defined Diane's abilities and disabilities; now the educational team analyzed those abilities and disabilities to design a specialized program and teaching strategies for the child. Once the program goals were set and the individual program was implemented, a plan was set up to measure Diane's progress at subsequent points to see if the objectives had been met.

THE INDIVIDUALIZED EDUCATION PROGRAM

One of the many innovations brought forth by the Education for All Handicapped Children Act is the requirement that every handicapped child have an individualized education program (IEP), a clearly documented and carefully monitored plan setting forth how to differentiate the curriculum and experiences of the exceptional child to meet the individual needs of that child. The instructional plan must include the following:

- The nature of the child's problem
- The program's long-term goals
- The program's short-term objectives
- The special education services the child will receive
- The criteria for gauging the effectiveness of those services

A literature review (Gallagher & Desimone, 1995) has shown evidence that the implementation of the IEP in school systems across the nation has had both positive and negative outcomes. On the positive side is evidence of better relations between teacher and family and improved understanding by the family of the special

The individualized education program describes the nature of the child's problem, the program's objectives and goals, the special education services the child will receive, and the criteria for gauging the effectiveness of those services. *(D and I MacDonald/The Picture Cube)*

Despite the additional time and effort required of teachers, implementing IEPs has increased family involvement in students' instructional programs.

education program; there is also more information for parents about academic achievement and gains made by their child, as well as general agreement between school and family about the goals and program directions for the child.

On the negative side is much evidence that the implementation of this idea has not gone smoothly in many places. The IEP is often seen as paperwork with no substantive meaning or use in the classroom. It places great demands on teachers' time, may replace the regular curriculum, and, in short, is seen as one more meaningless requirement that must be fulfilled.

Although there are voices calling for the abandonment of the IEP, few wish to abandon the gains it has brought. How can we get rid of the nonessentials of the process and keep the things that are good? A continual problem for educators!

Case Study: Frank

Frank, a 10-year-old fourth grader, could not concentrate on most tasks for more than two or three minutes at a time. Every ten minutes or so, he would turn around and bother the student behind him. His teacher had to stand over him and tap his desk every time he became disruptive. Writing was painstakingly difficult for Frank. It took him five minutes to write a five-word sentence. Most of the time he began sentences in the middle of the page. The letters were usually written very small, and some were written backward. His script *e* looked like an *l*, and he did not dot his *i*'s or cross his *t*'s. He often got frustrated and tore his paper up.

His teacher noted, however, that Frank was a "different boy" when he was working on his science lessons. He would sit quietly, read his assignment, and wait for his turn to present the information to the rest of the class. His teacher wanted an evaluation to determine why Frank performed so well in some areas and so poorly in others. She believed that Frank had the ability to do well in all subjects and wanted information that might help her to motivate him or accommodate his learning style. In addition, she thought that he might benefit from special education.

Frank's teacher felt he was having trouble in language arts and in maintaining attention. The teacher tried to introduce some special lessons and reward on-task performance. That helped a little, but Frank was referred for a comprehensive evaluation.

The Wechsler Intelligence Scale for Children (see Table 2.4) revealed Frank to be of average intelligence but with a wide variation of performance on various subtests. On the Vineland Adaptive Behavior Scales (see Table 2.5), Frank showed his adaptive scores about average, with some problems in social relationships. Tests of spelling and visual motor tasks, however, showed Frank to be two grades below his age, as was his low written language production. His pattern of performance suggested a child with learning disabilities.

On the basis of that pattern, Frank was placed in a resource room with a special education teacher for an hour a day. His special education teacher worked with the general education teacher to incorporate the resource room work with the regular classroom activities. No time limits were set on his tasks. Some of the goals and objectives in Frank's IEP are listed in Figure 2.3. After one year, Frank's progress toward the goals listed in his IEP will be evaluated and decisions about further steps made on the basis of that evaluation.

EDUCATIONAL RESTRUCTURING IN SPECIAL EDUCATION

The adaptations described earlier in this chapter are one aspect of school responses to the needs of exceptional children. Changes in societal structures, attitudes, and values in recent decades have led schools to accept their role more positively and often have resulted in new methods to carry out their responsibilities to exceptional children.

These changing attitudes come at a time when Americans increasingly believe that the public school system is not as effective as it should be and would benefit from new methods and approaches. Substantial efforts have been made to change or modify the overall system (Goodlad, 1985; Sizer, 1985). Reforms promise to change the educational landscape and create a very different educational environment for the exceptional child.

In many ways, special education has been defining its services to children with disabilities and to children with special gifts and talents on the basis of the established patterns of general education. Given the structure and programs of general education, special education has been defined by how it differs from the normal pattern of general education. Then major restructuring efforts in general education begun in the early 1990s made it necessary to redesign special educational services. This section briefly touches on some of the major elements of that restructuring effort.

The Inclusion Movement

Inclusion is the most significant movement in special education in the past two decades. As an educational philosophy, it essentially says that exceptional children

FIGURE 2.3   Goals and Objectives of Frank's IEP

Annual Goal	Evaluation Schedule
The student will increase his spelling scores from a grade level of approximately 2.5 to approximately 4.0.	Annual. Use a norm-referenced test.
General Objective	
When the examiner pronounces words that begin with consonants, the student will demonstrate his ability to recognize initial consonant sounds auditorily by writing the correct initial consonant for twenty-one out of twenty-one different consonants.	Every three months. Use a criterion-referenced test.
Immediate Short-Term Objectives	
(*Note:* Objectives of this type are changed and updated frequently and typically are found in lesson plans.) When the examiner pronounces fifteen words with initial blends *sw, sk,* and *cr,* the student will demonstrate his ability to recognize the initial blend by writing the correct two letters with 100 percent accuracy.	Weekly. Use a criterion-referenced test.
When presented with three printed stimulus root words and requested to add a designated suffix (*ing* with doubled consonants; *ed* with doubled consonants; *ed* to words ending in silent *e*) to that root word, the student will correctly write the requested word with 100 percent accuracy.	Weekly. Use a criterion-referenced test.

Source: Adapted from R. Taylor (1997). *Assessment of Exceptional Students.* Boston: Allyn & Bacon, pp. 510–519.

Supporters of the full-inclusion movement believe that all children, regardless of ability, should be educated in general classrooms.

should be *a part of,* not *apart from,* general education. The question that still bothers both special educators and general educators is how the philosophy of inclusion can be made operational in so many different schools in so many different communities. Additional questions include:

- Does inclusion mean that the exceptional child is always to be placed in the general education classroom?
- Does inclusion mean that the essential responsibility for the education of the exceptional child is in the hands of the general classroom teacher?
- Does inclusion mean that such children should receive special instruction only within the boundaries of the general classroom, or can they leave for special instruction for a period of time?

Previously, special education stood apart from general education, with separate administrators and specially prepared teachers. Are special education teachers now to be folded back into the general elementary and secondary programs and operate as consultants rather than hands-on teachers? If general educators are to have the additional responsibility for exceptional children, does that mean a change in their teacher preparation program? Where previously they left special instruction to the special educator, must they themselves now learn a new set of instructional approaches and strategies?

All those questions and more result from the fundamental change in educational philosophy called inclusion. They will be addressed in the chapters that follow. The basic principles undergirding the inclusion movement tell a lot about the movement and its purposes. Think about these core beliefs (Pearpoint, Forest, & O'Brien, 1996):

- All students belong in regular classrooms—no ifs, ands, or buts.
- General education teachers can teach *all* children.
- Necessary supports will be provided.
- Quality is a right, not a privilege.
- Outcomes must be success, literacy, and graduation for all.
- Creative alternatives will be available for populations who do not succeed in typical ways.

From this list, it is clear that inclusion is not only an educational strategy but a social movement, with proponents maintaining that anything but inclusion for children with special needs is morally and ethically wrong (Stainback & Stainback, 1996).

Stainback and Stainback draw a parallel between racial segregation and the segregation of children with special needs. They point out that similar arguments were made that "desegregation would not work," "it was not in the best interests of black children," or "we need more study." The proponents of inclusion see the same arguments being made opposing inclusion of exceptional children.

Like many analogies, the racial-segregation analogy breaks down on an essential point. The color of a person's skin has nothing to do with his or her learning ability, but serious impairment to the brain or the inability to see or hear certainly does. The opponents of full inclusion, meaning *all* children with disabilities in the general education setting (Fuchs & Fuchs, 1994; Kauffman, Lloyd, Baker, & Riedel, 1995) urge, as an alternative, a continuum of services, with the degree of inclusion determined by the needs of each individual child rather than automatically placing every child into the general classroom. Table 2.6 illustrates the limitations of inclusion.

Inclusion and the General Education Teacher

Part of the inclusion argument revolves around what resources will be available to help general education classroom teachers, who certainly need all the help they can get. Will special education specialists be available and in the classroom with the general education teacher for a significant amount of time to help with special instruction? Will paraprofessionals be present to provide necessary assistance to the children with special needs, particularly those with physical disabilities? Will general educators receive personnel preparation for their new roles concerning special needs children? The description in Table 2.7 of staffing for inclusion is desirable but hard to obtain.

TABLE 2.6 A School Principal Experiences the Limitations of Inclusion

Less than a month into the school year, Ronald started exhibiting behaviors that made him stand out from all the other students in the classroom. At first it was only the intensity of his behavior that was salient. He would scream, throw furniture, talk to himself, and hit other children with unmatched fervor. The classroom discipline plan called for consequences for each of these behaviors, and they were administered unemotionally by two exceptional teachers.

As this behavior developed, both of the teachers and their instructional aide watched Ronald closely in a heroic effort to catch him being good. When they did, they heaped praise and sometimes tangible rewards upon him. While he obviously enjoyed this positive attention, it did not suffice to maintain the good behavior, despite the fact that he was being reinforced almost continuously. It was as if there were another mechanism at work in his brain, saying, "I'll see your systematic efforts at behavior control and raise you random responses." We ended up enforcing the classroom discipline plan more as a model for the other children in the classroom than in the hope of changing Ronald's behavior.

As principal, I was called in almost daily to remove Ronald from the room to protect the other children. One of the three adults in the classroom was usually forced to deal with Ronald on an individual basis. Simple arithmetic would indicate that the mean instructional time per student was significantly affected by this fact alone. Add in the time it took for the teachers to keep a daily log of his behavior, write an individual behavioral contract, and meet with his mother and me to agree on appropriate rewards and punishments, and the loss of instructional time was even greater. . . . As I talked to my friends and colleagues about Ronald's conduct, they said such things as, "Oh yes, we see that, too. By the way, has he started licking other students' faces yet?" He had.

He had also rolled around on the floor, thereby delaying recess or lunch. He had eaten paste, paper clips, staples, and various other binding materials and had repeatedly stabbed himself in the arm with pencils. He had alternated between screaming and laughing raucously. In general, he pushed every button he could think of to make his teachers push the button on the wall that would summon me to come to the rescue.

I could continue this account, detailing how his teachers and I visited his home on several occasions in an effort to make him feel good about himself or how we provided transportation for his mother to make it easier for her to attend meetings with teachers. Food and gifts were provided anonymously during the holidays, and I even delivered a full set of the World *Book Encyclopedia* to his home for Christmas, compliments of our *World Book* sales representative. In short, we went more than a few extra miles in an effort to help Ronald fit in and feel a part of school. . . .

Readers may think that, in order to make my point, I chose the most difficult, cumbersome, and time-consuming case in our files. But the unfortunate truth is that Ronald's case was typical. It was not our most difficult or our most time-consuming or our most frustrating case. And in its very representativeness lies the real problem. No amount of explication on my part can ever do justice to the frustration, sense of abandonment, and feeling of demoralization that such cases bring to reachers.

In the case described here, the teachers and the paraprofessional involved were, indeed, the best and the brightest. They were extremely competent, dedicated, conscientious, warm, loving, and caring people who wanted nothing more than to practice their profession and help the children in their charge to learn and to grow. Their efforts were rewarded with nothing less than a full-scale attack on the orderly educational environment that they sought to establish in their classrooms. Their calls for help were answered with as cumbersome a bureaucracy as has been mustered in the history of educational bureaucracies.

Please understand that I do believe that the students who are protected by this bureaucracy have every right to that protection. But the other students in our classrooms have rights too. They have the right to a safe, orderly classroom. They have the right to a teacher's attention when they need help. They have the right to a teacher who is fresh and energetic enough to plan for them. They have a right to a teacher who feels respected and supported. And their parents have a right to know that their children's teacher is equally concerned about the education of their children.

Source: P. Idstein (1993). "Swimming against the Mainstream," *Phi Delta Kappan, 75,* pp. 336–340. Reprinted by permission of the author.

An alternative to full inclusion emphasizes providing a continuum of services based on each child's individual needs.

Those who support inclusion generally believe that supportive resources will be available for the general education teacher, whereas critics point to many situations where the support forces certainly are not there. More important, such support will likely not be there for some time to come, judging by the attitude of school boards and state legislators regarding the resources they are willing to put into inclusion programs.

"Portrait of Inclusion"

When anyone asks Lora about her son Mark's developmental problems, she usually looks the person straight in the eye and asks, "Why don't you ask my son? He's right here." Mark's response is, "My body has earthquakes."

Mark is an attractive 4-year-old boy with long, blond hair pulled back into a braided ponytail. He wears a helmet for protection in case of a seizure. In his Head Start classroom, Mark has frequent tantrums and shows a lack of compliance with classroom routines. He speaks rarely, but on occasion surprises everyone by issuing full, clear sentences. Mark uses sign language about half the time and verbal language the other half. Lora says that "when he needs to tell me something important, and when he's really serious, he'll sign." Mark also has delayed fine motor skills, and he is unable to zip or button his clothes. Yet his cognitive skills are two years advanced.

Mark and Lora have both learned that early childhood teachers are not necessarily prepared for inclusive programs. Lora removed Mark from a previous school program when she learned that Mark's teacher, after nine months with Mark in her classroom, did not know that Mark could talk. Lora reports that Mark was rarely involved in social activities in his previous classroom because his teachers "didn't know what to do with him and didn't want to upset him."

Recently in Mark's classroom, a boy took a truck Mark was playing with. Mark emphatically signed "stop" to the little boy. When the boy refused to return the truck, Mark resorted to wrestling with the boy. The teacher intervened, gave the truck back to Mark, removed the other boy, and seated him alone at a table. Lora would never tolerate that sort of behavior from Mark, whom she wants "to be treated the same as everyone else." Instead, a little boy was punished without understanding why, and without learning what Mark was trying to say. Mark's attempts to communicate were futile, and he missed an opportunity to learn the important art of negotiation. And the teacher remained lacking in competence.

When Lora is asked whether Mark has difficulty following directions, listening, and working in groups, Mark himself responds that he "doesn't really get that at school." Some things Mark would change about the program would be to have longer days and a summer program. Lora's ideal schedule would be a totally inclusive one, with therapy and behavior management available for all children in the classroom. Acknowledging that not all schools accept the responsibility to educate children like Mark, Lora says, "Well, they'd better become responsible because the world is inclusive."

Source: S. Janko and A. Porter (1997). *Portraits of Inclusion.* Bloomington, Ind.: Early Childhood Research Institute on Inclusion, Indiana University, School of Education. Reprinted by permission.

What Is the Context?

Mark is part of a Head Start classroom in which early childhood teachers include him just as they include all the other students in the classroom. Mark's mother took responsibility for finding a program where the teachers were prepared for an inclusive program. Ideally, Mark would receive all his services—including therapy and behavior management—in one classroom.

Pivotal Issues for Teachers

What kind of preparation do teachers need to successfully work in an inclusive setting? As a new teacher, what skills would you want to have to be able to work with students with disabilities in your general education classroom? What kind of support would you need from other professionals?

Social Relationships in the General Education Classroom

The overarching concern for those supporting the inclusion movement seems to be the social relationships of the child with disabilities, rather than mastery of certain academic and technical skills. This is the position of The Association for Persons with Severe Handicaps (TASH). The policy of full inclusion follows this path of reasoning: If we are to have, as a major goal, the *social integration* of persons with disabilities into adult society, then the school environment should foster the development of such skills, personal friendships, and relationships with children with disabilities. These skills are available to nondisabled persons in the natural course of their educational experiences (Snell, 1988).

Do friendships result from merely placing students in proximity to one another? Does the fact that some students are modeling appropriate behavior mean that the exceptional child will imitate such behavior? Probably not. Friendships generally grow between students who perceive similarities with each other. Students who are withdrawn gravitate toward others who are shy; an aggressive student often chooses another aggressive student to bond with (Dision, Andres, & Cosby, 1995). Reflect on your own youth. Did you always form friendships with peers with whom your parents wished you to be friends in the hope that they would be good role models for you? Or were your parents occasionally horrified to see whom you brought home, which friends stirred in you some bond of interest or some common feeling about the school or world around you?

One device that encourages closer social contact is the **circle of friends,** in which nondisabled children under the leadership of a teacher, counselor, or inclusion facilitator (Boathouse, 1993) take the responsibility for communicating with children with disabilities on a social level and spend time finding out about mutual likes and dislikes. To their surprise they may find little difference between themselves and the child with disabilities; that discovery is the beginning of wisdom and a degree of social acceptance.

An important question to be answered is how inclusion reform can be managed most effectively. In Table 2.7, Wood (1998) provides one version of the roles that general education and special education personnel working together might play. Wood points out that in practice distinctions between roles are fairly sharply defined. As the two teachers get to be more comfortable, the roles get blurred and overlap as the team members cooperate to get the job done.

How Much Inclusion Is "Included"?

The attitude of the Learning Disabilities Association of America (LDA) toward inclusion is quite different. LDA believes that the regular education classroom is

TABLE 2.7   Inclusion Team Roles: Division of Labor

General Education	Special Education
■ Present the regular curriculum with awareness of individual differences	■ Provide individual instruction for students as needed
■ Provide a setting of acceptance in the classroom; focus on student similarities	■ Model effectiveness instruction for exceptional children for teachers and aides
■ Maintain classroom standards of behavior and a structured routine that stresses fair treatment for all	■ Oversee responsibilities for paraprofessionals who work with children
■ Promote social interaction between children with disabilities and other students	■ Develop plan for coping with special behavior problems related to exceptionality
■ Be responsible for general class performance on accountability measures	■ Be accountable for IEP goals, paperwork, and concurrence with legal requirements

Source: Adapted from M. Wood (1998). "Whose Job Is It Anyway? Educational Roles in Inclusion." *Exceptional Children, 64*(2), p. 1. Copyright 1998 by The Council for Exceptional Children. Reprinted with permission.

not the appropriate place for many students with learning disabilities—those who may need alternative instructional environments or teaching strategies that cannot or will not be provided within the context of the regular classroom. Neither group denies the legitimacy of the other's priorities. The issue is which should have precedence.

Evans (1995) points out that the inclusion philosophy requires the application of a variety of other strategies that can maintain a diverse group of students in the general education environment. These strategies include consultant teacher models, collaborative consultation, collaborative teaching, cooperative professional development, and prereferral consultation. In other words, it is not enough merely to decree that all exceptional children will be placed in the general education environment. If inclusion is to work, there must be a wide variety of support personnel to help the general education teacher provide a healthy educational environment for *all* students. Table 2.8 describes the differentiated program advocated by proponents of inclusion. A special education teacher, two paraprofessionals, and considerable planning to meet individual needs would be necessary to achieve the results expected in this inclusive classroom. Few school systems at the present time could allocate this level of personnel to a general classroom.

How much inclusion is "included"? There has been a great deal of confusion about just how much time the child with disabilities must spend in the regular classroom to be considered "included." Must it be 100 percent of school time to justify the term *inclusion*? One answer is that the child with disabilities should be based in the regular class. Another is that the child is recognized to be a member of the class where he or she starts the school day. The child with disabilities need

TABLE 2.8   Necessary Conditions for the Integration of Children with Disabilities in Regular Classrooms

All of the school personnel have attended inservice training designed to develop collaborative skills for teaming and problem-solving. Mrs. Smith and the two paraprofessionals who work in the classroom also received special training on disabilities and on how to create an inclusive classroom environment. The school principal, Ben Parks, had worked in special education many years ago and has received training on the impact of new special education developments and instructional arrangements on school administration. Each year, Mr. Parks works with the building staff to identify areas in which new training is needed. For specific questions that may arise, technical assistance is available through a regional special education cooperative.

Jane Smith teaches third grade at Lincoln Elementary School. Three days a week, she co-teaches the class with Lynn Vogel, a special education teacher. Their 25 students include 4 who have special needs due to disabilities and 2 others who currently need special help in specific curriculum areas. Each of the students with a disability has an IEP that was developed by a team that included both teachers. The teachers, paraprofessionals, and the school principal believe that these students have a great deal to contribute to the class and that they will achieve their best in the environment of a general education classroom.

Mrs. Smith and Miss Vogel share responsibility for teaching and for supervising their two paraprofessionals. In addition to the time they spend together in the classroom, they spend 1 to 4 hours per week planning instruction, plus additional planning time with other teachers and support personnel who work with their students.

The teachers use their joint planning time to problem-solve and discuss the use of special instructional techniques for all students who need special assistance. Monitoring and adapting instruction for individual students is an ongoing activity. The teachers use curriculum-based measurement to systematically assess their students' learning progress. They adapt curricula so that lessons begin at the edge of the student's knowledge, adding new material at the student's pace, and presenting it in a style consistent with the student's learning style. For some students, reorganizers or chapter previews are used to bring out the most important points of the material to be learned; for other students, new vocabulary words may need to be highlighted or reduced reading levels may be required. Some students may use special activity worksheets, while others may learn best by using media or computer-assisted instruction.

In the classroom the teachers group students differently for different activities. Sometimes, the teachers and paraprofessionals divide the class, each teaching a small group or tutoring individuals. They use cooperative learning projects to help the students learn to work together and develop social relationships. Peer tutors provide extra help to students who need it. Students without disabilities are more than willing to help their friends who have disabilities, and vice versa.

Source: ERIC Digest (July 1993). "Including Students with Disabilities in General Education Classrooms." *Clearinghouse on Disabilities and Gifted Education.* Council for Exceptional Children. Reprinted with permission.

not spend all of his or her time with that class, but that class is the child's group, and everyone knows it (Brown et al., 1991). As Brown and his colleagues (1991) say, "It is better to be an 'insider' who goes out for short periods of time, than it is to be an 'outsider' who comes in" (p. 40).

RESTRUCTURING IN GENERAL EDUCATION: AMERICA 2000

The reform and restructuring movement of the 1990s has several elements that especially affect exceptional children. Table 2.9 describes Goals 2000, a set of eight goals for American schools endorsed by the President and the governors of all fifty states. It is not hard to see the special problems that would be created for exceptional children if the goals were taken seriously. These include possible changes in the administration of special programs, the location of special education services, and the training that special education teachers (and regular teachers) will receive. Reforms that affect special education are in middle schools, cooperative learning, site-based management, academic standards, effective assessment tools, accountability, and state and federal legislation.

Some Results of Restructuring General Education

MIDDLE SCHOOLS

Restructuring regular education also requires major changes in special education.

One result of the movement to restructure schools is a move away from the traditional junior high school program, with its imitation of the senior high school in establishing categorical content fields (such as chemistry and history), one-hour periods, and teachers who are prepared in those special content fields but rarely schooled in educational strategies or developmental psychology. Advocates propose to replace the junior high school with the middle school, which would emphasize (1) the affective life of the student (recognizing the major physical changes the student is undergoing in this time period), (2) an interdisciplinary curriculum to indicate how bodies of knowledge interrelate, (3) team teaching to allow for the use of the special skills and knowledge of the teachers, (4) flexible scheduling, and (5) the organization of small to large student groups, depending on the lesson and the time (George, 1988).

One current emphasis in middle schools is heterogeneous grouping, the deliberate mixing of all levels of students in the instructional program. This strategy raises serious concerns among special educators about whether the special needs of exceptional children will be adequately addressed (Oakes, 1985).

COOPERATIVE LEARNING

Although cooperative learning is a set of instructional strategies rather than a major administrative shift or structural change, it has come to symbolize a new emphasis in U.S. education toward cooperation, as opposed to competition or isolated learning. **Cooperative learning** organizes students into groups of three to six and gives them a task to solve cooperatively. The goal of such strategies is to help students learn problem-solving techniques and how to work with others in a constructive manner (Johnson, Johnson, & Holubec, 1990).

The child with exceptionalities can be expected to participate as a member of a cooperative learning team. In ideal circumstances, the task that is presented to the

TABLE 2.9   Goals 2000: Educate America Act

Title I: National Education Goals

Codifies into law eight National Education Goals and their objectives. The goals state that, by the year 2000,

1. All children in American will start school ready to learn.

2. The high school graduation rate will increase to at least 90%.

3. American students will leave grades four, eight, and twelve having demonstrated competency over challenging subject matter, including English, mathematics, science, arts, foreign languages, history and geography, civics and government, and economics.

4. The nation's teaching force will have access to programs for the continued improvement of their professional skills and the opportunity to acquire the knowledge and skills needed to instruct and prepare all American students for the next century.

5. U.S. students will be first in the world in math and science achievement.

6. Every American will be literate and will possess the knowledge and skills necessary to compete in a global economy.

7. Every school in America will be free of drugs, alcohol, and violence and will offer a disciplined environment conducive to learning.

8. Every school will promote partnerships that will increase parental involvement and participation in promoting the social, emotional, and academic growth of children.

Source: U.S. Department of Education.

group has a meaningful role for the exceptional child. A problem such as "How did our community come to be?" might provide the child with mental retardation the task of searching newspaper files for information, while the child with intellectual giftedness might go over courthouse records or conduct oral interviews of early residents. The use of cooperative learning has been reported to have increased the social acceptance of some exceptional children in regular classrooms (Johnson, Johnson, & Holubec, 1990). An emphasis in some cooperative learning programs on organizing the groups by heterogeneous mixing (Slavin, 1991) has caused some educators of gifted students to question the level of challenge that their students would meet in such groups (Robinson, 1991).

SITE-BASED MANAGEMENT

Many people in the reform movement believe in shifting the power of educational decision making back to the teacher and the local school and away from distant administrators in the "central office," who may not be aware of local issues or problems. With site-based management, the state department of education, the local school administrators, or institutions of higher education exercise less power and decision making. Site-based management is one of a number of attempts to empower teachers, to recognize their expertise, and to support them in their own decisions about what is best for the students in their charge.

Ideally the exceptional child has a meaningful role in cooperative learning activities. (© *David Pratt/Positive Images*)

How such a move will affect children with special needs probably will depend in large measure on whether a specific site has people knowledgeable about the special problems of such children and what educational strategies they can use to deal with those problems. If no one on the local site-based team knows about the special learning problems of children with learning disabilities, then there is concern that necessary services will not be delivered.

The Academic Standards Movement versus the Inclusion Movement

One of the fundamental parts of the educational reform movement involves the development of academic standards (National Council on Educational Standards and Testing, 1992). Such standards, which represent what students are expected to do at a certain level of schooling, are designed to counteract a supposed slippage of expectations in America's schools (Berliner, 1992). By establishing state or national standards for mastery of mathematics or history or science, we are able to assure ourselves that the schools in a community have been performing their educational job effectively.

Although the term *high academic standards* has an attractive ring to it, several questions should come to mind: How will we determine if students have met such standards? Are we calling for a major new testing program to determine if students meet minimal or challenging academic standards? Some people clearly hope that the establishment of standards and the tests to measure their attainment will be an effective motivator for upgrading school performance (Simmons & Resnick, 1993). It has not escaped the notice of educators that teachers will teach whatever is on *high-stakes tests* (tests whose results are translated into meaningful action by the schools, such as entrance to college or promotion to the next grade). How those new standards affect exceptional children is a key question that we need to concern ourselves with.

Two of the major educational reforms facing school systems today seem to be on a collision course. They are the standards movement and the inclusion movement in general education for special education. The issue has become so pressing that the National Academy of Sciences established a commission to study the matter (McDonnell, McLaughlin, & Morrison, 1997). The commission pointed out that the standards movement has made it clear that they expect all children to learn and achieve at high standards and that the term *all* includes children with disabilities (Goals 2000 legislation). Such expansive statements raise some serious questions for exceptional children. Does that mean that Barry, with severe cognitive impairments plus cerebral palsy, is expected to meet the same high academic requirements in math, science, language arts, and social studies as all other students? What about Mary, who has a serious pattern of autism?

Apart from the feasibility of applying such standards, there is the question of the desirability of such standards being applied to exceptional children. As the National Academy of Sciences report points out, many exceptional children take a secondary program that is vocationally oriented and directed to possible work practice and opportunities. "It is important that broader outcomes and school-to-work transition planning not be neglected in the move toward standards-based reform" (McDonnell et. al., 1997, p. 149).

Is Carl, with a severe learning disability, going to have to give up his school-to-work assignment with the local bus company in order to take the challenging American history course so he can get his high school diploma? It is clear that a lot of work needs to be done to bring together, in an operational fashion, the desirable goals from both of these reform movements on inclusion and standards.

The increasing concern about standards has raised an important point about what action should be taken with students who don't meet the standards. Suppose, in the interests of higher standards, the schools establish a minimum standard of performance to be achieved before a student moves on to the next grade. Many exceptional children will not be able to meet that standard. What happens then? All too often, the answer is retention or holding the student back a grade in the hope that the student will, with the extra time, be able to master the basic skills or knowledge. Retention, however, has been long demonstrated to be one of the least useful of techniques. In general, students who are retained tend to drop out of school more and do not learn the necessary material that was the goal of the retention in the first place. Such results are also found in a research synthesis with children with learning disabilities (McLeskey, Lancaster, & Grizzle, 1995). There is little reason to believe that mere retention will do anything to help the student. The standards issue promises to be problematical for children with special needs.

Effective Assessment Tools

There is also the important question of whether we have the correct tools for the tasks of program assessment and evaluation. Elaborate goals such as improving productive thinking or increasing the scope of knowledge structure sound impressive, but do we have the means of demonstrating that such goals have been met?

Some new approaches have appeared to take the place of the standard achievement tests. They bear names like *performance assessment*, *authentic assessment*, and *real-life assessment*. Because performance is knowledge in use, **performance assessment** is a measure of the applications of knowledge. If a student is asked to write an essay on a particular topic, that essay could form the basis for a type of performance assessment. If a student is asked to conduct a research project or produce an oral presentation on a topic, that assignment could be a basis for performance assessment (Wiggins, 1992).

Authentic assessment involves the regular classroom performance of the student, rather than a contrived task. Quite typically, it might be an examination of a student portfolio providing evidence of student performance over time. In this way, we have an assessment in real time, using classroom work and assignments as the basis for evaluation.

These forms of evaluation still leave the task of determining just what performance is acceptable or outstanding. Often such judgments are rather crude three-point or four-point scales ranging from *excellent* to *unacceptable*. Added to that would be a substantive critique of writing style or scientific procedures revealed through the authentic assessment. These approaches are good news for programs for gifted students because they give students considerably greater leeway to show what they know and what applications they can make of what they know than would be possible in a multiple-choice test. If these performance assessments or authentic assessments turn out to be high-stakes testing (an important decision regarding the student's life will be made as a result of their outcome), then considerable attention has to be paid to the scoring standards to ensure fairness and equity in the procedures from one place to another.

Accountability

The word *accountability* throws a mild chill into every educator. The general public tells us that we are to be held responsible for the products that we release from the educational system. No longer will the general public take the educator's word about what progress is being made in education; it wants to be shown. The public wants proof that education and special education produce good results, and it does not react well when told how hard it is to produce that proof, however valid the reasons (Gallagher, 1998).

In the field of exceptional children, the goals of the IEPs might be quite different from one child to another, and so aggregating results into a total report on the special education program may be hard. For example, if Mary is trying to achieve social acceptance goals and Sam is working on spelling, it would be hard to assess Sam's progress with a social acceptance scale or Mary's progress with a spelling test or to add up all the scores of the special students on these measures as a way of judging progress.

Currently, most standard achievement tests don't accurately measure the abilities of the exceptional child.

As currently constructed, standard achievement tests do not adequately measure the attainments of many exceptional children. The child with mental retardation may be learning many practical sets of skills and knowledge that are not covered by the standard curriculum and standard tests, and the gifted child will surely have his or her abilities and attainments underestimated because of the lack of depth and conceptual complexity of most of these measures. Programs for exceptional children must be accountable—as must all education programs—but special efforts must be made to ensure that the measurements fit the exceptional student's program goals.

STATE AND FEDERAL LEGISLATION

In many instances, what is happening in the schools with children with special needs has legislative ancestors. Many of the resources and finances that schools need to conduct special services for such children have come from state or federal legislation. While providing these resources, the legislatures sometimes make certain requirements about where and how to educate such children. To access those funds, local schools modify their programs to meet the demands of the legislation. Thus, what you are observing in the schools may be designed not so much by educators as by legislators eager to have their say about the best way to modify the general education program for children with special needs.

An Overview

One of the ways we express society's needs and intentions in a democracy is through legislation. At the turn of the century, individual states became involved in a limited way in subsidizing programs in public schools for children with sensory disabilities (blindness, deafness) and physical impairments. Some states helped organize and support classes for children who were mentally retarded or who had behavioral problems. After World War II, many states expanded their involvement, providing financial support for special classes and services in local schools for children with all types of disability. This expansion caused two problems that many believed could be solved only by federal legislation.

First, these new and larger programs created a personnel scarcity in the late 1940s and early 1950s. Professional special educators were in short supply, and the field of special education was not firmly established. Second, because not all states expanded their involvement in special education, organized parents' groups began asking why children with disabilities and their parents should be penalized through the accident of birth in a particular state or a particular region of a state.

Were not U.S. citizens (in this case, the parents of children with disabilities) entitled to equal treatment anywhere in the United States? Should parents, in addition to the burdens of having children with special needs, be forced to move their family to a community where special education resources were available, or to send their children to some institution far away from home and family because no local resources existed? The blatant unfairness of the situation called out for attention.

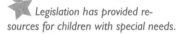
Legislation has provided resources for children with special needs.

Federal legislation clearly was needed, both to bring qualified people into special education and to equalize educational opportunities across the country. But that legislation was not easy to obtain. It violated the strong tradition in the United States that education is a state and local responsibility. Still, organized parents' groups with the support of other interested citizens convinced Congress that they needed help.

Public Law 88-164

After much debate, in the late 1950s Congress began to pass limited measures directed toward research and personnel training in the fields of mental retardation and deafness. In 1963, PL 88-164 authorized funds for training professionals and for research and demonstration. The law represented a strong initiative by President John Kennedy, whose interest was heightened by his sister's mental retardation. Those first efforts were followed by many others, and from that small beginning emerged thirty years of legislation to ensure that all children with disabilities have access to an appropriate education.

Public Law 94-142

That flood of legislation served notice that the federal government accepted responsibility for providing support and resources for children with disabilities and

By pressuring their representatives and speaking out themselves, exceptional individuals have been instrumental in getting new laws passed and new programs established. (© Rose Skytta/Jeroboam, Inc.)

for encouraging the states to carry out their basic responsibilities. Still, programs and resources were not consistent from state to state. To deal with that inconsistency and to help the states handle the costs of court-mandated programs, Congress in 1975 passed PL 94-142, the Education for All Handicapped Children Act. The measure, which took effect in 1977, was designed

> to assure that all handicapped children have available to them . . . special education and related services designed to meet their unique needs . . . to assure that the rights of handicapped children, and their parents or guardians, are protected, to assist states and localities to provide for the education of all handicapped children, and to assess and assure the effectiveness of efforts to educate handicapped children. (U.S. House of Representatives, 1975, p. 35)

Six key principles at the heart of PL 94-142 have shaped special as well as general education during the last two decades:

- *Zero reject.* All children with disabilities must be provided a free and appropriate public education. This means local school systems do not have the option to decide whether to provide needed services.

- *Nondiscriminatory evaluation.* Each student must receive a full individual examination before being placed in a special education program, with tests appropriate to the child's cultural and linguistic background. A re-evaluation is required every three years.

- *Individualized education program.* An IEP must be written for every student with a handicap who is receiving special education. The IEP must describe the child's current performance and goals for the school year, the particular special education services to be delivered, and the procedures by which outcomes are evaluated.

- *Least restrictive environment.* As much as possible, children who are handicapped must be educated with children who are not handicapped. The philosophy is to move as close to the normal setting (regular classroom) as feasible for each child.

- *Due process.* Due process is a set of legal procedures to ensure the fairness of educational decisions and the accountability of both professionals and parents in making those decisions. These procedures allow parents to call a hearing when they do not agree with the school's plans for their child, to obtain an individual evaluation from a qualified examiner outside the school system, or to take other actions to ensure that both family and child have channels through which to voice their interests and concerns.

- *Parental participation.* Parents are to be included in the development of the IEP, and they have the right to access their child's educational records.

To carry out the provisions of the law, the federal government authorized the spending of up to $3 billion by 1982, promising much larger sums of money to aid the states than had previously been provided. By 1990, the government was still spending about $1 billion a year. In return for that aid, states are required to show evidence that they are doing their best to help children with disabilities receive needed services. Specific provisions in the law placed substantial pressure on public school systems, demanding more in the way of assessment, parent contact, and evaluation than most school systems had been accustomed to providing.

Not surprisingly, many educators have protested the burden that these requirements place on them. But the law has become part of the educational landscape. In less than three decades, the federal government moved from little involvement in special education to become a major partner in local and state programs for students who have disabilities.

Public Law 99-457 and IDEA (Public Law 105-17)

The Education for All Handicapped Children Act was, in fact, misnamed. It wasn't for all children at all ages. As it became increasingly evident that early intervention was important, both for the exceptional child and for his or her family, pressure grew for a downward extension of the law.

PL 99-457 (Education of the Handicapped Act Amendments), passed in 1986, provided that opportunity by allocating federal funds for the states to develop plans and programs for children and their families from birth on. PL 105-17, passed in 1990, changed the title of the Education of the Handicapped Act to the "Individuals with Disabilities Education Act," or IDEA. As was true of the earlier legislation, embedded in these laws were numerous attempts to reform or restructure the service system. For example, PL 99-457 included the following:

- A requirement for an Individualized Family Services Plan (IFSP), which would provide a program of services to the child and family as appropriate and would recognize the rights of parents to influence their child's program.

- A call for the integration of various services. Agencies were required to work together so the resources of health, social, and family services and education could blend their efforts to the common benefit of child and family.

- A call for personnel preparation standards and plans, so that capable and well-trained persons would be working with these families.

■ A requirement that states pool existing sources of funds to provide for these programs (the federal government no longer took responsibility for paying more than a small part of the services bill).

IDEA added a requirement for transition services, a coordinated set of activities to promote movement from school to post-school activities such as secondary education, vocational training, independent living, and community participation. Many other provisions of this law provided services for preschool children with disabilities and their families and made clear that the service system for young children would be redesigned in a more appropriate fashion—with comprehensive services, in a multidisciplinary pattern with interagency cooperation.

Federal Actions for Students Who Are Gifted

The Javits Act, which provided resources for gifted students, pointed out the low incidence of cultural minorities identified as gifted.

Except for a brief period in the 1970s, there had been little movement at the federal legislative level to provide resources to aid in the education of children who are gifted. The Javits Act (Public Law 100-297), named after New York senator Jacob Javits, who showed early interest and support, provided a small sum of money to support research and demonstration programs that focused on the special needs of gifted students from economically disadvantaged circumstances, from different cultures, or with special physical disabilities. The new support of such programs seems linked to the general dismay of the American public at how far behind American students are in content fields such as mathematics and the sciences (see Chapter 4 for specific comparisons), when compared with students from other industrialized countries. This law also noted the limited number of gifted students being identified from cultural minorities and urged action on that issue.

THE ROLE OF THE COURTS

Courts have confirmed the right of children with special needs to a free, appropriate public education (FAPE).

Another important player in the establishment and design of programs for children with special needs has been the courts. The basic issue here is that children with special needs deserve a free and appropriate education, just as do all children in the United States. If that right is being abridged, or if other inequities are being created, citizens can appeal to the courts for justice and equity. During the 1970s and 1980s, a series of legal cases solidified the position of exceptional children and their right to a free and appropriate education.

For the last three decades the courts have assumed the role of protector of the rights of exceptional children. Their decisions, however, have not always been that favorable. Despite the rules for compulsory attendance to school that were in place during the first third of the twentieth century, there were court decisions that allowed schools to expel students with various disabilities.

As late as 1958, the State Supreme Court of Illinois did not require a free public education for children who were mentally deficient and who "could not reap the benefits of education" (Yell, Rogers, & Rogers, 1998). Even in 1969, North Carolina made it a crime for parents to force attendance of the child with disabilities after he or she had been excluded from school.

A landmark case that began a series of court decisions in favor of exceptional children and their right to a free public education was the *Pennsylvania Association for Retarded Children* (PARC) v. *Commonwealth of Pennsylvania* lawsuit and decision. In this case, the court decided that children with mental retardation did have a right to free, appropriate public education (FAPE) and that when the state constitution said all children are entitled to a free education, the term *all* did, in fact, refer to *all* children.

The movement toward judicial action was, in part, a recognition of the success of minority groups in using the courts to establish their educational rights. In 1954 with the classic school desegregation case, *Brown* v. *Board of Education,* the courts began to reaffirm the rights of minority citizens in a wide variety of settings. If court decisions could protect the rights of one group of citizens, they should do the same for another group: those with disabilities. Soon, supporters of people with disabilities were working to translate abstract legal rights into tangible social action through the judicial system.

Class action suits have been influential in changing the status of children with disabilities in the United States. A *class action suit* provides that legal action taken as part of the suit applies not only to the individual who brings the particular case to court but to all members of the class to which that individual belongs. That means the rights of all people with disabilities can be reaffirmed by a case involving just one child.

The rulings in several court cases have reaffirmed the rights of those who are handicapped and have defined the limits of those rights:

■ A child with disabilities cannot be excluded from school without careful due process, and it is the responsibility of the schools to provide appropriate programs for children who are different (*Pennsylvania Association for Retarded Children* v. *Commonwealth of Pennsylvania*, 1972; *Goso* v. *Lopez,* 1974; *Hairston* v. *Drosick,* 1974).

■ The presumed absence of funds is not an excuse for failing to provide educational services to exceptional children. If sufficient funds are not available, then all programs should be cut back (*Mills* v. *Board of Education,* 1972).

■ Children with disabilities who are committed to state institutions must be provided a meaningful education in that setting or their incarceration is considered unlawful detention (*Wyatt* v. *Stickney,* 1972).

■ Children should not be labeled "handicapped" or placed into special education without adequate diagnosis that takes into account different cultural and linguistic backgrounds (*Larry P.* v. *Riles,* 1979).

■ Bilingual exceptional children need identification, evaluation, and educational procedures that reflect and respect their dual-language background (*Jos P.* v. *Ambach,* 1979).

■ An individual with learning disabilities has a right to services whatever his or her age (*Frederick L.* v. *Thomas,* 1980).

■ A child with disabilities is entitled to an appropriate, not an optimum, education (*Board of Education* v. *Rowley,* 1982). The *Rowley* decision was the first court decision that suggested there was a limit to the resources that exceptional children could expect.

Recently, the attention of the courts has turned to the issues of *inclusion* and *least restrictive environment* and what an appropriate program for exceptional children should be. The results are a mixture of rulings, some supporting a strong version of inclusion and some supporting a continuum of services (McCarthy, 1994):

- A child with a hearing disability was allowed to attend a school several miles from home instead of a neighborhood school because the centralized program at the special school better met the child's needs (*Barnett* v. *Fairfax County Board of Education,* 1991).

- A child with a serious attention deficit and acting-out behavior should be placed in a special school rather than in the general education classroom (*Clyde & Shela K.* v. *Puyallup School District,* 1994).

- A child with Down syndrome was placed in a general education program rather than in a special education class because of the presumed priority of mainstreaming in IDEA (*Greer* v. *Rome City School District,* 1991).

- A court ruled that it is the responsibility of the school district to demonstrate that the child's disabilities are so severe that he or she will receive little benefit from inclusion or will be so disruptive as to keep other classmates from learning (*Oberti* v. *Board of Education of the Borough of Clementon School District,* 1993).

Clearly, these rulings reflect the specifics of each individual case and the interpretation of local or district courts. It may take a Supreme Court decision to provide more general guidance on the issue. Nevertheless, when the courts speak, people listen because court decisions represent the law as we currently know it and must be obeyed.

A recent trend has focused the courts on the financial formulas used by educators to provide services for exceptional children and for all students. Three states, Alabama, Wyoming, and Ohio, have had major parts of their school financing system declared unconstitutional (Verstegen, 1998). The basic reason for these decisions resided in the unequal funding by the school systems within the state and the inadequacy of funding for special education, which caused it to be a drain on local general education funds.

It seems clear that some alternative method of state funding may have to be devised that could go further toward guaranteeing a free, appropriate education for all students that is equitable from one system to another in a state, regardless of the differences in wealth from one district to another.

Numerous attempts have been made through court cases to determine just what the phrase *least restrictive environment* really means. Yell (1995) reviewed the many case decisions on least restrictive environment and concluded that

> for a school to survive a legal challenge to the placement of a student in a segregated setting, it must show that the student would not benefit academically or socially from an integrated placement, or that the student would disrupt classroom learning. (p. 402)

Just as laws have to be enforced and money has to be appropriated, so court decisions have to be executed. The court decisions created the expectation that something would be done, but they did not guarantee it. Closing down state institutions, reorganizing public schools, and providing special services to all children with disabilities were substantial and costly changes. They raised a serious problem for program administrators: From where would the money come for implementation? Ultimately, school and local leaders turned to Washington, pressuring Congress to appropriate funds to help pay for the changes that the courts were demanding. Even with federal assistance, implementation has come slowly.

Much of the change that has been formalized in legislation and court decisions protects the rights of youngsters with disabilities. But laws and court rulings are subject to interpretation. Special educators have a unique responsibility to see that laws and rulings are implemented as they were intended: to guarantee that all children receive an appropriate education.

▰▱ *Conclusion*

We discuss the education reform movement throughout this text. Because reforms were not specifically designed for exceptional children, however, their impact on such students was rarely considered in the initial stages of the intended reform.

The exceptional child must be viewed in a context that includes family, neighborhood, school, and society. All these forces impinge on the child and on his or her family, and they either enhance or inhibit the efforts of special educators to provide an appropriate education. The goal of special education teachers is to create the most favorable environment possible so that the child's capabilities are maximized.

In the next chapter, we focus on the early years of exceptional children. How these children and families develop during the period from birth to age 5 has a great deal to do with how the children react to later schooling.

Summary of Major Ideas

1. Changes in society's attitudes toward exceptional children are reflected in the processes that bring children closer to the regular classroom.

2. Instruction can be adapted to the individual needs of exceptional students in several ways: We can vary the learning environment, change the curriculum (lesson content), modify the skills taught, and adapt teaching strategies.

3. Many exceptional children come from different cultural backgrounds and have distinctive values, attitudes, and languages. It is the responsibility of special educators to take these differences into account in their special educational plans.

4. We can make innovative use of technology to meet the needs of exceptional students. Children with disabilities may face special challenges in living up to the newer adult role expected in their culture.

5. Teacher-assistance teams can sometimes help the regular class teacher deal with difficult students prior to their referral to special education and, perhaps, eliminate the need for such referrals.

6. Technology can serve two separate purposes for children with disabilities. Assistive technology enhances routine functioning and communication. Instructional technology aids in the delivery and support of instruction.

7. The assessment of exceptional children involves screening, diagnosis, classification, placement, and instructional planning.

8. An individualized education program (IEP) defines the nature of a child's academic situation, the program's long-term goals and short-term objectives,

needed services, and criteria for evaluation. The IEP has received positive comments (it improves relations between teacher and parent) and negative comments (it places time demands on the teacher without helping the child).

9. *Full inclusion* refers to educational situations where all children with disabilities are educated with same-age peers and the major goal is social integration.

10. Educational restructuring is changing the learning environment for exceptional children. Middle schools, cooperative learning, site-based management, and accountability proposed for all students are requiring changes in programs for exceptional children.

11. Legislation and court decisions have created a full range of educational opportunities for children with developmental disabilities.

12. National education goals (Goals 2000) indicate the national interest in the achievement of both equity and excellence in education.

13. Courts now require school systems to have strong documentation before moving a child with disabilities from the general education classroom.

Unresolved Issues

1. *Malleability of children.* We in education are in the business of trying to improve the status of children. How much can we expect children to change as a result of their experience in educational programs? We know that children are pliable, but what are the limits of their malleability? A quiet child is not going to be transformed into an extrovert by our efforts. A child who is mentally retarded is not going to become gifted by our efforts. We must limit our expectations to judge the success of what we do.

2. *Computers and individual instruction.* Computers present us with some tempting possibilities. They interact with children in ways that teachers cannot. The typical teacher can't respond instantly to every student, offering reinforcement and encouragement; a computer can. The teacher, however, is still the most influential element in the educational process—a source of thoughtful, flexible responses. Teachers must learn how to mix that humanity with technology in the classroom.

3. *Balancing least restrictive environment and inclusion.* A major dispute exists between those who support a continuum of services to educate children with disabilities and those who insist that all children with disabilities belong in the general education classroom. The impact of the exceptional child on the other children in the general classroom can be seen as both positive and negative. The fact that evidence for the benefits of either course of action is not currently available no doubt contributes to the intensity of the debate.

4. *Academic standards movement and inclusion.* At odds with each other are the academic standards movement and the inclusion movement. The academic standards movement expects all students to achieve at high levels, which may not be feasible. Many secondary exceptional students may prefer vocational training to academics as they prepare for the workplace.

Key Terms

Academic aptitude p. 50
assessment p. 49
assistive technology p. 46
authentic assessment p. 70
circle of friends p. 63
continuum of services p. 35
cooperative learning p. 66
diagnostic achievement tests p. 52
inclusion p. 35
individualized education program
 (IEP) p. 56

inert knowledge p. 46
instructional technology p. 46
inter-individual differences p. 50
least restrictive environment p. 42
performance assessment p. 69
resource room p. 42
standard (norm-referenced) achievement
 tests p. 52
transition services p. 39

Questions for Thought

1. Over time, attitudes in the United States toward individuals with disabilities have changed. Describe this change. p. 34

2. "Howe's belief that children need more than custodial care, that all children, whatever their circumstances, deserve an education, continues to guide current thinking." Support this statement with material from Chapter 2. pp. 35–39

3. In the transition from school to community, what are the three major components of adjustment? pp. 39–40

4. If good teaching is going on in the general education classroom, why are special education programs and services necessary? p. 42

5. What impact does the least restrictive environment have on the job of the general education teacher, on the quality of life for students with disabilities, and on students without disabilities? pp. 42–44

6. What specific advantages do computers offer in the education program for exceptional children? p. 47

7. Explain the five steps of the assessment process. p. 49

8. Explain the five components of the individualized education program. p. 56

9. How can the individualized education program contribute to the appropriate education of students with disabilities, and how can it help general education teachers? pp. 56–58

10. What are some of the current restructuring trends in education, and how might they affect special education? pp. 58–67

11. What two problems was federal legislation for special education intended to address? pp. 70–74

12. PL 94-142 was aimed primarily at the school-age population. Describe four major pieces of legislation that extended rights to children with disabilities. pp. 71–74

13. Identify and briefly explain the six key principles of PL 94-142, the Education for All Handicapped Children Act. pp. 72–73

14. How did passage of PL 94-142 place substantial pressure on public school systems? p. 73

Resources for Further Study

REFERENCES OF SPECIAL INTEREST

Biklin, D., Ferguson, D., & Ford, A. (1989). *Schooling and disability* (Pt. 2). Eighty-eighth Yearbook of the National Society for the Study of Education. Chicago: University of Chicago Press.

> This book is a strong statement in favor of major reforms in special education and an argument for mainstreaming. It describes how schools might perceive exceptional students differently and how they might develop programs and practices that would make schools the "inclusive communities" they ought to be.

Goodlad, J., & Lovitt, T. (Eds.). (1993). *Integrating general and special education.* New York: Macmillan.

> This book addresses a significant and knotty issue—how to bring together the two separate educational systems known as regular education and special education. Issues such as curriculum, financing, evaluation, and restructuring are dealt with in special chapters. There are some good summary chapters on the training of teachers and implementation.

McDonnell, L., McLaughlin, M., & Morrison, P. (Eds). (1997). *Educating one and all: Students with disabilities and standards-based reform.* Washington, D.C.: National Academy Press.

> A report from the National Academy of Sciences on the attempts to combine the educational standards movement with the special needs of the student with disability. How does one balance the "high standards for all" with the need for individual requirements for students with disabilities? The diversity of students with disabilities, the content standards, and the accountability and assessment issues are discussed in depth.

Paul, J., Rosselli, H., & Evans, D. (Eds.). (1995). *Integrating school restructuring and special education reform.* Fort Worth, TX: Harcourt Brace.

> This book spells out the various elements of educational reform and indicates how such elements will affect exceptional children. Some proposed changes call for personnel preparation, more research, and the geography of special education (for example, inclusion). Contributors deal in separate chapters with reforms beginning in general education (site-based management) and with reforms begun in special education (inclusion).

Remedial and Special Education [special journal issue on history]. (1998). *19*(4), 196–238.

> A series of articles that goes into interesting detail about the early years of special education and the identification and education of children with special needs. Most of the history begins in the nineteenth century and progresses to an increasing involvement of the educational system. Particularly interesting is a piece on the legal history of special education.

Stainback, S., & Stainback, W. (Eds.). (1996). *Inclusion: A guide to educators.* Baltimore: Paul H. Brookes.

> Twenty-six chapters and thirty-five contributors present the case for inclusion of children with special needs in the general classroom. Issues of basic strategies to establish inclusion policy, the collaboration with teachers and students, and special considerations of curriculum and behavioral concerns are the general foci of the text. This is a strong statement in favor of a broad policy of inclusion for the schools.

Taylor, R. (1997). *Assessment of exceptional students* (4th ed.). Boston: Allyn & Bacon.
A comprehensive and critical review of the various tests and informal procedures such as systematic observation, portfolio assessment, and curriculum-based assessment, with special reference to how these devices relate to exceptional children. There is a special section on the assessment of achievement in reading and mathematics and another on the special problems in early childhood education assessment and in vocational/transitional assessment.

Teaching exceptional children [Special issue]. (1998, May/June). *World Wide Web and Special Education 30*(5).
An entire issue devoted to explaining to teachers the multiple uses of the World Wide Web in the instruction of exceptional children. In addition to basic information such as how to access information through the Web, there are specific suggestions as to how the Web can be used for writing by students with learning disabilities, multimedia studies for deaf children, and coping with information access problems for students with visual disabilities, attention deficit disorders, and physical disabilities.

JOURNALS

Teaching Exceptional Children
   Council for Exceptional Children
   1920 Association Dr.
   Reston, VA 20191-1589
   1-888-CEC-SPED
   TTY 703-264-9446
   http://www.cec.sped.org/bk/abtec.htm

Remedial and Special Education
   PRO-ED Journals
   5341 Industrial Oaks Blvd.
   Austin, TX 78735-8809
   Fax: 512-451-8542
   http://www.proedinc.com/store/13.html

Journal of Early Intervention
   Council for Exceptional Children
   1920 Association Dr.
   Reston, VA 20191-1589
   1-888-CED-SPED
   TTY 703-264-9446
   http://www.cec.spec.org/

Educational Leadership
   Association for Supervision and
   Curriculum Development
   1703 North Beauregard St.
   Alexandria, VA 22311-1714
   703-578-9600 or 1-800-933-2723
   Fax: 703-575-5400
   http://www.ascd.org/

*Journal of the Association for Persons
   with Severe Handicaps* (JASH)
   11201 Greenwood Ave. North
   Seattle, WA 98133

PROFESSIONAL ORGANIZATIONS

Council for Exceptional Children
   1920 Association Dr.
   Reston, VA 20191-1589
   1-888-CED-SPED
   TTY 703-264-9446
   http://www.cec.sped.org/

3

Early Intervention: Priorities and Programs

FOCUSING questions

Why is there an emphasis on early intervention for infants with disabilities?

What is the meaning of the term *at-risk*?

How do we identify children who are in need of early intervention?

Who are some of the professionals involved in early intervention programs?

What is meant by family involvement?

Does early intervention improve the functioning of infants with disabilities?

Ann and Bryan were enthusiastically expecting their second child. Their first child, Suzi, was 3 years old and very bright. Both Ann and Bryan were 30 years old, active, and in good health.

When Ann and Bryan went to the hospital, a neighbor stayed with Suzi until the grandmother arrived. News was slow in coming, but at last Bryan called. Ann was fine, he said. The child was a boy, and his name was Colin. He said nothing more. Friends became concerned when Ann didn't return home with the baby as soon as they expected, and Bryan seemed unusually glum for a new father.

Meanwhile, Ann was in a state of despair. Colin had been diagnosed as having *Down syndrome,* a genetic disorder characterized by folds on the eyelids, some degree of retardation, and possibly other health problems. Neither Ann nor Bryan could understand how they, a vigorously healthy young couple with a bright 3-year-old, could have an infant with mental retardation.

Their physician contacted a local parent group and found another couple who had a child with Down syndrome. This couple went to the hospital to talk to Ann and Bryan and explain the realities of Colin's disabilities to them. They tried to convince Ann that all was not lost and that much could be done to help Colin develop, if not as fully as other children, at least to a higher level of functioning than had previously been believed possible for children with Down syndrome. The couple told Ann and Bryan about local programs that would help Colin strengthen his weak limbs and stimulate his intellectual curiosity. Through these programs, Ann and Bryan would meet other parents who could help them solve the problems they were facing.

After eight days, Ann took Colin home, somewhat reluctantly, and began the long process of working through her grief at having a child with disabilities rather than the ideal child she and Bryan had hoped to have. Ann knew her life had been markedly changed. As Colin grew, Ann and Bryan had to deal with grief and frustration many times, and they learned to work with hearing specialists, speech-language therapists, and physical and occupational therapists to begin the long process of helping Colin achieve as much of his potential as possible in spite of his disabilities.

This true story would have had a different ending thirty years ago. The physician would have told Ann and Bryan that there was little hope for most children with Colin's disabilities and probably would have recommended institutionalization. If Colin had been institutionalized, the long-term prediction would have been that he would be severely retarded by the time he was an adult. In addition, the physician possibly would not have been able to locate other parents of a child with Down syndrome; even if he could, they might not have been willing to talk to Ann and Bryan. Further, in the community there most likely would not have been early childhood programs in which therapists and educators could work with Colin to maximize his potential.

Ann and Bryan are just one example of the wide range of parents, families, and caregivers who are involved in early childhood intervention for children with disabilities. These people are old and young; they represent all the diverse cultures that make up our society. Many families do not know about services that are available to them—services that did not exist even a few years ago. In this chapter, we discuss the origins and significance of early diagnosis and intervention, why early intervention is important, who are the children at risk, how some disabilities can be prevented and detected, and the major programs and services that are available.

Overview of Early Intervention

DEFINITIONS AND GOALS

Early intervention is designed to prevent deficits or to improve an existing disability.

Early childhood intervention consists of sustained and systematic efforts to assist young, disabled, developmentally vulnerable children from birth to age 5 and their families (Meisels & Shonkoff, 1990). Early intervention is a term now used broadly to refer to a range of services provided to children, parents, and families during pregnancy, infancy, and/or early childhood (Dunst, 1996). Early intervention is designed to prevent deficits or to improve an existing disability by providing therapies (such as speech-language) or devices to help the child move (such as wheelchairs or braces for damaged limbs) and, most important in the new view of children with disabilities, by building strength through teaching and learning experiences. Early intervention cannot cure motor or sensory damage. However, it does work to prevent further loss and to improve functioning. For example, a child who is deaf may never hear sounds but can attain his or her cognitive and social potential through the use of sign language.

The time for early childhood intervention ranges from birth to 9 years of age and has become increasingly family directed (NICHCY, 1998). There is now an early intervention program in virtually every major community (Guralnick, 1998).

ORIGINS OF EARLY INTERVENTION

Early intervention programs are a logical extension of early childhood programs, which have a long history in the United States, beginning in the late 1930s (Safford, Sargent, & Cook, 1994). Early childhood programs, known as nursery schools or preschools, were an outgrowth of psychologists' concerns for children's mental health (Cairns, 1983), which psychologists believed was fostered by positive child-rearing practices in the early years of life (Anastasiow & Nucci, 1994). Children with disabilities, however, were excluded from most of these programs. Many children with severe disabilities or mental retardation were sent to live in large state-run, hospital-like settings. These institutions provided custodial care and little training. Parents who could afford the alternative of a private residential school sent their children with disabilities there.

The prevailing opinion was that little could be done for a child with disabilities because intelligence and skills potential were fixed at birth. However, programs were developed for children who were deaf, hard of hearing, blind, or experiencing some loss of vision. Before 1900, children usually entered such programs at age 10; thereafter, they started as young as age 5. Not until the 1930s and 1940s were programs initiated for children with physical disabilities and cerebral palsy (Safford et al., 1994). But these programs were not widely available throughout the United States.

The belief that nothing could be done for children with disabilities was challenged by the children's parents, special educators, and members of allied therapeutic professions. This belief changed markedly as a result of Skeels and Skodak's work with orphanage children in the 1930s. These researchers found that children who were placed in foster homes or were adopted fared much better than a comparable group who remained in the orphanage (Skeels, 1966). The adopted group

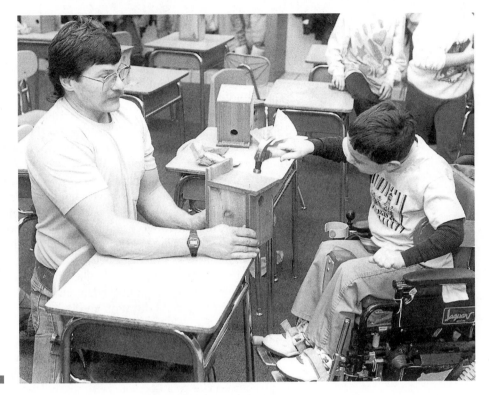

Early intervention programs are a logical extension of early childhood programs, which provide a sound base for the development of a secure and competent child who is ready for a successful regular school experience. *(© Michael Siluk/The Picture Cube)*

achieved normal intelligence, while many of the orphanage children were classified as mentally retarded. In addition, Kirk (1950) demonstrated that preschool experience could increase the rate of mental development and the social skills of children who were classified as mentally retarded (see also Bricker, 1993, for a more detailed history).

Hunt's book *Intelligence and Experience* (1961) was extremely influential because it summarized research studies. It led directly to the development of **Head Start,** an educational program for children living in poverty. One of the assumptions was that children from families with higher economic status had higher IQ scores because of their more privileged environments. Once Head Start was established, families of children with disabilities pressed schools, communities, and Congress to establish programs for their children as well. They cited the principle that had led to the creation of Head Start: If children with disabilities were taught early in their lives, then their lives could be improved. As a result of pressure exerted by the families of children with disabilities, early intervention was born.

LEGISLATIVE SUPPORT FOR EARLY INTERVENTION

Early intervention led to the development of early childhood special education.

Early intervention led to the development of early childhood special education, or the special training of teachers to work with infants and toddlers (from birth to age 2) and children from 3 to 5 years of age. Before 1968, few training programs prepared special educators or other specialists such as psychologists to work with infants and young children. In addition, few training programs prepared educators to work with speech-language therapists, physical therapists, physicians, and the host of other specialists who could intervene to improve the life outcome of a child with disabilities.

Congress established the Bureau for the Education of the Handicapped in 1967 and in 1968 passed the Early Childhood Special Education Assistance Act. Early intervention programs were first started by a separate act or law, but they soon became one of the bureau's ongoing responsibilities and became known as the Handicapped Children Early Education Program (HCEEP), later referred to as the First Chance Network (De Weerd, 1974). This act set up programs in every state of the United States to serve as models of how to work with children with disabilities and improve their lives. The programs usually were categorically oriented: There would be one program for children with visual losses, one for children with hearing losses, one for those with cerebral palsy, and so on. The intent was to demonstrate to others in the state how to work with children with disabilities early in their lives to make them to the greatest extent possible like children of the same age who do not have disabilities. HCEEP later became a regular program in the bureau, and by 1980 a budget of more than $20 million had been allocated to support early intervention programs throughout the United States. The bureau's name was changed to the Office of Special Education and Rehabilitation Services in the 1980s.

In more recent years, as we saw in Chapter 2, Congress passed Public Law (PL) 94-142, which provides services to all handicapped children between ages 6 and 21 in regular or special schools. PL 99-457 expanded the mandate to include children younger than 5 years of age (including newborns). Both laws were extended to provide service to all persons with disabilities through the Individuals with Disabilities Education Act (IDEA) of 1990. PL 99-457 (Part H), enacted in 1986, was a major national step to ensure that infants and toddlers who were at risk for disabilities, were developmentally delayed, or possessed an identifiable disability received the total range of services that they and their families required (Gallagher, Harbin, Eckland, & Clifford, 1994).

The U.S. Department of Education (1995) reports that Part H of PL 99-457 has been effective in the following areas:

- Creating and maintaining effective family-provider partnerships
- Ensuring quality of services
- Providing services in community-based inclusive settings
- Promoting seamless transitions for infants and toddlers to preschool

The fourth area is especially crucial because at the state level different agencies often handle the funding and administration of the 0–3 program and the preschool program. However, amendments to IDEA in 1991 (PL 102-119) were designed to provide effective transitions between Part H and the preschool grant program. More than half of the states passed special legislation to provide collaborative transitions between programs. Still unresolved is the setting in which the children should be served: an inclusive setting with children without disabilities or a school designed for children with specific disabilities.

In the current legislation, infants and toddlers with disabilities are located in **IDEA, Part C.** The new law encourages states to develop a system of services with multidisciplinary assessments and a plan that is family directed, and services are to be provided in a natural environment (NICHCY, 1998).

Early intervention markedly improves the functioning of children with disabilities

Current legislation encourages family involvement in the education plan and services that are promised in a natural environment.

Why Early Intervention?

From birth to the age of 3, the brain develops rapidly. Information from the environment is stored in pathways in the brain that are ready to receive it. During this period, the basic self develops in a transactional relationship with the caregivers in the environment and provides the foundation for autonomous emotional functioning (Schore, 1994). If information is not provided through experience, the pathways are unused and disappear. Enriched experiences build a better brain (Kolb, 1995). The purpose of therapies, training, and education of children with disabilities is to prevent further loss of function.

Because children are born able to learn and to respond positively to the effects of a supportive, stimulating environment, in this section we go into detail about why early intervention is important: to help children who are developmentally delayed achieve higher levels of intellectual and social function and to prevent secondary deficits in children with disabilities or sensory deficits. Then we look at some of the research that supports the effectiveness of early intervention.

AVOIDING DEVELOPMENTAL DELAYS

Infants develop at varying rates. Some sit at 6 months of age, others at 4 months, and still others at 8 months. Some walk early, and some walk late. These variations are the major reason for being cautious when deciding whether an infant is developmentally delayed. Delays must exist in more than one area to be considered a problem.

Delays in development are spotted by comparing an infant's development of physical, emotional, and intellectual skills with the development of other children of the same age.

Delays in development are identified by comparing an infant's development of physical, emotional, and intellectual skills with the development of other same-age children. The average ages of a task's accomplishment are put together in a **developmental scale.** If, for example, a child does not sit, stand, walk, or speak at the age when most children in his or her culture have acquired these skills, a disability or developmental delay is suspected.

It is well known that children with sensory deficits such as vision or hearing impairments, damaged limbs, or genetic disorders linked to mental retardation do not achieve all their developmental skills as quickly as nondisabled children. In fact, without extra help in the form of therapies or educational stimulation, the child with disabilities may develop very slowly and, as an adult, reach a much lower level of functioning than the child with disabilities who has had the benefit of early childhood special education. Because some deficits are irreversible, not all children with disabilities can achieve what the average child achieves easily (Capute & Accardo, 1996; Guralnick, 1996).

PREVENTING ADDITIONAL DEFICITS

Another major reason for early intervention is to avoid the development of secondary problems that can result from the lack of stimulation to the child because of a disability or sensory deficit. These secondary problems, which are usually called *self-stimulation* or *challenging behaviors* (such as hitting and biting), are discussed in Chapter 11.

Murphy (1983) warns that once aversive secondary problems are established, it is almost impossible to eliminate them. Murphy suggests that self-stimulation behaviors begin because of a lack of environmental input (for example, children with visual impairments cannot receive light; those with hearing impairments cannot receive sound) and serve to stimulate the parts of the brain near the pleasure areas. Thus, Murphy feels that self-stimulation is a self-induced pleasure for the child, and others in the environment must interact with the child early to enable him or her to find pleasure in the dual interaction of infant and basic caregiver. Touching the child and providing a great deal of physical contact will prevent the appearance of these behaviors in most children with visual impairments.

Effective child-rearing practices can sometimes greatly improve a child's development and help overcome at-risk conditions present at birth. One of the best sources of knowledge is the Kauai Longitudinal Study, conducted from 1952 to 1992 (Werner & Smith, 1992). In that study, the developmental courses of individuals were followed from the time their expectant mothers made their pregnancies known (usually at 2 to 3 months) to when they were 30 years of age (Werner & Smith, 1992). The Kauai study demonstrated that many children who are at risk for developmental delays from conditions such as lack of sufficient oxygen during birth (*anoxia,* usually occurring when the cord is around the baby's neck) or being born feet first (*breech birth,* highly associated with cerebral palsy) can achieve what the average child achieves, given a home that provides psychological warmth, low physical punishment, responsiveness, verbalness, and encouragement to develop. The phrase *encouragement to develop* can be defined as the knowledge the parent possesses about normal development and the parent's (or caregiver's) assistance to the child in achieving normal developmental milestones. Such childrearing practices tend to help heal the negative effects of abnormal birthing processes (Kolvin, Miller, Scott, Gazonts, & Fleeting, 1990; Werner, in press).

ARE EARLY CHILDHOOD INTERVENTION PROGRAMS EFFECTIVE?

Many authors have reviewed the effectiveness of early childhood intervention projects. We suggest *Handbook of Early Intervention* (Meisels & Shonkoff, in press) and *The Effectiveness of Early Intervention* (Guralnick, 1997) as good current sources of statistics and research results on early intervention. In general, mild retardation can be improved through early intervention programs so that these children can enter regular education classrooms (McNulty, Soper, & Smith, 1984). Therapy for a broad spectrum of communication disorders can be very effective in eliminating those disorders or at least minimizing their impact on later speech and language (McLean & Cripe, 1997, p. 403). Deaf infants who are taught a manual communication system in the first years of life do much better as adults than those who are taught later in life (Goldin-Meadow, 1998; Marschark, Simple, Lillo-Martin, & Everhart, 1998); social and behavioral problems can be controlled (Upsur, 1990); and motor problems can be improved (Shonkoff & Hauser-Cram, 1988).

Many studies support early intervention's effectiveness. Guralnick and Bricker (1987) reviewed studies of children with Down syndrome and concluded that these children made more significant gains in intervention programs than they would have made had they not experienced early intervention. In an extensive review Farran (in press) notes that although the results of intervention for groups of

What seems most important in the long run is the quality of physical and emotional care provided by the family in early childhood.

Child-rearing practices can help offset the effects of disabilities.

Early intervention is important because it provides quality physical and emotional care that promotes self-esteem and self-efficacy.

children are positive they are modest (Gallagher, 1997). However, when one looks at the results of individual children, the results vary widely, suggesting the need for looking more closely at individual children in the total context of their environment (Gallagher, 1998). That is the intent of the requirements of individualized family services plans and IEPs.

The importance of early intervention (besides lifesaving techniques) is to provide those protective factors of quality physical and emotional care that promote self-esteem and self-efficacy (Werner, in press). These factors are the keys to a positive outcome for children in any intervention program, whether it be for the disabled or nondisabled (Rutter, 1988; Kolvin et al., 1990). Once these elements are in place, they appear to provide individuals with the lifelong skills they need to face and deal with various kinds of adversity (Vaillant & Milofsky, 1980; Werner & Smith, 1992).

Intervention with children with disabilities needs to be individualized as much as possible and to focus on the ecology of the child—the broad range of issues affecting the child, the family, and the environment.

What Puts Children at Risk?

An **at-risk infant** is one who, because of low birth weight, prematurity, or the presence of serious medical complications, has a heightened chance of displaying developmental delays or cognitive or motor deficits (Rossetti, 1986, p. 2). Researchers have identified three general categories of conditions that put children at risk: genetic disorders, events occurring during pregnancy and birth, and environmental risks (Garwood & Sheehan, 1989).

GENETIC DISORDERS

More than one hundred genetic disorders are associated with lower developmental functioning and mental retardation (Kopp, 1983). They include mental retardation, Tay-Sachs (an incurable disease leading to early death), and Turner syndrome (a condition that occurs only in women—a missing X chromosome, which leads to short height and possibly mental retardation). Although children with these disorders require immediate attention, they account for less than 1 percent of the school-age population with disabilities. Of sixteen infants born with a disability, in only one can the disability be traced to genetic causes (Batshaw & Perret, 1992). One reason why few children are born with genetic defects is that fetuses with genetic defects usually result in spontaneous abortions (Batshaw & Perret, 1992). Most disabilities are caused by events that occur during pregnancy and birth.

EVENTS DURING PREGNANCY AND BIRTH

The second broad category of conditions that put infants at risk is events that occur in the womb during pregnancy or during the birth process. Prenatal care alerts mothers to the potential dangers of certain drugs as well as of infections and diseases. For example, German measles and chicken pox can cause damage to the fetus but can be prevented by currently available vaccines (Graham & Morgan, 1997). The most common maternal illness that can lead to fetal malformation is diabetes. Control of diabetes can prevent the occurrence of disabilities (Graham & Morgan, 1997).

ENVIRONMENTAL RISKS

Environmental risks—factors in the life of the infant or child that interfere with development—are the major cause of disabilities of children by age 6. Some well-known environmental factors that interfere with development are child abuse, poverty, and parental substance abuse. Parents who are unaware of the child-rearing strategies that facilitate development are particularly at risk in rearing low-birth-weight or premature babies, conditions that are known to be associated with disabilities. Other risks occur when family resources are too limited to provide adequate nutrition, medical care, and housing. These are briefly discussed in the following sections.

Child Abuse

Many of us may find it hard to understand the fact of child abuse, whether the child is with or without disabilities. How can an adult physically harm a baby or a young child, particularly one with disabilities? Yet most of us cannot imagine the stress that parents of children with disabilities endure. Imagine a child who screams constantly. For hours during the night, the parents try everything they can think of to calm him. They walk him, feed him, and bounce him, but nothing works. Throw into the equation a shaky marriage, pressures at work, and no prospect that tomorrow will be any better than today. If the child is perceived as the cause of all this, the formula for child abuse is in place.

Nothing justifies child abuse, of course, but by understanding what causes it, perhaps we can prevent it, which is far better than just condemning the adult who has lost control. Certainly if individuals or organizations are available to ease the daily pressure by counseling the parents or helping with the child, the likelihood of child abuse can be reduced. Zirpoli (1990) states that many studies have found relationships between specific disability groups and disproportionate incidences of abuse (p. 9). Money (1984) has shown that some severely physically abused children will stop growing physically, intellectually, and emotionally, not because of any genetic predisposition but because of extreme cruelty. When children are rescued from destructive environments, they begin to make rapid developmental gains.

Lower Socioeconomic Conditions (Poverty)

Prenatal care allows a physician to detect and treat potential disorders.

Women who live in poverty are likely to have insufficient medical care (including prenatal care), poor housing, and inadequate nutrition. A pregnant woman's poor nutrition rarely affects her fetus; a fetus acts like a parasite, drawing on the mother for what it needs (Batshaw & Perret, 1992). However, the poorly nourished mother may have an infant that is very small at birth.

In the absence of prenatal care, potential disorders that a physician could detect and treat are missed. For example, vitamin B_{12} or B (biotin) can cure one inborn defect in fetuses. If untreated, the child may be born with mental retardation and experience repeated episodes of vomiting (Batshaw & Perret, 1992, p. 165).

If the expectant mother is a teenager living in poverty, she is at great risk of having a premature or low-birth-weight infant, who itself is at great risk for a variety of disabilities. Teenage mothers who live in economically advantaged homes, have good prenatal care, and receive emotional support from their spouse or family are more likely to give birth to normal infants (Anastasiow, 1982).

Substance Abuse

Substance abuse by the mother or father can be linked to behavior problems and disabilities in children. A woman's heavy use of alcohol during pregnancy may result in her infant's having **fetal alcohol syndrome.** Such children have facial abnormalities, droopy eyelids, heart defects, small size, and usually some degree of mental retardation (Batshaw & Perret, 1992). Physical anomalies and growth deficiencies such as these persists in later childhood and adulthood.

Expectant mothers who use heroin may give birth to premature or low-birth-weight infants. The infant may go through severe withdrawal symptoms and will be at risk for disabilities. Heroin and cocaine appear not to cause disabilities in utero but may cause premature births. The problems associated with the conditions at birth of low birth weight and prematurity may lead to physical or behavioral irregularities as the child matures (Hansen & Ulrey, 1992). In their study of forty-nine children who were exposed to drugs prenatally, Cohen and Erwin (1994) found that half did not display any of the negative behaviors that one-quarter of the group did: anger, aggressiveness, and unoccupied behavior. It appears that there is wide behavioral variability among children prenatally exposed to drugs. Physicians and other health-care workers caution expectant mothers to avoid the use of drugs.

If the expectant mother smokes two packs or more of cigarettes a day, she risks giving birth to a premature or low-birth-weight infant. Major national campaigns have been mounted to discourage pregnant women from smoking and using substances that may harm their fetuses.

Caution, however, should be exercised in talking about any risk condition. A single risk factor may not be predictive of developmental delay. For example, a physically disabled child may make normal cognitive and emotional progress. In the Kauai Longitudinal Study, Werner and Smith (1982) found that some children with as many as four environmental or genetic risk factors managed to develop without debilitating disabilities. The concept of *invulnerability* has been constructed to describe those individuals who are at risk but do not acquire disabilities. For example, Werner and Smith (1982) found that the loss of a basic caregiver, usually the mother or father, was a high risk factor for young children. Some at-risk children, however, were able to overcome the loss and develop in a healthy manner. In examining the data, Werner (in press) found that in some cases a relative, teacher, neighbor, or friend helped the child adjust to the loss of the mother or other family member.

Prevention Before Birth

Prevention before birth involves genetic counseling and prenatal care.

The aim of prevention is to have a child without disabilities. Prevention involves two major activities: (1) genetic counseling, which includes an interview with the prospective parents to determine if the family has a history of disorder and, if so, what is the risk of their child having disabilities, and (2) prenatal care, which involves carefully monitoring the mother's health and fetal development to ensure that the infant is born healthy.

GENETIC COUNSELING

The first opportunity to detect potential disorders is **genetic counseling.** A counselor interviews the prospective parents about their families' histories of disabilities and analyzes samples of the clients' blood to determine if their gene pool contains defective genes that might be passed on to their children. Parents may choose to receive this counseling before the child is conceived. Some genetic disorders are most prevalent among certain racial groups, such as Tay-Sachs disease among Eastern European (Ashkenazic) Jews, Couley's anemia among Mediterranean Greeks and Italians, and sickle cell anemia among African Americans (Anastasiow, 1986). Individuals from populations at particular risk for these and other disorders may seek genetic counseling to determine the likelihood of their having a child with disabilities.

A genetic counselor can calculate the probability or odds of a couple's having a child with a disabling condition or genetic disorder (March of Dimes, 1990), but the counselor cannot confirm whether the child will be born with or without disabilities. If the parents have a high probability of having a child with disabilities, the expectant mother may choose to have a test that may detect if the child she is carrying has a disability.

PRENATAL CARE

Prenatal care can prevent some disabilities.

In providing **prenatal care,** the physician checks the mother's health, monitors the progress of her pregnancy, and warns her about dangerous practices such as the use of alcohol, tobacco, and other drugs that can harm the fetus. Prenatal care can significantly reduce the number of premature or low-birth-weight babies. Even benign neglect—if, for example, the mother does not take iron or vitamin supplements or have other medical assistance during pregnancy—can have an adverse effect on the health of an infant. The physician can detect some deficiencies in the expectant mother's diet and prescribe the vitamins and minerals she and her baby need.

Teaching prospective parents good child-rearing practices can prevent disabilities from developing, even when the infant is at risk. For example, parents can learn that paint containing lead should not be used where a young child can get at it. Ingesting chips of lead paint can cause lead poisoning and mental retardation.

In the United States armed forces, prenatal care is provided uniformly to all pregnant women in the service and to wives of servicemen. It has been found that these women have the lowest instances of prematurity, low-birth-weight infants, and infant mortality in the United States. Interestingly, there are no racial differences in the infant death rates in this population. This finding is atypical of all other populations in the United States, where large racial differences exist (Pear, 1992).

An integral part of prenatal care is the tests that are available to screen the fetus for various disabilities. Some of the major prenatal tests are discussed next.

Alpha-Fetoprotein Test

The **alpha-fetoprotein test** is a blood test that is offered to all pregnant women. Fetuses pass substances into the mother's blood, which can be examined to detect some disabilities. The blood sample is taken at sixteen weeks' gestation and can identify women who are at risk of having a fetus with a neural tube defect (a defect involving the spinal column or brain), Down syndrome, or some other birth defect (Batshaw & Rose, 1997; Blackman, 1983).

Because all women have some risk, however small, of having a child with a disability, some states require the alpha-fetoprotein test to alert the parents about the condition of their child before birth. If Ann and Bryan had taken the test, they would have known that their infant would be born with Down syndrome. They would have had time to decide how to deal with the situation. If the results of the alpha-fetoprotein test indicate the possibility of a disorder, two other steps—sonography and amniocentesis—are taken to determine whether the disorder actually exists.

If a neural tube defect is suspected, it is important to rule out twins. Because twins cause higher levels of spinal fluid than does a single fetus, extra fluid in the mother's bloodstream does not necessarily indicate a neural tube defect. Obstetricians often ask expectant mothers to have an ultrasound test in the third month of pregnancy to determine the position of the fetus, and another one at five months to monitor the progress of fetal development. If a disorder is suspected, it is usually confirmed by amniocentesis.

Sonography (Ultrasound)

Sonography, or ultrasound, is the use of sound waves to take a picture (like an x-ray) of the fetus. This picture allows specialists to determine the position of the fetus and possibly detect defects such as microcephaly (small head). It also detects the sex of the child and indicates whether there is more than one fetus.

Amniocentesis

Amniocentesis is a relatively safe test in which a needle is inserted into the placenta (with the help of ultrasound to ensure that the needle does not damage the fetus) at 14 to 17 weeks' gestation (Batshaw & Rose, 1997). The fluid can be analyzed to determine a number of (but not all) disabilities, such as Tay Sachs, Down syndrome, and spina bifida. If an incurable disability is detected, the prospective parents must choose between having the child and having an abortion, which is a personal family decision.

Chorionic Villus Biposy

A test usually not available or not recommended by many physicians is **chorionic villus biopsy.** In this procedure, some tissue is removed from the uterus of the pregnant woman during the first trimester. When the tissue is examined under a microscope, some disabilities, such as Down syndrome, can be detected. The major drawback of this procedure is that it increases the risk of miscarriage, and it can also lead to internal bleeding and infection in the expectant mother (Batshaw & Rose, 1997). Batshaw and Perret (1992), however, suggest that if these risks could be reduced, chorionic villus biopsy would be very useful. It can be performed early in pregnancy, it is less expensive than amniocentesis, and it is less emotionally traumatic for the expectant mother, who may be afraid of having a needle inserted into the placenta.

 Detecting Disabilities After Birth

If the infant is born with a defect that can be cured, treatment must begin early in life. For example, phenylketonuria (PKU) causes toxic accumulations of phenylalanine in the brain, which, if untreated, leads to multiple disabilities and mental retardation. Although infants have no obvious symptoms, PKU can be detected by a simple blood test, preferably when the infant is a week old. The treatment is to restrict the infant's diet to reduce the intake of phenylalanine. (Batshaw & Perret, 1992).

SCREENING AT BIRTH

Can a physician or other professional tell whether an infant is disabled or at risk for a disabling condition within the first few minutes of the child's birth? When a child is born, the physician administers the first screening test to determine whether the infant has any identifiable problems or abnormalities (Meisels, 1987). Screening tests are simple tests that are easy to administer and that separate infants without serious developmental problems from those who have a disability or are suspected of being at risk for a disabling condition (Anastasiow, Frankenburg, & Fandall, 1982). The first infant screening is done in the hospital at one minute and five minutes after birth. It is known as the **Apgar test,** after Virginia Apgar, who developed it in 1952.

In administering the Apgar test, the physician examines the infant's heart rate, respiratory effort, muscle tone, and general physical state, including skin color. A blue cast to the skin, for example, may indicate breathing or heart problems. Jaundice at birth is indicated by a yellow cast to the skin and eyes. A serious disorder, jaundice reflects the failure of the liver to process adequately because of its immaturity; as a result, bilirubin can accumulate. Many infants with jaundice recover in about a week. In more serious cases, the infant is placed under fluorescent lights for a day or two. This light treatment helps the infant process the bilirubin until the liver can function normally (Batshaw & Perret, 1992).

An infant with a below-average Apgar score at one minute or five minutes after birth is monitored by the physician to determine if a disability or medical problem exists and if medical intervention is needed. Lower-than-average Apgar scores are not necessarily predictive of disabilities, but they do serve to alert the physician that the infant may have special needs.

MEDICAL INTERVENTION

Additional medical screening includes blood and urine tests to determine if the infant has known curable disorders that should be treated immediately to prevent the occurrence of a disability. Hypothyroidism, or the failure of the thyroid gland to function, can lead to *cretinism,* an irreversible condition of severe mental retardation. If thyroid supplement is given at birth and continued throughout life, however, the condition can be prevented and the child will develop regularly. The success in preventing mental retardation associated with a thyroid gland deficiency has done much to encourage research in the prevention of occurrences of developmental conditions identifiable at birth.

DEVELOPMENTAL SCREENING

After the first screening tests, which are usually medical in orientation, other tests assess a broad range of infant capacities, including development in cognitive, social, emotional, physical, communicative, language, and self-help skills. Usually the tests are administered only if a problem is suspected.

Developmental screening is a brief assessment of a sampling of a child's developmental progress to determine whether the child is at risk for a delay, possesses an

When a child is born, the physician administers the Apgar test to determine if the infant has any identifiable problems or abnormalities.

Early screening tests can determine whether an infant has any identifiable problems. If the infant is born with a defect that can be cured, treatment must begin early in life. (© Bob Daemmrich/The Image Works)

identifiable disability, is delayed in development, or is proceeding at the expected pace for his or her age (Meisels & Provence, 1989). The critical dimension of any screening test is its accuracy in not identifying children as being at risk who are normal (false positives) or labeling children as normal who are at risk (false negatives).

There has been a proliferation of infant screening devices in recent years, but many of them fail to achieve acceptable levels of confidence. Many practitioners rely on the Bayley scales (Bayley, 1993) or on the Connecticut Infant and Toddler Assessment procedure (IDA), which provide more complete diagnostic assessments. Others administer some form of family assessment and gain critical information from the caregiver (Henderson & Meisels, 1994). There are a number of screening instruments for children 3 to 5 years of age. The Early Screening Inventory (Meisels, Marsden, Wiske, & Browning, 1997) is among the most accurate.

Early Intervention Programs

Children with Down syndrome reared in supportive homes and who receive early childhood special education have IQ scores much higher than untreated or institutionalized children with Down syndrome.

The goal of early intervention programs is to help children with disabilities develop to their maximum potential. An outstanding example of intervention is research with Down syndrome, a disorder associated with mental retardation (Guralnick & Bricker, 1987). Untreated children with this disorder who were placed in institutions rarely learned more than fifteen or twenty words, whereas those who were reared in supportive homes and received early childhood special education developed language to the level of persons without disabilities and a high degree of competence in all other developmental areas (Hayden & Haring, 1977).

Although this genetic condition does not go away, the child with Down syndrome who is reared in an enriched environment in the home or a center will have an IQ score as many as 30 points higher than the score of a child who is untreated or raised in an institution (Guralnick & Bricker, 1987).

In this section, we look at some intervention programs: where they take place and their strategies, how curricula are developed, and model programs. Some conditions can be prevented and others remediated, but many can be neither prevented nor remediated entirely. With most disabilities, however, improved conditions can be achieved through carefully planned and implemented intervention programs. The basis for planning intervention is the individualized family services plan.

THE INDIVIDUALIZED FAMILY SERVICES PLAN (IFSP)

Part H of PL 99-457 and IDEA, Part C require that an **individualized family services plan (IFSP)** be developed for each child from birth to 3 years of age who is diagnosed as disabled, developmentally delayed, or at risk for delay. When the child enters the public school early childhood special education services at 3 years of age, an IEP takes the place of the IFSP.

IDEA, Part C: Legal Requirements of the IFSP

IDEA, Part C requires that IFSPs be constructed to include the following:

- A statement of the infant's or toddler's present levels of physical development, cognitive development, communication development, social or emotional development, and adaptive development, based on objective criteria
- A statement of the family's resources, priorities, and concerns relating to enhancing the development of the family's infant or toddler with a disability
- A statement of the major outcomes expected to be achieved for the infant or toddler and the family and the criteria, procedures, and timelines used to determine the degree to which progress toward achieving the outcomes is being made and whether modifications or revisions of the outcomes or services are necessary
- A statement of specific early intervention services necessary to meet the unique needs of the infant or toddler and the family, including the frequency, intensity, and method of delivering services
- A statement of the natural environments in which early intervention services shall appropriately be provided, including a justification of the extent, if any, to which the services will not be provided in a natural environment
- The projected dates for initiation of services and the anticipated duration of the services
- The identification of the service coordinator from the profession most immediately relevant to the infant's or toddler's or family's needs (or who is otherwise qualified to carry out all applicable responsibilities under Part C) who will be responsible for the implementation of the plan and coordination with other agencies and persons
- The steps to be taken to support the transition of the toddler with a disability to preschool or other appropriate services (Council for Exceptional Children, 1998)

Because transition can be stressful, special transition efforts may be useful. An IFSP can address issues and goals related to the transition to an IEP for children 3 and older.

The individualized family services plan acknowledges that a child with disabilities is a child in a family and that family members may need educational, financial, or emotional support to help the child achieve his or her potential. *(© Jerry Speir/Design Conceptions)*

★ *The family may need help in locating, obtaining, and implementing the services specified in the IFSP.*

★ *The multidisciplinary team is a team of professionals who provide services to help a child with a disability.*

The focus on the *family* is an important outgrowth of the findings of early childhood intervention programs: A child with disabilities is a child in a family, and family members may need educational, financial, or emotional support to be able to provide the best setting, support, security, and stimulation to help the child with disabilities or developmental delays achieve his or her potential (Turnbull & Turnbull, 1989).

The Multidisciplinary Team

The law also recognizes that families need more than friendly neighbors or relatives to help them. They may need a variety of services from specialists as well as a service coordinator to help them locate, obtain, and implement the services specified in the IFSP. Children who qualify for services under IDEA must have been identified, screened, and diagnosed by a **multidisciplinary team** as having a disability known to be associated with developmental delays or be at risk for the occurrence of developmental delays. The term *multidisciplinary* means that more than one professional needs to work with the child. The child may need physical therapy for damaged limbs, speech-language therapy for poor control of the muscles involved in speech, and an educational program. Thus, a multidisciplinary team working in an early intervention program might include a member of each of those professions. Disciplines that are designated by law to be able to work with infants and children with disabilities are listed in Table 3.1.

An ideal team includes a physician or health-care worker who examines the child and reviews his or her medical record for any signs of disorder. A special educator or developmental psychologist assesses the child's physical, emotional, cognitive, language, and social development. A special educator, social worker, or

TABLE 3.1 Multidisciplinary Team Members	
Specialist	**Function**
Audiologist	Determines if hearing losses are present
Ophthalmologist	Determines if vision losses are present
Early childhood special educator	Plans and administers program for remediation of deficits and coordinates special therapies
Physician	Determines if a biological or health deficit exists and plans treatment
Nurse	Provides a plan for adequate health care
Occupational therapist	Promotes individual development of self, self-help skills, play, and autonomy
Physical therapist	Enhances motor development and suggests prostheses and positioning strategies; provides needed therapies
Psychologist	Provides a comprehensive document of the child's strengths and weaknesses and helps the family deal with the stress of having a child with disabilities
Social worker	Assists the family in implementing appropriate child-rearing strategies and helps families locate services as needed
Speech and language pathologist	Provides necessary assessment plan for needed therapies and delivers services in appropriate cases

psychologist interviews the family members to determine their health history, child-rearing practices, and concerns for the child. The ideal team also includes other specialists as necessary. For example, a physical therapist assesses muscle tone and development, a language pathologist determines whether speech patterns are abnormal or delayed, an audiologist evaluates the hearing function, and in some cases a geneticist determines if the child has a genetic abnormality not detected previously.

The assessment may also include a visit to the home to view the child's living space. Bradley and Caldwell (1984) have developed the Home Observation Measure of the Environment (HOME) scale, which examines the quality of the home-care environment and its potential for assisting or arresting development. The HOME scale assesses the basic caregiver's emotional and verbal responsiveness to the child, the amount of physical punishment administered to the child, the organization of the home, and the amount of play and stimulation that caregivers provide to the child. These factors are predictors of a child's developmental progress.

If negative factors exist, social workers or home visitors help the family develop facilitating strategies so the child can make the best possible developmental progress (Gottfried, 1984).

When all the information on the child and the child's family has been gathered, the multidisciplinary team, including family members, discusses the case. The specialists might prescribe therapy or recommend an early intervention program. Their conclusion might be that the child should be re-evaluated at a later age; if no disabilities or risk factors have been identified, perhaps the child should be discharged or monitored periodically. In cases in which the environment is the at-risk factor, the team may recommend parental counseling or identify sources of income assistance for the family.

The Americans with Disabilities Act (ADA) calls for public services (child-care programs) to make reasonable accommodations to prevent discrimination against children with disabilities. Child-care facilities may be required to do something different from their usual program or something additional to ensure full participation of all children in the program. These programs also need to be sensitive to the cultures and languages of families belonging to a nondominant group (Odom & McLean, 1996).

Child-care programs need to be sensitive to all cultures and languages.

The IDA (Erikson, 1989; Hutchinson, 1995), which uses a multidisciplinary team to assess the child's health, development, and family situation, meets the requirements of PL 99-457, Part H. A typical case might be handled as follows.

A pediatrician, a relative, or parents may raise concerns about a child's development. The family calls the state department of health, the state department of special education, or some other agency for help. The family is referred to a center where screening (a quick assessment of the child's current developmental status to determine whether the child needs further tests) is performed. (The child should not be labeled at any time, particularly after the screening.) Because the results suggest a potential problem, the IDA is administered by at least two persons from different professions. They conduct an interview with the family to collect a health history and a history of disabilities within the family. They request permission to examine the child's health records. They assess the child's motor, social, speech and language, and cognitive (intelligence) skills to determine whether the child can perform age-appropriate developmental tasks (such as stacking small colored blocks).

After collecting all the information from the family interview, the health history, and the developmental assessment, the team meets with the family to develop an IFSP and decide which of the following best describes the situation:

■ The child is all right and needs no special assistance.

■ The child appears to be somewhat delayed but not to such a degree that assistance is needed now; however, he or she should be brought back for another evaluation in three to six months.

■ The child has a particular problem and should be in an intervention program.

■ The family needs economic assistance, job training, or training in how to deal with the child and his or her disabilities.

The family may agree or disagree with the decision. If agreement is reached, a service coordinator is assigned to assist the family in finding the services they and their child need, such as an early intervention program for speech delays. This is the ideal situation and fulfillment of the hopes embodied in PL 99-457, Part H, and in IDEA, Part C. If the family disagrees, they may remove their child from services. Most states do not have mandatory education for children from birth to age 3, whether they are with or without disabilities. So the parents can decide not to place their infant or preschooler in early intervention.

SETTINGS AND STRATEGIES

An early intervention program can take place in a hospital, at home, or in an early childhood intervention center. The intervention strategies in each of these settings vary. A measure for assessing the characteristics of room environment, available curricula, staff training, and so forth is available from Harms and Clifford (1984). Early intervention programs can be operated privately, by national organizations such as United Cerebral Palsy, by religious organizations, or by means of government grants or state funds. Not all locations will have a program for a specific disability, and parents may have to search for an appropriate place for their child.

In a Hospital

Assistance for a child with disabilities may begin in a hospital on the first day of his or her life. Assistance may also begin in the early weeks through medical intervention such as surgery (for example, to close the open spine in cases of spina bifida), the administration of drugs, or the use of diagnostic tests to determine if a disability exists.

Hospitals provide medical intervention to premature and low-birth-weight, medically fragile, and sick infants until they can be sent home. The treatment in the hospital is usually lifesaving in that the child was born before he or she was biologically ready to be in an environment other than the womb. Most babies at the time of discharge should be able to survive without continuous medical treatment in a hospital, although sometimes it is necessary to prepare the home in some way, such as for an oxygen-dependent child (one who needs a tube to obtain extra oxygen from a tank).

Many hospitals have tried a variety of techniques to help premature infants, including providing an environment that simulates the womb by means of water beds, darkened rooms, and low stimulation. Most neonatal intensive-care units where at-risk infants are housed are noisy; contain many adult contacts for health, feeding, and hygiene services; and are generally overstimulating and aversive to the newborn (Field, 1984).

Als (1997) and her colleagues have developed a comprehensive intervention program in the hospital neonatal intensive-care unit for preterm infants. The program requires extensive training of the staff to implement the program and to attend to the infants' many needs. The philosophy of the program is to view the infant as a collaborator in the staff's efforts to help him or her survive and develop. The staff does that by engaging the infant in an ongoing relationship and determining through careful evaluation what supports the infant needs. Observations include behavioral interpretations and consistency of caregiving through establishing a multidisciplinary team, including a therapist for each infant. The team works collaboratively to enhance the child's development. The results of one study showed a marked decrease in the number of days invasive techniques, such as tube feeding, were needed, as well as a decrease in the length of hospital stay and hospital costs.

Assessment of a child's strengths help provide goals for a home or center program. *(© Elizabeth Crews/Stock Boston)*

★ *In a neonatal intensive-care unit, a multidisciplinary team should work collaboratively to enhance the child's development.*

A major movement is under way to establish intervention programs to follow the infant from the neonatal intensive-care nursery to the home. These programs aim to provide education to the parents, give them support, and help them find the services their infant requires (Affleck, Tennen, & Rowe, 1991; Beckwith, 1988; Infant Health and Development Project, 1990).

Home and Family

Therapists, teachers, and other interventionists often provide services in the home for a number of reasons. A common belief among many educators is that education should take place in the setting in which the skills will be used; hence the home is the functional setting for very young children. Infants spend most of their time sleeping, and it is not practical to take them to an early intervention program that offers educational and therapeutic practice. In addition, mothers who are going through the process of accepting their child's disability may not be ready to take the child into public places. In some rural areas, early childhood special education centers are a long way from the home, and mothers would spend much valuable time traveling instead of interacting with and caring for the child. Furthermore, the mother's or caregiver's primary responsibility is to establish in-the-home routines that will facilitate the child's development. Attachments grow out of joint interactions with the child and are of fundamental importance to the infant's well-being.

★ *Home programs emphasize helping the caregiver learn how to deal with the child in the child's setting.*

Home programs tend to offer comprehensive services (therapies and education) and are very effective in assisting families with children at risk, the developmentally delayed, and those with disabilities (Shonkoff & Hauser-Cram, 1988). The data from research on home programs indicate positive gains for children as well as their parents. These strategies emphasize helping the caregiver learn how to deal with the child in the child's setting, thereby establishing a daily routine that is therapeutic.

The first person to visit the home may be a social worker who works with the caregivers in the home and helps them locate services to facilitate the child's development. Home visitors provide caregivers with information about the child's disability, child development in general, parenting practices, therapies, and a curriculum for the child (Affleck et al., 1991; Beckwith, 1988). In the process, the home visitor provides emotional support and contact with the family. The home visitor can also act as a service coordinator and help the parents apply for additional services for the child or the family. An example of additional services is an occupational or physical therapist who visits the home once or twice a week to teach the caregivers to position, carry, sit, bathe, feed, and generally care for the child.

Rarely, if ever, does the home visitor act as a therapist. If the need for therapy is indicated, the home visitor will help the family locate the necessary personnel. Home programs tend to teach the mother to be the teacher or therapist for her child. Many home programs have declined as a consequence of the increased employment out of the house of women with young children (Moores, 1996).

EDUCATION PROGRAMS

Early Childhood Intervention Center

When the child is 3 to 6 months old, a popular solution is to combine parent and child home education with education at an early childhood intervention center. The best early childhood intervention centers have a well-trained staff sensitive to the needs of the children they serve and the needs of their parents, a well-developed curriculum, and appropriate multidisciplinary team therapies for the children. A center should be light and pleasant and not overcrowded with adults and children.

Early childhood centers provide families with a variety of personnel to assist them and their child. The infant program has the necessary therapists to work with the infant 30 to 45 minutes a day. A physical therapist works with children who have motor disabilities, and an occupational therapist might teach a child how to eat with a spoon or drink from a cup.

As infants move into the toddler stage, they usually need additional services. For example, it is expected that the children will begin to speak. Speech and language therapists are usually available to work with the child who has any identified problem. Because more infants and toddlers whose conditions require the use of technological equipment (oxygen tanks, respirators, and gastrostomy tubes) are entering public schools (this development is discussed more fully in Chapter 12), specialists who know how to regulate the equipment are needed, as are personnel trained to catheterize the child who is paralyzed from the waist down.

Centers offer supplies and resources to the family, providing ample toys for the child to manipulate and explore. The natural (genetic) manner in which all human beings learn is through play (Lerner, 1986). It is particularly crucial for young children, who are innately curious, to look at objects, manipulate (for example, shake or rattle) them to see what they will do, and then play with them. Play is used in most early childhood programs (Fewell & Rich, 1983; Linder, 1993a).

Part C of IDEA requires that services be provided in natural environments; for infants, that environment is the home.

Effective day-care and early childhood centers have low infant-teacher ratios and allow for child-initiated activities. *(© Elizabeth Crews/Stock Boston)*

Evidence indicates that children who enter a well-planned, intensively structured program during the first five years of life and stay in that program for a longer period of time make the greatest gains and suffer the least loss (Guralnick, 1998).

Developmentally Appropriate Practice (DAP)

Concern over the education of young children led the National Association for the Education of Young Children (NAEYC) and the National Education Association (NEA) to publish guidelines called **developmentally appropriate practice (DAP)** (Bredekamp, 1987). These guidelines encourage early childhood teachers to do the following:

1. Match early childhood practices to the ways children learn.
2. View the time of early childhood not as discrete age/grade levels.
3. Create classrooms that encourage exploration and facilitate learning and development.
4. Consider parent involvement as a critical and essential element in the curriculum.
5. Use ongoing evaluation for decision making and curriculum development. (Gullo, 1992, p. 11)

Following that effort, special educators met and developed a handbook of recommended practices for early intervention programs (Odom & McLean, 1996). These suggested practices include assessment, curriculum transitions, and teacher training.

Although special educators tend to agree with the goals of DAP, their list of suggested practices tends to include more teacher-directed suggestions. For example, the activity-based intervention program (Bricker & Cripes, 1992), though consistent with the goals of DAP, looks for opportunities for the teaching of specific skills that the child has not mastered (Novich, 1993). The major difference between the programs resides in how one engages the child. Child engagement is defined as the amount of time the child spends in developmentally and contextually appropriate behavior (Fox, Hanline, Vail, & Falant, 1994). Special educators recognize that children with disabilities do not always readily engage and have to be taught to do so.

Children with disabilities tend to be less active (passive) and less curious about the world around them (Field, 1989). They have fewer coping skills with which to respond to environmental demands (Zeitlin & Williamson, 1994). Thus, an interventionist may have to teach a child with disabilities how to play so the child can use play to learn (Anastasiow, 1996). Although the child with a disability may require more assistance than a child without a disability, great care must be taken to help the child with disabilities to develop independence, self-reliance, and critical skills for lifelong functioning (Wehmeyer, Agran, & Hughes, 1998).

Regular Day-Care and Early Childhood Centers

Day-care and early childhood centers are usually established for children who do not have disabilities. They vary greatly in quality, organization, staff-child ratio, and program orientation. The most effective centers have a low infant-teacher ratio (2:1), well-trained personnel, observational methods, child-initiated activities, access to other professions, a skilled administrator, and low staff turnover. Child-initiated structured play is available in the effective centers (Linder, 1993a).

In their longitudinal study, Schweinhart and Weikart (1998) found many positive personal and social effects among adults who as children had experienced a program oriented to intellectual, social, and physical development that encouraged them to make decisions, compared with adults who had attended a direct-instruction early childhood center.

These centers are required to accommodate infants and toddlers with disabilities. Many day-care and early childhood center teachers need additional training to accommodate and teach children with disabilities. The School of Nursing at the University of Colorado has made an effort to meet those needs by developing materials that provide information about infants and toddlers with a wide spectrum of disabilities and suggestions on how to work with them (Krajicek, Steinke, Hertzdeng, Anastasiow, & Skandel, 1997). Video tapes and other materials are available from PRO-ED and Paul H. Brookes publishing companies.

Assessment and Curriculum

Most children go through comprehensive assessments before they are assigned by a committee on special education. These assessments are conducted with a variety of instruments and personnel such as those we described earlier in the chapter. Teachers and therapists evaluate a child's progress in motor development, fine motor development, speech and language, social and emotional development, and self-help skills. The special education teacher's role is to coordinate therapies, provide age-appropriate in-class experiences, and assist the student to capitalize on his or her abilities to attain, insofar as possible, the skills of a child of the same age without disabilities.

The first curriculum issue is that most infants and toddlers with disabilities are subject to increased risks of health problems. Thus, they may need special equipment (such as wheelchairs, hearing aids, braces) and an individualized treatment

In school, teachers and therapists evaluate a child's progress in gross and fine motor development; speech and language; cognitive, social, and emotional development; and self-help skills.

program. In Chapters 5 through 12 we describe modifications for specific disabilities. What we want to stress here is that an effective curriculum that takes these needs into account must be designed and begun early in the child's life, as soon as the disability is diagnosed. The following curricula are frequently used as a basis for designing an individual child's curriculum.

Helping Babies Learn: Developmental Profile and Activities for Infants and Toddlers (Furuno, O'Reilly, Inatsuka, Hosaka, & Falb, 1995) is a well-designed developmental scale with suggested activities in five areas: Home Routines, Indoor Activities, Excursions, Social Development, and Health and Safety. These scales and activities are organized in three-month sections from birth to 3 years of age. The activities encompass a range of skills and describe situations in which the parent or teacher can observe and interact with the infant and facilitate his or her development.

The Hawaiian Early Learning Profile (HELP) (Furuno et al., 1989) has similar goals for 3- to 5-year-olds. The HELP contains nine scales and describes discrete tasks (such as drinking from a cup) and the average age at which most children accomplish the skill. By comparing an infant's or toddler's general profile across the nine areas, the teacher can pinpoint areas of delay and identify the areas that will constitute the curriculum.

The Carolina Curriculum (Johnson-Martin, Attermeier, & Hacker, 1990; Johnson-Martin, Jens, & Attermeier, 1991) is similar to the HELP in that it provides an assessment as well as a curriculum to assist the child in accomplishing skill development. It is now available in two volumes. The first is designed for children from birth to age 3, the second for children from ages 3 to 5.

These curricula are in essence large developmental scales, breaking down each area of development into small, discrete steps. The teacher presents each task and determines whether the child is able to accomplish it, such as identifying a cup and spoon and, later, naming objects presented in a series of pictures or actual toys. If the child is able to accomplish a task, the teacher moves on to the next task, until reaching a task the child is unable to accomplish. This process provides the teacher with information on where to begin instruction.

These scales are valuable because they were developed by multidisciplinary teams and established a sequence for skills reflecting the order in which a child who is not disabled would acquire those skills. For each curriculum, there are recording forms on which the teacher can enter the child's progress and share it with family members and with the next teacher. The major principle underlying these curricula is that the child moves from being a globally oriented infant to a youngster whose skills become more and more differentiated and complex. For example, an infant is expected to shake a rattle and, later, hold a cup and drink from it; a 3- to 5-year-old is expected to be able to pretend to give a doll a drink from a cup.

Play as Assessment. Transdisciplinary play-based assessment (Linder, 1993a) and transdisciplinary play-based intervention (Linder, 1993b) provide techniques for assessing children in their natural settings (usually a preschool) during play and curriculum suggestions. Play has long been known to involve children's thinking, their motivation, and their socio-emotional development. Linder's books help parents and the multidisciplinary team assess the child's functioning and, following assessment, provide curriculum suggestions for intervention if needed. Linder (1995) developed two training videos that demonstrate both assessment and intervention strategies through the medium of play. Forms are available to record the child's behavior.

"The Making of a Miracle"

My 3-year-old son started preschool this fall. Soon after, he started riding the bus. Significant but routine events in the life of an American child—unless the child has, as my son does, cerebral palsy.

For parents of disabled children, every "routine" milestone reached is a miracle, bringing with it excitement, joy and, at least in this case, a small degree of trepidation. And this particular miracle will seem unusual to many readers because of its source. It was planted by the social activism of special-needs parents in the 1960s and 1970s. Its roots grew from special-education legislation. And its cultivation can be attributed in large part to the hard work and dedication of publicly funded educators, as well as parents and others who care. It is an example of the good that can and does spring from legislative policymaking and government spending.

Ben is a smiling, energetic, funny little boy (also quite handsome according to this unbiased source) who cannot walk, cannot sit up by himself, cannot reach his arms very far, cannot feed himself and can speak only in difficult-to-understand single words. His disability was caused by a congenital defect; a small "drain" in his brain is too narrow, resulting in a condition commonly called hydrocephalus or "water on the brain." Doctors gave him an auxiliary drain (a "shunt") when he was 6 days old, correcting the underlying problem but leaving Ben with brain damage that occurred during pregnancy.

Trying to be a good parent—a challenge with any child—to a son who cannot communicate or learn the way typical children do can be a very frustrating and isolating experience. Not only do my husband and I have to attend to and contain our own feelings of guilt and grief; we also need to find ways to teach Ben things that typical children learn through their own physical independence. We are enormously proud of our Ben, but his birth drove home the reality that no matter how emotionally or financially independent you are, there are some challenges you cannot face alone.

Enter the special-education system, mandated by state and federal law. Upon diagnosing Ben, doctors referred us to an early-intervention center (serving children from birth to 3 years) in our home state of Massachusetts. We were referred to another one when we moved to New Hampshire several months later in order for my husband to take a new job. These centers are staffed by some of the most creative, bright, warm, and supportive people I have ever met. They helped us learn how best to teach Ben, how to motivate him and how to help him explore the world around him. Just before he began school, Ben's case manager, an occupational therapist, found a piece of equipment that helps him "crawl"—supporting his upper body on a sling so that his stronger legs can push the wheels attached to the sling's frame. Ben has begun to have the independent mobility that we had only dreamed of.

Prerequisites to Success

Ben's preschool, run by our town's school system, is building on Ben's experience with early intervention. Although it has been some time since the school has had a child with Ben's level of physical disability, the teachers and students have truly welcomed him to the school, a welcome that does not come cheap. Like all children, Ben needs a happy family life, a roof over his head, clean and appropriate clothes, good nutrition and caring teachers as prerequisites to success in school. But Ben's special needs don't stop there. He requires a full-time classroom aide to help him move, play and eat with the other children. He and some of his classmates receive physical occupation and speech therapy so that they can reach their maximum development.

The school will need to purchase special equipment. In a time of dwindling resources, educators, politicians, and parents of typical children may well ask whether the expense is worth it.

I can answer with an unqualified yes. Obviously, it's worth it to my family—especially to Ben. No child deserves a disability and Ben should be able to dream of being anything he wants to be, just as we encourage other children to do. But it is also worth it to Ben's community and especially to his peers. Ben has the potential to be a citizen in the true meaning of the word, very possibly a self-sufficient one who will not, as an adult, need to rely on the government for all or most of his financial support. But more important, Ben will provide his peers with a window to a world few of them would otherwise see, teaching them acceptance, tolerance, perspective and creativity. He may also turn out (and I hope this for him more than anything else) to be a best friend to someone who really needs his friendship.

The early reports from preschool are amazing, especially when compared with what Ben was able to do just a year ago. Ben is happy, watching his classmates closely, and in his fashion, participating in games, singing and story time. The other kids are curious about him, but once told that his muscles just don't work like everyone else's, they accept the information and figure out how they can play with him. They are happy that he likes to share his special equipment. The teachers and aides are warm, supportive, and, most important, very enthusiastic about Ben.

This small miracle of a routine beginning is not the stuff of made-for-TV movies, where the child walks despite the dire predictions of all the doctors. It is a miracle created by activists through government. And it is a miracle that requires money; without the dollars, the network of professionals who create and develop the information and experience that will cultivate a little boy like Ben into an integrated member of our society simply wouldn't exist. And it is a miracle that few parents could afford to create on their own, no matter how willing they might be.

Sometimes government spending does make a difference. Sometimes it can create miracles.

Source: Maggie Wood Hassan, "My Turn: The Making of a Miracle," *Newsweek*, January 6, 1992, p. 7. Reprinted by permission of the author.

What Is the Context?

This article discusses the importance of a supportive societal context that has been developed through the efforts of many parents and activists. In the author's view, the family cannot provide a self-sufficient environment; ideally, the family is a link to other support systems or contexts in the school or community. The author emphasizes to parents and families that "there are some challenges you cannot face alone." A major responsibility for families is understanding that they need support and finding out how to get it.

Pivotal Issues for Teachers

How does the family's experience with early intervention show the benefits to "regular" kids as well as to kids with disabilities? How does one become empathic and sensitized to the value of services for children with disabilities? How do the services described in this article demonstrate early childhood legislation in action?

With toddlers and children 3 to 5 years old, toys and play are the primary mode of teaching the names of objects and colors and the concepts of gravity, volume, and space and of overcoming weaknesses in motor skills and physical ability. (© Lydia Gans)

 Family and Lifespan Issues

A major movement in the United States is under way to give parents more authority in decisions related to their child with disabilities. Called *parent empowerment*, this movement aims to increase parents' control over decisions relevant to their child. For example, the UCLA Family Development Service Intervention Roles Profile for parents attempts to:

- Consolidate a helping working relationship between the interventionist and the caregiver
- Enhance communication of the caregiver and enhance the caregiver's personal adaptation
- Enhance alternative approaches to caregiver-child interactions (if needed)
- Provide direct affirmation and support (Heinicke, 1993)

One of the strongest movements in special education recently has been the *family-focused* or *family-centered* practices. The legislation IDEA calls for a family-oriented approach by requiring an individualized family services plan (IFSP), which spells out what services will be available for the family as well as for the child with disabilities (Turnbull & Turnbull, 1997).

CULTURE

Cultural relevance is one of the criteria established for the developmentally appropriate practices. These criteria are an important part of assessing the appropriateness of services for children and families from a variety of cultural backgrounds. Curricula need to be antibiased and culturally appropriate.

COPING WITH STRESS

All parents suffer from stress (Gallagher, Beckman, & Cross, 1983). Dryson (1991) found that parents of children with disabilities are under greater stress than are parents of children without disabilities. For the caregivers of children with disabilities, the key challenge is to develop the hope and conviction that they will need to cope with their stress as well as find the benefits they will need (therapeutic and educational services for the child, financial and emotional support for the caregiver) throughout the child's life. Several national programs are designed to teach parents how to cope cognitively, that is, to learn how to think positively about a problem and to enhance self-esteem (Turnbull & Turnbull, 1997).

Recall Colin's mother, whom we introduced at the beginning of this chapter. After eight days in the hospital, Ann accepted that her child was disabled. However, she was not ready to realize that her life would have to change completely to accommodate Colin's needs. During the next two years, she actively sought services for her child with disabilities. Not only did she seek and find the services he needed, she also attended to the needs of her nondisabled 3-year-old. Knowing that other families tend to avoid a family with a disabled child, Ann and Bryan planned backyard barbecues, birthday parties, mothers' get-togethers, and dinner parties without children present to maintain the social network they had enjoyed before Colin was born. Ann was even able to laugh when a friend said that Colin, who had facial abnormalities, looked just like his father.

It was not an easy process, because she had to give up her career aspirations to provide the attention that Colin needed. Her husband was very supportive and involved in Colin's development. The outcomes for Colin at 10 years of age were an inspiring example of what devoted parents and early childhood special education can accomplish. Colin speaks in clear, comprehensible sentences, skis and participates in other sports, and attends school with resource room help. The long-term prediction is that Colin will be able to work in supportive employment (see Chapter 11) and perhaps in independent competitive employment.

Affleck and associates (1991) suggest that the key to a mother's successful management of her disabled child appears to be the extent to which she perceives that she has control of the child's development, the degree of positive outcomes that she perceives, the finding of emotional support and needed services, and her acceptance of the child's disability without seeking to blame anyone for it. Mothers who cannot accept their child's disability are likely to seek a cause for it, and in most cases they attribute it to their own behavior (pp. 130–132).

Remember that the human body is genetically programmed to remain healthy and to ward off or overcome illness. Thus, children who are at risk have their body's systems helping them overcome their risk state. In addition, persons in the environment can greatly assist the child's biological system by providing support in the form of positive child-rearing practices (Werner & Smith, 1992). As Sandra Scarr (1982) writes,

> In this view, humans are made of the newer plastics—they bend with environmental pressure, resume their shapes when the pressures are relieved, and are unlikely to be misshapened by transient experiences. When bad environments are improved, people's adaptations improve. Humans are resilient and responsive to the advantages the environment provides. (pp. 852–853)

Similarly, Affleck and associates (1991) quote Taylor (1988) as follows:

> Despite serious setbacks . . . the majority of people facing such blows (e.g., personal tragedies) achieve a happy quality of life or level of happiness equivalent to or even exceeding their prior level of satisfaction. Not everyone readjusts, of course, but most do. (p. 142)

TRANSITION

In addition, care for at-risk or developmentally delayed children, or children with disabilities does not end in infancy. Many of these children require continual monitoring and support. For example, as children with disabilities grow, bigger wheelchairs or braces may be required. Although many children experience a diminishment of or outgrow their earlier at-risk states—particularly children with mild retardation who have the benefit of an early intervention program—most children with sensory disabilities will need long-term assistance. The employment rate of adults with disabilities is very low, less than 30 percent.

Another stress-inducing issue is that a child with disabilities is likely to outlive his or her parents, which poses the real problem of who will care for the child later in life. Fortunately, many national associations have been established to serve as guardians for children with disabilities when the need arises. Parents bequeath their estates to these associations to cover the cost of caring for their child, and the associations assume the responsibility for placing the individual in a foster home, group home, or independent living situation, and they monitor his or her needs as necessary.

Summary of Major Ideas

1. Early intervention programs can be very effective in facilitating the development of children who are at risk, developmentally delayed, or disabled.

2. Early intervention should begin as soon as the child has been diagnosed as having a disability or being at risk for a disability.

3. It is assumed that early intervention is effective because of the ability of the central nervous system to adapt early in life and its openness to environmental input in the early years. (The ability of the brain to adapt early in life is called *plasticity*.)

4. Some disabling conditions cannot be cured, but they can be improved to the point that the child can function in many environments and learn how to learn.

5. Early intervention is multidisciplinary in orientation at every step of the process: screening, diagnosis, therapies, and teaching.

6. Families of children with disabilities undergo stress as a result of not having the ideal child they expected. Some overcome this condition readily, but others need a great deal of help in accepting that their child has a disability. Family support groups are recommended as part of any early childhood special education service.

7. Low-birth-weight and premature infants are at high risk for disabling conditions. The increase in lifesaving techniques for very small babies is increasing the number of infants who have disabilities.

8. Parenting strategies can be very healing and do much to cure or improve the conditions of a child with disabilities.

Unresolved Issues

1. *New lifesaving techniques.* New lifesaving techniques are keeping very-low-birth-weight (under 1,500 to 2,000 g), low-birth-weight (under 2,000 to 2,500 g), and premature infants from dying. However, large numbers of these children acquire disabilities as a result of being born too soon and too small. This will mean an increase in the number of infants to be served by early intervention.

2. *Prenatal care.* Primary prevention through prenatal care is not available to all expectant mothers, particularly those who live in poverty. Even when it is available, some individuals—adolescents, for example—do not take advantage of it. If prenatal care were provided universally, as it is in the United States armed forces, it would markedly reduce the number of premature and low-birth-weight children, who are at risk for disabilities, thereby saving millions of dollars despite the costs of prenatal care.

3. *Inclusion.* Inclusion of children with disabilities in Head Start, day care, or private preschools for the nondisabled has been a slow process. To meet the requirements of federal law, massive training of Head Start staff must be undertaken.

4. *Difficulty of finding day care for children with disabilities.* Many women work outside the home because of preference or economic necessity. Among mothers of infants, 49 percent are employed outside the home. Among mothers of 3- to 4-year-olds, 55 percent are employed outside the home. Among mothers of 6- to 14-year-olds, 75 percent are employed outside the home. The primary caregiver of a child with disabilities, however, may not have the choice to continue working because of the difficulty of finding appropriate child care. Personnel of day-care centers usually are not trained to care for children with disabilities, and extended day care is not widely available.

5. *High turnover of early childhood staff.* Consistency is an important feature of successful intervention programs. Yet the yearly turnover of some staff is 100 percent in Head Start, 81 percent in licensed day care, 75 percent in private early childhood programs, and 63 percent in public schools. The high turnover is usually attributed to low pay. High turnover in early childhood special education is usually attributed to the stress and strain of working

with children with disabilities, particularly among those working with persons who have severe and profound disabilities.

6. *Teenage pregnancy.* Unmonitored teenage pregnancy (without prenatal care) continues at a very high rate, and these young mothers bear a great number of children who are disabled or at risk for developmental delays.

7. *Drug abuse.* The continued use of toxic substances (heroin, crack, alcohol, and tobacco) by many pregnant women places infants at risk for disabilities or developmental delays. Educational, drug treatment, and other programs are important to combat this problem.

Key Terms

alpha-fetoprotein test p. 92

amniocentesis p. 93

Apgar test p. 94

at-risk infant p. 89

chorionic villus biopsy p. 93

developmental scale p. 87

developmental screening p. 94

developmentally appropriate practice (DAP) p. 103

early childhood intervention p. 84

environmental risks p. 90

fetal alcohol syndrome p. 91

genetic counseling p. 91

Head Start p. 85

IDEA, Part C p. 86

individualized family services plan (IFSP) p. 96

multidisciplinary team p. 97

prenatal care p. 92

sonography p. 93

Questions for Thought

1. How has the history of early childhood programs influenced current ideas about early childhood special education? pp. 84–85

2. How effective are early intervention programs? pp. 88–89

3. What three conditions put children at risk? What are examples of each condition? pp. 89–91

4. Why is prenatal care important, and what does it involve? p. 92

5. What tests are currently available to screen the fetus? What disabilities can they detect? pp. 92–93

6. What does the Apgar test measure? When is it applied? p. 94

7. What does the IFSP contain? pp. 96–97

8. Who should be on a multidisciplinary team and why? pp. 97–100

9. What characteristics must early childhood intervention centers have, and what do they offer to families? pp. 102–103

Resources for Further Study

REFERENCES OF SPECIAL INTEREST

Krajicek, M., Steinke, T., Hertzdeng, D., Anastasiow, N., & Skandel, S. (Eds.). (1997). *Handbook for the care of infants and toddlers with disabilities and chronic conditions* and

Instructor's guide for the Handbook for the care of infants and toddlers with disabilities and chronic conditions. Austin, TX: PRO-ED.

> These materials cover a wide range of disabilities, providing information about conditions as well as techniques (such as positioning) for treating them. They were prepared under the leadership of Marilyn Krajicek, Ed.D., R.N., at the University of Colorado School of Nursing.

Furuno S., O'Reilly, K. S., Hosaka, C. M., Inatsuka, T. T., Allman, T., & Zeisloft, B. (1989). *Hawaiian early learning profile (HELP).* Vort Publishers, P.O. Box 60132, Palo Alto, CA 94306.

> A multidisciplinary team working in a model program in Hawaii constructed this comprehensive curriculum. The curriculum is divided into areas of development (self-help, cognition, communications, and so on). A teaching manual provides suggestions on how to work with a child who has been determined to be at a given level through the use of HELP. Also available from the same publisher is *Understanding My Signals: Help for Parents of Premature Infants.* This guide has many pictures to help parents note and reinforce the basic nonverbal communication system that leads to speech.

Furuno, S. F., O'Reilly, K. S., Inatsuka, T. T., Hosaka, C. M., & Falb, B. Z. (1993). *Helping babies learn: Developmental profile and activities for infants and toddlers.* Tucson, AZ: Communication Skill Builders, The Psychological Corporation.

> This manual contains activities and developmental scales in five areas: Home Routines, Indoor Activities, Excursions, Social Development, and Health and Safety. The five areas are further organized in sections according to age: 0–3, 3–6, 6–9, 9–12, 12–15, 15–18, 18–21, 21–24, 24–27, 27–30, 30–33, and 33–36 months. Developmental charts are available to help track a baby's development. The activities encompass a range of skills and describe situations in which the parent or teacher can observe and interact with the infant and facilitate his or her development.

Johnson-Martin, N., Jens, K. G., & Attermeier, S. (1991). *The Carolina curriculum for handicapped infants and infants at risk.* (2nd ed.). Baltimore: Paul H. Brookes.
Johnson-Martin, N., Attermeier, S., & Hacker, B. (1990). *The Carolina curriculum for preschool children with special needs.* Baltimore: Paul H. Brookes.

> These two comprehensive curricula are prepared so that each item is clearly stated and in small steps for children with disabilities to master, and each section is based on sound development of nondisabled children. The books are oriented not toward therapies but toward education in the domains of cognition, communication, self-help, motor development, and independence. They can be purchased separately from Paul H. Brookes, P.O. Box 10624, Baltimore, MD 21285-0624. Booklets to record progress are available with the curricula and can be purchased separately for each child.

Odom, S. L., & McLean, M. E. (1996). *Early intervention/Early childhood special education: Recommended practices.* PRO-ED, 8700 Shoal Creek Boulevard, Austin, TX 78757-6897

> This book contains a discussion and a comprehensive list of recommended practices, including assessment, development of IFSPs and IEPs, curriculum and intervention strategies, evaluation, transition, and personnel preparation. It is an essential source for all phases of program development and implementation.

JOURNALS

Infants and Young Children
Aspen Publishers, Inc.
7201 McKinney Circle
Frederick, MD 21701

Journal of Early Intervention
Council for Exceptional Children
1920 Association Dr.
Reston, VA 20191-1589
1-888-CEO-SPED
http://www.cec.sped.org/

Topics in Early Childhood
Special Education
PRO-ED Journals
5341 Industrial Oaks Blvd.
Austin, TX 78735-8809

PROFESSIONAL ORGANIZATIONS

The Beach Center (information for parents)
3111 Haworth Hall
University of Kansas
Lawrence, KS 66045
http://www.lsi.ukans.edu/beach/
beachhhp.htm

Division for Early Childhood of the
Council for Exceptional Children
14444 Wazec St., Suite 230
Denver, CO 80202
http://www.dec-sped.org

March of Dimes Resource Center
Birth Defects Foundation
P.O. Box 1657
Wilkes Barre, PA 18703
http://www.modimes.org

Parents Helping Parents Resource Center
3041 Olcott St.
Santa Clara, CA 95054
http://www.php.com

4

Children Who Are Gifted and Talented

FOCUSING questions

How do public schools define children who are gifted and talented?

What have studies shown to be some of the characteristics of children who are gifted and talented?

How can we modify curriculum content to accommodate a student's special gifts and talents?

What are some special problems of girls who are gifted?

How has the educational reform movement affected programs for students who are gifted?

Ever since a senior member of the tribe brought a few children into the cave to teach them about survival in prehistoric times, it has been evident that some youngsters learn faster than others, remember more easily than others, and are able to solve problems more efficiently and creatively than others. It has also been obvious that these youngsters are often bored with the pace of instruction, a pace geared to "average" children, and that they pose a challenge to their teachers, occasionally an embarrassing one. Picture a bright child in the prehistoric cave innocently asking, "What happens if the spear misses the saber-toothed tiger?"

Society has a special interest in children who are gifted, both as individuals and as potential contributors to society's well-being. As individuals, they have the same right to full development as do all children. In addition, many of the leaders, scientists, and poets of the next generation will come from the current group of children who are gifted and talented. Few societies can afford to ignore that potential.

In this chapter, we discuss the special characteristics that set these students apart from average students. We explore how the schools attempt to adapt programs to meet the special needs of students who are gifted, in what ways educational reform movements have been affecting their education, and what is currently being done to find "hidden giftedness" in our schools to help those students reach a higher level of proficiency.

One of the strong motivating forces supporting special educational opportunities for students who are gifted has been the flood of negative reports about how U.S. students perform in comparison with students of other countries. One can add to these findings a devastating comparison of U.S. students with Chinese and Japanese students in mathematics in 120 classrooms in Taiwan, Japan, and Minneapolis. Among the top 100 first graders in mathematics, there were only 15 American children. And only 1 American child appeared in the top 100 fifth graders (Stevenson, Chen, & Lee, 1994). Many observers are calling for more emphasis and excellence in the mathematics instruction for all students, especially for those with exceptional talents.

Of special interest to us is that when the performance of the top 1 percent of students from each group is compared, we see the same discouraging findings: Our best students, in an academic sense, do not compare favorably with the best students from other countries. We have come to assume that Americans are in first place in everything. However, a series of international comparisons indicates that that assumption is far from accurate. Ross (1993) reports in a study on national excellence the following:

> Americans assume that our best students can compete with the best students anywhere. This is not true. International assessments focused attention on the relatively poor standing of all students. These tests also show that our top-performing are undistinguished at best and poor at worst when compared with top students in other countries. (p. 8)

Another wake up call to American educators came with the publication of the results of the Third International Mathematics and Science Study (TIMSS) (Takahira, Gonzales, Frase, & Salganik, 1998). This study, which involved about 15,000 schools around the world in tests of their mastery of mathematics and science at the fourth-, eighth-, and twelfth-grade levels, revealed disturbing results for American students.

At the fourth grade, American students appeared to be performing above average for the fourteen countries that participated in the study. That result changed, however, at the middle-school level, with American students falling below average in both subjects. The twelfth-grade results were even more devastating, with the American students at or near the bottom of the over twenty countries with which they were compared.

Clearly, there needs to be concern about the performance of all our students in these critical curricular areas. The students who will be expected to go on to higher education and graduate education would be of particular concern, if they have not mastered the basics of mathematics and science in their elementary and secondary years.

Also of particular educational relevance is that when a task demands higher-level thinking processes, a domain in which students who are gifted supposedly have the greatest advantage over average students, additional poor results are reported by the National Assessment of Educational Progress. One natural question about these results is, "Do the other countries have programs for students who are gifted?" Although the answer varies from country to country, almost all countries funnel students into separate educational channels at or around early adolescence, creating in effect ability and performance grouping for their higher-ability students. The total portrait is one of students in the United States, both those who are gifted and those who are not, not being well prepared for our complex, information-based world.

Definitions

American middle school students are below average in math and science compared with students in other countries.

The term *gifted* traditionally has been used to refer to people with intellectual gifts, and we use it here in the same way. Each culture defines *giftedness* in its own image, in terms of the abilities that culture values. Ancient Greeks honored the philosopher and the orator, and Romans valued the engineer and the soldier. From a society's definition of giftedness, we learn something about the values and lifestyles of the culture. We also learn that the exceptional person often is defined by individual ability and societal needs.

Children from all cultural groups, economic levels, and areas of human endeavor show outstanding talents.

In the United States, early definitions of giftedness were tied to performance on the Stanford-Binet Intelligence Test, which Lewis Terman developed during World War I. Children who scored above an agreed-upon point—such as 130 or 140—were called gifted. They represented from 1 to 3 percent of their age-group population.

Essentially, a high score on the Stanford-Binet or on other intelligence tests meant that children were intellectually developing more rapidly than their age-mates. What was unique was not so much *what* they were doing as *when*, developmentally, they were doing it. A child playing chess is not a phenomenon, but a child playing chess seriously at age 5 is. Many children write poetry, but not at age 6, when most are just learning to read. Early rapid development is one of the clear indicators of high intellectual ability, and that is what intelligence tests measure.

Over the past few decades, periodic efforts have been made to broaden the definition of giftedness to include more than abilities directly related to schoolwork. Table 4.1 presents a recent federal definition of children who are gifted. Within the definition in Table 4.1 are many phrases that reveal our current thinking about

TABLE 4.1   Federal Definition of Students Who Are Gifted

Children and youth with outstanding talent perform, or show the potential for performing, at remarkably high levels of accomplishment when compared with others of their age, experience, or environment.

These children and youth exhibit high-performance capability in intellectual, creative, and/or artistic areas, possess an unusual leadership capacity, or excel in specific academic fields. They require services or activities not ordinarily provided by the schools.

Outstanding talents are present in children and youth from all cultural groups, across all economic strata, and in all areas of human endeavor.

Source: P. Ross (Ed.). (1993). *National Excellence.* Washington, DC: U.S. Department of Education.

 Teachers need to be aware of special talents present in children from all cultures and economic backgrounds.

gifted students. The phrase "show the potential for performing" means we accept the idea that children can be gifted without showing excellent performance. "Compared with others of their age, experience, or environment" means we accept the important role of environment and context in producing gifted students. The phrase "require services . . . not ordinarily provided" means we expect that school systems will and should modify their services and programs to take into account the different levels of development of these students. "Outstanding talents are present in children . . . from all cultural groups, across all economic strata" means teachers should be encouraged to seek special talent from all cultural groups.

Other definitions of giftedness try to include the way an individual defines and then tackles a problem—the ability to *problem-find* and *problem-solve* (Gardner, 1985; Getzels, 1978; Siegler, 1986; Sternberg, 1986). In the real world, problems do not come in neat packages ready for solving. Usually, they are hard to define and organize—they are what Simon (1979) called *ill structured*. The ability to take an ill-structured problem and organize it so the issue is clear is one indicator of giftedness.

Despite the addition of creativity, problem-finding and problem-solving skills, and different types of intelligence to our definition of giftedness, emphasis is still placed on intelligence tests as one means of identifying children who are gifted. Why? Because these tests have been effective in predicting performance in school-related activities.

Components of Intellectual Competence

What are the components of intellectual competence? What does a student who is gifted need to be productive, and what must the schools offer to such a student? As noted in Chapter 1, Perkins (1995) believes that competence reflects three major factors:

- The power of a person's neurological computer
- The tactical repertoire or cognitive strategies that a person can bring to bear
- Context-specific content and know-how

The term *giftedness* refers to exceptional ability in academic areas and to exceptional creativity, artistic talent, leadership capacity, and problem-solving abilities. *(© Nita Winter/The Image Works)*

Students who are gifted appear to have advantages across the full range of information processing. They tend to grasp new ideas faster, they see more associations between ideas, and they have a rich storehouse of concepts and systems of ideas to apply to individual problems. They also have a superior ability to use cognitive strategies, which increases their ability to cope with difficult assignments. In most instances, their ability to reason—that is, to use existing information to generate new information—is at a level two to three years or more beyond that of their agemates.

It is the responsibility of the schools to help students develop a tactical repertoire and content mastery. The notion that the student who is gifted will automatically learn these strategies or knowledge, however, is an idea that dies hard. The tactics or strategies that these students employ as they try to cope with difficult problems must be explicitly taught because they will rarely be spontaneously discovered. This collection of strategies is often referred to as the *executive function*.

The student will not naturally stumble on the process of multiplication (which, after all, is a strategy for processing information), principles of logical analysis, problem finding, and a number of other devices that are useful tools to the serious thinker. All these strategies must be taught. Occasionally, a student who is gifted will intuitively solve a problem in an innovative fashion, but unless the student explicitly recognizes the method, he or she will not likely have full use of the strategy (Glaser & Rabinowitz, 1986). Schools should deliberately attempt to teach the use of thinking strategies in many different content areas and tasks, because the conceptual transfer of a thinking strategy from one task to another is not as easy as many people think.

Schools need to teach thinking strategies in a variety of content areas and tasks.

One Gift or Many?

Should giftedness be regarded as one overriding mental ability or as a series of special abilities? Howard Gardner is one of the latest of a group of psychologists to view giftedness as a series of special abilities (1985). He has proposed a list of seven distinct and separate abilities that need specific educational attention (Table 4.2).

TABLE 4.2   Gardner's Multiple Intelligences

Linguistic intelligence	The ability to use language in written and oral expression to aid in remembering, solving problems, and seeking new answers to old problems (novelist, lecturer, lawyer, lyricist)
Logical-mathematical intelligence	The ability to use notation and calculation to aid with deductive and inductive reasoning (mathematician, physicist)
Spatial intelligence	The ability to use notation, spatial configurations; important in pattern recognition (architect, navigator, sculptor, mechanic)
Bodily-kinesthetic intelligence	The ability to use all or part of one's body to perform a task or fashion a product (dancer, athlete, surgeon)
Musical intelligence	The ability to discriminate pitch; sensitivity to rhythm, texture, and timbre; the ability to hear themes; production of music through performance or composition (musician)
Interpersonal intelligence	The ability to understand other individuals—their actions and motivations—and to act productively on that knowledge (teacher, therapist, politician, salesperson)
Intrapersonal intelligence	The ability to understand one's own feelings and motivations, cognitive strengths, and styles (just about anything)

Source: From H. Ramos-Ford and H. Gardner (1997). Giftedness from a multiple intelligences perspective. In N. Colangelo and Gary Davis (Eds.), *Handbook of Gifted Education,* Boston: Allyn & Bacon. Copyright © 1997 by Allyn and Bacon. Adapted with permission.

There seem to be several types of intelligence. A student may be gifted in one area, such as linguistic intelligence, but not be gifted in other ways.

Everyone knows persons who are particularly good at one or two of the abilities listed in Table 4.2 but who are not superior in them all. Think of a student who is a math wiz but is not expert in linguistic or interpersonal intelligence. Some students seem to be particularly gifted in spatial intelligence but have only above-average ability in other areas. Whereas all these abilities seem to be positively correlated with one another, and students who have outstanding talents in one area are usually good in the other areas as well, we can find concrete examples of specialists in outstanding performance. Consequently, the educational issue becomes not only how to plan one *overall* program for students who have talents in many of these areas but also what should be done with students who have specialized talents in a single area such as mathematics, visual perception, or interpersonal perception.

Students who are gifted provide a fine example of the need to view exceptional children *in context*. Although abundant evidence suggests that we are born with differing neurological systems that are differentially responsive to outside experience (Plomin & McClearn, 1993), factors within the family and the society also help determine the full extent of the development of the child who is gifted. (See the discussion in Chapter 1 on heredity versus environment.)

Students with high native ability still need support and help from the family, schools, and society to make the most of their outstanding abilities. The failure of these outside forces to provide support may result in such a reduction of usable talent that the student may no longer be referred to as "gifted" (Frasier, 1987) and no longer be eligible for special services.

All other exceptional children have deficits in one or more areas of development. Children who are gifted are the only group of exceptional youngsters with a surplus of ability or talent in certain areas of development. That very surplus can create unique educational challenges for these children, their families, and their school systems.

Factors That Contribute to Giftedness and Talent

Are children born gifted and talented? Do outstanding abilities emerge no matter what opportunities or education a person has? What role does heredity play in giftedness? How important is the context of the child who is gifted?

HEREDITY AND ENVIRONMENT

More than one hundred years ago, Francis Galton, in a study of outstanding Englishmen, concluded that extraordinary ability ran in families and was genetic in origin. (Galton overlooked the environmental advantage of being born into an upper-class family.) Ever since, there has been a strong belief in the powerful role that heredity plays in producing mental ability. Certainly, studies of twins and the close relationship of the abilities of adoptive children to the abilities of their natural parents demand that we recognize a hereditary element (Plomin & McClearn, 1993).

Students who are gifted appear to have both favorable hereditary and favorable environmental factors in their early development.

Although researchers make a strong case for the importance of heredity in giftedness, environment, or the context of the child, is important as well. Extraordinary talent may be shaped by heredity, but it is nurtured and developed by the environment. We've discussed the role that society plays in defining gifts and talents and rewarding them. A more powerful influence, because it is closer, is the family.

Benjamin Bloom (1985) attempted to uncover the factors that are linked to extraordinary ability. Bloom conducted a retrospective study of the early lives of world-class swimmers, pianists, mathematicians, and other gifted persons. He identified the participants through consultations with authorities in the fields and evidence of success (awards in national and international competitions, special prizes, fellowship awards). In interviews with the subjects, their parents, and their former teachers, he found that several general characteristics seem important whatever the talent area:

- Willingness to do great amounts of work (practice, time, effort) to achieve a high level or standard

Extraordinary talent may be shaped by heredity, but it is nurtured and developed by the environment—by how society and the family define and reward gifts and talents. (© Elizabeth Crews)

Family encouragement is critical to the emergent talent of the gifted child.

- Competitiveness with peers in the area of talent and determination to do the best at all costs
- Ability to rapidly learn new techniques, ideas, or processes in the area of talent

Bloom suggested that the group's high motivation was stimulated in a powerful way by the early recognition of talent by parents and friends, who went out of their way to obtain special instruction and to encourage and nurture the talent. The enthusiasm and support of the family seemed to be a critical element in the emergence of these gifted persons into world-class performers. A study of eight extremely high IQ students (Morelock & Feldman, 1997) confirmed the important role played by the families, who were described as more cohesive and more expressive than "average" families in ideas and feelings.

Studies of Students Who Are Gifted

What sets students who are gifted apart from their agemates? How do those characteristics affect the way teachers plan their education? To answer these questions, we look for general patterns among youngsters who are gifted and for deviations from those patterns (the variance of characteristics within the group). Our objective is to identify and study, over time, groups of students who are gifted to see what form their development takes.

After his revision and the publication of the Binet-Simon Tests of Intelligence in 1916, Lewis Terman, a professor of psychology at Stanford University, turned his attention to children who are gifted. In 1920, he began a study of 1,528 such children, which was to continue for more than sixty years as he and his colleagues followed them into maturity and old age.

Terman conducted his search for children who were gifted in California's public schools. He used teacher nominations and group intelligence tests to screen subjects. (Those procedures are now thought to limit the findings because they tended to eliminate children whose behavior irritated teachers, children who underachieved, and children who showed gifts in realms other than academic work.) Terman based the final selection of children on their performance on the Stanford-Binet Intelligence Scale. Most had IQ scores of 140 or higher; the average IQ score for the group was 151. Table 4.3 summarizes Terman's findings. The results, on average, were favorable in practically every dimension. The group did well not only in school and career but also in areas such as mental health, marriage, and character.

Until recently, the follow-up on the Terman sample gave us the only systematic data available on what happens to gifted children when they grow up. Now the findings of another longitudinal study is helping us determine whether gifted children fulfill their early promise. The Speyer School, a special elementary school in New York, was established through the work of Leta Hollingworth (1942), a pioneer in the education of gifted children. White and Renzulli (1987) conducted a forty-year follow-up of graduates of the school. Twenty-eight students were found; twenty of them returned questionnaires, and eight were interviewed in depth. Like the subjects in the Terman study, the majority of the men had entered professions, while the women tended to combine career and family. Their memories of the school were vivid. And "they all believed that their experience at Speyer School was instrumental in providing them with peer interaction for the first time, exposing them to competition, causing them to learn and like school for the first time, giving them a strong desire to excel" (p. 90).

Although no one in the group had made an earth-shaking discovery or contribution, most seemed to be contributing substantially to the quality of society in what they were doing. (Remember that individuals can be extraordinarily successful in their own field, such as business, science, the arts, or religion, and still be virtually unknown to the general public. Can you name three of the country's outstanding biochemists? Can you name one?)

Terman unbalanced his sample of gifted individuals through his identification process of young children. By using his own IQ test, the Stanford-Binet, as the tool for selecting gifted students for his sample, he eliminated many potentially bright youngsters from low-economic or immigrant status from the sample. As a consequence, what we are looking at in these lifespan results are largely what happens to gifted students from already well-established professional or managerial families.

One of the recurring questions regarding longitudinal studies such as the one that Terman and his associates did is, "Are the results due to the students or to the culture and times (the context) in which the study took place?" A more recent study provides some information on this issue (Subotnik, Kassan, Summers, &

TABLE 4.3   Characteristics of Students Who Are Intellectually Gifted: The Terman Longitudinal Study

Characteristics	Findings
Physical	Above-average physique and health; mortality rate 80 percent that of average
Interests	Broad range of interests in abstract subjects (literature, history, mathematics)
Education	Rates of college attendance eight times that of general population; achieved several grades beyond age level throughout school career
Mental health	Slightly lower rates for maladjustment and delinquency; prevalence of suicide somewhat lower
Marriage and family	Marriage rate average; divorce rate lower than average; group's children obtained an average IQ score of 133
Vocational choice	Men chose professions (medicine, law) eight times more frequently than did the general population.
Character	Less prone to overstatement or cheating; appeared superior on tests of emotional stability

Source: Adapted from *Genetic Studies of Genius* (Vols. 1, 4, 5), by L. Terman (Ed.), 1925, 1947, 1959, Stanford, CA: Stanford University Press. Used by permission.

Wasser, 1993). In the 1940s, a special elementary school was established at Hunter College in New York City. The school was highly selective of the students it enrolled. Each year, fifty students with IQ scores ranging from 122 to 196 were enrolled (the average IQ score was 157). A survey closely following the Terman questionnaires was taken of the six hundred students who attended the school from 1948 to 1960. Researchers found 210 persons who had attended and who completed the questionnaire. They interviewed 74 members of this group.

In educational attainment, the results were similar to those reported by the Terman group. Over 80 percent held a master's degree, and 68 percent of the men and 40 percent of the women held a doctorate in medicine, law, or some other area. They were in good health, mentally and physically, and were earning an income as impressive as their educational attainments would suggest. Over half the sample mentioned receiving one or more awards for professional work or community service.

One major difference between the Terman and the Hunter Elementary samples was in the activities of the women. The vast majority of the women in the Hunter Elementary sample were employed and were satisfied with their careers. Fewer than 10 percent were homemakers exclusively. The interviews made it clear that the women's movement (context again!) had had a decided effect on their becoming more oriented to work outside the home.

Subotnik and the other authors of the study were somewhat disappointed by the lack of drive for success or for extraordinary achievement that they found in the Hunter Elementary group. Most members of the group seemed content to do their professional job and enjoy their social life and the opportunities their vocational success provided. The well-rounded students had become well-rounded, complacent adults. One of them remarked,

> This is a terrible thing to say, but I think I'm where I want to be—terrible because I've always thought that there should have been more challenges. I'm very admired and respected where I work. . . . I don't want to be a senior vice president. . . . I want to have time to spend with my family, to garden, to play tennis, and see my friends. I'm very happy with my life. (p. 78)

The authors raise the interesting point that perhaps some degree of unhappiness or dissatisfaction may be necessary to create the obsessive concern with a particular goal and the single-minded drive and motivation to achieve that goal that lead to great attainments. On the other hand, the vast majority of these students became productive and useful citizens, and we might well ask if we should expect more of them than that. What might schools, parents, and the community do to foster greater creative productivity in the lives of highly able learners?

 On average, children who are gifted grow up to become well-adjusted adults, successful in their chosen careers.

The Challenges Associated with Giftedness

Despite their demonstrated ability to make friends and generally to adapt well, people who are gifted may shoulder some problems or challenges that stem from their exceptionality.

Increased attention has been paid to the personality of gifted students. One popular theory about self-development comes from a Polish psychologist, Dabrowski (Silverman, 1993). Dabrowski maintains that some persons have what he calls "overexcitabilities," by which he means a heightened capacity to respond to stimuli of various types. He identifies five major areas—*psychomotor, sensual, imagination, intellectual,* and *emotional*—that can be stimulated. These superstimulations carry positive connotations, such as an unusual capacity to care for others, an insatiable love of learning, vivid imagination, and so on. Therefore, overexcitability means an abundance of energies in these five areas. Many students who are intellectually gifted also reveal emotional overexcitability and are referred to as "sensitive." Two examples from Silverman's files at the Gifted Child Center illustrate these feelings:

> R had early awareness and empathy with others' feelings. . . . She has amazing tolerance and was emotionally beyond her age. She wears her heart on her sleeve and is honest with her feelings with adults as well as with other children (age 4).
>
> M is a very loving and compassionate child, cannot stand to hear a baby crying, puts his hands over his ears if he hears anything too loud or too violent, his feelings are hurt in an instant. Concerned about the welfare of others (age 3¾). (p. 16)

One common adjustment problem of many students who are gifted is dealing with the boredom that comes from sitting through classes in which something they already know is being taught. Imagine yourself faced with learning the multiplication tables over and over, and you might begin to understand their dislike of a nondifferentiated educational program.

One interesting insight into the minds and concerns of gifted students was highlighted when the same study was conducted twice, with an interval of twenty years. In 1975, George and Gallagher (1975) compared thoughts about "the future" of groups of gifted fifth graders with those of regular fifth graders in a small community in North Carolina. The interesting result of the study was that the gifted students were more pessimistic about the future than the regular students, but they were able to produce a greater variety of possible solutions to the problems they saw ahead.

In 1995, George and Scheft (1998) conducted the same study in the same community, at the same grade level, and asking the students the same questions. What, if anything, had changed? The gifted students were even more pessimistic than they were twenty years earlier, and they were now joined by the regular students, who had been rather optimistic in 1975. With the Cold War over and the economy booming, what were these students worried about? The issues that gained special prominence were the "quality of the environment" and "crime." Education was still seen as a mild plus by both groups. While the overall "quality of life" was seen positively by the regular students, the gifted students saw it as slightly negative in the future. Further, the gifted students did not give as many solutions in 1995 as they had in 1975. Issues raised the second time that weren't on the first list were AIDS, school violence, personal computers, homelessness, and the future quality of work. George and Scheft suggested an emphasis of curriculum on problem finding and problem solving, which might help reduce the depressed view of the future that so many of these youngsters appear to have.

A less recognized issue facing many students who are gifted is selecting from among their many talents. Table 4.4 presents a passage from a Thinking Log entry by a girl who recognizes that problem with a sense of humor.

The adjustment of students who are gifted to peer groups not interested in intellectual subjects or excellence has been the subject of several investigations (see Cross, Coleman, & Terharr-Yonkers, 1991). Gifted students were given the scenario of having completed a test that they felt was easy and then facing peers who complained that the test was unfair, that it was very hard, and that they probably had failed. The question was how the gifted students would respond to their peers' complaints. Several coping options were available:

TRUTH: "I thought it was kind of easy."

PLACATE: "I probably studied as hard as you did, but the test wasn't that hard."

COPOUT: "How long did you study?"

COVER-UP: "I probably studied as long as you did."

LIE: "Yeah, that exam was a pain."

Gifted students may wish to not identify themselves as being gifted by using a coping style that denies interest in excellence and even by making fun of other gifted students (Coleman, 1985). It is interesting that at special schools for advanced students, the social norm is that it is OK to be interested in intellectual and academic goals (Kolloff, 1996). Under this social environment, students who are gifted find it comfortable to reveal their true selves and interests.

Gifted students can be more pessimistic about the future than other students.

The social pressures gifted students feel to conform to the dominant peer norm is very strong.

TABLE 4.4	Excerpt from the Thinking Log of a Gifted Girl

I wish I could still draw. When I was in grammar school (junior high school included), I used to draw pretty decently. I still have some stuff I drew then. I love to draw—in pencil and in chalk. Art of all kinds intrigues me. I love music, paintings, carpentry and metal working, dancing, sewing, embroidery, cooking. I miss this stuff at school. I would love to take art classes again. I want to *so* badly. But I have my college-bound electives (I like these, too, they just don't leave time for anything else!), foreign language (German), and Band. Sometimes I want to draw so badly, or play with clay, or work in metal shop or wood shop, that it almost hurts I can feel it so much. But it's really hard to make myself sit down and draw. I'm so out of practice and I don't like to mess up! It's really scary to draw after a few months of not drawing at all. I'm so jealous of people like Todd, who bring their sketch pads everywhere with them; they take lots of art classes like I wish I could.

I want to dance in my old ballet class, play my clarinet, draw thousands of pictures (*good* ones), create beautiful pieces of woodwork, cook and sew for my children, decorate my home, be an astrophysicist, go to Mars, and understand all of my questions about life. That's not so much to ask, is it?

Source: S. Morris, *Thinking Log.* Copyright © 1991. Reprinted by permission of Illinois Mathematics and Science Academy.

Some additional difficulties that gifted students often have are coping with unrealistic expectations placed on them by people who believe that everything comes easily to them and finding people who share their interests.

Developmental Profiles

We would like you to meet two children, Cranshaw and Zelda. Both are 10 years old and in the fifth grade. Cranshaw probably meets the criteria for intellectual, creative, and leadership giftedness; Zelda, the intellectual criteria. Their developmental profiles are shown in Figure 4.1.

Cranshaw is a big, athletic, happy-go-lucky youngster who impresses the casual observer as the "all-American boy." He seems to be a natural leader and to be enthusiastic over a wide range of interests. These interests have not yet solidified. One week he can be fascinated with astronomy, the next week with football formations, and the following week with the study of Africa.

His past history in school has suggested that teachers have two very distinct reactions to Cranshaw. One is that he is a joy to have in the classroom. He is a cooperative and responsible boy who can not only perform his own tasks well, but be a good influence in helping the other youngsters to perform effectively. On the other hand, Cranshaw's mere presence in the class also stimulates in teachers some hints of personal inferiority and frustration, since he always seems to be exceeding the bounds of the teachers' knowledge and abilities. The teachers secretly wonder how much they are really teaching Cranshaw and how much he is learning on his own.

"On Going to College Early"

Two years ago, I had the great fortune to interview the poet and author Dr. Maya Angelou. Something she said to me has come back to me over and over since we first met: "Everybody born is born with talent. They may not know it, they may not show it, but they are born with it. It's the rare person, however, who has the intelligence, the discipline, the forthrightness, and the perseverance to architect a dream."

What I think I got out of going to college early and, in particular, attending Simon's Rock College, is not so much any single intellectual achievement. What I believe I gained was a positive focus for my considerable energies; through the professors, mentors, and friends I met here I was given the tools with which to architect my dreams.

It is imperative that, as educators and concerned citizens, we not forget the needs of black and Latino students who are gifted and talented. On a recent show about black men Oprah Winfrey poses the question, "Why is it easier for black men to get into San Quentin than it is for them to get into Stanford?" So I pose the question to you—why is it easier for 15- or 16-year-old black youths to get into the criminal justice system than it is for them to get into Simon's Rock, Johns Hopkins, or the University of Chicago?

Some of the typical questions posed about early college entrance are: Do you miss not attending the prom? Does going to college early make you grow up too fast? Let me say this: When there are guns in your school and metal detectors at the front door, then I would suggest that, no, missing the prom is not a big deal. As to the question of growing up too fast, I believe that the elements of racism, poverty, the hustle of the inner city—one or some combination of all three—rob far too many kids of their childhood. I know because I was one of them. And

for me, going to college early was a chance to do what I couldn't do at home—focus on my school work and socialize like the teenager I was.

Expectation plays a large part in all of our development. Too often, the expectation of young black people is criminality and stupidity. I grew up in the New York City public school system. One thing I remember very clearly is that the gifted and talented classes were always the ones with the most white kids. My friend Retha, who grew up in Queens, remembers exactly the same thing. More was expected of the white students. Period.

We moved often. Every time we did, I was put into the C or average class despite the fact that I'd always been in the gifted and talented classes before we began moving so much. After a couple of weeks, I would go up to my teacher and ask if there was a "harder class," and I would be moved. I was only 9 and 10 years old, but would have, somehow, to find a humble way to point out to a teacher that I wanted to be challenged more. No teacher ever asked why I, sitting in the C class, completed the math test in 10 minutes and sped through my reading assignments. "Did you do this yourself?" was a frequent and upsetting question. The expectations for me were low, and as long as I didn't cause trouble my overworked teachers ignored me. I had to challenge myself. And for that desire to learn I don't credit any sort of super-intelligence, but instead a high self-esteem that I was able to nurture and protect despite my circumstances. But think of how many young black students sit in C classes, needing more work but not receiving it! After all, they are just kids. Maybe some of them say, "Cool. This is gonna be a breeze." And it is. Maybe some of them don't want to be seen as a smarty pants, so they play it low-key. Maybe some of them play dumb to fit in with their friends. Regardless, if you're poorly tracked by the fourth grade, you stop trying so hard. You don't go to college early. Perhaps, you don't go to college at all.

Like many black parents, like many immigrant parents, my mother and father trusted the school system to do right by their kids. All of us here know that lack of involvement can be a trust misplaced. Standing at the elevator bank at the *New York Times,* where I work, the other day I overheard two women, both white, both upper class, discussing their children's education. "We're trying to get our son into a lab school," said one woman, "but there's also a gifted and talented class we could get him into. And if worse comes to worse, thank God we've got the money for private school." Think about it. Then ask yourself why it is easier for young black persons to get into jail than it is for them to get into Simon's Rock. The answer shouldn't be because jail is free.

I urge you to do better by students of color. And I do not ask of you what I don't demand of myself. If there is something I can do on behalf of your students or your institution, call me. Our African-American neighborhoods are always more full of basketball recruiters than college recruiters. These days, record producers are also a known force—searching the streets for the next great gangsta rapper, the next platinum-selling Snoop Doggy Dogg. A message is being sent to our young black people that there are only three trades open to them—the dope trade, the basketball trade, and the rap trade. College recruiters need to make their voices heard and let these kids know that their gifts and talents are not limited to the streets, the basketball courts, and the rap studios.

I know there are many, many students like me—poor and black—who are biding their time for college while struggling with difficult situations. The ability to go to college early is the ability to keep your dreams alive before they are snuffed out by any number of traps that await children in urban areas—teenage pregnancy, drug dealing, under-education, and under-employment. For students like me, going to college early was not about missing the prom but about saving our own lives.

I come from a race of people that has given this country some of its best and brightest leaders: Children's Defense Fund head Marian Wright Edelman, attorney and White House insider Vernon Jordan, writers James Baldwin, Rita Dove, and Toni Morrison, astronaut Mae C. Jemison. When you are in your classrooms and universities, ask yourself: Where are the black faces, the Latino faces, the poor and the disadvantaged of all races? Then ask yourself what you can do to get these students what they need. We know where talent can go when it is nurtured, and we know what happens when the gift sits idle.

Source: Veronica Chambers, "On Going to College Early," speech presented at the Conference on Adolescence, Acceleration, and National Excellence at Simon's Rock College of Bard, Great Barrington, MA, June 19, 1994. Reprinted by permission of the author.

What Is the Context?

In this speech, a young woman who is gifted addresses the many challenges she has faced in her neighborhood, in school, and in college. The constant tumult of the inner city and exposure to racism, drugs, and poverty force children to grow up very fast. College became the sanctuary where she could concentrate on studying and have the opportunities to socialize. Negative expectations by society for inner-city youths become self-fulfilling prophecies. Veronica Chambers came to understand that it was vital to protect and nurture her self-esteem and to assert herself whenever teachers assumed that she belonged in unchallenging classes. Faced at times with conflicting pressures from violent neighborhoods and schools, she has come to understand herself as a talented, focused, whole person and to take responsibility for improving the opportunities of poor, inner-city children.

Pivotal Issues for Teachers

What are some of the pressures that black and Latino students who are gifted face when placed in low-level classes? What other pressures, difficulties, and needs do black and Latino students who are gifted and talented face? Why are they more highly regarded for their athletic and musical ability than for their academic ability? How did the accelerated academic program help Veronica Chambers?

Cranshaw's family is a well-knit, reasonably happy one. His father is a businessman, his mother has had some college education, and the family is moderately active in the community. Their attitude toward Cranshaw is that he is a fine boy, and they hope that he does well. They anticipate his going on to higher education but, in effect, say that it is pretty much up to him what he is going to do when the time comes. They do not seem to be future-oriented and are perfectly happy to have him as the enthusiastic and well-adjusted youngster that he appears to be today.

Zelda shares similar high scores on intelligence tests to those manifested by Cranshaw. Zelda is a chubby girl who wears rather thick glasses that give her a "bookish" appearance. Her clothes, while reasonably neat and clean, are not stylish and give the impression that neither her parents nor Zelda have given a great deal of thought to how they look on this particular child. Socially, she has one or two reasonably close girl friends, but she is not a member of the wider social circle of girls in her classroom and, indeed, seems to reject it.

Teachers respond to Zelda with two generally different feelings. They are pleased with the enthusiasm with which Zelda attacks her schoolwork and the good grades that she gets. At the same time, they are vaguely annoyed or irritated with Zelda's undisguised feeling of superiority toward youngsters who are not as bright as she is; they tend to repel Zelda when she tries to act like an assistant teacher, or to gain favors that are more reserved for the teachers.

Zelda and her family seem to get along very well with each other. The main source of conflict is that the family has values which Zelda has accepted wholeheartedly but that are getting her into difficlty with her classmates. Her father is a college professor and her mother has an advanced degree in English literature. They seem to value achievement and intellectual performance almost to the exclusion of all other things.

Their social evenings are made up of intellectual discussions of politics, religion, or the current burning issue on the campus. These discussions are definitely adult-oriented, and Zelda is intelligent enough to be able to enter occasionally into such conversations. This type of behavior is rewarded much more by the parents than is the behavior that would seem more appropriate to her age level. (Gallagher & Gallagher, pp. 11–12, reprinted by permission)

Cranshaw's adjustment is as good as his academic achievement; Zelda has social difficulties. She is not accepted by her agemates and doesn't understand why. The pattern of development is different for each of these students because of differing environmental factors.

The teachers of gifted students face several basic challenges: holding the interest of youngsters whose abilities are several years beyond their grade level, encour-

Figure 4.1
Profiles of Two Gifted Students

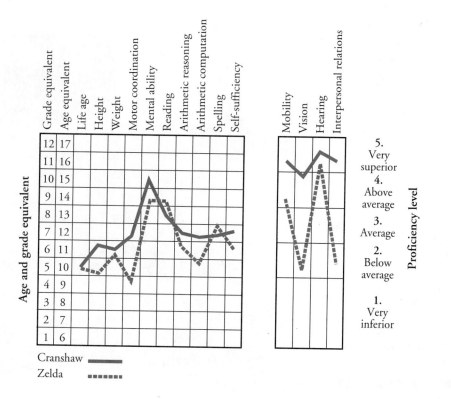

Cranshaw ——————
Zelda ▪▪▪▪▪▪▪

aging them to work in areas that may not interest them, and helping them deal with the social problems that may be linked to being gifted.

Identification

Before we can provide children who are gifted with special services to match their special needs, we have to find them. Identification is not an easy task! In every generation, many such children pass through school unidentified, their talents uncultivated.

We generally expect that teachers can spot these children and do something for them. But studies have shown that teachers do not always recognize children who are gifted, even those with academic talent (Parke, 1991). The identification of these students requires an understanding of the requirements of the program for which they are chosen. If we want to choose a group of students for an advanced mathematics class, our approach would be different than if we are looking for students with high aptitude for a creative-writing program. Specific program needs and requirements shape the identification process.

Any program for identifying children who are gifted in a school system should include both subjective and objective methods of evaluation. Classroom behavior, for example, can point up children's ability to organize and use materials and reveal their potential for processing information, sometimes better than can a test. Products, such as superior essays and term projects, that can be kept in a student portfolio can serve as an indication of special gifts.

Any program for identifying children who are gifted in a school system should include both subjective and objective methods of evaluation. Classroom behavior, for example, can point up children's ability to organize and use materials and can reveal their potential for processing information. *(© Thomas Cheek/Stock Boston)*

The visual and performing arts use expert judgment to identify talented students.

In the visual and performing arts, talent usually is determined by the consensus of expert judges, often in an audition setting. Experts in the arts are not enthusiastic about tests of artistic ability or musical aptitude. They trust their own judgment more, although their judgment is susceptible to bias. Sometimes, it is possible to judge the quality of a series of products or a portfolio of drawings or compositions that students produce over a period of time (Clark & Zimmerman, 1998).

Most schools have test scores available from group intelligence tests or group achievement tests. Such data can serve as a starting point for selecting candidates for a special program, but they do have limitations:

- Group intelligence tests are not as reliable as individual tests.
- Group tests seldom differentiate abilities at the upper limits, because they have been designed largely for the average student.
- Group tests rarely measure creative thinking or cognitive areas beyond academic aptitude.
- Some children do not function well in a timed testing situation.

Despite those limitations, group intelligence tests are a practical means of screening large numbers of students, although the scores of students from culturally diverse settings are likely to be underestimated. It is financially prohibitive, however, to give all children individual examinations.

Achievement tests are even less discriminating. They detect only the children who are achieving well academically. Emotional disturbance, family problems, peer-group values, poor study habits, a foreign-language background, and many other factors can affect a child's ability to perform academically. And because of family pressures, good study habits, or intense motivation, some children may achieve at a higher educational level than is consistent with their other abilities or their apparent mental level.

Another approach used to identify students who are gifted is to start with a particular program and find youngsters with the special abilities that meet program requirements. Stanley (1989) used this method to initiate a talent search for mathematically and verbally precocious youngsters—the Study of Mathematically Precocious Youth, now referred to as the Center for Talented Youth at Johns Hopkins University.

The Scholastic Aptitude Test and other aptitude tests are used to screen students who are extraordinarily capable in mathematics. Other characteristics—motivation and academic efficiency—determine the type of special attention suitable for those who score at the highest level on these tests. Most special education programs for students who are gifted now use a combination of aptitude tests, teacher ratings, nominations, portfolios, and scholastic records to help identify eligible students. A committee of teachers and other specialists often will try to match the child's talents with the special services that are available.

Identifying children who are gifted should be the first step to a differentiated program. It also can be used to determine eligibility for state financial aid that may provide a subsidy for local programs or to satisfy state or federal guidelines.

Special Groups of Children Who Are Gifted

The category of children who are gifted and talented contains many subgroups. How well individuals in these groups are adapting depends to a major degree on how their families raise them, how their schools utilize their special gifts, and how society sees them.

GIRLS WHO ARE GIFTED

It seems strange in one respect to identify girls who are gifted as a "special" group, because girls make up more than 50 percent of the student population. But sufficient evidence shows that members of this group differ meaningfully on a number of indices from their male counterparts. The differences appear to rest in their perceptions of the world around them, often formed by the attitudes of those close to them. If trusted Aunt Millie tells her niece that girls are not supposed to be good in mathematics, and if other family members or other persons whom the child trusts share that viewpoint, then what is the girl likely to believe—particularly if such a stereotype is repeated in the popular media and in the girl's peer group?

The limited number of girls being identified as gifted seems to be the result of societal preconceptions that girls do not have special abilities.

Gender differences in self-perception appear to limit girls' intellectual performance, so it is extremely important for teachers to be aware of such differences and try to do something about them. These differences appear to be related to societal expectations. Although there is reason to believe (Hollinger, 1995) that attitudes toward girls and women are changing, the forces at work to limit achievement of girls appear still powerful.

One study (Cramer & Oshima, 1992) places the key at about sixth through ninth grade, finding that girls who are gifted began at that level (but not before) to attribute math success to greater ability on the part of males and less to effort than males did. Such a belief can have a smothering effect on girls' efforts to achieve in mathematics. Another study showed a relationship between the mathematics

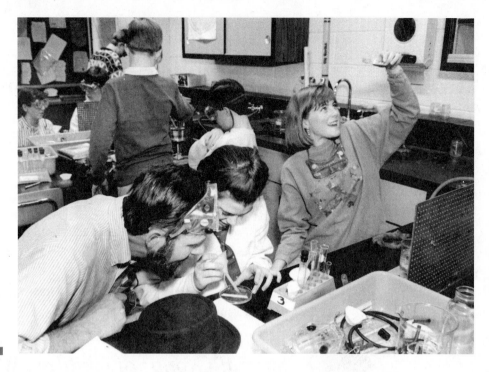

The belief is growing that girls who are gifted represent one of the largest groups of untapped intellectual potential in this country. (© Jerry Howard/Positive Images)

Career development counseling and internships give gifted girls direct experience with career options.

self-concept of high-ability girls and their parents' belief in the ability of their daughters (Dickens & Cornell, 1993). Girls with a high mathematics self-concept had parents who had a similarly high perception of their daughters' ability and high expectations for their performance. This finding seems to indicate the importance of high parental expectations in dampening the societal bias against girls doing well in mathematics.

The fact that society still has a long way to go is made clear by Reis and Callahan (1989). They point out the relative absence of women in positions of power and prestige in our society—in business, the media, the Supreme Court, Congress, corporations, universities, symphony orchestras, and so on. The relative scarcity of female role models is another stumbling block, although that problem is easing now as more women become visible in desirable occupations. Van Tassel-Baska (1998) has suggested that the use of successful women as adult role models and mentors can help girls set goals and consider career decisions. She also advises the use of career development counseling and internships so gifted girls have some direct experience with various career areas. Bright girls should also be helped to begin to confront the balancing act between career and family, which may affect their future.

Several experimental programs have been designed to overcome this societal bias. Some have grouped girls who are gifted for special instruction in mathematics (Rand & Gibbs, 1989). By using female role models and keeping the intimidating element of male students out of the classroom, these programs hope to build students' confidence in their own abilities. It is too early to judge the impact of gender-linked segregation on this kind of instruction. The goal is to ensure that girls who are gifted receive the education that will allow them to choose what they want to do, not what others believe they should do. Table 4.5 reveals a set of rules proposed to aid girls in their science interests. These suggestions are designed to aid the girls' self-concepts and mastery of necessary skills.

TABLE 4.5	**Strengthening the Science Interest of Girls Who Are Gifted**

1. *Remember: Do not overhelp young girls.* Let them gain valuable experience by thinking through a problem and trying various solutions. Encourage self-reliance or independence.

2. *Encourage girls to trust their own judgment.* Discourage girls from seeking constant approval or verification from others before making decisions or moving to the next step. They need to develop confidence in their own abilities.

3. *Insist that girls use tools and equipment.* They should feel confident in their ability to identify and use equipment from basic hand tools to sophisticated computers and microscopes.

4. *Introduce female role models whenever possible.* This includes historical as well as women currently in science fields. Remember also that women such as mothers and teachers exert a strong influence on a young girl's life; examine your own approaches to the areas listed above.

Source: D. Rand and L. Gibbs (1989). "A Model Program for Gifted Girls in Science." *Journal for the Education of the Gifted, 12*(2), p. 153. Chapel Hill: The University of North Carolina Press.

CHILDREN OF EXTRAORDINARY ABILITY

It is generally accepted today that superior intellectual ability predicts high academic performance and personal adjustment. But doubts linger about the youngster of extraordinary ability—the 1 in 100,000 at the level of an Einstein. What happens to the student who is seven or eight years ahead of his or her age group in development?

Is there a relationship between extraordinary intelligence and later development? As IQ scores increase, do we see an increase in later accomplishments? Feldman (1984) compared two groups of adults among Terman's subjects. As children, one group obtained IQ scores of more than 180; the other, randomly selected from the average range of scores, had IQ scores in the area of 150. There was some evidence that men in the "very high IQ" group had accomplished more than men in the "high IQ" group. For example, one was an internationally known psychologist, another a highly honored landscape architect. Still, many of the men in the lower group were successful, if not eminent. Feldman also found a difference between the women in the two groups. Those with IQ scores around 180 tended to have full-time careers; those in the lower group tended to be homemakers. Despite the difference he found between the groups, Feldman concluded that *genius* is not solely a function of intelligence but rather reflects a combination of intelligence, personality, motivation, and environmental variables.

Certainly Feldman's conclusions seem accurate when we look at the stories of two American prodigies, William Sidis and Charles Fefferman. Sidis was a mathematical prodigy who knew algebra, trigonometry, geometry, and calculus by age 10. He was admitted to Harvard University at age 11 and graduated cum laude at age 16. Despite his scholastic success, Sidis's emotional adjustment was always a problem. He retreated into social isolation, strenuously avoiding all academic life and publicity. He died in his middle forties, penniless and alone (Montour, 1977).

Many people believe that that is what happens to prodigies: "The faster the rocket goes up, the faster it comes down" and "Early ripe, early rot." Much more typical, however, is the story of Charles Fefferman, the youngest person in recent history to be appointed to a full professorship at a major university. He received that appointment at the University of Chicago at age 22. Encouraged by his father, a Ph.D. in economics, he was taking courses in mathematics at the University of Maryland by the age of 12 and entered college as a full-time student at age 14. He combined his studies with a normal social life; his friends were in junior high at the time. He won a number of prizes for his work in mathematics and at age 27 was the first recipient of the $150,000 Allan Waterman Award of the National Science Foundation (Montour, 1977).

The great developmental distance between these youngsters and their age peers necessitates individual programs for them, not unlike the IEPs proposed for children with disabilities. Such programs and services would consider acceleration, moving the student through the system more rapidly, and some form of tutoring or mentoring by adults with special knowledge in the student's area of special interest (Silverman, 1998).

Extraordinarily precocious students represent one of our greatest and rarest natural resources. We must learn more about them to understand the origin of their giftedness and ways to help them adapt to an often difficult social environment.

UNDERACHIEVERS WHO ARE GIFTED

One of the many myths surrounding children who are gifted is the cannonball theory. The idea, simply put, is that such children can no more be stopped from achieving their potential than a cannonball once fired can be diverted from its path. Like most simplistic ideas about human beings, this one, too, is wrong. There is a subgroup of children referred to as **gifted underachievers,** students whose academic performance consistently falls far short of expectations (e.g., a consistent C average).

A substantial proportion of children never achieve the level of performance that their scores on intelligence and aptitude tests predict for them. In the Terman longitudinal study, the researchers identified a group of 150 men who had not achieved to the level of their apparent ability and compared them with 150 men who had done well (Terman & Oden, 1947). In their self-ratings and in ratings by their wives and parents, four major characteristics separated the underachieving men from the achieving men: greater feelings of inferiority, less self-confidence, less perseverance, and less of a sense of life goals. More striking was an examination of teacher ratings made on the men twenty years earlier, while they were in school. Even at that time, their teachers believed that the underachievers lacked self-confidence, foresight, and the desire to excel.

Whitmore (1980) summed up the literature on the distinctive personality and behavioral traits that describe many underachievers:

> A negative self-concept, low self-esteem, expectations of academic and social failure, a sense of inability to control or determine outcomes of his efforts, and behaviors that serve as mechanisms for coping with the tension produced by conflict for the child in school. (p. 189)

Most teachers are able to describe at length the characteristics of underachievers. But what they really want to know is what to do about them. Whitmore reported on a special program at the primary-grade level. A group of twenty-seven under-achievers who were gifted was placed in a special class where the children were encouraged to express their feelings and concerns. The teacher met monthly with each child and his or her parents. After a year, twelve of the students had gained from 1½ to 3 years in reading scores; only three failed to reach grade level in reading or arithmetic. Social behavior and work habits also improved. Whitmore pointed out that many of the children had shown signs of emotional disturbance, but the creation of a warm, accepting environment apparently had overcome the outward symptoms of those problems.

In a carefully designed experiment with elementary school students, Butler-Por (1987) placed thirty-six underachievers in a program that stressed three elements:

- Acceptance of the individual child
- Recognition by the child and the parents that a change in the school situation was necessary
- Willingness of the child to take responsibility for change

Each of the twelve teachers in the study used diagnostic profiles to help the students recognize the need for change. At weekly meetings, teachers and students agreed to individual written contracts that spelled out goals for the coming week and rewards for achieving them. Goals included preparing homework, organizing a social event, and reducing classroom disruptions. At the end of the program, teachers and students evaluated the success of their joint efforts and agreed that progress would continue without structured individualized meetings. In comparing the students in the experimental group with a similar group of youngsters who received no special attention, Butler-Por found that the experimental group showed improvement in grades, in positive social experiences, in attitudes, and in school attendance.

Both Whitmore and Butler-Por have shown that carefully designed programs over an extended period of time can make a positive difference in the academic and social performance of underachievers. Yet very few school systems offer these programs. Why? Because underachievers who are gifted do not often come to the attention of special educators. They don't fail in school, yet they can't perform at the level that would place them in programs for students who are gifted (see also Supple, 1990).

A different approach to underachievement, one using the Renzulli Enrichment Triad model, seems to have some promise (Baum, Renzulli, & Hebért, 1995). For that model, seventeen underachievers in grades 3–9 were selected by their teachers as students who would qualify for the gifted and talented program but who were judged to be underachievers. The basis for the underachievement was judged in different children to be social and emotional problems, poor self-regulation, or negative response to the standard curriculum.

The teachers engaged each of the seventeen students in a Type III enrichment activity, the goal of which was to provide an opportunity for the student to actually investigate real problems through suitable means of inquiry and to bring his or her findings to bear on realistic audiences. (Note the similarity to the problem-finding approach described earlier in this chapter.)

The authors reported positive gains in attitude, interviews, achievement tests, and other areas, although the magnitude of the change was unspecified. The authors felt

A warm, accepting, supportive environment can significantly improve the academic and social performance of underachievers.

Gifted students who are seen as underachievers may benefit from enrichment activities based on investigating real problems.

Students can be challenged by participating in Outward Bound activities, such as these high schoolers sailing in Boston harbor. (© *Walter S. Silver/The Picture Cube*)

that taking part in Type III activities, which encouraged positive relationships with adults, practicing self-regulation behaviors, and using an interest-based curriculum, plus addressing real-world problems, played a role in helping the underachieving students make progress.

CULTURALLY DIVERSE CHILDREN WHO ARE GIFTED

One way to expand the number of culturally different children who are identified as gifted is to adopt alternative policies for state and local schools. Coleman and Gallagher (1992) analyzed the special changes that the fifty states made in their standard identification procedures to try to discover in nontraditional families and cultural groups children who are gifted. These strategies included

- Developing student profiles and case study examples of nontraditional gifted students
- Using multiple identification criteria with the clause "no single criterion should prevent identification"
- Using portfolios of student work samples to document giftedness

Such measures seemed necessary because cultural diversity often masks outstanding talent, at least to those who are not members of that culture.

Wolf (1981) used a unique approach to qualify urban minority students for advanced work in the visual and performing arts. The identification process was in two stages. First, the top 15 or 20 percent of the student body was identified by performance on standard tests. That group was enrolled in a theater techniques program that emphasized expressive and communication skills. At the end of the program, the staff rated the students along a number of dimensions. Those who rated high graduated to an independent study and seminar program at the Educational Center for the Arts, which provides training in music, dance, theater arts, and graphic arts.

Once culturally diverse students who are gifted are found, by whatever method, we must develop an educational plan for their special needs and circumstances. One objective for minority-group youngsters is to encourage their understanding of and respect for their own cultural background. Biographies and the works of noted writers or leaders from the particular cultural group are often the basis of special programs. Because there are so many groups with such diverse backgrounds, these programs are usually unique (Baldwin, 1987; Bernal, 1979).

Children who come from very different family cultures and values face not only the limited opportunity to learn the knowledge that the school feels is important but also a psychological struggle over whether they want to become part of mainstream America and participate in the same fashion as middle-class white children. Figure 4.2, a poem written by a Native American girl, is an expression of this conflict and of the desire to hold on to the values of another culture. Such ambivalence is not favorable to achievement in the traditional school sense.

As minority groups gradually assimilate into the larger community, educational programs carry the difficult task of encouraging youngsters to respect their cultural heritage and, at the same time, to take on those characteristics of the larger society that can help them succeed within that society. The balance is a delicate one.

One of the most difficult issues for culturally diverse students to cope with is their own self-identity, particularly if there appears to be a gap between the majority white culture and the culture of the family from which the student comes. Black students who are gifted and who are perceived as acting white are likely to have a difficult time achieving good peer adjustment (Ford, Harris, & Schuerger, 1993) or finding a way to feel good about themselves.

Some special counseling has been suggested as a means of helping individual students come to terms with the differing values, attitudes, and norms of the dominant culture and their parent culture. Special multicultural counseling strategies are needed, together with use of mentors and role models. The ordinary school counseling program by itself does not seem adequate for this special task. Gifted students from culturally diverse families may need special career counseling so they are aware of the range of opportunities that are available to them (Perrone, 1997).

One of the major controversies in the early 1990s pitted the *assimilation approach* against the *pluralistic approach*. Proponents of the assimilation approach believed that students who are gifted and from minority backgrounds should learn about the majority culture and what behaviors and knowledge are necessary to make an academic and economic success within the rules of the majority culture (Frasier, 1991). Proponents of the pluralistic approach focused on how to modify the majority culture to better take into account the needs of the various subcultures (Kitano, 1992). It is likely that elements of both positions will find a way into the school curriculum and into programs for nontraditional students who are gifted. (See Figure 4.2.)

Maker (1989, p. 301) summarized the program suggestions from a wide variety of specialists concerned with children from different cultural backgrounds:

Figure 4.2
"Sadness in My Heart,"
by Vena Romero, 13 years old

My thoughts flow vigorously
through my mind
as I see the tears fall endlessly
because we, the younger generation, are
blind.
Blinded by the white world
and what it brings,
we forget about our world
and all our sacred native things.
We have held our tradition
for so very long.
The elders are praying, wishing,
that it will live on.
We're forgetting about them
and our future.
Slowly we're losing them
and our culture.
We can't see how we're hurting ourselves
by losing our identity,
our culture, tradition, heritage, and ourselves.
We are not Native Americans
without our world.
We are just dark-skinned Americans
in a white world.

Source: Vena Romero (1994), in C. Callahan and J. McIntire, *Identifying Outstanding Talent in American Indian and Alaska Native Students.* Washington, DC: U.S. Department of Education, p. i.

1. Identify students' strengths and plan a curriculum to develop those abilities.
2. Provide for the development of basic skills and other abilities students may lack.
3. Regard differences as positive rather than negative attributes.
4. Provide for involvement of parents, the community, and mentors or role models.
5. Create and maintain classrooms with a multicultural emphasis.

CHILDREN WITH DISABILITIES WHO ARE GIFTED

Through the remainder of this book, we discuss children who have various disabilities. They may not be able to see or hear or walk, but such a limitation does not mean they are not intellectually gifted. It only means that they stand a good chance of having their special talents overlooked. Whitmore (1981) described a child who not only went unrecognized as gifted but was actually considered mentally retarded:

Kim. At seven years of age, this child with cerebral palsy had no speech and extremely limited motor control. In a public school for severely handicapped students, she was taught only self-help skills. Her parents, who were teachers, observed her use of her eyes to communicate and believed there was unstimulated intellect trapped in her severely handicapped body. Upon parent request, she was mainstreamed in her wheelchair into an open-space elementary school. After two months of stimulation and the provision of a mechanical communicator, Kim began to develop rapidly. She learned the Morse code in less than two days and began communicating continuously to the teacher and peers through her communicator. Within four months, she was reading on grade level (second), and subsequent testing indicated she possessed superior mental abilities—an exceptional capacity to learn. (p. 109)

It is not hard to imagine what Kim's world would have been like if she had not been given the opportunity to learn and communicate.

A gifted student might also have a learning disability.

One of the areas of disabilities to which researchers have given particular attention is the child who is both gifted and learning disabled. Some students can be gifted and also have neurologically based attention problems or visual perceptual problems that can cause reading or spelling errors.

Coleman (1992) studied the coping strategies used by students with learning disabilities who were gifted, as opposed to average students with learning disabilities. She found that the students who were gifted had many more constructive coping strategies—that they developed problem-solving plans—whereas the average student with learning disabilities often displayed *learned helplessness* ("there's nothing I can do"), *escape/avoidance* ("go out and play instead of do homework"), or *distancing* ("just shrug it off"). Coleman recommended that all students with learning disabilities be directly instructed in coping strategies as a way of helping them survive the educational environment.

Education Reform and Its Effects

Many changes are taking place in the schools today. Even though most are not initiated for students who are gifted, they are having a profound effect on them. Education for these students is a relatively small part of the huge U.S. educational establishment. Whenever major change takes place in the overall educational establishment, it reverberates through the system and affects all of the smaller parts. This is true of the educational reform efforts of the 1990s (see Chapter 2).

Table 4.6 summarizes some of the major movements in that reform effort and their apparent effects on education for students who are gifted. The *excellence movement* was designed to combat international economic competition and stirred interest and influenced a key national goal: taking steps to ensure that the United States was first in the world in mathematics and science by the year 2000. This goal, plus the realization that American students were substantially behind students from other countries in science and mathematics, energized a variety of special programs for talented students, from the establishment of state residential schools (like the Illinois Mathematics and Science Academy) to summer enrichment programs. Various curriculum reform movements also began.

Ironically, two of the other reform elements, *cooperative learning* (Slavin, 1989) and the *middle schools movement* (George, 1988), stress the importance of heterogeneous grouping. Although these movements were not formed with gifted students as the focus, the programs provide students who are gifted with the opportunity to experience and understand students at all levels of ability and cultural backgrounds. As a result, many schools have reduced the number of advanced classes or honors classes, which previously had served and stimulated children who are gifted.

TABLE 4.6 Educational Reform and Students Who Are Gifted

Reform	How Reform Is Revealed	Implications for Education of Students Who Are Gifted
Excellence movement	Concern that U.S. has lost competitiveness and we, as a nation, need to encourage our best and brightest students	Emphasis on strengthening curriculum in math and science; raising standards
Cooperative learning	Techniques for group or team learning, often stressing diversity of ability or cultural background in group formation	Gifted students often placed in tutorial roles in small-group work, may not be challenged by tasks
Middle schools movement	Focus on affective learning, interdisciplinary content, thinking processes, team teaching, and flexible scheduling; features heterogeneous grouping in many schools	Potential loss of advanced classes, honors programs; academic challenge may be lessened unless vigorous provisions are made in heterogeneous classrooms
Site-based management	More key educational decisions made at school level; teachers empowered	Will children with special needs be recognized? Will district-wide programs (e.g., magnet schools) be discontinued?
Accountability	Schools expected to demonstrate or display the results of their work	Usual measures grossly underestimate gifted students' performance; too low a ceiling

Source: Adapted from J. Gallagher (1991). "Educational Reform, Values, and Gifted Students." *Gifted Child Quarterly, 35*(1), pp. 12–19.

Site-based management—making many educational decisions at the school level, where students are best known and planned for—is a reform that can work well if educators at the site understand the special needs of exceptional children. In a backhanded way, *accountability* (the last reform listed in Table 4.6) may increase attention to students who are gifted. The results of an evaluation can reveal the poor results on achievement tests for all students and put pressure on the schools to raise standards and challenge the best of the students. As is the case with many complex movements to change the schools, the overall impact of accountability on the education of students who are gifted remains uncertain.

Educational Adaptations

Children Who Are Gifted and Talented

A school program for students who are gifted involves modifications to the learning environment, to curriculum content, and to cognitive strategies.

Consider the following three general educational objectives for special programs or services for students who are gifted and talented:

- Mastering important conceptual systems that are at the level of their abilities in various content fields
- Developing skills and strategies that enable them to become more independent and creative
- Developing pleasure in and excitement about learning that will carry them through the routine that is an inevitable part of the learning process

Although regular classroom teachers, in collaboration with other teachers and specialists, can help children who are gifted meet some of these goals, special programs are deemed essential to consistently achieve in all three of them. We can modify the school program for any group of exceptional children in three areas: learning environment, content, and cognitive strategies. A special type of change in learning environment involves moving the student more rapidly through school—educational acceleration. In this section, we explore these topics, focusing on children who are intellectually gifted.

ADAPTING THE LEARNING ENVIRONMENT

Teachers can change the learning environment in many ways, but most of those ways are designed to bring children who are gifted together for instruction for a period of time. Our aim is threefold:

- To provide students who are gifted with an opportunity to interact with one another and to learn and be stimulated by their intellectual peers
- To reduce the spread of abilities and performance within the group on instructionally relevant dimensions (past achievement, for example) to make it easier for the teacher to provide instructionally relevant materials
- To place students who are gifted with an instructor who has expertise in working with such students or in a relevant content field

Because changes in the learning environment affect the entire school system, they have received more attention at the school district level than have changes in skills and content, which remain primarily classroom issues. Still, the three elements are closely related: Changes in the learning environment for students who are gifted are often necessary to meet the instructional goals of special skills and differential content development.

Table 4.7 summarizes some of the adaptations that educators can make for students with special gifts and talents: flexible pacing, grouping, and organization of special courses. The choice of which, if any, of these options to implement depends on the characteristics of the student and the context in which he or she is placed.

Flexible Pacing

Flexible pacing allows students to move through material at their own pace. Sometimes this accelerates the student to a level in the school program that is higher than the level of his or her agemates. If Cranshaw (whom we met earlier in this chapter) is in a school where few of the other students have aptitudes similar to

TABLE 4.7   Placement Options for Educating Students Who Are Gifted

Flexible Pacing	Flexible pacing is any provision that places students at an appropriate instructional level and allows them to move forward in the curriculum as they achieve mastery of content and skills.
Early entrance	Students enter elementary, middle, or high school or college earlier than their agemates.
Continuous progress	Continuous progress allows students to progress at their own rate. It requires a high level of individualization.
Course acceleration (subject skipping)	Students are allowed to "test out" and bypass specific subjects or skill levels. They might receive some instruction at a higher level with another group of students yet remain with their peer group for most of their instruction.
Grade acceleration	Students move ahead one or more years, skipping levels in the normal sequence of promotion. This has traditionally been used successfully with students who are highly gifted.
Concurrent (dual) enrollment	Students can be enrolled in two levels of schooling at the same time. This option is appropriate for secondary students who might be enrolled in courses at postsecondary institutions.
Credit by examination	Students are allowed to "test out" of a course and receive credit on satisfactory completion of an examination or certification of mastery.
Compacted courses	Course content is covered in a shortened period of time, leaving students to pursue projects of special interest.
Grouping	Grouping by performance or aptitude has been used to meet individual instructional needs since the late 1800s. There continues to be a need for some grouping to meet the diverse needs of students who are gifted.
Cross-age grouping (multiage)	Multiage students are grouped within a school by interests or skills, but by no more than a two-year age span.
In-class flexible grouping	Students in each class are assigned to a small group for instruction. The groups may be homogeneously grouped according to skill level.
Cluster grouping within a regular class	A cluster group of six to ten students who are gifted is assigned to a regular heterogeneous class. The cluster teacher receives extensive training in gifted education and works closely with a specialist in giftedness.
Subject grouping	Students are grouped for specific subjects based on their aptitude or performance. Grouping may not be limited to identified gifted students but may include other high achievers.

TABLE 4.7   Placement Options for Educating Students Who Are Gifted (cont.)

Part-time special class with integration	Students who are gifted attend classes for enriched or accelerated work part-time, and they attend regular classes the rest of the day. This allows them to receive differentiated instruction in the appropriate academic area.
Full-time special class	Students who are gifted are assigned to a special class for all of their instruction. It is important that the curriculum in such classes be truly differentiated.
Magnet school	Special programs may be designed to have a special focus or be of particular interest to students. Students may be bused into a school from other schools.
Special Courses	
Honors courses	Honors courses are advanced courses that cover traditional content but also focus on issues, problems, and themes related to topics. They are designed to help students apply knowledge at an advanced level.
Advanced Placement courses	The Advanced Placement program consists of college-level courses and examinations for high school students. AP courses are usually taught by teachers who have received special training.
International baccalaureate courses	International baccalaureate programs provide an excellent opportunity for acceleration. They are usually designed as two-year high school programs that emphasize international concerns and foreign language.
Special school	Selected students attend a special school all day. Eligibility requirements may be based on aptitude and performance or on interest, depending on the nature of the program.
Residential high school	Such schools offer advanced courses or specialized curriculum not available in most high schools. Such schools are committed to having a culturally diversified student body and consider geographic representation.

his, then some form of course or grade acceleration might be considered, especially in view of Cranshaw's good social and personal adjustment.

Grouping

Grouping by performance or aptitude usually is done to reduce the range of ability that the teacher must face in teaching subject matter. Having all students with high-performance ability in one group allows the teacher to proceed much more swiftly and in greater depth than otherwise might be possible. There is a continuing debate in American education about the advantages and disadvantages of

Changes in the learning environment for gifted students are necessary to meet the instructional goals of special skills and differential content development. *(© Elizabeth Crews)*

profit from such arrangements even though other students might not—an outcome that creates a considerable dilemma for the school administrator (Kulik & Kulik, 1997).

The magnet school, which draws students who excel in a given subject, is a recent addition to the options available to bright students and is a type of performance grouping. Magnet schools often specialize in subject matter such as mathematics or in an activity such as art, and they encourage interested and qualified students to attend. Students who are gifted are interested in magnet schools that allow them to study at advanced levels and with other highly motivated students.

Special Courses

At the secondary school level, various **special courses** often address the increasing diversity of achievement and aptitude found in that student body. Honors courses or Advanced Placement courses for which students may earn college credit are common and popular. Over ten states have advanced residential schools for high-performing students. The North Carolina School of Science and Mathematics, the Illinois Math and Science Academy, and other schools focus on math and science (Kolloff, 1997).

Regardless of the attractiveness of the context of learning, unless there are clear modifications in content and process (for example, in thinking strategies), not much is likely to be accomplished by merely grouping youngsters of high ability together (Kulik & Kulik, 1997).

Inclusion

The great current interest in the strategy of **inclusion** for children with disabilities has also influenced the education for the students who are gifted. Educators have renewed efforts to find strategies for effectively teaching students who are gifted within the framework of the general classroom (Maker, 1993; Parke, 1989). Devices such as *cluster grouping* (the practice of placing six to ten gifted students in one classroom) and the use of a *teacher-consultant* have been revisited in an effort to avoid the physical separation of students who are gifted from their peers, particularly at the elementary level. Despite efforts at inclusion, many school systems rely on pull-out programs and resource rooms conducted by specially qualified teachers to modify the regular program in important ways to meet the educational needs of students with special gifts and talents.

All these strategies can be useful in the right circumstances. If a school system is near a major computer company, the availability of knowledgeable mentors could lead local schools in that direction. If experienced master teachers are available, the teacher-consultant approach could work well. A middle school program using teams of teachers with differing skills can be helpful (George, 1988).

ADAPTING CURRICULUM

Effective Education Programs

Effective education programs support the cognitive and affective needs of all gifted students.

An important question to raise in the education of gifted students—and in all education—is "Are the practices we are using beneficial, or do they just represent established practice, which through repetition becomes the established way of doing things?"

Shore and his colleagues (Shore, Cornell, Robinson, & Ward, 1991) took 101 widely advocated practices for educating gifted students and did a detailed literature review to indicate which practices had research backing and which did not. As a follow-up on that effort, Shore and Delcourt (1996) included more recent studies, as can be seen in Table 4.8.

While a number of practices such as problem solving and use of microcomputers can be used effectively with all students, acceleration and high-level curriculum seem to be especially relevant to gifted students.

Curriculum Compacting

Suppose you were told again and again how to write simple noun-verb combinations, or you had to practice simple spelling lists after you had mastered all the words. You'd be bored. Boredom is a real problem for children like Cranshaw and Zelda, who are often forced to "learn" material they already know.

Renzulli, Smith, and Reis (1982) describe a process called **curriculum compacting,** which allows gifted youngsters to move ahead. The process has three steps:

1. Find out what the students know before instruction.
2. Arrange to teach, in a brief fashion, the remaining concepts or skills.
3. Provide a different set of experiences to enrich or advance the students.

TABLE 4.8   Desirable Practices in Gifted and General Education

Uniquely Appropriate for Gifted	Effective with Gifted and General Education
Acceleration	Enrichment
Career education (girls)	Inquiry, discovery, problem solving, and creativity
High-level curriculum	Professional end products as standards
Differential programming	Microcomputers

Source: Adapted from B. Shore and M. Delcourt (1996). "Effective Curricular and Program Practices in Gifted Education and the Interface with General Education." *Journal for the Education of the Gifted, 20*(2), pp. 138–154.

Renzulli and his colleagues used Bill, a sixth-grade student with a straight-A average in math, as a case in point:

> After two days in math class Bill explains to the teacher that he knows how to do the math. He describes his interest in working on logic problems and shows his teacher the beginning of a logic book that he is putting together for other students.
>
> Bill's teacher administers the chapter tests for units 1–3 . . . [and] Bill scores 100 per unit. (p. 190)

Educators can use content acceleration, enrichment, sophistication, and novelty to individualize a student's curriculum.

The teacher responds to Bill's needs by arranging time for him to work on his logic book and to meet with people from a nearby computer center to develop his logic capabilities further. What Bill's teacher was doing was creating a differentiated curriculum for him. Gallagher and Gallagher (1994) described how teachers can use *acceleration, enrichment, sophistication,* and *novelty* (Table 4.9) to individualize the curriculum of the student who is gifted.

Content Acceleration and Enrichment

The purpose of **content acceleration** is to move students through the traditional curriculum at a fast rate. The process allows students to master increasingly complex sets of ideas. For example, by learning calculus in ninth grade, students have the foundation to begin physics and chemistry, subjects that require the skills of calculus. Table 4.9 shows how content can be accelerated in mathematics and other subject areas.

Content enrichment gives students the opportunity for a greater appreciation of the topic under study by expanding the material for study (exploring additional examples, using specific illustrations). Having students read the diaries of Civil War soldiers on both sides, for example, enriches their perspective on the war. This form of differentiated content for students who are gifted is often used

TABLE 4.9   Curriculum Modifications for Students Who Are Gifted

Modification	Math	Science	Language Arts	Social Studies
Acceleration	Algebra in fifth grade	Early chemistry and physics	Learning grammatical structure early	Early introduction to world history
Enrichment	Changing bases in number systems	Experimentation and data collecting	Short-story and poetry writing	Reading biographies of persons for historical insight
Sophistication	Mastering the laws of arithmetic	Learning the laws of physics	Mastering the structural properties of plays, sonnets, etc.	Learning and applying the principles of economics
Novelty	Probability and statistics	Science and its impact on society	Rewriting Shakespeare's plays to give them happy endings	Creating future societies and telling how they are governed

Source: From J. Gallagher and S. Gallagher (1994). *Teaching the Gifted Child* (4th ed.). Copyright © 1994 by Allyn and Bacon. Adapted by permission.

in the regular classroom because it requires no change in content, just additional assignments.

Content Sophistication

Content sophistication challenges students who are gifted to use higher levels of thinking to understand ideas that average students of the same age would find difficult or impossible to comprehend. The objective is to encourage children who are gifted to understand important abstractions, scientific laws, or general principles that can be applied in many circumstances. One example is *values*, an area rarely explored in regular educational programs. The diversity in our society often causes us to overlook important common principles that we share with one another. This oversight can lead idealistic youngsters to believe that they live in a valueless society, a society dominated by selfish people acting against the public interest.

How would you go about teaching values? You could assign students to look for those ethical standards held in common by classmates or neighbors and then discuss how common values bind the nation together. For example, Gardner (1978) identified several fundamental values held in common in our society:

- *Justice and the rule of law.* The attempt to provide justice for all, though often falling short in practice, represents one of the most common themes of U.S. society.

- *Freedom of expression.* The right to speak one's mind, regardless of who is offended, is another proud tradition. Without it, many of our other freedoms would likely vanish.

- *The dignity and worth of each person.* Equality of opportunity—giving all a chance to reach their potential—is a consistent theme. The insistence on special education for all children with disabilities is a clear reflection of this value.

- *Individual moral responsibility.* Each of us is responsible for the consequences of our actions. Even making allowances for differences in background and opportunities, in the end we are assumed to be the captains of our fate and are judged as such by our friends, neighbors, and communities.

- *Distaste for corruption.* The larger purposes of society may be betrayed by hatred, fear, envy, the misuse of power, or personal gain. We agree that they should not be, and we array our legal and social institutions to protect the larger society against personal frailty.

You can encourage vigorous discussions about clashes involving these accepted values in the "real world."

Content Novelty

Content novelty is the introduction of material that normally would not appear in the general curriculum because of time constraints or the abstract nature of the content. Students who are gifted are often able to see relationships across content fields. Because of this ability, a teacher could describe one or two examples and have the students think of others.

The distinction between *content enrichment* and *content novelty* is that enrichment is linked to the standard curriculum and takes off from that curriculum, whereas novelty can be totally apart from the standard curriculum.

ADAPTING COGNITIVE STRATEGIES

One of our goals in educating gifted students—and all students—is to capitalize on skills they already have, that is, the ability to generate new information from existing information. If I tell you that "Mary is taller than Joyce and Joyce is taller than Betty," you most likely will generate the new information that "Mary is taller than Betty." You have generated new information from old knowledge, just as you would if I asked you to solve 34×42.

The ability to generate new information from old is extremely valuable. The cognitive processes for doing so can be simple exercises like the examples above, or they can lead to a new solution for global warming, the discovery of genes linked to cancer, or an improved transportation system. All students need to increase their ability to generate new information from old, but particularly gifted students, who have the capability for dealing with problems of greater complexity than do their agemates.

Focusing instructionally on the enhancement of thinking skills and dimensions such as creativity, problem solving, problem finding, and so on addresses higher-level thinking skills. Few students, no matter how bright, will be likely to discover, on their own, calculus, the scientific method, or the creation of depth perspective in art. These must be taught, and we expect students to produce findings and results that will demonstrate that they have learned the skills required for the generation of new knowledge or information.

Students need to be taught higher-level thinking skills such as creativity, problem solving, and problem finding.

Enrichment Triad Experiences

One of educators' favorite adjustments to both content and process is Renzulli's *enrichment triad* (Renzulli, 1992). It consists of three steps that the teacher can take a class through. An example is shown in Table 4.10. Step 1 is the introduction of the topic to be studied—in this case, "How did our city or town begin?" In step 1, the teacher designs exploratory activities such as field trips and interviews with citizens with special knowledge to intrigue and pique students' interest with stories about the beginnings of the city. In step 2, students learn methods by which they can find answers to questions that they themselves have posed as a result of Step 1. They might learn how to search for the early records of the town or for early newspapers that may have ceased publication and how to handle historical information and check the validity of information. In step 3, students choose a real problem using the skills they learned in step 2. The teacher can accommodate individual differences by encouraging students like Cranshaw and Zelda to tackle problems more difficult than the problems other students in the class work on. Such enrichment triad experiences can be exciting to students, encouraging active rather than passive learning. They also place a considerable burden on the classroom teacher to monitor and supervise the students' various projects.

The enrichment triad is a device for encouraging active learning.

Problem Finding and Problem Solving

Gallagher (1994) defined **problem finding** as "the ability to review an area of study and to perceive those elements worthy of further analysis and study." **Problem solving** is "the ability to reach a previously determined answer by organizing and processing the available information in a logical and systematic fashion."

The approach to enhancing problem-finding and problem-solving skills, which can be taught in the regular classroom, resource room, or special class, is to provide students with a set of strategies by which they can attack a problem more efficiently. For example, to help students increase their problem-finding skills, we can have them ask questions like these:

To enhance problem-finding skills, ask students what negative things will happen if a problem isn't solved.

- How many people will be helped by the solution to this problem?
- What negative things will happen if the problem is not solved?
- What are the benefits of solving this problem?

Parnes, Noller, and Biondi (1977) developed a model for creative problem solving that has been much used. The creative problem-solving steps are as follows:

1. *Fact finding:* Collect data about the problem.
2. *Problem finding:* Restate the problem in solvable form, using data from step 1.
3. *Idea finding:* Generate many possible solutions.
4. *Solution finding:* Develop criteria for the evaluation of alternatives.
5. *Acceptance finding:* Convince the audience who must accept the plan that it can work.

The creative problem-solving model might be used to think about the need to conserve energy resources in this country, for example.

TABLE 4.10   The Renzulli Enrichment Triad: How Did Our City or Town Begin?

Step	Teacher Activity	Student Activity
1.	General exploratory activities introduce students to a major topic. Field trips, special speakers, etc., help to stir students' interest.	Students are asked to consider why their town started and developed here. They may read old newspapers and documents to stir their curiosity.
2.	Students are introduced to methods by which they can find answers to these questions.	Students learn how to find historical documents, how to use school and community libraries, how to deal with conflicting information.
3.	Students take a real problem and conduct an independent investigation using some of the skills they learned in step 2.	Cranshaw uses diaries and other reports to study the role played by the initial settlers in establishing the community. Zelda studies the role played by trade via the roads and rivers that shape and determine community growth.

The Importance of Knowledge Structure and Its Stimulation.   Do certain personal characteristics help us find and solve problems? The ability to store and access complex networks of associations seems to be an important basis for productive thinking. A set of experiments comparing the memory of children who were skilled chess players with adults who had little or no experience with the game yielded important information (Chi, 1978). In one experiment, chess pieces were placed on a chessboard in various combinations. Each person was allowed to look at the board for a short time and then was asked to remember which pieces were on the board and where they were placed. The chess-playing children outperformed the adults on this task. Did the children have a special ability in memory? Was that why they were so good at chess? To answer these questions, researchers tested the youngsters and adults on short-term memory ability. The purest test of short-term memory is the ability to reproduce a string of numbers—such as 4-7-2-8-3-9—given orally. When the participants were given this kind of test, the adults did better than the children. Clearly, simple memory alone was not at work. Did the children's familiarity with the chess pieces give them the advantage? In another experiment, the chess pieces were placed on the board randomly, not as they would be placed in a game (deGroot, 1965). Under those conditions, the adults outperformed children.

By eliminating alternative theories, we begin to see why the chess-playing children did better than the adults on the original task. They were not remembering just the individual chess pieces; they were remembering *patterns of pieces,* pieces in recognizable game positions. They had a **knowledge structure,** or a bank of interrelated information in long-term memory, that helped them recognize and recall patterns to use in solving problems. In this case, the patterns consisted of patterns of chess pieces.

Studies comparing the problem-solving capabilities of experts and novice professionals in the fields of engineering, computer programming, physics, medical diagnosis, and mathematics all yield similar results. The experts relied on their past knowledge structure to solve problems, whereas the novices were limited to the specific elements of the problem presented. Effective problem solving depends strongly on the nature and organization of knowledge available to the problem solver (Bransford, Sherwood, Vye, & Rieser, 1986).

The way to develop problem-solving skills in individuals who are gifted and those who are not is *not* to drill them on unconnected facts but to help them build a knowledge structure of interrelated information. And the key to this is

> practice, thousands of hours of practice. . . . There may be some as yet undiscovered basic abilities that underlie the attainment of truly exceptional performance . . . but for the most part, practice is by far the best predictor of performance. (Chase & Chi, 1981, p. 12)

Building a usable knowledge structure that is more complex and sophisticated than the knowledge structure of one's agemates is one of the marks of a student who is gifted. The investigations of the differences between experts and novices illustrate one type of difference between students who are gifted and students who are average. The experts may be persons experienced in medical diagnostics, persons knowledgeable about physics, or veteran chess players. Whatever their expertise, they have in common many characteristics that separate them from novices in their domain of expertise. According to these studies (see Gallagher, 1994), students who are gifted can see large, meaningful patterns in the problem or in the information available to them. These students have superior long-term and short-term memories and can draw on their knowledge to solve problems.

Suppose the teacher presents a problem related to the Battle of Saratoga in the Revolutionary War. The average student (likely unknowledgeable on the subject) is limited to the materials the teacher makes available. By contrast, Cranshaw has read much about the Revolutionary War and can draw on a number of sources to enrich his answers and products. Developing these knowledge structures and linking them with one another are a teacher's prime goals with all students. The developed knowledge structures of students who are gifted and the ease with which these students add to existing structures make such tasks relatively easy and quick for them.

Problem-Based Learning

★ *An important part of problem-based learning is for the students to feel they are specialists as they search for information.*

Problem-based learning (PBL) originated as an alternative method for teaching medical students (Barrows, 1988). Instead of formal courses in anatomy and physiology, students were presented with patients and asked to solve the problems the patients presented. Subsequent examination revealed that the students who had to cope with a real patient learned as much formal knowledge as students in traditional courses and were much ahead in patient skills and enthusiasm.

The PBL approach has been adopted in education (Stepien, Gallagher, & Workman, 1993). There are three critical features to the PBL approach:

1. Learning is initiated with an ill-structured problem.
2. The student is made a stakeholder in the situation.
3. The instructor plays the role of metacognitive coach.

An ill-structured problem lacks the necessary information one needs to solve it; there must be a search for more information. Students can be made stakeholders by being told, for example, that they are specialists in highway safety and that a truck with a sign that reads DANGER: CORROSIVE MATERIAL has overturned. The students are on their way to the crash site and must decide what to do.

The instructor, playing the role of coach, helps students to understand the problem and organize how to attack the problem and provides resources that can help the students in their quest. Table 4.11 is a *need-to-know* table that summarizes (1) what students know about the wrecked truck, (2) what they need to know, and (3) how they propose to find it out. The material in Table 4.11 represents what one group of students came up with as a result of their discussions about the situation. Devices like need-to-know tables are extremely useful in trying to cope with any complicated problem.

There are several manifest advantages to the PBL approach, beginning with heightened student interest. Students become intrigued with the question and spend a substantial amount of time working on the discovery of the real problem and the design of a solution. They also experience various types of incidental learning about how to organize an attack on a problem and how to shape a problem into manageable size.

The disadvantage is time. Students often need a great deal of time to organize themselves into a working group and to find relevant information. For students who are gifted, time constraints are less likely to be a serious matter because the students probably have completed the regular unit or have shown mastery through curriculum compacting. Time limitations are much more serious in a heterogeneous class, in which the teacher worries about whether the average students have mastered the basic learning expected of that grade level.

Creativity

Superior intellectual talent enables students to generate new and better solutions to problems.

Creativity is "a mental process by which an individual creates new ideas or products, or recombines existing ideas and products in a fashion that is novel to him or her" (Gallagher, 1985, pp. 268, 303). More attention has probably been paid to creativity than to any other single objective in the education of children who are gifted and talented. We expect that superior intellectual development or talent gives students the ability to generate novel and better solutions to problems.

Gallagher (1992) reported that the recipe for creative production in students depended on the presence of four main ingredients:

- A strong knowledge base
- High motivation for distinctive achievement
- Willingness to be different, to oppose the status quo
- Cognitive strategies for solving difficult tasks

Even the most facile mind cannot operate without a strong knowledge base. A student may be asked a classical divergent-thinking question such as, "How many ways can we suggest to save the salmon in the Columbia River?" If the student has

TABLE 4.11 Need-to-Know Table for Hazardous-Spill Problem

What's going on? The driver of a truck carrying hazardous material had an accident. People around the accident could get sick.

What Do We Know?	What Do We Need to Know?	How Do We Find Out?
Truck is overturned.	What spilled?	Find out about spills.
A clear liquid is coming from it.	Why are police and fire officials there?	Learn what a corrosive is.
Traffic is stopped.	What is a corrosive?	Learn about transporting hazardous materials.
There is a gash in the side of the truck.	Why transport it?	
The truck lost one wheel.	Do I use it?	Learn about hazardous materials.
Fire trucks are there.	Is it safe?	Learn about the material that has been spilled in this problem.
"Corrosive" is written on the side of the truck.	What could happen?	
Rescue squad is there.	What will this do to the environment?	Give the driver an alcohol test.
We are in charge of the situation.	If there is danger, how far does it go?	
	How are spills handled?	
	Is the driver drunk?	

Source: S. Gallagher, W. Stepien, B. Sher, and D. Workman (1995). "School, Science and Mathematics: Implementing Problem-based Learning in Science Classrooms," *School Science and Mathematics, 95*(3), pp. 136–146. Reprinted by permission.

no knowledge of salmon or the Columbia River, no matter how intelligent or creative the student is, he or she will have a hard time generating many "creative" answers. Even if a lot of off-the-top-of-the-head answers are produced, they are unlikely to be of any serious use. One must begin creative thinking with a good knowledge base.

Although it has been traditional to picture a creative person working independently at his or her craft or special product, many researchers believe that it is impossible to consider most acts of individual creativity apart from the culture and environment in which the creator works (Csikszentmihalyi, 1990; Gardner, 1993; Starko, 1995). Csikszentmihalyi views creativity as an interaction among persons, products, and environment. This change from focusing intense attention on the creative individual to focusing on the interaction between individual and environment helps us focus more on how to create a more fruitful environment for the creative child. We realize that by teaching children how to behave independently, and how to search for new ideas, we can help many students to become more creative, not merely the few with the highest measured intelligence.

The stimulation of creativity in the classroom has to be arranged with the context in mind. A creative student is not necessarily a solitary student left alone in a

Students use brainstorming to extend their intellectual fluency by discussing a particular problem and suggesting as many answers as possible for the problem. During brainstorming, criticism and evaluation are delayed until all ideas have been presented. *(© Elizabeth Crews)*

Creativity can be seen as an interaction among persons, products, and environment. Creativity can be stimulated by small-group activities.

corner with his or her creative muse. Creativity is a product that can be stimulated by appropriate small-group work and interaction with other people and by additional resources. For example, a student working on the "How Did Our City or Town Begin?" project could be encouraged to produce creative work on what the city might have been like if it did not have a major river flowing through it. Innovative ideas can be stimulated by the reports of other students and the research that the class has done.

Starko (1995) presented a series of topics devoted to the preparation of students to be more independent:

- Uses of independent work time
- What to do if you are stuck and don't understand a task
- How to signal a teacher for assistance or for a conference
- Choice of activities and what to do when tasks are completed

It is increasingly clear that many general education classrooms with their standard curricula, worksheets, and restrictive management are destined to impede the development of independent thinking without meaning to do so. It is also clear that if one of your instructional goals is student independent thought, you will need to plan carefully to bring about this desired result.

Encourage students to come up with as many ideas as possible when brainstorming.

Another accepted practice for extending intellectual fluency is **brainstorming** (Osborn, 1957). A group of people or a whole class that is brainstorming discusses a particular problem (for example, how to improve local government) and suggests as many answers as possible. You can use this activity with students of a wide range of abilities because many answers are "right" or acceptable. Here are some ground rules for brainstorming:

1. *No criticism is allowed.* Nothing should stop the free flow of ideas. Neither teacher nor students should criticize or ridicule a suggestion. Let students know in advance that evaluation comes later.

2. *The more ideas the better.* When a lot of ideas are suggested, it is increasingly likely that a good one is among them. Place a premium on unusual or unique solutions.

3. *Integration and combinations of ideas are welcomed.* Be sure everyone understands that it's acceptable to combine with or add to previous ideas.

4. *Evaluation happens after all ideas have been presented.* Judge when the fluency or inventiveness of the class is lagging. At that point, encourage evaluative thinking by students.

Divergent thinking requires fluency, flexibility, and originality.

Notice that evaluation becomes an important part of the process after the **divergent thinking**—that is, producing many different answers to a question—takes place. Once the ideas are produced, the group can choose those that seem most likely to solve the problem. Brainstorming, then, requires divergent thinking; judgment is more evaluative.

Our exploration of how to allow the human spirit and imagination to soar in the classroom while achieving other educational objectives is only beginning. We know what *not* to do (lecture interminably, ridicule fresh ideas, discourage alternatives), but we still have much to learn about the most effective ways to stimulate productive thinking.

The ability of a gifted student to reason, to remember, to find and solve problems is not sufficient to produce a productive or creative student. The emotional side of the student will often determine how productive that student or adult will be. Goleman (1995) describes *emotional intelligence,* by which he means such characteristics as self-awareness, impulse control, persistence, empathy, and social deftness, which will go a long way toward determining how efficiently individuals can utilize their superior brain power.

Csikszentmihalyi (1990) describes a recognizable phenomenon he calls *flow,* which is a state in which "people are so involved in an activity that nothing else seems to matter; the experience itself is so enjoyable that people will do it even at great cost; for the sheer sake of doing it" (p. 4). Many creative artists and scientists report such experiences. It becomes a matter of importance as to whether we can individually create the conditions for such experiences for ourselves or for our students. Csikszentmihalyi reports some components of the flow experience:

- The experience usually occurs when we confront tasks we have a chance of completing.

- We must be able to concentrate on what we are doing.

- Concentration is possible because the task undertaken has clear goals.

- The task undertaken provides immediate feedback.

- We act with a deep but effortless involvement that removes from our awareness the worries and frustrations of everyday life.

- Enjoyable experiences allow us to exercise a sense of control over our actions.

- Concern for the self disappears, yet paradoxically the sense of self emerges stronger after the flow experience is over.

■ The sense of duration of time is altered; hours pass by in minutes, and minutes can stretch out to seem like hours.

We need to reflect as to whether the design of our educational environment and curricula will easily allow these experiences to occur.

INSTRUCTIONAL TECHNOLOGY

The rapid development of educational technology has made mountains of knowledge easily accessible to every student who has access to a computer. This development is a boon for gifted students, who now use the Internet for more and more of their assignments. An entire encyclopedia is available on a single small disk—it's like having a library inside their home. The challenge for the teacher is to ensure that students do not succumb to the temptation of playing video games instead of using the computer as a learning tool.

One of the half-truths about education has been that teachers cannot teach concepts and ideas any more complicated than they themselves understand, that they cannot instruct students in, say, Newton's laws or postimpressionism art if they themselves don't know about those topics. That perception is pessimistic and generally incorrect. If teachers know how to access major references or sources of information, they can open the door to more knowledge for their students, who can then explore for themselves. (Students who are gifted can—and often do—surpass their teachers in understanding selective fields.) Of course, teachers have access to these new sources of information as well and, by using the same technology, can become continuous learners themselves.

Another limitation to many gifted students, particularly those in rural areas, is the lack of teachers to teach certain advanced classes in mathematics or science (for example, genetics). Several attempts are now being made to establish *distance learning*—interactive television—to bring complex ideas to the bright students in remote areas. The North Carolina School of Science and Mathematics, a special statewide school for highly talented students, engaged its highly educated faculty to construct a precalculus course and beam it to all areas of the state (Wilson, Little, Coleman, & Gallagher, 1997). There will be much more use of distance learning in the near future, to the great advantage of gifted students.

The role of the local teacher will change from one of *direct instruction* to that of *instructional coach* of individual students. Teachers also need to help students evaluate information they obtain from such sources as the Internet. The largely unscreened communications on the Internet allow many outrageously incorrect statements to be widely broadcast. A new challenge is teaching students the difference between legitimate information and spurious information.

TIME

The failure to recognize *time* as the enemy of teachers and teaching is at the heart of many teachers' disputes. The question is often posed, "Cannot the average student learn what is being taught to students who are gifted?" The answer is "Yes," if you disregard the time factor. For example, middle school students who are gifted can be taught about the solar system and the various theories about its origin in an enrichment lesson because they have already mastered the required cur-

Teachers can help gifted students explore new areas of knowledge by teaching them to distinguish between legitimate information on the Internet and less credible information.

Limited time often prevents teachers from presenting a sophisticated curriculum to students.

riculum in less than the time allotted. Could average students also master these theories? Of course, if they are given enough time. But they have not yet mastered the required lessons of the regular curriculum, and they also have greater difficulty with the concepts of distance, of orbits, and of centrifugal force—difficulty that will extend further the time they need to master the theories.

Time is a fixed constant. Between 180 and 200 days are available in a school year, so there is not an unlimited period in which students can master needed knowledge and skills. Youngsters who learn faster than others will be able to master more knowledge and practice more of the necessary skills than will other students in the same amount of time. Such differences are a fact of life that we, as educators, must adjust to, instead of pretending that they don't exist.

STUDENT ACCELERATION

We can also adapt the educational program by abandoning the traditional practice of going from grade to grade and varying the length of the educational program. Because more and more knowledge and skills must be learned at the highest levels of the professions, students who are talented and gifted can find themselves still in school at age 30 and beyond. While skilled workers are earning a living and starting a family, students who are gifted are often dependent on others for a good part of their young adult life. The process of **student acceleration**—passing students through the educational system as quickly as possible—is a clear educational objective for some children. Stanley (1989) described six ways of accelerating students:

- *Early school admission.* The intellectually and socially mature child is allowed to enter kindergarten at a younger-than-normal age.
- *Skipping grades.* The child can be accelerated by completely eliminating one semester or grade in school. The primary drawback here is the potential for temporary adjustment problems for the student.
- *Telescoping grades.* The child covers the standard material but in less time. For example, a three-year middle school program is taught over two years to an advanced group.
- *Advanced Placement.* The student takes courses for college credit while still in high school, shortening the college program.
- *Dual enrollment in high school and college.* The student takes college courses while still in high school.
- *Early college admission.* An extraordinarily advanced student may enter college at 13, 14, or 15 years of age.

Stanley (1989) found that acceleration, particularly through dual enrollment in high school and college and early admission to college, is most effective for many students who excel in mathematics. In a field like mathematics, in which the curriculum content can be organized in sequential fashion, it is possible for bright students to move quickly through the material. Stanley developed a program for accelerating students in mathematics courses and for awarding college credit to children from 12 to 14 years of age. He described one student:

Sean, who is 12½ years of age, completed four and one-half years of pre-calculus mathematics in six 2-hour Saturday mornings compared with the 810 forty-five or fifty-minute periods usually required for Algebra I through III, plane geometry, trigonometry, and analytic geometry. . . . [D]uring the second semester of the eighth grade he was given released time to take the introduction to computer science course at Johns Hopkins and made a final grade of A. . . . While still 13 years old, Sean skipped the ninth and tenth grades. He became an eleventh-grader at a large suburban public high school and took calculus with twelfth graders, won a letter on the wrestling team, was a science and math whiz on the school's television academic quiz team, tutored a brilliant seventh grader through two and one-half years of algebra and a year of plane geometry in eight months, played a good game of golf, and took some college courses on the side (set theory, economics, and political science). (p. 175)

All this work allowed Sean to enter Johns Hopkins University as a sophomore with 34 credits at the age of 14. And Sean was just one example. Stanley reported that a number of youngsters with extraordinary talent in mathematics had academic programs that were shortened by accelerating either the student or the content.

Many students who are gifted can be moved ahead a year or two without serious negative effects.

From early admission to school to early admission to college, research studies invariably report that children who have been accelerated, as a group, have adjusted as well as or better than children of similar ability who have not been accelerated. Despite these findings, some parents and teachers continue to have strong negative feelings about the practice, and some educational administrators do not want to deal with these special cases. The major objection to the strategy is the fear that acceleration can displace individual children who are gifted from their social and emotional peers, affecting their subsequent social adjustment (Southern, 1991). The result of these misgivings is that many students who are gifted spend the greater part of their first three decades of life in the educational system, often locked in a relatively unproductive role, to the detriment of themselves and society.

Family and Lifespan Issues

The economic and vocational futures for most individuals with gifts and talents are bright. The vocational opportunities awaiting them are diverse, including the fields of medicine, law, business, politics, and science. Only in the arts, where a limited number of opportunities exist to earn a comfortable income, do people who are gifted encounter major social and economic barriers to their ambitions.

It is virtually certain that when most students who are gifted finish secondary school, they will go on to more school. They often have from eight to ten *more* years of training before they can expect to begin earning a living. This is especially true if they choose careers in medicine, law, or the sciences. The delay in becoming an independent wage earner creates personal and social problems that researchers are just beginning to study. Prolonged schooling means that individuals who are gifted must receive continued financial support. The most common forms of financial support are assistance from family and subsidies from private or public sources. If financial aid takes the form of bank or government loans, then a man or woman who is gifted can begin his or her career with a substantial debt. This period of extended schooling also tends to cause gifted invididuals to postpone marriage and raising a family.

The psychological problems that result from remaining dependent on others for financial support for as much as thirty years remain unexplored. We need to consider these issues before we burden students who are gifted with more schooling requirements intended to meet the demands of this rapidly changing world.

Summary of Major Ideas

1. Children who are gifted may show outstanding abilities in a variety of areas, including intellect, academic aptitude, creative thinking, leadership, and the visual and performing arts. They also can show talent in superior self-knowledge and interpersonal relationships.

2. Intellectual giftedness appears to be created by a strong combination of heredity and environment, with a close and continuing interaction between these two major forces over the developmental period.

3. Longitudinal studies indicate that most children who are identified as gifted are healthy and well adjusted and achieve well into adulthood. There are some exceptions (called underachievers).

4. A series of international comparisons of U.S. students with students from other countries in mathematics and science revealed that even top-level U.S. students lag behind top-level students of other countries.

5. The great differences in the motivation, experience, and family and cultural backgrounds of students who are gifted require flexibility in the schools in choosing the appropriate learning environment, content, and cognitive strategies to teach.

6. Ability grouping, combined with a differentiated program, has been demonstrated to be an effective strategy that results in improved performance by students who are gifted.

7. Cognitive strategies—problem finding, problem solving, and creativity—are the focus of many special programs for students who are gifted. Effective problem-finding and problem-solving skills depend on the individual's flexible use of his or her knowledge structure.

8. Creativity depends on the individual's capacity for divergent thinking, a willingness to be different, strong motivation, and a favorable context.

9. Society's traditional expectations for girls have limited their willingness and opportunities to succeed and the areas in which they try to succeed. Many efforts are now being tried to counteract those limited expectations.

10. The characteristics of underachievers who are gifted (feelings of inferiority, low self-confidence, expectations of failure) can be modified through carefully planned and intensive educational programs that focus on the child's interests and allow the child to take control of his or her learning.

11. Many students possess giftedness that is "hidden" by differing attitudes, values, and interests. A multifaceted approach using a wide variety of tests, observations, and performance indicators seems necessary to discover these "hidden" students who are gifted.

12. Children with physical and sensory disabilities can be intellectually gifted, but often their abilities are undiscovered because of the lower expectations held for such children.

13. Prolonged schooling (perhaps as much as twenty-five years) can create personal and social problems for the individual who is gifted. It also denies society the contributions of that individual while he or she is in school.

Unresolved Issues

1. *Equity versus excellence.* The conflicting educational priorities between equity and excellence has resulted in negative feelings being expressed against gifted students in some quarters. Their rights to an appropriate education are seen as endangering the cause of equity. Such feelings are predominantly found at the elementary and secondary levels, rarely at the higher-education levels.

2. *Do gifted students require specially trained teachers?* The diversity of students in regular education makes it difficult for general education teachers to meet the needs of gifted students or even to master the special strategies and skills and the differentiation of curriculum that are necessary. Most observers of this issue propose additional preparation for teachers who will be concentrating on gifted students.

3. *Undiscovered and underutilized talent.* For many reasons, some students who are gifted or potentially gifted are being overlooked in public schools. Standard tests for identification are not helping the situation to any significant degree. We need more and better approaches to discover this hidden talent and, just as important, special programs to enhance it.

4. *Young children who are gifted.* Very little is being done on a systematic basis to help young (preschool) children who are gifted, even though the parents of these children are aware of the need and are asking for help. Most of these children are not allowed to enter public schools before a certain age—whatever their intellectual maturity—and often are unable to go beyond their grade level despite manifest achievements.

Key Terms

brainstorming p. 156
content acceleration p. 148
content enrichment p. 148
content novelty p. 150
content sophistication p. 149
creativity p. 154
curriculum compacting p. 147
divergent thinking p. 157
flexible pacing p. 143

gifted underachievers p. 136
grouping p. 145
knowledge structure p. 152
problem-based learning (PBL) p. 153
problem finding p. 151
problem solving p. 151
special courses p. 146
student acceleration p. 159

Questions for Thought

1. How do heredity and environment interact in those with special talents? pp. 121–122

2. What is the significance of Terman's longitudinal study? pp. 122–123

3. From the developmental profiles, list five characteristics each for Zelda and Cranshaw that are associated with giftedness. pp. 127, 130

4. In what ways has social bias affected the achievement of girls who are gifted? pp. 133–135

5. How might the definition of giftedness differ from culture to culture? How can students who are gifted be discovered in diverse cultural groups? pp. 138–140

6. Describe four ways in which teachers can adjust curriculum content to meet the needs of students who are gifted and talented. pp. 147–150

7. Briefly explain the six ways Stanley described to accelerate students. p. 159

References for Further Study

REFERENCES OF SPECIAL INTEREST

Colangelo, N., & Davis, G. (Eds.). (1997). *Handbook of gifted education* (2nd ed.). Boston: Allyn & Bacon.

> Over forty well-known authors in the field of gifted education have contributed chapters to this volume, which includes sections on instructional models, creativity and thinking skills, and psychological and counseling services.

Gallagher, J., & Gallagher, S. (1994). *Teaching the gifted child* (4th ed.). Boston: Allyn & Bacon.

> A widely read general textbook on the education of gifted students. Topics such as differentiated curriculum, thinking processes, and administrative adjustments are discussed, along with several case studies.

Perkins, D. (1995). *Outsmarting IQ: The emerging science of learnable intelligence.* New York: Free Press.

> This readable book describes current thinking on the development of intelligence. Perkins concludes that people can improve their intelligence and gives suggestions as to how to achieve that goal.

Ross, P. (Ed.). (1993). *National excellence.* Washington, DC: U.S. Department of Education.

> This report on the status of the education of students in the United States who are gifted and talented points out that studies have indicated American students fall behind students from other countries in areas such as mathematics and science and that the provisions for such students in the United States are fragmentary and not well supported. Recommendations for improving the situation are included.

Shore, B., Cornell, D., Robinson, A., & Ward, V. (1991). *Recommended practices in gifted education: A critical analysis.* New York: Teachers College Press.

This volume reviews 101 common practices in use for educating students who are gifted and the available research to support each practice. The authors also provide implications of the state of knowledge for the implementation of each practice and suggestions about what research is needed to improve the knowledge base for that particular practice.

Starko, A. (1995). *Creativity in the classroom.* White Plains, NY: Longman.

This fine review of the theories of creativity contains many useful translations of those theories into practical classroom use. There is a particular attempt to blend changes in process and in instructional strategies with important content ideas. The author's belief that creativity is influenced by culture and surroundings, as well as by the characteristics of the creative person, is a relatively new idea.

Van Tassel-Baska, J. (1998). *Excellence in educating gifted and talented learners* (3rd ed.). Denver: Love Publishing Company.

This general textbook focuses on curriculum differentiation and provides a number of good suggestions for teachers and administrators.

JOURNALS

Educational Leadership
Association for Supervision &
Curriculum Development
1250 N. Pitt Street
Alexandria, VA 22314-1453

Gifted Child Quarterly
National Association for
Gifted Children
1707 L Street NW, Suite 550
Washington, DC 20036

Journal for the Education of the Gifted
Prufrock Press
P.O. Box 8813
Waco, TX 76710-2032

Journal for Secondary Gifted Education
Prufrock Press
P.O. Box 8813
Waco, TX 76710-2032

Parenting for High Potential
National Association for
Gifted Children
1707 L Street NW, Suite 550
Washington, DC 20036

Roper Review
The Roper School
P.O. Box 329
Bloomfield Hills, MI 48303-0329

PROFESSIONAL ORGANIZATIONS

National Association for
Gifted Children
1707 L Street NW, Suite 550
Washington, DC 20036
http://www.nagc.org

The Association for the Gifted
Council of Exceptional Children
1920 Association Dr.
Reston, VA 20191-1589

5

Children with Mental Retardation and Developmental Disabilities

FOCUSING questions

How do educators define mental retardation and developmental disabilities?

What are the two major groups of children with mental retardation or developmental disabilities?

What four areas of instruction generally comprise the special education programs for students with mild or moderate mental retardation?

How has the push for inclusion influenced the education of children with mental retardation or developmental disabilities?

How can teachers prepare students with mental retardation or developmental disabilities to function in the workplace?

How has the standards movement influenced children with mental retardation or developmental disabilities?

How do we help families cope with the presence of a child with mental retardation or developmental disabilities?

Awareness of the existence of children with mental retardation or developmental disabilities—children who learn more slowly than their agemates and have difficulty adapting to social and educational demands—has been present for centuries, but the exact nature of the condition, its identification, and societal attitudes toward it have been constantly changing. Above all, we are trying to discover what can be done educationally for children and youth with the condition. Ideas about appropriate educational adjustments change as we add to our knowledge of the condition and what can be done to cure or ameliorate it.

 *Definition*

Definitions of what constitutes mental retardation and developmental disabilities (MR/DD) are not cast in concrete. As we learn more about a condition and its treatment, we modify how we refer to it and to the individuals the condition affects. Table 5.1 highlights the current definition of mental retardation set forth by the American Association on Mental Retardation (AAMR). It refers to two separate domains where limitations must be found before we refer to a person as having mental retardation. The first is significantly subaverage intellectual functioning; the second domain reflects limitations in two or more of ten separate indicators of adaptive skills.

Four key assumptions are essential to the definition. Any assessment of an individual needs to take into account the following:

- Cultural differences in individual circumstances
- The influence of community environments on the development of adaptive skills
- Individuals' relative strengths in various domains of development
- The improvement in life functioning that can occur with appropriate supports

The context of the child affects his or her ability to adapt positively.

In short, the context of the child can determine his or her eventual ability to adapt, positively or negatively. The term **developmental disabilities** includes mental retardation plus other conditions of mental and physical impairment likely to need lifelong help from a variety of health, social, and educational agencies.

INTELLECTUAL SUBNORMALITY

The definition of mental retardation/developmental disabilities must include retardation in intellectual development and in adaptive behavior.

No definition, no matter how comprehensive, is worth much unless we can translate its abstractions into concrete action. Intellectual subnormality has traditionally been determined by performance on intelligence tests. Children with mental retardation are markedly slower than their agemates in using memory effectively, in associating and classifying information, in reasoning, and in making sound judgments—the types of performance measured on intelligence tests. One of the earliest of these tests was developed by Alfred Binet for the express purpose of finding children who were not capable of responding to the traditional education program in France at the turn of the twentieth century.

Later on, individual tests of intelligence developed by David Wechsler (1974) became popular and widely used. Part of the popularity of the Wechsler scales is

TABLE 5.1   Definition of Mental Retardation

Mental retardation refers to substantial limitations in present functioning. It is characterized by significantly subaverage intellectual functioning existing concurrently with related limitations in two or more of the following applicable adaptive skills areas: communication, self-care, home living, social skills, community use, self-direction, health and safety, functional academics, leisure, and work. Mental retardation manifests before age 18.

Application of the Definition

The following four assumptions are essential to the application of the definition:

1. Valid assessment considers cultural and linguistic diversity as well as differences in communication and behavioral factors.

2. The existence of limitations in adaptive skills occurs within the context of community environments typical of the individual's age peers and is indexed to the person's individualized needs for supports.

3. Specific adaptive limitations often coexist with strengths in other adaptive skills or other personal capabilities.

4. With appropriate supports over a sustained period, the life functioning of the person with mental retardation generally will improve.

Source: Adapted from R. Luckasson, D. Coulder, E. Polloway, S. Russ, R. Schalock, M. Snell, D. Spitalnik, and I. Stark (1992). *Mental Retardation: Definition, Classification, and Systems of Support.* Washington, DC: American Association on Mental Retardation, p. 1.

that they provide for ten subtests (for example, similarities, information, and block design) and scale scores that allow psychologists to develop a profile of the skills of the individual tested and allow teachers to distinguish between verbal IQ and performance IQ (see chapter 2). Other group tests of intelligence were designed to test large numbers of students in a shorter period of time. Though considerably less expensive than the individual tests, they are also less reliable and less valid and should be used only for screening.

ADAPTIVE BEHAVIOR

The current emphasis on the environment and the context of the child has resulted in an extended attempt to distinguish among various categories of adaptive behavior. Table 5.2 lists ten areas of adaptive skills that can be described and rated. To be considered to have mental retardation, a child or adult must be significantly deficient in at least two of these areas. This delineation of ten areas of adaptation is much more extensive than past efforts to define adaptive behavior and reflects the growing concern for adaptive skills as a key element in special education programs. Thus, it is possible to have a low IQ score and still possess usable adaptive skills, be self-sufficient in the community, be able to interact reasonably with other citizens, and maintain a part-time or full-time job. Under such circumstances, an

The identification of ten areas of ability in assessing mental retardation shows the emphasis now put on adaptive behavior.

TABLE 5.2   Adaptive Skills and Mental Retardation

Category	Skills
Communication	Skills involving the ability to comprehend and express information through symbolic behaviors (e.g., spoken word, written word/sign language) or nonsymbolic behaviors (e.g., facial expression)
Self-care	Skills involved in toileting, eating, dressing, hygiene, and grooming
Home living	Skills related to functioning within a home, which include clothing care, housekeeping, food preparation, and home safety
Social	Skills related to social exchanges with other individuals, including initiating interaction and terminating interaction with others; responding to pertinent situation cues; recognizing feelings
Community use	Skills related to the appropriate use of community resources, including traveling in the community; shopping at stores and markets; purchasing or obtaining services (e.g., gas stations, doctor's and dentist's offices); using public transportation and public facilities
Self-direction	Skills related to making choices; following a schedule; initiating activities appropriate to the setting; completing necessary or required tasks
Health and safety	Skills related to maintenance of one's health in terms of eating; illness, treatment, and prevention; basic first aid; sexuality; basic safety considerations (e.g., following rules and laws)
Functional academics	Cognitive abilities and skills related to learning at school that also have direct application in one's life (e.g., writing, reading, using basic practical math concepts, awareness of the physical environment and one's health and sexuality)
Leisure	The development of a variety of leisure and recreational interests (i.e., self-entertainment and interaction) that reflect personal preferences and choices
Work	Skills related to holding a part- or full-time job or jobs in the community in terms of specific job skills, appropriate social behavior, and related work skills (e.g., completion of tasks, awareness of schedules, ability to take criticism and improve skills)

Source: Adapted from R. Luckasson, D. Coulder, E. Polloway, S. Russ, R. Schalock, M. Snell, D. Spitalnik, and I. Stark (1992). *Mental Retardation: Definition, Classification, and Systems of Support.* Washington, DC: American Association on Mental Retardation, pp. 40–41.

individual would still be considered intellectually subnormal but would not be considered mentally retarded.

Whether deficits in adaptive behavior are seen as a key component in the definition of mental retardation or as merely one of the characteristics that many of these children possess, adaptive behavior is a critical element in their adjustment as adults. Bruininks, Thurlow, and Gilman (1987) summarized the available literature and estimated that "20–40 percent of mentally retarded people in various samples and service programs consistently exhibit behaviors that are perceived by others in their environment as serious problems" (p. 76). Further, they observed that "deficiencies in social skills are frequently primary factors in the failure of handicapped individuals to be successfully integrated into community and work settings" (p. 78). These factors of adaptability clearly call for a strong emphasis on the development of constructive social skills and the elimination of maladaptive behaviors as a key part of any educational or training program for these children.

Despite the problems that the AAMR definition poses, most educators and psychologists see the wisdom of using the dual criteria—*intellectual subnormality/ developmental delay* and *deficits in adaptive behavior*—as important to identifying mild mental retardation.

LEVELS OF MENTAL RETARDATION

Historically, psychologists and educators distinguished among levels of intensity of mental retardation by assigning students to various categories (first *idiot, imbecile,* and *moron;* later *educable, trainable,* and *dependent;* then *mild, moderate, severe,* and *profound*). *Mild* indicated development at between one-half and three-fourths of the normal rate; *moderate,* development at about one-half of the normal rate; *severe,* development at slightly more than one-fourth of normal cognitive growth; and *profound,* less than one-fourth the normal rate. Psychologists and educators assess how well these children are adapting to their environment in the ten categories of adaptability listed in Table 5.2, as well as their level of measurable intelligence.

The formal definition places the issue of mental retardation or developmental disabilities within the individual, but another way of viewing the individual is to define the level or intensity of support necessary to allow the child or individual to operate effectively. The intensity of support is measured as *intermittent, limited, extensive,* and *pervasive. Intermittent* refers to support as needed but not necessarily present at all times. *Limited* refers to support provided on a regular basis for a short period of time. *Extensive* support indicates ongoing and regular involvement. The *pervasive* level of support describes constant high-intensity help provided across environments and involving more staff members than the other categories. While these four terms line up well with the *mild, moderate, severe,* and *profound* AAMR categories, it places the emphasis on what will be needed to provide necessary supports for the individual (Luckasson et al., 1992).

Although there has been a movement away from the designation of a child by level of development (educable, trainable, and so on), there remains a division of children with mental retardation into two groups (Hodapp, Burack, & Zigler, 1990). The *organically injured group* consists of children whose retardation can be attributed to some specific organic damage. The *familial retarded group* consists of individuals whose retardation is not accompanied by any known organic

Intensity of support—intermittent, limited, extensive, pervasive—emphasizes the level of support needed by a person who has mental retardation.

The child who has mild retardation because of delayed mental development has the capacity to develop academically, socially, and vocationally. (© Jerry Howard/Positive Images)

insult. These individuals appear to come predominantly from families at the lower socioeconomic levels, and their problems seem to stem from lack of stimulation or opportunity to learn rather than from, or in addition to, a fundamental defect within the individuals themselves.

The reason for the division between the organically injured and the familial retarded groups is that evidence seems to indicate that developmental processes are somewhat different for the two groups and different even in the various subgroups within the organically injured classification. It has been observed, for example, that Down syndrome children are more delayed in language development than in other areas of development; children with fragile X syndrome seem to have a decline in IQ scores around puberty, and autistic children have more severe delays in psychosocial development (Dykens & Leckman, 1990).

Teachers, in particular, need to be alert to the specific developmental patterns to be expected from the etiology of a child with mental retardation. Students in the group with mild retardation have problems with understanding and interpreting their context—their surrounding environment. For mental structures to grow, there must be psychological and educational nourishment, just as there must be nourishment for physical growth (Sameroff, 1990). Familial retardation, as it reveals itself in the schools, probably represents a combination of lack of experiences plus limited genetic potential (Plomin & McClearn, 1993). The lowest score on an IQ test that a child with an intact, undamaged nervous system (the familial group) would achieve is not zero but about 60 or 70. Any score lower than that is generally an indication of some type of organic pathology.

As noted in Chapter 1, there has been a major reduction in the number of children identified as mentally retarded in the schools. Such reduction in numbers seems to reflect the unwillingness or reluctance of educators to label students "mentally retarded." Those children labeled as having mild mental retardation (MMR) already seem qualitatively different from those who have a variety of pathological conditions that have limited their intellectual development.

Accordingly, there have been some attempts to find a term more in keeping with our current understanding of the condition. One recent suggestion has been to refer to such children as those with *generalized learning disabilities* (MacMillan, Siperstein, & Gresham, 1996). Such a term would indicate an "across-the-board" developmental delay in academic and cognitive abilities and distinguishes it from children with specific learning disabilities, which would indicate a specific deficit in a particular area such as processing auditory signals. Under such a category many youngsters now being called learning disabled could be included in the *generalized learning disabilities* label. And the *specific learning disability* term could be restricted to those youngsters that have a clear deficit in the information processing domain.

Changing the name of a well-established group (MMR) is no small matter. It would mean changing the name of journals, professional societies, and two generations of legislation, so the term "mild mental retardation" will likely be with us for a time to come.

Biological Factors That Contribute to Mental Retardation

CHROMOSOMAL ABNORMALITIES

The question of how a tiny gene can influence the complex behavior of children and adults has puzzled scientists for many years. The breakthroughs of James Watson and Francis Crick helped to explain the functions of DNA and RNA, and it is now possible to provide a general answer to that question. According to McClearn (1993), "Genes influence the proteins that are critical to the functioning of the organ systems that determine behavior" (p. 39). Thus, genes can influence anatomical systems and their functions—the nervous system, sensory systems, musculature, and so on.

Do certain patterns of genes predetermine certain types of behavior? Are we unwittingly automatons driven by mysterious bursts of chemicals? Not really. No particular gene or protein forces a person to drink a glass of whiskey, but some people have a genetic sensitivity to ethanol that may increase their tendency to become alcoholics if they drink a lot. The relationship between genes and behavior is complex, and environmental influences are almost always an important factor.

According to Plomin, DeFries, and McClearn (1980), human genetic abnormalities are common, involving as many as half of all human fertilizations. They don't show up in the general population because most genetic abnormalities result in early spontaneous abortion. About 1 in 200 fetuses with genetic abnormalities survives until birth, but many of these infants die soon after they are born. So although many deviations occur, most are never seen. More than 100 genetic disorders have been identified. Fortunately, most of them are relatively rare. Here we look at three of the most common ones: Down syndrome, phenylketonuria, and fragile X syndrome.

Down Syndrome

One of the most common and easily recognized genetic disorders is **Down syndrome.** Down syndrome occurs once in every 600–900 live births (Schachter & Demerath, 1996). Although clearly genetic, the condition is not hereditary, with the problem existing in the chromosome division. The vast majority of Down syndrome children are produced through *nondisjunction,* which is the failure of some chromosomes to divide properly, resulting in forty-seven chromosomes instead of the normal forty-six (Lejeune, Gautier, & Turpin, 1959) (Figure 5.1). The condition in most instances leads to mild or moderate mental retardation and a variety of hearing, skeletal, and heart problems. The presence of Down syndrome is related to maternal age; the incidence increases significantly in children born to mothers age 35 and older. According to current figures, more than 50 percent of children with Down syndrome are born to mothers older than 35. We do not know exactly why age is related to the condition. We do know, however, that the mother is not the exclusive source of the extra chromosome. The father contributes the extra chromosome in 20 to 25 percent of all cases (Abroms & Bennett, 1980). The age of the father does not seem as significant as the age of the mother. Down syndrome can also be caused by a chromosomal abnormality called *translocation.* The child may have forty-six chromosomes, but one pair breaks, and the broken part fuses to another chromosome.

Before the 1970s, the diagnosis of Down syndrome and a number of other pathological conditions was not made until the child was born or even later. **Amniocentesis,** a procedure for drawing a sample of amniotic fluid (the fluid that surrounds the fetus in the uterus) from the pregnant woman, has made earlier diagnosis possible. Fetal cells in the fluid are analyzed for chromosomal abnormality by **karyotyping,** a process in which a picture of chromosomal patterns is prepared (see Figure 5.1). Tests of prenatal maternal alpha-fetoprotein and ultrasonography can also reveal the presence of a fetus with Down syndrome. Such early diagnosis has posed a major dilemma for families and physicians (Pueschal, 1991). It allows

Figure 5.1

Chromosomal Pattern of a Girl with Down Syndrome, with an Extra Chromosome in Pair 21

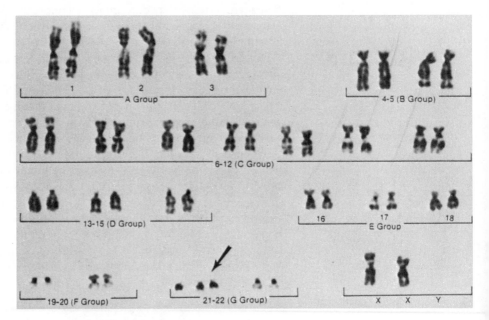

Source: From S. Pueschel (1983), "The Child with Down Syndrome," in M. Levine, W. Carey, A. Crocker, and R. Gross (Eds.), *Developmental-Behavioral Pediatrics.* Philadelphia: Saunders. Copyright 1983 by W. B. Saunders & Co. Reprinted by permission.

Figure 5.2
Child with Down Syndrome Before and After Plastic Surgery

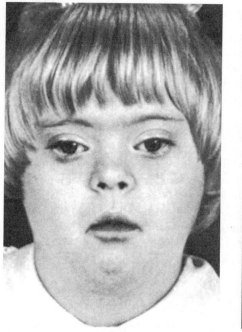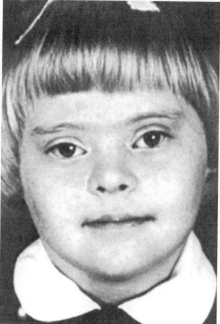

Source: C. Turkington (1987), "Special Talents," *Psychology Today* (September), pp. 42–46.

parents to decide whether the pregnancy should be terminated. The decision is not an easy one, generating questions about the right to life and genetic selection.

The effects of Down syndrome extend well beyond the child's early development. School-age children with Down syndrome appear to have higher social and adaptive skills than would be expected given their slow intellectual development and less developed language and communication skills. Adults with Down syndrome seem particularly disposed to depression, dementia, and Alzheimer's disease (Loveland & Tunali-Kotoski, 1998). Systematic efforts to prevent or control these later risks have yet to be made (Epstein, 1988).

Part of the context of the child with Down syndrome is the distinctive physical appearance of the child, which may evoke negative responses from other children and adults. Recently, suggestions have been made for plastic surgery to remove some of the distinctive physical features (Figure 5.2).

Phenylketonuria

Normal growth and development in the embryo and fetus depend on the production of enzymes at the right time and place. When enzymes are not produced or fail to perform their normal functions, a number of unfavorable developmental conditions can result. These conditions are called *inborn errors of metabolism.* One of them is **phenylketonuria (PKU)**, a single-gene defect that can produce severe retardation. In PKU, the absence of a specific enzyme in the liver leads to a buildup of the amino acid *phenylalanine.*

PKU is an unusual genetic disorder in that it can be modified by environmental treatment, a special diet. The diet is very strict, however, and many families have difficulty holding to its requirements. PKU can be detected at birth, and some states have established a screening program to identify such children so they can be started on a nutritional regime early (Simonoff, Bolton, & Rutter, 1998).

Fragile X Syndrome

Although basically undiscovered until 1969, **fragile X syndrome** (so named because of a constriction near the end of the X chromosome) is now recognized as one of the leading causes of mental retardation and developmental disabilities (Simonoff, Bolton, & Rutter, 1998). The frequency in males is about 1 in 3,000; in females, it is about 1 in 4,000. Its most serious influence is on males, although females can carry the genetic basis for the disorder. Girls seem not affected in general IQ scores, as are males, but girls may reveal specific learning disabilities in their school performance.

The major effect of fragile X syndrome is impaired intellectual performance. A study of 250 males with the syndrome found only 13 percent with IQ scores over 70, and there was a tendency for the IQ scores of males with this disorder to decline in measured ability over time (Hagerman et al., 1989). Some physical characteristics that appear with the syndrome include a slightly larger-than-normal head together with a long, narrow face, loose connective tissue, and a high, arched palate. Such physical anomalies do not show up until two years or more after birth.

There is considerable diversity in the behavior patterns of children with fragile X syndrome. But there are consistent problems with social relationships, delays in communication skills, and marked tendencies toward perseveration (repetition of words or phrases). There have been associations of fragile X syndrome with autism, but no more than 5 percent of children with this condition are also identified as having autism.

Prenatal tests can now determine if a fetus has any genetic abnormalities.

TOXIC AGENTS

The remarkable system whereby a pregnant mother transmits nutrients through the umbilical cord to her fetus is also the highway by which many damaging substances can pass to the developing child. Our increasing ability to monitor fetal development and the rapidly growing body of research from studies of animals have raised concerns about the effects on the unborn child of substances ingested by the mother. A **teratogen** (from the Greek, meaning "monster creating") is a substance that adversely affects fetal development. Drugs (including alcohol) and cigarette smoke are prime examples of teratogens. The heavy use of alcohol or other drugs creates a prenatal and postnatal environmental context that is unfavorable for the infant's and child's early development.

Fetal Alcohol Syndrome

For centuries we have been generally aware of the unfavorable effects that alcohol consumption by the mother has on her unborn child. But only in the past few decades have those general concerns been substantiated with specific statistics and detailed descriptions of the consequences of what is now referred to as **fetal alcohol syndrome (FAS).** Most of these findings have stirred even more alarm and concern. About 7 out of 10,000 births result in FAS, with greater frequencies in African-American and Native American families (Baumeister & Woodley-Zanthos, 1996).

Obviously, not every fetus is affected by maternal drinking; otherwise we would be awash with children with FAS. It is sufficiently prevalent, however, to be a major cause of concern. Milder effects of alcohol consumption during pregnancy, known as *fetal alcohol effects (FAE),* include distractibility and hyperactivity,

According to the "least restrictive environment" principle, children should be moved from the mainstream of education only as far as necessary to meet their special needs. (© Lydia Gans)

which may go unnoticed because they do not have FAS's catastrophic impact on the child.

One of the distressing aspects of FAS is that it directly affects the development of the brain, and its results last long into adulthood. FAS is currently considered one of the leading causes of moderate or severe organic mental retardation (Menke, McClead, & Hansen, 1991).

FAS is a leading cause of organic mental retardation.

Heavy Metals

Ingesting heavy metals, such as lead, cadmium, and mercury, can result in severe consequences, including mental retardation. Most attention is currently focused on lead, and much of the lead that enters the brain comes from the atmosphere. One of the most effective steps that has been taken, on a societal level, was the reduction of lead amounts permitted in gasoline. This reduction resulted in a lowering by one-third of the average lead levels in the blood of U.S. men, women, and children. The reduction in lead levels paralleled the declining use of leaded gasoline (Mahaffey, Annest, Roberts, & Murphy, 1982).

Also, legislation has restricted the use of lead in paint and mandated that lead paint be removed from the walls and ceilings of older homes—a common source of lead poisoning in youngsters. Some children are born with high levels of lead in their blood (prenatal exposure to lead can be determined by examining the umbilical cord). On tests of intelligence, these children scored 8 percent below children who had lower levels of lead in their blood (Bellinger, Leviton, Waternaux, Needleman, & Rabinowitz, 1987). Children, who will place anything in their mouths, are known to ingest peeling paint chips with some regularity. Davis (1988) pointed out that good nutrition can prevent lead-related damage by reducing lead absorption in the body. The susceptibility of many children from low economic backgrounds to lead poisoning may, in part, reflect a combination of poor nutrition and the greater availability of lead in their environment, another contextual feature. Medications can be prescribed that can have the effect of flushing the system of lead, once it has been discovered (Pueschel, Scola, Weidenman, & Bernier, 1995).

INFECTIONS

The brain begins to develop about three weeks after fertilization. Over the next several weeks, the central nervous system is highly susceptible to disease. If the mother contracts **rubella** (German measles) during this time, her child will likely be born with mental retardation and other serious birth defects. A rubella vaccine that is now available has reduced the number of rubella children. Children and adults are also at risk of brain damage from viruses that produce high fevers, which, in turn, destroy brain cells. Encephalitis is one virus of this type. Fortunately it is rare, as are other viruses like it.

One of the viruses that is having an enormous effect on the entire world in the last decades of the twentieth century is acquired immune deficiency syndrome (AIDS). As the name implies, this virus interferes with the body's immune system, allowing it to become vulnerable to a host of fatal infections that the body is normally able to ward off (Scola, 1991). The AIDS virus is spread through sexual contact with an infected person, through exposure to infected blood or blood products, and from an infected mother to her child before and during birth. At this writing, there is no known cure.

The AIDS virus, HIV, can spread from an infected mother to her child before and during birth.

Although the presence of human immunodeficiency virus (HIV), the virus that causes AIDS, is often a death sentence to adults, it is not certain whether the same discouraging statement can be said about children with HIV. Many individual cases, however, demonstrate that children with the virus can become mentally retarded, although the extent to which this occurs is not yet known. What is known is that children with AIDS and their families need massive help from the health and educational communities.

Environmental Factors That Affect Mental Retardation

There has long been an enormous gap between what we know about the brain and its function and the set of behavioral symptoms by which we define mental retardation. With current advances in understanding the central nervous system, we are able to make some reasonable assumptions about the links between that system and behavior. Huttenlocher (1988) suggested that experience influences the development and maintenance of certain structures in the brain. The implications are exciting. If the development of the nervous system is not preset at fertilization by genetic factors, the nervous system can grow and change as the individual experiences new things. That means environment and human interactions can play a role in neurological and hence intellectual development.

Sameroff (1990) raised the issue of possible biosocial influences on the child, or the effect of the interaction of the environment with the biological state of the child. He pointed out that many children with birth complications actually grow up to show no evidence of their unhappy start, and he concluded that "social conditions were much better predictors of outcome for those children than either their early biological status, as measured by birth and pregnancy complications, or their psychological status, as measured by developmental scales" (p. 95).

When children who tested in the "low" or "mentally retarded" range as preschoolers are retested at ages 10 to 12, the correlation between the two measurements tends to be very high. Researchers have often interpreted this high correlation as an indication of the consistency with which the slow developmental rate of intellectual growth is maintained. When Sameroff tested the influences of external environment over time, he found similarly high or higher correlations between the preschool child's unfavorable environmental conditions and the preadolescent's environmental conditions. So the environmental conditions that the child experienced were as consistent as the measurements taken of the child's intellectual performance. Sameroff observed (1990):

> When predictions on how children will turn out are based on their early behavior, the predictions are generally wrong. When such predictions are based on their life circumstances, the predictions are generally right. In this domain, an understanding of the context may have greater developmental importance than an understanding of the child. (p. 97)

Sameroff (1990) identified a set of ten environmental risk factors (such as breadwinner employed in unskilled work, poor maternal health). Only in families with *multiple risk factors* did the child's competence seem to be in jeopardy. The multiple pressures of (1) the amount of stress from the environment, (2) the family's resources for coping with that stress, (3) the number of children who must share those resources, and (4) the parents' flexibility in understanding and dealing with their children play a role in fostering or hindering the child's intellectual and social competencies.

Life circumstances, or the child's environment, are a strong predictor of how well a child will do in school and in society.

Characteristics of Children with Mental Retardation or Developmental Disabilities

Special programming for children with mild and moderate MR/DD is shaped in part by the characteristics that distinguish these children from their agemates. There are marked differences in factors linked to level of intellectual development, such as the ability to process information, the ability to acquire and use language, and emotional development.

ABILITY TO PROCESS INFORMATION

The most obvious characteristic of children who have mild or moderate retardation is their limited cognitive ability, a limitation that inevitably shows up in their academic work. These children may lag by two to five grades, particularly in language-related subjects (reading, language arts). To help children who are not learning effectively, we must understand what is preventing them from learning. To do this, we must understand how they think—how they process information.

Many children who have mental retardation have problems in **central processing,** or the classification of a stimulus through the use of memory, reasoning, and evaluation. *Classification*—the organization of information—seems to be a special problem for children who have mental retardation. School-age children quickly

To help children learn, teachers need to know how children with mental retardation or developmental disabilities process information.

With organized training programs and support services, many young people with mental retardation or developmental disabilities can adjust well in employment and community settings. (© Frank Siteman/The Picture Cube)

learn to cluster (or group) events or things into useful classes: A chair, a table, and a sofa become "furniture"; an apple, a peach, and a pear become "fruit." Children who have mental retardation are less able to group things. They have difficulty telling how a train and an automobile are alike.

Memory, another central-processing function, is also difficult for children who have mental retardation. Memory problems can stem from poor initial perception or poor judgment about applying what has been stored to a given situation. Most children use "rehearsal" as a memory aid, saying a string of words or a poem to themselves until they remember it. Children with retardation are less likely to rehearse information because their ability to use short-term memory appears limited.

Executive function—the decision-making element that controls reception, central processing, and expression—is a key factor in the poor performance of children who have mental retardation (Baumeister & Brooks, 1981; Borkowski & Day, 1987; Sternberg, 1982). It is not so much that these children cannot perceive a stimulus as it is that they cannot pay attention to the relevant aspects of a problem. It is not so much that they cannot reason as it is that they do not have the metathinking strategies to organize information to a point where reasoning can take place. And it is not so much that they do not have a repertoire of responses as it is that they too often choose an inappropriate response. Their teachers often say that they lack good judgment.

A common way to refer to the difficulty in processing information is to say there is a lack of good judgment.

For these children, learning problems are not limited to a specific cognitive function; instead, the whole information-processing system substantially breaks down. Most children whose IQ score is 50 or lower suffer from neurological damage that can make information processing very difficult.

ABILITY TO ACQUIRE AND USE LANGUAGE

The ability to develop language is one of the great achievements of humans, and there always has been curiosity as to how, if at all, language development is changed or modified in children and adults with mental retardation. The close link between language and cognition has long been noted (Cromer, 1991) as well as its reciprocal interaction. Not only is language limited by cognition, cognition (especially thinking, planning, and reasoning) is limited by language (Fowler, 1998). In addition, there is the problem of limited input and an impoverished database during the language learning years that can add up to an impoverished linguistic system (Locke, 1994).

Recently, the study of language in persons with mental retardation has become more complex in two specific ways. First, an increasing attempt has been made to study the elements of language for such children separately so that *semantics* (meaning and comprehension) is separated from *pragmatics* (the use of language for communication) and *phonology* (speech expression), and also the study of language development of children with specific etiologies. Children with Down syndrome can be compared with children with Williams syndrome, for example (Tager-Flushberg & Sullivan, 1998).

The question as to whether language develops in the same fashion, only slower, with children with mental retardation or in a special fashion has been answered largely in favor of the first choice. It is largely just slower; for example, a child at age 5 would match in linguistic skills a mentally retarded child of 10 whose mental age was 5.

Yet there are intriguing variations on this generalization. Some persons with undeniable mental retardation seemed to have developed language far beyond their general mental ability (see References of Special Interest, Rondal, 1995), and we don't know precisely what to make of such a phenomenon. Children with Down syndrome have retardation in language (pragmatics and semantics) even lower than that of their general mental deficit, while children with Williams syndrome seem to have advanced language beyond their general mental abilities. This puzzle guarantees that there will be much more research on these topics in the near future (Fowler, 1998).

EMOTIONAL PROBLEMS AND SOCIAL ACCEPTANCE

For many years, there has been a modest understanding of the link between emotional and social problems and the condition of mental retardation. But what that link signifies and what should be done about it remain issues of some dispute (Korinek & Polloway, 1993). We know that emotional and social difficulties can undermine vocational and community adjustment. We are also aware that emotional and behavioral problems probably lower the level of social acceptance experienced by children with mental retardation in comparison with their peers in the classroom. It is entirely possible that this low level of social acceptance is related to the behavioral and social problems rather than to the condition of mental retardation.

Recent studies attempt to separate the ability to use language for communication and language for comprehension.

Emotional and behavioral issues associated with mental retardation probably lower social acceptance by peers in the classroom.

The current stress on main-streaming and inclusion makes it particularly important to find ways to improve the social relationships of children with mental retardation—one of the main goals of inclusion.

IEP objectives need to include social skills.

To be socially accepted, children need to know certain social skills, such as sharing, smiling, and following directions, and when to use them.

As has been the case with language development, recent studies on social development have focused on the specific problems of children with special etiologies such as Down syndrome (Kasari & Bauminger, 1998). A range of studies reveal many problems in peer relationships for children with mental retardation. With the current stress on mainstreaming and inclusion, it becomes particularly important to find ways to improve the social relationships of children with mental retardation, since that is one of the key reasons for the inclusion in the first place.

Certain skills appear to be important for social acceptance. They include sharing, turn taking, smiling, attending, and following directions. A person with social competence uses such skills appropriately in social situations. Despite the widespread acknowledgment of the problems of social adaptation and social skills development that confront young mentally retarded students, IEPs often do not address those problems. McBride and Forgnone (1985) found that fewer than 5 percent of the IEP objectives written for middle school students with mild retardation reflected either a career vocational or a social behavioral emphasis. This situation seems particularly serious in light of research indicating that a minority of the graduates of programs for students with mild mental retardation are employed (Edgar, 1987; Wagner et al., 1991). We may be missing a real opportunity to help others make good adjustments to adulthood.

Korinek and Polloway (1993) have called for a major emphasis in the curriculum on the development of social skills and social competencies. This means a goal not only to improve social adaptability to increase academic efficiency but also to develop social skills for their own sake and because of their importance in adult adjustment. Indeed, students who do not have social skills are ill prepared to adapt to the inclusive classroom or school. One serious remaining problem involves the specific curriculum for teaching social skills. How can such a program fit into the regular classroom activities and objectives? If most of the general students have already learned these skills without specific instruction, then how can the teacher take the time to engage in this training with just a handful of students with mental retardation?

Developmental Profiles

Figure 5.3 shows the developmental profiles of Bob, a child with mild familial retardation, and Carol, a child with moderate organic retardation. Both children are 10 years old. The patterns revealed in the figure are not unusual for children of their intellectual development, although individual differences from one child to another within each of these groups may be great.

Bob's physical profile (height, weight, motor coordination) does not differ markedly from the profiles of others in his age group. But in academic areas such as reading, arithmetic, and spelling, Bob is performing three and four grades below his age group. Depending on his classmates and the levels at which they are performing, Bob would fall at the bottom of the regular class group or be placed in a special program in a resource room. Bob's mobility, vision, and hearing are average, but he is having problems with interpersonal relationships. Although he is a likable boy under nonthreatening conditions, he is quick to take offense and fight on the playground. In the classroom, he has a tendency to interrupt other children at their work and to wander aimlessly around the room when given an individual assignment. All these characteristics add up to a situation in which

Figure 5.3

Profiles of Two Children with Mental Retardation

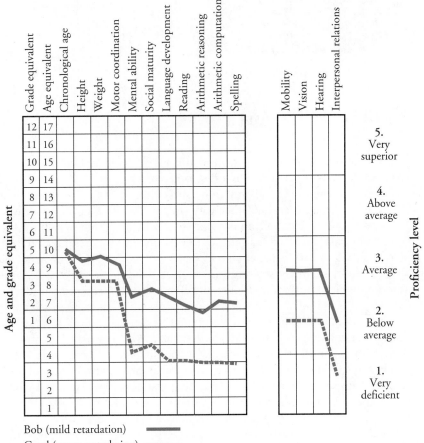

Bob (mild retardation) ————

Carol (severe retardation) ▪▪▪▪▪▪▪

Bob has only a few friends, although he is tolerated by his classmates. With special help, he is able to maintain a marginal performance within the regular class.

Carol has severe retardation and a much more serious adaptive problem. Her development is at the level of a 4-year-old (her IQ score is in the 40s). Like many other children with Down syndrome, she shows poor motor coordination and some minor vision and hearing problems that complicate her educational adaptation.

Carol's developmental profile shows that her academic performance is well below first-grade level; indeed, at maturity, Carol's reading and arithmetic skills may not exceed a first- or second-grade level. She can learn important skills or concepts in an educational setting, but the standard academic program is clearly inappropriate for her. To develop her capabilities to their maximum potential, Carol will need some special experiences with specially trained personnel.

 ## *Prevention of Mental Retardation*

As we learn more about the causes of mental retardation, we are in a better position to prevent it. Scott and Carran (1987) described three levels of prevention: *primary*, *secondary*, and *tertiary*. Table 5.3 lists objectives for each level and strategies for achieving them.

"Jon Will's Aptitudes"

Jon Will, the oldest of my four children, turns 21 this week and on this birthday, as on every other workday, he will commute by subway to his job delivering mail and being useful in other ways at the National Institutes of Health. Jon is a taxpayer, which serves him right: he voted for Bill Clinton (although he was partial to Pat Buchanan in the primaries).

The fact that Jon is striding into a productive adulthood with a spring in his step and Baltimore's Orioles on his mind is a consummation that could not have been confidently predicted when he was born. Then a doctor told his parents that their first decision must be whether or not to take Jon home. Surely 21 years later fewer doctors suggest to parents of handicapped newborns that the parental instinct of instant love should be tentative or attenuated, or that their commitment to nurturing is merely a matter of choice, even a question of convenience.

Jon has Down syndrome, a chromosomal defect involving varying degrees of mental retardation and physical abnormalities. Jon lost, at the instant he was conceived, one of life's lotteries, but he also was lucky: his physical abnormalities do not impede his vitality and his retardation is not so severe that it interferes with life's essential joys—receiving love, returning it, and reading baseball box scores.

One must mind one's language when speaking of people like Jon. He does not "suffer from" Down syndrome. It is an affliction, but he is happy—as happy as the Orioles' stumbling start this season will permit. You may well say that being happy is easy now that ESPN exists. Jon would agree. But happiness is a species of talent, for which some people have superior aptitudes.

Jon's many aptitudes far exceed those few that were dogmatically ascribed to people like him not long ago. He was born when scientific and social understanding relevant to him was expanding dramatically. We know much more about genetically based problems than we did when, in the early 1950s, James Watson and Francis Crick published their discoveries concerning the structure of DNA, the hereditary molecule, thereby beginning the cracking of the genetic code. Jon was born the year before *Roe* v. *Wade* and just as prenatal genetic tests were becoming routine. Because of advancing science and declining morals, there are fewer people like Jon than there should be. And just in Jon's generation much has been learned about unlocking the hitherto unimagined potential of the retarded. This begins with early intervention in the form of infant stimulation. Jon began going off to school when he was three months old.

Because Down syndrome is determined at conception and leaves its imprint in every cell of the person's body, it raises what philosophers call ontological questions. It seems mistaken to say that Jon is less than he would be without Down syndrome. When a child suffers a mentally limiting injury after birth we wonder sadly about what might have been. But a Down person's life never had any other trajectory. Jon was Jon from conception on. He has seen a brother two years younger surpass him in size, get a driver's license and leave for college, and although Jon would be forgiven for shaking his fist at the universe, he has been equable. I believe his serenity is grounded in his sense that he is a complete Jon and that is that.

Shadow of Loneliness

Some of life's pleasures, such as the delights of literature, are not accessible to Jon, but his most poignant problem is that he is just like everyone else, only a bit more so. A shadow of loneliness, an irreducible apartness from others, is inseparable from the fact of individual existence. This entails a sense of incompleteness—we *are* social creatures—that can be assuaged by marriage and other friendships, in the intimacy of which people speak their hearts and minds. Listen to the wisdom whispered by common locutions: We speak of "unburdening ourselves" when we talk with those to whom we talk most freely.

Now, try to imagine being prevented, by mental retardation and by physical impediments to clear articulation, from putting down, through conversation, many burdens attendant on personhood. The shadow of loneliness must often be somewhat darker, the sense of apartness more acute, the sense of incompleteness more aching for people like Jon. Their ability to articulate is, even more than for everyone else, often not commensurate with their abilities to think and feel, to be curious and amused, and to yearn.

Because of Jon's problems of articulation, I marvel at his casual everyday courage in coping with a world that often is uncomprehending. He is intensely interested in major league baseball umpires, and is a friend of a few of them. I think he is fascinated by their ability to make themselves understood, by vigorous gestures, all the way to the back row of the bleachers. From his season-ticket seat behind the Orioles dugout, Jon relishes rhubarbs, but I have never seen him really angry. The closest he comes is exasperation leavened by resignation. It is an interesting commentary on the human condition that one aspect of Jon's abnormality—a facet of his disability—is the fact that he is gentleness straight through. But must we ascribe a sweet soul to a defective chromosome? Let us just say that Jon is an adornment to a world increasingly stained by anger acted out.

Like many handicapped people, Jon frequently depends on the kindness of strangers. He almost invariably receives it, partly because Americans are, by and large, nice, and because Jon is, too. He was born on his father's birthday, a gift that keeps on giving.

Source: "Jon Will's Aptitudes," copyright © 1993 by George F. Will, from *The Leveling Wind* by George Will. Used by permission of Viking Penguin, a division of Penguin Putnam, Inc.

What Is the Context?

This article discusses Jon Will's capabilities, wants, and joys as he progresses from the inner circle of family to the outer circle of community. His father describes Jon's abilities and inabilities, joys and frustrations, but above all shows how Jon's life is simple but whole. Jon copes with a difficulty in articulating his thoughts by showing resolve and gentleness in adversity.

Pivotal Issues for Teachers

What does the author value about Jon and his abilities? How is Jon's personality affected by Down syndrome? How has the way Jon's family raised him affected Jon's current abilities and attitudes? How does Jon's love of baseball give a sense of wholeness to his life? Now that Jon has reached adulthood, what does he contribute to the community, and in what other ways might he contribute?

Primary prevention focuses on the developing fetus. The objective is to reduce the number of children born mentally retarded or with conditions that could lead to mental retardation. Good prenatal care—teaching pregnant women about the dangers of drugs, alcohol, and smoking, for example—is one important strategy. Genetic counseling for couples whose children are at risk is another. Research is essential to finding causes of and possible treatments for conditions that can lead to retardation. The effects of rubella, for example, have been largely eliminated through antibody screening and immunization programs (Crocker & Nelson, 1983).

TABLE 5.3 Preventing Mental Retardation		
Prevention Level	**Objective**	**Strategy**
Primary	Fewer children born with mental retardation	Prenatal care Genetic counseling Scientific research Improved family planning
Secondary	Early identification and effective treatment	Intensive neonatal care Parental education Long-term social services Screening Diet management
Tertiary	Adaptations to achieve maximum potential and highest quality of life	Increased educational and social services over lifespan

Source: Adapted from K. Scott and D. Carran (1987). "The Epidemiology and Prevention of Mental Retardation," *American Psychologist, 42*(8), pp. 801–804. Used by permission.

Preventing harmful environmental, family, and social conditions may help reduce mild mental retardation.

Primary prevention of mental retardation occurs before birth, secondary prevention occurs in early childhood, and tertiary prevention occurs throughout the lifespan.

The objective of *secondary prevention* is to identify and change environmental conditions that could lead to retardation. By screening newborns for PKU, we can begin treatment and prevent retardation. By eliminating sources of lead, we can reduce brain damage from lead poisoning. By providing youngsters from disadvantaged homes with strong preschool programs, we can begin to counteract the elements that can cause environmental retardation.

Tertiary prevention focuses on arranging the educational and social environment so people who are born with or who develop mental retardation can achieve their maximum potential and highest quality of life. Early intervention programs start with youngsters who seem to be at risk for retardation at an early age and try to sharpen their perceptual abilities, encourage the use of expressive language, and give practice in classification and reasoning. Some programs urge parents to continue and extend these activities at home. All attempt to strengthen the thinking processes of young children who are delayed in development, and all succeed to a degree.

What proportion of the child's social and cognitive development depends on biology and what proportion on the social environment remains a major issue. Horowitz and Haritos (1998) pointed out that few intervention programs with the goal of improving the social and cognitive experiences of young children born into poverty showed large increases in IQ scores. Most of those programs did show benefits in areas of school achievement, behavioral functioning, and personal adjustment. They concluded that the growing body of evidence points to biological factors strongly controlling the developmental outcomes but that environmental intervention can result in modest improvement.

Educational Adaptations

Children with Mental Retardation or Developmental Disabilities

Organized attempts to help children who learn slowly began less than two hundred years ago, when Jean Itard, a French physician, tried to educate a young boy who had lived by himself in the woods—the so-called Wild Boy of Aveyron. Although Itard failed to achieve all his objectives, one of his students, Edward Seguin, later developed Itard's approaches and became an acknowledged leader of the movement to help mentally retarded children and adults.

Over the years, the care and education of children with mental retardation have moved gradually from large state institutions to the public schools and within the schools to the least restrictive environment.

One other person worth noting is Maria Montessori (1912), who worked with retarded children in the physiological tradition, using what is now called *sense training*. Her work was so successful that her teachings were applied to the teaching of young normal children. Today she is best known for her educational play materials and methods, even though her original work was with children who were retarded.

Since the 1970s, thanks to major investments in research by the federal government, there have been significant advances in discoveries and attempts to find ways to aid in the development of the children with disabilities and in the support available to their families (see Chapter 2). The context in which children with mental retardation have been growing up also has changed. The context of modern life, with its increasing emphasis on advanced education and complex understandings, has not always been kind or favorable to children and adults with mental retardation. Opportunities for employment seem to be shrinking at the same time that acceptance of such individuals as a part of our society appears to be growing.

ADAPTING THE LEARNING ENVIRONMENT

Identifying Students with MR/DD

The first step in adapting the standard educational program to meet the needs of children with mental retardation or developmental disabilities is to identify those children who need special help. How does a child find special education services? Although referrals can come from many different sources, most students with mental retardation or developmental disabilities come to the attention of special education services because they fail in school. The inability of the child to adapt academically or socially to the expected standards of his or her age group sets off alarm bells in the teacher and calls for action.

Until recently, the response to such alarm bells was a diagnostic examination by the school psychologist to determine if the child was eligible for some form of special education. Now, many school systems use a *prereferral team,* which includes the classroom teacher, the principal, someone from special education, and relevant other special personnel. The team tries to see if it can help the classroom teacher devise some adaptation of the regular classroom program to cope with the student's problems without more intensive (and more expensive) intervention (Chalfant, 1989). If the student makes no apparent gain as a result of the recommendations of the prereferral team, the child may then be referred for more detailed diagnostic examination by the psychologist and, if found eligible, placed in more intensive special education services with an IEP decided by the multidisciplinary IEP team working with the child's parents.

The diagnostic examination assesses the child's intellectual development and adaptive behavior, the two key elements in the AAMR definition of mental retardation. The individual intelligence test remains the most common instrument used to determine intellectual subnormality. A student whose scores fall below those of 98 percent of his or her agemates is considered intellectually subnormal, unless cultural differences call the results into question.

Adaptive behavior is more difficult to assess because behavior can differ depending on the environment. Adaptive rating scales may indicate that a child is adapting well to the larger environment, but the child is acting out in the classroom. The Adaptive Behavior Scales of the American Association on Mental Retardation (AAMR) and the Adaptive Behavior Inventory for Children (ABIC) measure adaptation to the community (Leland, 1991). Most children do well on these and similar scales because they are not asked to perform academically and constraints on their behavior are minimal. But a total measure of adaptation should measure how well students respond in the school environment, where they spend five or six hours a day, five days a week. The school edition of the AAMR scale does focus on behavior in the school setting (Lambert & Windmiller, 1981; Salvia & Ysseldyke, 1988) and therefore may be the more appropriate measure to use.

An addition to the measures of adaptive behavior has been the Vineland Adaptive Behavior Scales (Sparrow, Balla, & Cicchetti, 1984). The scale covers four domains and appears to have good reliability and validity:

- *Communication:* What the individual understands (receptive), says (expressive), and reads and writes (written)

- *Daily living skills:* How the individual eats, dresses, and practices personal hygiene; performs household tasks (domestic); and uses his or her time, money, telephone, and job skills (community)

- *Socialization:* How the individual interacts with others, plays, uses leisure time, and demonstrates sensitivity and responsibility to others

- *Motor:* How the individual uses arms and legs for movement and coordination and uses hands and fingers to manipulate objects (Leland, 1991)

Despite the availability of such formal tools for assessing adaptive behavior, the school assessment may still depend on the judgment of teachers and other educators who have had direct experience with the child.

Many of the current methods of identifying children with retardation are based on medical procedures for diagnosis, which include identification, diagnosis, and treatment. Today, many educators want to bypass most of the diagnostic and classification procedures and get right to work educating the child. As Forness and Kavale (1984) pointed out: "The essential diagnosis of a child's needs usually takes place only *after* the special education teacher or resource specialist has worked with the child in the special or regular classroom over a period of weeks" (p. 243).

Fuchs and Deno (1992) introduced an interesting alternative to the use of intelligence or aptitude tests to determine the student's performance level. Their curriculum-based measurement uses readings from various textbooks and asks

Despite the availability of formal tools to assess adaptive behavior, assessment may still depend on the judgment of teachers and counselors.

students to read aloud from a hundred-word passage from the text. The number of words said correctly in one minute is the index of performance of the student. A variety of texts of differing levels of difficulty can fix the approximate reading level of the child. Such a simple method seems to correlate highly with standard measures of reading skills. It also provides the teacher with a clear sense of the student's developmental level of reading. If the teacher uses material of several grade levels to determine the proper reading level for the student, then the teacher should be able to adjust the difficulty level of the lessons that he or she provides to the student.

Before 1970, an additional category was used, *borderline mental retardation,* which basically meant that although the student's IQ score was not below 70, the student still seemed to be in educational difficulty. Students with borderline mental retardation were considered to be children whose IQ scores fell within the 71–85 range. That category was dropped largely because it was so disproportionately composed of minority group children that it became an embarrassment for the schools. Recently, the issue was raised as to what happened to those borderline youngsters and what were they doing in school now. The answer was that they are not doing very well. They continue to struggle academically even though they are not being actively sought out by special educators (MacMillan, Gresham, Bocian, & Lambros, 1998). This concerns educators, who worry about the fate of children with mental retardation or developmental disabilities in the regular classroom. If the borderline group is having trouble, what will happen to students with lower IQ scores in the same setting?

Issues of Inclusion

How should the educational program be adapted to meet the needs of children with mental retardation? One intriguing aspect of the reform movement for inclusion is that it highlights principles of interpersonal interaction that are designed for life in the larger society. Proponents of inclusion wish the child with disabilities to be welcomed into a community of equals in the classroom, no one to speak disparagingly about others, everyone to be helpful to one another, and no one to be put down by others because of an inability to do certain things. But can such a philosophy of fairness and love be implemented in the school as we know it, particularly when the school has a number of competing academic goals that may make achieving such interpersonal goals difficult? Implementation would be particularly difficult in the absence of support personnel to assist the classroom teacher, who otherwise would have to bear sole responsibility for inculcating such values.

The U.S. Congress left little doubt as to their preference for education in the regular classroom for all special needs children with the following language (from the Individuals with Disability Education Act amendments of 1997):

> To the maximum extent appropriate, handicapped children, including children in public or private institutions or other care facilities, are educated with children who are not handicapped, and that separate schooling, or other removal of handicapped children from regular educational environment occurs only when the nature or severity of the handicap is such that education in regular education classes *with the use of supplementary aids and services* cannot be achieved satisfactorily. [20 U.S.C. §1412(5)(B)]

Stainback, Stainback, and Johnson (1992, p. 13) describe the way inclusion should be. Teachers in inclusive classrooms should be able to call on reading specialists, compensatory education personnel, students in the classroom, school counselors, physical and speech therapists, other classroom teachers, math and science teachers, and a variety of other people to provide suggestions or participate in the classroom to make classes more flexible and relevant to the needs of all students.

Those who worry about a terrible traffic jam as these counselors, special teachers, and psychologists bump into one another trying to get to the classroom teacher need not be concerned just yet. The availability of these personnel is uncertain, to say the least. It is not the ideals of inclusion that are being argued, but the ability to achieve or implement them. All three of the major areas of change—learning environments, curriculum content, and skills mastery—seem to require attention for students with mental retardation.

Individualized Education Programs (IEPs)

The IEP has brought both positive and negative effects to the education of children with mental retardation or developmental disabilities.

One of the first efforts to develop long-range plans for child and family came forth from the IEPs, mandated in 1975 by the Education for All Handicapped Children Act (PL 94-142) to increase the collaboration between professionals and parents and to ensure some thoughtful consideration about how children would be served within the special education program.

The case study of Tanisha, a mildly retarded child, shows the annual goals and short-term objectives on her IEP. The objectives are written in such a way that we can easily tell if they have been achieved. Tanisha's IEP in Table 5.4 provides goals and measurable objectives along three major dimensions: academic, social, and physical. The academic goals are written to meet Tanisha where she is developmentally, so she can perform at some level in school. The social and physical goals are designed to improve Tanisha's behavior and enable her to interact with peers in recreational activities. Whenever these short-term objectives have been achieved, a new and more advanced set can be designed. It is important that the written IEP includes the nature of the supplementary aids and services to be provided, who will provide the services, anticipated benefits for the child, and how data are to be collected to gauge achievement of objectives (Etscheidt & Bartlett, 1999).

A new concept in use for children with mental retardation is the development of social supports that are necessary to help the individual move toward independence and interdependence in the community. They may include, for older children, everything from financial planning, to technology assistance, to carpooling, to mobility training.

General Education Classroom

In special education, it often appears necessary to change the learning environment to provide the special curricula or skills required to meet students' special needs. According to the "least restrictive environment" principle, the child should

	TABLE 5.4 Tanisha's IEP	
Tanisha (CA = 7–3, IQ = 58)		
Area	**Annual Goals**	**Sample Short-Term Objectives**
Academic	1. Tanisha will count out any number of items between 1 and 20.	Given 5 items on the computer screen, Tanisha will press the correct number in 4 out of 5 trials.
	2. Tanisha will decode new words.	When presented with a new, one-syllable, printed word consisting of familiar letter sounds, Tanisha will say the word correctly in 4 out of 5 trials.
	3. Tanisha will print her full name.	When instructed to print her first name, Tanisha will print all the letters legibly in the correct order in 9 out of 10 trials.
Social	Tanisha will stay in her seat unless given permission to leave it.	During reading period, Tanisha will ask permission before leaving her seat without exception on 4 out of 5 days.
Physical	Tanisha will play kickball.	When instructed to kick, Tanisha will kick the ball in 7 out of 10 trials.

Source: From *Mental Retardation: Foundations of Educational Programming*, by L. Hickson, L. Blackman, and E. Reis. Copyright © 1995 by Allyn & Bacon. Adapted by permission.

be moved from the mainstream of education only as far as necessary to meet those needs. Nevertheless, many students continue to be removed from the regular program for part or all of the school day, and that practice has generated major controversy within and outside special education.

One of the main concerns of many special educators about the inclusion strategy that brings children with disabilities into the regular classroom is placing students back into the very environment in which they failed in the first place (Keogh, 1996). These students found their way into special education by being referred by the general education teacher as not being able to adapt to the general education classroom.

Those stressing the inclusion strategy point out that the classroom situation will be much different, with support personnel and a specific plan (IEP) designed to meet the needs of individual students (Stainback & Stainback, 1996). So one of the keys is, "How much support is actually being given?" The answer may well be different from one school system—indeed, from one school—to the next.

Teacher Consultants or Facilitators

Just about everybody agrees that simply placing a child with special needs into a regular classroom, without making additional and necessary resources available to the classroom teacher, is a recipe for failure. A *support facilitator* can help broaden regular education curriculum by

- Encouraging and organizing support networks for the child with special needs
- Serving as a resource locator for the regular classroom teacher
- Playing the role of *team teacher*.

The curriculum in mainstream education requires expansion to meet the needs of all students. Curriculum areas, such as daily life and community living skills, competitive and supportive employment, sign language, braille, speech reading, and other similar areas, need to become an inherent part of regular education. (Stainback & Stainback, 1988, p. 76)

Statements like that, as well as the following, may be making regular educators somewhat nervous about the implications of inclusion, given the diverse responsibilities they already have:

Because a student cannot read, multiply, or write does not necessarily preclude the functionality of, and importance of, him or her taking core regular education high school courses such as science, history, and literature. (Stainback & Stainback, 1988, p. 81)

Few high school teachers would willingly take into their science or history classes students who could not read or write, even if doing so were socially beneficial for those students.

The acceptance of any new child into a classroom group is rarely an easy process. When various characteristics make a child discernibly different from the other children, as a child's special needs would, the task requires special attention. Therefore, the mainstream placement of children like Bob or Carol needs careful planning.

A device that seems to encourage children to develop an accepting attitude toward a child with special needs is the use of "Circles." Figure 5.4 shows a sample dialogue that might take place as a facilitator tries to prepare the way for May, the new child. Read the dialogue carefully. You will see that the facilitator (1) acknowledges May's differences; (2) accepts the child; and (3) allows the students time to express their own ideas of how to facilitate the acceptance.

Nor is the task done when the initial acceptance has been completed. May is not an easy person to get along with, and the children in the classroom may react negatively to her; those negative feelings must then be counteracted. The use of team learning strategies such as cooperative learning can foster feelings of acceptance and belonging (Johnson & Johnson, 1986).

There is also the task of helping May adopt more constructive coping skills. It is the rare classroom teacher who has the training or the time to devote to such objectives. This calls for a team of professionals working together.

How to Use the Resource Room

A resource room provides children with mild or moderate retardation an opportunity to work with special education teachers and focus on particular

Figure 5.4
Circles of Friends:
A Support Network

Consultant (C): Hi. I've come to talk to you about May, who is coming to your class next week. You met her last week when she visited with her mother. For years, May has gone to a segregated school or been in a self-contained life skills class. What does that mean?

Students (S): Places for retarded people.
Schools for kids who are really bad.
Like the one near my house where all the wheelchairs go.

C: Well, May is coming here and I'll tell you a secret. Everyone is really scared. Her mother and father are scared, Mr. Gorman [teacher] is scared. Mr. Cullen [principal] is scared. I'm scared. Why do you think all of us are so scared?

S: You all think we'll be mean to her.
You think we'll tease her and be mean to her.
You think she'll be left out.

C: There are some things we don't want you to do when she arrives. What do you think these are?

S: Don't treat her like a baby.
Don't pity her.
Don't ignore her.
Don't feel sorry for her.

C: Why are we doing this? Why is May coming to this class?

S: Why not? She's our age, she should be here.
How would you feel if you were 12 and never were with kids your own age?
It's dumb for her not to be here.
She needs friends.
She needs a boy friend.

C: What do you think we want you to do?

S: Treat her like one of us.
Make her feel welcome.
Help her make friends.
Help her with her work.
Call her and invite her to our parties.

C: I want to switch gears for a few minutes and ask you to all do an exercise with me called "circle of friends." I do this very same thing with teachers and parents and I think you are all grown up enough to handle it.

(The consultant handed out a sheet with four concentric circles on it. After the first circle, each circle was a little larger and farther away from the center of the page, where a stick person was drawn.)

There are four circles. On each circle, you are to list people you know. I want you to think about whom you would put in your first circle. These are the people closest to you, the people you really love. You can do this privately or in pairs, and you can tell us or keep it private.

Source: From S. Stainback, W. Stainback, and M. Forest. (1989). *Educating All Students in the Mainstream of Regular Education*, (pp. 47–48). Baltimore: Paul H. Brookes. Reprinted by permission.

learning problems that are interfering with their performance in the regular classroom. These children leave the classroom for about an hour a day to take part in special lessons. The number of children in the resource room at any one time is usually much less than the number in the regular classroom, giving the resource room teacher an opportunity to work individually or in small groups with children who have retardation. In some schools, resource room programs combine other children with mild handicaps who are at a comparable developmental level with the children with mild retardation, allowing the teacher to plan for them in small groups. Although the resource room has come under increasing criticism, it still is a highly popular model for delivering special educational services.

Special Classes

The greater the degree of disability, the more likely a child is to need a special learning environment to learn distinctively different material. In the special class, a trained teacher provides a distinctive curriculum for a small group of children, typically no more than fifteen. The curriculum may include exercises in personal grooming, safety, preprimary reading skills, or any subject not appropriate for the normally developing child in the regular classroom but highly appropriate for a child like Carol, whose cognitive development is half or less of what is normal for her age. The argument against the special class is that such a setting does not allow for social interaction with general education students.

ADAPTING CURRICULUM

What Are the Goals?

There has been much discussion about the most desirable curriculum for children with mental retardation. Should the content be different from that given to the average child? If so, where in the educational sequence should the branching take place? In secondary school? In middle school? Or should the curriculum be different right from the beginning? The important questions to be answered in the development of curricula for students with mental retardation are, "What are our goals? What are our immediate objectives to reach that goal?"

For students who have moderate or severe retardation, reasonable goals are to:

- Learn to read at least to the "survival words" level (*stop, poison, restroom,* and so on)
- Do basic arithmetic and understand the various denominations of money
- Learn social skills, such as the ability to work cooperatively with others
- Have some leisure-time skills
- Communicate with persons such as storekeepers and community helpers
- Learn some work skills to be partially or fully self-supporting in adulthood, if possible

The more difficult curriculum decision involves children with mild mental retardation, who can be expected to reach a medium-to-high elementary school level of skills and knowledge. This decision is particularly difficult if the child is mainstreamed. The curriculum will be the mainstream curriculum—which may or may

Children with mild mental retardation can be included in regular activities. *(© Elaine Rebman/Photo Researchers)*

not meet the needs of the child, except for the social contacts the student will be having in the regular program. Patton (1986) suggested that it is possible to infuse relevant career education topics into regularly assigned lessons. Though possible, such a process would require more knowledge and teamwork between special education and regular education than are often present.

At what point does the student with mild mental retardation branch off into a separate secondary school program that is designed to provide work skills rather than help the student reach the next level of education? Even inclusion advocates do not expect students with mild or moderate retardation to take advanced high school physics or calculus. It is in the secondary program where attention is traditionally paid to community adjustment and work skills.

Oddly, the recent national emphasis on educational excellence may be a special problem for marginal students such as Bob. They may face academic difficulties when confronted with policies that do not tolerate academic mediocrity and insist on a minimal competence level in order to continue in middle school or secondary school programs.

Educational Reform and Students with MR/DD

One of the distinctive characteristics of the educational reform movement is its commitment to high standards and accountability. "High standards" generally refers to high conceptual learning in traditional subjects such as language arts and mathematics. This is surely not good news for students with mental retardation or developmental disabilities who do not do well on high-level conceptual material and whose secondary program may even be focused on learning community living. Yet the reform movement increasingly insists on including children with disabilities in these districtwide assessments following those principles:

- All students should have access to challenging standards.

- Policymakers and educators should be held publicly accountable for every student's performance. (McDonnell, McLaughlin, & Morrison, 1997)

As yet, little is know about the performance of children with disabilities on accountability measures, because many of these students, particularly students with mental retardation or developmental disabilities, have been exempted from the exams by local school systems (Vanderwood, McGrew, & Ysseldyke, 1998). But there is increasing call for testing *all* students in a school system, so we have another issue emerging as to what to do with students who do not perform well on the tests, even if their educational program departs somewhat from the traditional.

Differential Instruction

In most programs for children with mild and moderate retardation—particularly for those who are grouped with other students of limited abilities or performance—differential instruction takes place in four major areas:

- *Readiness and academic skills.* With preschoolers and elementary school children, basic reading and arithmetic skills are stressed. Later, these skills are applied to practical work and community settings.

- *Communication and language development.* The student gets practice in using language to communicate needs and ideas. Specific efforts are directed toward improving memory skills and problem-solving skills at the level of the student's ability.

- *Socialization.* Specific instruction is provided in self-care and family living skills, beginning at the preschool level with sharing and manners, then gradually developing in secondary school into subjects like grooming, dancing, sex education, and avoiding drug abuse.

- *Prevocations and work-study skills.* The basis for vocational adjustment through good work habits (promptness, following through on instruction, working cooperatively on group projects) is established. At the secondary level, this curriculum can focus on career education and include part-time job placement and field trips to possible job sites.

We will examine each area separately. Because of current awareness of the value of early intervention, many of these skills are being included in the school curriculum at various levels.

Basic Academic Skills

To develop a curriculum for primary-grade children with mental retardation, we use **task analysis**—breaking down a complex task into simple subtasks that are within the child's abilities. Reading, for example, combines auditory perception (auditory discrimination and sound blending) and visual perception (matching letters and letter-word recognition) (Wolery & Brookfield-Norman, 1988). By helping the child master these basic skills, we are preparing the child to read.

In much the same way, we prepare the child to think about numbers in sets and to match numbers and objects by first teaching the child how to count. And we prepare the child to write by focusing on simple visual-motor activities (imitating a specific stroke, then tracing letters). The process offers dual benefits. First, the subtasks are the source from which academic skills will develop. Second, mastery of the subtasks gives the child with retardation an opportunity to succeed and gain self-confidence.

When we teach reading to Carol and other children with moderate retardation, we focus on functional reading (Snell, 1987). Although these individuals are unlikely to ever read for comprehension or recreation, they need to be able to:

- Identify key words in simple recipes
- Develop a protective vocabulary (*walk, don't walk, stop, men, women, in, out*)
- Recognize the skull and crossbones that denotes poisonous substances.

Traditionally, we use the whole-word method to teach students with mental retardation. It helps them recognize words in context. Students may be asked to "read" television schedules or directions on food boxes or to travel around their community looking for key words.

Children such as Carol, with moderate retardation, are not often taught the formal arithmetic usually presented in the primary grades. They can learn quantitative concepts (*more* and *less, big* and *little*) and the elementary vocabulary of quantitative thinking. They can be taught to count to 10 and to identify quantities in small groupings. As they grow older, these children can learn to write numbers from 1 to 10 and understand time concepts, especially the sequence of activities during the day, telling time, and an elemental understanding of the calendar. They often show surprising mastery of television schedules. Some can recognize and remember telephone numbers, their own ages, and simple money concepts. In general, the arithmetic they are taught, like the reading, is related to everyday living.

Language and Communication

There is a substantial effort in elementary schools to help children with moderate retardation use language as a tool for communication. Students may be asked to describe a simple object such as a table (it is round; it is hard; you put things on it; it is brown). And they may learn to communicate feelings of happiness, anger, and sadness by using language.

The functional use of language is a critical goal for children with mental retardation.

Language exercises for children with moderate retardation aim to foster the development of speech and the understanding and use of verbal concepts. Communication skills such as the ability to listen to stories, discuss pictures, and tell about recent experiences are stressed. Two important areas of study are the home and the community. Children learn about holidays, transportation, the months of the year and days of the week, and contributions to home life. Classes make use of dramatization, acting out a story or a song, playing make-believe, engaging in shadow play, and using gestures with songs, stories, and rhymes.

For the youngsters with moderate retardation, there may be an expectation of mastery of reading and arithmetic to the second- or third-grade level. That means special attention should be paid to their learning key words that operate in our society to start or stop actions. Such "survival words" (and phrases) are listed in Table 5.5. Direct instruction in these words can help the child with moderate retardation exhibit proper behavior in the community even without extrinsic mastery of more complex reading skills.

	TABLE 5.5	**A Functional Reading Vocabulary**	
Go	Up	Dynamite	School
Slow down	Down	Explosives	School bus
Stop	Men	Fire	No trespassing
Off	Women	Fire escape	Private property
On	Exit	Poison	Men working
Cold	Entrance	Wet paint	Yield
Hot	Danger	Police	Railroad crossing
In	Be careful	Keep off	Boys
Out	Caution	Watch for children	Girls

Source: C. Drew, M. Hardiman, and D. Logan (1996), *Mental Retardation: A Life Cycle Approach, 6/e.* © 1996. Reprinted by permission of Prentice-Hall, Inc. Upper Saddle River, NJ.

Socialization

Social skills are a critical component of the primary school curriculum for children who are mentally retarded, but instruction at this level should be informal. Children can learn to take turns, share, and work cooperatively as part of their daily activities. The lunch table is an excellent location for teaching social skills. Here, youngsters learn table manners as well as how to pass and share food, help others (pouring juice, for example), and wait their turn. The lunch table is also a good place to review the morning's activities and talk about what is planned for the afternoon or the next day. Although the teaching is informal, it is both effective and important to the child's social development.

Children with retardation have difficulty transferring or applying ideas from one setting to another. Thus, we teach needed social skills directly. We do not expect the children to automatically understand these skills and apply them from experience.

Part of the process of growing up is gradually mastering social skills to establish effective communication and relationships with others. We rarely think about these skills because they emerge through adult and peer modeling without our being conscious of them. If we are asked how we meet strangers, break unpleasant news, communicate with someone we haven't seen for a long time, or tell someone that he is intruding on our space and time, it is likely that we will have to think for a while before we can recall the coping strategies that we use without conscious effort. These skills are the lubrication that allows each of us to move smoothly through our daily contacts and tasks. Someone who is markedly deficient or awkward in such skills stands out in a crowd. Many children with mental retardation lack these social skills and need direct instruction in them if they are to establish a useful personal and community adjustment.

Bob, for example, usually got too close to the person he was speaking to. He made the other person uncomfortable but was not aware of this reaction. Through role-playing a number of social situations with Bob and others, the teacher was able to establish that each person has a personal space that is not to be invaded without permission (for example, to kiss an aunt good-bye). Such social rules may seem trivial, but their importance is magnified substantially when they are violated.

It is important that the sense of privacy is established and understood when the child begins to cope with sexual relationships. Parents and other adults worry about the susceptibility of young people with mental retardation to sexual abuse or unwanted sexual contact merely because they lack the skills to fend off others in sexual encounters. The closer the student is brought to the mainstream, the more likely he or she is to have a variety of contacts with members of the opposite sex. Therefore, some type of counseling and role-playing of relationships or situations with the opposite sex are often part of the curriculum for students with mild or moderate retardation.

The **social learning approach** (Bandura, 1989) aims to foster critical thinking and independent action by those with mild retardation. Lesson experiences focus on psychological needs (for self-respect, mastery), physical needs (for sensory stimulation), and physical maintenance and social aspects (for independence, mobility). For example, in the middle school, lesson experiences teaching the importance of economic security could include the following objectives: (1) choosing a job commensurate with skills and interests, (2) locating and acquiring a satisfactory job, (3) maintaining a job, and (4) effectively managing the financial resources earned from a job.

An important issue related to full-inclusion schools is the social status of children with disabilities. In a research project conducted in a large western community, when researchers asked students whom they liked best and whom they liked least in the class, children with disabilities received significantly more negative choices and significantly fewer "liked" choices than children without disabilities in the comparison group (Sale & Carey, 1995). When interpreting those results, we should take care, because they are from a single school system; they are consistent, however, with previous findings of a relative lack of acceptance of exceptional children. The results of that study remind us that the task of gaining social acceptance for children with disabilities in the inclusive class is not easy and requires special planning.

The Socialization Agenda of Inclusion. One of the distinguishing features of inclusion is the emphasis on socialization of the child with disabilities within the inclusive setting. This is the primary objective of the schools, from the standpoint of inclusion advocates, and in their view is more important than academic achievement.

> Children need to go to school in their own neighborhood, to attend classes with typical children their own age, and to be involved with kids in activities outside of school. Adults should not interfere but at the same time should understand that some children may need help in being introduced to others, in sharing their gifts with them and in making personal connects (Strully & Strully, 1997, p. 153).

To meet this socialization goal, those educators endorsing inclusion have devised a series of activities that enhance social contact and learning. In *peer-buddy systems,* a classmate may help a classmate with disabilities negotiate the school day; *peer support networks* help students become part of a caring community; and in *circles of friends,* an adult facilitator helps potential peer buddies sensitize peers to the friendship needs of students with disabilities (Villa & Thousand, 1997).

One of the strategies designed to enhance socialization is the creation of a MAP (for *making an action plan*). This may seem similar to an IEP, but is different in that it is constructed by those students and adults directly involved in the person's life instead of by a team of professionals constructing an IEP. The key question in the design of a MAP is, "What do the child and the family want?" Goals are established, along with the means to reach them.

A person identified as an *integration facilitator* may have the skills necessary to help relevant individuals create a MAP for Bob or Carol. Emphasis is placed on the individual strengths of the children and what actions need to be taken to allow them to achieve their dreams. The focus is not on academic learning but on the social skills that will serve the children in adult life (Pierpoint, Forest, & O'Brien, 1997). Supporters of these activities point out that students without disabilities have some important learning to do to realize the diversity of the general population and the importance of being a part of a caring community.

Prevocations and Work-Study Skills

When students with mental retardation reach middle school, their special education programs often begin to emphasize work skills.

As the child with mild retardation reaches middle school or junior high school, many special education programs focus on the development of work skills. The skills may be related to a specific occupation (assembling transistor radios) or to general work skills (cooperation, punctuality, persistence).

For the preadolescent child, lessons often take the form of prevocational experience, focusing on the knowledge and skills that are the basis for vocational competence. For example,

- Given a road map, the student can demonstrate the route from one point to another.
- Given an assigned work task involving two or more students, the participants work together until the task is completed.
- Given a newspaper, the student demonstrates the ability to find specific information when requested to do so (Kolstoe, 1976).

Such specific, observable behaviors often are the crux of the individualized education programs that must be completed for all children with mental retardation.

Table 5.6 presents important knowledge and skills to be mastered in five areas—consumer economics, occupational knowledge, health, community resources, and government and law. Listed in the table are examples of the concrete and practical knowledge that persons with mental retardation need, such as how to fill out forms, read a city or town map, and get a driver's license. This approach is preferable to teaching generalizations or abstract principles that the child then has to apply to specific situations—a skill in which children with retardation are not proficient. The problem for the teacher comes when other students in the classroom are learning different materials more appropriate for their age level. It takes a good deal of joint planning with the classroom teacher or the middle school teaching team to integrate functional competencies with the standard educational program.

Vocational training focuses on dimensions beyond the job itself: banking and using money, grooming, caring for a car and obtaining insurance, interviewing for

TABLE 5.6	Model of Junior High School Functional Competency: Examples of Tasks				
	Consumer Economics	**Occupational Knowledge**	**Health**	**Community Resources**	**Government and Law**
Reading	Read an ad for a sale locating name, location, and phone number of store and price of item	Read a job description	Locate poison control numbers in telephone book	Use telephone book to locate recreational program in community	Locate and read lists of members of state government and of U.S. Congress
Writing	Fill out a magazine order form completely	Practice writing abbreviations for words.	Write a menu for a balanced diet	Write a letter to television station about a canceled program	Fill out voter registration card
Speaking, writing, viewing	Discuss saving versus spending money	Discuss reasons why we work	Listen to positive and negative feedback on personal appearance	Call library to find out if it has a certain book	Discuss why we need to vote
Problem solving	Given $10 for the evening, choose an activity, e.g., movies, bowling, or pizza	Decide on job environment: inside, outside, desk, travel, etc.	Role-play appropriate behavior for various places (movies, church, restaurant)	Locate the skating rink on a city map and decide the best way to get there	Decide what items have state or local tax
Interpersonal relations	Ask a salesperson for help in purchasing jeans	List questions to ask in job interview	Discuss honesty, trust, and promise; define each	Call skating rink to inquire about hours	Call to find out what precinct you live in
Computation	Compute the sales tax on a pair of jeans	Compute net income	Calculate and compare the prices of hair-grooming products	Calculate bus fare to and from the teen center	Calculate the cost of getting a driver's license (fee, gas)

Source: G. Robinson, J. Patton, E. Polloway, and L. Sargent (1989). *Best Practices in Mild Mental Disabilities*, Reston, VA: Council for Exceptional Children. Used by permission.

jobs, and using leisure time. Adjustment to the work world involves adapting to the demands of life as well as to a specific job.

Some programs try to build a set of vocational skills progressively over time, involving a variety of social agencies in the educational activities. Fundamental activities and skills are taught in a special class setting. Then specific areas of prevocational and vocational training, including on-the-job training, are covered in the adolescent years. Finally, with the help of vocational rehabilitation, attempts are made to provide a useful work experience in either a sheltered workshop facility or a competitive employment setting. This plan has the merit of establishing developmental tasks and long-range goals that those who are moderately retarded can approach step by step.

The recent movement toward the inclusion in regular classes of children who have mild retardation has created a difficult conflict. As long as children with retardation are in regular classrooms, they are receiving the regular curriculum or some variation of it. But the secondary school curriculum of content subjects (English, history, science) may not be the most appropriate for them. These students could profit more from a program that emphasizes the practical and vocational skills needed for independent living.

ADAPTING TEACHING STRATEGIES

Special education draws heavily on learning theory to help children achieve a level of constructive behavior. Many of the learning principles we use to help children with retardation associate ideas or remember events have been used intuitively in classrooms and families for years. One popular approach, Premack's principle (Premack, 1959), is to attach a wanted but low-probability behavior to a high-probability behavior, which then becomes a positive reinforcer. Practically, the teacher says, "If you clean up your workplace on time, you can do a puzzle or listen to records." (Premack's principle has been called "Grandma's law": "First you eat your vegetables, then you get dessert.")

The special learning problems that children with mental retardation have required special teaching strategies. Two of these strategies are scaffolding and reciprocal teaching. In **scaffolding**, the teacher models the expected behavior and then guides the student through the early stages of understanding. As the student's understanding increases, the teacher gradually withdraws aid (hence the name "scaffolding"). The goal is to have the student internalize the knowledge and operate independently. The goal is unlikely to be reached, however, without the teacher's help and assistance, which is gradually withdrawn (Brown & Palinscar, 1989). For example, in teaching division, the teacher does some problems and talks about the steps she or he is taking. When the student first attempts the problem, the teacher is at hand to prompt but then gradually moves away to allow the student to do the problems on his or her own.

In **reciprocal teaching**, small groups of students and teachers take turns leading a discussion on a particular topic. This exercise features four activities: questioning, clarifying, summarizing, and predicting. In this strategy (as in scaffolding), the teacher models how to carry out the activities successfully. The students then imitate the teaching style while the teacher plays the role of the student. In this way, students become active players in a role they find enjoyable.

Behavior Modification

Behavior modification is a term describing techniques designed to reduce or eliminate obnoxious or nonadaptive behaviors and to increase the use of socially constructive behaviors. It is based on principles developed by B. F. Skinner (1953), who found that the systematic application of **positive reinforcement** after a behavior tends to increase the likelihood of that behavior occurring in the next similar situation. **Negative reinforcement** (the application of a negative stimulus immediately after a behavior) causes unwanted behaviors to decrease. The absence of reinforcement, either positive or negative, causes a behavior to disappear or be extinguished. The quickest way to eliminate an unwanted behavior, then, is to ignore it while responding positively to a more acceptable behavior.

The educational strategy here is to arrange the environment so that the particular behavior the teacher wants the child to repeat will occur. When the behavior does occur, it receives a positive reward (food, praise, a token, or some other symbol of recognition). If possible, the teacher does not respond to the unwanted behavior.

Gresham (1981) noted a variety of techniques that use these principles:

1. *Differential reinforcement.* **Differential reinforcement** follows the basic behavior modification procedures by rewarding behaviors that are appropriate and ignoring the target behavior (for example, aggressive behavior). In a variation of this approach, the teacher provides rewards if the student can increase the time between displays of unacceptable behavior. If the child is acting out a great deal, the teacher rewards a ten-minute period of acceptable behavior if it reflects an increase in the elapsed time between periods of unacceptable behavior.

2. *Time-out.* **Time-out** is the physical removal of a child from a situation for a period of time, usually immediately after an unwanted response. A child who has shown unacceptable aggressive behavior in the classroom may be asked to leave the classroom or may be moved to a section of the classroom in which he or she is left alone with some reading or work materials, essentially isolated from the group for a period of time. The child is asked to return when he or she feels in control of the unacceptable behavior. This procedure has proved effective in decreasing disruptive, aggressive, and inappropriate social behaviors.

3. *Contingent social reinforcement.* Some teachers who work with young handicapped children use **contingent social reinforcement**, or a token system, to teach appropriate social behavior. Tokens are handed out in response to the appropriate use of certain social skills (greeting another child, borrowing a toy in an acceptable manner). If a child displays unacceptable behavior, tokens may be taken away. Children save tokens and cash them in for toys or time to do a puzzle or play a game. This kind of extrinsic reward program appears to be effective in controlling social behavior within special groups of children and, to some extent, within the context of a mainstreamed class.

The use of behavior modification techniques with exceptional children has helped increase academic response rates and attendance, achievement, and grades and has encouraged verbal interchange and the following of instructions (Sabatino, Miller, & Schmidt, 1981). Despite these positive results, however, the procedures are controversial because they accomplish the goal without the cooperation of the child and thus strike some observers as being overly manipulative.

Figure 5.5

Tanisha's Self-Instruction Training Sequence

CASE STUDY: Tanisha (CA = 7–3, IQ = 58)

Self-Instruction Training Sequence

Student *Tanisha*   Date *December 3, 1992*

Short-Term Objective *During reading period, Tanisha will ask permission before*

leaving her seat without exception on 4 out of 5 days.

Training Sequence

1. *Cognitive Modeling.* The trainer sits in a student seat in the classroom and raises her hand, saying aloud, "Each time I want to leave my seat, I must raise my hand and ask the teacher for permission." Then the trainer says to the teacher, "May I go to the water fountain?"

2. *Overt External Guidance.* The trainer instructs and verbally prompts Tanisha to raise her hand and ask the teacher for permission to go to the water fountain.

3. *Overt Self-Guidance.* Tanisha raises her hand, saying to herself aloud, "Each time I want to leave my seat, I must raise my hand and ask my teacher for permission." Then Tanisha says to the teacher, "May I go to the water fountain?"

4. *Faded, Overt Self-Guidance.* Tanisha raises her hand, whispering to herself, "Each time I want to leave my seat, I must raise my hand and ask my teacher for permission." Then Tanisha says to the teacher, "May I go to the water fountain?"

5. *Covert Self-Instruction.* Tanisha raises her hand, and says to the teacher, "May I go to the water fountain?" This time, she uses private, nonvocal speech to remind herself that she must raise her hand and ask permission to leave her seat.

Source: From *Mental Retardation: Foundations for Educational Programming* by L. Hickson, L. Blackman, & E. Reis. Copyright © 1995 by Allyn & Bacon. Adapted by permission.

Fading and Self-Instruction

Earlier in this chapter, we presented the IEP goals and objectives for Tanisha. To achieve those objectives, though, it often would be necessary to adopt special instructional strategies to adjust to Tanisha's limited ability to generalize or to maintain desired behaviors even after they have appeared.

Figure 5.5 is a sequence of self-instruction training designed to aid Tanisha's ability to reach the objective that "Tanisha will ask permission before leaving her seat without exception on 4 out of 5 days." The trainer or aide first models the desired behavior by raising her hand and asking the teacher permission to go to the water fountain, then encourages Tanisha to do the same. Tanisha is taught to say aloud to herself, "Each time I want to leave my seat, I must raise my hand and ask my teacher for permission," then to whisper it to herself, then finally to use private, nonvocal speech to remind herself to ask permission. The process of going from speaking aloud to whispering to nonvocal speech is known as *fading.*

This long and involved sequence may strike some as a complicated series of events for the "simple" task of getting a student to raise her hand before leaving her seat, particularly since most students learn this behavior automatically. We have learned through sad experience, however, that unless this systematic and sequential system is followed, children with mental retardation, like Tanisha, may not learn the social and academic skills necessary to their adaptation to the classroom and the community. It also should be clear that a teacher, without support persons and with the host of other duties he or she has in the classroom, would find it difficult to carry out this sequence for a single child.

Intrinsic Motivation

Some maintain that students who are intrinsically motivated work harder and longer on tasks than do students who are extrinsically motivated.

It is generally accepted that children with mental retardation seem to be motivated more by **extrinsic motivation** (If you are good, I will buy you an ice cream cone) than by **intrinsic motivation** (If you do your homework, you will feel much better about yourself). This finding is translated into educational strategies through the use of various extrinsic rewards—such as positive social reinforcement by means of praise, gold stars, or tokens to be cashed in for toys—to motivate the student to greater effort. Some, however, maintain that an intrinsic motivational approach is helpful to children with special needs (Switzky & Schultz, 1988). They maintain that children with intrinsic motivation work harder and longer on tasks than do those with extrinsic motivation and that therefore it is important to help instill an attitude of intrinsic motivation in youngsters. The problem with extrinsic motivation, they point out, is that someone will not always be present and ready to give immediate and tangible rewards for proper behavior. Then what will extrinsically motivated youngsters do?

A number of educators have devised approaches to stimulate intrinsic learning (Feuerstein, Rand, & Hoffman, 1986; Haywood, Brooks, & Burns, 1986). These approaches require extensive modeling of task-intrinsic behavior by the teacher and positive motivation. They attempt to foster in students an active learning style and to correct problem-solving deficits by having the teacher use a mediational teaching style and teach cognitive processes and strategies even if they are not among the students' strong points at the outset.

Classroom teachers cannot do everything. They often need the help of support personnel, special educators, counselors, and school psychologists. Most schools now recognize that special programs for children with retardation are the responsibility of a team that includes classroom teachers, special education teachers, and other professional personnel working together to help these children learn and adapt.

Cooperative Learning

Interestingly, emphasis has switched from a focus on a one-on-one type of instruction for the individual student with special needs, as represented in the policies for an IEP, to the importance of student participation in *cooperative learning* or *team-assisted individualization*. With the inclusion of many children with special needs in regular classrooms has come the need to develop strategies that will help the teacher integrate students with disabilities with the other students. Cooperative learning is one of these strategies. There are many versions of it (Johnson & Johnson, 1992; Kagan, 1994; Slavin, 1993), but all have some characteristics in common.

In **cooperative learning,** the teacher gives a task to a small group of students (typically four to six), who are expected to complete the task by working cooperatively with one another. The teacher may assign different responsibilities to different members of the group or ask each child to play a specific role (such as recorder, reporter, searcher, or praiser). Although group members are expected to work cooperatively, most advocates of cooperative learning insist that the students be evaluated individually. The child with disabilities may have the same overall objective as other students but be operating with a lower level of task expectations, a reduced workload, or partial participation. As long as the child feels a part of the enterprise, some good social interactions can occur.

Group instruction may actually be more advantageous than one-on-one instruction because of the economy of teacher effort, students learning how to interact with peers, and students learning from peers. Small-group instruction is the mode for the regular classroom if the students are to be mainstreamed (Collins, Gast, Ault, & Wolery, 1991).

Skills Mastery

One of the most important questions facing the teachers of children with mental retardation and developmental disabilities is how to motivate these children to learn. There are a lot of reasons for them not to be motivated in school. Bob, for example, comes from a home in which there is little interest in school learning. He is 10 years old and has had a few years' experience in school. But those years have not been full of positive experiences. Bob has known a lot of failure, and failure is a distinct turnoff for most children and adults.

People who believe they are likely to fail can develop a condition known as *learned helplessness.* They think, "I can't do anything about my situation, and I know things are going to turn out badly" (Dweck & Leggett, 1988). Students who experience this feeling tend to avoid situations in which they think they probably will fail. They avoid the very learning situations that they need to experience if they are going to improve their situation. Such individuals need a strong dose of *self-efficacy* (Bandura, 1989), the belief that they are competent at some tasks. But if failure is their constant diet, how can they develop feelings of competence? Finding an answer to that question is the basic challenge facing the educator who will work with Bob.

Carol, however, faces a different situation. Many special educators believe that their students' fundamental goal is not the mastery of knowledge or skills but the mastery of adaptive behaviors such as social skills, communication skills, and work skills. After all, they ask, who cares very much if Carol reaches third-grade or fourth-grade mastery of academic skills? What is important is that Carol develop adaptive skills that will serve her well in adulthood and in the world of work. Thus, it is important for Carol to participate in cooperative learning exercises, not necessarily to learn what the other students learn, but to experience positive social interaction and learn how to work constructively with others. Many special educators are less interested in the middle school academic curriculum and more interested in how they can help students like Carol become effective workers.

A large part of the positive experience of school stems from success in learning how to learn and learning how to work constructively with others. Such skills, if they become habits, serve the individual well beyond the school years. So the mastery of social skills becomes a major objective of programs for exceptional children. It is unwise to assume that students with mental retardation absorb these skills any more readily than they do academic skills. It is much more likely that teachers need to design activities to help students achieve social skills and replace disruptive behavior such as aggression, excessive talking, and out-of-seat behavior with prosocial skills.

One goal of teachers is to help students develop a sense of competence. Self-confidence comes in part from being able to do well the work that is expected of you. The teacher can build students' self-confidence by presenting lessons that are challenging but within the range of their ability to perform.

Teachers also need a variety of skills that will help them nurture positive, prosocial skills and diminish negative patterns of behavior that a student may be showing.

TECHNOLOGY

Instructional technology in the classroom has many applications for students with mental retardation, as well as for other students. Table 5.7 lists some instructional uses of computers. Serna and Patton (1989) indicated that the computer can be used for *drill and practice*—in reading and arithmetic particularly—*tutorials, simulations,* and *problem solving.* A disadvantage of using computers is that the teacher cannot merely point to the computer and say, "Bob, go and do your exercises." Students with mental retardation need consistent monitoring, and some need considerable instruction in the use of the computer and in the use of some of the simulation and problem-solving programs.

Parette (1991) pointed out that state-of-the-art *hypermedia*—an information storage and usage design that enables text, graphics, animation, and sound to be combined to suit individual needs—can be adapted for use with children with mental retardation. Such approaches may help students who otherwise would have problems linking ideas and thoughts.

This increasingly available technology can be a valuable adjunct to the well-prepared teacher, particularly when the student becomes stuck in the mastery of a particular skill or set of information. It has the additional social value to students with retardation of signaling their ability to use sophisticated equipment, just as the other students do (Gardner & Bates, 1991).

Can Special Education Make a Difference?

Researchers have made numerous efforts to assess in students with mental retardation the nature and level of the change that accompanies changes in their learning environment, curriculum, or skills mastery. Does the type of learning environment make a difference in the academic achievement, adaptive behavior, or cognitive development of children with mild and moderate retardation? Research findings suggest that changes in the learning environment alone do not make a striking difference. A large number of studies have tested the effectiveness of mainstreaming children with mental retardation (Gottlieb, Alter, & Gottlieb, 1991), but the information derived from such studies is not often educationally significant. Few of the studies discuss the nature of the program the students received, and that surely is just as important as, if not more important than, "where" the student has been placed.

The diversity of programs included under the "mainstreaming" umbrella is probably another reason for the disparity of results obtained. Studies rarely found major differences in academic achievement between students in mainstreamed versus those in special education programs. In addition, there was often poor social acceptance of special education students in the mainstream. We do not know, however, whether there was careful preparation for the entry of children with mental retardation into the classrooms or whether they were assigned to the classes without the preparation that mainstreaming and inclusion advocates insist is necessary.

Although most of the intervention programs that have been assessed have focused on children with mild mental retardation, some assessments have attempted to test the impact of programs for children with moderate mental retardation as well. In one such program, eleven centers in Washington State were devoted to the education of children with Down syndrome and other developmental delays (Delwein, Fewell, & Pruess, 1985). The eleven centers emphasized enhancing five skill areas: gross motor, fine motor, cognitive, communicative, and social/self-help. The Developmental Sequence Performance Inventory (DSPI), a developmental checklist for children from birth to age 8, was used to test the effectiveness of the program. The children with Down syndrome exceeded developmental expectations in cognitive and communication areas and showed modest progress in the gross and fine motor areas. Only in the social/self-help areas were no substantive developmental gains noted.

It seems that teachers can accelerate developmental trends by giving specific instruction to children with moderate handicaps. This point is echoed by Castro (1987), who reviewed seventy-four intervention studies for all levels of disabling conditions and found evidence supporting the usefulness of special intervention programs for a wide variety of students.

Intervention programs result in moderate improvement in the development of adaptive behaviors.

TRANSITION

From School to Work

In the not-too-distant past, little or no information was available about the progress of students with mental retardation after they left school. Today, a growing number of studies indicate how these students are doing in adult life. The news is mixed.

A major study looking at 8,000 youths with disabilities, the National Longitudinal Transitional Study of Special Education Students (Blackorby & Wagner, 1996), was begun in 1987. Researchers used a careful sampling design to ensure that their sample was nationally representative and generalizable to the population as a whole as well as to students in eleven disabilities categories. Large samples of youngsters with disabilities from 300 public school districts and from 25 state-operated schools for children who are deaf or blind were surveyed and interviewed. In addition, a subsample of more than 800 parents of youth who had been out of secondary school between two and four years was interviewed.

What happened to youths identified as having mental retardation? Let's look first at performance in secondary school. Half of the students with mental retardation graduated from high school; the rest either dropped out or aged out of school. The reasons for dropping out of school appeared to be related to behavior rather than to

| TABLE 5.7 | Computer Applications for Students with Mental Retardation |

Type of Use	Description	Features	Cautions
Drill and practice	Reinforces previously learned information and provides student with practice	Many students need extra practice; best used as adjunct to ongoing instruction	Does not teach new concepts; best to have students work independently
Tutorial	Presents new or previously presented material and then assesses the student's understanding of the information	Additional instruction for those who need more time to grasp concepts	Not the most effective way of presenting new information to special learners
Simulation	Allows students to experience vicariously real-life events not easily shown in a traditional setting	Powerful; can provide more concrete examples of abstract concepts	Possible problems if students do not possess prerequisite knowledge, skills, or both; students may need help in generalizing computer-displayed events to real world
Problem solving	Use of the computer to solve real-life problems; can include programming	Helps students understand problems and the processes needed to solve them	May be too difficult; often requires teacher assistance and monitoring

Source: Adapted from L. Serna and J. Patton (1980), *Science*, in G. Robinson, J. Patton, E. Polloway, and L. Sargent (Eds.), *Best Practices in Mild Mental Retardation* (Vol. 5). Reston, VA: Council for Exceptional Children, pp. 197–199. Used by permission.

academic performance. Twenty-eight percent of the students with disabilities who dropped out were identified as individuals having serious discipline problems.

What about social relationships? About 1 out of every 4 individuals with mental retardation was identified as a social isolate in school. But the percentage of students with mental retardation who regularly saw friends was no lower than the percentage among those who were visually impaired, speech impaired, or learning disabled. Children with mental retardation were less likely than other students with disabilities to be members of organized groups such as the Boy Scouts, religious youth groups, or sports teams. Only about 1 out of every 3 of the students with mental retardation was identified as belonging to, or having some regular membership in, a group.

What about the arrest rate of youth with disabilities? Children with mental retardation ranked fourth in the eleven categories of youth with disabilities who were arrested while they were in secondary school, and they ranked fifth in the "out of school" arrest category. Roughly 1 out of every 10 of the school youth with mental retardation had an arrest record. A factor significant to the arrest record was gender: Males were arrested four times more often than females.

What about responsibilities at home? Out-of-school youth with mental retardation had roughly the same amount of household responsibilities as youth in other disability categories. Although the number of students with mental retardation who were performing in an unsatisfactory fashion was not encouraging, their adaptation seemed to be similar to that of students with other disabilities.

What about living independently? In the first or second year after secondary school, fewer students with mental retardation were living independently than were students with other disabilities. For example, 9 percent of the mentally retarded students, 22 percent of the students with learning disabilities, and 26 percent of the visually impaired students were living independently. These figures improve, however, three to five years after high school. Then, 24 percent of adults with mental retardation were living independently. There also were encouraging increases in employment rates and wages (Blackorby & Wagner, 1996).

Adulthood

Figure 5.6 compares the employment rates of people in all eleven categories of disabilities with the rates of people in the specific category of mental retardation. The figure shows that 56 percent of the adults with mental retardation and 70 percent of those in all eleven categories "had a paid job last year." So adults with mental retardation are somewhat less likely than others to secure a paid job. But, on the positive side, more than half of these former students did secure a paid job and thus demonstrated their capability to have a productive vocational adaptation.

Figure 5.6 also shows 46 percent of those in the "all conditions" and 28 percent of those in the "mentally retarded" category to be "currently competitively employed." On the plus side, 1 out of 4 individuals with mental retardation is "currently employed" and another 9 percent are "employed for pay at a sheltered workshop." Such figures highlight the importance of special educational programs in both the vocational/academic and the social domains.

The lesson here is that we cannot release young people with retardation from school and expect them to adjust to a working environment without help and planning. With organized training programs and support services, many of these individuals can adjust well. The support resources that can be brought to bear fall into four categories:

Children with mental retardation can and do make good adaptations in adulthood.

- *Individuals:* skills, competencies, the ability to make choices, money information, spiritual values
- *Other people:* family, friends, coworkers, cohabitants, mentors
- *Technology:* assistive devices, job/living accommodations, behavioral technology
- *Services:* habilitation services that can be used when natural resources are not available

We should think of the total resources for helping young adults present in the community instead of merely the resources of the school system. Attention to the individual's adaptive skills at adolescence may yield the best chance for a meaningful adult adjustment.

Of course, society has changed and with it the workplace. With technological advances, both are becoming far more complex. But adults with mental retardation can still make an important contribution in many areas. Edgerton (1988) proposed one set of interesting ideas:

First, there is an obvious need for expanded day care facilities for the children of working parents. I can see no reason why many mentally retarded adults would not be able to make a helpful contribution to day care centers. Second, nursing homes

Figure 5.6
Employment Rates of Youth
with Disabilities and with
Mental Retardation

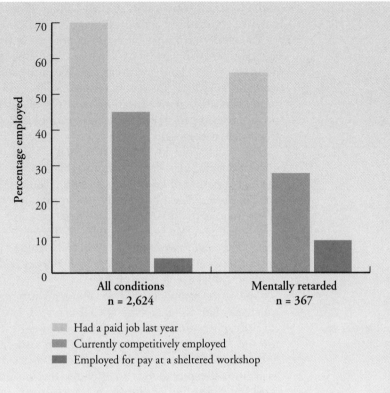

Source: M. Wagner, L. Newman, R.
D'Amico, E. Jay, P. Butler-Nalu, C. Marder,
and R. Cox (1991), *Youth with Disabilities:
How Are They Doing?* Washington, DC:
U.S. Department of Education, Office of
Special Education Programs.

are understaffed; retarded persons could push wheelchairs, serve meals, help with
patient care and provide human contact and conversation to infirm and aging patients too often alone. Third, retarded persons could help serve meals to infirm persons who live at home; they could also provide other helpful services and could offer
companionship. Fourth, they could help with many jobs in what are now all-too-
often moribund social and recreational programs designed for handicapped children
or adults. (pp. 338–339)

Helping adults with mental retardation find employment and social opportunities
surely will be an important goal in the twenty-first century.

 Family and Lifespan Issues

What happens to children with mental retardation when they finish their schooling? Do they find work? At what kinds of jobs? Where do they live? What kinds
of support do they need to adapt to society?

FAMILY SUPPORT

For the family of a child with mental retardation, the traditional roles of nurturer,
breadwinner, and mentor are extended to include guardian of the child's health
and safety, perhaps supporter of other parents in the Parent to Parent program,

and advocate for the rights of their child and other children with similar disabilities, as described in Figure 5.7.

The family's role in creating the context or environment in which the child with mental retardation grows up depends on whether the child is in the organically injured or the familial retarded group. When the child is at the low end of the intellectual distribution but is without observable pathology, the family often creates a context in which poor education, poverty, and a barren neighborhood create additional problems for the child, who in turn creates problems for the teachers trying to educate him or her.

The impact on the family of having a child with mental retardation can be great. Some families seem to mourn the death of the child-that-was-to-be and go through a period of grief (Farber, 1986). The stress that families experience is evident in an increased rate of divorce in families with a child with retardation or other handicaps (Bristol, 1987). There are numerous accounts of the problems that families suffer from (Turnbull & Turnbull, 1994), but not all families collapse. The majority of families seem to be able to cope well if they receive reasonable professional support services and support from extended families and friends (Bristol, Gallagher, & Schopler, 1988).

One of the strategies that professionals use to help families cope with the extra stress that often accompanies living with children with disabilities is respite care. **Respite care** is the provision of child-care services so the parents are freed, for a few days, of their constant care responsibilities. Parents who may not have had a "day off" from child-care responsibilities for years greatly appreciate such assistance. Respite care is an effective way of reducing parental depression and stress and enabling parents to be more effective in their role (Botuck & Winsberg, 1991).

There is little doubt that many of these parents are under an additional burden of stress, and one of the responsibilities of professionals who interact with family members is to recognize and support the family members with understanding and empathy. One of the ways to accomplish that goal is to reflect the feelings of the parent as a way of showing understanding and sympathy with what the parent is facing.

Family member: Everything seems to be a burden these days, doing the housework, taking care of the kids, paying the bills. I just don't know how much longer I can keep up the pace.

Professional: All your responsibilities really cause a drain on your time and energy.

Family member: Ever since Eliot was born, my family and friends have put a wall up between me and them. I guess they don't want to do the wrong thing, but what they don't realize is that the worst thing of all is doing nothing and staying away. I have no one to turn to and feel my "resentment gauge" going up by the day. It really hurts me and makes me angry when I've always tried to be there for them, and now when I need them most, they just seem to back away.

Professional: You're feeling very let down by family who you thought would always be there for you. (Turnbull & Turnbull, 1997, p. 66)

Another role for the professional is to help the family in establishing a sustainable daily routine (Gallimore, Bernheimer, & Weisner, 1998). Many parents react

Respite care is one of the simplest and most effective aids to families.

Figure 5.7

Lessons Learned "from the Trenches"

Judy Engleman has been a warrior and a winner. Her battle against an insurance company to pay for the special nutritional supplement essential to her daughter Haley's survival has been chronicled in *Exceptional Parent* (February 1996). Here, in an open letter to *Exceptional Parent* and its readers, she speaks directly to the dangers of burnout and how one mom learned to protect herself—despite herself— along the way.

Dear Exceptional Parent,

I have come a long way, from a frightened, intimidated, unknowledgeable, sedentary parent of a special needs child, to an assertive, aggressive, educated and physically active happy person. In addition to all of my family's needs, I now take care of myself and see myself— for who and what I am—as a worthy and interesting person. No longer do I allow myself to be known solely as the parent and caregiver of a unique child with rare disorders and obscure syndromes. Unfortunately, we—as parents and advocates—are often made to feel that way.

It is we who are at our children's bedsides when they are hospitalized—no matter how frequently or for how long they remain in-patients. We are the ones who take our children to their medical appointments. We advocate for them when they are unable to do so themselves. We make certain that their needs are met.

Along the way, our identity often gets lost. We become an offset of the environment we are in. Medical personnel call us "mom" and/or "dad," even when asked to call us by our names. This sends a clear message: You, as individuals, do not matter to us. Concerned friends and relatives ask how our children are; but never how we are doing. Our self image is gradually shattered. We are so busy trying to keep up and get through another day, we do not even see it happening.

My compassion and concern for others in similar settings is enormous. I will forever strive to help anyone in any way that I am able. It is not just me who can enact change within an insurance company. Perhaps my struggle can help yours. I am not the only one who can dramatically change my physical body from overweight and out of shape to fit, active, and healthy. Perhaps my struggle—and success—in this area, too, can help others.

We all have the right to think of ourselves and take the time to take care of us! It is not only our special needs children who need special care. We, as parents and caregivers, do also. All of us deserve the best possible lives we can make for ourselves!

You may print my name, address and e-mail. Keeping in touch with others is crucial to opening the doors of our alienated lives.

With my gratitude,
Judy Engleman

to their stressful situation by saying that they are merely going "one day at a time"—all the more reason to emphasize the importance of developing a daily routine that meets the needs of each family member in some optimal way.

As difficult as this life situation may be for the two-parent family, it becomes even more of a strain when only one parent is present or if the family unit is in poverty. One should not overlook the role of available resources or money to pay for child minding, laundry appliances, and cleaning services to relieve the parents of certain household tasks.

Too often in the past, when we said we were involved with the family, we really meant the mother. We now realize the importance of relating to the father as part of the family unit. This is especially true since there is evidence that the typical father tends to play less of a family role when there is a child with disabilities (Gallagher, Cross, & Scharfman, 1981). Some direct counseling and support for the father in his role may be important to achieve the sustainable daily routine that seems so necessary to keep the family on an even keel.

We used to assume that every family who has a child with disabilities was in a crisis situation. We have since discovered that many families adapt well to these special pressures (Bristol, Gallagher, & Shopler, 1988), while others require special attention. A popular program called Parent to Parent matches a trained "veteran parent" (someone who has experience as a parent with a child with disabilities) and a "referred parent" (one who is dealing with the issues for the first time). Although only twenty years old, there are 550 Parent to Parent programs serving nearly 30,000 parents (Turnbull & Turnbull, 1997). An example of just what such a program can mean comes from a referred parent:

> Parent to Parent has been my lifeline. When I first heard the diagnosis, I was devastated. Well-meaning doctors and nurses, as well as friends and family, simply did not understand. It was only when I finally connected with another parent through the Parent to Parent program that I could begin to hope for a future for us all. My veteran parent was gently there for me whenever I needed her. (Turnbull & Turnbull, 1997, p. 181)

INTERACTION WITH THE COMMUNITY: THE SPECIAL OLYMPICS

A goal of almost everyone, regardless of their educational philosophy, is to increase community contacts and interaction for students with mental retardation and developmental disabilities. Whether it is on-the-job vocational training, boarding a community bus to an athletic event, or field trips to various community sites, there is a manifest advantage in these students interacting in the community where they will live as adults.

One of the most successful of these ventures is a program called Special Olympics, which uses the format of the Olympic Games, but in which all the persons participating have developmental disabilities. The program was begun in 1968 by Eunice Kennedy Shriver, the sister of President John F. Kennedy. It has grown to an international event, with several thousand participants and many thousands of spectators. The purpose of the games is to allow children with disabilities to participate in races, swimming meets, field events, and team games and to feel what other athletes feel in competition, in winning and losing—an experience they rarely are able to achieve elsewhere. It has received substantial community support and is now touted as the largest athletic event now operating besides the traditional Olympics.

Interestingly, some negative voices are heard about the Special Olympic games—they are not designed to integrate the students into the mainstream but are special games only for children with disabilities, emphasizing that they are different from the general public. Of course, most of these youngsters could never

One outstanding bridge between children with disabilities and mainstream society is the Special Olympics program. Its national and international meets encourage children with disabling conditions to compete in races, field events, and games. (© Jonathan A. Meyers)

compete for the basketball or track and field teams of their mainstream schools, so the idea of integration is not possible anyway. The sheer joy that these youngsters and their parents get from their Special Olympics experience is obvious to any observer.

Summary of Major Ideas

1. The AAMR's current definition of mental retardation/developmental disabilities focuses on two major components: intelligence and adaptive behavior. An educational diagnosis of mental retardation depends on the characteristics of the child and on the demands of the social environment.

2. In recent years, the number of children in the public schools identified as mentally retarded has dropped. Although prevention and early intervention play a part in this decline, most of the change stems from changes in classification procedures and the establishing of a top limit to subnormal intelligence.

3. Many factors contribute to the cause of mental retardation. They include chromosomal abnormalities, toxic agents, infections, and environmental factors.

4. There are three levels of prevention. The objective of *primary prevention* is to reduce the number of children born with mental retardation. *Secondary prevention* focuses on early identification and treatment of conditions that, if ignored, could lead to mental retardation. Education is a form of *tertiary prevention;* its objective is to help students with mental retardation and developmental disabilities achieve their maximum potential and highest quality of life.

5. Early intervention programs are one means of preventing retardation caused by environmental factors, but they are not a cure-all for the effects of poverty and social disorganization in the home.

6. Children with mental retardation have difficulty processing information. For many, the problem lies in limited memory, perception, and the way they organize information and make decisions.

7. Children with mental retardation have a general language deficit and specific problems using interpretative language.

8. Educators identify students with mental retardation by their performance on intelligence tests and adaptive scales and from the reports of teachers and other educators who have direct experience with the youngsters.

9. The learning environment in which the child with mental retardation is placed is less important than the curriculum and skills taught there.

10. The elementary and secondary curricula for students with mental retardation stress academic skills, communication and language development, socialization, and prevocational and vocational skills. The emphasis, particularly for students with moderate retardation, is on functional learning.

11. By reducing failure, increasing success, and modeling appropriate behaviors, teachers can improve the attitudes and behaviors of children with mild and moderate retardation.

12. Social learning theory is generating teaching strategies to help youngsters with retardation to learn.

13. A strong effort is being made to build intrinsic motivation for students with mental retardation as a way of improving their learning skills when no adults are present.

14. Planning and vocational training are needed to ease the transition from school to work of those with mental retardation.

15. Families with a child with mental retardation may need support and assistance to function at an expected level.

Unresolved Issues

1. *The culture of poverty.* We still are not sure what factors in the culture of poverty are responsible for the slow development of children with mild retardation. Until we can determine the nature of the problem (lack of motivation, poor language, inattention and hyperactivity, lack of effective adult models), it is difficult to design effective methods for preventing it.

2. *The changing job market.* The future of students with mental retardation depends as much on the environment or context in which they live as on their education and training. The increasing complexity of modern society

casts a shadow over the goal of independence for these youngsters, although they may be able to get jobs in the service sector. Do individuals with mild or moderate retardation have a place in a shrinking job market, or will they be part of a "surplus" population?

3. *The resilient family.* Some families are able to adjust to the problem of having a child with moderate or severe retardation; others are shattered by it. Why? What gives some families the strength to adapt to the stress? There are two quite different approaches to the families of the handicapped: One wants them to be teachers of their children with disabilities; the second stresses professional help and respite care to allow periodic relief from the daily burden of care. Which approach is more appropriate for which families?

4. *Secondary education.* By mainstreaming youngsters with mild mental retardation at the secondary level, we limit them to a standard curriculum. Yet these students need special instruction in prevocational and survival skills. How do we balance the benefits of mainstreaming against these special vocational needs?

Key Terms

amniocentesis p. 172
behavior modification p. 200
central processing p. 177
contingent social reinforcement p. 201
cooperative learning p. 204
developmental disabilities p. 166
differential reinforcement p. 201
Down syndrome p. 172
executive function p. 178
extrinsic motivation p. 203
fetal alcohol syndrome (FAS) p. 174
fragile X syndrome p. 174
intrinsic motivation p. 203

karyotyping p. 172
mental retardation p. 167
negative reinforcement p. 201
phenylketonuria (PKU) p. 173
positive reinforcement p. 201
reciprocal teaching p. 200
respite care p. 210
rubella p. 176
scaffolding p. 200
social learning approach p. 197
task analysis p. 194
teratogen p. 174
time-out p. 201

Questions for Thought

1. Why is the concept of adaptive behavior important to identifying mild mental retardation?   pp. 167–169

2. Compare the development of children with mild retardation with the development of those with moderate retardation.   pp. 169–171

3. How do toxic agents influence the development of mental retardation? pp. 174–176

4. How does the language acquisition of children with mild retardation differ from that of children who do not have mental retardation?   p. 179

5. Explain the roles of central processing and executive function in information processing.   pp. 177–179

6. What is being done to prevent mental retardation at the primary, secondary, and tertiary levels?   pp. 183–184

7. Why is adaptive behavior difficult to assess?   pp. 185–187

8. What roles do the prereferral team and the diagnostic examination play in identifying children who need special help?   pp. 185–187

9. Describe the usefulness of each of the following environments for students with mental retardation: regular classroom, resource room, special class. pp. 188–192

10. Why is intrinsic motivation important for persons with mental retardation? p. 203

11. Do intervention programs for children with mental retardation make a long-term difference?   pp. 204–205

Resources for Further Study

REFERENCES OF SPECIAL INTEREST

Bradley, V., Ashbaugh, J., & Blaney, B. (Eds.). (1994). *Creating individual supports for people with developmental disabilities.* Baltimore: Paul H. Brookes.

This work is an attempt to present a new approach to developing individual supports for exceptional children. A push is made for an expanded partnership between many disciplines, for parents to design an individualized program, and for detailing the individualized planning process. The book has chapters written by professionals from different fields to illustrate a fundamental change in service delivery.

Burack, J., Hodapp, R., & Zigler, E. (1998). *Handbook of mental retardation and development.* New York: Cambridge University Press.

An important book that synthesizes what we know about the development of children with mental retardation. Major chapters are devoted to cognitive and linguistic development, social and emotional development, and the effects of environment and family. There is little stress on education, but the global portrait of children with mental retardation provides a good basis for discussing these children's special needs.

Hickson, L., Blackman, L., & Reis, E. (1995). *Mental retardation: Foundations of educational programming.* Boston: Allyn & Bacon.

This texts places a special emphasis on educational planning for children with mental retardation from early childhood until the child leaves the system. Includes a number of case studies to help the reader gain a true-to-life context in which to anchor general principles.

Rondal, J. (1995). *Exceptional language development in Down syndrome.* New York: Cambridge University Press.

This book is devoted to a case study of the language processes of a woman with Down syndrome. Its significance lies in the woman's having normal productive and receptive language even while showing the standard cognitive deficits expected of her condition. This suggests that some linguistic processes can exist and develop apart from the central cognitive processes and that people like her may be educable even with central damage.

Simeonsson, R. (Ed.). (1994). *Risk, resilience and prevention.* Baltimore: Paul H. Brookes.
This is a detailed description of the concept of prevention. Several professionals define what primary prevention is and discuss how to modify service delivery in ways that can enhance primary and secondary prevention. The text covers topics ranging from physi-

cal injury and child abuse to internalizing affective disorders and preventing school failures and dropouts.

Stainback, S., & Stainback, W. (1996). *Inclusion: A guide for educators.* Baltimore: Paul H. Brookes.

The authors defend the inclusive school movement by presenting suggestions about how school curricula should be modified to take into account the presence of children with special needs. They attempt to answer the questions of critics of the inclusive classroom approach by presenting practical suggestions for curriculum adaptations in the classroom for exceptional children.

Turnbull, A., & Turnbull, H. R. (1997). *Families, professionals and exceptionality: A special partnership* (3rd ed.). Upper Saddle River, NJ: Prentice Hall.

A rich text that focuses on the many roles played by the family members of a child with disabilities. It is designed to help professionals understand families, collaborate with families to help family empowerment, and aid family roles in the community and educational system improvement. Many practical quotes from family members bring the issues to life.

JOURNALS

American Journal on Mental Retardation
444 N. Capitol St., NW
Washington, DC 20001-1570

Education and Training in Mental Retardation and Developmental Disabilities
Division on Mental Retardation and Developmental Disabilities
The Council for Exceptional Children
1920 Association Dr.
Reston, VA 20191-1589

Mental Retardation
1719 Kalorama Rd., NW
Washington, DC 20009

Research in Developmental Disabilities
Elsevier Science, Inc.
660 White Plains Rd.
Tarrytown, NY 10591-5153

PROFESSIONAL ORGANIZATIONS

American Association on
Mental Retardation
444 NW, Capitol St., Suite 846
Washington, DC 201-1512
http://www.aamr.org

The Arc
500 E. Border St., Suite 300
P.O. Box 1047
Arlington, TX 76010
http://www.TheArc.org/welcome.html

National Down Syndrome Society
666 Broadway, 8th Floor
New York, NY 10012-2317
http://www.pcsltd.com/ndss

United Cerebral Palsy Association
1660 L St., NW, Suite 700
Washington, DC 20036-5602
http://www.ucpa.org

6

*C*hildren with
*L*earning *D*isabilities

FOCUSING
questions

How are learning disabilities defined by law?

What are neuropsychological/developmental and academic/achievement learning disabilities?

Is there one known primary cause of learning disabilities?

How do we identify children with learning disabilities?

What are some of the important issues in working with the parents of children with learning disabilities?

In what setting are children with learning disabilities instructed?

Not all learning problems are learning disabilities.

Perhaps no area of special education is generating so much multidisciplinary research and stimulating so much debate as learning disabilities. Researchers are intrigued by learning disabilities because children who possess them have near-average or higher IQ scores but do not succeed in areas that the IQ scores predict, particularly in learning how to read and write. Essentially, persons with learning disabilities belie one fundamental assumption about human beings: If you do not experience mental retardation, mental disturbances, visual or hearing impairments, or environmental deprivations, you should be able to do well in school. Why children with learning disabilities do not do well has fascinated and baffled researchers in the fields of reading, cognition, speech and hearing, neurology, learning, vision, audition, and special education in general. Although not all evidence is in, some appealing hypotheses are being discarded for lack of research support, and others are gaining stronger support. What is clear is that there is no one cause of the difficulties experienced by all persons who are said to have learning disabilities. There appear to be multiple causes, and not all children with learning disabilities have the same set of deficits. Most have trouble learning to read and write. Others have trouble with math. Some have trouble with all three.

A Historical Overview

Children who have normal intelligence and no classifiable disability yet do not succeed in school have been a concern to teachers, parents, researchers, and the children themselves. Researchers began investigating the causes of the conditions now known as learning disabilities in the 1800s, and research continues today. Poor teaching and lack of effort by the student have been ruled out as causative factors, but many questions remain.

A number of intriguing hypotheses have been proposed to account for the disorder. Orton (1937) believed that the difficulty resides in the failure of the left hemisphere of the brain to take on the role of language as it typically does in human beings. He called students who had difficulty learning "minimally brain damaged." Kirk and Kirk (1971) and Myklebust (1954) perceived the problems as a specific language disorder and followed that line of reasoning in their research. Frostig, Lefever, and Whittesey (1964), Getman (1965), and others investigated perceptual and motor processes as possible factors. Fernald (1943) and Gillingham and Stillman (1960) believed that the disorder is primarily in the area of written language. These differences in opinion produced a fragmented body of research and no consensus among researchers as to the causes of the disorder or what to call it. At a meeting of concerned parents, Samuel Kirk (1963) proposed the term *learning disabilities* to describe the condition; the term was widely adopted and is still used.

Today most of the older hypotheses about learning disabilities involving brain damage have been abandoned or revised, but the causes of the disorder are still largely unknown (Lyon, 1994; Stanovich, 1986; Torgesen & Wong, 1986). Many researchers are working to devise tests to determine the source of the disorder and curricula to remediate academic problems.

⬤⬤ *Definitions*

The label *learning disability* refers to a category of children and does not describe the specific deficit or dysfunction of the child or the specific academic or achievement problem of the child (National Information Center for Children and Youth with Disabilities [NICHCY], 1997). The label assists persons in identifying and classifying children who need special help.

Children with learning disabilities are children with unusual ways of perceiving the world. Their neurological patterns seem somewhat different from those of children of the same age without disabilities. Persons with learning disabilities have in common some type of failure in school or in the community. They are not able to do what others with the same level of intelligence are able to accomplish.

The *Federal Register* (1977) includes the regulations for identifying and defining students with learning disabilities under the Education for All Handicapped Children Act of 1975 (PL 94-142):

> "Specific learning disability" means a disorder in one or more of basic psychological processes involved in using language, spoken or written, which may manifest itself in an imperfect ability to listen, think, speak, read, write, spell, or to do mathematical calculations. The term includes such conditions as perceptual handicaps, brain injury, minimal brain dysfunction, dyslexia, and developmental aphasia. The term does not include children who have learning problems which are primarily the result of visual, hearing, or motor handicaps, of mental retardation, of emotional disturbance, or of environmental, cultural, or economic disadvantage. (Federal Register, 1977, p. 650; NICHCY, 1997)

The *Federal Register* definition has four criteria that teachers must consider when identifying students with learning disabilities:

1. *Academic difficulties.* The child with learning disabilities has difficulty learning how to read, write, spell, organize thoughts, or do mathematical calculations, compared with other children of the same age.

2. *Discrepancy between potential and achievement.* The child with learning disabilities experiences a serious discrepancy between intellectual ability and achievement in school; this is known as an **aptitude-achievement discrepancy.**

3. *Exclusion of other factors.* A person may not be classified as having learning disabilities if the learning problem is caused by visual or hearing impairments, mental retardation, motor disabilities, emotional disturbance, or environmental factors.

4. *Neuropsychological disorder.* Basic learning disabilities are the result of some type of neuropsychological disorder.

The revised regulations of the Individuals with Disabilities Education Act (IDEA) define "a learning disability in one or more basic psychological processes involved in using spoken or written language, which may manifest itself in an imperfect ability to listen, think, speak, read, write, spell, or to do mathematical calculations" (NICHCY, 1997).

The National Joint Committee for Learning Disabilities (1991) proposed the following definition:

⭐ *Learning disabilities are indicated by a great discrepancy between intellectual ability and actual school achievement.*

Learning disabilities refers to a heterogeneous group of disorders manifested by significant difficulties in acquiring and using listening, speaking, reading, writing, reasoning, or mathematical abilities. *(© Gale Zucker)*

Learning disabilities is a generic term that refers to a heterogeneous group of disorders that are manifested by significant difficulties in the acquisition and use of listening, speaking, reading, writing, reasoning, or mathematical abilities. These disorders are intrinsic to the individual and are presumed to be due to central nervous system dysfunction. Even though a learning disability may occur concomitantly with other handicapping conditions (e.g., sensory impairment, mental retardation, social and emotional disturbances, insufficient/inappropriate instruction, psychogenic factors), it is not the real result of those conditions or influences. (p.16)

"Central nervous system dysfunction" is currently more commonly called *neuropsychological dysfunctioning* and/or *differences*. These terms mean that the definition assumes that the brain or perceptional systems or both are not damaged but work in a way that is different from the way they function in children without learning problems. Learning disabilities are suspected to arise out of differences in brain and perceptual functioning rather than from specific damage to these systems.

Both definitions point to the need to present an alternative set of lessons to match the unusual neurological patterns of these children. Much of the special education designed for these children focuses on strategies to help them master lessons they cannot learn from the traditional curriculum.

It is important to bear in mind the following:

- All children with learning disabilities have learning problems.
- Not all children with academic problems have learning disabilities.

One should not say, for example, that children with Down syndrome have learning disabilities, although they may need special help because of their lower cognitive abilities caused by the disorder. And children who have trouble learning in academic settings because of the disorganized environment in which they live or emotional trauma they have experienced are not considered by definition to have learning disabilities.

At this time, we can make the following general statements about learning disabilities:

- *Learning disabilities* is a general term that refers to a heterogeneous group of disorders that includes different subgroups.
- Learning disabilities must be viewed as a problem not only of the school years but also of early childhood and adult life.
- A learning disability is intrinsic to the individual; the basis of the disorder is presumed to be a central nervous system dysfunction.
- Learning disabilities may occur with other handicapping conditions as well as within different cultural and linguistic groups (Kavale, Forness, & Bender, 1987, Vol. 1, p. 6).

Prevalence

Ninety-eight percent of the states exclude from the learning disability criteria children with mental retardation and low academic achievement due to environmental disadvantage. However, MacMillan and Speece (in press) report that the evidence reveals that between 52 percent and 70 percent of children identified by schools as learning disabled do not meet the standard established by state and federal criteria. Gottlieb, Alter, Gottlieb, and Wishner (1994) note that in the urban areas they studied many of the children classified as learning disabled previously would have been classified as educable retarded because of their lower IQ scores.

Over 39 percent of students with learning disabilities are served in the regular classroom.

Cramer and Ellis (1996) report that 15 percent of the U.S. population has learning disabilities and that 2.3 million students are classified as learning disabled. Of the total population of students in special education in the United States, 52 to 54 percent are considered learning disabled. In its *18th Annual Report to Congress,* the U.S. Department of Education (1997) states that 39.3 percent of students with learning disabilities are served in regular classrooms, 41 percent in resource rooms, 18.8 percent in separate classes, and less than 1 percent in separate schools, residential facilities, and hospitals. The distribution in the United States is not geographic and varies from state to state. For example Rhode Island reported that 63 percent of the special education population in the state had learning disabilities; Alabama reported that 26 percent of its special education population had learning disabilities.

The problem with prevalence figures lies in the lack of a uniform definition of learning disabilities across the states and a failure to administer a complex multidisciplinary assessment that encompasses social, genetic, cultural, and educational

Because reading and arithmetic are similar in many ways (e.g., numbers and words stand for concepts), a child with language difficulty is likely to have difficulty in learning to calculate. *(© Alan Carey/ The Image Works)*

factors. Because there is no single cause of school failure, some factors have to be ruled out (such as severe hearing impairments or cultural deprivation) before a child is considered as having learning disabilities (Interagency Committee, 1990, p. 140). The category of learning disabilities contains the largest number of students in special education (Kavale & Forness, 1997). Some schools tend to identify all students in academic trouble as having learning disabilities.

Keep in mind the concept of individual and intra-individual differences when thinking about children with learning disabilities. These children have some disabilities in common; for example, 75 to 80 percent of students with learning disabilities have reading or language deficits (Council for Exceptional Children [CEC], 1997; Cramer & Ellis, 1996). However, some students have other disabilities that are idiosyncratic characteristics of only a small subgroup of the population with learning disabilities. Although children in a subgroup may have characteristics in common, they will differ from one another on some dimension, some having several problems and some having only one. For example, Snowling and Perrin (1988) found that some children with learning disabilities have problems in reading, spelling, and writing, whereas others are excellent readers but poor spellers. Learning disabilities may be of a verbal or a nonverbal nature (Rourke, 1995).

Is There a Single Cause?

No one has discovered a single cause of learning disabilities. Rather, studies that focus on subgroups within the larger population of children with learning disabilities have identified some neurological differences and sensory deficits associated with their learning problems (Hynd, 1992; Lyon, 1995; Rourke, 1994).

For example, although visual-perceptual-motor deficits do not appear to be a single cause of learning disabilities when researchers look at a large group overall, they do appear to be a factor for a small sample within the group. Satz and Morrison (1981) wrote that "virtually all subgroup studies have revealed a subgroup of children with learning disabilities who have relatively intact language processing abilities but impaired performance on visual-perceptual-motor tasks" (p. 34).

Research now clearly supports the rejection of a single cause or a single deficit. The field recognizes multiple problems and teaches each child, keeping his or her particular deficit clearly in mind. Instruction varies from child to child, depending on the problems he or she faces.

The search for the cause of a learning disability in one child or in many children is similar to a detective story in which many suspects must be eliminated one after another until the real perpetrator is found. This detective story has multiple solutions, however, because the true cause of learning disabilities for one child can be quite different from that of another child so labeled.

It is one thing to say that something is wrong with the way a child processes information and another thing entirely to expect that the same defect will appear in every child categorized as having a learning disability. Perhaps for one child the problem lies in how visual information available to that child is processed. Perhaps it may lie in auditory perception. Perhaps it is in how the information is stored and how the child organizes stored information. One must assume that every student with learning disabilities must be approached as if his or her problems are unique, idiosyncratic, and personal.

This major detective story is complicated because the child with learning disabilities is likely to have failed frequently in schoolwork in the past, and some of the presenting problems relate to that history of failure and the child's reaction to it as well as to the original condition.

 Learning disabilities result from a variety of causes.

Characteristics of Children with Learning Disabilities

Children with learning disabilities, until they begin to fail in school, usually are happy. In school, they have difficulty making friends (Vaugh, McIntosh, & Spencer-Rowe, 1991), and they do not seem to hear all that is said or respond quickly to questions (Curtis & Tallal, 1991). They have trouble learning the rules of games, but once they learn them, they insist on strict adherence to them (Valletutti, 1987).

In the literature on learning disabilities, authors have used many negative terms to describe children with learning *disabilities*. These terms, however, are equally descriptive of children with learning *problems*. The main point to keep in mind is that children with learning disabilities have normal intelligence and have difficulty in one or more school subjects—difficulty that is *not* associated with a known disability such as cerebral palsy or mental retardation. It is hoped that the earlier we identify a child with learning disabilities and institute a successful educational program, the less likely are boredom, lack of motivation, and lack of interest to set in. But if a child continues to fail in elementary school, problem behaviors may be established by adolescence.

Classification of Learning Disabilities

Researchers generally take one of two perspectives on learning disabilities: developmental or academic achievement. Those who take a neuropsychological/developmental perspective seek an underlying cause for students' difficulties in academic subjects. The upper part of Figure 6.1 contains the hypothesized neuropsychological/developmental disorders: biological/genetic, perceptual-motor, visual, auditory, memory, and attentional disorders. A large number of researchers are pursuing the source or causes of these disorders (Kavale, Forness, & Bender, Vols. 1–3, 1987).

Researchers who take the academic perspective investigate the specific problems that students have with the content and processes (executive functions) they need to learn to master academic subjects. The middle part of Figure 6.1 lists the academic areas that teachers are most concerned with: language and reading, writing, spelling, mathematics, and executive functions. A large group of researchers are focusing on how to solve these difficulties by developing teaching strategies and curriculum (see Adelman & Taylor, 1993; Lenz, Ellis, & Scanton, 1996; Sturomski, 1997).

The developmental-academic model implies that the child with learning disabilities comes to school with a set of developmental problems in processing information. **Developmental learning disabilities** (also called **neuropsychological learning disabilities**) include attention problems, memory problems, and disorders in thinking and using language. These problems are rarely detected before the child enters school because few serious demands are made of the preschool child in these areas. The downward extension of schooling to ages 3 and 4 may result in more systematic observation and earlier identification of such children (see Wolery, 1992).

These developmental learning disabilities lead to **academic achievement learning disabilities** in reading, spelling, writing, or arithmetic. Again, not everyone who has these academic problems has a learning disability, but a thorough examination can determine the presence of developmental learning disabilities (Lyon, 1994).

NEUROPSYCHOLOGICAL/DEVELOPMENTAL LEARNING DISABILITIES

Inherent in the term *learning disabilities* is the understanding that the disorder or disorders exist in the person, not in the environment. Hence, the first hypotheses proposed that these individuals suffered from brain damage, brain dysfunction, or brain differences resulting in disordered thinking skills, poor memory, poor attentive skills, and challenging behaviors (for example, lack of motivation, passive aggression). The neuropsychological/developmental model assumes that learning disabilities are due to the following:

- Something wrong with or different in the child's brain or perceptual systems
- Some type of neurological dysfunction
- Disturbances in perceptual-motor functioning
- An imbalance of intelligence abilities and academic achievement from some type of damage to the brain (Kavale, Forness, & Bender, Vol. 1, 1987; Rourke, 1994)

Learning disabilities occur within the child, not within the environment.

Figure 6.1
Types of Learning Disabilities

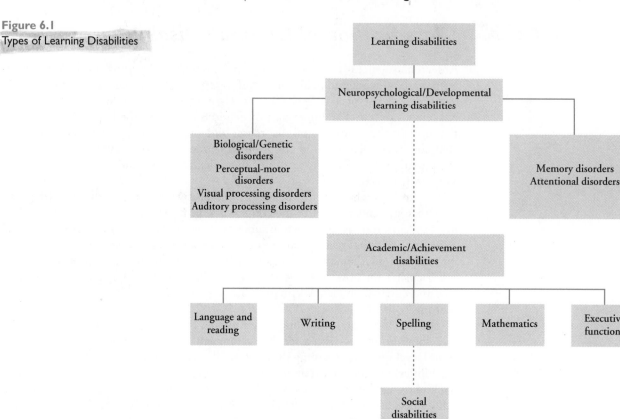

We have already mentioned that most children with learning disabilities have trouble learning to read. Herein may be the source of many of the disputes about learning disabilities. Learning to read depends on several perceptional systems: vision, hearing (matching one's auditory system to print), attention, previous experience, and so on. Thus, a researcher who pursues one of these topics may come to assume that one particular disability is the major source of learning disabilities. What is being discovered is that a researcher who makes this assumption is both right and wrong, overgeneralizing that all children with learning disabilities have vision problems, for example, and accurately perceiving that some of them actually do.

In the following sections, we look at attempts by researchers to discover a cause (or causes) of learning disabilities.

Biological and Genetic Explanations

Researchers have reported biological, hereditary, and genetic explanations for some subtypes of learning disabilities. Pennington (1995) demonstrated that some learning disabilities have a genetic base and are inherited. Greschwind (1985) proposed elevated hormone imbalances as a source of learning disabilities. Several researchers have demonstrated relationships between brain damage and some types of learning disabilities (DeFries and Alarcón, 1996; Rourke, 1994).

It has been known for a long time that persons with damage to the frontal lobe of the brain have problems in planning and using appropriate strategies in solving problems, but it is not correct to assume that persons who display these problems have frontal lobe damage. By analogy, if a baseball player who is nearsighted misses a ball hit to him, that does not mean everyone who fails to catch a fly ball is nearsighted. A player may or may not be nearsighted, just as students with learning disabilities may or may not have brain damage. The student's disability may be a brain dysfunction or a way of operating different from that of most other children.

Perceptual-Motor Problems

Recall that early researchers perceived perceptual-motor disorders as a major cause of learning disabilities. The hypotheses were that learning disabilities were due to disordered motor skills, perception, perceptional integration, balance, and tactile and kinesthetic disorders (Cruickshank et al., 1961; Frostig et al., 1964; Getman, 1965; Gillingham & Stillman, 1960; Kephart, 1964). Many remedial activities were suggested to increase perceptual-motor integration. Modern concern, how-ever, tends to focus on techniques for remediating specific deficits—such as reading, spelling, or mathematical disorders—rather than on activities to increase proposed lacks in body integration. It is "unexpected underachievement" that is at the core of today's thinking about learning disabilities (Lyon, 1994, p. xv).

Visual Processing Deficits

Because reading depends partially on vision, many people assumed that visual deficits are the cause of learning disabilities. Children with visual deficits were observed to have difficulty moving their eyes from left to right to follow printed text, and they moved their eyes frequently back and forth across a line. These visual processing deficits were perceived to signal not a problem in seeing but instead a problem in how visual information was processed in the brain and how the children used their eyes to gain information. Visual processing deficits should not be ignored. Testing for them should be part of the diagnostic process so children with these deficits can be identified and receive appropriate remediation (Atkinson, 1993; Satz and Morris, 1981; Swanson, 1987).

Auditory Processing Deficits

Curtis and Tallal (1991) and Tallal, Miller, and Fitch (1993) suggested that auditory processing is slower in children with language delays. Language delays are common in children with learning disabilities. These children take longer to process auditory as well as visual information (Blakeslee, 1991). If the information takes longer to get into the short-term memory, it may not get into long-term memory. In addition, these children take longer to respond to questions or to solve problems. They differ from their peers in the rate at which they process sensory information (Curtis & Tallal, 1991). The impairments are perceived to be in the rate of processing (Torgesen, 1988) as well as slower access to long-term memory for response. These deficits have strong educational relevance, as we shall explain later in the chapter.

Children with learning disabilities are thought to have attentional deficits and to be easily distracted, impulsive, hyperactive, or poor listeners. (© Alan Carey/The Image Works)

Memory Disorders

A deficit in auditory processing affects storage in short-term memory (Curtis & Tallal, 1991). The slower auditory processing doesn't allow enough time for information to be entered into short-term memory. Hence, much of what is presented to the learner is lost, does not enter short-term memory, and therefore is not transferred to long-term memory (Tallal, Miller, & Fitch, 1993; Vellutino, 1987). The deficit related to learning disabilities appears to occur in semantic memory and affects encoding, cataloging, and recalling information that one has been taught (Interagency Committee, 1990; Mann & Liberman, 1984).

Attentional Deficits and Hyperactivity

It has long been thought that children with learning disabilities have attentional deficits and are easily distracted, impulsive, hyperactive, or poor listeners (Berger, 1978; Krupski, 1986; Torgesen & Licht, 1983). Some of the professionals who identify children as having learning disabilities prefer to regard the condition as an **attention-deficit hyperactivity disorder** (**ADHD**) (see Chapter 7). The basic assumption was that attention deficits and **hyperactivity** (impulsivity, acting before thinking, excessive moving about) were the source of the academic problems. Silver (1990) suggested that *learning disability* should be used to describe persons whose brains interfere with their learning, not persons unavailable for learning because of their increased activity and inattention. There is no conclusive evidence that children with learning disorders are fated to develop antisocial behavior. Rourke (1994) suggests most students with learning disorders appear to achieve adequate behavioral control.

Those who believe that ADHD causes learning disabilities might agree to use drugs to calm the individual. The most commonly used drugs are Ritalin and

Dexedrine (Gadov, 1985; Mercer, 1992). Although many professionals in the field of learning disabilities object to the use of these drugs, Forness and Kavale (1988) reported positive results in improving academic learning, and Hallahan and Kauffman (1995) found that the effect of these drugs in improving learning is conclusively documented. Some believe, however, that the student's failure to learn at the same rate as his or her peers is the source of the behavioral problems.

ACADEMIC ACHIEVEMENT LEARNING DISABILITIES

Lerner (1997) defined academic achievement learning disabilities to include deficits in school subjects such as reading, writing, spelling, and mathematics. How to teach these subjects to students with learning disabilities has been the subject of a long debate; there is no general consensus about which model is best.

Language and Reading Disorders

Language disorders is a general term referring to difficulties in listening, speaking, phonological mastery, word recognition, reading, spelling, and writing (see Lyon, 1994, for a discussion of each area and its measurement). The most common difficulty identified for children with learning disabilities is mastery of phonological systems, which leads to deficits in reading, spelling, and writing (Cramer & Ellis, 1996; Liberman & Shankweiler, 1985; Tallal, Miller, & Fitch, 1993).

About 80 percent of children with learning disabilities have difficulty in word and letter recognition or reading comprehension (Lerner, 1997). Becoming a skilled reader is so important in our culture that an unskilled reader is at a great disadvantage in school and the workplace. The following problems may prevent a child with learning disabilities from learning to read:

- Faulty auditory perception without hearing impairment
- Slow auditory or visual processing
- Inability to perceive words (dyslexia)
- Lack of knowledge of the purpose of reading
- Failure to attend to critical aspects of the word, sentence, or paragraph
- Failure to understand that letters represent units of speech (Clark, 1988; Curtis & Tallal, 1991; Liberman & Liberman, 1990)

Dyslexia

Currently, dyslexia is accepted as a subgroup disorder within the learning disability population, and it has been widely studied (Clark, 1988; Deshler, Ellis, & Lenz, 1996; Liberman & Shankweiler, 1977). The major conclusion is that children with **dyslexia** have a variety of deficits resulting from brain dysfunction (that is, the brain is not damaged, but it operates differently from the brain of a child without dyslexia) (Rourke, 1991).

Children identified and classified as **dyslexic** have a combination of problems learning the relationships between sounds and letters (the abstract code representing sounds). Thus, they have difficulties recognizing letters, learning the names of letters, and breaking words down into the sounds of letters and letter combinations (phonemes); they also have difficulties with spelling and writing (Clark,

1988). While persons with dyslexia have difficulties in language-based tasks (reading, spelling, writing, and phonological awareness), they have well-developed abilities in visual, spatial, motor, and nonverbal problem solving (Dickman, 1996). They are not mentally retarded (Gray & Kavanaugh, 1985).

In the opinion of many professionals, dyslexia is simply a severe reading disability (Mercer, 1992). The term is still used, however, particularly among those who are medically oriented, and the condition does appear to have a genetic base (Pennington, 1995; Rourke, 1991).

Despite the enormous problems children with dyslexia face, the general consensus among researchers and teachers is that they can learn (Clark, 1988; Deshler, Ellis, & Lenz, 1996). When the diagnosis of dyslexia is made in the first two grades, more than 80 percent of the children are brought up to grade level. However, if it is not made until fifth grade, only 10 to 15 percent are helped (Fletcher & Forman, 1994, p. 187).

It is important to remember that not all children with learning disabilities have dyslexia. Dyslexia is an extreme form of learning disability. The term *dyslexia* is overused in the popular press, which gives the inaccurate impression that everyone with reading or literacy problems is dyslexic.

Eighty percent of dyslexic children diagnosed in first and second grades are brought up to grade level.

Writing Disorders

A disorder affecting handwriting is technically called *agraphia,* and its neurological basis is unknown. Other writing problems include difficulty in composing a cohesive story, organizing a written composition, or outlining in a logical sequence (Zipprich, 1995).

Spelling Disorders

Many children with language and reading problems are poor spellers. However, that is not always the case; some excellent readers are poor spellers. This finding suggests that the skills involved in spelling and reading may not be connected (Moats, 1994). Moats suggests that prior research has shown spelling to be a complex process that is not simply mechanical. A sign that a child may be learning disabled and not have a learning problem is the ability to read well coupled with poor spelling ability.

A sign that a child may be learning disabled is an ability to read well but an inability to spell well.

Mathematics Disorders

Mathematical learning disabilities have been studied far less than reading difficulties. The technical term *dyscalcula* refers to selective impairment in mathematical thinking or in calculation skills (Fleishner, 1994). Often mathematical learning disability occurs without deficits in reading or in other verbal skills. However, mathematics can be thought of as a language system with numeric symbols instead of words or letters. The brain's mathematic-arithmetic system is located in the same hemisphere as spoken, gestural, and other language systems (Bellugi, 1988). Reading and arithmetic are similar in many ways: Numbers and words stand for concepts; rule systems govern the correct use of the numbers and words, and so on. Thus, a child with a language difficulty may also have difficulty in learning to calculate.

"A Student Helps Other Dyslexics"

Writer's block was more than a passing problem for Joan Corsiglia. The only way she could write a paper was to cut out each sentence of the laborious first draft, put the sentences on a table like pieces of a jigsaw puzzle and sort them under topics to form coherent paragraphs.

Only when she was a junior at Harvard did she learn why it took her ten times as long as other students to do reading and writing assignments. She had assumed that she was not trying hard enough.

She was diagnosed by tests at the Harvard health office as a dyslexic, one of average or better intelligence who has difficulty learning to read, write and organize language because of abnormal interactions in the brain. But her problems did not stop there. She found that there was no policy of remedial counseling or help, such as untimed exams, for dyslexic students.

"The deans and the tutors congratulated me on my strategies of coping, and the Bureau of Study Skills people told me that my skills were as good as any, but I was concerned that there was no help for students who had the same problems. Two percent of each entering class at Harvard have dyslexia."

The determined student organized a group of students with the same disorder to talk with faculty on what to expect from them and how to accommodate their needs. She turned to the Orton Dyslexia Society for speakers and films about the disorder, which affects some 15 percent of the nation's schoolchildren.

Then, during her senior year at Harvard and while she was preparing for medical school, Corsiglia was tutored by Jeanne Chall, professor of education at the Harvard Graduate School of Education, and one of her students, Martha Freeman.

Now a third-year medical student at Dartmouth, Corsiglia has helped to develop support policies there for dyslexics. More than 150 educators from 20 colleges met at Dartmouth in mid-April for a symposium that she organized on dyslexia and learning disabilities, and many more were turned away for lack of space.

Corsiglia's success at Harvard and Dartmouth in establishing support policies for dyslexics earned her an award from the New England Branch of the Orton Society at a dinner April 25 to raise $200,000 for dyslexia research. Dr. Drake D. Duane of the Mayo Clinic in Minnesota told her that any medical residency program will be lucky to have such a highly motivated person.

She calls herself lucky to have had so much help from her parents, Joseph and Sharon Corsiglia of Darien, Conn., and teachers who gave her confidence to overcome her learning handicaps.

"My father owns his own business, so his hours were flexible," says Corsiglia. "He and my mother took us to historic sites all over New England on three-day weekends so that we could learn history that way, as well as by reading. He had a horrible time in school, and so did my brothers, but they weren't diagnosed as dyslexic until after I was.

"My biggest thing was how do things work and why things are the way they are. I asked a lot of questions in school." Corsiglia says teachers told her that she was careless with her spelling, although she spent hours memorizing words, but they praised her for good ideas and extensive reports that gave her a chance to build models and do creative artwork to supplement her essays. Her mother checked her homework and sent her to the dictionary. "But my biggest problem was getting as far as the first draft of a paper," she says.

In the ninth grade, teacher Joan Burchenal sparked Corsiglia's interest in biology. She and her husband, Dr. Joseph Burchenal, an oncologist, helped Corsiglia build an incubator in her basement for experiments on the effects of chemotherapeutic drugs for leukemia on chick embryos.

Determination and fascination with learning won high marks for Corsiglia and helped get her into Harvard, but, by her junior year, her coping strategies began to break down. There wasn't enough time to do every assignment over and over again.

Carroll Williams, her biology adviser, was helpful in getting a diagnosis because he has a son with the same disorder. He had recognized the discrepancy between her laboratory work and written work, and encouraged her. She worked in his laboratory on her honors thesis on "Hormonal Control of Molting in the Tobacco Hornworm." "He helped me to get back my confidence," she says.

Another mentor was Martha Freeman, a graduate student of Jeanne Chall's at the Harvard School of Education.

Corsiglia talks of the tutoring given by Martha Freeman. "She set me to reading editorials in the *Boston Globe* and the *New York Times* and writing summaries." Corsiglia says, "Then I had to turn my summaries into paraphrases without going back to the originals." Medical papers and literate essays such as those of Dr. Lewis Thomas' "Lives of a Cell" captured her attention during long hours of tutoring.

Sports are an important outlet for Corsiglia. She runs from 3 to 5 miles a day and makes time for varsity cross-country track as well as skiing, basketball, soccer, tennis and golf.

With her record of advocacy for and interest in dyslexia, Corsiglia has been doing research on the anatomical differences between dyslexic and nondyslexic brains. She has been working with Albert Galaburda, associate professor of neurology at the Harvard Medical School and director of the Orton Society's Dyslexia Neuroanatomical Laboratory at the Beth Israel Hospital. She plans to specialize in neurology and direct her efforts toward research and clinical practice.

"I want to work with patients as well as in the laboratory," she says. "I feel it is terribly important for young people with dyslexia to get help early so that they won't be discouraged from fulfilling their potential."

Source: Phyllis Coons, "A Student Helps Other Dyslexics," *Boston Globe*, June 14, 1987. Reprinted courtesy of The Boston Globe.

What Is the Context?

Joan Corsiglia's support system at Harvard included organized advocacy groups like the Orton Society as well as her family and professors. The supportive context promoted the development of alternative methods of learning and evaluation to accommodate her dyslexia. Joan's experience demonstrates the importance of finding an approach to education that is tailored to the particular needs of students with learning disabilities and that focuses on their strengths rather than their weaknesses.

Pivotal Issues for Teachers

Discuss the various methods of learning and evaluation that Joan and her teachers used. Why were they effective for Joan? How can teachers learn to adapt their teaching to the needs of individual students with learning disabilities?

Deficits in Executive Function or Cognitive Strategies

To be able to solve the problems that schools present as learning, children must master a set of skills known as **executive function, metacognition,** or **cognitive strategies;** these are the internal processes that children use to select, control, and monitor the strategies they use to solve problems or to learn (Torgesen, 1994). They include monitoring one's behavior, planning how to learn, and self-regulation (keeping oneself on task and not becoming distracted). These strategies are gained from experience, being taught, or learning and are stored in long-term memory. For most adults, they seem automatic. They are the way a person thinks about how to learn. Previous knowledge is essential for appropriate problem solving; for example, one must know the times tables to be able to multiply (Flavall, 1993). Some children with learning disabilities do not possess or do not use these strategies to solve problems and must be taught them (Denckla, 1994; Stone & Conca, 1993).

SOCIAL DISABILITIES

Children with learning disabilities are, by definition, intelligent but have difficulties in learning what the school expects them to learn. This failure, when often repeated, leads to depression, lack of motivation, oppositional behaviors, and a poor self-concept. These side effects are often interpreted to be part of the syndrome of learning disabilities, but evidence suggests they are not (Rourke, 1994). Children with learning disabilities are likely to attribute their failure to their lack of ability, which lowers their feelings of self-esteem (Stone & Conca, 1993).

Some children with learning disabilities may have mild-to-severe disturbances in socioemotional development. Most children with learning disabilities appear to achieve adequate psychosocial adaptation. There is no uniform pattern of personality characteristics, psychological adaptation, social competence, self-concept, or other indicators of socioemotional functioning (Rourke, 1994). Thus, social disorders of children with learning disabilities are *related* to learning disabilities and are not included in the syndrome of learning disabilities (Voeller, 1994).

Teachers can do much to help children with learning disabilities recognize that their academic problems are not due to a lack of effort or intelligence. Early intervention and identification of learning disabilities can do much to decrease social deficits.

Developmental Profile

★ *Learning problems are often confused with learning disabilities.*

Distinguishing students who have learning disabilities from those who have learning problems is not always easy. Individuals in both groups often present similar academic problems.

Massie, a fifth grader, had serious academic problems in all areas of the curriculum (Figure 6.2). She had occasional outbursts of anger and rarely participated in group activities or outdoor play. The exception was her love of creative dance, in which she excelled.

Discussions with the principal and previous teachers revealed a history of academic failure and a very troubled home life. The parents considered her retarded in spite of excellent intelligence test scores. Further psychological testing indicated serious emotional problems. A health evaluation determined that she was grossly overweight and nearsighted. Her parents refused to come to school or to allow a

Figure 6.2
Developmental Profiles of
Two Children

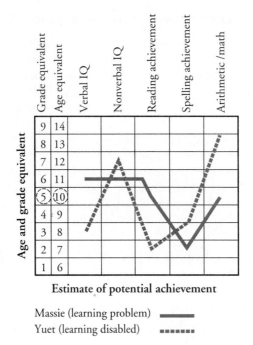

Massie (learning problem)
Yuet (learning disabled)

home visit to discuss these problems. The psychologist and other evaluators considered Massie maladjusted but not learning disabled. Her learning problems stemmed from environmental issues, not neurological ones.

Yuet, a fifth-grade student, could read only extremely frequently appearing words such as her name, street signs, and the names of comic strip characters. Yet she was a talented artist and an excellent oral problem solver, and she possessed excellent fine motor skills. Her nonverbal IQ score was well above average, whereas her verbal IQ score was near the retarded range (see Figure 6.2).

Yuet was completely unmotivated to do most classroom work and, if allowed, spent her time drawing masterful three-dimensional pictures to accompany the current social studies lessons. A meeting with her parents revealed that they were as puzzled about Yuet as the teacher was.

The psychologist's report noted superior fine motor skills and suggested that Yuet be taught reading with a nonaural method that took advantage of her visual capacity, using pictures, stories, and a whole-word approach. This nonaural approach was effective with Yuet, and after two years of specialized help in the resource room her reading greatly improved, as did her self-esteem and motivation.

Yuet has a learning disability. The wide difference between her nonverbal IQ and verbal IQ scores is often a sign of the disability. Her superior art work along with her poor reading are other signals of her disability. Yuet probably falls into the subgroup of children with learning disabilities who have damage to their left hemisphere.

Identification and Assessment

Identifying children with learning disabilities is not easy. First, learning disabilities must be distinguished from other conditions, then the difference between potential and achievement must be evaluated. How large a discrepancy is acceptable?

Must a child have an identifiable developmental learning disability that has contributed to educational underachievement? Who makes the decision?

School systems, according to the provisions of PL 94-142 and PL 101-476, are required to assemble a multidisciplinary team of professionals to examine the child psychologically, mentally, socially, and educationally and, with the parents, come to a decision about whether the child is eligible for special education. The identification process that most school systems follow includes these steps:

1. Someone such as a teacher or parent refers the child for evaluation.

2. A committee that includes the educational evaluator, the special education teacher, and the parent evaluates the referral to determine whether a multidisciplinary team should assess the child.

3. Once an assessment is approved, parental permission for the assessment is obtained.

4. A multidisciplinary team that includes psychologists, social workers, the classroom teacher, and the special education teacher conducts the evaluation.

5. Team members hold a conference and decide whether the child is eligible for special education.

6. If the child is eligible, an IEP is formulated, and the child is placed in the appropriate service.

To adequately assess the child with learning disabilities, specific deficits, dysfunctions, or difficulties, skilled personnel are needed to select the appropriate measure, whether it be in the neuropsychological domain or the academic achievement domain. Lyon's book (1994) is a valuable tool for selecting specific measures in all the subtypes of learning disabilities currently identified. Great care must be taken, because all too frequently the test does not measure what the title of the test suggests.

DIAGNOSIS

A **differential diagnosis** is used to pinpoint an atypical behavior, explain the behavior, and differentiate it from similar problems of other children with disabilities. A differential diagnosis allows teachers to determine the remedial program best suited to correcting or improving the disability. Methods of identification and diagnosis are somewhat different for preschool children and school-age children. Preschoolers are identified through developmental discrepancies, or measured strengths and weaknesses in their developmental abilities. Schoolchildren are identified through discrepancies between aptitude and school achievement.

Educational diagnosis is different from identification of the type of a disability. As a teacher, you will need to know what the academic deficit is and then plan a strategy to remediate it. Achievement tests based on national norms are the most commonly used and readily available in most school districts. A Curriculum-Based Measurement (Deno, 1985) is a technique in which the assessment is based on what has been taught specifically in the classroom (Fuchs, Fuchs, Hamlett, Phillips, & Bentz, 1994). A newer, comprehensive approach, the Work Sampling System (Meisels, Jablon, Marsden, Dichtelmiller, & Dorfman, 1994), offers guidelines about what to sample of children's classroom work and compares the sample to developmental age norms. These methods avoid the pitfalls of achievement tests that contain items and content that may not have been taught.

A differential diagnosis pinpoints an atypical behavior, explains it, and differentiates it from similar problems of other children with disabilities. *(© Jerry Howard/ Positive Images)*

EARLY INTERVENTION

Obviously, the earlier we identify children with learning disabilities, the sooner we can begin intervention programs to help them. More important, if we can identify youngsters who are at risk for learning disabilities, we may be able to prevent those disabilities (Fletcher & Forman, 1994; Wolery, 1992).

Badian (1983, 1988) found that two tests—the information subtest and the sentences subtest of the Wechsler Preschool and Primary Scale of Intelligence—predict with a fairly high degree of accuracy the long-term performance of students in reading. (The information subtest assesses factual knowledge; the sentences subtest assesses the ability to repeat increasingly complex sentences.) Moreover, certain characteristics—troubled birth history, family history of learning disabilities, late order of birth among siblings, delayed speech development, and lower socioeconomic status—differentiate poor readers from good readers (Badian, 1983, 1988).

The identification of learning disabilities in preschool children depends on our being able to observe behavior on age-appropriate tasks. These tasks often involve preacademic readiness skills (cutting with scissors, holding a crayon, sharing an experience with a classmate). Some children have trouble with fine and gross motor development. Others are slow to develop oral language and reasoning abilities. These delays in information processing can affect the child's learning, ability to communicate, and social and emotional adjustment. The most common disorders among preschoolers are delayed language development, poor perceptual-motor skills, and lack of attention.

Current research suggests that many students' reading difficulties stem from such factors as poor instruction, lack of reading readiness, or cultural differences. For these students, their reading deficits can be ameliorated by intensive reading instruction, particularly in phonological awareness and processing (Council for Exceptional Children, 1997; Cramer & Ellis, 1997; Lyon, 1995).

In diagnosing preschool children, examiners rely on the observations of parents and teachers, rating scales, informal clinical diagnoses, and norm-referenced and criterion-referenced tests. They function like detectives, gathering clues and formulating and discarding hypotheses until they arrive at the solution that best fits the available evidence.

Language Disabilities

Language disabilities are the most common learning disabilities among preschoolers.

The most common learning disabilities noted at the preschool level are language disabilities. To diagnose a language disability, psychoeducational examiners follow a series of steps:

1. Obtain a description of the language behavior as observed by the parent, the preschool teacher, or both.

2. Review the medical record to see whether the disability can be explained medically.

3. Study the family situation to determine whether factors in the home contribute to the disability.

4. Using formal and informal tests, examine the child's abilities and disabilities in understanding language, relating things heard to past experiences, and talking.

5. Determine what the child can and cannot do in a specific area. For example, if the child functions well in most areas but does not talk, the next step is to find out if he or she understands language. If the child does not understand oral language, the next step is to find out if he or she can discriminate among words, among phonemes, or among common sounds in the environment.

6. Organize a remedial program that moves the child step by step into areas in which the child could not initially perform.

To identify potential language difficulties early, an assessment of the infant's or young child's *prelinguistic* behaviors must be made. These behaviors before words are spoken include eye contact, mutual gaze, prespeech vocalization, and gesture (Dromi, 1993).

Perceptual-Motor Disabilities

Youngsters with **perceptual-motor disabilities** have difficulty understanding and responding to the meaning of pictures or numbers. In diagnosing perceptual-motor disabilities in a preschooler, psychoeducational examiners ask the usual questions about medical and home background, and through ratings, interviews, and formal tests they try to discover the contributing factors and areas in which the child experiences major difficulties. In the process, examiners try to answer several questions:

The appropriate instruction is based on the child's individualized needs. *(© Michael Zide)*

- Can the child interpret the environment and the significance of what he or she sees?
- Can the child match shapes and colors?
- Can the child recognize visual objects and pictures rapidly?
- Can the child assemble puzzles?
- Can the child express ideas in motor (nonverbal) terms through gestures and drawings?

Attentional and Other Disabilities

Examiners use observation and formal and informal tests to diagnose attentional and other disorders. They are trying to answer these kinds of questions:

- Can the child sustain attention to auditory or visual stimuli?
- Is the child easily distracted?
- Does the child persevere in the face of difficulty or initial failure?
- Can the child discriminate between two pictures or objects (visual discrimination), between two words or sounds (auditory discrimination), or between two objects felt or touched (haptic discrimination)?
- Is the child oriented in space? Does he or she have right-left discrimination?
- Can the child remember immediately what was heard, seen, or felt?
- Can the child imitate the examiner orally or with gestures? Can the child mimic?
- Does the child have adequate visual-motor coordination? Is the child clumsy?

Educational Adaptations

Children with Learning Disabilities

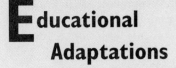

Children with learning disabilities require an individualized teaching plan.

A large group of researchers in the field of learning disabilities have been focusing on the academic problems of children with learning disabilities. Their focus: to analyze what the children must learn and to identify the problems they have in mastering the material. Although this trend has many proponents, there are major differences in recommendations about how to adapt the educational process to help each child.

Historically, approaches to remediation of learning disabilities were based on multiple sensory techniques such as teaching children how to read, spell, write, and compute by using pictures, tracing letters in sand, and drill and practice. Many teachers in remedial instruction still use these techniques for children with learning disabilities and children who are developmentally delayed or mentally retarded. As Clark (1988) writes: "Despite the widespread inclusion of multisensory techniques in remedial programs for dyslexic students and the almost unanimous conviction among practitioners using these techniques is that they work, we have little empirical data to validate their effectiveness" (p. 49). From an educational point of view, the best help for teachers working with children with learning disabilities is to provide teachers with tools for identifying the academic and social problems that children with learning disabilities possess and a curriculum with strategies and materials that will help these children use their strengths to overcome their weaknesses (Lerner, 1997; Yule, Rutter, Berger, & Thompson, 1974).

ADAPTING THE LEARNING ENVIRONMENT

Where should students with learning disabilities be taught? The answer to this question is subject to lively debate about **inclusion.** (See Kauffman & Hallahan, 1995; Stainback & Stainback, 1992.) Several professional organizations argue for full inclusion of all students with disabilities in general education classrooms (see Chapter 11). However, the Council for Learning Disabilities, the National Joint Committee on Learning Disabilities, and the Hearing Disability Association of America do not support full inclusion for all students with learning disabilities (Lackaye, 1997). They suggest that while many students with learning disabilities may profit from the general education classroom, others may need alternative instructional environments and teaching strategies that cannot be provided within the context of a general education classroom.

Depending on the teacher's support system, students with learning disabilities can learn as much in a regular class as they can in a special class.

Whether children with learning disabilities are educated in regular education classrooms, resource rooms, or special education classes depends on what state they live in. In its *18th Annual Report to Congress,* the U.S. Department of Education (1997) reported that 94 percent of children with learning disabilities in Vermont, 86 percent of those in New Mexico, and 68 percent of those in Idaho are educated in the regular education classroom. However, 84 percent of the students with learning disabilities in Minnesota, 72 percent of those in Kentucky, and 78 percent of those in Colorado are educated in resource rooms. In 39 states, more than 40 percent of students with learning disabilities are educated in resource rooms.

Issues of Achievement

One of the studies supportive of inclusion demonstrated that students with learning disabilities in regular classrooms achieved as much as students with learning disabilities in special classrooms (Affleck, Madje, Adams, & Lowenbrau, 1998).

Other studies have not supported inclusion. Zigmond and Baker (1990) reported that students with major learning disabilities did not make progress in academic subjects in regular classrooms. In a further study, Zigmond et al. (1995) concluded that the achievement outcomes of 40 percent of the students with learning disabilities did not reflect gains. In fact, the students fell further behind.

One reason for the failure may be that teachers tend to teach the total class but the student with learning disabilities does not profit from group instruction (Fuchs, Fuchs, Hanlett, Phillips, & Korn, 1995). Guterman (1996) found that the consumer—the student with learning disabilities—viewed the classroom as unrealistic. In general, students with learning disabilities believed the regular classroom was better for social reasons but the resource room was better for learning (Kettman et al., 1998). Early childhood and elementary classrooms may be more successful in educating children with learning disabilities, but high school teachers are under greater pressure to cover course content (Schuman et al., 1995), and the culture of the school is content oriented (Tralli et al., 1996). Crockett and Kauffman (1998) and Keogh (1996) recommend tutorials, one-on-one teaching, and specialized instructional arrangements for students with learning disabilities. One model currently regarded as a solution is the collaborative model.

Collaboration and Inclusion

Collaborative team models composed of a regular education teacher and a special educator bring together the former's knowledge of content and grade-level expectations with the latter's expertise in strategies and skills designed for the student with learning disabilities.

Successful collaboration requires good problem-solving and interpersonal skills and knowledge of the goals and vocabulary of all team members.

Successful inclusion requires patience, perseverance, and time. Teachers, both regular and special education, who work in collaborative arrangements need to develop clear-cut responsibilities to be effective. When a collaborative team is first established, the members should receive training in small-group interpersonal skills and problem solving and review each other's vocabulary and goals (Wood, 1998).

Garnett and Lackaye (1993) have prepared a manual to help teachers adapt material by academic subject area to aid inclusion of the student with learning disabilities. These suggestions complement and repeat many of the suggestions made in this text. They highlight the need for careful diagnosis of the learning needs of the student and selection of the appropriate teaching strategy to remediate academic and social deficiencies. There are no conclusive answers. The student with learning disabilities has the right to be in the regular classroom, but the following question should be answered unequivocally: Is this the most appropriate place for a student to acquire the skills he or she needs to learn an independent life?

ADAPTING CURRICULUM

The curriculum for students with learning disabilities is the regular school curriculum. The major challenge facing teachers is how to organize and present instruction to students with learning disabilities based on the diagnosis and evaluation of their strengths and weaknesses. The teachers' task is to familiarize themselves with the school's required curriculum and to organize it so students with learning disabilities master as much of it as possible. Table 6.1 contains many suggestions on

Curriculum for students with learning disabilities is the same as for all non–learning disabled students in the general education classroom.

how to adapt the curriculum for students in inclusive classrooms as well as techniques for individualized instruction. Many students with learning disabilities do not profit from large-group instruction (Zigmond, 1997). Crockett and Kauffman (1998) suggest a focus on specially designed instruction to improve academic functioning and to select the strategies and best place to instruct.

For some students, one-on-one tutoring is the most appropriate instructional strategy, designed after the evaluation is complete and the IEP has been written. For others, the resource room can provide a person specially prepared to work with students with learning disabilities. In the resource room or regular education classroom, augmented communication devices and computers can be useful, but most of them require the student to be able to read and follow directions. Strategy learning (see Pressley et al., 1990) may be required before instructional technology is introduced.

In junior and senior high schools, some students have not yet mastered the basic skills sufficiently to cope with content subjects. English, mathematics, science, social science, and history require reading, and most of that reading is beyond the ability of youngsters with learning disabilities. These students also continue to have difficulty with tasks that require specific types of information processing. Many of them need the developmental programs that are appropriate for their age. Most schools offer these programs in resource rooms and self-contained special education classrooms.

Another technique is to modify the textbook (Meese, 1997), which can be done by highlighting the basic information to be learned or by recording the textbook. Adult volunteers can be asked to record the text. In the process of recording, a helpful device is to stop at times and summarize what has been covered. A student with specific reading difficulties can be integrated into a regular classroom utilizing this individualized technique.

Supportive Inclusion

Tralli et al. (1996) have proposed a model of supportive inclusion for the secondary school. Students with mild learning disabilities are given intensive instruction in strategy learning in the resource room on a daily basis until they achieve mastery. Following mastery of learning strategies, students are then taught content enhancement routines the teacher uses in the classroom. When the students have mastered those skills, they are taught empowerment skills geared to enable them to perform their best, make friends, and interact in positive ways with teachers and peers (Tralli et al., 1996, p. 205).

The success of supportive inclusion depends on the ability of teachers to plan and work collaboratively to support the students with their newly acquired skills. Some individuals with learning disabilities have become very successful, such as President Woodrow Wilson and Governor (and later Vice President) Nelson Rockefeller. For others, although they may have graduated from high school, employment opportunities have been mixed. Recent results show marked gains for persons with learning disabilities, who are employed at nearly equivalent rates as members of the general population (Blackorby & Wagner, 1996). However, many hold jobs that are low paying, for instance, dishwashing, clerking, and working in the fast-food industry. Some need on-site job training or job coaches. IDEA requires that transition services be included in the IEP when the student is 14.

TABLE 6.1　Adaptations for Students with Learning Disabilities in Inclusive Classrooms

General Adaptations	Textbook Adaptations

General Adaptations

Approaching the Students

Respect students as individuals with differences.
Provide reinforcement and encouragement.
Establish personal relationships with students.
Help students find appropriate ways to deal with feelings.
Communicate with students, the special education teacher, and parents.
Establish expectations for students.

Learning Environment

Establish routines appropriate for students.
Adapt classroom management strategies that are effective with students.
Adjust physical arrangement of room for students.

Instruction

Make adaptations for students when developing long-range plans.
Make adaptations for students when developing daily plans.
Plan assignments and activities that allow students to be successful.
Allot time for teaching learning strategies as well as content.
Monitor the students' understanding of directions and assigned tasks.
Monitor the students' understanding of concepts presented in class.
Provide individual instruction.

Materials

Adapt general classroom materials for students.
Use alternative materials for students.
Use computers to enhance learning as a tool for practicing skills.

Grouping Students

Pair each student with a classmate.
Involve students in small-group activities.
Involve students in whole-class activities.

Evaluation and Assessment

Provide extra time for students.
Adapt pacing of instruction.
Keep records to monitor students' progress.

Textbook Adaptations

Approaching Reading Assignments

Determine students' reading levels to identify students with potential problems with textbooks.
Read textbook aloud to students.
Create interest in reading assignments to motivate students.
Teach reading strategies to improve comprehension of text.
Provide students with questions to guide their reading.
Preview reading assignments with students to orient them to a topic and budget reading and study time.
Substitute or supplement textbook reading assignments with direct experiences.
Provide students with purposes for reading.
Reduce length of assignments.
Introduce key vocabulary before a reading assignment.

Varying Media and Visuals

Use film, videotapes, and recordings to supplement or substitute for textbook reading.
Use computer programs to supplement or substitute for textbook reading.
Use different colors to mark key words, definitions, and important facts throughout textbooks.
Teach students to use graphic aids.
Avoid use of textbooks.
Audiotape textbook content.

Adapting Teaching Strategies

Teach study strategies to improve retention of text material.
Work with students individually or in small groups to master textbook material.
Provide assistance for answering text-based questions.
Structure postreading activities to increase retention of content.
Summarize and reduce textbook information to guide classroom discussions and independent reading.
Demonstrate and model effective reading strategies and comprehension techniques.
Determine level of difficulty of textbooks.

TABLE 6.1 Adaptations for Students with Learning Disabilities in Inclusive Classrooms (cont.)

General Adaptations (cont.)	Textbook Adaptations (cont.)
Evaluation and Assessment (cont.) Provide students with ongoing feedback about performance. Adapt evaluations for students. Adapt scoring/grading criteria for students.	**Adapting Teaching Strategies (cont.)** Explain textbook information thoroughly in classroom lectures and presentations. Pair students to master textbook content. Construct abridged version of textbook content or use publisher's abridged version. Develop a study guide or study outline to direct learning from text. Preview textbook with students to orient them to textbook organization and learning tools. Place students in cooperative learning groups to master textbook content. Use multilevel, multimaterial approach. Teach comprehension-monitoring techniques to improve ongoing understanding of text.

Source: Adapted from Schumm, J. S., & Vaughn, S. (1995). "Getting Ready for Inclusion: Is the Stage Set?" *Learning Disabilities Research and Practice 10*(3), 169–179 (pp. 178, 179). Reprinted by permission of Lawrence Erlbaum Associates, Inc.

ADAPTING TEACHING STRATEGIES

The approaches presented here can be adapted to subject matter, including mathematics, writing and spelling, and reading or dealing with dyslexia. These techniques can be used in the regular classroom, resource room, or special class.

Applied Behavioral Analysis

Applied behavioral analysis (ABA) is frequently called *behaviorism* because it grew out of earlier work on the modification of challenging behaviors and emotional disturbances. Behaviorism is based on the work of Skinner (1953) and has been used widely to control or modify unacceptable behavior in school. The same techniques are used for teaching academic skills and subjects (Trieber & Lahey, 1983). In theory, ABA is concerned with the causes of disorder only insofar as they help teachers to formulate a treatment plan (Tindal & Marston, 1988). The learning programs are based on individual analyses of the child's functioning rather than on the child's assumed biological problems. Before the steps of ABA can be implemented, the task to be learned must be thoroughly analyzed (*task analysis*), and the child's skill and academic strengths and weaknesses must be thoroughly assessed (Trieber & Lahey, 1983).

Koorland (1986) suggested the following steps in ABA:

1. Pinpoint the child's behavior to be targeted for change.

Researchers recently have focused on analyzing what children must learn and identifying the problems children with learning disabilities have in mastering the material. *(© Paul S. Conklin)*

Applied behavioral analysis uses demonstration, modeling, and feedback to teach and reinforce desired behavior.

2. Measure the behavior directly and repeatedly.

3. Institute a change in events antecedent and consequent to the behavior (what happens in the environment immediately before and after instruction).

4. Evaluate and record results.

5. Try again if goals are not attained. (Koorland, 1986)

To those five steps, we add four more:

6. If the child is successful, reward or reinforce the success.

7. If the child is successful, increase the demand with additional or more complex tasks.

8. Chart the results of the child's work.

9. Involve the child in identifying target behaviors.

Demonstrating, modeling, and feedback are recommended antecedent and consequent strategies in ABA. The instruction is always direct and focused on the specific fact or skill to be learned. At times, prompting or cueing is used to help the student focus on the task (Koorland, 1986). Direct instruction can be used with individual children or with small groups of children who have similar problems. Evaluation and recording of results are conducted for individual children, however, and are not combined for group results.

The following is an example of how to apply this approach to teach arithmetic:

1. Teach the concept of 5.

2. Identify for yourself what are the smallest units of 5: $1 + 4$; $4 + 1$; $3 + 2$; $2 + 3$; if zero is known, $5 + 0$ and $0 + 5$.

3. Present the concepts directly to the child, step by step (one at a time).

4. If necessary, use aids such as sticks or objects that can be placed in groups of five and counted.

5. Record results and reward or reinforce success.

6. Review and reteach any concept that is not mastered, such as $0 + 5$ or $5 + 0$.

7. If the child is successful, move on to the concept of 6.

8. Follow the steps used in teaching the concept of 5.

Programs have been developed to teach students how to multiply and solve word problems (Cramer & Ellis, 1996). In summary, teaching strategy programs fall into two main categories: (1) teaching strategies that can be applied to all content areas and (2) those that apply to specific areas.

Diagnostic Prescriptive Model

The diagnostic prescriptive model (Pressley et al., 1990) is designed to remediate *executive functions, metacognitions,* or *organizational strategies.* The model, which focuses on the teacher's behavior as well as the student's, can be applied to all academic areas and to children with and without learning disabilities. The approach uses many behavioral principles and includes teaching children strategies for approaching learning problems. Psychologists refer to these strategies as **metacognition,** or the ability to think about one's own thinking and monitor its effectiveness. Pressley's overall plan is presented in Table 6.2.

Learning strategies are techniques, principles, or rules that help students learn how to solve problems, complete tasks, self-regulate, and use past learnings (Lackaye, 1997). A learning strategy program teaches the students strategies that can be used in a variety of content areas as well as with specific content, for example, mathematics or reading (Deshler, Ellis, & Lenz, 1996). If the child is not successful in the task, the strategy may have to be repeated. It may also be advisable to reconsider and perhaps modify the behaviors of the teacher, change the setting of the learning, or change the nature of the reinforcement (to ensure that it is rewarding).

The diagnostic prescriptive model approach can be applied to all subject areas from elementary to high school. It emphasizes self-monitoring by the teacher and the student. Facts, skills, and strategies may be taught in tutoring sessions, through peer teaching, or in small groups (Clark, 1988). The teacher may use prompts such as pictures of a word or of the idea of a story, object aids for counting or understanding fractions, or the actual object when introducing a word such as *ball.*

There are several other models for teaching strategies to help students learn new materials and integrate new information with what was previously taught (Sturomski, 1997). DEFENDS (Deshler, Ellis, & Lenz, 1996) reads as follows:

Decide on audience, goals, and position.

Estimate main ideas and details.

Figure best order of main ideas and details.

Express the position in the opening.

Teaching strategies are often modified for children with learning disabilities.

	TABLE 6.2 General Model of How-to-Teach Strategies

- Teach a few strategies at a time, intensively and extensively, as part of the ongoing curriculum.
- Model and explain new strategies.
- Model again and re-explain strategies in ways that are sensitive to aspects of strategy use that are not well understood.
- Explain to students where and when to use strategies.
- Provide plenty of practice, using strategies for as many appropriate tasks as possible.
- Encourage students to monitor how they are doing when they are using strategies.
- Encourage continued use of and generalization of strategies.
- Increase students' motivation to use strategies by heightening students' awareness that they are acquiring valuable skills that are at the heart of competent functioning.
- Emphasize reflective processing rather than speedy processing; do all possible to eliminate high anxiety in students; encourage students to shield themselves from distraction so they can attend to academic tasks.

Source: From M. Pressley and Associates (1990). *Cognitive Strategy Instruction That Really Improves Children's Academic Performance.* Cambridge, MA: Brookline Books, p. 18. Reprinted with permission.

Note each main idea and supporting points.

Drive home the message in the last sentence.

Search for errors and correct.

Other strategies include questioning and paraphrasing, reciprocal teaching, questioning to find the main idea, and story mapping (NICHCY, 1997). An approach that is supported by research evidence is the Strategies Intervention Model (SIM) (Deshler, Ellis, & Lenz, 1996). First, the teacher selects a strategy or strategies to be taught, then follows these steps:

STRATEGIES INTERVENTION MODEL

1. Pretest students and get them interested in learning the strategy.
2. Describe the strategy and give examples of ways it can be used.
3. Model the strategy, for example, talking aloud as one works on a real task.
4. Practice the strategy; have the student think aloud.
5. Provide feedback.
6. Provide generalization; show how the strategy can be applied to a different problem.

Guided practice and generalizing the strategies to new problems and different contexts assist the student with learning disabilities in mastering and using the strategy independently (Sturomski, 1997).

Mnemonic Devices

A **mnemonic** is a device or rhyme that helps people to remember words or concepts. The use of mnemonics is a popular way to help children with learning disabilities (Snowman, 1991). One simple example is this mnemonic sentence that helps us remember the planets in order of distance from the sun: Mary's (Mercury) violet (Venus) eyes (Earth) make (Mars) John (Jupiter) sit (Saturn) up (Uranus) nights (Neptune) period (Pluto). More sophisticated examples can be found in Snowman (1991).

Cooperative Learning

In cooperative learning, students of all levels of ability work together to solve a problem.

Cooperative learning is a teaching strategy that involves students of varying ability levels working together to solve a problem. The students may ask the teacher for help if necessary, but for the most part the group works on the problem without the teacher. When used appropriately, cooperative learning has positive results. Students with difficulties are assisted by others who have mastered the skills needed to solve the problem; those students in turn have their understanding of the problem reinforced by helping others in the group.

Another form of cooperative learning is **peer tutoring,** in which a capable student works with a student who needs help on a specific topic. The success of peer tutoring depends on balanced interaction between the tutor and the student, with the tutor teaching, rather than telling, the student what to do. Care should be taken with peer teaching. Many students with learning disabilities have difficulty understanding new concepts, to the frustration of themselves and their peers in these cooperative settings. This can lead to further social rejection of the student with a learning disability.

Mastery Learning

Mastery learning breaks instruction into learnable units at each individual's level.

Mastery learning was developed in the educational reform movement of the 1960s. It is a combination of ideas of Bloom (1971), Gagne (1985), and others. The basic concept is to begin instruction at the student's current level of functioning and to break the instructional tasks into learnable units based on the individual student. In addition, continuous evaluation of the student's progress is conducted, and students proceed at their own learning rate. Guskey, Passaro, and Wheeler (1997) suggest that by applying mastery learning strategies in regular classrooms, teachers can effectively deal with the larger range of achievement levels inclusion presents to them.

Cognitive Instruction

Other approaches for teaching students with learning disabilities are based on cognitive (information-processing strategies) and cognitive-learning theory (a combination of ABA and cognitive principles). The distinction between ABA and cognitive approaches is becoming blurred because they use similar techniques. The major difference is that cognitive approaches rely more on theories of how children process information, along with direct and indirect teaching.

Wong (1986) emphasized that all cognitive approaches attempt to have the child with learning disabilities become aware of his or her own learning processes. Thus, in learning how to read, the child first focuses on the knowledge that words have meaning, that they are made of letters that stand for sounds, and that the sounds are part of the child's auditory system. Cognitive approaches combine knowledge of letter recognition, phonemes, syntax, word knowledge, and strategies for abstracting meaning from the printed page (metacognition) (Baker & Brown, 1984; Short & Ryan, 1984). Wong (1986) suggested that basic knowledge of four cognitive strategies aids reading:

- Awareness of the purpose of reading
- Knowledge of reading strategies
- Self-monitoring comprehension
- Spontaneous looking back while reading (p. 21)

Teaching cognitive strategies has been popular with both cognitive and behaviorally oriented curriculum planners. One major project (Kline, Deshler, & Schumaker, 1991) teaches educators how to teach the strategies and also presents a curriculum for teaching students with learning disabilities.

Learning how to learn has long been a goal of modern education, because it provides students with the ability to be lifelong learners. Many students without disabilities acquire these strategies quickly; for students with learning disabilities, the teaching has to be more direct, explicit, repetitive, and in smaller steps (NICHCY, 1997). Students with learning disabilities usually need daily and sustained instruction and multiple opportunities for practice (Tralli, Columbo, Deshler, & Schumaker, 1996).

Approaches to Content Instruction

Preschool curriculum for those at risk for learning disabilities is not too different from the regular preschool curriculum. The major difference is the mode of presentation, which focuses directly, in a supportive manner, on the child's strengths as well as on deficits, allowing the child ample time to engage in the tasks. The tasks may need frequent repetition and review for the child with potential learning disabilities. Tasks include the following (see Lerner, 1997, for other ideas):

PRESCHOOL CURRICULUM

- *Gross motor:* walking forward, backward, and sideways; line walks
- *Fine motor:* cutting, pasting, buttoning, tracing, throwing, and assembling puzzles
- *Communication:* listening, talking, explaining, rhyming, and engaging others
- *Visual:* recognizing similarities and differences in pictures, objects, shapes, and letters
- *Auditory:* phonological awareness, word games, rhyming games
- *Cognitive:* learning relationships and differences; classifying objects by use, color, and shape
- *Social:* communication with peers and adults, sharing, turn taking, cooperative play

Reading.   A child first learning to read matches his or her own auditory sound system to an abstract system of print. In English, the twenty-six letters of the alphabet are abstract symbols of a sound system consisting of consonants and vowels. The vowels (*a,e,i,o,u,* and sometimes *y*) combine with the consonants to make up forty-eight *phonemes,* the smallest units of sound meaning. Thus, "bat" has three phonemes (*b a t*), which are blended together. "Boat" also has three phonemes, because the *a* is silent and serves only to make the *o* long, or sound its name.

To read, a child must have a rich store of auditorially perceived words that have meaning, such as knowing that a bat can be a flying rodent or a stick used in baseball. The child must next break the abstract code. Although words contain letters, it is not knowing the alphabet in sequence that helps in reading but understanding the relationship of the letters as phonemes and being able to decode (figure out the sound the letter stands for) and blend the letters into words (Liberman & Shankweiler, 1985; Mann & Liberman, 1984). Deficit in phonology appears to be the major problem causing children with learning disabilities to fail in reading (Lyon, 1996).

Approaches to teaching reading to students with learning disabilities are based on one of three philosophies of how children learn to read: bottom-up, top-down, and interactive. The *bottom-up approach* attempts to teach children phonics, letter-sounds combinations, and isolated words, and then how to use those skills to decode text. The *top-down approach* uses the child's prior knowledge and experience to construct meaning from a text. Programs that use whole-language or literature-based methods are examples of the top-down philosophy, which emphasizes that meaning and understanding can be generated only from within the reader in the context of working with real literature. The *interactive approach* combines the top-down and bottom-up philosophies. The student might be encouraged to use top-down strategies when the text is familiar and bottom-up strategies when the text is unfamiliar (Mercer, 1992, p. 501).

Many schools use basal readers in reading instruction. Basal readers are prepared by grade level and provide material for the development and practice of reading skills and reading comprehension. Stories are selected that will appeal to the age of the child and introduce skills in a sequential fashion. There usually is a teacher's manual for each grade that contains suggestions on how to present the story. Basal readers generally take an interactive approach; however, some series introduce bottom-up activities earlier than others.

Most basal readers suggest a *directed teaching approach;* the teacher introduces new words contained in the story, motivates children to read by telling them what kind of story it is (fairy tale, mystery, and so on), and lets know in advance what to look for in the story. Students read silently, sometimes reading the story aloud after reading it silently. The teacher questions them about the content of the story and plans follow-up activities.

In the *language experience approach,* students dictate stories based on their experiences. The stories are usually written on a large chart, then students copy from the chart into their own storybooks. The approach can be used with small groups, the members of which dictate a story. The goal is to have students read the words dictated from their own vocabulary and use them to make connections with the rules of phonics. Teachers can build more complicated stories by providing in-school experiences or field trips that can become the subject for students' stories.

Later, as writing and reading skills improve, students may write their own stories and read them to the class or teacher. Burns, Roe, and Ross (1992) suggested that the language experience approach can be used effectively with bilingual students who are able to understand the stories they dictate and whose oral skills are reinforced by the use of written language.

For students with learning disabilities, any of these approaches may need to be used with one-to-one instruction so the teacher can identify a student's learning style and the particular difficulties the student is experiencing.

Many techniques have been used to teach children with dyslexia to read: tracing over letters, using the sense of touch, showing pictures along with the word, using toys along with the word, and using a general language enrichment program. Persons with dyslexia usually have deficits in the ability to process information into language or cognitive systems. Some teachers rely on tape recordings of books. After the tape has been played, the teacher asks the child a series of oral questions about its content. If the child has major problems with audition as well as dyslexia, however, this method may not work. Teachers need to try different approaches to determine which works best with the individual student.

Using the spell check on the computer is a legitimate way to solve problems with spelling.

Spelling and Writing.   Spelling is a more difficult skill to master than reading, because there are no clues, such as context, to help students spell (Lerner, 1997). In addition, the English language contains many exceptions (for example, *tough, through, thorough*) to orderly phonetic rules, and each exception must be taught separately. Word processors with spell checks are invaluable for students with spelling difficulties. Remember that the resource the child uses to achieve the correct spelling is not as important as the fact that the child was able to select an appropriate source and solve the problem (this is equally true in mathematics and other subjects).

If a motor writing problem is also present, the teacher may ask an occupational therapist for techniques to help the child hold and control the pencil as well as techniques to make writing legible.

The student who has difficulty in composing a story needs to be taught the strategies for composition: planning what is to be written, making an outline of the story's sequence, considering the parts of the story. Discussing the story with the teacher or the tutor before writing may aid the student in avoiding sparse, uninteresting one-paragraph compositions. Table 6.3 presents the Internet-Expanded Writing Process, which is available on the World Wide Web (Boone & Higgins, 1998).

Mathematics.   Most children with math learning disabilities profit from working with basic counting, matching, and measuring activities with real objects. Tongue depressors, small discs, and water pitchers are useful objects. Repeated counting to obtain the correct numerical sequence is basic. Recognizing how many objects are present without having to count them is a good exercise. Most arithmetic manipulatives help students gain a firm foundation for later arithmetic operations. Once children have learned the basic signs of the four basic arithmetic operations, a simple calculator can be useful to assist them in accomplishing the calculations needed to solve mathematical concepts (Lerner, 1997).

	TABLE 6.3 The Internet-Expanded Writing Process	
Writing Process Phases	**Typical Activities**	**Internet Activities**
Prewriting	■ Brainstorming ■ Outlining ■ Clustering ■ Collecting information	■ Keyword searches ■ Browsing ■ Downloading information
Writing	■ Series of drafts	
Revision	■ Peer response ■ Teacher response ■ Editing ■ Revision	■ E-mail drafts to other kids for response ■ E-mail drafts to experts for response ■ Final draft reviewed for possible hypertext links to other WWW sites ■ Additional searches made for possible links ■ Story is pasted into a WWW creation program ■ Hypertext links added
Publishing	■ Final drafts ■ Bound into a book ■ Can be read by others in class ■ Parents can read it	■ Story file is transferred to a classroom WWW site on a networked computer ■ URL address is established ■ The story WWW page is registered with search page, Yahooligans!, for international access

Source: From S. Smith, R. Boone, and K. Higgins. (1998, May/June). "Expanding the Writing Process to the Web," *Teaching Exceptional Children, 30*(5), p. 25. Copyright 1998 by The Council for Exceptional Children. Reprinted with permission.

Children with reading problems may need to have word problems read to them. This can be easily accomplished by a peer or in a cooperative learning group.

INSTRUCTIONAL TECHNOLOGY

Although there are many software programs designed for students with disabilities (check the Web site http://www.cec.sped.org/pd/exhibit.htm), some students with learning disabilities have difficulty learning how to use the computer. Many are not trained. Tony is a case in point. Like 72 percent of students with learning disabilities (Barnett, Clarilo, & Payette, 1997), he repeated one grade in high school and dropped out before graduating. He successfully completed a training

Teaching techniques use multi-sensory strategies to assist learning. *(© Paul S. Conklin)*

program and secured a job as a skilled mechanic. His success brought difficulty because his employer upgraded him to a position that required the use of a computer. Rather than fail, Tony quit his job and took a lower-paying position that did not require sophisticated skills. Wong (1998) reports that many women on welfare have previously undiagnosed learning disabilities and are untrained and thus unable to meet the demands under many current work-welfare programs. As technology increasingly dominates the workplace, instruction designed to assist students with learning disabilities to acquire computer skills is essential.

TRANSITION

Transition to the workplace may require a job coach and job training.

Individuals with learning disabilities have their disabilities throughout their lives. They may graduate from high school with a special diploma that indicates they attended but did not meet all requirements, and they have very low employment rates (Kavali, Forness, & Bender, Vol. 3, 1987). The U.S. Vocational and Rehabilitation Department has developed programs on the national and local levels to assist persons with learning disabilities in making a successful transition from school to work.

One effort to assist persons with severe and profound disabilities is *supportive employment*. Supportive employment places the individual in an actual work setting and provides a supervisor to assist in mastery of the required tasks. As the person masters the tasks, coaching is diminished, and the supervisor gradually is removed but may remain available for counseling and emotional support. Supportive employment grants pay for this on-the-job preparation and for the supervisor's time. Although strategies vary, most of these programs have a common goal: to enable the person with learning disabilities to be independent and self-supporting. Bear in mind that persons with learning disabilities vary greatly in skill performance. Some function quite adequately, others need a great deal of help.

With students whose learning disabilities are severe, a variety of strategies are used: peer tutoring, functional skills development (at the work site), counseling about social skills (how to dress, how to talk to coworkers and supervisors), and counseling about good work habits (low absenteeism, punctuality).

Some students with learning disabilities may enter community colleges or four-year colleges. Persons with learning disabilities who have mastered the acquisition of strategy skills and academic subjects are able to pursue higher education. Some may need extra support to complete academic tasks. Professors may allow those who have difficulty writing to dictate their responses to examinations. Garnett (1989) prepared a handbook of suggestions for college students with learning disabilities as well as an excellent handbook for teachers (Garnett, 1996).

Family and Lifespan Issues

The parents of a person with severe learning disabilities are constantly challenged to make adjustments. They must consider their own needs as well as the special needs of their child, needs that change as the child moves into adolescence and adulthood. Some people with learning disabilities may continue to live in their parents' home until early middle age (Schearn & Todd, 1997), while others go on to independent living.

Parents play an integral part in any plan to assist their child with learning disabilities. At times, parents and other family members need help to become fully empowered to make decisions for themselves. O'Hara and Levy (1987) suggested the questions listed in Table 6.4 to help practitioners determine who can best assist the student to function independently.

 Families need to be informed that the child's problems are not due to lack of effort.

Families must be intimately involved in every aspect of the life of the child with a disability, from diagnosis and intervention programs to transitional services, not only because of the law's requirements but because the family is key to the child's success. This is particularly true of families with children with learning disabilities. These children do not function as other children do, and they confuse the family. Too often the child is seen as lazy, not working hard enough, or resistant to instruction. From the earliest days of the child's life, children with learning disabilities tend to be less consistent, less flexible, unpredictable, and prone to temper outbursts (Breske, 1994).

The quality of the child-parent transactions, the extent to which the family provides diverse activities, influences the child's progress. Families of children with learning disabilities are at risk themselves if they lack social support and are undergoing stress due to having a child with disabilities. They may fall into the trap of teaching by being more "demanding" than "interacting" and using meaningless drills rather than *transacting* (taking turns in conversation, for example).

Harbin (1993) pointed out that families with children with disabilities have an ever changing source of stress that affects the entire family. For children with

TABLE 6.4   Questions to Help Practitioners Determine How Best to Assist Parents of Children with Learning Disabilities

- How do parents describe their child? Do they use primarily positive or negative terms?
- What is their statement of the problem?
- What do parents expect from professionals? Remediation or cure?
- What do parents understand about the cause of the problem? Do they think it is their fault their child is learning disabled? The fault of one parent? Is it genetically linked? Are the parents blaming each other? Are they blaming professionals?
- What do parents understand about the child's ability to influence the problem?
- What diagnostic information have they heard previously?
- What is their understanding of learning disabilities?
- What is their perception of their own relationship to the ongoing nature of the problem? To what extent do they believe they can influence the course of the disability? How have they tried in the past to influence the situation?
- What has their experience been with other persons presenting problems similar to those of their child?
- What is the parents' assessment of how this problem affects their lives?
- How do they regard previous experiences associated with this problem? What was it like for them to take this child for diagnostic testing? Was their pediatrician supportive? What was diagnostic counseling like for them? How was the information presented? Were both parents present for the informing session? Were they able to support one another? What have their experiences been like with the school system thus far?
- What are their expectations for their own performances in relation to the problem?
- How do the parents feel about this situation? Are they angry or sad? Are they able to express any feelings at all?

Source: Adapted from D. O'Hara and J. Levy (1987), "Family Intervention," in K. Kavale, S. Forness, and M. Bender (Eds.), *Handbook of Learning Disabilities*. Boston: College-Hill, p. 215. Reprinted by permission of the author.

learning disabilities, the struggle can be, and usually is, lifelong. Parents may feel guilty that they have genetically passed on the disability. However, families are unique and may display amazing strengths as well as needs. Many recognize that their children with learning disabilities need to be taught strategies (executive functions) for learning as well as information and facts. Families are key to convincing their children with learning disabilities that they are not "stupid" or "lazy," and families need to find ways to motivate their children to persist in the face of academic failure.

Teachers working closely with families can develop an individualized learning program appropriate for the child. Teachers can do much to help families use the appropriate teaching strategy for the particular child. At times, this may require a revision of the family's child-rearing techniques; at other times, it may require a reinforcement of the effective techniques the family has been using. Regardless, transaction occurs in four areas: (1) teacher-family, (2) teacher-child, (3) family-child, and (4) parent-teacher. Each influences the other as progress is made. The task, as Heinicke (1993) suggested, is to consolidate a helping working relationship in three areas: (1) encouraging communication, (2) providing mutual support, and (3) revising and evaluating child instruction and progress.

There is a particular distinction between families of children with learning disabilities and families of children with other disabilities. Learning disabilities are diagnosed later in life, and the child may exhibit emotional problems growing out of difficulties in learning that occur before his or her condition is known (O'Hara & Levy, 1987). The family's way of life may therefore have to be altered once the diagnosis is made, and the change can disrupt the functioning of the family and its flow of development. Whereas the family of a child with other kinds of disabilities usually has to make changes early in the child's life, the family of a child with learning disabilities has to make changes much later.

Summary of Major Ideas

1. Although the cause or causes of learning disabilities are largely unknown, the most commonly accepted cause is a dysfunction in processing information at the neurological level (not damage to the system).

2. Many researchers are attempting to investigate subgroups of children with learning disabilities and to design teaching strategies that match specific deficits.

3. There is major movement in the field toward accepting of the intelligence-achievement deficit and designing instructional strategies that capitalize on the individual's strengths.

4. Accurate diagnosis of a student with a learning disability who has academic deficiency is key to planning appropriate instructional remediation.

5. In most cases, a student with a learning disability will need, regardless of instructional setting, individual, tutorial, peer, or cooperative instruction to become academically successful.

6. A student with a learning disability can be integrated best in regular class settings in the areas of his or her competence.

7. All students with learning disabilities require a full range of support for their disability as well as instruction designed to utilize their strengths to resolve their academic deficits.

8. Most major approaches for teaching students with learning disabilities include teaching strategy as well as specific subject matter.

9. Transitional programs are needed for persons with moderate-to-severe learning disabilities.

10. Persons with learning disabilities face a lifelong problem, because the deficits are at the neurological processing level, and dysfunction will continue throughout the lifespan.

Unresolved Issues

1. *Definition of learning disabilities.* The definition of *learning disabilities* is not uniform across the country. Some states may include the mildly retarded in this group, thereby inflating the prevalence figure.

2. *Cause of learning disabilities.* There is no consensus about the cause or causes of learning disabilities.

3. *Early intervention.* Techniques have not been fully developed for the early identification of individuals with learning disabilities. At present, we do not know if the development of deficits associated with learning disabilities can be prevented early in life. For effective intervention, attention must be given to indications of potential problems during the earliest stages of the brain's plasticity.

4. *Transitional programs.* There is a need for more programs throughout the United States to help individuals with learning disabilities make the transition from high school to work or college.

5. *Appropriate placements.* There is strong debate as to the appropriate instructional setting for students with learning disabilities. Some argue for full inclusion in the regular classroom. Others suggest partial inclusion with remedial instruction in the resource room. For some, individualized tutoring is deemed advisable. For others, the special class is still maintained in some settings. There is no consensus on where to most effectively educate students with learning disabilities.

6. *Full range of services.* Students with learning disabilities are a heterogenous group with a wide range of individual needs. For schools to provide the multiple range of services for individual students strains financial resources. In addition, there are shortages in available trained personnel.

Key Terms

academic achievement learning
   disabilities p. 225
applied behavioral analysis (ABA) p. 243
aptitude-achievement discrepancy p. 220
attention-deficit hyperactivity disorder
   (ADHD) p. 228
cognitive strategies p. 233
cooperative learning p. 247
developmental learning disabilities p. 225
differential diagnosis p. 235
dyslexia p. 229
dyslexic p. 229

executive function p. 233
hyperactivity p. 228
inclusion p. 239
learning disabilities p. 221
metacognition p. 233
mnemonic p. 247
neuropsychological learning disabilities
   p. 225
peer tutoring p. 247
perceptual-motor disabilities p. 237

Questions for Thought

1. How does the *Federal Register* define *specific learning disability*?   p. 220

2. What four criteria must teachers consider when identifying students with learning disabilities?   p. 220

3. Briefly compare the characteristics of a child who is mildly retarded (see Chapter 5) with the characteristics of a child who is learning disabled. pp. 220–222

4. Describe the differences between neuropsychological/developmental and academic achievement perspectives on learning disabilities. p. 225

5. According to the neuropsychological/developmental model, what are the causes of learning disabilities? p. 225

6. Briefly describe how each of the following contributes to learning disabilities: biological and genetic factors, perceptual-motor problems, visual processing deficits, auditory processing deficits, memory disorders, attentional deficits, and hyperactivity. pp. 226–229

7. Define *dyslexia* and describe some of the techniques used to teach dyslexic children. pp. 229–230, 249–250

8. In preschool children, the identification of learning disabilities is directly related to behavior on age-approximate tasks. What are these tasks, and how does the examiner get the information necessary for identification? pp. 236–237

9. What are the most common learning disorders among preschoolers? How are they diagnosed? p. 237

10. What steps are involved in applied behavioral analysis? pp. 243–244

11. What are some effective teaching strategies? pp. 243–248

12. Describe three approaches to reading instruction for students with learning disabilities. pp. 249–250

 Resources for Further Study

REFERENCES OF SPECIAL INTEREST

Adelman, H., & Taylor, L. (1993). *Learning problems and learning disabilities.* Pacific Grove, CA: Brooks/Cole.
> The authors distinguish between students with learning problems and those with learning disabilities. This comprehensive text is a rich source of instructional techniques and intervention strategies.

Clark, D. B. (1993). *Dyslexia: Theory and practice of remedial instruction.* Parkton, MD: York Press.
> The author presents a comprehensive view of dyslexia and the designing of educational strategies to assist dyslexic individuals.

Garnett, K., & Lackaye, T. (1993). *Modifying and adapting methods and materials for students with disabilities in mainstreamed classrooms.* New York: Hunter College.
> In this valuable resource of techniques organized by academic subjects, specific suggestions are presented for teachers to use in a regular classroom with a child with learning disabilities.

Kavale, K. A., Forness, S. R., & Bender, M. (Eds.). (1988). *Handbook of learning disabilities: Vol. 1. Dimensions and diagnoses. Vol. 2. Methods and interventions. Vol. 3. Programs and practices.* Boston: College-Hill/Little, Brown.

The articles in these volumes cover all areas of the various theories and practices in the field of learning disabilities.

Lerner, J. L. (1997). *Learning disabilities: Theories, diagnosis and teaching strategies* (6th ed.). Boston: Houghton Mifflin Company.
This text is a comprehensive introduction in the teaching of students with learning disabilities. Its balanced coverage of theory and practice has made it a standard in its field.

Lyon, G. R. (Ed.). (1993). *Understanding learning disabilities*. Baltimore: Paul H. Brookes.
This book is an exploration of the theories and implications of practice for persons with learning disabilities.

Pressley, M., & Associates. (1990). *Cognitive strategy instruction*. Cambridge, MA: Brookline Books.
This is an excellent source of strategies for teachers and students and of ways to design and conduct instruction for all children.

Rourke, B. P. (Ed.). (1995). *Syndrome of non-verbal learning disabilities*. New York: Guilford Press.
The writings in this collection constitute a comprehensive overview of subtypes of learning disabilities whose assets and deficits have predictable academic outcomes.

Wong, B. Y. L. (1996). *The ABC's of learning disabilities*. San Diego, CA: Academic Press.
A concise summary of the research, teaching, methodologies, and issues in the field of learning disabilities. This book is an excellent combination of research findings and practical applications.

JOURNALS

Annals of Dyslexia
International Dyslexia Society
Chester Bldg., Suite 382
8600 LaSalle Rd.
Baltimore, MD 21204-6020

Journal of Learning Disabilities
PRO-ED Journals
8700 Shoal Creek Blvd.
Austin, TX 78757

PROFESSIONAL ORGANIZATIONS

International Dyslexia Society
(formerly Orton)
Chester Bldg., Suite 382
8600 LaSalle Rd.
Baltimore, MD 21204-6020
http://www.interdys.org

Learning Disabilities Association (LDA)
4156 Library Rd.
Pittsburgh, PA 15234
http://www.ldanatl.org

National Center for Learning Disabilities
381 Park Ave., Suite 1401
New York, NY 10016
http://www.ncld.org

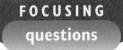

7

Children with Emotional and Behavior Disorders

FOCUSING questions

What are several potential causes of emotional and behavior disorders?

What can we do to deter an attitude of learned helplessness?

What techniques do we use to teach children to manage and control their own behavior?

How does functional assessment differ from other treatment programs?

How successful are special education programs in helping youngsters with emotional and behavior disorders make the transition from school to workplace?

ew experiences are as disturbing to teachers as trying to teach children who are chronically unhappy or driven to aggressive, antisocial behavior. The teachers feel distressed, knowing there's a problem but feeling unable to do anything about it.

Children with behavior problems carry a burden that youngsters with other disabilities do not. We don't blame children who are mentally retarded or who have cerebral palsy for their deviant behavior. But many people assume that children with behavior disorders can control their actions and could stop their disturbing behavior if they wanted to. The sense that they are somehow responsible for their disability colors these children's interactions with those around them: their families, their agemates, their teachers.

Definition

It is not easy to define behavior and emotional problems in children. Most definitions assume that a child with a **behavior disorder,** or serious emotional disturbance, reveals consistent "age-inappropriate behavior" leading to social conflict, personal unhappiness, and school failure.

A behavior disorder implies that the child is causing trouble for someone else. Serious emotional disturbance can be merely manifesting personal unhappiness. But almost all children reveal age-inappropriate behavior at one time or another. Moreover, a child's behavior is not the only variable that determines classification in this category. The person who perceives the child's behavior as "inappropriate" plays a key role in the decision. Clearly, some kinds of behavior, such as physical attacks, constant weeping or unhappiness, and extreme hyperactivity, are unacceptable in any setting. But the acceptability of a wide range of other behaviors depends on the attitude of the perceiver.

In our pluralistic society, behavior that is acceptable in some groups or subcultures is unacceptable in others. Our definition, therefore, must allow for cultural differences. Can we say that a child's behavior is deviant if the behavior is the norm in the child's cultural group, even though we may find the particular behavior socially unacceptable?

Wood (1982) suggested that a definition of *problem behavior,* or a set of actions that follows from the definition, should include four elements:

- *The disturber element.* What or who is perceived to be the focus of the problem?
- *The problem behavior element.* How is the problem behavior described?
- *The setting element.* In what setting does the problem behavior occur?
- *The disturbed element.* Who regards the behavior as a problem? (pp. 7–8)

These elements clearly suggest an environmental basis for the definition. The term *problem behavior* refers not just to the behavior itself but to the context in which the behavior is observed or judged. Debate continues among the various professionals who encounter children with behavior problems about how much environment and how much personal characteristics influence the classroom and interpersonal problems.

A definition of acceptable behavior must allow for cultural differences.

Because practically all children exhibit inappropriate behavior from time to time, criteria for identifying problem behavior depend largely on the frequency and intensity of specific behaviors. *(© Lilyan Aloma/Monkmeyer Press Photo Service)*

Context often plays a role in defining problem behavior.

The federal government's definition of children with serious emotional disabilities is important because it determines who receives federal funds to help with their exceptionality. In the Individuals with Disabilities Education Act (IDEA), PL 101-476, that definition is as follows:

> . . . a condition exhibiting one or more of the following characteristics over a long period of time and to a marked degree that adversely affects educational performance—
>
> A. An inability to learn that cannot be explained by intellectual, sensory, or health factors;
>
> B. An inability to build or maintain satisfactory interpersonal relationships with peers and teachers;
>
> C. Inappropriate types of behavior or feelings under normal circumstances;
>
> D. A general pervasive mood of unhappiness or depression; or
>
> E. A tendency to develop physical symptoms or fears associated with personal or school problems. [*Code of Federal Regulations*, Title 34, §300.7(b)(9)]

As defined by IDEA, a serious emotional disturbance (SED) includes schizophrenia but does not apply to children who are socially maladjusted, unless it is determined that they have a serious emotional disturbance. The history of that exclusion strongly suggests that the lawmakers' intent was to prevent adjudicated delinquents from receiving special education services, on the grounds that they were being cared for under the provisions of other laws (Maag & Howell, 1992). Nevertheless, this exclusion causes much confusion within the school community.

As an example, consider Pete, a 13-year-old doing quite poorly in school (third- or fourth-grade-level proficiency).

Pete has been a constant trial to his middle school teachers. He belongs to a gang known as the Griffins who, on occasion, terrorize other students in the school. They are suspected of stealing from local stores and perhaps marketing drugs in the school. But Pete does not appear to be depressed or anxious or show any of the other symptoms of seriously emotionally disturbed students; instead he seems quite satisfied with himself. He just does not like school. He does not appear to be upset—his role in life seems to be to upset other people.

Pete would fit the definition of being socially maladjusted without question, but is he emotionally disturbed? If not, he will be excluded from special education services. This is the importance of definitions that otherwise would receive little attention from working teachers.

The definition of SED has another problem that seems to be even more serious. A number of observers have pointed out that the federal definition places *all* responsibility for the problem on the child and none on the environment in which the child exists, thus making it the responsibility of the special education program to change the *child* but not the *learning environment*—which can be considerably flawed (Maag & Howell, 1992; Nelson, Crabtree, Marchand-Martella, & Martella, 1998).

The learning environment may be exactly what is at issue for youngsters who come to school from very different cultures with different lifestyles and values (Rueda, 1989). Juan, a newly arrived Hispanic child, has trouble with the different ways he is supposed to react to authority. He is expected to look teachers in the eye when they are talking to him ("Look at me when I am speaking to you!"). But if he did that at home, he would be severely reprimanded because such eye contact would be considered defiance of parental authority. Juan's reaction to this very different environment may cause him to exhibit behavior within the range of the current definition of behavior disorder. That behavior would be due not to some underlying pathology but to the clash of cultural values of the school and of the home (Harry, 1992; Webber, 1992).

What treatment is prescribed for such a child? Should Juan be made to change his behavior patterns to fit the new environment or try to reach an accommodation between the two? The issue of an individual child with maladaptive behavior may turn out to be an issue of clashing societies with a very different prescription for social remediation that extends far beyond the reach of special education.

Even the student caught between two cultures can still manifest behaviors that are certain to cause him trouble now and in the future in the school environment and in the community. In short, the problem may start out as a cultural clash, but it is transformed into a personal adjustment problem. Should the child receive some type of intervention to help in that situation? In this situation, it is appropriate to think of the entire family as the focus of attention. Increasingly, the family unit is involved in the attempts at behavior change in the child.

There is a disturbing gap between the number of children being served in the schools and the number of children who have both serious emotional disturbance and behavior disorders (variously estimated between 5 and 15 percent) (Knitzer, Steinberg, & Fleisch, 1990). This category lacks the quantitative character of an index like IQ scores, and many of the judgments are subjective and left to local personnel. This is not to say, however, that there is not a core of youngsters who can readily be identified as having an emotional or behavior disorder. A child who attacks another child with a weapon such as scissors, a knife, or a hammer leaves little doubt; neither does a child who weeps five or six times a day without apparent cause. As always, confusion about whether a child is eligible for special services exists at the margin of the category.

Does it make any difference whether children with emotional or behavior disorders are identified? Could we be dealing with a temporary developmental immaturity that will go away with time? The clear answer is, unfortunately, no. The presence of emotional or behavior disorders in school strongly predicts future school failure, school dropout, delinquency, and adult psychiatric problems (Robins, 1966; Walker, Shinn, O'Neill, & Ramsey, 1987). Although not every child who is aggressive and violent in school will show such behavior in adulthood, it is hard to find an aggressive and violent adult who did not show that behavior in his or her youth (Simpson, Miles, Walker, Ormsbee, & Downing, 1991). It is in everyone's best interests that such youngsters are screened and identified early in their school career and positive steps are taken to modify maladaptive behavioral patterns.

A child's emotional or behavior disorders in school are strong indications of future difficulties in school and society.

Factors Related to Behavior Problems

Parents and professionals looking for the reasons why some children show disturbed behaviors must examine an array of potential influences, including the individual's biological makeup and cognitive ability and the family and its relationship to the larger society. Some ideas are harder to accept than others. One hypothesis is that future behavior is determined at birth. The essential unfairness of such a concept repels us and makes genetic research findings harder to accept. Fortunately, we can now say that the final determination of behavior is a mix of genetics and environment, so that delinquency or criminal behavior is *not* fixed at birth. What the genetic evidence does tell us, though, is that some youngsters have a predisposition toward behaviors such as hyperactivity, attention problems, or impulsiveness. Those behaviors may call for some special educational or social environments to ensure that such predispositions do not flower into real behavioral problems (Rutter, 1997).

More than adequate evidence has been collected about factors that predict whether a child is at risk for emotional disturbance. Figure 7.1 shows some of the factors that affect the lives of more than 30 percent of the children identified as emotionally disturbed (Nelson & Pearson, 1991).

Strong family-related factors put children at risk for behavior disturbance.

BIOLOGICAL RISK FACTORS

For a quarter-century, sociologists and psychologists pointed to the environment as the key factor in behavior disturbance. But today, a growing body of knowledge suggests that much abnormal behavior has a genetic base. Studies comparing the behavior of monozygotic (identical) and dizygotic (fraternal) twins clearly indicate that children who share an identical genetic background (the monozygotic twins) are more alike in terms of aggressive behavior—even when reared apart—than are the dizygotic twins (even when reared in the same environment) (Cantwell, 1982; Gershon, Hamovit, & Guroff, 1983).

Many behavioral disturbances have a biological origin.

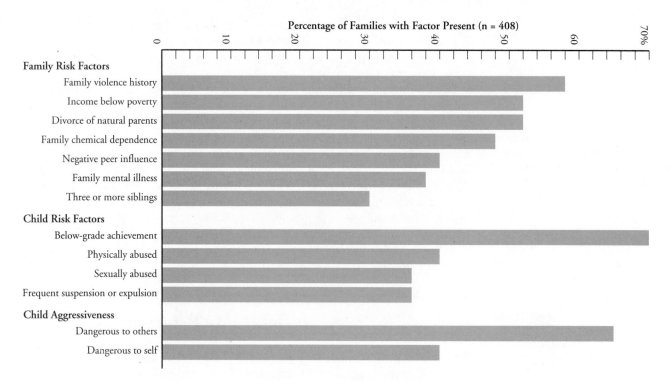

Figure 7.1 Factors That Put Children at Risk for Social and Emotional Disorders

Source: Adapted from C. Nelson and C. Pearson (1991). *Integrating Services for Children and Youth with Emotional and Behavioral Disorders.* Copyright © by The Council for Exceptional Children. Reprinted with permission.

The Influence of Genes

McClearn (1993) also found credible evidence of the important role that heredity plays in shaping behavior and personality, specifically the sex-linked differences in many behavioral conditions. Infantile autism, hyperactivity, and conduct disorders (alcoholism, antisocial behavior) occur in males four to eight times more often than they do in females. Depression and social phobias appear in postpubescent females two to three times more than they do in males. Of course, we can tie these differences—at least in part—to the very different ways in which society treats males and females. But they also suggest that a sex-linked genetic factor may be at work.

To what extent are deviant behaviors hereditary? To what extent are they environmental? We probably can say that all behaviors reflect some combination of heredity and environment. The task of behavioral geneticists is to sort out the contribution of these forces in specific behavioral areas.

The evidence of the genetic influence on behavior has been traced through the study of identical twins (identical heredity), adoptive children (Is the child more like the biological parents or the adoptive parents?), and statistical analyses of the prevalence of conditions in certain families or populations over generations (Plomin & McClearn, 1993).

Interaction Between Genes and Environment

Behavior is both genetically and environmentally controlled. According to Kagan, Arcus, and Snidman (1993),

No human quality, psychological or physiological, is free of the contributions of events both within and outside the organism. No behavior is a first-order, direct product of genes. . . . Every psychological quality is like a pale gray fabric woven from thin black threads, biology; and thin white ones, experience. But it is not possible to detect any quite black or white threads in the gray cloth. (p. 209)

It is one thing to identify genetic characteristics in various areas of exceptionality and another to conclude that they are final determinants of behavior. Although there clearly is some genetic influence in conduct disorders, particularly those associated with hyperactivity, inattention, and poor peer relationships (Rutter, Silberg, & Simonoff, 1993), there is no reason to believe that environmental experiences cannot counteract those influences. After all, if you can get a lion to sit on a chair and a bear to ride a bicycle (hardly gene-driven behavior), as happens in many circuses, you can control the behavior of a child with tendencies to hyperactivity.

Perhaps the only condition in the field of behavior disturbance in which genetics plays an overwhelming role is autism (see Chapter 11). Strong evidence from family and twin studies indicates that genetics play a significant role in the unusual behavior shown by children with autism. Even so, intensive treatment programs have been successful in ameliorating many of the symptoms of that condition (Rutter, Bailey, Bolton, & Le Couteur, 1993).

The Interaction of Factors

Practitioners in many different disciplines—pharmacologists, neurologists, psychologists, and educators—are conducting studies of behavior disorders and aggressive behavior. However, knowledge obtained from any one line of investigation has not been readily shared with the other disciplines.

What does seem clear is that there are two-way interactions between the various forces at work. That is, while aggression can change psychosocial factors, so can psychosocial factors change levels of aggression. Similar interactions occur with biological factors. Grisso (1996) provided a useful illustration of one potential sequence of events:

For example, Ritalin may reduce the aggression of an attention-deficit, hyperactive-disordered child, but the reduction in aggressive behavior may also produce a change in the family's response to the child. Whether that response is positive (e.g., interpersonally rewarding) or negative (e.g., the child is suddenly ignored) may influence the continued benefits of the biological intervention. (p. 6)

Such complex interactions have resulted in an increase in multidisciplinary research and treatment since these problems spill over into the domains of many disciplines.

FAMILY RISK FACTORS

The family risk factors shown in Figure 7.1 clearly indicate that problems within the family may help produce a child who is disturbed. One interesting indicator is family violence, which includes child abuse. Violence against children is a behavior that the children themselves are likely to display when they are old enough to inflict violence on those weaker than they.

The intergenerational aspect of this disorder is distressing. A child with serious emotional disturbance rarely comes from a stable home with warm and loving

Children who are victims of abuse and violence often learn to inflict those behaviors on others.

parents. And the child who is abused is likely to be an abusive parent and to re-produce the entire negative pattern unless the school or community intervenes.

Ramsey and Walker (1988) compared two groups of boys drawn, as pairs, from the same fourth-grade classrooms. The thirty-nine boys in one group exhibited an-tisocial behaviors; the forty-one boys in the other group did not. Data that came from structured family interviews confirmed that the antisocial children lived in an unstructured, negative environment where discipline was harsh and inconsis-tent. Although these factors may not have "caused" the antisocial behavior, they certainly did not contribute in a positive way to the child's social development. These factors, once again, indicate the importance of involving the entire family when possible.

A generation ago, feelings were strong that parents were in large part responsi-ble for their child's behavior problems. Today, many believe that the child's atypi-cal behavior may cause parents to react in ways that are inappropriate and make the condition worse in a downward spiral of unfortunate sequential events.

SCHOOL RISK FACTORS

As Figure 7.1 indicates, the child risk factor most frequently associated with social and emotional disturbance is below-grade achievement in school. Do these chil-dren act out *because* they are academically slow and not able to keep up with their classmates? Is their acting out a reaction to their failure in school? The idea is an interesting one, but the evidence does not seem to support it. For one thing, stud-ies that measure the abilities of children with conduct disorders consistently find that, as a group, they score in the below-average range of intelligence (Kauffman, 1997). For another, the aggressive behavior that gets these youngsters into trouble in school is clearly observable *before* they enter school (Thomas & Chess, 1984).

Jim, for example, was in trouble in school right from kindergarten. His school records are peppered with teachers' statements: "He seems bright but doesn't want to apply himself." "He's unmotivated and an angry little boy." "This boy will not take the time necessary to learn the basics."

In the general education literature, *time on task* is a well-established predictor of school success (Berliner, 1990). In other words, the common-sense conclusion that the more time you spend on learning a topic the more likely you will be to master it turns out to have solid research backing. This principle is relevant to the school performance of children who are seriously emotionally disturbed because they spend less time engaged in academic activities in the classroom—and proba-bly outside the classroom as well (Walker, Stieber, & O'Neill, 1990).

Children with serious emotional disturbance probably spend less time on task, so they may be less likely to master the subject matter.

SOCIAL RISK FACTORS

Violence in the Schools

One of the continuing concerns of school administrators and teachers is the pres-ence of violence in the schools. While individual instances of school violence can be newsworthy and dramatic, we are left with the question as to whether the trends toward drugs, gangs, and violence are on the rise or receding.

The National Center for Educational Statistics conducted a survey in 1989 and another in 1995 of representative samples of 10,000 students ages 12–19 and was able to compare the trends that were revealed (Chandler, Chapman, Rand, & Taylor, 1998). There appeared to be an increase in students reporting violent victimization while at school (3.4% to 4.2%). There was a slight increase in the availability of drugs at school during that time (63% to 65%) and, perhaps most disturbing, an almost doubling of the presence of street gangs at school (15% to 28%). All these trends appear to confirm a growing unlawfulness in the schools that needs sustained attention.

Family and Culture

Bronfenbrenner (1979) focused on the family as a child-rearing system, on society's support or lack of support for that system, and on the effects of that support or lack of support on children. He maintained that the alienation of children reflects a breakdown in the interconnected segments of a child's life—family, peer group, school, neighborhood, and work world. The question is not "What is wrong with children with emotional or behavior disorders?" but "What is wrong with the child's social system?"

Although many of these children do not have feelings of anxiety or guilt about their behavior (especially children with socialized aggression or aggression stimulated by peer group actions or neighborhood values), the conflict between the values of those in authority in society (and in the school) and the values of their subculture can create tension. For example, what does a child do who sees a friend cheating? Honesty—a valued societal ethic—demands that the child report the incident. But loyalty—a valued subcultural ethic—demands silence. Even more serious in its impact is the situation in which the subgroup devalues education or pressures the individual to use drugs or violence.

What are the origins of delinquency? Does it lie within the characteristics of the young child, the family, the neighborhood, or the peer group? Apparently the answer is "all of the above." When an age cohort of 1,037 children from a New Zealand community were followed into adolescence (White, Moffitt, Earls, Robins, & Silva, 1990), early behavior problems at ages 3 to 5 were clearly predictive of later delinquency, although the prediction was not perfect. The authors concluded that early antisocial behavior is the best predictor of later antisocial behavior.

On the other hand, from another large sample of 1,271 second through fifth graders, when divided into middle and low socioeconomic status (SES) neighborhoods, the middle-class neighborhood seemed to operate as a protective factor for reducing aggression from children in high-risk families (Kupersmidt, Griesler, Derosier, Paterson, & Davis, 1995). Low-income African-American children living in a single-parent home in a low-SES neighborhood were more aggressive than other combinations of child–social class–income variables. They show that the neighborhood context was associated with childhood aggressiveness over and above family characteristics. When IQ scores were compared with delinquency for 13-year-old boys in a longitudinal study of high-risk boys, low IQ scores seemed to predict delinquency, as did school failure (Lynam, Moffitt, & Stouthamer-Loeber, 1993).

Lynam, Moffitt, and Stouthamer-Loeber (1993) suggested that school failure plays a more important role in the delinquency of African-American boys from low-income families because the school provides a source of social control that is lacking in the neighborhood. The boy who finds school so frustrating that he rejects it and what it represents is removing himself from its control and influence.

Neighborhood delinquencies and pressures are free to rush in and fill the void (p. 195). So we have evidence that the school, the neighborhood, the social class, and the family as well as some individual characteristics of the child are all implicated in delinquency.

THE CHALLENGE OF SUBSTANCE ABUSE

One of the serious side problems of many children with behavior disorders is substance abuse. The public's attention is often directed to the use of exotic drugs, but the use and abuse of alcohol and tobacco are much more common. There is evidence (Elmquist, Morgan, & Bolds, 1992; Leone, Greenberg, Tricket, & Spero, 1989) that children with behavior problems have rates of substance abuse much higher than the rates of their peers in special education or in general education. Despite this information, there appears to be little systematic effort to include prevention programs in the school curriculum for these students.

Does the presence of behavior or emotional problems predispose an individual to use drugs? If you are anxious, depressed, or angry, are you more likely to take drugs? Common sense would answer "Yes," but research is not clear.

Substance abuse is a growing problem in U.S. schools (Hawley, 1987). The prevalence of alcohol abuse and drug use is substantial, and Johnson (1988) theorized that exceptional children may be overrepresented among those who use drugs and alcohol. Think about the characteristics of drug users: low self-esteem, depression, inability to handle social experiences, and stress. These are the same characteristics that mark children with behavioral disorders. Johnson suggested a dual diagnosis: The primary handicap is a behavioral disturbance; the secondary handicap is a chemical dependency. Special educators, then, must know the signs of chemical dependency, what to do when they suspect drug abuse in their students, and how to work with drug treatment programs.

A number of forces are inhibiting a direct educational attack on substance abuse for such students (Genaux, Morgan, & Friedman, 1995). Among those factors are limited interest shown by parents, lack of curriculum materials, and lack of time and funding. There appears to be a need to focus general education and special education teachers on the whys and hows of drug abuse and what they can do about it.

 Classifications and Characteristics

Within the broad category of children with behavior disorders, many subgroups are educationally relevant. The purpose of classifying is to produce subgroups that either (1) improve our understanding of the origin or causes of a condition or (2) provide the basis for differential education and treatment. For example, Jim seems sullen and has angry outbursts. Molly is an anxious and withdrawn child. Both can be classified as "children with behavior disorders," but they belong in different subcategories and would probably receive very different educational programming. (We discuss Jim's and Molly's developmental profiles later in this chapter.)

In the past, classification systems for children and adults with behavior problems emerged from psychiatry in response to the diagnostic patterns described by professionals in fields like clinical psychology and psychiatric social work. Two major classification systems were developed from that clinical perspective: the *Diagnostic and Statistical Manual of Mental Disorders,* fourth edition (*DSM IV*) (1994), and the classification system of Psychopathological Disorders in Children from the Group for the Advancement of Psychiatry (GAP). These systems also contain subgroups—for example, personality and developmental disorders, motor coordination disorders, and psychoneurotic disorders. But as useful as these designations may be from a psychiatric standpoint, they hold little value for educators.

A somewhat different approach involves the use of statistical techniques that isolate patterns of interrelated behaviors. By using checklists, rating scales, and other measuring devices to evaluate large numbers of children, it is possible to sort out clusters of responses that separate one group of characteristics or symptoms from another. This approach has yielded patterns of deviant behavior in children such as conduct disorders (including attention-deficit hyperactivity disorder) and anxiety-withdrawal (Quay & Werry, 1986).

CONDUCT DISORDERS

We find a common pattern in the families of children with conduct disorders. Often the father is aggressive and hostile and uses physical force for discipline. Jim's father treated what he thought was Jim's misbehavior with spankings that verged on beatings. Apparently hostility breeds hostility, and Jim became even more of a problem when his father walked out on the family, leaving Jim's mother to cope with Jim. Also, the mothers of these families tend to be inconsistent with discipline and preoccupied with financial survival (Wood, Combs, Gunn, & Weller, 1986). Obviously, the entire family can benefit from treatment, and attempts are made to involve key family members in treatment where possible.

There are many different opinions about the causes of the aggressive behavior that is typical of conduct disorders. One opinion based on social learning theory has gained wide acceptance. Patterson (1980) argued that, over time, children with conduct disorders (usually boys) learn that aggressive behavior is a way of getting what they want. They see it first at home, when parents give in to the aggressive youth. They use the response again and again in other situations, usually getting their way there, too. Parental punishment here is sporadic and ineffective and simply provides another model of aggressiveness. In short, these children are rewarded for aggressive behavior and thus continue to act out.

Children with conduct disorders are a serious problem in a school setting. They are easily distracted, unable to persist at tasks, and often disrupt class. Their inability to follow directions and maintain attention on a specific task is a source of constant irritation to teachers. As education has become more directly involved with these children, increasing concern has been expressed about their academic status. The problems of asocial and antisocial behavior, unless dealt with vigorously in childhood, can lead to antisocial behavior in adulthood, which in turn can create a new generation of antisocial children. And so the cycle continues.

Children with conduct disorders learn that aggressive behavior is a way of getting what they want, particularly when parental punishment is sporadic and ineffective and provides another model of aggressiveness. (© Michael Weisbrot)

Attention-Deficit Hyperactivity Disorder

As we learn more about conditions that we wish to study, we establish different descriptions of those conditions. We tend to separate out conditions such as infantile autism for the purpose of understanding their specific causes and identifying the most effective treatment. For **attention-deficit hyperactivity disorder (ADHD)**, the intent of establishing a new condition is to distinguish ADHD from other conditions that belong to the general category of developmental disorders or delay.

A child with ADHD, such as Dave, a compact and energetic 6-year-old, displays significant signs of inattention, distractibility, and disorganization but does not show the typical signs (such as delayed cognition) of a child with mental retardation. Such patterns of behavior show up typically in the preschool age. Dave's parents describe Dave like this: "He hits the floor running every day and has us all worn to a frazzle by midmorning." "He seems driven by some unseen force to be always on the go." "I never seem to be able to catch his attention to read him a story or get him to slow down to pay attention to what I want to tell him." It is not clear what the cause of such a condition is, but whether the cause is nutritional or neurological or an imbalance of neurotransmitter chemicals, the impact on the family and the teacher is predictable. Dave is hard to teach because he won't pay attention long enough for a person to communicate meaningfully with him.

To help students with ADHD, teachers might supplement verbal instructions with visual instructions.

One standard possible treatment for ADHD is medication, primarily to slow the child down so that someone can catch his or her attention long enough to teach needed information. Drugs such as Ritalin, Dexedrine, or Cylert are prescribed, often with the desired result of increasing the child's control of his or her own behavior (Pueschel, Scala, Weidenman, & Bernier, 1995). Dave's parents are reluctant to give such powerful medicine to a 6-year-old, but his uncontrollable behavior may cause them to eventually give in.

Children who are anxious and withdrawn have problems with excessive internal control and often feel helpless and unable to be spontaneous. (© Elizabeth Crews)

Whether or not Dave responds positively to such medical intervention, he needs special educational programming, because he will miss many important educational experiences while he engages in this whirl of physical activity that can be so wearing on his parents and teachers.

Children with ADHD find it difficult to settle down to a particular task, particularly deskwork. Such students have been called learning disabled or even emotionally or behaviorally disturbed. Sometimes there is a case for classifying them under "other health impaired." But whatever the classification, some standard intervention techniques can help teachers respond to such students.

- Provide a structured learning environment.
- Repeat and simplify instructions about in-class and homework assignments.
- Supplement verbal instructions with visual instructions.
- Use behavioral management techniques.
- Use tape recorders.
- Teach organization and study skills.
- Post daily schedules and assignments.

ANXIETY-WITHDRAWAL

Children who are anxious or withdrawn are more likely a danger to themselves than they are to others.

Children who are anxious or withdrawn are likely to be more of a threat to themselves than to others around them. Because they usually are not disruptive, they generally do not cause classroom management problems. But they are a source of concern for teachers.

In contrast to children with conduct disorders, who show too much behavior, children who are anxious and withdrawn show too little (Quay, 1979). Their problems are with excessive internal control; in all settings they maintain firm control over their impulses, wishes, and desires. Children who are anxious and withdrawn may be rigid and unable to be spontaneous.

Where do fearful children come from? We know that many of them have parents with similar problems. In addition, most professionals agree that chronic anxiety in children comes from being in a stressful situation, not being able to get out of the situation, and not being able to do anything to improve it. This inability to change the situation adds to feelings of helplessness and reinforces low self-image.

For college students, a crucial examination looming on the horizon can create chronic anxiety. For younger children, anxiety can stem from homes where they feel unwanted or are abused. Children are often too young to understand that their parents may be working out their own problems or that their parents' actions have little to do with them. All they understand is that no matter what they do they are not getting praise or love from their parents.

One serious outcome of a prolonged intense period of anxiety or depression is suicide (suicide is also a problem among youngsters with other disabilities). Concern is growing about the prevalence of suicide in schoolchildren. It is the third leading cause of death in the 15-to-24 age group and the sixth leading cause for ages 5 to 14 (Guetzloe, 1991). Even these figures may be low, because many suicides are listed as accidental deaths. If a teenager drives into a tree or off a bridge, it is difficult to know whether the crash was accidental or deliberate. Even accidents that are alcohol related may be a form of suicide if the use of alcohol was stimulated by depression.

Guetzloe (1991) reported a series of risk factors identified by many psychologists and psychiatrists to alert the observer to the possibility of suicide. One list points out that it is not just the *presence* of the characteristics; they should be in evidence nearly every day for a two-week period. At least five of nine factors should be present:

- Depressed or irritable mood
- Loss of enjoyment or interest in normally pleasurable activities
- Change in weight, appetite, or eating habits
- Problems with sleeping (insomnia or hypersomnia)
- Psychomotor agitation or retardation (hyperactivity in children)
- Loss of energy or feelings of fatigue
- Feelings of worthlessness or excessive or inappropriate guilt
- Diminished ability to attend, think, or concentrate (indecisiveness)
- Recurrent thoughts of death or suicide

Although the list gives a strong impression that the problem rests within the individual, context factors can play a part. For example, there can be a significant increase in youth suicide following a front-page story on suicide or fictional accounts of suicide (Phillips & Carstensen, 1986). It is clear that some individuals are figuratively standing on a roof edge and can be pitched off by events in the community that cause them to lose control.

One effort to thwart suicide attempts has been the formation of crisis teams at both the school and the district levels. Team members learn procedures to cope with suicidal individuals, and the team has access to resources that it can bring to

Children develop chronic anxiety when they are frequently exposed to stressful situations and are unable to control or remove themselves from those situations.

bear quickly (Guetzloe, 1989). A teacher who sees the danger signs has the immediate task of providing relief from the feelings of helplessness or hopelessness that the student may be expressing and instilling in the student some feeling of being in control (Guetzloe, 1988). Some positive change, no matter how small, must be made to prove to the student that the situation is not hopeless. Shneidman (1985) called this change a "just noticeable difference."

Long-range treatment may demand services from community and mental health agencies, and teachers should be aware of good referral sources. For schools, the best method of prevention is an educational program that enhances feelings of self-worth and self-control. Explicit instruction in positive coping skills can be one way of providing feelings of self-control.

All of us have felt depressed at one time or another. Why do these feelings persist in some individuals and not in others? Schloss (1983) had three separate theories: learned helplessness, social skills deficiency, or coercive consequences. For each of these theories there is a predictable intervention technique. In the case of *learned helplessness,* we must convince children that they are capable of influencing their own environment. In the case of *social skills deficiency,* we can teach and reinforce effective interpersonal skills. In the case of *coercive consequences,* we can avoid reinforcing children's dependency and helplessness, focusing instead on positive aspects of their personality and performance.

Learned helplessness in children is the belief that nothing they do can stop bad things from happening. Learned helplessness results in severe deterioration in performance after failure, as though the children have said to themselves, "It's all happening again." These children often have such low self-concepts that failure in a school task or a social setting only confirms for them their worthlessness and helplessness in the face of an unfriendly environment (see Seligman & Peterson, 1986). These children's poor performance in the classroom may be much worse than they are capable of doing, simply because they are so pessimistic about themselves and their abilities. Low self-esteem seems to be at the heart of much of the underachievement of children who are anxious and withdrawn.

Learned helplessness comes from low self-esteem and depression.

Developmental Profiles

Figure 7.2 shows the profiles of the two youngsters mentioned earlier, Jim and Molly. Both have behavior problems, and both are experiencing academic difficulties. The two children, however, manifest these problems in different ways.

Jim is an 11-year-old who seems sullen and angry most of the time. He rarely smiles and has a history of temper outbursts. When he is frustrated, he sometimes blows up and attacks the nearest person with such frenzy that other children give him a wide berth and hesitate to interact with him.

Stories in the neighborhood recount Jim's cruelty to animals, how he has tortured and killed cats and dogs. His language borders on profanity, and he has been known to challenge his teachers by asking, "What are you going to do about it?" Jim is a threat not only to his peers but also to his teachers' sense of their own competence. His physical skills are advanced, even though his interpersonal skills are not, which tends to complicate the situation. As he grows older, he will become less manageable physically. Although we can tolerate the temper tantrums of a 5-year-old, the same outbursts from a 15-year-old are frightening.

Figure 7.2

Profiles of Two Children
with Behavior Disorders

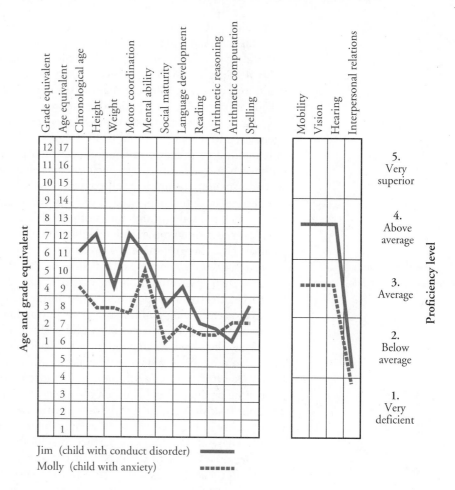

Jim (child with conduct disorder)

Molly (child with anxiety)

School personnel are actively seeking alternative placement for Jim on the grounds that they are not capable, either physically or psychologically, of coping with his problems. Jim comes from a father-absent home; his mother is somewhat disorganized and seems to have given up trying to control her son. Attempts have been made to coordinate the program for Jim with mental health services for his mother in hopes of strengthening the family as a viable social unit. Although some progress has been made, the situation remains difficult. His social contacts are limited to a few other youngsters who have similar propensities for acting out when they become angry. Those who are close to Jim are worried about his future. Jim's performance in school, as shown in the profile, is from two to five grades below his grade level, and his hostility and unwillingness to accept correction or help have caused his teachers much anxiety.

The second profile in Figure 7.2 is of Molly, a 9-year-old girl in the fourth grade who is having a difficult time at school. In contrast to Jim, who tends to externalize his problems, Molly seems to internalize hers. She is in tears and depressed much of the time. She is not able to make friends with the girls who have formed the major social group in the classroom, and she seems lonely and alone. Molly is so quiet that if it were not for the manifest unhappiness that shows in her face and physical demeanor, she would likely go completely unnoticed in school. She, like Jim, is seriously behind in her academic work. Jim is clearly externalizing his problems and, in the process, is causing problems for others. Molly is internalizing her problems and making herself miserable but is not directly confronting others.

Molly's middle-class parents are concerned about her and have taken many different steps to help her, including therapy from a psychiatrist in the community, but so far their efforts have met with little success. She is a source of great frustration to her parents, who cannot understand why she is not like her older sister, who seems to succeed effortlessly in both academic and social spheres. Molly is not the personal threat to teachers that Jim is because she does not challenge their ability to control the classroom. But she does challenge those teachers who want the children in their classes to be happy in school and who are upset by their inability to modify her sadness and low self-concept.

Identification and Placement

The decision to refer a child for special education services is an important one; it must be made carefully. It is often difficult to distinguish between children with behavior disorders and those who just have a series of **transient adaptation problems**: Each child shows unacceptable behavior, but one shows it longer and more intensely than the other.

For example, Larry has become increasingly disruptive and irritable in class, far beyond what the teacher was used to from Larry, who had always been a reasonably friendly and happy boy. A further discussion with parents revealed that Bart, Larry's older brother, had gone off to college. Bart had been a true role model and friend to Larry, and they did many things together. Larry is having trouble adjusting to Bart's absence, but given some patience combined with firm application of the rules, this transient adaptation problem will likely fade away.

The placement of a disproportionate number of minority students in special education programs has raised questions about the process that many school systems use to identify students with behavior problems. Are these systems mistaking cultural differences for aberrant behavior? Are the personal biases of some decision makers playing a role in decision making? Or are some subgroups especially likely to show the symptoms of behavior problems?

Whatever the answer may be in individual circumstances, it is clear that some testing and an interview with the school psychologist are not enough to support a placement decision. Wood and Smith (1985) developed a five-step response and assessment process:

1. *Classroom or home adjustments.* The first level of response to a child's problems is the home or the classroom teacher. Usually a parent or teacher deprives a child of privileges or reprimands the child following asocial or antisocial behavior. If the problem is transitory, this action may be as far as the issue needs to be taken.

2. *Prereferral activities.* If a problem persists in the classroom, some school systems use a *prereferral team*—a group of specialists (e.g., psychologist, principal, speech-language therapist)—to work out a plan that the teacher can implement in the regular classroom with the help of the team. If the plan fails after a reasonable time, additional steps are necessary.

It often is difficult to distinguish between children with behavior disorders and those who just have a series of transient adaptation problems. *(© J. Greenberg/The Image Works)*

3. *Referral for special education services—collecting information.* With the parents' consent, information is gathered about the child. In addition to the standard intelligence achievement data and health information, direct observational data about the child in the classroom should be collected so the problem is seen in the environment in which the solution must be implemented. Data are assembled through interviews, teacher rating scales, tests, and observations and usually are synthesized in a case study team approach.

4. *Referral for special education services—placement.* At this stage, the assessment team determines that the child is not profiting from the current placement and makes new recommendations. These can include a change in physical environment, different treatment schedules, or the employment of supportive services. The IEP is developed at this stage.

5. *Implementing the IEP.* The plan developed during the earlier steps of the assessment is put into operation. Evaluative data on the child's progress continue to be collected.

The IEP, when used properly, is an effective guide for teachers who are trying to cope with children who show emotional or behavior problems. The IEP is shaped not only by the student's specific problem but also by available resources. The presence of professional consultants in the mental health area or an active remedial program in the school gives both the assessment team and the parents more options to consider.

Despite a liberal definition of children with behavior problems that includes the perceiver as well as the child, most diagnostic instruments now in use focus exclusively on the characteristics of the child and do not take into consideration the nature of the environment. Judgment about the role of the environment still is left to the discretion of the individual observer, clinician, or special educator.

Family and Community

"Parents Involved Network Gives Families Support"

Almost immediately after adopting 3½-year-old Chris, parents Kathy and Vincent Minnucci said, they had a gut feeling something was wrong. The parents of six, they said they knew that Chris' destructive behavior—breaking things, lying and temper tantrums—were not the actions of a typical toddler. At first, Vincent Minnucci said, pediatricians tried to convince the couple that Chris was simply "active."

Within a year of his arrival, Kathy Minnucci said, a growing list of doctors diagnosed him with a range of severe emotional problems, including trauma anxiety and detachment disorder—the inability to bond emotionally with anyone.

"We had professionals say, 'Sign the kid back over [to state authority].' But we couldn't. We love him; he is in our hearts," Kathy Minnucci said. "He had lived in 12 foster homes or shelters before the age of 3, and we didn't want him to go through that anymore. . . . We felt alone and frustrated trying to find help."

That changed, she said, when the couple found Christina Corp, "who has been like a guardian angel to us." Corp is coordinator of the Delaware County Parents Involved Network (PIN), a self-help advocacy organization for parents of children who suffer from a variety—and often a combination—of emotional, behavioral and mental disorders.

The Delaware County group held its first meeting when eight parents gathered in October 1987 at Corp's Havertown home. It has grown to about 1,500 members. Corp said she became interested in PIN when she was seeking help for a family member.

"These children are like purple rice. They don't fit anywhere on the shelf. I found help, but I needed support for myself," Corp said.

"PIN is an umbrella voice. We network with other support groups, and we work for parents by giving them support and helping them find information, so they can make the best choice for their child.". . .

The organization's most important tasks . . . are to assure families dealing with mental-health issues that they are not alone and to help those struggling with misplaced blame for children's problems.

"People will say, 'There must be something wrong with your family life,' or, 'You need to take a parenting class,' or, 'Give me one weekend, or a week, and I'll straighten your child out,' when a child has a biological mental illness," Corp said.

Kathy and Vincent Minnucci said they heard those and other, more destructive, comments while trying to find help for Chris, now 8. Chris is a brilliant student, Kathy Minnucci said, but his disruptive behavior had school special-education officials calling them daily with complaints. By talking with PIN members, she said, she learned about Chris' rights to specialized treatment and found a school designed for his needs. Anita Anderson of Wallingford said that when her adopted daughter was diagnosed with depression at age 12, members of PIN's adoptive parents' subcommittee offered a friendly voice.

"You hear from other parents who are in the same situations, and you are reassured that nothing you have done has caused this," Anderson said. In the Minnucci household, Kathy Minnucci said, every day is a challenge with Chris and his 5-year-old half-brother, Gabe, who is mildly retarded and has other mental impairments. Thus, she said, having PIN members to lean on is a blessing.

"I see beautiful little souls," Kathy Minnucci said of her two sons. "To meet someone else who feels the same way, parents with the same issues and needs, takes away the feeling of being so alone."

Source: "Parents Involved Network Gives Families Support" by Gloria Hoffner. Reprinted with permission from the *Philadelphia Inquirer,* October 31, 1988.

What Is the Context?

Chris's parents provided a supportive family environment. In addition, they reached out to a community organization for additional resources.

Pivotal Issues for Teachers

As a teacher, how could you provide resources to parents of students with emotional and behavioral disorders? What questions would you have for Chris? For his parents?

 Intervention Strategies

In earlier chapters, we discussed the various ways that educators can modify the standard educational program to meet the special needs of exceptional children. They can change the *learning environment* in which the child is currently placed, they can change the *content* of the lessons provided to the child, and they can teach the child *skills* to process information and to work effectively with peers and adults. In addition, teaching personnel must be given intervention strategies as well as training to accomplish these differential tasks. It is important to think of modifications in all these areas for children with behavioral disorders.

Educators are using a wide variety of approaches to try to change behavior. Their objectives are to change behavior patterns, encourage constructive behaviors, and help children develop effective strategies for coping with their disorder.

Major strategies in this area have a base in what we have learned about operant conditioning and ecological strategies. Drug therapy may also be an option. Intervention strategies often are used in combination with one another.

POSITIVE REINFORCEMENT

One of the most commonly used strategies has been that of **positive reinforcement.** This is the application of a positive stimulus immediately following the response that we wish to strengthen. If the child is paying attention for a set period of time, the child will be rewarded with praise or with a tangible reward, such as a token to be later turned in for something the child wants. There have been objections to this approach saying that we shouldn't be rewarding students for doing what they are expected to do. But such rewards are only a temporary condition that can be reduced or faded when the response that we wish (e.g., attention to teacher) is well established.

One of the key elements of a positive reinforcement system is providing some type of external reward (extra time at recess, free time, a field trip) when the child exhibits the target behavior (Paul & Epanchin, 1986). Once the student starts behaving appropriately, the teacher can begin to use positive reinforcement. But a teacher can't reinforce behavior that isn't there. As one teacher commented, "I am more than ready to give positive reinforcement. When is *he* [the student] going to show some positive behavior that I can reinforce?"

One program designed to elicit positive behavior is called a *levels program* because it features identifiable levels of rewards and privileges that are available for students who behave appropriately. Mastropieri, Jenne, and Scruggs (1988) reported an example of the approach used in a secondary education resource program. Fifteen high school students identified as behaviorally disturbed were placed in an English program. The teacher identified four different behavioral levels, and colored nametags identified the level at which each student was performing. As the students' behavior improved—as judged by their peers—their privileges increased, and the colors of their nametags were changed.

At the lowest level, students with a blue nametag were expected to be prepared for their lessons, to raise their hands before speaking, and to be in their seats at all times. Students who showed appropriate behavior moved up to the next level. At the highest level (a red nametag), students were allowed to move around the room, study in a special room, and monitor their own behavior.

Did the program work? The students' academic and social behavior improved substantially during the four-week program, and a follow-up two weeks after the program was discontinued showed the same improvement.

Some object to the use of such reinforcement techniques because they treat the child like a slot machine (insert a quarter, get good behavior) and have little impact on the child's basic personality. This criticism is not fair. The educational objective is to create in the child a positive response that can be expanded and used for better overall social adjustment.

To help children experience success, teachers can establish goals and organize tasks in small steps.

The usual procedure for shaping behavior in the classroom is to establish goals and organize tasks in small steps so the child can experience ongoing success. This procedure is referred to as *task analysis*. The child receives positive reinforcement for each step or part of the total task as he or she completes it (arithmetic, reading, or spelling, for example). Assignments are programmed in easy steps. After the child completes a task in a specified period of time, the teacher checks the work, praises the child (social reinforcement), and rewards the child with a mark, a grade, a token, or some other tangible reinforcement. In this way the child is able to work at assignments for longer and longer periods and to accept increasingly more difficult tasks.

FUNCTIONAL ASSESSMENT

Functional assessment is another intervention strategy to use with children with behavioral disorders. A functional assessment is a multistep procedure carried out for the purpose of understanding the intended objective or intent of the student's behavior as well as describing that behavior (Gibney & Wood, 1994). It is different from operant conditioning, which deals directly with the behavior itself regardless of what the behavior might signify to the individual.

◼◼◼ **TABLE 7.1 Functional Assessment About Shoplifting**
I: Hello, Melissa. Would you tell me what happened yesterday at the store. **M:** (*Looks surprised.*) Oh, you heard. **I:** Yes. I'd like to hear more about it. **M:** Well, I was walking through the store with my friend, Tim. He dared me to steal a leather jacket. That's all. **I:** Shoplifting is no big deal? **M:** You sound like my mom. Shoplifting isn't like regular stealing. You aren't hurting a person, and the store won't miss one stupid jacket. **I:** So, it's O.K. to take something if you aren't hurting someone? **M:** Yeah, I guess so. **I:** But you got caught. **M:** Yeah, so what? I know my mom told you to talk to me about this. What does it matter to you if I got caught? **I:** Well, you know your mom is going to ask me about our talk. I think stealing is serious stuff, and I'm going to have to tell her about this. **M:** I know, but she won't care. Ever since the divorce she hasn't been the same. She doesn't care what I do.

Source: C. Gibney and F. Wood (1994). *Why Would Anyone Do Something Like That?* Minneapolis: University of Minnesota, p. 23. Developed through a Joint Project of the University of Minnesota and the Osseo Public Schools. Reprinted by permission.

Understanding the behavior can aid teachers in knowing how to respond to a student's provocative behavior.

Starting from the premise that even puzzling and self-destructive behavior has a rational purpose, functional assessment aims to shed light on that purpose. Much aberrant behavior is a reaction to fear or anger, but if we don't know precisely what the fear or anger refers to, we have difficulty knowing how to respond to the sometimes provocative behavior.

Table 7.1 presents a conversation in which a teacher uses some functional assessment methods to determine what might be behind a shoplifting incident in which Melissa was involved. It soon becomes clear that the incident involves not merely the theft of a jacket but complex relationships between Melissa and her boyfriend and between Melissa and her mother. The teacher attempts to see the world through the eyes of the child in order to understand what this otherwise puzzling behavior means to the child. After all, we all react to the world as we see it, not as others see it.

ECOLOGICAL STRATEGIES

Environmental modification is the deliberate creation of a more responsive environment in which the children work. Ecological strategy assumes that the child is an inseparable part of a small social system, of an ecological unit made up of the child, family, school, neighborhood, and community. Supporters of this model maintain that behavior problems are a result of destructive interactions between the child and this social system, or the environment (family, agemates, teachers, cultural subgroups). Treatment consists of modifying elements in the ecology, including the child (through counseling), to foster more constructive interactions between the child and the environment.

Project Re-Ed

Hobbs (1970, 1979, 1982, 1996) and his colleagues implemented the ecological strategy with programs for emotionally disturbed children. They called their program Project Re-Ed (re-education). Two residential schools in the Re-Ed program were organized to house approximately forty children each, ages 6 to 12. The plan was to re-educate these children for a short period of time (from four to six months) and at the same time, through a liaison teacher, to modify the attitudes of the home, school, and community. The program was oriented toward re-establishing the children as quickly as possible in their own homes, schools, and communities.

In general, a program of re-education follows a number of principles:

1. *Life is to be lived now.* Every hour of the day children engage in purposeful activities and in activities in which they can succeed.

2. *Trust is essential.* How to inspire trust, according to Hobbs, is not something that can be learned in college courses. It is something that those working with emotionally disturbed children "know, without knowing they know."

3. *Competence makes a difference.* The arrangement of the environment and learning tasks must be structured so that children are able to gain confidence and self-respect from their successes.

4. *Symptoms can and should be controlled.* The treatment of symptoms, not causes, is emphasized.

5. *Community is important.* Purposeful attempts need to be made to help the child be part of community groups and to teach the child responsibility, as a citizen, to contribute to the community.

6. *A child should know joy each day.* Furthermore, the child should look forward, with eagerness, to some joy-giving event tomorrow. (Edgar, 1998)

The teacher-counselor is the key staff person in re-education programs and is qualified not only in special education but also in counseling methods designed for children who are disturbed. A liaison teacher-counselor works in the program to form effective alliances among home, school, and child. When a child is removed from a regular school and placed in a Re-Ed school, the liaison teacher-counselor keeps the school aware of the child's progress in the program and prepares the child and the school for his or her re-entry when the time approaches.

Time-Out

One of the techniques used most frequently to control the behavior of children with behavior disorders is the **time-out**—sending students who have violated classroom rules to a secluded place in the room or in a space nearby with instructions

The time-out is frequently used to control the misbehavior of children.

A cooperating teacher can often speak with the student during a time-out to help diffuse a tense situation. *(© Elizabeth Crews)*

The Think-Time strategy is similar to a time-out but includes a cooperating teacher who talks with the student.

to come back when they feel they have regained control of themselves. Time-out takes the student away from possibly negative interactions with other students and gives him or her a chance to cool off.

One version of the time-out approach is the Think-Time strategy (Nelson, Crabtree, Marchand-Martella, & Martella, 1998). This approach requires the cooperation of another teacher who can provide the think-time area. The student engaging in disruptive behavior is sent to an area in another classroom previously designated in cooperation with another teacher. This enables the teacher to cut off a negative social exchange or a power struggle and provides the student with time to think about future performance. Once the student has calmed down, the cooperating teacher can get the student to review the inappropriate behavior, what the student was trying to do, and what he or she needs to do on returning to the regular classroom. Such an intervention cuts short what could be a serious situation and allows all parties time to cool off.

DRUG TREATMENT

One of the supplementary strategies for coping with children with ADHD has been the administration of drugs to dampen the hyperactivity or inattention so the student is in a better personal context for learning. Forness (1992) studied seventy-one boys with ADHD and the effect of methylphenidate (Ritalin) over a five-week period on their reading comprehension. The effects on measured ability and achievement were quite modest. The only group that responded consisted of boys who had "ADHD with conduct disorders"; and their reading comprehension improved. It does not seem that a magic pill will solve the academic problems of such students, although medication may be helpful in individual cases.

It was once thought that drug treatment was going to be an important answer. It is still clear that the right dosage of the right drug can result in marked improvement in the behavior of a hyperactive student (Kauffman, 1989, p. 239). The problem is that the effects of medication are highly idiosyncratic and cannot be predicted in advance of trial. Also, enough negative side effects, such as adverse effects on learning, growth, and health, and even a reducing of the students' sense of self-control ("It is the drug that is improving behavior, not me"), have been reported that caution and careful clinical monitoring are needed. Kauffman concluded:

> Responsible clinicians use drugs carefully as one approach to treatment when other solutions to the problem of hyperactivity are not feasible or when there is reason to suspect that drugs, in addition to other interventions, will produce a better result. (p. 239)

It seems to be increasingly clear that under the right circumstances and with certain individuals, drug therapy can be an important part of a total program of help. But it rarely, if ever, can be the sole method of treatment.

TREATMENT COMBINATIONS

Each skills mastery technique or intervention strategy brings some benefits to children with behavior disorders and their families. Hinshaw, Henker, and Whalen (1984) studied the effects of combining several treatments into one multidisciplinary approach. Twenty-four hyperactive boys were taught how to work by themselves on academic tasks, how to control their anger, and how to evaluate themselves. In addition, they were given medication to control their hyperactivity. The results suggested that the educational program in combination with medication worked best.

There are few easy answers in the search for good educational programs for exceptional children. But we do know that we have to match the characteristics of the child with the characteristics of his or her environment, and we need to look for a variety of treatment options that will match the characteristics of individual students.

To be effective, teachers must tailor treatments to the individual child's characteristics.

Educational Adaptations

Children with Emotional and Behavior Disorders

ADAPTING THE LEARNING ENVIRONMENT

The learning environment for children with behavior disorders who passed through the prereferral stage and are determined eligible can include inclusion in the regular classroom, a resource room, a special class, and special residential schools where a total therapeutic environment is provided for children who do not seem able to cope with the regular school program or vice versa.

Understanding Emotional and Behavior Disorders

There are two elements in any disruptive behavior in the classroom. The first element is the *immediate crisis,* which is often of interpersonal conflict; the second is the *underlying dynamics* that nudged the students to the immediate crisis.

> Paul is engaged in a verbal exchange with Mike in which he couldn't convince Mike to do things his way. Suddenly, Paul leaps on Mike, pounding him to the floor.

There is no question that the immediate crisis must be dealt with quickly and decisively. No matter the provocation, physical violence is unacceptable, and Paul must be taken aside and reminded that he has broken the rules of the classroom and the school and that sanctions will have to be applied.

Once the immediate crisis is over and relative peace has been restored, we need to pursue the underlying reasons for Paul's outburst. Unfortunately, such an outburst gives us few clues as to the cause except that Paul has fragile control over his impulsive behavior. Perhaps Paul is worried about a forthcoming test, was abused by his father before school today, or was humiliated at recess by a bigger boy. Unless we are able to tease out these dynamics, which are different for each individual incident, we will be hard pressed to help Paul avoid a similar episode in the future. The value of the multidisciplinary team is that different members may be able to fit together more pieces of the puzzle, and together they can plan for a longer-range strategy to help Paul in the future.

Collaboration: The Role of the Multidisciplinary Team

Prior to 1975, children with behavior disorders were seen as the clients of the mental health community. Then the schools took over the major responsibility through vehicles like the Education for All Handicapped Children Act (PL 94-142). Recognition is now growing that these multifaceted problems need multifaceted solutions and the professional services of many different fields.

One realization that has emerged from experiences with children with behavior disorders or emotional disturbance (or both) is that various professional skills are required to make a difference in the life situation for such students. Multidisciplinary teams that may include educators, counselors, social service personnel, mental health personnel, paraprofessionals, and parents are increasingly popular (Simpson, Miles, Walker, Ormsbee, & Downing, 1991).

The multidisciplinary team is coordinated by a *case manager* (also known as a *service coordinator*). This person may come from any of these professions and is directly responsible for seeing that the treatment program is carried out. Among the case manager's functions are

- Coordinating the various services going to child and family
- Providing follow-up to ensure that goals are being met
- Guiding the work of paraprofessionals and volunteers who work with the child

It is a substantial advantage to have one person who knows all aspects of the treatment program and who has responsibility to see that forward progress is being made (Johnson, 1989).

This may seem to be an enormous expenditure of staff for one student, but it has become increasingly clear that this type of approach is necessary to obtain positive results. Minor tinkering with one or another part of a student's environment is not likely to effect major changes in students prone to aggressiveness and violence.

One thing is certain. Failing to act can be very expensive in human lives and in scarce resources. Although the cost of treatment is substantial, it is nowhere near the cost of not treating the child and family. As of 1990, the state of Kentucky estimated that institutionalization in a psychiatric hospital cost taxpayers $72,000 per child per year. Similarly, the cost of incarcerating a juvenile is estimated at $30,000 per year (Allen-Hagen, 1991). Society is faced with a serious set of choices of the "pay me a little now, or pay me a lot later" variety.

The Helping Teacher

The helping teacher concept fits well into the inclusive classroom.

One innovative suggestion for helping classroom teachers is the **helping teacher,** a person who comes into the general classroom and provides the teacher with support for children with special needs. Obviously, a classroom teacher with twenty-five or thirty children cannot cope with all aspects of the classroom environment without help. Who can provide that help? The strategy rests on five assumptions and principles:

- Even a child who has serious behavior problems is not disturbed all the time. There are *only certain periods* when the pupil cannot function in the larger group setting. These periods may be at certain regular times or in the press of a crisis. But most of the time, the child can benefit from and fit into the regular class.

- Teachers need direct assistance. Consultation is one thing, but real help is something else. Psychologists and similar professionals might offer advice, but they do not know what it is like to try to administer a classroom that includes children who have behavior disorders.

- The direct-service helping teacher should work full-time in the school to which he or she is assigned, should not be itinerant, and should be trained as a special teacher. The helping teacher should be able to respond to the child who is in crisis but also be able to help all children with academic and emotional problems. Many of these youngsters need direct counseling help with issues such as self-concept, but just as many can achieve growth through therapeutic tutoring.

- Sometimes the helping teacher can assist best by taking over the classroom while the regular teacher works through a phase of a problem with a youngster.

- Help should be based on the reality of how the child is able to cope with the classroom and not on categories, labels, or diagnostic criteria. Morse (1976) pointed out that many normal children need help during a crisis in the classroom or in their lives, just as the chronically and severely variant youngster does (pp. 1–2).

The helping teacher generally uses techniques that are an extension of regular education procedures, emphasizing support and encouragement. In addition, the helping teacher is able to provide important liaison services that are not within the capabilities of the heavily burdened classroom teacher. Children with behavior problems often need the help of pediatricians, psychologists, and paraprofessionals, and the helping teacher can coordinate these sources of assistance. Morse (1976) summed up the nature of the relationship as follows:

The plan envisions co-team teaching of the special and regular teacher. There is no intent to replace, only to supplement. The best staff education will come as a result of offering direct help; through service comes change. The job is overwhelming, all agree, but the direction has stood the test of time. (p. 8)

The concept of the helping teacher gains particular relevance with the emergence of the inclusion philosophy. It offers an alternative to resource rooms and brings needed assistance to an already heavily burdened classroom teacher.

The Wraparound Approach

One of the newer approaches in designing service programs for children with behavior disorders is referred to as the *wraparound approach*. Services that are needed by the particular student are brought *to* the student and "wrap around" the student's needs. This often requires the multidisciplinary team.

The plan focuses on the strengths of the student as well as on attempts to mute any deficits in performance that the student may have. Although it is often used as a vehicle for maintaining the student in the regular classroom by bringing additional resources into that classroom, services might be delivered in a resource room or a self-contained special class if that is what represents the least restrictive environment for that student (Kerr & Nelson, 1998).

Inclusion

The goal of special education has been to place children with behavior disorders in the least restrictive environment, which is the regular education program, whenever possible. The reasons are to give these students a chance to:

- Interact with children who do not have disabilities
- Have constructive models of behavior
- Keep in step academically

Although teachers may desperately wish to remove some disruptive children from their classrooms, educators who stress inclusion as a strategy wish to keep them in.

One of the most serious barriers to the proper educational and mental health programming for students with behavior problems is that the intensity of the treatment does not match the intensity of the problem. Students did not acquire their dysfunctional patterns of behavior overnight. The dysfunctional patterns have been years in the making, and it is not realistic to believe that they can be eliminated and positive responses substituted for them as a result of an hour of remedial education two times a week. We often shortchange such children because of staff or financial limitations and then wonder why they don't show more immediate improvement.

On the basis of phone interviews with over 130 programs across the country and site visits to twenty-six programs, Knitzer, Steinberg, and Fleisch (1990) concluded that the resource room strategy has generally been nonproductive. They recommended that it be replaced with direct supportive services brought into the general classroom, together with substantial collaboration between mental health services and educators.

There has been an unfortunate tendency for general education teachers to refer children to special services or special education to get themselves out of an awkward situation. The prereferral strategies mentioned in previous chapters (see Chalfant & Pysh, 1989) seem to be a preferred strategy, with a team of personnel in the school building meeting with the teacher to see what adjustments or adaptations might be made in the regular classroom before a referral is made to special education. Substantial questions have been raised about whether sufficient support services will be available to support the general educator. Kauffman (1994), for example, worried about whether there are sufficient general classroom resources to cope with the most violent or disturbed children in an inclusive classroom:

> Special education is intellectually bankrupt and morally derelict to the extent that it embraces a philosophy that insists on the same placement decision for all students. A second topic for discussion is how does this philosophy of inclusion and the practices derived from it fit with the nature of schools as they exist now, their changing priorities, and the processes of reform? At the same time that teachers are faced with increasingly difficult tasks, they are being asked to do more and to do better with less.
>
> Many of the students now identified for special education because of their emotional or behavioral disorders are kids with very serious problems who require intensive sustained services from many well-trained people who are continuously available. (p. 14)

The issue surrounding inclusion of children with behavioral disorders essentially boils down to whether one has confidence that the schools will be able to provide the support personnel necessary to allow a particular child, the teacher, and other students to have a positive and constructive experience. Clearly, the consensus that emerges from the current literature is that necessary social skills instruction and behavior management support are not in place in many general education environments, and general educators are not prepared at this time to accept and teach students with challenging behaviors (Lewis, Chard, & Scott, 1994, p. 288).

It is possible to create a positive social environment through instruction and prior preparation, so that children in general education classrooms can reach out to children with disabilities in an informed, empathic way.
(© Elizabeth Crews/Stock, Boston)

It is productive to have a life space interview with the student immediately after a crisis situation.

One technique that emerged from the field of mental health and has been used successfully by teachers is the **life space interview**, originally designed by Redl (1959) and updated by Wood and Long (1991). A life space interview with the student occurs directly after a particular crisis situation or event, so the child faces the consequences of the behavior immediately instead of waiting a day or more for a regular counseling session or a visit to the principal, by which time the child has forgotten or has built sufficient defenses around the event for self-protection. Let's look at how it works.

> On the playground Jim has been unmercifully teasing another youngster, Paul, who did something to irritate Jim in the classroom. Finally, out of desperation, Paul strikes out at Jim, giving Jim an excuse to hit back. The teacher immediately sits down with Jim quietly in a private setting and discusses the incident in detail. The teacher might ask Jim to describe what happened and his role in creating the event. Jim would have full opportunity to verbalize his own attitudes about the situation and to express his feelings about Paul.

Ideally, a life space interview ends with specific steps for resolving the problem or for preventing similar problems in the future. Some evidence supports life space interviews as a means of reducing maladaptive behavior, not only by inhibiting undesirable behavior but also by generating alternative solutions.

It is not always possible for the regular class teacher, or even a team of teachers untrained in the special instructional strategies, to cope with students with behavior disorders in the regular education setting. In such instances, the student spends a part or all of the school day with a specially trained teacher so that both social and academic goals can be met.

ADAPTING CURRICULUM

Emphasis is often placed on the nonproductive behavior and what to do about it. This can downplay the importance of the academic performance of the student with emotional or behavioral problems. The failure to deal also with academic problems can start a downward spiral and a lack of self-confidence that are hard to break. The more the student fails, the unhappier he or she gets; the unhappier the child gets, the more likely he or she will respond in nonproductive ways; the more the student responds in nonproductive ways, the more likely he or she will fail some more; and down the spiral goes.

A student's IEP needs to include plans for dealing with academic problems when they are present (e.g., a tutor will help Paul with his reading difficulties), in addition to the strategies for modifying the nonproductive behavioral response patterns that have brought the child to the attention of the school staff.

For children with behavior disorders, the path toward academic success is likely to be difficult and uncertain. Not only do they often have poor relationships with many of their teachers, but their personal and social problems distract them from academic tasks. Consequently, these children often find themselves far behind in their academic work and in need of remedial attention (Kerr & Nelson, 1998). The content of their curriculum may not be different from that of other children, but because they may be at an earlier developmental level, the curriculum may need to be two or three grade levels below their current grade level. The special education teacher in a resource room where a child with behavior problems may come for an hour a day often spends much time in a combination of remedial reading and arithmetic and empathic counseling.

Mark is an 8-year-old boy who was referred to a special class for emotionally disturbed children because his mother was concerned about his immaturity and learning problems. After a thorough evaluation, the special services committee in his school agreed that Mark was excessively rigid, inhibited, and anxious. Even after the evaluation, however, it was not clear why he was having learning problems. Mark was placed in a special class for academic work. His teacher formulated an IEP that involved remedial work in reading and math. The teaching materials included stories about children and how they felt in various circumstances. In addition, the teacher tried, whenever possible, to give Mark psychological permission to express his feelings.

One day when the teacher was very late getting to him, she said, "I'm sorry I'm late. If I had to wait as long as you've had to wait, I'd be upset. Are you a little upset?" On another day, when a child ripped Mark's paper off the bulletin board, she said, "It's too bad about your paper. That upsets me!"

Gradually, Mark began to express his feelings, and as he did it became increasingly evident that once he had vented his frustrations, he was learning and producing more efficiently. With this realization, the teacher began to teach Mark about himself—about how he behaved and how he could monitor himself.

Though Mark's problems were emotional in nature, they led to serious academic problems that could not be ignored. Even if, through some combination of drug treatment and psychotherapy, those emotional problems could have been "solved," Mark still would have been left with serious academic deficiencies that needed remediation.

One way to adapt a program content for children with behavior problems is to design a self-awareness curriculum that provides students with an opportunity to learn more about their own feelings and those of other children. The teaching tools include carefully chosen literature, role-playing, and class discussions in which the teacher stresses feelings and attitudes.

ADAPTING TEACHING STRATEGIES

Skills Mastery Techniques

The difficulties of teaching students with emotional and behavioral disorders does not lie in knowing what should be done, but in the ability of the teacher to carry out these principles in the face of resistance and misbehavior. Some of the established principles are (Wehby, Symons, & Canale, 1998)

- Provision of appropriate structure and predictable routines
- Positive teacher-student interaction with adequate praise and systematic response to problem behavior
- Frequent implementation of instructional sequences that promote high rates of academic engagement and high levels of student response.

But when the teacher, Mrs. Casey, approaches Jim, a disruptive student, with a reading assignment and is confronted with, "No, I won't do it!" the teacher is thrown back on her personal resources to cope with such outright defiance. It is not surprising that the evidence shows that teachers tend to avoid students like Jim and have fewer interactions with them than with other students. This is particularly true when the giving of assignments typically is followed by disruptive behavior. It is not clear that additional preservice training would help, but some form of mentoring of new teachers by teachers who have been there can be more effective.

Specialists working with children who have behavior disorders have focused much of their attention on behavior change, which can occur with or without the child's participation. That means reducing some unacceptable behavior or encouraging proactive, socially desirable behavior. Behavior change that occurs without the child's participation results from operant conditioning. Specialists apparently can also help youngsters to actively change their behavior. They can help youngsters (1) to see the signals in their environment that trigger their unacceptable behavior, (2) to inhibit the impulse to respond immediately, and (3) to develop a plan of action to meet different situations. In many respects, the goal of learning those three skills is as important to the education of youngsters with behavior disorders as are the academic goals of reading and arithmetic. Until these children are able to exercise self-control and to develop other social skills, they are unlikely to learn traditional academic skills.

Teachers can use various strategies with students who have behavior disorders, but each strategy imposes costs or demands on the teachers, whether they are trying to communicate with students, support desirable behavior, or control problem behavior. In the list of strategies in Table 7.2, those preceded by an asterisk are unusually costly in time or additional effort. For example, reminding a student about the rules of the classroom costs the teacher less in energy or effort than does conducting a group meeting on a problem behavior. High-cost teacher behavior, however, may be needed to bring some benefits to the situation. Teachers often find

TABLE 7.2   Strategies for Managing the Behavior of Students with Emotional or Behavior Disorders

Communication Strategies

Structure schedules, which communicates expectations about the use of time.

Structure expectations that link behavior and reward—"If you choose to do this, you will receive this reward."

Define the relationship between unacceptable behavior and sanctions—"If you choose to do this, you will be penalized in this way."

Establish classroom procedures and routines, "rules of the road."

*Discuss with students the meaning/value of what is to be learned. Solicit and respect a student perspective.

*Communicate regularly with students—conversations, notes, journals. (At secondary level, each student should be assigned to at least one teacher.)

*Communicate regularly with parents—notes, phone conversations, conferences.

Supporting Desirable Behavior

Verbally praise a student who is behaving appropriately.

Verbally encourage appropriate behavior.

Give grades and other recognition for achievement.

*Accommodate individual instructional needs by grouping.

*Organize "buddy" or peer tutoring assistance.

*Reward using individualized token/points system (entire group).

Controlling Problem Behavior

Remind student of expectations and rules being violated.

Use gesture or signal alert.

Move closer to student (proximity control).

Use verbal humor.

*Reinforce another student who is behaving appropriately as a reminder of expectations (also a support strategy for the student whose behavior is appropriate).

*Promise reward for return to appropriate behavior.

*Conduct tension-release activities.

*Conduct group meeting focused on problem behavior that has just occurred.

*Supervise time-out at special place in classroom.

*Involves extra time or effort by the teacher.

Source: F. Wood (1991). Cost/benefit considerations in managing the behavior of students with emotional/behavior disorders. *Preventing School Failure,* *35*(2), pp. 17–23.

themselves having to decide whether to use these high-cost strategies, and all sorts of factors—professional and personal—can affect the final decision. A variety of strategies have been developed to cope with children who manifest these disorders.

Cognitive Strategy Approaches. There is a family of strategies currently known as the *cognitive strategy approach*. Whether called *self-monitoring, self-instruction,* or *self-control,* these methods rely on the cooperation of the child and encourage the development of effective conscious coping skills. With the development of the child's skills comes more self-confidence and a more positive self-image as the child achieves greater control over his or her impulses.

Self-management for behavior change has received much favorable comment. One attraction of self-management techniques is that students who successfully apply them assume greater responsibility for their behavior, instead of being externally controlled or "forced" to change by various kinds of conditioning.

Students using self-management assume greater responsibility for changing undesired behaviors.

Suppose Jim has trouble staying in his seat. The first step is to teach him to recognize the behavior and then to record its frequency. Next, Jim negotiates a reward that is satisfying to him (perhaps some time to work a puzzle) for staying in his seat for a specified period. Once he has shown the ability to control the behavior, he can be given the opportunity to control his own schedule and make decisions about the content or skills he would like to work on in the time slot.

There are several self-management techniques:

- *Self-monitoring* requires students to determine whether a target behavior has occurred and then record its occurrence. For example, if Jim feels an aggressive attack coming on, he can note it in a journal. This helps him become increasingly aware of the clues identifying a potential outburst.

- *Self-evaluation* asks the student to compare his or her behavior to some criteria and make a judgment about the quality of the behavior being exhibited, for example, "On a scale of 1 to 5, am I paying attention to the teacher?"

- *Self-reinforcement* means that the student rewards himself or herself with a token or a tally after meeting some performance standard, such as avoiding aggressive outbursts for a set period of time. For example, a timer set for ten minutes that goes off without an aggressive outburst earns for the student a token that he or she can cash in later for game-playing time or a specially designed activity.

- *Self-instruction* is a method by which students can, in essence, talk to themselves, encouraging themselves with verbal prompts to persist in solving an academic or social problem.

Those techniques are designed to increase students' awareness, competence, and commitment to eliminating negative behaviors and to encourage the acquisition of constructive ones. For Jim, this means the teacher works with him to improve self-awareness skills that will enable him to increase his own control over his hyperactivity or distractibility. One practical way of increasing the student's personal responsibility is to let the student participate in developing his or her own IEP.

A review of eleven studies regarding the effectiveness of self-management has determined that such techniques were universally successful in changing the behavior of students with behavior disorders (Hughes, Ruhl, & Misra, 1989). The majority of the behaviors that changed, however, involved fairly simple tasks, such as increasing on-task performance. Whether these techniques work as well with changes in more complex behaviors or last over an extended period of time remains to be determined.

The greatest advantage of this approach is that the child gains self-confidence by exerting control of his or her previously out-of-control behavior. There is an important additional advantage. Many children with behavior disorders spend part of their time in the regular classroom as a result of the least restrictive environment and inclusive philosophies. Many regular classroom teachers do not wish to, or feel they cannot, engage in the complex monitoring and recording of individual student behaviors that some of the other behavior-shaping techniques require. Therefore, because students who use self-management monitor themselves, once the students learn what they are to do in a self-management program, they can proceed with only modest teacher supervision.

Student Contingency Contracts. Figure 7.3 shows a contingency contract with a student, constructed with the student's help, that contains both rewards for successful completion of the tasks and sanctions for violation of the proposed contract. Note also the signature of the parent as a participant in the contract and the short time period before it is re-evaluated. The evidence on the usefulness of such contracts in modifying the behavior of students with emotional and behavioral problems has been quite good (Kerr & Nelson, 1998).

A written contract between the student and the teacher can also aid in developing social skills. This contract is developed by the teacher and the student, who agree on a particular goal toward which the student is striving. For example, Robert might agree to try to go a week without a major temper outburst; the teacher might then agree to provide some free time for him to read any book that he likes if that happens. The advantage of a contract is that it is written down and can be referred to in the future to see if an agreement has been kept. If Robert succeeds at this level, then a new contract might be written focusing on his writing skills and mentioning other contingent rewards for successful performance.

Developing Social Skills. Many children with behavior disorders not only engage in nonadaptive behaviors that cause them trouble with their peers and teachers but also lack positive social skills. One specific goal of a special education program, therefore, is to enhance the use and practice of socially acceptable behaviors.

Molly's periodic weeping "turned off" her peers, and she had few positive skills to re-establish social contact with her classmates. One positive skill that can be introduced to Molly is how to approach another child with a request to play or talk.

Kerr and Nelson (1998) described a sequence of activities by which such skills might be developed:

1. *Modeling.* The skill can be introduced through live, audio, or video modeling. Peers can demonstrate such skills.

2. *Role-playing.* The skill can be played out in a pretend real-life situation. The role-play can be highly structured so the person has a good chance of performing acceptably.

> Students can use self-management to monitor their own behavior, allowing only modest teacher supervision.

Figure 7.3
Student Contract

I, _____Helen Alison_____, understand that I have a problem with these behaviors:

1. _Talking back to my teachers when they tell me to do something._

2. _Refusing to do or finish my schoolwork._

3. _Getting into fights with other kids at lunch and at recess._

This week I am going to work on these behaviors:

1. _Talking back to my teachers._

2. _Finishing my homework in the resource reading room._

I know that if I do either one of these behaviors I will lose _my shopping trip Saturday_

to the mall with my friends

to remind me that what I did was not right.

But, if I control these behaviors and have a week without them, I will get to

Go to a movie with Jeanie, or get an extra 50¢ allowance

as a reward.

Signed: _____Helen Alison_____ Date: _____11/20_____
                        (Student)

            _____Mrs. Blouze_____ Date: _____11/20_____
                        (Teacher)

            _____Mr. Sider_____ Date: _____11/20_____
                (Resource Teacher)

            _____Mrs. P. Alison_____ Date: _____11/20_____
                        (Parent)

We have read and discussed this contract in an after-school meeting on ___11/20___

And we hereby sign as a way of making our commitment to this arrangement.

We will all meet on ___11/28___ to reevaluate the contract.

Source: M. Kerr and C. Nelson (1998). *Strategies for Managing Behavior Problems in the Classroom* (3rd ed.), p. 277. © 1990. Reprinted by permission of Prentice-Hall, Inc. Upper Saddle River, NJ.

3. *Performance feedback.* Just as drama students are critiqued for their performance of a scene, so the teacher can discuss with the student the pluses (always first) and the minuses of the performance. The student might be asked to do the scene again after the critique, and the performance is almost always improved.

4. *Generalization and maintenance.* The student must be able to use the skill in a variety of situations. Self-monitoring techniques can be helpful in keeping the skill foremost in the student's mind.

The supportive atmosphere that teachers and peers can establish in this process usually is extraordinarily helpful in its own right. This means that the teacher takes pains to set the situation up as a helping situation with perhaps more than

Social skills can be developed through modeling, role-playing, performance feedback, and generalization and maintenance. (© Michael Weisbrot)

one student as the focus of the social skills practice. Such extensive efforts require much time and attention on the part of the teacher and are best done with a teacher consultant in the classroom or in a small-group setting such as a resource room or special classroom. The increased pressure to place students in the least restrictive environment means that many children with behavior disorders will be in the regular classroom and raises the question of how much the regular classroom teacher can or will do to aid in these situations unless provided with professional support.

Inclusion in the General Education Classroom: Modeling Acceptable Behavior.
One of the strongest issues related to inclusion and children with behavioral problems has been the modeling of acceptable behavior. Those supporting the inclusion model ask, "How can a child learn acceptable behavior in a group that is displaying a large amount of unacceptable behavior, as might be true in a special class with behavior problems?" Stainback and Stainback (1996) pointed out that the behavior of a person with normal behavior patterns can be made abnormal if the person spends all day with persons with abnormal behavior. The Stainbacks suggested that placing children with maladaptive behavior patterns in a regular class, in which many students reveal acceptable behavior patterns, will encourage the child with deviant behaviors to seek a more socially acceptable pattern. This would be done through **vicarious learning**—that is, learning from observing other children being positively reinforced even though they themselves are not part of the event.

By being included in a regular classroom, children who have behavioral difficulties can learn the desired behaviors vicariously by observing those behaviors in their classmates.

Activities such as participating in a community project or helping a charity give students an environment where they can observe and model positive behavior.

Such conclusions, however, have been brought into question by Halenbeck and Kauffman (1995), who reviewed the literature on observational learning and its effect on student behavior. They point out, among other things, that the child with behavior disturbance probably came from a classroom of students performing in a socially acceptable manner. Why hadn't the student learned the proper behavior through observing his or her classmates there? These three questions need answering in such a situation:

- Under what circumstances will students imitate the desirable behavior of typical peers?
- What types of models are these students most likely to imitate?
- Under what conditions will models have vicarious effects on such students?

The answers to these questions are complex but basically confirm the notion that merely placing a youngster in a classroom in which much desirable behavior is being presented does not guarantee that the child with deviant behavior will imitate it. Data from observation suggest that people most readily imitate those whom they perceive to be similar to themselves in significant ways (Bandura, 1986). Indeed, within the regular classroom such a preference can lead to the formation of a subgroup of antisocial boys who see the youngster who is misbehaving as being more closely aligned to themselves than to the more properly behaved students.

The issue in the regular classroom is complicated by some other observations. Once a student has received negative judgments from other students, it is very difficult for that student to rid himself or herself of an undesirable reputation even if his or her behavior changes. Also, teachers' attitudes toward disruptive students do not necessarily change even when the students decrease their disruptive behavior.

Halenbeck and Kauffman (1995) concluded that children with emotional or behavior disorders, particularly those displaying aggressive behavior, need specific interventions and reinforcement programs. If they are to benefit from observing peer models, they will need instruction on what to pay attention to, how to remember and rehearse model behavior, and how to judge whether to produce imitative responses. These require an intensity of treatment unlikely to be available in the regular classroom, in their opinion.

In other words, students do not imitate every behavior that they observe. The imitation is selective and related to their own identification of similarity to the model and also to their own predetermined view of themselves. Students who have been told that they are aggressive and disruptive seem especially likely to model themselves after other students with the same label. Halenbeck and Kauffman (1995) suggested that a student with behavior disorders is more likely to imitate other students with behavior disorders who are making an attempt to modify and improve their behavior than they are to imitate peers with whom they think they have little or nothing in common.

An IEP plan agreed upon by parents and school personnel can help in developing social skills. (See sample IEP in Chapter 2, p. 59.)

The Needs of the Individual Student. The emphasis in programs stressing positive reinforcement is that "work comes before play." This means that highly preferred activities (play) are contingent on less preferred activities (work). When successful, these programs have an additional advantage in that a sense of pride emerges in the child for accomplishing valued tasks—if the teacher is skilled enough to present tasks that Hobbs (1974) referred to as "just manageable difficulties" (JMD), or tasks of sufficient difficulty that the student has a true sense of accomplishment when they are completed.

Are our treatments or educational interventions effective? Which methods appear to be more effective than others? One of the difficulties in answering those questions is that the treatment of youngsters with behavioral disorders is individual and based on the needs of a particular child, making comparisons among children difficult.

An innovative attempt to bring together the results of sixty-four single-subject studies (reporting the results of one student at a time from a beginning baseline to performance after treatment) revealed moderate positive results for social skills training (Mathus, Kavale, Quinn, Forness, & Rutherford, 1998). Delinquent students seemed to respond better to social skills instruction than do emotionally or behaviorally disturbed children or autistic children. The modest nature of the impact of social skills instruction suggests that further work needs to be done to improve such training and also reminds us how difficult it is to change patterns of human behavior once they have been established.

A summary of the research on social skills training to produce socially acceptable learned behaviors such as cooperation, assertion, responsibility, empathy, and self-control revealed a modest positive gain for that training (Gresham, 1998).

There was even some suggestion that improvement in academic skills instruction might improve the behavior of many students as well as the social skills instruction itself. One of the biggest problems was that there was a failure of *generalization*, that is, the student might learn a skill in one setting (e.g., proper greeting) but be unable to generalize it to other settings, such as the playground. Gresham has proposed a contextual approach to teaching social skills that would take advantage of events that occur naturally in the school environment; most social skills instruction in home, school, and community settings can be characterized as informal. Thousands of behavioral incidents occur in these settings, creating numerous opportunities for successful learning experiences (p. 22).

TECHNOLOGY

Computers: Aiding Content Mastery and Avoiding Negative Response

A computer can be an especially useful learning tool for a student with behavior problems because it provides an objective, neutral response to the child's sometimes provocative or challenging behavior. Children with a long history of social interaction problems may respond poorly to teacher feedback, particularly when criticism or correction is involved. The child who is adept at manipulating others can quickly change the focus of a discussion from his or her inadequate academic performance to the teacher's behavior. "Why are you always picking on me?" is a common theme. With a computer, however, the student must find a different approach.

Obviously, a computer isn't able to interact emotionally with the child. If the student has difficulty solving a problem, he or she must find out why and determine the right answer to proceed with the computer program. The student cannot resort to emotional manipulation or accuse the machine of being unfair.

Children who are hyperactive or who have an attention-deficit hyperactive disorder often have difficulty concentrating and can be helped by a computer. When working with a computer, they must pay some degree of attention to get results. The orderliness and sequence of the software programs can provide a systematic structure for students who have very little cognitive structure or self-discipline. Given the extensive possibilities for the use of computers with students who have behavior problems, it is surprising that little research on their impact with such students has been published.

Students with ADHD may benefit from working on a computer.

⬤▬ *Family and Lifespan Issues*

One of the major questions facing special educators is what happens to their students in secondary school and beyond. To what extent do they find jobs? To what extent are they personally independent?

TRANSITION FROM SCHOOL TO WORK

Several studies have been conducted that look at the transition experiences from school to work of youth with disabilities. One study in the state of Washington tracked more than 4,000 students who graduated between 1978 and 1986 (Neel, Meadows, Levine, & Edgar, 1988). One hundred sixty of these students had behavior disorders, and the researchers compared them with more than 500 nonhandicapped students of the same ages and from the same schools. Only 60 percent of the students with disabilities were currently working, compared with 70 percent of the nondisabled group. Moreover, those who were working had found their jobs themselves or with the help of family. No social or rehabilitation agency was actively working on their problems.

The authors concluded that school programs are not teaching children with behavior disorders the skills they need to find jobs. And a large number of parents agreed. One-third were dissatisfied with the programs their children had in school or with the jobs their children found. One of the most important responsibilities special educators have is helping students cope with the transition between school and the workplace. The main function of school is to prepare youngsters to live as independent adults. Mithaug, Martin, and Agran (1987) identified four skills that should be part of the secondary curriculum for exceptional children:

1. Choosing among available job options
2. Performing independently (a learning-to-learn strategy that allows students to respond to a new task without relying on others to help)
3. Self-evaluation (so students can measure their own performance)
4. Adjustment (deciding what to do the next time they work at a task)

None of those skills is easy to master. Students need extensive practice with them if they are going to make an effective transition from school to work.

The National Longitudinal Transitions Study of Special Education Students included more than 8,000 youths from ages 13 to 21 and was a nationally representative sample (Wagner et al., 1991). Persons who were classified as emotionally disturbed had adjustments to school that were manifestly unsuccessful. They had lower grade point averages than students in other disability categories and the highest dropout rate of all students with disabilities.

Students with behavior disorders have lower grade point averages than students in other disability categories.

One in five secondary school students with the designation "seriously emotionally disturbed (SED)" had been arrested, and 35 percent of the persons older than school age had been arrested. This group was least likely to belong to social and community groups after high school. Outside school, however, their adaptation was another matter. Students with emotional disturbances had among the highest employment rates while in school and earned wages comparable to the wages of students with learning disabilities who were living independently.

ADULTHOOD

What happens to individuals with emotional or behavioral disorders when they reach adulthood? Figure 7.4 compares the employment rates of youth with emotional problems with the rates of youth in eleven categories of disability (Wagner et al., 1991). The figure presents some modest good news and motivation for

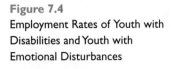

Source: M. Wagner, L. Newman, R. D'Amico, E. Jay, P. Butler-Nalu, C. Marder, and R. Cox (1991). *Youth with Disabilities: How Are They Doing?* Washington, DC: U.S. Department of Education, Office of Special Education Programs.

Figure 7.4

Employment Rates of Youth with Disabilities and Youth with Emotional Disturbances

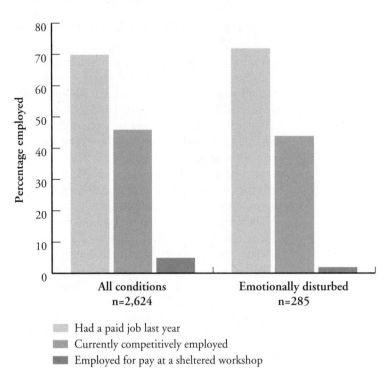

the establishment of effective and intense programs for students with emotional problems.

Figure 7.4 shows that about 72 percent of youth with emotional disturbance "had a paid job last year"; the corresponding percentage among youths in the "all conditions" group was slightly lower—70 percent. This is a positive and somewhat unexpected finding. About 45 percent in each group are "currently competitively employed." Half or more of the emotionally disturbed youth are employed in some fashion, and there is little doubt that more effective and more efficient training programs and support features could improve those figures.

Something about the school environment appears to be particularly unsuitable for these students. Research with smaller samples seems to yield consistent findings. Feldman, Denhoff, and Denhoff (1984) carried out a ten- to twelve-year follow-up study on forty-eight adults who had been diagnosed as hyperactive children. The researchers found that by age 21, 91 percent were in some form of school or special training or working and seemed to be performing in a reasonably effective manner, although they had lower self-esteem and less educational achievement than their nonhyperactive siblings who made up the control group.

Hechtman and Weiss (1985) studied seventy-six youngsters originally seen in a psychiatric department of Montreal Children's Hospital, where they were diagnosed as hyperactive at 6 to 12 years of age. These children were compared in young adulthood with forty-five control subjects, who were matched for gender, IQ score, and socioeconomic status with the hyperactive subjects. The control subjects had no observable behavior or academic problems. Hechtman and Weiss found that the hyperactive subjects in young adulthood attained lower academic grades, had more car accidents, and received somewhat more court referrals. On self-report scales they indicated higher levels of anxiety, grandiosity, and hostility. The researchers concluded that few hyperactive children become grossly disturbed or chronic offenders of the law when they become adults, but they do have adjustment problems related to their impulsiveness and inability to concentrate, two characteristics that created problems for them in school.

What seems to emerge from these studies is that early problems such as a difficult temperament or hyperactivity increase the risk of poor adult adjustment but do not, in any sense, guarantee it. Our treatments can be effective, and favorable environmental circumstances help a child cope more effectively with impulsiveness, lack of attentiveness, and feelings of hostility.

Summary of Major Ideas

1. Unlike children with other disabilities, youngsters with emotional and behavior disorders are often blamed for their condition. This affects their interactions with the people around them.

2. The definition of *emotional and behavior disorder* takes into account the intensity and duration of age-inappropriate behavior, the situation in which the behavior is exhibited, and the individual who considers the behavior a problem.

3. Although fewer than 1 percent of schoolchildren are receiving special education services for emotional and behavior disorders, studies show that the number of children who actually need those services is at least 5 percent and may range as high as 15 percent.

4. Conduct disorders include aggressive behavior, hyperactivity, and attention deficits. They are far more common in boys than in girls. Often the punishments children receive for these kinds of behaviors actually serve to reinforce them.

5. Intervention for the child who is anxious and withdrawn should have as its primary objective instilling a sense of self-worth and self-control. Positive experiences play an important role in preventing suicide—a serious problem among youngsters who are deeply depressed and withdrawn.

6. Both genetic and environmental factors interact in complex ways to produce problem behavior in children.

7. The decision to place a child in a special program should be considered only after adjustments have been made in the general classroom and home, prereferral activities have been carried out, and information has been gathered.

8. We currently lack a graduated intensity of treatment programs and settings to cope with the various levels of behavior disorders.

9. Because computers do not react emotionally to children's behavior and force users to pay attention, they can be an effective tool for students with behavior disorders.

10. Inclusion appears to offer a viable setting for some students with behavior disorders, if the classroom teacher has received training in special instructional strategies, the other students have been alerted to the special needs of

the student with behavior problems, and adequate support services are made available.

11. Ecological strategies focus on the interactions between children and their environment and attempt to design therapeutic settings for the children. Social skills training has been only a modest success and should focus on the need for generalization.

12. Drug therapy, in combination with educational intervention, is effective in the treatment of many hyperactive youngsters, although the reaction to drugs is a highly individual matter that needs careful monitoring.

13. A key component of the special education program for students with behavior disorders is the development of skills to help these individuals make the transition from school to the workplace.

Unresolved Issues

1. *Increasing uses of multidisciplinary teams.* One serious condition limiting the delivery of quality educational services to children with behavior problems is the need for highly trained personnel. Unless a way can be found to use paraprofessional personnel, as has been done in behavior shaping programs, it will not be possible to provide the help needed by the large number of youngsters identified as having behavior problems.

2. *Need for intervention.* Longitudinal studies of children who are socially maladjusted and act out their aggressive feelings suggest strongly that they do not outgrow these tendencies. Unless something significant is done with these children or with the environment surrounding them, we can predict that aggressive children who hurt people will become aggressive adults who hurt people. The need for large-scale intervention within the school, family, and neighborhood is clear.

3. *Understanding the causes of emotional and behavioral problems.* Since World War II, the predominant thinking about causes of problem behavior has focused on psychological or sociological causes. Either the child was mentally ill because of unusual or bizarre psychic processes or was showing abnormal behavior as a result of some negative sociological or ecological condition. Now, with increasingly sophisticated analysis, the role of genetics in causing or influencing emotional behavior has been reintroduced. We need to sort out the roles that these various forces play in the creation of unproductive behavior.

4. *Placement of children with emotional and behavioral disorders.* Within the field of special education, there is considerable disagreement about the feasibility of inclusion for children with emotional and behavioral disorders. On the one hand, the classroom teacher without special education training is ill equipped to cope with such students. On the other hand, the clustering of students with behavior disorders often removes models of positive behavior from their view. Some careful descriptions of programs that have achieved success seem required.

5. *Social reform.* A number of specialists in the emotional and behavior fields have urged professionals to become more involved in significant social issues that surround their students (Walker et al., 1998). They point out

that while professional interventions have been successful in reducing out-of-seat behavior and the number of times aggressive students hit each other at recess, they have not responded to critical policy issues such as the following:

- How do parents know their child is safe in school and on the way to and from school each day?
- How do we accommodate students who are clearly a danger to others?
- How do we prevent students from bringing weapons to school?

The inability of special educators to confront those social issues has caused a public loss of faith in the ability of professionals to be effective, despite their positive results in the more limited sphere of the classroom.

Key Terms

attention-deficit hyperactivity disorder (ADHD) p. 270
behavior disorder p. 260
environmental modification p. 280
functional assessment p. 279
helping teacher p. 285

learned helplessness p. 273
life space interview p. 288
positive reinforcement p. 278
time-out p. 281
transient adaptation problems p. 275
vicarious learning p. 295

Questions for Thought

1. What five characteristics exhibited to a marked degree over a long period of time does PL 94-142 identify as behavior disabilities?   p. 261

2. What is the apparent relationship between substance abuse and behavior disorders?   p. 265

3. What family risk factors may contribute to producing a child with a behavior disorder?   p. 266

4. What are the common patterns in families of children with conduct disorders?   p. 269

5. What is the relationship, if any, between anxiety and adolescent suicide? pp. 271–272

6. Briefly describe the five-step assessment process that Wood and Smith developed for identifying and placing children who are behaviorally disturbed.   pp. 275–276

7. Describe the use of drug therapy to treat academic problems.   p. 283

8. Describe steps that students can take to monitor their own behavior. pp. 292–293

9. List the sequence of activities by which socially acceptable behaviors might be developed, according to Kerr and Nelson.   p. 293

10. Give two reasons why computers are an effective teaching tool for children with behavior problems.   p. 298

11. Identify the four skills that can help exceptional children make the transition from school to the workplace.   p. 299

Resources for Further Study

REFERENCES OF SPECIAL ÏINTEREST

Bullock, L., & Gable, R. (1996). *The mini-library series on emotional/behavioral disorders*. Reston, VA: Council for Exceptional Children.

> A series of short (50 pages) monographs on topics designed to help the classroom teacher cope with youngsters with severe emotional disabilities. Discussions of best practices, planning effective programs, behavior management strategies, and coping with youth violence are included.

Harry, B. (1992) *Cultural diversity, families, and the special education system*. New York: Teachers College Press.

> This volume focuses attention on the special situation of an increasing number of minority families who have children referred for special education services. Harry emphasizes the issues of power and responsibility in the relationship of school systems and the families, who are often poor and uninformed about special education and its implications for their children.

Illback, R., & Nelson, C. (Eds.). (1996). *Emerging school-based approaches for children with emotional and behavioral problems*. New York: The Haworth Press, Inc.

> This book contains a variety of reports of how schools have tried to bring comprehensive planning and collaborative treatment programs for children with behavior problems within the framework of the public schools. The integration of mental health services and education is a well-recognized but often unrealized goal. Many of the chapters provide individual illustrations of these wraparound services in school systems and how they are implemented.

Kauffman, J. (1993). *Characteristics of behavior disorders of children and youth* (5th ed.). Columbus, OH: Merrill.

> This popular basic text provides a comprehensive portrait of the history of, characteristics of, and treatment options for children with behavior disorders. The author provides a strong review of the literature and has some special suggestions for teachers.

Kerr, M., & Nelson, C. (1998). *Strategies for managing behavior problems in the classroom* (3rd ed.). Upper Saddle River, NJ: Merrill.

> This book is rich in the wide varieties of strategies and techniques for dealing with children with behavior problems. It includes principles for selecting interventions and for dealing with specific behavior problems, aggressive behaviors, and psychiatric problems. It also presents survival skills for the teacher.

Knitzer, J., Steinberg, Z., & Fleisch, B. (1990). *At the schoolhouse door*. New York: Bank Street College.

> This report details a major study on the effectiveness of various educational programs and practices designed to cope with children with behavioral and emotional problems. The authors point out that many of the traditional methods of providing services for such children have not demonstrated their effectiveness, and they describe programs that coordinate mental health and educational services to good effect. They also recommend ways to improve programs for such children.

Quay, H. (1994). *Disruptive behavior disorders in childhood*. New York: Plenum Press.

> The author has written a solid review of the various issues relating to the special prob-

lems of students and children who violate societal norms and pose a special problem for teachers and parents. The book reviews past methods for coping with such children and provides suggestions about how teachers should attempt to deal with them. A strong scholarly and research base makes this book particularly authoritative.

JOURNALS

Behavioral Disorders
Council for Children with
Behavioral Disorders
Council for Exceptional Children
1920 Association Dr.
Reston, VA 20191-1589
http://earthvision.asu.edu/BD/
index.html

Exceptional Children
Council for Exceptional Children
1920 Association Dr.
Reston, VA 20191-1589
http://www.ccc.sped.org/

Journal of Applied Behavior Analysis
Department of Human Development
University of Kansas
Lawrence, KS 66045-2133
http://www.envmed.rochester.edu/
wwwrap/behavior/jaba/jabahome.htm

*Journal of Emotional and
Behavioral Disorders*
PRO-ED, Inc.
8700 Shoal Creek Blvd.
Austin, TX 78757-6897

Teaching Exceptional Children
Council for Exceptional Children
1920 Association Dr.
Reston, VA 20191-1589
http://www.nscee.edu/unlv/Colleges/
Education/ERC/tec.html

PROFESSIONAL ORGANIZATIONS

American Psychological Association
750 First St., NE
Washington, DC 20002-4242
(202) 336-5500
http://www.apa.org/

Council for Children with
Behavioral Disorders
Council for Exceptional Children
1920 Association Dr.
Reston, VA 20191-1589
http://earthvision.asu.edu/BD/
index.html

National Alliance for the Mentally Ill
200 N. Glebe Rd., Suite 1015
Arlington, VA 22203-3754
http://www.cais.com/vikings/nami

National Mental Health Association
1021 Prince St.
Alexandria, VA 22314-2971
http://www.nmha.org

Society for Research in Child Development
505 E. Huron, Suite 301
Ann Arbor, MI 48104-1522
http://www.journals.uchicago.edu/
SRCD/srcdhome.html

8

Children with Communication Disorders in Speech and Language

FOCUSING questions

How are communication disorders classified?

What are the elements of spoken language?

What are some other ways of communicating besides oral language?

What is the sequence of language development?

What can teachers do to assist stutterers?

Why should language intervention begin early, when a disorder is identified?

Nothing is more exciting to parents than their infant's amazing ability to begin to acquire speech and language in the first year of life. So it is not surprising that parents are often devastated if their infant fails to acquire verbal language and to speak in a manner that is understandable.

Communication through speech and language is a complicated but natural human process that grows out of the child's prelinguistic communication through cries, grunts, smiles, and gestures (Dromi, 1993). It involves cognition (thinking) and audition (hearing). It means receiving information and sending information back. It means learning how to control air for sound production and muscles of the mouth for articulation and speech in a fashion that another person of the same culture can understand.

Speech and language development occurs in most individuals who are not disabled. Thus, failure to learn to produce sounds (words) that have meaning in a given culture (language) is indicative of almost all major communication disabilities. When such a disability is suspected, it must be identified and appropriate remediation initiated as early in the child's life as possible so the child will be able to communicate with others and, at school age, learn to read and write.

Definitions

Communication is the exchange of thoughts, information, and ideas. Most commonly, we think of verbal communication as occurring through speech or talking. Messages can be transmitted in other ways, however: through writing, reading, telegraphy, and the electrical impulses of the telephone (using a computer and a modem). Communication can be nonverbal, through gestures and facial expressions. Sign language uses an ordered form of gestures to convey meaning. Necessary for communication to take place are a sender, a message, and a receiver (Figure 8.1).

Speech is the systematic oral production of the words of a given language. Sounds become speech only if they produce words that have meaning. Speech has a rhythmic flow with stress and intonation and words with stressed and unstressed syllables. Figure 8.2 presents a simplified overview of the production of speech. A thought occurs in the brain; it is translated into symbols and sent to the larynx area for phonation and resonation, which takes place in the vocal tract; then air is sent to be modified by movements of the tongue and passage over the teeth and lips, which combine to form the sounds, words, and sentences of a particular language (articulation). The thought transformed into words is received by a listener through hearing, in a process called **audition.**

The following four processes are involved in the production of speech:

- **Respiration** (breathing) generates the energy that produces sound.
- **Phonation** is the production of sound by the vibration of the vocal cords.
- **Resonation** gives the voice a unique characteristic that identifies the speaker. It is the product of sound traveling through the speaker's head and neck.
- **Articulation** is the movement of the mouth and tongue that shapes sound into phonemes (the smallest unit of sound), which make speech.

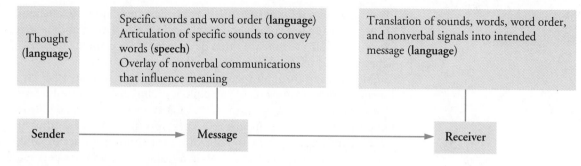

Figure 8.1   The Communication Process

Damage to any of these processes can result in a speech disorder but does not necessarily interfere with language learning or reading and writing. Hearing losses can also cause speech disorders. A child will fail to produce speech if he or she cannot hear it spoken or hear his or her own sound production. Fortunately, most children with hearing losses have some audition, and they can learn to speak when provided with amplification through hearing aids (children who are deaf or hard of hearing are the subject of Chapter 9).

Language is an organized system of symbols that humans use to express and receive meaning (Jusczyk, 1997). Language systems evolved over time and largely replaced the innate communication system of emotions by means of gestures and facial expressions, which convey meaning, though the range of meaning they convey is limited. When a given community selects a series of sounds to convey meaning, it creates speech. Spoken language has many advantages over the expression of emotions: It can convey meaning through speech and writing, and it can express the past and future as well as the present.

An infant is innately programmed to communicate through smiles, eye contact, sounds, and gestures (the prelinguistic system). The language system uses these talents, and parents teach the child that people and objects have names and particular sounds to identify them. Because they are rational beings, children learn early in life that things have names (Bower, 1989) and are genetically prepared to learn a language (Stromswald, 1996). The language they learn is the one spoken in the home.

Differences Between Speech Disorders and Language Disorders

Communication may be oral (speech), gestural, or written.

A **communication disorder** is a disorder in speech and/or language. It is important to distinguish between disorders in speech and disorders in language because they have different origins and require different interventions. A **speech disorder** is a disorder affecting articulation, voice, or fluency. A **language disorder** is the impairment or deviant development of comprehension or use (or both) of a spoken, written, or other verbal symbol system. Cromer's 1978 definition is still a standard. Cromer defined a language disorder as a disorder that exists without other disabilities, such as

Figure 8.2
Processes Involved in the
Production of Speech

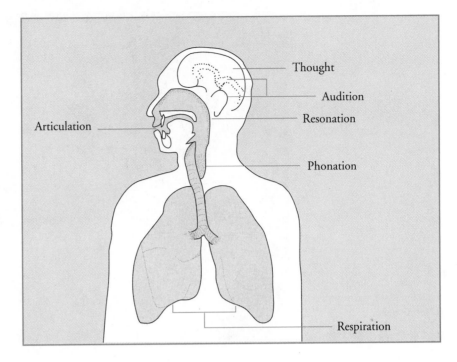

deafness, mental retardation, motor disabilities, or personality disorders. Language problems can coexist with all those deficits, however, and need to be treated.

The definitions of communication disorders in speech and language presented in Table 8.1 are those of the professional organization of specialists in speech and hearing, the American Speech-Language-Hearing Association (ASHA).

The Elements of Verbal Language

 Most verbal languages have elements in common.

Verbal language is language expressed in words, through speech and in writing. To be considered a verbal language, spoken or written words must have several elements in common so that members of the culture in which the words are used are able to understand what the speaker or writer wants to communicate.

There must be agreement about **semantics** (what the words mean) and **phonology** (how to pronounce the words). If the language is written, the words must be spelled in conformity with the alphabetic system and phonemes of the language.

All human infants have language mechanisms that enable them to figure out the rules (syntax) and sounds (phonology) of their language (Pinker, 1991). The mechanisms that enable an infant to identify the sounds of his or her language begin to operate when the infant is about 6 months of age. The mechanisms that enable the infant to figure out the rules of the language (morphology, syntax, and pragmatics) begin to operate shortly before the child's second year of life (Bloom, 1991; Jusczyk, 1997). These mechanisms may be similar to cognitive mechanisms; however, they can exist when a child has mental retardation and faulty cognitive mechanisms but

Speech therapists encourage production and understandable articulation. *(© Joel Gordon)*

is linguistically sophisticated, as children with Wallace syndrome are (Bellugi, 1988; Pinker, 1991).

In summary, the production of meaningful spoken and written language depends on a multitude of working parts of the biological system. It also requires the child to learn rules of pronunciation, grammar, and usage. Children without disabilities generally master spoken language quickly and display an amazing competence by the third year of life. Because our culture highly values proficiency in spoken language and expects everyone to master it, a great deal of research has been conducted to identify discrete disorders of language, specialists are trained to remediate them, and curriculum is devised to improve them. Spoken language is considered the hallmark of human functioning, and when it does not come naturally, a great deal of attention is paid to correcting it.

▬▬ *Prevalence of Communication Disorders*

Because of the many systems and processes in which communication problems can originate, it is difficult to get an accurate picture of how many communication disorders are speech deficits and how many are language deficits. Speech and language impairment affected over 1 million children in 1994–1995, composing 21% of the total number of children with disabilities (U.S. Department of Education, 1997). Not all children with language disorders are in special education classes. In fact, 87.5 percent of children with speech and language impairments are served in regular classes; only 7.6 percent are in resource rooms and 4.5 percent in separate classes. Children with speech and language disorders are more likely than children with other disabilities to be served in the regular classroom.

TABLE 8.1 ASHA Definitions of Communication Disorders and Variations

I. A *communication disorder* is an impairment in the ability to receive, send, process, and comprehend concepts or verbal, nonverbal, and graphic symbol systems. A communication disorder may be evident in the processes of hearing, language, and/or speech. A communication disorder may range in severity from mild to profound. It may be developmental or acquired. Individuals may demonstrate one or any combination of communication disorders. A communication disorder may result in a primary disability or it may be secondary to other disabilities.

A. A *speech disorder* is an impairment of the articulation of speech sounds, fluency, and/or voice.

   1. An *articulation disorder* is the atypical production of speech sounds characterized by substitutions, omissions, additions or distortions that may interfere with intelligibility.

   2. A *fluency disorder* is an interruption in the flow of speaking characterized by atypical rate, rhythm, and repetitions in sounds, syllables, words, and phrases. This may be accompanied by excessive tension, struggle behavior, and secondary mannerisms.

   3. A *voice disorder* is characterized by the abnormal production and/or absences of vocal quality, pitch, loudness, resonance, and/or duration, which is inappropriate for an individual's age and/or sex.

B. A *language disorder* is impaired comprehension and/or use of spoken, written, and/or other symbol systems. The disorder may involve (1) the form of language (phonology, morphology, syntax), (2) the content of language (semantics), and/or (3) the function of language in communication (pragmatics) in any combination.

   1. Form of Language
      a. *Phonology* is the sound system of a language and the rules that govern the sound combinations.
      b. *Morphology* is the system that governs the structure of words and the construction of word forms.
      c. *Syntax* is the system governing the order and combination of words to form sentences, and the relationships among the elements within a sentence.

   2. Content of Language
      a. *Semantics* is the system that governs the meanings of words and sentences.

   3. Function of Language
      a. *Pragmatics* is the system that combines the above language components in functional and socially appropriate communication.

C. A *hearing disorder* is the result of impaired auditory sensitivity of the physiological auditory system. A hearing disorder may limit the development, comprehension, production, and/or maintenance of speech and/or language. Hearing disorders are classified according to difficulties in detection, recognition, discrimination, comprehension, and perception of auditory information. Individuals with hearing impairment may be described as deaf or hard of hearing.

   1. *Deaf* is defined as a hearing disorder that limits an individual's aural/oral communication performance to the extent that the primary sensory input for communication may be other than the auditory channel.

   2. *Hard of hearing* is defined as a hearing disorder, whether fluctuating or permanent, which adversely affects an individual's ability to communicate. The hard-of-hearing individual relies on the auditory channel as the primary sensory input for communication.

(continued)

TABLE 8.1   ASHA Definitions of Communication Disorders and Variations (Cont.)

D. *Central auditory processing disorders* (CAPDs) are deficits in the information processing of audible signals not attributed to impaired peripheral hearing sensitivity or intellectual impairment. This information processing involves perceptual, cognitive, and linguistic functions that, with appropriate interactions, result in effective receptive communication of auditorily presented stimuli. Specifically, CAPD refers to limitations in the ongoing transmission, analysis, organization, transformation, elaboration, storage, retrieval, and use of information contained in audible signals. CAPD may involve the listener's active and passive (e.g., conscious and unconscious, mediated and unmediated, controlled and automatic) ability to do the following:

- attend, discriminate, and identify acoustic signals;
- transform and continuously transmit information through both the peripheral and central nervous systems;
- filter, sort, and combine information at appropriate perceptual and conceptual levels;
- store and retrieve information efficiently; restore, organize, and use retrieved information;
- segment and decode acoustic stimuli using phonological, semantic, syntactic, and pragmatic knowledge; and
- attach meaning to a stream of acoustic signals through use of linguistic and nonlinguistic contexts.

II. Communication Variations

A. *Communication difference/dialect* is a variation of a symbol system used by a group of individuals that reflects and is determined by shared regional, social, or cultural/ethnic factors. A regional, social, or cultural/ethnic variation of a symbol system should not be considered a disorder of speech or language.

B. *Augmentative/alternative communication* systems attempt to compensate and facilitate, temporarily or permanently, for the impairment and disability patterns of individuals with severe expressive and/or language comprehension disorders. Augmentative/alternative communication may be required for individuals demonstrating impairments in gestural, spoken, and/or written modalities.

Augmentative communication devices such as hearing aids assist individuals with hearing impairments.

Source: American Speech-Language-Hearing Association Ad Hoc Committee on Service Delivery in the Schools. (1993). "Definitions of Communication Disorders and Variations." *ASHA, 35* (Suppl. 10). 40–41. Reprinted with permission.

Prevalence figures also tend to be distorted because mental retardation, cerebral palsy, and many other disabilities affect communication. Although a communication disorder may be secondary to another disability, it still requires treatment and therapy as part of a total special education program (Table 8.2).

Some patterns in communication disorders have been found. Tallal, Curtis, and Kaplan (1988) demonstrated that speech-language problems tend to run in families. They occur in about 33 percent of the children whose mothers have such problems and 18 percent of the children whose fathers have such problems. Knowing that a member of the family has a specific language problem alerts parents to the risk of their children having a similar problem.

TABLE 8.2 Disabilities That Communication Disorders May Accompany	
Disability	**Characteristic of Communication Disorder**
Mental retardation	Delayed language is a universal characteristic; disorders may be present in all aspects of language production and reception.
Cerebral palsy	Poor muscle control and impaired breathing of the child with cerebral palsy result in communication difficulties ranging from language delays and voice disorders to the inability to speak.
Learning disabilities	Major problems in learning to read, write, spell, and do arithmetic. The most likely hypothesis is that an unknown brain dysfunction interferes with auditory and visual perception and thus with all language reception and production.
Severe and profound multiple disabilities	Inability to speak; possibly able to learn a limited number of receptive words. Those without mental retardation may have no difficulties or may experience delays in language development; the child with severe physical disabilities may need a head pointer to type or some other form of augmented communication device to communicate by pointing to pictures, letters, or words.
Autism; childhood mental disturbance	Spoken language may not be present, but some can learn to communicate by using augmented and alternative communication devices. Autistic children with mental retardation and other severe mental disturbances may have disordered language in terms of syntax and semantics.

Language Development: A Brief Overview

It is far beyond the scope of this chapter to list all aspects of language development. As you read this overview, keep in mind that a child is a hypothesis maker and an active creator of theories about his or her world and language (Bower, 1988). When children hear speech, they try to figure out the rules of speech. They do so without explicit instruction, because they are motivated to learn language on their own, and they monitor their own learning (Pinker, 1991; Shantz & Ebeling, 1991). Chomsky (1988) states it well: "Language learning is not really something the child does, it is something that happens to the child placed in an appropriate environment" (p. 62).

In this chapter, we discuss spoken language (speech). Gestural languages are covered more fully in Chapter 9.

CHARACTERISTICS OF LANGUAGE DEVELOPMENT

In most, if not all, societies, children who are not disabled learn to speak the language of their culture very early in life. The sequence in mastering a language is similar across cultures. Language is social in origin, and it arises in the context of a close interaction with basic caregivers (usually the child's parents). Linguists generally agree that the infant learns language during interactions with his or her basic caregivers.

The caregiver's sensitive responsiveness to the child and to the child's requests greatly facilitates the child's acquisition of language. The interaction of caregiver and child in games such as "peekaboo" and "I'm going to get you" is enjoyable play for the child and encourages the child to fulfill his or her genetic push to learn language. Children learn language when interacting with caregivers in a setting (usually the home) in which they are provided with psychological warmth and encouragement. At first, the child's contribution may be smiles, gestures, and babbling, and the caregiver's role is to take turns and provide words.

Most caregivers use what psycholinguists call *motherese* to talk to their children. Motherese is a form of language in which the adult uses a high-pitched voice, which infants seem to respond to, speaks in simple sentences, repeats words and sentences, uses the present tense, and asks a lot of simple questions about what is going on in the context. Examples of these questions are "Where's Daddy?" "See the doggie?" "Where did the doggie go?" "More milk?" and "More cookies?" Motherese is spoken slowly and pronounced carefully. The clear pronunciation may help babies learn sound categories, and the questions may help babies identify objects by name. The use of motherese seems to be widespread; it has been found in fourteen different languages.

Thus, nature (genes) and parents combine to enable the child to master the language of his or her home.

THE SEQUENCE OF LANGUAGE DEVELOPMENT

By 2 to 3 months of age, infants begin to coo, make eye contact with their caregivers, and emit a socially communicative smile. By 2 months of age, they can detect the rhythm of the language of their home (Garrett, 1996).

Around 5 to 6 months of age, infants babble and parents begin to match the sounds the infants produce to words in the home language. When the infant produces sounds such as "ba ba, da da, na na, ma ma," the mother will tend to select "ma ma" and reinforce it. Thus, the infant "learns" to say "ma ma." At 6 months of age, babies change from being "universal linguists" who can learn any language of the world into specialists in their own language (Bloom, 1991). By 7 months, infants appear to recognize major features of their home language (phonology, syntax, and phrases) and lose the ability to distinguish sounds not found in their own language (Leonard, 1997).

Most adults simplify their language (spoken or gestural) when communicating with a young child.

Parents in many cultures use motherese to communicate with infants and toddlers.

The caregiver's sensitive responsiveness to the child and to his or her requests greatly facilitates the child's acquisition of language.
(© Jonathan A. Meyers)

Learning language involves a combination of genetic and environmental inputs.

Language development proceeds like this: Infants are programmed genetically to make sounds, and the caregivers give meaning to these sounds and repeat them. Consequently, the infant learns to repeat the sounds made by their caregivers in the way the caregivers say them. Caregivers tend to select sounds that occur in their home language. The most common babblings considered words by caregivers are the sounds the infant genetically produces at about 7 to 9 months of age. Most cultures have come to accept these sounds as terms for parents—*Mama, Dada, Tata,* and so on.

At this point, the infant learns (cognitively) a major fact about the world: People and objects have names (Bower, 1989; Brown, 1958). The child appears to be able to abstract meaning from the environment and figure out the words associated with objects at home by looking where the caregiver is looking while saying a word—for example, the name of an object like *ball.* At this point in the infant's development, usually by the age of 9 months, the child's speech or oral sounds take on meaning, and they become language by the time the child is 12 months of age, when the first words appear.

When the first word appears, the child may string together a series of nonsense syllables with the word. The child seems to understand that one word isn't enough, but combining words is beyond his or her ability at this age.

The child's first sentences are one-word sentences that convey the total meaning of what the child is trying to communicate. Thus, the word *ball* may mean "See the ball," "I want the ball," "Throw me the ball," or "Where is the ball?" For parents, deciphering meaning is a guessing game. They have to be in the same context as the child to determine what the child is communicating. Words have meaning only in a particular context.

Around 18 months, most children are speaking in two-word sentences, usually a verb and a noun, such as "See doggie," or "Daddy go." The verb in the two-word sentence conveys much of the meaning (Bloom, 1991). By 3 years of age, most children are speaking in multiple-word sentences and using generally correct syntax, although some common errors are present, such as overgeneralizations ("I runned" instead of "I ran") and errors in making plurals (*sheeps* for *sheep* and *deers* for *deer*). By 6 years of age, the child is a good communicator with a knowledge of several thousand words. He or she is using speech and language in various logical forms and has mastered most of the phonology of the community's language. Learning the rules of how to pronounce all the sounds of the home language extends through infancy and childhood into adulthood (Gleason, 1993). Remember that children go through these language acquisition stages at roughly the same ages but with some degree of individual variation.

It is important to understand language development, because it is in the early stages of language development that disorders appear. Some elements of language, such as correct pronunciation and articulation, will improve with age. Problems with other elements indicate the need for early therapy if they are to be remediated.

Classification of Communication Disorders

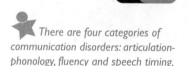

There are four categories of communication disorders: articulation-phonology, fluency and speech timing, voice, and language.

Communication disorders usually fall into four broad categories: (1) disorders of articulation-phonology, (2) disorders of fluency and speech timing, (3) disorders of voice, and (4) disorders of language. The first three classifications are traditionally considered speech disorders.

We want to emphasize that these classifications are not mutually exclusive. Individuals with one kind of disorder are by no means protected from having another. The relationship between articulation-phonology disorders and language disorders is well established, and researchers are exploring other connections among these areas.

DISORDERS OF ARTICULATION-PHONOLOGY

Articulation-phonology disorders are misproductions of speech sounds. They are the most common communication disorder among children in public schools. Although historically these disorders were considered speech disorders, they can be considered language disorders as well. We discuss them here as a distinct category of disorder and later as a subcategory of language disorders.

In recent years, the terminology used to describe articulation-phonology disorders has become more precise (ASHA, 1993). Today, the term **articulation errors** indicates misproductions associated with speech motor activity, such as saying "ring" for "king." The term **phonological errors** indicates misproductions of speech sounds associated with the dysfunctional use of the sound system of the language (Paul, 1996a). There is a strong relationship between phonological errors and reading problems, which will be discussed more fully later in this chapter.

The number and kinds of misproductions and their effect on intelligibility are among the criteria for judging the disorder on a continuum ranging from mild to severe. Articulation-phonology disorders may range from a mild frontal lisp, a fleeting hesitation in words, to mispronunciations of speech sounds so severe that the speaker is unintelligible to listeners in his or her own community. Persons with severe and profound disabilities may never develop speech and must rely on learning how to use their prelinguistic system for communication (Dromi, 1993). Tallal, Galaburda, Llinas, and Von Euler (1993) proposed that some children are unable to process auditorially the rapidity of speech. This failure to be able to process and integrate speech begins with phonological difficulties and eventually leads to defects in language development and difficulty in learning to read.

The Nature of Articulation-Phonology Disorders

Imprecise phoneme production or articulation errors are described as substitutions, distortions, omissions, and, infrequently, the addition of extra sounds (McReynolds, 1986). When the intended phoneme is replaced by another phoneme, the error is one of *substitution*. Common examples are *w* for *r* (*wight* for *right*), *t* for *k* (*toat* for *coat*), and *w* for *l* (*wove* for *love*). The influence of multiple substitutions on intelligibility becomes apparent when *like* becomes *wite*. In other instances, a misproduction makes a phoneme sound different, but the difference is not enough to change the production into a different phoneme. These productions are known as *distortions* (for example, *brlu* for *blue*). When a disorder involves *omissions*, certain sounds are omitted entirely (*pay* for *play*, *ka* for *cat* or *cap*).

Misarticulations are not always consistent. In some phoneme sequences, sounds are articulated correctly; in others, they are not. Often the position of a sound (at the beginning, middle, or end of a word) or the position of a word influences the production.

Disabilities Associated with Articulation-Phonology Disorders

Obvious handicaps associated with disordered articulation are cleft palate, hearing loss, cerebral palsy, and other disorders of the central nervous system.

Cleft palate is a structural deficiency caused by the failure of the bone and soft tissue of the roof of the mouth to fuse during prenatal development. It is often associated with cleft lip. Historically, these clefts have been of special interest to speech-language pathologists. Hypernasality (excessively nasal-sounding speech) is the most familiar speech characteristic of children with clefts. Children with palatal clefts also make particular kinds of articulation errors related to impaired palatal function.

Sometimes an articulation-phonology disorder is associated with another speech disorder (for example, stuttering) or is part of a basic language disorder. Although researchers have examined many different causal factors, they have not reached a consensus.

DISORDERS OF FLUENCY AND SPEECH TIMING

Fluency is the flow of speech. The most common fluency disorder is **stuttering,** which is characterized by repetitions and prolongations of sound, syllables, or words; tension; and extraneous movement. Stuttering is a complex behavioral disorder with a variety of assumed causes. For some children who stutter, there is a genetic component (Yairi, Ambrose, & Cox, 1996). Many children who stutter have spontaneous recovery by school age (Bloodstein, 1995). What is clear is that early intervention (begun by the age of 3) is very effective in reducing stuttering (Onslow, Costa, Andrews, Harrison, & Packman, 1996).

DISORDERS OF VOICE

Voice is the production of sound in the larynx and the selective transmission and modification of that sound through resonance and loudness. When we talk about voice, we usually think of three characteristics: quality, pitch, and loudness. We evaluate these characteristics in terms of the speaker's age, sex, and culture (Moores, 1996). A **voice disorder** is an inappropriate variation in voice quality, pitch, or loudness.

Disorders of voice quality, generally called **dysphonia,** can be related to phonation, resonation, or both. Breathiness, hoarseness, or harshness are disorders of phonation. Problems with resonation include hypernasality (excessively nasal-sounding speech) and hyponasality (speech that sounds as if the speaker has a bad cold). Often phonation and resonation disorders are present in the same person, but they can be separate disorders.

Pitch indicates whether the speaker is male or female, young or old. Pitch breaks, a common problem, occur in adolescents and affect boys particularly. High-pitched and variably pitched voices are common among children with severe hearing impairments or cerebral palsy (Boone & McFarlane, 1988).

DISORDERS OF LANGUAGE

As we explained earlier, culturally determined rules of correct usage govern the elements of language. Each element—phonology, morphology, syntax, pragmatics, and semantics—is a potential source of language disorder. For example, some children are able to express age-appropriate ideas in correct sentence structures but are not able to use accepted rules of morphology; they might have difficulty with pluralization (*foot-feet*), with verb tenses (*run-ran, walk-walked*), or with the use of prefixes (*pre-, anti-*).

Language involves both *reception* (taking in information) and *expression* (giving out verbal information). In some manner, language is processed internally during both reception and expression, but language production and language comprehension do not always proceed at the same pace. Some children will speak but do not seem to understand the meaning of the sentence (Miller & Paul, 1995). Processing errors interfere with all types of learning, including language learning.

The stages and sequences of normal language acquisition give clues to language disorders. But it is often difficult to determine a specific cause for a specific language disorder in a specific child. Speech problems, developmental disorders, or other disabilities may all influence the child's ability to use language.

In summary, any deviation from linguistic competence involving the following is considered a disorder (revised and adapted from Dore, 1986, p. 4):

- Producing understandable sounds (articulation and pronunciation)
- Creating well-formed sentences and understanding grammatical structures (syntax and morphology)
- Creating sentences with meaningful content (semantics)
- Constructing logical sentences with appropriate knowledge (for example, saying "I see a bird," when the child sees a bird, not an airplane)
- Speaking appropriately in context (pragmatics)

Developmental Delay in Communication

Some children are slow talkers and with an enriched environment are able to achieve average scores by kindergarten age (Leonard, 1998). Other children, however, are slow to develop and possess a disability. The following categories describe different groups of slow developers.

Children with *slow expressive language development* (SELD) have fewer than the average 50 words in their vocabulary by 24 months of age. However, they usually move into the normal range of language expression by school age (Paul, 1995). SELD is a risk factor, not a disorder.

Children from lower socioeconomic conditions tend to have significantly lower vocabulary scores (Hart & Risley, 1995). Adults in lower-class environments tend to use and encourage language less than middle-class adults do.

Some children who have slower acquisition rates have difficulty in auditory processing sounds in the normal pace of speech (Curtis & Tallal, 1991). This difficulty manifests itself in the child's failure to distinguish among phonemes such as "ba" and "da." The slower auditory processing does not allow enough time for the sound to enter short-term memory and then be stored in long-term memory. Thus, accurate recognition and production of phonemes do not occur, which leads to reading problems (Tallal et al., 1996).

Families with a history of language impairments tend to have children with language impairments. There appears to be a genetic component that manifests itself in 50 percent of the children in such families (Tallal, Ross, & Curtis, 1989). These children tend to have significantly lower language scores in comparison to their matched-age peers.

Children with *specific language impairment* (SLI) have a limited language ability for which there are no known sensory, motor, emotional, psychosocial, or general cognitive deficits (Leonard, 1998). These children have a slow rate of language development that persists over time. They need to be carefully evaluated so they are not confused with risk groups such as children with SELD, who require enrichment rather than therapy. Children with SLI are at least one standard deviation below norms on language-production measures (Nelson, Camarata, Welsh, Butskovsky, & Camarata, 1996). These children require therapy, and as many as 50 percent of them will have trouble learning how to read (Leonard, 1998).

 Developmental Profile

Figure 8.3 shows the developmental profile of Michele, a 10-year-old girl who has a moderate articulation-phonology disorder (she mispronounces specific sounds). Careful evaluation indicates that Michele also has a language deficit. (Often a speech disorder signals an underlying language impairment.) Academically, she is performing below grade level on skills that require language mediation. Her sound substitutions and omissions are not so severe that she cannot be understood, but oral productions call attention to her speech and set her apart from her peers.

Figure 8.3

Profile of a Child with a Mild
Speech and Language Disorder

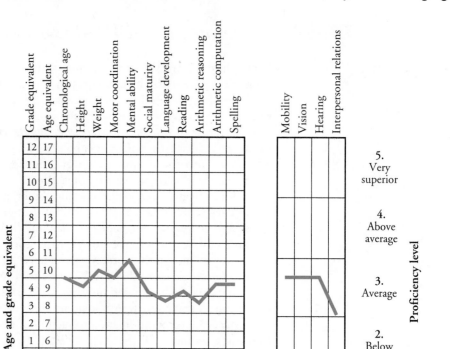

Michele's speech is characterized by consistent sound substitutions (*w/r* as in *wabbit* for *rabbit; t/k* as in *tome* for *come*). She also sometimes omits sounds at the ends of words, including the sounds that represent verb tense and noun number (for example, the final /s/ in *looks* and *cats*). Careful listening to her conversational language reveals that she omits articles and that her sentence structure is not as elaborate as that of most 10-year-olds.

Michele is in a regular classroom but seems reluctant to participate in class. It has not been determined whether this reluctance stems from her sensitivity to others' reactions, an inability to formulate speech and complex language to express her ideas, or both.

In contrast to Michele, many children with mild speech disorders seem to develop normally in other areas and do not differ markedly from other children in educational performance or social skills. Young children often make developmental articulation errors that continue into kindergarten or first grade and then disappear as the child matures and acquires reading skills. Children whose misarticulations persist until about age 8 are less likely to correct inaccurate sound productions themselves. The teacher can do much to help Michele feel comfortable in spite of her disorder. The suggestions listed on page 332 to help children who stutter would also help Michele develop a more positive self-esteem.

When misarticulations continue until age 8, the child probably needs the help of a speech-language pathologist.

Identification and Assessment

PRESCHOOL CHILDREN AND EARLY INTERVENTION

Although much of language development begins before a child says his or her first word, most tests for language delays or disorders are not administered until the child is 2 years of age (Leonard, 1992). Leonard stated that the criterion for administering diagnostic tests is the failure of the child to master fifty words by age 2. Mastery of fewer than fifty words may indicate that the child has a communication disorder or a hearing impairment.

Attention recently has been given to the nonverbal communication system (the prelinguistic system) that is a precursor to speech. Prior to the emergence of words, infants point to objects, respond to the caregiver's pointing, look at what the caregiver is looking at, and interact in basic play activities (Dromi, 1993). Infants also use gestures to make requests and to respond. If these prelinguistic competencies fail to develop at the expected time, a communication deficit may exist.

Irregularities in an infant's production of sound, sucking, swallowing, or breathing may portend a problem in the infant's development of spoken language.

Irregularities in the early nonverbal sound system (such as a strange infant cry) or in the sucking, swallowing, or breathing systems may predict a problem in spoken language development (Oller, 1985; Schiefelbusch, Sullivan, & Ganz, 1980). These difficulties will interfere with speech production. Deficient sucking or choking on fluids is an indicator of potential disorder, as is the child's swallowing excessive air or failing to chew by 18 months of age (Schiefelbusch et al., 1980). A pediatric neurologist should be consulted to determine if a disorder exists. A physician or surgeon may need to determine if abnormalities are present in the mouth, throat, or breathing apparatus.

Otitis media, a middle-ear infection almost universal in children of school age, can lead to hearing and language impairments. Preschool teachers can assist youngsters with frequent otitis media in critical language learning by utilizing the techniques listed in Table 8.3. These techniques are useful for the child identified as hearing impaired as well as for children in general.

A multidisciplinary team composed of speech-language pathologists, physical therapists, physicians, audiologists, occupational therapists, special education teachers, parents, psychologists, and social workers may be formed to plan early intervention services. Because speech disorders so commonly accompany other disabilities, the speech-language pathologist has a role in many different therapies. That role may be major or minor in the delivery of service, but it is always major in assessment, diagnosis, and planning a program for the remediation or improvement of a communication disorder.

The speech-language pathologist primarily should be responsible for the identification, diagnosis (as part of a multidisciplinary team), and design of the treatment plan and curriculum for children with language and speech deficits. The speech-language pathologist sits down with the teacher and suggests or designs lessons to include in the IEP or IFSP. The speech-language pathologist may formulate plans to encourage the spontaneous flow of language and assist non-English-speaking children in learning the English language. He or she may suggest activities for all children to encourage phonological discrimination and acquisition through rhymes and jingles that contain words with consonant and vowel combinations that are troubling the student. For example, the jingle "Polly put the popcorn in a big iron pot until it went pop, pop, pop" introduces the child to the

TABLE 8.3 Listening and Language Strategies for a Child with Frequent Otitis Media

Make speech louder or clearer.

- Get down on the child's eye level to talk whenever possible. Get close (no more than 3 feet away) and face the child to provide clear visual and auditory information.
- Gain the child's attention before speaking to make sure that the child is listening. Remind the child to listen when necessary.
- Speak clearly and repeat important words but use a natural speaking intonation or pattern.
- When possible, use visual support to help the child understand what he or she is hearing. For a young child, point to objects, pictures, or people and gesture when talking. For an older child, give written as well as verbal instructions.
- When there is a speaker in the classroom, seat the child close to the speaker but where the child also can see other children (e.g., at the side of the room).

Minimize background noise.

- Turn off record players, radios, recorders, and television playing in the background, which can interfere with children hearing ongoing conversation.
- Repair noisy appliances (e.g., air conditioners, heaters, fans, vacuum cleaners) that make it hard to hear speech clearly.
- Reduce distractions by using movable barriers (e.g., bookshelves, flannel boards) to create small areas in a classroom where small-group and one-to-one interactions can take place.
- Hang washable draperies over windows to absorb sound, and close doors and windows if there is noise that makes it hard to hear.

Promote language learning.

- Show an interest in what the child is talking about and in things that interest the child, and follow the child's topic.
- Play interactive games with children to encourage turn taking (e.g., peekaboo).
- Model desired language by describing ongoing activities.
- Respond immediately and consistently to a child's communication attempts.
- Pause to give the child time to talk.
- Check with the child to see if directions and new information are understood.
- Give positive feedback for language attempts.
- Elaborate on what the child says by adding words to the child's utterances.
- For older preschoolers, encourage discussions that explain things, predict what will happen next, describe feelings, and refer to children's own experiences.

Increase children's attention to language.

- Sing simple songs with repeated words and phrases (e.g., "The Wheels on the Bus").
- Play word and listening games (e.g., I Spy) in which children listen to familiar patterns and fill in words.
- For older preschool children, play rhyming games (e.g., cat, fat, bat).
- Read frequently with children, labeling and describing pictures and referring to children's own experiences.

Source: From J. E. Roberts & I. Wallace (1997). *Otitis Media in Young Children: Medical, Developmental, and Educational Considerations,* p. 155. Baltimore: Paul H. Brookes. Reprinted with permission.

The IFSP may include activities for the parent to model with the child.

sounds of *p* with vowels in initial and end positions. The IFSP may include plans for the therapist or teacher to send home simple activities such as this for the parent to model for the child.

The teacher's primary role may be to encourage talk, expand talk, and model correct forms and usage. Rarely should children with speech and language disorders be placed in a special class. These children will be part of the regular preschool classes (inclusion) and perhaps have extra instruction outside class several times a week in a resource room.

SCHOOL-AGE CHILDREN

Many school systems use four procedures to identify children who have communication disorders (Neidecker, 1987):

1. Screening children who are suspected of having communication disorders and who may need additional testing or a full evaluation
2. Evaluating those identified during screening and from referrals with appropriate audiological, speech, and language assessment tools
3. Diagnosing the type and severity of communication disorder according to the criteria of the evaluation data
4. Making appropriate placement decisions for children who need speech or language intervention and developing an IEP or IFSP for them

Rarely should children with speech and language disorders be placed in a special class.

Screening

Most school systems have formal screening programs for vision, hearing, and communication disorders. Often parents or teachers request that a child be screened. Speech-language pathologists may conduct screening in selected grades at the beginning of each year to identify children suspected of having disorders of articulation, fluency, voice, or language. Screening is sometimes a yes-no process: Yes, this child needs further evaluation; no, this child does not need further evaluation *at this time*. If there is any doubt, an assessment is conducted. The purpose of rapid screening is detection, not diagnosis; it must be well planned, fast, and accurate.

Federal regulations do not require a parent's permission before group screening; however, some school districts and some states require that parents be notified. Children who are identified through screening are then evaluated more thoroughly.

Evaluation and Diagnosis

Evaluating children who are suspected of having communication disorders and diagnosing those disorders usually involve the following steps:

1. *Obtaining parental permission.* Federal law requires that parents or legally designated caregivers give permission before a child is formally tested for communication disorders.
2. *Taking a case history.* During the evaluation process, the speech-language pathologist often obtains information about other people's opinions of the child's communication abilities and disabilities. This history may include background information about the child's development, a health history, family information, a social history, school achievement records, and data from earlier evaluations.

3. *Assessing the disorder.* The clinician assesses the type and severity of the disorder with formal audiological, speech, and language tests and informal procedures (language sampling, analysis of conversation). The speech-language pathologist also evaluates the structure and function of the speech mechanism.

4. *Assessing other areas.* Assessing intellectual development may be particularly important for children with language deficits. Psychologists usually are responsible for intelligence testing. Often psychological tests are administered to evaluate cognitive skills and identify differences between verbal and nonverbal abilities. Educational assessment and its consistency with other assessment data are important. Physical therapists, occupational therapists, and other health professionals may also contribute important assessment information.

5. *Making a diagnosis.* Diagnosis has been called the art and science of distinguishing one disorder from another according to the signs and symptoms that characterize each disorder. The speech-language pathologist makes a written report about the kind of disorder(s) observed and describes the symptoms of the disorder(s) on which the diagnosis is based.

Developing the IEP

The speech-language pathologist may lead the school team in developing an IEP for the child with a communication disorder. Parental permission is required for the plan to be implemented. Intervention for the communication disorder outlined in the IEP is based on assessment data, the diagnosis, and other characteristics of the child (intellectual function, learning deficits).

LINGUISTIC DIVERSITY

Children learn to speak the language that is spoken in their homes and neighborhoods. They tend to use language to express their needs and thoughts in the same way as their parents or caregivers do. In some homes, parents use language in ways that are different from the language some teachers expect students to use. For example, teachers may demand explicitness in language (Anastasiow, Hanes, & Hanes, 1982). Whereas the two sentences "He took it" and "Arthur took my truck" convey the same meaning, the listener has to be in the immediate environment to understand the former, less explicit communication. Children who have not been exposed to explicit communication in the home may have difficulty when they encounter a teacher who expects it. Teachers must be aware that differences in language usage such as this are not treated as disorders. Such differences can be addressed by teaching rather than by therapy. Comparing the child's communication skills with the skills of peers from the same cultural background avoids labeling the child as language impaired rather than language different (Roseberry-McKibbin, 1997).

Assessment of Non-English-Speaking Children

Children from homes in which English is not the primary language are likely to encounter difficulty in using English in school. Language differences can and should be identified early, and language skills (how to relate to and speak to the teacher) should be taught to avoid failure by the child due to cultural differences

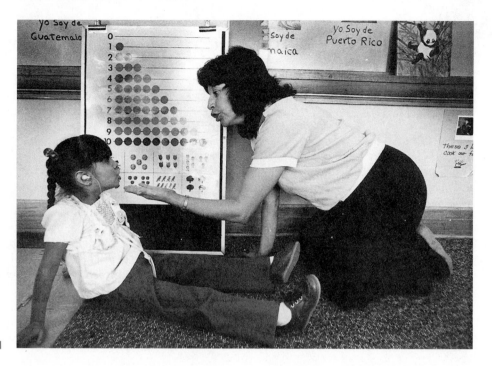

Children from communities that speak a language other than American English need assessments by speech-language pathologists who are skilled in the child's primary language. (© Michael D. Sullivan/Texas Stock)

Assessments of bilingual children should include a specialist who is bicultural and bilingual.

in talking with adults. Children from communities that speak a language other than American English need assessments by speech-language pathologists who are skilled in the child's primary language.

Children who are bilingual vary in their English competence. Any assessment of these children should involve a specialist who is bicultural and speaks the language of their home and who can answer three basic questions (Metz, 1991): Who speaks what language? When is that language spoken? For what purpose is that language spoken?

Great care must be taken that children from different cultures who speak a different language receive an accurate assessment by a person well versed in the children's language and cultural mores. Naglai (1991) reported that a child was referred for a hearing test and failed not because of hearing loss but because of the child's "inability to follow simple instructions in English" (p. 15). Situations such as that must be avoided.

Another issue is that the child may not understand the so-called native language. For example, Metz (1991), a person of Mexican-American Spanish background, reported that when she assessed a child from Puerto Rico, the child could not understand her dialect of Spanish because it lacked the intonation patterns of Puerto Rican Spanish. Spanish speakers use many variations of Spanish. The assessor and the child being assessed must be from the same Spanish-speaking subgroup. When a native speaker of the child's language is not available to conduct the assessment, a mediator who speaks the child's language can be hired as a neutral person to assist the evaluator and the family. During the evaluation, the mediator can relieve the family's stress by keeping the family informed about what is taking place (Metz, 1991). Language differences between Black English and Spanish-influenced, Native American, and Asian dialects and standard American speech can be found in Paul (1996, pp. 154–159).

Educational Adaptations

Children with Communication Disorders in Speech and Language

ADAPTING THE LEARNING ENVIRONMENT

The organization of programs for speech and language disorders in the schools varies with the size of the district and other local factors. Most children with communication disorders are in regular classrooms. Special language classes and other alternatives are available in some school systems, and school services may be offered in various combinations of delivery models.

Inclusion

Inclusion has been the general trend for children with communication disorders. The major shift is that speech-language pathologists increasingly are working directly with children in the regular classroom, supporting the academic program. They may alert students to pay attention to verbal or written instructions, encourage them to ask fitting questions and to participate in discussions, and assist them in responding in a culture- and classroom-appropriate fashion (pragmatics). Inclusion is an important option for the child with communication disorders. Children with primary speech disorders typically respond to the regular education program if they receive additional help for their special communication needs.

Consultative Service

Consultative service provides a school system with a speech-language pathologist who serves as a consultant to regular classroom teachers, special class teachers, aides, curriculum specialists, administrators, and parents in organizing a speech and language development program. Specialized materials and procedures, inservice education, demonstrations, and other activities help educators, administrators, and parents improve the communication skills of children in natural settings—the classroom and the home. The educational audiologist is becoming more involved in assisting teachers in working with children with communication disorders (English, 1995). (See Chapter 9 on children who are deaf or hard of hearing.)

Itinerant Service

In the past, the most common delivery system was the itinerant service provider, that is, a therapist who went from room to room or took children out of the classroom. In some areas, a speech-language pathologist still travels from school to school to give direct service to children in regular and special classrooms.

Intensive-Cycle Scheduling

Another method of service delivery is the *intensive cycle*, sometimes called the *block system*, in which children are scheduled for therapy four or five times a week for a concentrated period, usually for four to six weeks. This type of scheduling is sometimes used in combination with the itinerant service provider, particularly where more than one speech-language pathologist is on the staff (Neidecker, 1987).

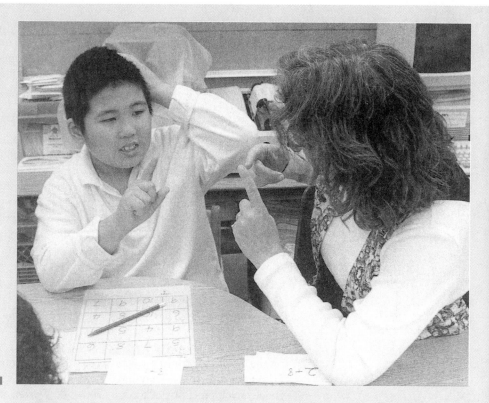

Most children with communication disorders are in regular classrooms. Speech-language pathologists give direct service to these children individually, in resource rooms and in regular and special classrooms. (© Elizabeth Crews)

Educational Setting

In the school year 1994–1995, more than forty-seven states predominantly used the regular classroom with resource room backup as the educational setting for children with speech and language disorders. Three states predominantly used the resource room as the place of service with the regular classroom as backup. Separate classes are infrequently used as the educational setting (U.S. Department of Education, 1997).

ADAPTING TEACHING STRATEGIES

Speech and Language Therapy

The speech-language pathologist brings to each therapy session a considerable knowledge base and set of skills to recognize and remediate each child's specific problem (such as errors in articulation, syntax, and voice). The choice of therapy depends on the assessment of the child's need. The most common therapeutic procedure for most young children with deficits is play (sometimes called role-playing). Play, as we mentioned earlier, is the way all children learn speech and language. In the therapy sessions, therapists model the way children who are not disabled learn language. For example, the therapist introduces an age-appropriate toy, talks about it, and encourages the child to examine and manipulate the toy and discover its aspects and the word for it. The therapist asks questions about the toy ("What will it

If the child's language is not perfectly pronounced, the therapist (or teacher or parent) does not correct the form but recasts it into a correct form in the reply.

do?" "Can you push it?" "What color is it?" "Can you make it go?") and encourages the child to respond. If the child responds in one word, the therapist expands the child's response and models the correct pronunciation and language form (Fey, Catts, & Larrivee, 1995; McCune-Nicolich, 1986; Ogura, 1991). Attempts are made to encourage the child to initiate the conversation and the adult responds and amplifies (Leonard, 1998).

Rarely is it advisable to break a word into syllables or to stop the child's communication to correct the pronunciation. If the therapist can understand the meaning the child intends to convey, expansion and modeling are called for. If the therapist cannot understand the child, the adult may query the child about what he or she wished to communicate. If the word did not communicate (for example, if the child had said "cookie" instead of "juice"), the therapist would correct the response. Because a portion of the treatment and intervention program may be delivered by parents or the teacher, the speech-language therapist may be responsible for training the parent or teacher and modeling correct behavior for them. For example, if the child says "Wa doo," the parent may say, "I don't understand; tell me again." The child repeats "Wa doo," looking at the refrigerator. The parent then says, "Oh, you want some juice," and gives it to the child (Camarata, 1995, p. 70). Camarata also calls it *recasting* when the parent models correct pronunciation without correction. For example, a child says "a wion," and the parent says, "yes, a lion." At no time does the parent or teacher interrupt the child and tell him or her, "Say lion." These responses by the adult that build on what the child is communicating are also referred to as *following directives.* They have been shown to be positively associated with language development (McCathren, Yoder, & Warren, 1995).

Parents also need to be taught that their child with disabilities needs everything a child without disabilities needs and perhaps something more in the form of aids or extra time.

The speech-language pathologist and the teacher must work closely together to ensure that a child's disorder is treated appropriately.

The Speech-Language Pathologist.   Speech-language pathologists have specific terminology for some of the major disorders. These terms are listed in Tables 8.4 and 8.5. The terminology is necessary information for teachers. During the preparation of the IEP or the IFSP, speech-language pathologists use these terms to refer to common speech-language disorders, and teachers need to work closely with the speech-language pathologist to decide how to approach the child's disorder. Often the speech-language pathologist works individually with the child outside the classroom as well.

Speech-language pathologists use many techniques to promote the carryover of newly acquired communication skills into the classroom and everyday conversation. These techniques include children's notebooks prepared by therapists that are kept in the classroom for the teacher's regular review, weekly conferences with teachers regarding specific objectives, the use of devices and props as reminders, and carefully planned in-class "talking" activities. A major task of the communication specialist is to help the classroom teacher use these tools effectively, because the teacher's help is vital to success.

Many children outgrow articulation problems when they are between 5 and 6 years of age. The teacher needs to be aware of what therapies the child has received in kindergarten and work with the speech-language pathologist to determine which therapies to continue. The multidisciplinary team should determine what therapies (if any) to include in the IEP or IFSP.

TABLE 8.4	Terms That Speech-Language Pathologists Use to Describe Disorders
Term	**Disorder**
Apraxia	Severe irregular and persistent speech disorder
Aphasia	Impairment in the ability to communicate due to brain damage
Dysarthria	Articulation or voice disorder due to impaired motor control problems of throat, tongue, or lips
Anarthria	Loss of the ability to speak
Dysphonia	A disorder of voice quality
Stuttering	A disorder of fluency: repetitions, prolongations, and hesitations of sounds and syllables

General education teachers need to cooperate in scheduling out-of-class time for students' speech therapy.

The success of intervention depends on the teacher's cooperation in scheduling time out of class for therapy and sending children to "speech lessons" regularly. Some speech and language changes (the production of particular sounds, language targets, fluency patterns) are best learned in individualized structured therapy sessions; however, the teachers' creativity in adapting classroom opportunities to foster ways of talking will help the student to generalize new skills. The classroom is often the most appropriate setting for incidental and interactive functional teaching (Fey, Windsor, & Warren, 1995).

The speech-language pathologist and the regular classroom teacher often work side by side in the regular classroom.

Teachers often participate in innovative alternatives to traditional speech-language lessons. It is common practice for the speech-language pathologist and classroom teacher to work side by side each day in a classroom, focusing on the language components of reading, language arts, and socialization (Cole, 1995).

Teachers recognize that there are differences between speech-language programs at the elementary and secondary levels. Often young children have therapy in their classroom, and older students have individual therapy. Because fewer standardized materials are available for students at the secondary level, the speech-language pathologist may have to design and develop or adapt materials for older students with speech and language disorders. Computer programs are very useful in helping high school students master a wide variety of language skills (Schery & O'Connor, 1995).

A speech-language pathologist must be able to deal with a wide variety of disorders.

Additional Roles of the Speech-Language Pathologist. From the variety of settings and options for delivery of services to children with speech and language disorders, it's obvious that a speech-language pathologist must be able to serve in more than one capacity. An itinerant speech-language pathologist must be prepared to deal with a broad range of disorders—primary articulation, fluency,

TABLE 8.5	Terms That Speech-Language Pathologists Use to Describe General Disorders of Speech and Associated Behaviors
Disorder	**Behavior**
Voice disorder	A variation of speech from accepted norms in voice quality, pitch, and loudness (dysphonia)
Articulation-phonology	Mispronunciation, lisping, substitution (*toat* for *coat*)
Fluency	Stuttering (breaks in the flow of speech caused by repetitions and tensions in the speaking mechanisms)
Pitch	Voice too high or too low
Cerebral palsy and physical disabilities	Articulation deficits in as many as 80% of persons with these handicaps
Cleft palate	Nasal voice, articulation errors; multidisciplinary team needed to correct split lip, loss of teeth, or potential hearing loss; language learned in normal fashion
Social disorders	Autism; failure to relate and develop speech and language

voice, and language disorders—as well as the problems found among children with cleft palate, mental retardation, cerebral palsy, learning disabilities, and emotional disturbance.

Speech-language pathologists often work with parents of children with other disabilities. Researchers have found that parents may not talk to a child with disabilities as much as they would talk to a child without disabilities, or they may overwhelm their child with talk. They appear to be more anxious about their child's progress, especially the progress of a low-birth-weight premature child who is less responsive to the parent and generally less fun to interact with than a child without disabilities (Field, 1983). Mothers of children with hearing-language impairments may need help in being flexible and encouragement in communicating with their child.

Speech language pathologists assist children who have communication disorders in many ways:

- They provide individual therapy.
- They consult with the child's teacher about effective ways to assist the child in the classroom.

- At times they may work with the entire class.
- They work closely with the family.
- They work with vocational teachers and counselors to establish goals for work.
- They work with individual children in the classroom, cuing them when to ask questions and encouraging them to participate in discussion and interact verbally.

Interactive Approaches

It was once quite popular to use operant conditioning to train a child to repeat words spoken to him or her. (*Operant conditioning* is a technique of behavior modification that works by controlling the stimulus that follows a response.) If the child repeated the word correctly, he or she was rewarded for doing so. Some interventionists achieved success in having the child master a list of words, but they were disappointed when the child did not use the words in his or her own free speech. The material learned in the training sessions did not transfer or generalize to other settings (Warren & Kaiser, 1988). Bloom (1991) noted that these modeling procedures failed in part because children without disabilities imitate far less than was previously believed.

Operant conditioning and most other behavioristic approaches to teaching language have been replaced. Teachers and therapists now focus on the social use of language (pragmatics) and stress functional communication in natural language environments (Kaiser & Gray, 1993). Most interventions have changed from didactic, learning-principle orientations to ones based on natural language acquisition (Camarata, 1995).

A more popular form of treatment is the *interactive approach*. The interventionist—the parent, special education teacher, or speech-language pathologist—tries to capitalize on the natural inclination of the child to talk about what he or she is doing, plans to do, or wants to do. To encourage correct word use and language use, interventionists provide remediation sessions while the child is eating, playing, or visiting community settings such as a fast-food restaurant (Warren & Kaiser, 1988).

This natural approach is frequently referred to as *functionalism*, which means using speech and language in a functional way to acquire and satisfy one's needs. Other terms for this technique are *incidental teaching* and *social language learning*. The intent of these techniques is to increase the child's amount of talk (Bloom, 1991). The more the child talks, the more the child will gradually gain accuracy and increase his or her vocabulary.

Intervention for Fluency Disorders

Since the 1970s, intervention programs based on learning theory and principles of behavior have had a tremendous impact on all speech and language therapy, particularly for stuttering. Although parent counseling and training to change environmental stress continue to be important therapeutic tools for young children, direct speech intervention programs for children as young as age 2 have been developed and are working (Fey, Windsor, & Warren, 1995).

Many successful therapies recognize the importance of motivation, attitudes toward speech and self, and environmental interactions. In one successful approach developed many years ago by pioneers in speech-language disorders at the University of Iowa, stutterers are taught to control stuttering, to reduce extraneous behaviors, and to stutter "normally." They are taught to face the problem rather than try to cover up their dysfluencies. The approach makes use of outside speaking activities (shopping, asking for directions, making telephone calls).

Classroom teachers can be particularly helpful to the child who stutters by working with the speech-language pathologist to plan opportunities for the child to participate in speaking activities that are appropriate for practicing newly acquired fluency skills at increasing levels of complexity. The following lists of suggestions can help teachers (Blance, Stedal, & Smith, 1994).

SUGGESTIONS FOR TEACHERS OF STUDENTS WHO STUTTER

- Reduce the rate of speech.
- Create silence in interactions.
- Model sample vocabulary and grammatical forms.

SUGGESTIONS TO IMPROVE STUDENTS' SELF-ESTEEM

- Disregard moments of nonfluency.
- Show acceptance of what the child has expressed rather than how it was said.
- Treat a child who stutters like any other member of the class.
- Acknowledge nonfluency without labeling the child.
- Help the child feel in control of his or her speech.
- Accept nonfluency.

Focused Stimulation

Focused stimulations are procedures held in a naturalistic environment in which the therapist recasts a child's sentences to highlight desired language, particularly grammar. The naturalistic environment provides an opportunity for play and the stimulation of language, as in this example (Fey, Cleave, & Long, 1997):

Child: I can play, too?
Adult: Oh, you played it, too.
Child: Him like that.
Adult: Does he like that?

Phonological Training

Phonological awareness, the best predictor of reading achievement, is the ability to recognize that words can be divided into smaller units, such as syllables and phonemes (Leonard, 1998; Rivers, Lombardino, & Thompson, 1996). Children

A speech therapist can engage a child in play in a naturalistic environment as an opportunity to stimulate language. (© Bob Daemmrich/Stock Boston)

who have difficulty recognizing and mastering phonemes will have difficulty learning how to read.

Slow Auditory Processing

For the child with slow auditory processing, Tallal et al. (1997) have developed a computerized presentation of phonemes at a slower than normal speech rate. The program allows the child to distinguish and accurately store the phonemes correctly, which in turn leads to improved reading performance.

Regardless of the method, phonological impairments must be improved if the child is to become a successful reader. Swank (1997) cautions that phonological awareness should be taught in the context of meaning; that is, always present the phoneme in a word the child understands (for example, *ba,* as in *baby* or *baby doll*).

Augmented and Alternative Communication

At times, children with severe motor problems cannot produce intelligible speech. A common instructional strategy is called *augmented and alternative communication*. **American Sign Language (ASL)**, a system of gestures that contain meaning, is one example of this strategy. Another gesture system that is sometimes used is

Signed English. Sign language is taught to some visually or motor-impaired children (Bower, 1989).

Other aids include communication boards of varying complexity, with letters or pictures to which the child can point to spell out a word or select a picture of the word (Beukelman & Mirenda, 1992). The use of these aids has been shown to assist the child in acquiring language—many times without speech, but not always (McLean & Cripe, 1997).

ADAPTING CURRICULUM

Intervention Priorities

School systems must provide appropriate services to all students, and they can make decisions about types of services and where to offer them. A number of professionals are concerned about the priorities in providing speech and language services within the educational program. Neidecker (1987) suggested the following continuum of services based on a model developed by ASHA:

- *Communication disorders.* Children with moderate-to-severe articulation, fluency, voice, or language disorders require intensive intervention. These disorders often interfere with academic achievement and social adjustment, and a variety of professionals may be needed to plan a treatment program.
- *Communication deviations.* Children with communication deviations have less severe handicapping disorders, but their communication can cause adaptation difficulties in school. Youngsters with developmental lags and mild mental retardation often are in this group.
- *Communication development.* All children may need some effort by speech-language pathologists to prevent the progression of mild speech problems and to improve their primary linguistic skills and enrich their language.

Dialects

The use of a dialect is a sign not of a speech disorder but of the linguistic diversity of the society at large.

Variations in word usage, pronunciation (**phonology**), word order (**syntax**), and meaning (**semantics**) influence the child's use of language (**pragmatics**). A *dialect* is a variety of language differing in pronunciation, vocabulary, or syntax from the literary form of the language. A dialect is used and understood by a group within a larger community. Dialects reflect regional, social, occupational, and other differences: "He done sold his car." "We be there tomorrow." "She be sick to her stomach."

A dialect is very much a part of a child's self-concept, and teachers must react to it carefully. They need to model standard literary usage and encourage children to use it when reading aloud and writing, but they should allow children to use dialect in their informal speech if communication is clear.

A major problem for teachers is that the existence of a dialect may mask a delay or disorder that will become increasingly difficult to diagnose the longer it remains undetected. A major failing of language assessment tools is that they are based on the average child's use of language, which is not necessarily the way lan-

Evaluating children who are suspected of having communication disorders involves assessing the disorder with formal speech and language tests and with informal procedures such as language sampling and analysis of conversation. (© Michael Weisbrot)

guage is used, taught, and encouraged in all families and communities. Therapists and teachers need to learn what a specific community considers accurate pronunciation and usage, and they need to teach children to respond to questions fully. Through "show and tell" and by dictating creative stories, with teachers encouraging expansion and explicitness, children can be encouraged to speak in sentences, to use standard American English, to be explicit, and not to overuse pronouns (as persons in noninclusive settings tend to do).

★ *Saying "warsh" for "wash" is a regional dialect, not a speech disorder.*

Saying "warsh" for "wash" is not a sign of a speech defect but a regional dialect. If a child says "dog" for "cow," then a disorder may be suspected (though it may be that the child has not learned the new term).

TECHNOLOGY

★ *Speech-language pathologists must be computer literate to be able to use some therapeutic tools.*

Speech-language professionals are using computers as therapeutic tools. Today it is essential for speech-language pathologists to be computer literate. ASHA and the national group Computer Users in Speech and Hearing (CUSH) both provide information about technological advances.

Instructional Technology

Computer programs are designed for a variety of specific purposes, for example, phonological evaluation and teaching children sentence structure. Another important use is word processing, which frees children from the burden of organizing

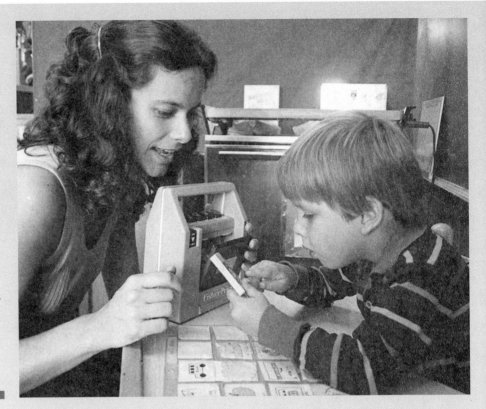

For children with severe motor problems who cannot produce intelligible speech, a common instructional strategy is augmented and alternative communication by means of American Sign Language, Signed English, and communication boards. (© Alan Carey/The Image Works)

bits and pieces of written language on the spatial confines of a page. There are several benefits of word-processing systems for children with disorders of written language (and for others as well):

- There is no penalty for revising.
- It is easy for students to experiment with writing.
- Interest in writing is maintained.
- Editing is simple: Spelling, punctuation, and grammar can be checked and corrected.
- Writing and editing are less time consuming.
- Frustration is minimized.
- It is easy to produce perfect copy.

Computers provide highly structured, totally consistent stimulus materials and response acceptance. They give students independence in routine activities, and they help maintain interest in practice and drill, areas that traditionally have bored both students and clinicians. They are also designed to provide specific communication skill training (Schery & Connor, 1995).

Word-prompt programs provide a list of words based on the letter being typed. For example, if the user types *b*, all the words beginning with *b* appear on the screen (Wood, Rankin, & Beukelman, 1997). More sophisticated programs pro-

◀▬▬▬ **TABLE 8.6** Software Programs for Users with Language-Related Disabilities
Co: Writer. Don Johnston Developmental Equipment Co. Inc., P.O. Box 639, Wauconda, IL 60084
Cue-Write. Communication Skill Builders, 3830 E. Bellevue, P.O. Box 42050, Tucson, AZ
EZ Keys. Words+, Inc., 40012 Sierra Highway, Palmdale, CA 93550
HandiWORD. Microsystems Software, Inc., 600 Worcester Road, Framingham, MA 01701
Mindreader. Brown Bag Software Inc., 2155 South Bascom Ave., Suite 113, Campbell, CA 95008
Predict-It. Don Johnston Developmental Equipment Co. Inc., P.O. Box 639, Wauconda, IL 60084
Telepathic II. Madenta Communications Inc., 9411 A 20 Ave., Edmonton, AB Canada T6N1E5
WriteAway. Institute of Applied Technology, Boston's Children's Hospital, 300 Longwood Avenue, Fegan Plaza, Boston, MA 02115
Write OutLoud. Don Johnston Developmental Equipment Co. Inc., P.O. Box 639, Wauconda, IL 60084.

Source: From L. Wood, J. Rankin, & D. Beukelman (1997, August). "Word Prompt Programs: Current Uses and Possibilities," *American Journal of Speech-Language Pathology*, 6 (3), p. 64. Reprinted with permission.

vide words from a vocabulary list, others from dictionaries, and some by context. The programs listed in Table 8.6 are useful writing aids for children with a number of different language-related disabilities.

TRANSITION

For a young child in a preschool program and in therapy, transition may be a daily occurrence (Bruder & Chandler, 1996). Care must be taken that communication from the two sources is consistent and involves parents. Because articulation and stuttering respond well to early intervention, when the child moves from preschool to regular school, he or she may no longer need therapy. If therapy does need to be continued into grade school, records detailing the therapeutic approach and diagnosis as well as the child's progress must follow the child to the new setting.

"Joining In on the Conversation"

Have you ever wondered what it would be like not to be able to communicate? It's very frustrating. It's very lonely. It hurts.

Think about it. You feel, you think, you know and understand the words yet you cannot speak them. You hear everyone around you in an interesting conversation, but you cannot join in.

You cannot express any of the feelings or emotions that are just as deep inside of you as anyone else. You are furiously angry and you have to hold it in; or you are extremely happy and you can't show it. Your heart is so full of love you could just burst, but you can't share it. I know what it is like because for years I could not communicate or express myself. I am a 19-year-old girl. I have cerebral palsy and cannot talk. I do not have coordination in my hands to write or use sign language. Even a typewriter was out of the question when I was younger. I know what it is like to be fed potatoes all my life. After all, potatoes are a good basic food for everyday, easy to fix in many different ways. I hate potatoes! But then, who knew that but me?

I know what it is like to be dressed in reds and blues when my favorite colors are mint greens, lemon yellows and pinks. I mean really, can you imagine?

Mama found me one night curled up in a ball in my bed crying, doubled over in pain. I couldn't explain to her where or how I hurt. So, after checking me over the best she could, she thought I had a bad stomachache due to constipation. Naturally, a quick cure for that was an enema. It didn't help my earache at all!

Finally, help came! I was introduced to Blissymbols.

My life changed! Blissymbols were originally developed for a universal language but they have been a miracle for me and others like me. Blissymbols are a combination of the written word and a symbolized picture that anyone can learn, which are displayed in a way that can be easily used. There was a tray strapped to my wheelchair. It was covered with a sheet of paper which was divided into little blocks of words to form sentences. At last, I could communicate!

Naturally, one board could not hold all the words needed. I had to learn to make up my own, combining two or more words to mean another. As in "story sleep" for dream or "bad night horse" for nightmare.

My teachers started me on ten words a day to see if I could learn them. I learned as fast as they could give me new words. I was ready to communicate! I could even stutter! That's what my uncle calls it when it takes three or four tries to point to one word.

Once I mastered Blissymbols I left the symbols behind and changed to words and sentences. I got my first computer. It was an Autocom™. I programmed my Bliss board into it and much more. It also had a printer. Finally, I could write!

I didn't stop there. I went on to a more advanced system. I had fun learning about computers by using my Express III™. I was doing the programming all by myself and even did some of the "funny" spelling.

The first thing I learned about computers was to think of them as "hotel." My "Hotel Express III™" had 99 floors or levels. Each floor had 128 rooms or spaces for programming. In each room I could put one person as in a letter or a number, or a whole family as in a sentence; or I could just throw a wild party with several paragraphs. So you see my "Hotel Express III™" had almost unlimited accommodations.

Did I stop there? Surprise, I got a new device. It is called a Touch Talker™ with Mindspeak software. This one has the same basic features as my Express III™, but I can connect it to an Apple computer to either store the memory on a disk or just use the screen to make my paragraphs all in one instead of having to say bits and pieces at a time. Everything in it is coded like my Express III™, but it is much easier to get the words or sentences out because everything is coded by pictures instead of numbers and it is a lot easier to remember pictures. The Express III™ had number levels and it was harder to remember where I put everything, so as you can see, the Touch Talker™ makes it a lot easier for me to communicate with you or anyone else.

Communicating for me has opened a lot of doors. It even let me act in a play. I have been a guest speaker at a Kiwanis Club meeting. It has done a lot more, too. There's help out there, just don't give up.

Source: Reprinted by permission of the American-Speech-Language-Hearing Association, Rockville, MD, from its brochure *I Can Even Stutter Now!* © ASHA.

Note: *Let's Talk. . . ,* a publication for people with special communication needs, is published by the Consumer Affairs Division of ASHA, 10801 Rockville Pike, Rockville, MD 20852, (800) 638-TALK.

What Is the Context?

It is difficult to be part of any community if you can't communicate. Sara can now make a difference by expressing her ideas and feelings to others. Prior to using Blissymbols, she had no way to communicate many important messages to her family, friends, and teachers. Basic needs were difficult to communicate, and her knowledge and ideas were nearly impossible to get across. Since Sara started using Blissymbols and other assistive technology, she can communicate her basic needs as well as more complex thoughts and desires. What activities can Sara participate in now that she couldn't previously? Does this allow her to be a part of the community—to join in and make a difference? How?

Pivotal Issues for Teachers

Students like Sara need assistive technology to be able to speak about what they already know but don't have the ability to communicate. Assistive technology makes it possible for students like Sara to learn and grow. Notice that Sara has excellent writing skills as she tells her story in this article. That is one of her strengths. Identify the strengths of children in your classroom who have communication disorders. Are there students in your class who would benefit from assistive technology to help them communicate? What professionals can you ask about advances in technology that might help your students?

 Family and Lifespan Issues

What lies ahead for the child who has a communication disorder? The answer to this question depends on the nature and severity of the disorder. Children who have primary articulation disorders (that is, a speech or language disorder not associated with other disabilities) seem to have few special problems as adults. In contrast, follow-up studies of children with severe disorders show that those with language deficits, in spite of early intervention, continue to have problems in academics, interpersonal relationships, and work. Intelligence seems to be an important variable in determining the outcome among children who have language disorders from brain damage or mental retardation.

Families are concerned by any and all irregularities in their child's spoken language. They need information about their child's condition, and they need to be taught appropriate techniques to use at home. Teaching parents to recast the child's pronunciation, articulation, or incomplete sentences is critical. Parents will tend to correct communications that are understandable but not correct in form. The techniques for teachers that we suggested in the Educational Adaptations section under "Intervention for Fluency Disorders" need to be taught to parents. Language learning proceeds best in a setting in which language is used naturally (Fey, Windsor, & Warren, 1995).

Contemporary research is giving us evidence that speech and language intervention programs decrease the severity of communication disorders. In 1987, forty-three studies were analyzed with special techniques to assess the overall effectiveness of language intervention with individuals who have language-learning disabilities. The composite results indicated that the average child with language disorders moved from the 50th to the 85th percentile as a result of language intervention (Shriberg & Kwiatowski, 1988).

The prospect for stutterers to learn good communication skills also seems to be brighter than it once was. For at least two professional generations, very little direct therapy was provided for young children who stuttered. An important outcome of that practice was that most therapy was carried out with older, confirmed stutterers, and success with permanent fluency carryover into social communication remained elusive. We know now that "the therapeutic success record is enviably better with children and best with preschoolers" (Shames & Rubin, 1986). Therapy with stutterers should begin by 3 years of age, at the first appearance of stuttering. Since the 1980s, serious research has focused on the problems of maintaining fluent speech and preventing relapse. Evaluation of these studies and others indicated that scientifically based therapy is clearly effective (McLean & Cripe, 1997). Rates of spontaneous recovery from stuttering are reported to vary from approximately 45 percent to 80 percent (Shames & Rubin, 1986). Early intervention for stuttering has become so widespread that some authors refer to it as prevention in which the family plays the critical role (Culattla & Goldberg, 1995).

Important changes have come about in helping students with language disorders make transitions from high school to college and the workplace. Many colleges and universities have support services and special programs for these students. Special clinics and help sessions are staffed by speech-language pathologists, learning disabilities specialists, and psychologists, and individualized techniques for note taking, class participation, and writing are available to help students who have written-language deficits.

Summary of Major Ideas

1. Communication can be verbal, nonverbal, or a combination of both. A sender, a message, and a receiver are necessary for communication to take place. Language is the system of symbols used to express and receive meaning. Speech is the systematic oral production of the words of a given language.

2. The processes needed to produce sound are respiration, phonation, resonation, articulation, audition, and symbolization/organization.

3. Communication disorders include speech disorders of articulation, fluency, and voice, and language disorders. Hearing loss can also cause speech disorders.

4. Impaired speech is conspicuous, usually unintelligible, and considered unpleasant. A child who is language impaired shows skills in the primary language that are markedly below the skills expected for the child's chronological age.

5. The prevalence of language disorders in the school-age population in the United States is between 5 and 10 percent. But data collection methods and classification procedures raise questions about the accuracy of this estimate.

6. Communication disorders can be secondary to other disabilities.

7. An understanding of normal patterns of language acquisition is an important part of identifying children with language disorders and developing remediation programs for them.

8. The process of identifying and assessing schoolchildren with communication disorders involves screening, evaluating, diagnosing, and making appropriate placement decisions.

9. Common models for the delivery of language and speech services are consultative services, itinerant services, intensive-cycle scheduling, and resource rooms—all of which fit well within the concept of mainstreaming—as well as training parents and teachers to deliver services.

10. The role of the speech-language pathologist has expanded. In the schools, this professional is a member of the multidisciplinary team that develops and monitors the child's IEP or IFSP.

Unresolved Issues

1. *Individual versus group therapy.* Children with major speech disorders need one-on-one therapy. However, recent emphasis on inclusion raises questions on how individual therapy can take place in the classroom without disrupting the classroom program. The problem of incorporating full inclusion with individual therapy is still unresolved.

2. *Implementing early intervention.* Most speech disorders are not identifiable until a child reaches 2 years of age, when verbal language ability usually appears. Unfortunately, parents frequently do not recognize early signs of potential speech disorders in the prelinguistic stage as signs of a potential problem. How to make this information more available to both pediatricians and parents remains an issue.

3. *Multicultural language issues.* The large number of immigrants from many different non-English-speaking cultures has introduced major problems for U.S. schools. Because the number of languages sometimes can be as many as eight different ones, some schools find it difficult to cope with the demands of this diversity. How schools can locate personnel who speak these languages and how the schools can afford to hire them are unresolved issues.

Key Terms

American Sign Language (ASL) p. 333
articulation p. 307
articulation error p. 316
audition p. 307
cleft palate p. 317
communication p. 307
communication disorder p. 308
dysphonia p. 318
fluency p. 317
language p. 308
language disorder p. 308
phonation p. 307

phonological error p. 316
phonology p. 309
pragmatics p. 334
resonation p. 307
respiration p. 307
semantics p. 309
speech p. 307
speech disorder p. 308
stuttering p. 317
syntax p. 334
verbal language p. 309
voice disorder p. 318

Questions for Thought

1. Explain the roles of speech and language in the communication process. pp. 307–308

2. Between 5 and 10 percent of school-age children are receiving services for speech or language problems. What two factors contribute to the uncertainty of that figure? What patterns of prevalence of speech-language problems have been documented?   pp. 310, 312

3. What is motherese, and how does it help children learn language?   p. 314

4. Briefly describe the four broad categories of communication disorders. p. 316

5. Briefly describe the causes of voice disorders.   p. 318

6. What prelinguistic irregularities may signal the existence of a communication disorder?   p. 321

7. What steps are involved in evaluating and diagnosing children who are suspected of having communication disorders?   pp. 323–324

8. Briefly describe some intervention strategies.   pp. 327–334

9. Briefly describe six general disorders of speech.   p. 329

10. What can a classroom teacher do to help a student who stutters?   p. 332

11. What service options are available for dealing with communication disorders?   p. 334–335

 ## Resources for Further Study

REFERENCES OF SPECIAL INTEREST

Bloodstein, O. (1987). *A handbook of stuttering* (3rd ed.). Chicago: National Easter Seal Society.

The text is a comprehensive easy-to-read overview written by an authority. The author summarizes history, theory, and treatment.

Fey, M., Windsor, J., & Warren, S. (Eds.). (1995). *Language intervention: Preschool through elementary years.* Baltimore: Paul H. Brookes.

> In this collection, authorities in the field offer teachers many practical suggestions based on sound research.

Kaiser, A., & Gray, D. (Eds.). (1993). *Enhancing children's communication.* Baltimore: Paul H. Brookes.

> The articles in this collection offer a rich array of intervention techniques, such as parent-implemented language intervention, for dealing with language disorders.

Lahey, M., & Bloom, L. (1988). *Language disorders and language development.* Columbus, OH: Merrill.

> The first edition was a classic in the field, and this edition (with the title reversed) is equally valuable. The authors provide a clear and succinct description of speech and language disorders and how to deal with them in the classroom and in special therapy situations. Highly recommended.

Neidecker, E. (1987). *School programs, in speech and language* (2nd ed.). Englewood Cliffs, NJ: Prentice-Hall.

> A guide to designing and implementing speech and language services in the schools, this book contains information on caseload selection, programming and scheduling, team participation, and record keeping.

Paul, R. (1995). *Language disorders from infancy through adolescence: Assessment and intervention.* St. Louis, MO: Mosby.

> A comprehensive presentation of assessment strategies for a wide array of speech-language disorders as well as suggestions for intervention.

Watkins, R., & Rice, M. (Eds.). (1994). *Specific language impairments in children.* Baltimore: Paul H. Brookes.

> This research-oriented collection sheds light on the genetic basis of language disorders and suggests intervention strategies.

JOURNALS

Journal of Speech, Language, and Hearing Research
American Speech-Language-Hearing Association
10801 Rockville Pike
Rockville, MD 20852

Journal of Speech-Language Pathology and Audiology
130 Albert St.
Ottawa, On. KIT5G4 Canada

PROFESSIONAL ORGANIZATIONS

The American Speech-Language-Hearing Association (ASHA)
10801 Rockville Pike
Rockville, MD 20852
http://www.asha.org/

National Stuttering Project
5100 E. La Palma Ave., No. 208
Anaheim Hill, CA 92807
http://members.aol.com/nsphome/index.html

9

Children *Who* Are *Deaf* or *Hard* of *Hearing*

FOCUSING
questions

What three factors are critical elements in the definition of hearing losses?

How do we identify children with hearing losses?

How do hearing losses affect a child's language development, and what can be done to maximize communication potential?

What are the trends in school placement for students who have hearing losses?

What is the deaf community, and how can it help a student who is deaf or hard of hearing?

Why is it critical to teach a gestural language to a person who is deaf and to his or her family?

Children who are deaf or hard of hearing have a much greater chance of achieving a communication system (gesture-manual, speech, or both) and academic success than at any time in the past. There is now much broader acceptance of persons who are deaf or hard of hearing in society. In the past two decades, an actress who is deaf won a Tony award for her performance in a Broadway play, and another actress received an Oscar for her performance in the motion picture based on that play, as well as an Emmy for the leading role in a television series about a lawyer who is deaf. Miss America of 1995 is deaf. There is a player who is deaf on a major league baseball team, and one who plays professional football. Moreover, there are now doctors, lawyers, directors of government agencies, and other professionals who are deaf. The president of Gallaudet University is deaf. There are many students who are deaf or hard of hearing in regular schools and more adults who are hearing impaired in the workplace.

Children who are not hearing impaired are more likely to play, interact, and make friends with children who are hearing impaired in regular schools and in their communities. There are now more than 3,000 interpreters in the public schools to translate from speech to gestural language and vice versa (U.S. Department of Education, 1997).

These advances have been greatly assisted by government mandates. Commissions established by Congress in 1986 and 1988 led to the establishment of the National Information Center on Deafness and the Helen Keller National Center for Technical Assistance and to rules and regulations requiring statewide telephone relaying systems. In addition, all television sets sold in the United States now must be equipped to receive captioned broadcasts. The Individuals with Disabilities Education Act (IDEA; PL 101-476), the Americans with Disabilities Act (PL 101-336), the Rehabilitation Act (PL 102-569), and other laws and regulations have increased public awareness of the talents and educational needs of persons who are deaf and hard of hearing. Identification during infancy and early childhood has led to progress for parents and their children through early intervention and educational and communication training.

In spite of the gains, there is a lack of agreement in the field on several major issues, two of which are critical: what to teach and how to teach it. Our speech-language-oriented society has not readily accepted a gestural-language system. Thus, some educators of persons who are deaf and hard of hearing strongly advocate oral-speech language. Others advocate gestural language or some combination of both. There is a strong movement to consider persons who are deaf or hard of hearing as a sociocultural language minority rather than as individuals who are disabled (Parasnis, 1997).

While reading this chapter, keep in mind that the essential deficit is a partial or total lack of auditory reception and that language can be communicated orally (speech) or by means of gestures (manual-movement, visual).

 There is a strong movement to consider persons who are deaf or hard of hearing as a sociocultural language minority rather than as individuals who are disabled (Parasnis, 1997).

Definitions

Hearing losses are defined in terms of the degree of loss, the age at which the loss occurs, and the type of loss.

DEGREE OF HEARING LOSS

The term *hearing impairment* has different meanings for different authors. For some, it describes a slight-to-moderate hearing loss (Moores, 1989, p. 1). For others, it describes any hearing loss, mild or severe (Paul & Quigley, 1994). We use the terms **deaf** to refer to a profound or complete inability to hear and **hard of hearing** to refer to all other categories of loss.

The severity of hearing losses is determined by the individual's reception of sound as measured in **decibels (dB)**. A loss between 15 and 25 dB is considered slight; increasing degrees of loss range from mild to severe and profound hearing impairment or, to use a more common term, deafness (Moores, 1996). Table 9.1 presents the range of degrees of hearing impairments and their descriptive classification, etiology, and potential needs.

Individuals classified as hard of hearing may be able to hear and understand speech, or they can be assisted to do so with hearing aids. Persons who are severely hard of hearing may be able to hear speech with the assistance of some form of hearing aid. Only a small percentage (less than 1 percent) of persons who are deaf are unable to hear speech under any conditions.

To give you an idea of how to relate hearing losses to noises and sounds in the environment, Table 9.2 lists the levels of common environmental sounds. As the table indicates, a person with a hearing loss of 60 dB and without amplification such as a hearing aid provides has difficulty hearing conversational speech. An individual with a loss of 100 dB is not able to hear a power lawnmower without amplification.

AGE OF ONSET OF LOSS

Children experience hearing loss before they acquire speech when their hearing loss is genetic or is caused by an event during pregnancy; this phenomenon is called **prelinguistic deafness**. Loss after the child has acquired some speech and language is called **postlinguistic deafness**.

THE STRUCTURE OF THE EAR AND TYPES OF HEARING LOSS

The ear is a complicated structure (Figure 9.1), and it functions in a complex way. The middle ear is composed of the tympanic membrane, or eardrum, and the three ear bones: the malleus, the incus, and the stapes. The stapes lies next to the oval window, the gateway to the inner ear. The inner ear contains the cochlea and the vestibular apparatus, collectively called the labyrinth (Steinberg & Knightly, 1997).

Although defects are possible in structure and function, they can be classified into four categories: conductive losses, sensorineural losses, mixed losses, and central losses.

A **conductive hearing loss** reduces the intensity of sound reaching the inner ear, where the auditory nerve begins. Sound waves must pass through the ear canal to the tympanic membrane (eardrum), where vibrations are picked up by the three bones of the middle ear (the malleus, the incus, and the stapes) and are then passed

TABLE 9.1 Degrees of Hearing Impairment

Level of Hearing Loss	Description	Etiology	Sounds Heard	Degree of Disability	Possible Needs
15–25 dB	Slight hearing loss	Serous otitis perforation, monmeric membrane sensorineural loss, tympanosclerosis	Hears vowel sounds clearly; may miss unvoiced consonant sounds	Mild auditory dysfunction in language learning	Hearing aid, lip reading, auditory training, speech therapy, preferential seating
25–40 dB	Mild hearing loss	Serous otitis perforation, tympanosclerosis, monmeric membrane sensorineural loss	Hears only some louder-voiced speech sounds	Auditory learning dysfunction, mild language retardation, mild speech problems, inattention	Hearing aid, lip reading, auditory training, speech therapy
40–65 dB	Moderate hearing loss	Chronic otitis, middle ear anomaly, sensorineural loss	Misses most speech sounds at normal conversational level	Speech problems, language retardation, dysfunction, inattention	All of the above plus therapies
65–95 dB	Severe hearing loss	Sensorineural or mixed loss from a sensorineural loss plus middle ear disease	Hears no speech sounds of normal conversation	Severe speech problems, language retardation, learning dysfunction, inattention	All of the above plus sign interpreter
More than 95 dB	Profound hearing loss	Sensorineural or mixed loss	Hears no speech or other sounds	Severe speech problems, language retardation, learning dysfunction, inattention	All of the above

Source: Adapted from N. J. Roizen (1996). "Hearing Loss." In A. J. Capute & P. J. Accardo, *Developmental Disabilities in Infancy and Childhood, Volume II; The Spectrum of Developmental Disabilities*, p. 481. Baltimore: Paul H. Brookes. Reprinted with permission.

on to the inner ear. Any condition that impedes the sequence of vibrations or prevents them from reaching the auditory nerve causes a loss in conduction. The sequence of vibrations can be held up anywhere from the external to the inner ear. Wax or a malformation can block the external canal, the eardrum can be broken or punctured, or the movement of the bones in the middle ear can be obstructed. Conductive defects seldom cause losses of more than 60 to 70 dB. These losses can be effectively reduced through amplification, medical treatment, or surgery (National Information Center on Deafness [NICD], 1989).

TABLE 9.2 Hearing Threshold Levels and Some Common Environmental Sounds

Hearing Threshold Levels	Decibels	Environmental Sounds
Pain	140	Shotgun blast
Discomfort	130	Jet takeoff
	120	Loud rock music
	110	Power lawnmower
	100	
	90	
	80	Party with 100 guests
	70	
Conversational speech	60	
	50	
	40	
	30	Inside a library
Whisper (5 feet)	20	
	10	
Threshold of hearing (1,000 Hertz)	0	

Source: P. V. Paul & S. P. Quigley (1990). *Education and Deafness.* White Plains, NY: Longman, p. 31. Based on Bess & McConnell (1981). Copyright © 1990 by Longman Publishing Group. Reprinted by permission of the authors.

Sensorineural hearing losses are caused by defects in the inner ear (cochlea) or the auditory nerve, particularly in the delicate sensory hairs of the inner ear or in the nerves that supply them. Those nerves transmit impulses to the brain.

Tests with an audiometer can determine whether a hearing loss is conductive or sensorineural. Figure 9.2 shows the audiogram of a child with a conductive hearing loss. On the audiometer, the child heard airborne sounds at the 40-dB level at all frequencies; using a bone-conduction receiver, the child responded in the normal range. Notice that the hearing loss is fairly even at all frequencies.

We see a very different pattern in Figure 9.3. The audiogram in this figure is of a child with a sensorineural hearing loss. The youngster shows a profound loss of high frequencies (about 1,000 cycles) and a severe loss of low frequencies. In this case, the bone-conduction receiver gave no better reception because the defect is in the auditory nerve, not in the middle ear structure that carries the sound vibrations to the nerve. Even with amplification to increase the sound level, persons with this pattern may perceive speech sounds as distorted (NICD, 1989).

Mixed hearing losses result from problems in the outer ear as well as in the middle or inner ear (NICD, 1989). Persons with this type of loss may hear distorted sounds as well as have difficulty with sound level. **Central hearing losses** result from changes in the reception of hearing areas in the brain or damage to the pathways of the brain (NICD, 1989). Central hearing losses are not frequently encountered.

Figure 9.1
Structure of the Ear

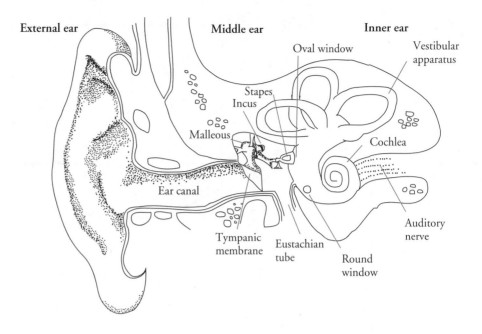

Source: M. L. Batshaw (Ed.) (1997). *Children with Disabilities* (3rd ed.). Baltimore: Paul H. Brookes, p. 323. Used by permission of the author.

Prevalence of Hearing Loss

About 21 million persons in the United States, or 8 percent of the general population, have some degree of hearing loss. Of these, about 1 percent are deaf (Paul & Quigley, 1994; NICD, 1989). During the school year 1994–1995, 65,568 students were listed as deaf or hard of hearing. They accounted for 1.3 percent of students with disabilities (NICHCY, 1997). Of these students, 31 percent were served in regular classes, 20 percent in resource rooms, 31 percent in separate classes, and 19 percent in separate or residential schools (U.S. Department of Education, 1997). Because of the impact of the Education for All Handicapped Children Act (PL 94-142) and IDEA, the education of children who are hard of hearing or deaf has moved from residential and day schools to local schools.

More students who are deaf are now being educated in local schools.

Causes of Hearing Loss

The causes of deafness and hardness of hearing are estimated to be one-third genetic, one-third environmental or acquired, and one-third unknown (Steinberg & Knightly, 1997). Some authorities divide the causes into one-half genetic and one-half environmental (NICD, 1989). There are 70 documented genetic syndromes as well as many other single genetic causes of deafness and hardness of hearing. Environmental causes include exposure to bacteria, viruses, toxins, and trauma, as well as infection during the course of pregnancy or in the birth process (Steinberg & Knightly, 1997). Table 9.3 lists some common causes of hearing losses. Note the number of illnesses, infections, or accidents that can lead to hearing losses after birth.

Figure 9.2
Audiogram of a Child with a
Conductive Hearing Loss

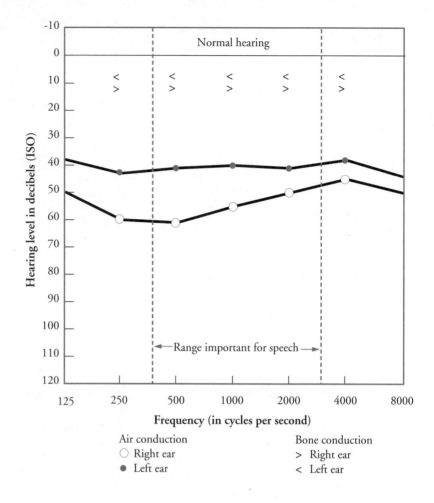

GENETIC CAUSES

The genetic causes are disorders inherited from one or both of the parents. More than two hundred different types of genetic deafness have been identified and can be inherited from either a hearing parent or a nonhearing parent (NICD, 1989).

Children with other genetic defects may have associated hearing disorders. For example, children with Down syndrome (a genetic disorder associated with mental retardation) have narrow ear canals and are prone to middle ear infections, which may cause hearing losses. Individuals with cleft palates (an opening in the lip and aboral ridge) also may have repeated middle ear infections, which can result in conductive hearing losses (Roizan, 1997).

Rh (hyperbilirubinemia) can develop incompatibility when a mother who is Rh-negative carries a fetus that is Rh-positive. The mother's immune system begins to destroy the fetus's red blood cells when they enter the mother's circulatory system. As a result, the fetus may become anemic and die in utero. If the child survives, he or she is likely to have a high-frequency hearing loss. The drug RhoGAM is available to block the formation of antibodies in the mother's system. Usually, the first

Figure 9.3
Audiogram of a Child with a
Sensorineural Hearing Loss

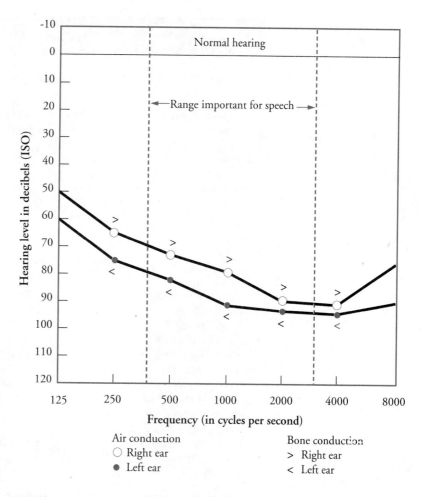

Air conduction
○ Right ear
● Left ear

Bone conduction
> Right ear
< Left ear

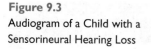
Some genetically based hearing losses occur during childhood and adolescence.

pregnancy is not affected, but all subsequent ones are if the condition is not identified and treated.

Boothroyd (1988) reminds us that not all hearing losses due to genetic defects appear at birth. Babies born with perfectly normal hearing may lose it in months or years as a result of heredity (p. 50). Teachers who suspect that a child may be exhibiting signs of a loss should be aware that loss can occur in a child who previously exhibited a normal range of hearing.

ENVIRONMENTAL CAUSES

Some infections that the mother has during pregnancy can cause deafness in her child.

The environmental effects that begin before birth are associated with illness or infections the mother may have had during pregnancy. For example, uncontrolled diabetes in the mother may cause a hearing loss in her child. More specifically, a group of infections that affect the mother but cause severe hearing losses in the fetus have been labeled *TORCHS*. The *TO* stands for toxoplasmosis, a parasitic disease common in Europe that may be contracted by handling contaminated cat feces or eating infected lamb that has not been cooked sufficiently (Batshaw &

TABLE 9.3   Some Causes and Conditions Associated with Hearing Loss in School-Age Children

Conductive Hearing Impairment

Otitis media (including middle ear fluid)	Impacted cerumen (wax)
Otitis externa	Blockage of the external auditory meatus by foreign object
Discontinuity of the ossicles	
Congenital malformation of the outer ear	Cholesteatoma
Congenital malformation of the middle ear	Cleft palate
Genetic syndromes (e.g., Down syndrome, Hunter's syndrome)	Traumatic head injury
	Eustachian tube dysfunction
Perforation of the tympanic membrane	

Sensorineural Hearing Impairment

Congenital viral infections	Meningitis
Maternal rubella	Encephalitis
Cytomegalovirus	Scarlet fever
Prematurity and low birth weight	Measles
Perinatal anoxia or hypoxia	Mumps
Hyperbilirubinemia	Influenza
Rh-factor incompatibility	Other viral infections
Maldevelopment of inner ear	Cerebrovascular disorders
Hereditary familial hearing impairment (congenital or acquired)	Drug ototoxicity
	Congenital syphilis
Noise-induced hearing loss	Unexplained high fever
Genetic syndromes (e.g., Waardenburg's syndrome, Hunter's syndrome)	Auditory nerve tumors (e.g., neurofibromatosis)

Source: B. Friedrith (1987). "Auditory dysfunction." In K. Kavale, J. Forness, & M. Bender (Eds.), *Handbook on Learning Disabilities, Vol. I.* Austin, TX: PRO-ED. Copyright © 1987. Used by permission of the publisher, PRO-ED, Inc.

Perret, 1992). The *R* stands for rubella (German measles), which, if contracted by the mother, can cause not only serious hearing losses in the child, but also blindness and retardation as well. With the advent of the rubella vaccine, very few cases are occurring (Steinberg & Knightly, 1997). This vaccination must be renewed periodically. The *C* stands for cytomegalovirus (CMV), an infection in the mother's uterus, which is a major environmental cause of deafness in the United States. CMV can go undiagnosed, or it can be misdiagnosed (sometimes as the flu). A particularly harmful virus, it can pass through the placenta and affect the fetus. Specialists believe that some children with hearing losses caused by rubella may actually have been exposed to CMV (Gothelf, 1991). CMV is so strongly associated with low-birth-weight and premature infants that it has been considered as a possible cause of prematurity as well as of the resulting hearing loss (NICD, 1989). While the incidence of rubella has decreased 1 percent, CMV has increased from 1 percent to 2 percent (Holden-Pitt & Diaz, 1998). The *HS*

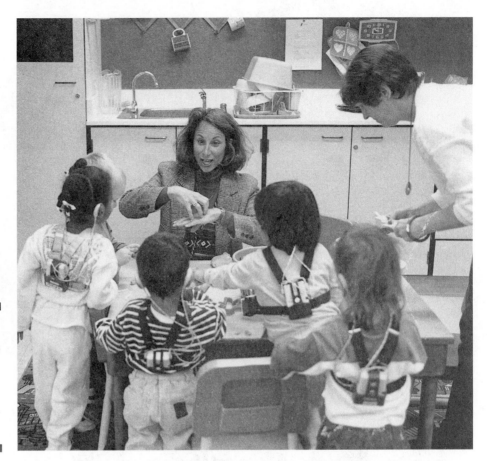

The identification during infancy and in early childhood of children who are deaf or hard of hearing means these children have the opportunity for early access to instruction and assistive technology. This increases their potential for communication development and academic success. *(© Elizabeth Crews)*

stands for herpes simplex virus, which, if untreated, can lead to the death of 60 percent of infected infants. Those who survive may have serious neurological problems and potential hearing loss. Some believe that CMV is a form of herpes virus (Pappas, 1985).

Noise pollution, particularly loud and persistent noises, can cause hearing loss. It is suspected that the noise produced by isolettes for premature babies is related to hearing loss, but this has not been proven (Batshaw & Perret, 1988).

Infections after birth, such as *meningitis* (an inflammation of the membranes covering the brain and spinal cord), can damage the auditory nerve. Because the antibiotics given to treat the infection may also cause damage to the auditory nerve, the dosage for the infant must be measured carefully (Batshaw & Perret, 1992). All infants should be inoculated against meningitis.

Otitis media, a universal infection of the middle ear, may cause a hearing loss if it is persistent or recurrent and untreated. It is generally associated with mild-to-moderate hearing losses. This is discussed more fully in Chapter 8.

Asphyxia (lack of oxygen) during the birth process may bring about a hearing loss.

Premature and low-birth-weight infants weighing less than 4 pounds are at greater risk of hearing loss. Because of increasingly successful lifesaving techniques

When reading is taught visually or by a gestural method, deaf children are better able to learn how to read, write, and use language logic forms and to succeed in school. (© Betty Medsger)

now being used in neonate nurseries, we are seeing an increase in the number of infants with hearing losses (Robertson & Whyte, 1983).

Characteristics of Children with Hearing Loss

COGNITIVE DEVELOPMENT

⭐ *Most children who are deaf or hard of hearing possess normal intelligence.*

The most important thing to remember about children who are deaf or hard of hearing is that most of them possess normal intelligence. They are not deficient or deviant in their cognitive abilities; they are simply children who cannot hear as well as children with normal hearing. Hearing loss is a silent disability. It is not accompanied by pain, fear, or physical problems. It is only when verbal demands are made on the child that it becomes apparent (Lillo-Martin, 1997). Children with hearing losses follow the same sequence of cognitive development as children without losses, but sometimes at a slower rate.

One of the major problems in the past in determining the intellectual level of children with hearing losses was that the intelligence tests used to measured their abilities were not appropriate for children with hearing losses. Orally (speech) administered intelligence tests greatly underestimate the abilities of a child whose primary language is gestural (Paul & Quigley, 1994). To assess children who are deaf or hard of hearing in written English is like testing a monolingual English-speaking child with Chinese characters (Marshark & Harris, 1996, p. 127). When nonverbal tests are used with a sign system familiar to the child, these children perform well within the normal range (Bellugi & Studdert-Kennedy, 1984).

A child who has not heard the sounds of the language will not be able to decode print if taught in the usual method of matching sounds to print. If reading is taught visually (Moores, 1996) or by a gestural method (such as American Sign Language [ASL] or finger spelling, which are discussed later in the chapter), however, children who are deaf or hard of hearing are able to learn how to read, write, and use language logic forms (for example, past tense, questions, and logical propositions such as if-then or either-or) and will be successful in school. Depending on the degree of hearing present, the child may learn how to use both the gestural system and the oral system of language. Thus, cognitive ability is present in persons with hearing losses, but if they do not do as well as expected in acquiring reading, writing, and literacy skills, it is probably because the manner in which they are being taught is inappropriate for students with hearing losses.

Why most children with hearing losses do not develop literacy skills commensurate with their intelligence is suspected to be a consequence of the hearing impairment not having been identified early. Children who are identified as being deaf and taught a sign language before the age of 2½ perform much better on all tasks than those identified after reaching 2½ years of age (Mauk & White, 1995). This fact is the basis for the position advocating universal auditory screening of infants. Hard-of-hearing children who are fitted with hearing aids before 3 years of age do better than those who receive them after age 3 (Calderon & Greenberg, 1997). What is clear is that children who are deaf or hard of hearing, who have parents who are deaf or hard of hearing, and who are taught a sign language (usually ASL) early usually do far better in school than other such children who have first been taught an oral system.

Let us look at some information from linguistics about how all children acquire language and the implications for effective teaching of children who are deaf or hard of hearing.

LANGUAGE DEVELOPMENT

Children who are born deaf or hard of hearing are no different from children born hearing (Lillo-Martin, 1997). During the first year of life, which is called the prelinguistic period (meaning without speech), they will exhibit the same behaviors, such as crying, making comfort sounds, and babbling to parents. In babbling, the child produces his or her first sounds that resemble words (*baba, dada*), and the parents reinforce these sounds and transform them into words. What many parents do not realize is that these behaviors are innately programmed and will appear whether the infant can hear or not. Infants who can hear typically produce their first word around 12 months of age. For the infant who is deaf, babbling does not develop into words. However, Petitto and Marentette (1991) found that children with severe hearing losses gesture at about the same developmental age as non–hearing impaired children babble. They concluded that infants are innately predisposed to learn language and do so by stimulating the environment by babbling; if they cannot hear, they use babbling-like hand gestures that are sign equivalents of speech sounds. These signs are not words, but they are similar to the babbling sounds. Parents who are deaf recognize these signs and begin teaching a gestural/manual/visual system, usually ASL. Each language, spoken or gestural, proceeds in similar fashion. If the parents do not help the child form gestures into language, the child may develop his or her own sign system, called *home sign*.

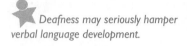

Deafness may seriously hamper verbal language development.

The point is that the innate language mechanism is so strong that children who hear will develop a spoken language and children who are deaf will develop a gestural one. Each will develop the language of his or her home. For the child who can hear, it will be English, French, Spanish—whatever language is spoken in the home. For the child who is deaf, it will be the sign system taught in the home or one developed by the child (Goldin-Meadow, 1997).

Thus, for all children, language begins before birth and proceeds during the first year of life well in advance of the production of the first word at around 12 months of age. The gestures of infants with hearing losses are precursors to learning language in the form of manual signs. Parents must recognize and reinforce these gestures in much the same way that they would reinforce oral sounds. The major problem is that 90 percent of children who are deaf or hard of hearing are born into homes with hearing parents who do not recognize the child's deafness or his or her attempts at a manual language.

These babbling-like gestures are seen in children of parents with severe hearing losses, who tend to reinforce them. Thus, the presence of both babbling and gestures tends to support the position of those who believe there is a strong, innate push to learn how to communicate in one's home, using the same mode of communication as the adults in the home (Goldin-Meadow, 1997).

The language learning patterns of children who are deaf or hard of hearing and of children who can hear are the same. As noted, most children produce their first word by 12 months of age. By 18 to 22 months of age, they master the logic forms of the language used in their home (Bloom, 1991), and they begin on their own to figure out the rules of language from the spoken examples provided by their environment (Pinker, 1991; Shantz & Eberling, 1991). This ability to independently generate the rules of grammar (particularly syntax or word order) tends to disappear after 6 years of age. If the child masters these rules of grammar by the age of 6, he or she can build on them through instruction. If the child has not acquired them by then, it is extremely difficult or almost impossible to teach them to the child.

Children with severe prelinguistic hearing losses who are not provided with amplification and early childhood special education are seriously deprived of the experience they need to use their innate mechanisms to figure out the grammar (syntax) and use (pragmatics) of their language. Not surprisingly, grammar and syntax are two aspects of language that children with prelinguistic hearing losses have difficulty mastering (Paul & Quigley, 1994).

For those who can hear no sounds, the introduction of sign language during the first year of life does much to encourage normal gestural language, which has most of the features of American English.

Our basic argument is that all children have a genetic push to acquire language (Chomsky, 1988). They can do so in rich language environments and in poor ones. If they cannot hear, they can develop an equally adequate system of gestural language (Goldin-Meadow, 1997). If a speech or gestural system is not provided for children to master, however, each child develops a system that is unique, which is not considered normal (Paul & Quigley, 1994).

The NICD (1989) stated the following:

> Deaf children have unique communication needs; unable to hear the continuous repeated flow of language interchange around them, children with severe hearing impairments are not exposed to the enormous amounts of language stimulation

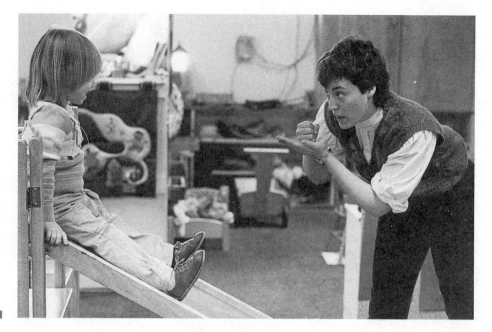

All children have a genetic push to acquire language. For those with severe and profound hearing losses, the introduction of sign language during the first year of life does much to encourage normal gestural language, which has most of the features of American English.
(© Steven Stone/The Picture Cube)

experienced by hearing children during the early years. For children with severe hearing losses, early, consistent, and conscious use of visible communication modes (such as sign language, finger spelling, and cued speech) and/or amplification and aural/oral training can help reduce this language delay. Without such assistance *from infancy,* problems in the use of English typically persist throughout the child's school years. With such assistance, the language learning task is easier but by no means easy. (p. 21; emphasis added)

These results point to the importance of *every* parent or teacher of a student who is deaf learning a signed system, particularly in infancy and the preschool years, when the child's central nervous system is ready to learn language. The language of the child's culture, whether it be expressed in gestural or oral form, must be provided with strong parental involvement if the child is to learn to communicate (Solnit, Taylor, & Bednarczyk, 1992). The teacher's and parents' abilities to sign not only will aid the child in developing a communication system but also will enhance the child's social skills, peer interaction, and play (Luetke-Stahlman, 1994).

SOCIAL AND PERSONAL ADJUSTMENT

A hearing loss often brings with it communication problems, and communication problems can contribute to social and behavioral difficulties:

Personality inventories have consistently shown that deaf children have more adjustment problems than hearing children. When deaf children without overt or serious problems have been studied, they have been found to exhibit characteristics of rigidity, egocentricity, absence of inner controls, impulsivity, and suggestibility. (Meadow, 1980, p. 97)

People with serious hearing losses develop a sense of community and an awareness of their needs as a group, which have been translated into political and social action to protect their individual and group rights. (© Bob Rashid/Monkmeyer Press Photo Service)

Lack of verbal language makes it difficult for children who are deaf to make friends with children who speak and do not sign.

Consider the boy with prelinguistic hearing loss who wants a turn on the playground swings. He cannot simply say, "I want my turn" or "It's my turn now." What does he do? He may push another youngster out of the way. Obviously, this kind of behavior is going to cause the child difficulties with interpersonal relationships. And when it is repeated many times, it can create serious social adaptation problems.

Several factors should improve the social adjustment of children who are deaf or hard of hearing.

- Early identification and intervention markedly improve the child's overall functioning, thus giving him or her increased feelings of self-esteem.
- Increased parent training teaches families the most effective ways to interact with their child and facilitate his or her development, thereby reducing family stress and increasing the child's acceptance.
- The availability of sophisticated technological aids such as the Internet and the World Wide Web provides access to information and social contacts.
- The increasing number of sign-language interpreters in public schools gives these children an outlet for making friends and engaging in a larger variety of activities.

In the meantime, it is not surprising that many children with severe hearing losses prefer to be with children like themselves, with whom they can feel socially accepted and comfortable (Anita, 1982).

The desire to cluster extends into adulthood, and in many large cities there is a culture of people with severe hearing losses, a group of individuals who socialize

Computer-generated programs provide meaningful practice for people who are deaf in learning a sign language. (© NR Rowan/The Image Works)

Interpreters in the general education classroom sign oral instruction as a way to support children who are deaf.

with one another and intermarry—the deaf community. This tendency to band together is not unusual. Most adults and children feel most comfortable with people like themselves. This does not mean that people who are deaf do not want to be or cannot be integrated into society. Nor does it mean that all people who are deaf are alike.

Interpreters

Interpreters can greatly assist the successful inclusion of students who are deaf into the regular classroom. Interpreters have not necessarily been trained as teachers, so they need to be in close communication with the classroom teacher to be able to understand the teacher's goals and preferred way in achieving them. In some schools the interpreter is a regular member of the multidisciplinary team (Moores, 1996). In some classrooms, the interpreter may work individually with one or more children; in most cases, however, the interpreter's role is to sign oral instruction. In any event, good communication acquired through frequent meetings with the classroom teacher and discussing the individual child's needs and progress are recommended. The NICD publishes a booklet, *Becoming a Sign Language Interpreter,* which can be obtained for a nominal fee. (See the address at the end of this chapter.)

The Deaf Community

The deaf community exists as a separate cultural group within our society and has exhibited considerable cohesiveness for more than a century (Moores, 1996). Its members share similar values and traditions, and they have a common language, ASL. As we have noted, parents who are deaf teach ASL to their children who are deaf. Many adults who are deaf learned ASL from their peers in residential schools.

The deaf community has state and local networks, holds world games for the deaf and a Deaf Miss America Pageant (Moores, 1996), and publishes a newspaper as well as other material. The community is strongly bonded, and most deaf adults in the United States move toward membership and involvement in it. The deaf community has the status of a minority group within the mainstream culture. Its members are bilingual, using ASL for communication with others and American English for reading and writing. They provide one another with a sense of belonging and pride, and they help one another overcome their isolation from mainstream society.

The cohesive deaf community helps its members overcome a sense of isolation from the mainstream society.

Some Special Services

Numerous social service agencies extend their programs to clients with severe hearing losses. In addition, various agencies and organizations—related either to hearing losses or to disability in general—provide specific services to people with severe hearing losses.

Captioned Films for the Deaf.　Captioned Films for the Deaf lends theatrical and educational films captioned for viewers with severe hearing losses. It is funded by the Captioning and Adaptations Branch of the U.S. Department of Education. Its aim is to promote the education and welfare of people with severe hearing losses through the use of media. The Captioning and Adaptations Branch also provides funds for closed-captioned television programs, including the live-captioned ABC television news (NICD, 1989).

Registry of Interpreters for the Deaf, Inc.　A professional organization, the Registry of Interpreters for the Deaf (RID) maintains a national listing of persons skilled in the use of ASL and other sign systems. The organization also provides information on interpreting and evaluation and certification of interpreters for people with severe hearing losses (NICD, 1989).

State Departments of Vocational Rehabilitation.　Each state has specific provisions for the type and extent of vocational evaluation, financial assistance for education and training, and job placement help (NICD, 1989).

National Information Center on Deafness.　NICD is located at Gallaudet University, 800 Florida Avenue, NE, Washington, DC 20002-3695. It is a centralized source for information about hearing loss and deafness. NICD has a wealth of information available in a variety of written and visual forms and at nominal cost.

Signaling Devices.　Signaling devices that add a flashing or vibrating signal to the existing auditory signal are popular with hearing impaired users. Among devices that use flashing lights are door "bells," telephone-ring signalers, baby-cry signals (which alert the parent that the baby is crying), and smoke alarms. Alarm clocks may feature either a flashing light or a vibrating signal.

Figure 9.4

Profiles of Three Children with Different Degrees of Hearing Loss

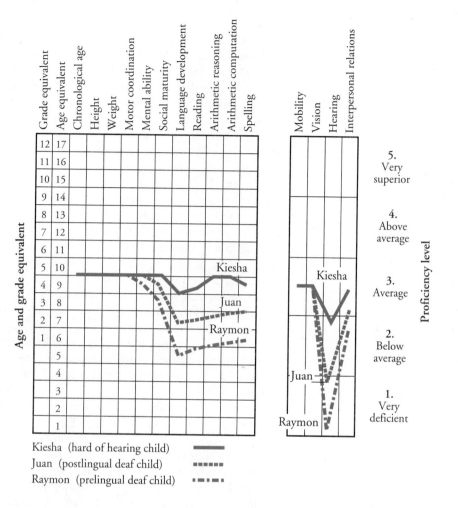

Kiesha   (hard of hearing child)
Juan   (postlingual deaf child)
Raymon   (prelingual deaf child)

Telecommunications for the Deaf, Inc. Telecommunications for the Deaf (TDI) publishes an international telephone directory of individuals and organizations that own and maintain telecommunication devices for the deaf (TDDs) for personal or business use (NICD, 1989).

Developmental Profiles

Figure 9.4 shows the developmental profiles of three children: Kiesha, Juan, and Raymon. All three children are 10 years old. Their profiles are similar in shape, but their intra-individual differences increase with the severity of hearing loss and age at the onset of deafness. Kiesha is hard of hearing, Juan has a postlingual hearing loss, and Raymon has a prelingual hearing loss.

The upper profile in the figure is Kiesha's. She has a moderate hearing loss of 45 dB. Like Juan and Raymon, Kiesha is of average height, weight, and motor co-ordination. She also shows average mental ability and social maturity for her age. Her speech development is slightly delayed. She has some difficulty in articulation and needs speech remediation. This speech problem has affected Kiesha's reading skills, but her achievement in arithmetic and spelling is at grade level.

When Kiesha was first fitted with a hearing aid, her special education program included instruction in its use. Now an itinerant speech-language pathologist gives her speech remediation, auditory training, and speech-reading lessons once a week.

Even though Kiesha's development and educational achievement are close to those of her peers, she does need some special attention from the classroom teacher. Her hearing aid makes her feel different from her friends, which could become more of a problem when she is an adolescent. Kiesha's hearing fluctuates somewhat when the weather changes or when she has a cold. Teachers who are not aware of this fluctuation may think that she is deliberately ignoring them when in fact she simply cannot hear them.

The middle profile in Figure 9.4 shows the developmental pattern of Juan, who has a severe hearing loss. He was born with normal hearing but suffered a severe hearing loss in both ears at age 4. He is classified as having postlingual severe hearing loss. Although Juan is approximately normal in physical ability, intelligence, and social maturity, his speech and language have not developed normally. On an audiometer test, he showed a hearing loss of 75 dB even after he was fitted with hearing aids. Fortunately, Juan learned to talk normally before his loss of hearing and developed considerable language ability. That means he can learn through the auditory channel with the help of hearing aids. Still, his reading and other academic achievement scores are at a second-grade level. His hearing loss has interfered considerably with his educational progress, but with hearing aids, speech habilitation, and other special education services, he is moving ahead.

Juan relies a good deal on his speech-reading skills. For that reason, and to use his hearing aids to best advantage, he sits at the front of the classroom, facing the teacher. He needs extra help in developing social skills and making friends.

The bottom profile in Figure 9.4 is of a child with a profound hearing loss. Raymon was born with a severe hearing impairment. He has never heard a spoken word. Hearing aids might make him aware of environmental sounds but cannot help him develop speech and English. Because of the severity of Raymon's hearing loss—it tested at more than 95 dB—he is in a self-contained special class. He would need intensive tutorial services if he were integrated into the regular classroom.

Raymon's speech is difficult to understand. His English language development has not followed the pattern of hearing children. In reading and other academic subjects, he is about four grades behind his agemates.

Raymon's communication with his family and peers is limited; so are his sources of information and his social experiences. He often reacts to social situations in ways that are characteristic of a much younger child. If he were placed in the regular classroom, he would need help in making friends.

 The School's Role in Identification

Children with severe hearing losses are usually identified through public health screening or pediatric examinations before they enter school. Children with mild or moderate hearing losses often go undiagnosed until academic performance indicates a problem. Even then, an accurate diagnosis is not automatic. Many of the symptoms of a hearing loss are also indicative of other disorders. A child who stares blankly at the teacher may not be able to hear or may not understand what is being said.

THE GENERAL EDUCATION TEACHER

★ *A general education teacher can help identify a child with a possible hearing loss by observing his or her articulation, need for a higher volume of sounds, requests that information be repeated, and inattentiveness or unresponsiveness.*

How does the classroom teacher identify a child with a possible hearing loss so the child can be referred for comprehensive examination? Stephens, Blackhurst, and Magliocca (1982, pp. 43–44) suggested that teachers watch for several things:

- *Does the child appear to have a physical problems associated with the ears?* The student may complain of earaches, discomfort in the ear, or strange ringing or buzzing noises. Teachers should note these complaints and also be alert for signs of discharge from the ears or excessively heavy waxy buildup in the ear canal. Frequent colds and sore throats are occasional indicators of infections that could impair hearing.

- *Does the child articulate sounds poorly and particularly omit consonant sounds?* Students who articulate poorly may have a hearing problem that is preventing them from getting feedback about their vocal productions. Omission of consonant sounds from speech is often indicative of a high-frequency hearing loss.

- *When listening to radio, television, or records, does the student turn the volume up so high that others complain?* Because it is much in vogue among young people today to turn up the amplification of rock music almost "to the threshold of pain," this determination will sometimes be difficult to make. Teachers can get clues, however, by observing students listening to audio media that are not producing music, such as instructional records and sound-filmstrips.

- *Does the student cock the head or turn toward the speaker in an apparent effort to hear better?* Sometimes such movements are obvious and may even be accompanied by a "cupping" of the ear with the hand in an effort to direct the sound into the ear. In other cases, actions are much more subtle. Teachers often overlook such signs, interpreting them as symbols of increased inquisitiveness and interest.

- *Does the student frequently request that what has just been said be repeated?* Although some students pick up the habit of saying "Huh?" as a form of defense mechanism when they are unable to produce what they perceive as an acceptable response, such verbalizations may also indicate a hearing loss. When a particular student frequently requests repeated instructions, teachers should further investigate the possibility of hearing loss.

- *Is the student unresponsive or inattentive when spoken to in a normal voice?* Some students who do not follow directions or do not pay attention in class are frequently labeled as "troublemakers," which results in negative or punitive treatment. Often, however, these inappropriate school behaviors are actually caused by the student's inability to hear. They can also be caused if the sounds that are heard appear to be "garbled."

■ *Is the student reluctant to participate in oral activities?* Although reluctance to participate orally may be symptomatic of problems such as shyness, insecurity with respect to knowledge of subject matter, or fear of failure, it also may be due to hearing loss. The child might not be able to hear the verbal interactions that occur in such activities.

THE AUDIOLOGIST

With the passage of the Education for All Handicapped Children Act, the presence of the audiologist on the multidisciplinary team had an impact on the services that audiologists provide in the school setting (English, 1995). Audiologists continue to provide traditional clinical services: evaluating hearing level, recommending and fitting devices, and offering counsel on hearing conservation and room acoustics. In addition, they are involved in instruction in speech and in reading (listening skills as well as checking and monitoring all types of amplification devices), and they assist teachers in recognizing and resolving psychological issues of the child who is hard of hearing or deaf (English, 1995). In essence, audiology has developed a subspecialty: educational audiology.

Means of Testing Hearing Loss

AUDIOMETRY

Pure-Tone Audiometry

An audiologist is critical in assessing the degree, type, and extent of hearing loss.

Pure-tone audiometry, which is the most common means of determining hearing loss, can be used in children about 3 years of age and older. The **audiometer**—an instrument for testing hearing acuity—presents pure tones (not speech) to the individual, who receives the tones in a headset. The audiometer presents a range of sounds and measures the frequency (vibrations) and intensity (pitch) that the individual is able to hear through the earphones. The individual being tested responds to the sounds by raising his or her hand (or speaking into a microphone) if he or she can hear the tone. These responses are recorded on a graph called an **audiogram.** From an examination of the results, an audiologist can determine the degree and range of hearing loss. More elaborate audiometers can present and measure speech reception and discrimination (Paul & Quigley, 1994).

Behavioral Observation Audiometry

Audiologists use behavioral observation audiometry to test hearing in children younger than 3 years of age. The child is placed in an environment with attractive toys, and an outside observer notes the child's reactions as sounds are introduced into the room. Head turning, eye blinking, smiles, movements toward the sound source, and lack of response to presented sounds are recorded.

Play Audiometry

Play audiometry tests are conducted in a pleasant environment with toys that move and make sounds. The toys are used to elicit responses, such as eye blinks and changes in respiration or heartbeat (slower heartbeats indicate attention).

The child is brought into a room with his or her caregiver. An examiner distracts the child with an attractive toy. Sounds are piped into the room. A change in sound indicates that a curtain will be raised to reveal a more attractive toy. The child is not told that this will happen. Children without hearing losses hear the change of sound and turn to look at the hidden toy before the curtain is lifted to reveal it. If the child does not turn when the sound is changed, hearing losses are suspected.

Other play behavioral assessments are based on principles of conditioning children to respond to sound by rewarding them when they indicate that they hear it. The reward is usually allowing them to play with the toy. Paul and Quigley (1994) reported that play-conditioning audiometry is both reliable and an acceptable technique for assessing hearing in young children (p. 37). However, it is not suitable for infants (ASHA, 1991).

AUDITORY BRAINSTEM RESPONSE

Auditory brainstem response is the preferred method for testing an infant's hearing.

Auditory brainstem response (ABR) is currently the preferred method of evaluating whether or not an infant can hear. It is based on the fact that as sounds move through the ear canal to the middle ear, they will stimulate thousands of hair cells, causing them to vibrate and emit a sound. By using a small microphone, it is possible to receive and record this sound in the external ear (Mauk & White, 1995). If no sound is received, further evaluation is indicated.

BONE-CONDUCTOR TEST

With infants and preschool children younger than 3 years of age, it is common to use both a **pure-tone test** and a **bone-conductor test,** which measure the movement of sound through the hearing system to the brain. The reception of sound in the brain (auditory brainstem recognition) is recorded on a graph that charts the brain's response in vibrations (Linden, Kankkunen, & Tjellstrom, 1985). The vibrations are received by electrodes placed on the child's ear. By comparing the test taker's responses to the responses of a population of hearing persons, the audiologist can ascertain hearing abilities of losses (Linden et al., 1985).

COCHLEAR IMPLANTS

Cochlear implants involve a surgical procedure in which electrodes are inserted into the cochlea. A microphone worn behind the ear receives environmental sounds and sends them through the auditory system (Steinberg & Knightly, 1997). Cochlear implants do not restore hearing, but they do provide a sound system that can assist the user in understanding incoming auditory stimuli (Marschark, 1993). They appear to be effective over a longer period of use if worn consistently. Cochlear implants are still controversial, particularly in the deaf community.

"Talking Back"

My name is Brittany Sinclair and I am a 14-year-old student who is deaf. For as long as I can remember, I have worked with my mother to help develop my lip-reading skills. As I grew up, I was able to participate fully in the hearing world. My skills in lip-reading were already strong at a very early age, and so by the time I was six, doctors refused to believe that I was deaf.

My mother and Dr. Geraldine Detosta, who was the head of the child study team at a local hospital, arranged for a brainstem audio test. . . . It . . . produced evidence that erased all doubt—I have severe profound neurosensory deafness.

One of the major obstacles my family and I had to overcome was the ongoing dispute between whether I should attend the mainstream versus the deaf school, as well as signing versus oral communication. While I can sign, I have always been able to speak and read lips. It was difficult when I was very small to sit by as doctors told me that I should be mute and my lack of hearing would cause me to be delayed in my academic development. So each day, I go to school with my hearing aids, FM (a device that works with hearing aids which relays the voice of the teacher who is using a microphone), and my bookbag. Mainstreamed in the Walter T. Bergen public school in Bloomingdale, New Jersey, I attend honors classes and participate as if I were a hearing adolescent. I was invited to attend the summer gifted project at Boys Town, in Omaha, Nebraska, in the summer of 1995. This fall, I will start high school.

Learning from the Best

My Mom and Dad have always encouraged me. They are my biological grandparents who adopted me at birth. They have always made me feel that I can do whatever I want to, without letting my deafness stand in my way. . . .

I love music and I play several instruments. The eight instruments that I play are the flute, piccolo, trumpet, piano, organ, drums, guitar, and clarinet. I come from a family with a gift for music, as my mother is also talented. With my heaing aids in and from the vibrations of the instrument, I can tell that I am playing the right notes. I play with the Butler High School Band and I was appointed to the State Regional Band. . . .

Last year, I achieved the Excellence in Art award for my school. I also gained recognition at the state "Mini-Model Congress" for excellence in bill writing. I authored and debated a bill to have captioning put in movie theaters so that people who have hearing impairments could enjoy the latest movies without using an interpreter. I feel strongly that closed captioning should be available in all theaters.

Motivation

I am fueled by my desire to help students with disabilities feel safe and secure in the hearing world. The great financial burden of the many devices needed for the hearing impaired led me to request the Lions Club to obtain flashing fire alarms for the hearing impaired at little or no cost to them, thus hopefully saving lives. 2,000 people die in fires each year because they did not hear the alarm. This is devastating. Being deaf makes you feel vulnerable. No one wants to feel unsafe. When you feel safe, it gives you hope and makes you feel that you are not at a disadvantage. It makes you feel that you are as important as anyone else.

I am very social and love to be the center of attention. At the moment, I am between boyfriends, but that is not a problem because I have good friends to spend time with. . . .

Making my friends laugh is one of my favorite things. Because of my deafness, my voice sounds a little different and people who don't know me will ask me what country I am from. I sometimes say France, but I will say any country that pops into my head. I answer this way because whenever I explain that I am deaf, I notice a change in the way strangers act toward me; they are astonished and want to know how I can talk. I have a good sense of humor about everything. I don't mind that I sound like "The Nanny" from television! . . .

Speaking Up

In the future, I hope to graduate law school. Since I enjoy problem solving, like the idea of protecting people, and need to have action in my life, I will probably become either a lawyer or an FBI agent. My music and acting are something that I can keep as a secondary pursuit.

I have learned from my parents that I can do anything I set out to do. I would say to other parents of kids with disabilities, do not hold them back! If your children are discriminated against, stand up for them, since they cannot do it themselves. My parents also taught me that if there is anything that you have to do that is difficult, deal with it head on and don't dodge it. Then it doesn't seem so hard after all.

Source: "Talking Back" by Brittany Sinclair, *Exceptional Parent*, July 1998, p. 45. Reprinted with the expressed consent and approval of *Exceptional Parent*, a monthly magazine for parents and families of children with disabilities and special health care needs. Subscription cost is $36 per year for 12 issues. Call 1-877-372-7368. Offices at 555 Kinderkamack Rd., Oradell, NJ 07649.

What Is the Context?

Brittany is an active part of her community. She plays in the high school band, contributes to the Lions Club, and participates in sports and many other school activities. Through her own motivation and the support of family, friends, and community, Brittany successfully carries out her interests and participates fully in the community.

Pivotal Issues for Teachers

What factors contribute to how well Brittany has adjusted socially and personally? What kind of educational adaptations might Brittany need to accommodate for her deafness? What types of communication methods does Brittany use? What types of assistive devices or instructional technology might be useful to her?

Educational Adaptations

Children Who Are Deaf or Hard of Hearing

★ *Involving parents in early intervention programs for the deaf or hard of hearing assists both child and parent.*

★ *Many parents won't recognize their child is deaf until the child is 2 years old.*

ADAPTING THE LEARNING ENVIRONMENT

Although approximately 22 percent of children with severe hearing losses are still being educated in residential settings, most are in public or private day schools or classes (segregated classes held in regular public or private schools). Of the children who are in residential settings, many are day students. A large majority of students with severe hearing losses in the United States are enrolled in programs that allow them to live at home. Some states—Texas, for example—have regional day schools for children with severe hearing losses.

Parent Involvement and Early Intervention

Teachers of students with severe hearing losses all agree on the importance of early intervention. Infants learn about communication from the facial expressions, lip and head movements, gestures, touch, and vocal vibrations of those around them. That is why it is so important for the parents of children who are deaf or hard of hearing to establish effective communication as early as possible.

During infancy and early childhood, the innate language mechanism propels infants to learn a language. For the hearing child, it is the language of the home. For the child who is deaf and has parents who are deaf, it is a manual/sign/visual system. The critical factor is for the child to make at least 50 words (speech or manual) before 18 months to 2 years of age, when the innate grammar acquisition mechanism begins to function.

It is clear that children who are hard of hearing and those who are deaf with parents who can hear must receive early intervention if they are to accomplish these learnings during the critical language learning period. If the child has residual hearing, hearing aids or other technological devices are needed to allow the child to hear the language of the home and master it. Some professionals advocate both prostheses, such as hearing aids, and sign language. However, proponents of the oral-only orientation do not encourage sign learning for those with some residual hearing.

Many of the early education programs for preschoolers with severe hearing losses focus on the parents. Some provide counseling to help family members accept and adjust to the diagnosis of the severe hearing losses and to understand the condition. Others train parents to take an active role in teaching their children, carrying out in the home developmental tasks that are part of the overall program. The extent of the parents' involvement is a function of their readiness to participate and the willingness of educators to include them. Most parents of children who are deaf are not deaf themselves and have little or no experience with persons who are deaf. Many of them will not recognize that their child is deaf until he or she is 2 years of age or older. What most intervention programs for infants and toddlers who are deaf have come to stress is teaching the parents effective strategies for teaching their children. Some of these strategies are listed here.

STRATEGIES FOR PARENTS OF DEAF INFANTS

- Develop a perception that is accepting of deafness.
- Learn a sign system, preferably ASL.

Good emotional and behavioral adjustment is one of the greatest challenges for deaf children, who may experience social difficulties (© Freda Leinwand/Monkmeyer Press Photo Service)

- Use gentle facial touch to gain the infant's attention.
- Use facial expressions to help the infant understand the sign.
- If the infant looks away, allow him or her to do so before trying to continue communication.
- Use signs at a slower rate than you would for spoken language to an adult.
- Sign near the object to be identified or move the object into the infant's gaze. (Adapted from Jamieson, 1995; Koester, Karkowski & Traci, 1998; Lylte & Rovins, 1997; Masataka, 1996; Waxman, Spencer, & Poisson, 1996)

Parent training and programs for very young children with severe hearing losses are often provided in the home by appropriate therapists and special education teachers. These programs are also available in nursery schools, day-care centers, and some public schools. Their primary objectives are as follows:

- To train parents
- To develop communication skills
- To give children with severe hearing losses opportunities to share, play, and take turns with other children
- To help children with hearing losses use their residual hearing (through auditory training or with hearing aids)
- To develop readiness in basic English, reading, and arithmetic

Intensive preschool training is a fundamental step in preparing children with severe hearing losses for school. One important part of that preparation for children and their parents is learning to use sign language.

Inclusion in Elementary School

The increasing popularity of inclusion, or integrating children with disabilities into the regular classroom, has triggered controversy among teachers of children with severe hearing losses. Obviously, any academic program that attempts to mainstream children with severe hearing losses must provide trained supplementary personnel, such as interpreters, speech-language pathologists, and audiologists, who are accessible to parents as well as to children. The teacher must be skilled at some form of gestural communication (Solnit, Taylor, & Bednarczyk, 1992). The child's major responsibilities during the elementary years are to develop reading, writing, arithmetic, science, and social studies skills.

The trend in reading instruction for the deaf is to use a whole language approach, which includes guided reading, language experience approaches, sustained reading, shared reading, and writing in journals. It includes both the bottom-up technique (word identification, phonemes, and syllables) and the top-down technique (comprehension and knowing what the word means) (LaSasso & Mobley, 1996).

Knowledge of the alphabetic principle, which is essential for understanding the relationship among phonemes (vowels and consonants) and intonation, pause, and rhythm, is critical if the student is to learn the grapheme (print) of letters and words (Paul, 1996c). This is not an easy process for the child who is deaf or hard of hearing, and specialists need to provide intervention to enable the child to acquire these skills. Decisions about the type of school placement and curriculum should be based on the needs of the individual child at his or her particular stage of development.

In addition, there is a movement to teach reading by the whole word method. First, students learn to read words that stand for persons or things with which they are familiar, for example, *ball*. Then, after students have acquired a basic reading vocabulary, the teacher introduces phonics as a part of a continuing emphasis on teaching whole words (Abrams, 1991).

Inclusion in Secondary School

It is difficult to mainstream high school students with serious hearing losses because they often are several grade levels behind their agemates in achievement. When they are mainstreamed, these students need sign language interpreters in the classroom as well as supplementary resource assistance. Moores, Kluwin, and Mertens (1985) reported a tendency to mainstream children with severe hearing losses more in mathematics than in English, history, or science. Interviews with teachers and administrators revealed a consensus that there are fewer problems in mathematics achievement than in other academic areas.

A number of large metropolitan and suburban school districts offer a wide range of special services by centralizing programs (Moores, Kluwin, & Mertens, 1985). Schools within a district or several districts working together can combine

With the growing impact of inclusion, the importance of using interpreters in the classroom cannot be overemphasized.

their resources to provide special services to accommodate students with severe hearing losses within a large, comprehensive high school. This setting allows a range of environmental options, from self-contained classes for youngsters with severe hearing losses to mainstreaming in all academic courses.

The Education Team

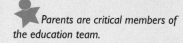
The education team includes an audiologist, speech therapist, and special education teacher.

A child with a significant hearing loss faces problems that are so varied that no single professional can deal with them all. The child's needs demand a team of professionals to produce a comprehensive program of education and therapy. A clinical audiologist must carefully assess the hearing loss and its physical and functional dimensions. A speech therapist must help the child reach his or her potential in speech reading and production. A special education teacher trained to work with children with severe hearing losses must develop an individualized education program (IEP) and a sequence of lessons to help general education teachers understand the special needs of the child.

That list is not exhaustive. The education of children with severe hearing losses is changing. Because of the recognition that instruction must adapt to the students' needs, and because their needs appear to include some form of manual interpretation, we find interpreters in the classroom and teachers trained not only in special education but in subject areas as well.

Parents are critical members of the education team.

One critical segment of the education team is not professional at all. Less than 50 percent of the families of children who are deaf or severely hard of hearing use signs in the home (Trybus, 1985). In more than 90 percent of these families, parents and siblings do not have hearing losses. In addition, family members are providing important reinforcement and even training throughout the critical preschool years. For individuals in the deaf community, hearing aids, cochlear implants, and oral approaches emphasize the negative aspects of deafness. They believe that parents of children who are deaf should communicate with them through a sign system, thereby demonstrating acceptance of them (Lane, Hoffmeister, & Bahan, 1996).

ADAPTING CURRICULUM

Academic Achievement

Three factors are related to the academic achievement of children with hearing losses: the degree of hearing loss, the presence of language, and experiences in the environment with people and things. If the child who is deaf is taught signing in infancy, or if he or she has some auditory perception and amplification is provided before the age of 2, and his or her environment is rich in terms of experiential language and activities, the child need not fail in school.

Most children who are deaf do not read at the average national norm.

National trends in the reading achievement of children with hearing losses are exciting. Moores (1996) reports that each year children who are deaf continue to make gains in reading scores, compared to the scores in previous years of those who are deaf. However, most children who are deaf do not read at the average national norm. New technology should help these students attain their age-appropriate academic levels.

Moores (1996) attributed some of these gains to the movement toward teaching reading and writing in a more functional (practical) and semantic (knowledge/meaning) manner. Many also affirmed that mainstreaming (placing children with hearing losses in regular classrooms) has increased students' academic achievement.

About 65 percent of the graduates of Gallaudet College are going on to graduate school and doing as well as their classmates who do not have hearing impairments (Moores, 1996). However, this is not to say that the academic achievement problem has disappeared. Several factors should be mentioned for persons with hearing losses at all age levels:

- Peer play and interaction are limited, because peers who can hear usually cannot communicate gesturally.

- Not all family members can use gestural communication. Although 70 percent of students with hearing losses use some form of signing, only 35 percent of their families use it at home (Paul & Quigley, 1994).

- The experiences of young children with hearing losses are limited. They cannot go into the environment without supervision because they cannot hear approaching cars or other dangers and the general populace cannot communicate with them.

Components of Successful Programs

In addition to fostering the teacher's individual efforts, programs should concentrate on the following components, which research has found to be desirable:

- *Reading training.* Over and above conventional reading instruction, a special program should train students with severe hearing losses in adjusting reading strategies for various purposes. After reading is mastered, emphasis should be placed on reading to learn (Kelly, 1995; Moores, 1996).

- *Cognitive strategies.* The teaching of cognitive strategies should be an important part of the curriculum (Moores, 1996). Students use these strategies to select, control, and monitor how they learn and solve problems. According to Moores, they are frequently neglected in programs for students who are deaf or hard of hearing. (See Chapter 6 for specific techniques for teaching strategies.)

- *Special programs.* Students with severe hearing losses who have high potential should be identified and should receive accelerated training.

- *Tutoring.* Even if a one-to-one situation cannot be maintained, with careful planning a low student-teacher ratio in programs for persons with severe hearing losses can lead to significant one-to-one and small-group instruction.

- *Cooperative parent programs.* The alterable curriculum of the home can be manipulated to foster school achievement.

Encouraging Academic Achievement at Home

The idea behind the use of the alterable home curriculum is not to place the total reseponsibility for teaching on parents but to encourage academic achievement.

Students who are deaf and also gifted should receive accelerated instruction.

The results have been excellent. Basic things parents are asked to do include the following:

- Keep television viewing to moderate levels (twelve hours per week or less).
- Monitor homework to see that it is completed.
- Encourage leisure reading.
- Discuss school with the child.
- Express interest in the child's progress.
- Learn a sign or gestural communication system if the child has a severe hearing loss.

Many programs at homes or with therapists and early intervention programs focus on teaching words and phonemes (the smallest units of sound with meaning) rather than on the broad set of literary skills. Children with hearing losses must be taught the following concepts (after Paul & Quigley, 1994, pp. 181–186):

- *Word meanings:* multiple meanings of the same word, such as *mole,* an animal, and *mole,* a spy whose task it is to collect classified information within an organization
- *Syntax:* variety of word order, such as in questions, declarative statements, and possessives
- *Figurative language:* similes ("he has a head like a rock"), metaphors ("she is a vixen"), and onomatopoeia ("the whir of the engine")
- *Idioms:* for example, "he pulled himself up by his bootstraps"
- *Inferences:* for example, "the cold wind blew snow around the house," from which it can be inferred that it is winter

ADAPTING TEACHING STRATEGIES

Communication Skills

The dispute over how to teach language to a child with hearing losses began in Europe, with Samuel Heinicke in Germany stressing oralism (speech) and Abbé de l'Eprée in France stressing manualism (gestures). A conference held in Milan in 1880 stressed oralism and claimed that gestural language impeded language development (Paul & Quigley, 1994).

In the United States, the gestural approach was taken up by Thomas Hopkins Gallaudet, who founded the first school for the hearing impaired in Hartford, Connecticut, in 1817. The school was moved to Washington, D.C., in 1884. The oral approach was advocated by Alexander Graham Bell, inventor of the telephone and the audiometer. Interestingly, both men had mothers with severe hearing losses, and each was firmly convinced of the correctness of his position.

Not until the 1970s did Bob Holcomb (Gannon, 1981), a college graduate with a severe hearing loss, advocate the use of both systems, oral and gestural, and coin the term *total communication method* to describe this dual approach. In total communication, some type of sign system is used simultaneously with speech.

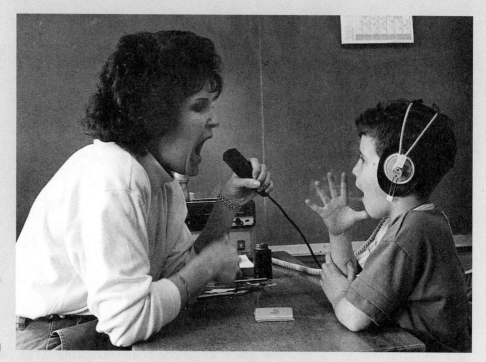

The combination of gestural and oral systems in a total communication approach is now being widely recommended for those with hearing losses, regardless of whether the impairment is moderate or severe. (© Grant LeDuc/Monkmeyer Press Photo Service)

However, according to Paul and Quigley (1994), many educators of persons who are deaf or hard of hearing do not use a sign system as an instructional technique. The simple fact is that our culture prefers that people learn to speak with correct pronunciation, correct word order, and interpretable meaning appropriate to the setting in which speech is spoken. Given this strong societal bias, educators of students who have hearing losses stress oral language, although the children do not succeed as well as expected. Many specialists in educating persons with hearing losses argue that it is more important to teach a communication system that the child can master, regardless of whether it is gestural or oral. The combination of gestural and oral systems in a total communication approach is now being more widely recommended for those with hearing losses, regardless of whether the loss is moderate or severe (Moores, 1996).

As mentioned earlier, there is a movement to consider ASL as the primary language for persons who are deaf and English as a second language. The position is that persons who are deaf constitute a language minority group and should be entitled to bilingual education (Lane, Hoffmeister, & Bahan, 1996; Parasnis, 1997). Given the importance of cultural diversity in the U.S. population, teachers and specialists may be confronted with students whose first sign language may be influenced by Spanish, Chinese, or some other spoken language. This population may sign (or speak if there is residual hearing) in a language that is not English; by learning ASL and English, they become trilingual. Technology may be the key for assisting members of other language groups who are deaf (Gallaudet Research Institute, 1997).

★ Many individuals in the deaf community believe in communicating with a signing system (such as ASL) rather than using hearing aids or the oral approach to communicating.

Communication Methods

Oral methods of communication for persons who are deaf or hard of hearing use whatever hearing and speech abilities a person has. Oral methods include the oral-aural method and the auditory method. **Manual methods** include the various signing systems (ASL, for example) and finger spelling. The effectiveness of all these methods depends on the severity of the hearing loss and the availability of early intervention.

Oral-Aural Method. The **oral-aural method** uses residual hearing through amplified sound, speech reading, and speech to develop communication skills. Oral-aural programs do not use or encourage the use of sign languages or finger spelling, believing that manual communication impedes the child's adjustment to the hearing world.

One important skill in the oral-aural method is **speech reading,** the visual interpretation of spoken communication (also known as *lip reading*). It is one means by which people with severe hearing losses receive communication from those who can hear. Because few hearing people go to the trouble to learn a complex system of manual communication, individuals with severe hearing losses who want to keep in meaningful contact with the hearing world must learn to speech-read.

Speech reading is possible because many sounds in the English language bring a particular expression to the speaker's face. For example, the *n* sound looks very different from the *k* sound. A major problem, however, is sounds that are homophones—they are articulated in similar ways and look the same on the speaker's lips and face (for example, *cite, height, night*). The fact that half of the words in the English language have homophones is one reason why speech reading is so difficult.

The approach that is used to teach youngsters speech reading depends on the child's age. When the child is young, the teacher or parent talks in whole sentences. At first the child may not pick up any clues, but as the teacher or parent repeats the same expression over and over in the same relationship to something that the child is experiencing—an object, an action, a feeling—the child begins to get an idea of what is being said. At a later stage, these vague whole impressions are converted into lessons that emphasize details and into exercises that help the child discriminate among different words and sounds. Eventually, the special education teacher uses speech reading to present lessons in school.

Auditory Method. The **auditory method** (or **aural method**) makes extensive use of sound amplification to develop listening and speech skills. It involves auditory training—teaching the child to listen to sounds and to discriminate among different sounds. Although the method is used widely with school-age youngsters who have mild or moderate hearing losses, it has been most effective with preschoolers, particularly children with a severe loss. Parents play an important part in the early training process, and one of the goals of hearing specialists is to instruct parents and include them in the training.

The effectiveness of any communication method depends on the severity of a person's hearing loss and how early the loss is diagnosed and intervention is begun.

American Sign Language is the only signing system of communication that is a distinct language with its own grammar and syntax, which are both very different from English grammar and syntax. (© Arlene Collins/Monkmeyer Press Photo Service)

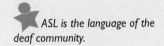
ASL is the language of the deaf community.

The auditory method is also called the **acoustic method,** the **acoupedic method,** and the **unisensory method.** Calvert and Silverman (1983) called it the **auditory global method** and claimed that the approach makes maximum use of residual hearing. They also recommended that it be used with amplification as early as possible.

Signing Systems.　There are several signing systems of communication: **American Sign Language (ASL),** Pidgin Sign English (PSE), Seeing Essential English (SEE I), and Signing Exact English (SEE II). Of these, ASL is the only distinct language (Bellugi & Studdert-Kennedy, 1984). The others are manual codes based on English.

Like all languages, ASL has its own grammar and syntax. It is very different from the "home" language, be it American English, an Asian language, or Spanish as it is spoken in different parts of North and South America. The language of the deaf community, ASL is not easily learned by adults who learned another language first.

Because there are very few teachers who are deaf in intervention, school, and college programs, teachers who can hear face the challenge of teaching ASL to students who are deaf.

Each sign has three elements: the position of the hands, the configuration of the hands, and the movement of the hands to different positions (Moores, 1996). Moores reports that Gallaudet University requires faculty members to attain proficiency in ASL within six years. He feels it may be unreasonable to expect parents who hear to learn ASL in a short period of time.

Differences in grammar and syntax between ASL and English have created a controversy over the use of ASL with students with severe hearing losses. Many educators believe that ASL inhibits the acquisition of English. Others, principally researchers, believe that ASL is (or should be) the native language of children with severe hearing losses and they should learn it *before* they learn English.

PSE, SEE I, and SEE II are manually coded systems that preserve the syntactic patterns of English. Of the three, PSE comes closest to ASL. It uses the same signs and occasionally omits English function words and inflections. SEE I and SEE II are similar. Both systems maintain strict English structural patterns. In both, one morpheme equals one sign. (For example, the word *cats* would be signed with two morphemes: *cat* plus *s*.) The major difference between SEE I and SEE II is the way each treats compound words (such as *babysit, cowboy*). SEE I borrows signs from ASL; SEE II treats each part of the word (*baby, sit*) separately.

Finger Spelling. **Finger spelling** is writing in the air. The signs are presented in Figure 9.5. Instead of writing with a pencil, the child writes with his or her finger, spelling out each letter of the word. The practice was very common in the USSR in the 1970s and 1980s among preschool children who were hearing impaired; finger spelling was used in conjunction with speech (Gallagher, 1974; Moores, 1996). In the United States, finger spelling with speech is commonly known as the **Rochester method** (NICD, 1989). In Russia, finger spelling is a common way to begin teaching speech to preschoolers who are deaf or hard of hearing. In the United States, it is used to establish the letter-phoneme correspondence to reading.

Approaches to Teaching Communication

Total Communication Method. The **total communication method**, also known as the **simultaneous method** or **combined method**, combines finger spelling, signs (one of the several signed English systems), speech reading, speech, and auditory amplification. The Conference of Executives of American Schools for the Deaf (1976) defined *total communication* as a "philosophy requiring the incorporation of appropriate aural, manual, and oral modes of communication in order to insure effective communication with and among hearing impaired persons" (p. 358).

Combining the oral and aural (auditory) methods, total communication is the most common method of classroom communication; the oral-aural method is the next most common. The two procedures together were used by more than 90 percent of the schools surveyed. Manual communication by itself was not reported as a major mode of instruction in any school (Paul & Quigley, 1994).

Bilingual Approach. Some specialists in teaching people with hearing losses advocate postponing the introduction of speech. They believe that children should first be taught a gestural system and be introduced to oral language later, as if it were a second language (the first being the gestural one). Children with hearing losses who were taught in this manner would be considered bilingual. Children who are deaf would use ASL as their first language and the written or oral form of English as their second language. It should be noted that

Students who know ASL and written and oral English may be more proficient in ASL.

Figure 9.5
The Alphabet of Finger Spelling

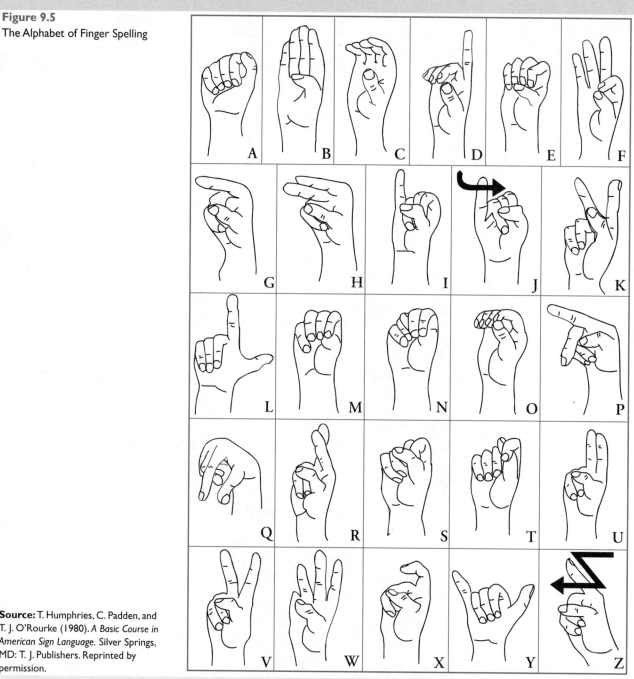

Source: T. Humphries, C. Padden, and T. J. O'Rourke (1980). *A Basic Course in American Sign Language*. Silver Springs, MD: T. J. Publishers. Reprinted by permission.

studies of persons who are bilingual indicate that they may develop full proficiency in only one of the two languages they speak. Therefore, an individual who is able to code-switch from ASL to the written or oral form of English with considerable linguistic skill may still be more proficient in the first language, in this case, ASL.

Teacher Strategies

Strategies under the control of the teacher are knowledge of subject matter and skill in communicating with children with severe hearing losses. The following additional instructional strategies also enhance the teaching and learning process:

- *Reinforcement.* The teacher should provide appropriate reinforcement and positive feedback.

- *Mastery learning.* The addition of teaching and feedback procedures to conventional instruction enhances learning.

- *Graded homework.* Meaningful homework that is assigned, graded, and responded to will increase learning.

- *Time on task.* There is a positive correlation between the time spent on a subject and the amount learned. This may seem a rather simplistic statement, but many teachers—particularly teachers of students with severe hearing losses in academic content areas—spend surprisingly little time on task.

- *Class morale.* Teachers should strive to maintain cohesiveness, satisfaction, and goal direction in the classroom.

- *Support.* Someone who can sign (the teacher or an interpreter) needs to be in the classroom.

An interpreter or a teacher who can sign needs to be in the general education classroom to support any students who are deaf or hard of hearing.

TECHNOLOGY

Assistive Technology

Assistive technology is any equipment or product that assists the learner with a disability. Federal law requires that assistive technology be considered for every student with a disability (U.S. Department of Education, 1997).

Hearing Aids. One of the most important developments in this century for those with hearing loss is the electronic hearing aid. Paul and Quigley (1994) explained how a hearing aid works:

> Three basic units are common to all amplification systems—the microphone, the amplifier, and the receiver. The microphone converts acoustic sound waves into a weaker but similar electrical energy. The amplifier driven by a power supply (usually a battery) increases the amplitude of the electrical signal. (pp. 45–47)

Thus, the receiver in the ear receives an electrical signal, which is transformed into speech.

The development of the transistor transformed hearing aids from heavy, cumbersome units to easily portable devices. And directional microphones have cut down on background noise, amplifying only the sounds coming from directly in front of the listener (Northern & Downs, 1978).

The following devices also facilitate hearing:

- Bone-anchored hearing aids.

- Augmentative communication devices (symbolic black-and-white outline drawings, pictorial symbols, pointers) (MacDonald & Gillette, 1986).

- Assistive listening devices (ALDs), which increase the volume of the voice received and reduce other sounds in the environment. They are wired or wireless and are small enough to be portable for use in vocational or recreational settings (Armstrong, Carr, Houghton, Belanich, & Mascia, 1995).

- A hardware device with a direct line to the earphone set and to the microphone.

- An induction loop device, which is an audio loop system that surrounds a seating area connected to a microphone and amplifies the sound received by the hearing aid. The loop may be small enough to be worn around the neck or as large as a room.

- Infrared devices, which transmit sound via invisible light waves. They can be directly connected to a hearing aid, to the ear without a hearing aid, or to a neck loop.

The teacher should receive information from the multidisciplinary team about each child who wears a hearing aid as to its operation and how to be sure the child is receiving sound. The audiologist is skilled in this area and will be an invaluable resource for the teacher. The audiologist will periodically check to be sure the aid is in good working order (English, 1995). Because some children will lip-read in addition to wearing their aid, the teacher should make every effort to look at these children when speaking.

Speech Viewer III. Speech Viewer III provides a variety of visual displays, such as a balloon getting larger in proportion to the loudness of the speaker's voice. The program is designed to improve voicing, pitch, timing, and sustained production (Mahshie, 1998). Another program, the CyberSign project, provides students with line illustrations of a number of signs (Nakamura, 1997). The ERIC Clearinghouse on Disabilities and Gifted Education is an excellent source in this rapidly evolving field.

TTY. A major advance in technology for children and adults with serious hearing losses is the teletypewriter-printer device (**TTY** or **TT**), which was developed in 1964 by an orthodontist and a physicist who were deaf. This machine enables persons with severe hearing losses to communicate by using a typewriter that transforms typed messages into electrical signals, then retranslates them into print at the other end of a telephone connector. To make a TTY call, the individual places an ordinary telephone receiver on a coupler modem or interface between the typewriter and the telephone. The acoustic coupler transforms the electrical signals into two sounds at different frequencies that are then transmitted over the telephone and converted back into printed letters on the receiving end (Compton & Brandt, n.d.). More sophisticated units that can work with a computer are available, and research is under way to determine how the TTY can be used to im-

Modern technology greatly facilitates communication for the deaf and hard of hearing.

prove social language skills (Rittenhouse, 1985). Telephone relay services are in every state. Their locations and telephone numbers are listed in the NICD bulletin *What are TTY's, TT's, and TDD's?* (1994).

A series of similar systems, known as telecommunication devices for the deaf (**TDDs**), have been generated over the past two decades. Currently, more than fifty thousand stations send, receive, and print messages on TDD systems. Although costs for the machines and the messages are high, the systems provide a very effective way for people with severe hearing losses to communicate across long distances (NICD, 1994).

Instructional Technology

Software programs to assist instruction are being developed at a rapid rate. High-speed computers make it possible to combine print, videos, sounds, and signs to help the student who is deaf or hard of hearing understand instruction. Multimedia programs are available that contain video dictionaries of sign language (usually ASL). When the user encounters an unfamiliar word, he or she moves the mouse and clicks the appropriate key, and a video appears with a person signing the word (Andrews and Jodron, 1998).

The usefulness of computers for children with hearing losses is comparable to their usefulness for those who have learning disabilities (see Chapter 6). Applied computer technology has advanced to such an extent that special word-processing systems can be used to translate written English into graphic finger spelling signed on the computer screen. The computer enables the student with severe hearing losses to practice both signed and written English.

Clymer and McKee (1997) report that 70 percent of the schools serving students who are deaf or hard of hearing have access to the Internet and the World Wide Web. Therefore, these students can have access to Web pages related to deafness, ASL, and deaf culture.

The majority of schools serving students who are deaf or hard of hearing have Internet access to Web pages related to deaf culture, sign language, and other deafness-related topics.

TRANSITION

Postsecondary Programs

In the mid-1960s, surveys of the vocational status of adults with severe hearing losses revealed some disturbing facts. The unemployment rate among the population was four times greater than that of hearing adults, and the level of employment was primarily fixed at unskilled or semiskilled positions (for example, see Moores, 1989). At about the same time, an effort to locate all persons with hearing losses who had enrolled in or graduated from regular colleges and universities was under way. It yielded just 653 persons, only 133 of them graduates, who had prelinguistic hearing losses (Quigley, Jenne, & Phillips, 1968). Clearly, one factor affecting the kinds of jobs that adults with severe hearing losses were finding was their limited educational opportunities.

Since the 1970s, the situation has changed. There are an increasing number of vocational programs for young adults with severe hearing losses. In 1967, the National Technical Institute for the Deaf was established in Rochester, New York. The institute, supported by the federal government, was founded to provide technical and vocational training for adolescents and adults with severe hearing losses.

New job opportunities come with educational opportunities. One academic alternative for students with severe hearing losses is Gallaudet University in Washington, D.C., the only college in the world devoted to the liberal arts education of students with severe hearing losses. The school is supported by the federal government. It is an accredited four-year liberal arts college and now includes a graduate school for deaf, hard-of-hearing, and hearing students. Gallaudet also operates the Kendall Demonstration Elementary School and the Model Secondary School for the Deaf.

Many state universities now have students with moderate-to-severe hearing losses on their campuses. They provide interpreting and note-taking services for these students. The impact of new educational opportunities is yet to be determined, but much depends on the quality of early education.

National Information Center on Deafness

The National Information Center on Deafness (NICD) is located at Gallaudet University, 800 Florida Avenue, NE, Washingotn, DC 20002-3695. It is a centralized source for information about hearing loss and deafness. NICD has a wealth of information available in a variety of written and visual forms, and at nominal cost.

Many universities provide students who have hearing losses with interpreters and other support services.

Family and Lifespan Issues

The most important inclusion required by law in educational programs for the deaf and hard of hearing is the family. Family-oriented approaches have resulted in children who are deaf or hard of hearing attaining better communication skills. Moreover, when stress is reduced within a family, better interaction usually occurs among its members (Moores, 1996). IDEA stresses that the family is central to intervention programs.

Focusing on the family system requires recognition of its strengths and respect for its values, beliefs, choices, and aspirations. It helps the family to recognize the critical role that sign language plays in the development of children who are deaf or severely hard of hearing. The child's development is facilitated when family members adopt interactive strategies, encouraging the child to request, respond, and take the initiative. All these interactive patterns are important factors in effective learning (Jamieson, 1994). They also stimulate the child to use language rather than shifting to the visual mode.

The teacher is faced with a dual problem—how to recognize the strengths of the family and how to improve (when necessary) the transaction patterns if parents are not aware of how they should be used to maximize the development of a child who is deaf or hard of hearing.

When the parents of a child who is deaf are also deaf, they are likely to prefer having the child learn a sign or manual language, usually ASL, first. Children in this situation are fortunate because they learn a language early and probably develop more quickly than children who are deaf and born to hearing parents, who may not recognize their child's condition for some time.

Most parents who can hear have little or no experience with deafness and may not know how to proceed with a child who is deaf. Feelings of guilt and helplessness are common. In many instances, they initially misperceive the condition, believing it to be an inability to speak rather than an inability to hear. They tend to resort to spanking more often (the child cannot hear other commands) and exhibit a great deal of frustration. In turn, they also tend to be overprotective of the child, and the child tends to be more dependent.

Summary of Major Ideas

1. Children with hearing losses fall into several categories: those with mild hearing loss, some residual hearing (hard of hearing), and severe hearing losses, usually prelinguistically impaired (deaf). With sound amplification, the child who is hard of hearing can understand speech; the child with severe hearing losses (deaf) usually cannot and must depend on a sign system.

2. Prelinguistic deafness is the loss of hearing before speech and language develop; postlinguistic deafness is the loss of hearing after speech and language develop. The child who has prelinguistic severe hearing losses faces the most serious learning problems.

3. A conductive hearing loss reduces the intensity of sound reaching the inner ear. A sensorineural hearing loss is caused by a defect of the inner ear or auditory nerve. Conductive losses can be reduced through sound amplification; sensorineural losses cannot.

4. Severe and profound hearing losses are usually identified before the child enters school, but a mild loss may go unnoticed. Teachers should be aware of certain behaviors that could indicate a child has a hearing loss.

5. The causes of hearing losses are equally divided between genetics and the environment. Environmental causes include complications during pregnancy and birth, childhood diseases, infections, and injuries.

6. Only one child in one thousand has a severe hearing loss (deafness), and only three or four in one thousand are hard of hearing.

7. Studies show that most children with serious hearing losses are cognitively normal. Their poor reading performance stems from their difficulty in reading and writing in English.

8. The difficulty children with severe hearing losses have in understanding the complex structure of the English language is a function of their limited opportunities to use that language on a daily basis.

9. The social adjustment of youngsters with severe hearing losses can be impeded by a lack of communication with those around them.

10. Most early intervention programs for youngsters with severe hearing losses make the parents a critical part of the process. Most elementary and secondary programs bring children who have severe hearing losses into the public schools, either in general education classrooms or in special classrooms.

There are a limited number of postsecondary programs for young adults who have severe hearing losses. Most offer vocational training.

11. Methods of teaching communication skills to students with severe hearing losses include the oral-aural method, the auditory method, and manual methods. Approaches to teaching communication include the total communication method and the bilingual approach. The total communication method combines oral and manual communication and is currently the most popular approach.

12. The use of signs and auditory training during the child's early developmental years have a positive effect on academic performance and adjustment.

13. Technology is having an impact on children with mild-to-severe hearing loss. The electronic hearing aid is used extensively, and computers give students the individual attention they need. Advances in telecommunications are allowing people with severe hearing losses to communicate across long distances. Cochlear implants offer the promise of increased hearing in some individuals. And captioned films and television programs are making visual channels more accessible.

14. Many of the problems facing adults with severe hearing losses in our society are job related. Limited language skills, poor educational and vocational training, and employer prejudice make finding appropriate jobs difficult. The underemployment and low-level employment of adults with severe hearing losses gives them a financial handicap in addition to their physical disability.

Employment Issues

1. *Employment prospects.* With respect to unemployment, occupational level, wage earnings, and opportunities for advancement, in all groups persons with severe hearing losses fare worse than the general U.S. population.

2. *Job performance.* The favorable reports of most supervisors regarding the job performance of their employees who have severe hearing losses indicate that employed young adults who have severe hearing losses perform well in their jobs, as does the supervisors' willingness to have more subordinates who have severe hearing losses and to advance them if they receive further training.

3. *Resources.* The vocational preparation resources for persons who are deaf are limited.

4. *Opportunities.* The opportunities for young adults with severe hearing losses to advance are limited. In spite of their employers' ratings of "average" or "above average" in the performance of their jobs, only a few of the employed young adults with severe hearing losses can advance beyond their present occupational levels without retraining or relocation (or both).

5. *Training and services.* An updating and upgrading of vocational training and ancillary services for young adults with severe hearing losses is long overdue.

6. *Postsecondary training.* A majority of current and former students who have severe hearing losses and their parents perceive a need for postsecondary training and indicate that they would support such programs if the opportunity were available. A majority of parents would prefer that postschool training for young adults who have severe hearing losses be provided in a facility for hearing students, with modifications including addi-

tional staff introduced to serve trainees who have severe hearing losses. Approximately 40 percent of the young adults with severe hearing losses have a preference for being educated with peers who have severe hearing losses (Moores, 1989).

Unresolved Issues

1. *Educating the multiply handicapped child with a hearing loss.* Approximately one of every four children with severe hearing losses has some other impairment. It is essential to design educational programs for these youngsters. At present, only a handful of pilot programs provide systemic education for children who are emotionally disturbed and have severe hearing losses or those with learning disabilities and severe hearing losses. If we want to see a change here, we must begin training teachers in the special needs of students who have multiple and profound disabilities as well as hearing losses.

2. *Stimulating language development.* The growing popularity of the total communication method reflects the importance of language to the academic performance of a child with a severe hearing loss. Our teaching of the structural and conceptual aspects of language must be organized in sequence so that youngsters can move from preschool to elementary to secondary programs that build on and reinforce earlier learning.

3. *Increasing occupational opportunities.* Although people with severe hearing losses are working, they are working at low-level, low-paying jobs. Even the availability of postsecondary vocational programs has not had a substantial impact on their employment. In a world where communication and language have become increasingly important, how do we broaden the opportunities of people with severe hearing losses so they can communicate in the hearing world? Most people who have severe hearing losses still find that interaction with the hearing world is both painful and difficult. As a consequence, they segregate themselves as adolescents and as adults. If we believe that integration is a valuable goal, we must provide the means by which those with severe hearing problems can be integrated successfully, both vocationally and socially.

4. *The factors that facilitate speech reading.* We must determine what factors are at work in the speech-reading process. "Speech reading, the hallmark of education for those with severe hearing losses, remains an enigma. Even those persons with severe hearing losses who are proficient lip readers are unable to explain how they acquired the ability or what factors enable them to use this method to understand speech" (Farwell, 1976, p. 27). Obviously, it is impossible to teach a skill efficiently if we do not understand the factors that operate in helping the individual master the skill.

5. *Improving teacher-training programs.* Most teacher-training programs reflect traditional philosophies and methodologies, not the innovative educational approaches suggested by research findings. All too often, the preparation of teachers and the operation of research programs are mutually exclusive functions. Until teacher-training programs begin to integrate preparation and research through faculty appointments and university emphases, the students who graduate from traditional programs may continue to use methods that are not working.

6. *Teaching reading and English language to children with severe hearing losses.* Many adolescents who have severe hearing losses graduate from high school today with little control over the English language. Although the education of those with severe hearing losses has changed markedly over the course of this century, more improvements are needed. With new findings in language and cognitive research and new materials, we may see some changes in the achievement of youngsters with severe hearing losses. Of course, this means that new findings and materials must be assimilated directly into teacher-training programs if we want them to be implemented as soon as possible.

Key Terms

acoupedic method p. 376

acoustic method p. 376

American Sign Language (ASL) p. 376

audiogram p. 364

audiometer p. 364

auditory global method p. 376

auditory method p. 375

aural method p. 375

bone-conductor test p. 365

central hearing loss p. 348

combined method p. 377

conductive hearing loss p. 346

deaf p. 346

decibels (dB) p. 346

finger spelling p. 377

hard of hearing p. 346

manual method p. 375

mixed hearing loss p. 348

oral-aural method p. 375

postlinguistic deafness p. 346

prelinguistic deafness p. 346

pure-tone test p. 365

Rochester method p. 377

sensorineural hearing loss p. 348

simultaneous method p. 377

speech reading p. 375

TDD p. 381

total communication method p. 377

TTY p. 380

unisensory method p. 376

Questions for Thought

1. Explain the difference between a conductive hearing loss and a sensorineural hearing loss.   pp. 346–347

2. What are three causes of conductive hearing loss and three causes of sensorineural hearing loss?   p. 352

3. To be able to identify possible hearing problems, what should the classroom teacher watch for?   pp. 363–364

4. What are the primary objectives of early intervention programs? pp. 368–370

5. What three factors still hinder the academic achievement of students who are deaf or hard of hearing?   pp. 371–372

6. What are several things that parents can do at home to help encourage the academic achievement of their child who is deaf or hearing impaired? pp. 372–373

7. Explain how speech reading is taught and why it is an important skill.   p. 375

8. What is the bilingual approach to teaching persons who are deaf or hard of hearing, and how does it work?   pp. 377–378

9. How are hearing aids, TTYs, TDDs, used?   pp. 379–381

10. How have computers and other technological advances helped persons who are deaf or hard of hearing?   p. 381

Resources for Further Study

REFERENCES OF SPECIAL INTEREST

American Speech-Hearing-Language Association. (1991). *ASHA, Supplement H, 33*(3). This guide to position statements on children with hearing impairments or speech and language disorders is a must for all speech-language and hearing pathologists as a professional guide to practice.

Batshaw, M. L. (Ed.) (1997). *Children with disabilities: A medical primer.* Baltimore: Paul H. Brookes. A comprehensive guide to all disabilities, with a focus on medical causes and treatments, this book includes both genetic and environmentally induced dysfunctions. It is amply illustrated with photographs and diagrams of aids for children with disabilities.

Dolnic, E. (1993). Deafness as culture. *The Atlantic Monthly, 272,* 37–53. In an accessible article, the writer explains the meaning and importance of the deaf culture in American society.

English, K. (1995). *Educational audiology across the lifespan.* Baltimore: Paul H. Brookes. The author describes the role of audiologists in the education of persons with hearing disabilities. The text includes suggestions for practice as well as ways in which an audiologist can contribute to collaborative teams.

Moores, D. (1996). *Educating the deaf: Psychology, principles, and practices* (4th ed.). Boston: Houghton Mifflin. This comprehensive textbook on children with severe hearing losses provides a rich historical background and up-to-date reports on current research, educational trends, and preschool and postsecondary programs.

Moores, D., & Meadows-Orlan, K. P. (Eds.). (1990). *Educational and developmental aspects of deafness.* Washington, DC: Gallaudet University Press. The articles in this collection cover a wide variety of topics on deafness.

Paul, P., & Quigley, S. (1994). *Language and deafness* (2nd ed.). San Diego: Singular. This is a comprehensive, readable report on the various issues and controversies surrounding the education of children with mild-to-severe hearing losses. The authors offer an especially good review of essential research over the past decade and present the findings on the effectiveness of different communication systems in an evenhanded way.

JOURNALS

American Annals of the Deaf
Gallaudet University, KDES, PAS-6
800 Florida Ave., NE
Washington, DC 20002

The Volta Review
3417 Volta Place, NW
Washington, DC 20007

PROFESSIONAL ORGANIZATIONS

Alexander Graham Bell Association for the Deaf
3417 Volta Place, NW
Washington, DC 20007
http://www.agbell.org

ERIC Clearing House on Disabilities and Gifted Education
The Council for Exceptional Children
1920 Association Drive
Reston, VA 20191-1589
1-888-CEC-SPED
TTY 703-264-9449
http://www.cec.sped.org/bk/ec-jour.htm

Gallaudet University
800 Florida Ave., NE
Washington, DC 20002-3695
http://www.gallaudet.edu

National Association of the Deaf
Captioned Film/Video Program
814 Thayer Ave.
Silver Springs, MD 20910
http://www.nad.org/
http://www.cfv.org/

National Information Center on Deafness (NICD)
Gallaudet University
800 Florida Ave., NE
Washington, DC 20002-3695
http://www.gallaudet.edu/~nicd

10

Children with Visual Impairments

FOCUSING
questions

What effects do limited visual experiences have on the development of children with visual impairments?

Why is learned helplessness a problem for many children who are visually impaired?

How do we adapt the instructional program for youngsters with visual impairments?

What effects has technology had on the communication skills and mobility of children and youth with visual impairments?

How does the philosophy of inclusion affect the education of these special students?

About one child in ten enters school with some visual impairment. Fortunately, most of these problems can be fully corrected with glasses and have little or no effect on social or educational development. But for one child in a thousand, visual impairments are so severe they cannot be corrected. In this chapter, we discuss the special needs of children who are visually impaired and the educational adaptation that are—or should be—made for them.

Definitions

Visual impairments fall along a continuum ranging from normal vision to profound visual disability (blindness). The smallest number of children are found at the blindness end of the continuum. Visual impairments can be classified in several ways. Legally, a definition distinguishes blind and partially sighted or low-vision children on the basis of tests of visual acuity. A child who is legally blind can see, with correction, at only 20/200 or less. This means that the child can see only at 20 feet what someone with normal sight can see at 200 feet. Legal blindness does not necessarily mean that a child has no visual stimulation at all; the child may be able to sense light and darkness and may have some visual imagery. A child who scores between 20/70 and 20/200 on tests of visual acuity, with correction, is legally partially sighted. The term *low vision* refers to children and adults whose vision is 20/200 or less and who read print or braille when assisted by a variety of devices.

More and more, levels of visual impairment are being defined in educational terms, which are very different from legal terms that focus on distance of effective sight. Educational classifications are *moderate, severe,* and *profound* and are based not on tests of visual acuity but on the special educational adaptations that are necessary to help these children learn (Table 10.1).

A **moderate visual disability** can be almost entirely corrected with the help of visual aids, either in the regular classroom or in a resource room. A **severe visual disability** is helped only somewhat with visual aids; still, the child can use vision as a channel for learning. This classification is equivalent to the definition of a child with partial sight. A child with a **profound visual disability** cannot use vision as an educational tool. For this child, touch and hearing are the predominant learning channels.

Visual Interpretation and the Human Eye

Vision or visual interpretation is a function of the brain, experience, and the adequacy of the sense organ that receives stimuli from the outside world: the eye. Faulty visual interpretation can result from a defect in the brain, inadequate experience, or a defective eye. The process of visual interpretation is as follows: Light enters the eye, focuses on the retina, and is transmitted along the optic nerve to the brain, where visual information is interpreted. Two people with well-functioning sense organs can interpret a visual experience differently, depending on their training and experience.

Educators of children with visual impairments are concerned primarily with adapting instruction to the impairment. To accomplish this, they need to under-

TABLE 10.1	Educational Characteristics of Children with Visual Disabilities
Level of Visual Disability	**Performance Capability**
Moderate	With use of special aids and lighting, child can perform visual tasks almost like students with normal vision.
Severe	In performance of visual tasks, child may need more time and energy and be less accurate even with visual aids and modifications.
Profound	Performance of even gross visual tasks may be very difficult, and detailed tasks cannot be handled visually at all.

Source: Adapted from N. Barraga (1986). "Sensory Perceptual Development." In G. Scholl (Ed.), *Foundations of Education for Blind and Visually Handicapped Children and Youth*, p. 86. New York: American Foundation for the Blind. Adapted from A. Colenbrander (1977). "Dimensions of Visual Performance," *Transactions of the American Academy of Ophthalmology and Otolaryngology, 83*, pp. 332–335.

Vision is a function of the sensation and perception of light.

stand how healthy eyes operate and what some of the conditions are that can cause problems.

THE HUMAN EYE

The human eye is a complex system of interrelated parts (Figure 10.1). Any part can be defective or become nonfunctional as a result of hereditary anomaly, disease, accident, or other causes.

The eye has been called a camera for the brain. Like a camera, the eye has a diaphragm, the **iris.** The iris is the colored muscular partition that expands and contracts to regulate the amount of light admitted through the central opening, or **pupil.** Behind the iris is the **lens,** an elastic biconvex body that focuses onto the retina the light reflected from objects in the line of vision. The **retina** is the light-sensitive innermost layer of tissue at the back of the eyeball. It contains neural receptors that translate the physical energy of light into the neural energy that results in the experience of seeing.

As Figure 10.1 shows, other protective and structural elements in the eye can affect vision. The **cornea** is the transparent anterior (front) portion of the tough outer coat of the eyeball. The **ciliary muscles** change the shape of the lens so the eye can focus on objects at varying distances. In the normal mature eye, no muscular effort is necessary to see clearly objects 20 feet or more away. When the eye looks at an object closer than 20 feet, the ciliary muscles increase the convex curvature of the lens so that the closer object is still focused on the retina. This change in the shape of the lens is called **accommodation.**

Figure 10.1
The Human Eye

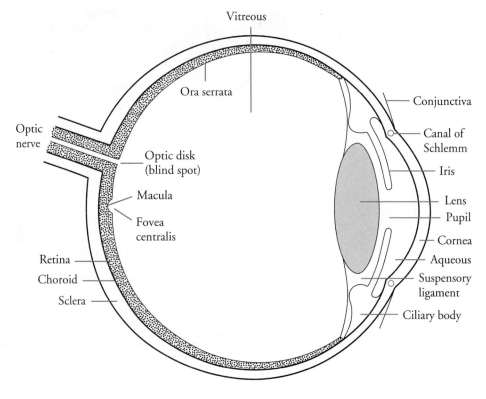

Source: From Prevent Blindness America. (1994). Vision problems in the U.S. (pamphlet). Schaumburg, IL: Author; reprinted with permission of Prevent Blindness America®.

Extrinsic muscles control the movement of the eyeball in the socket. The change made by these muscles is known as **convergence.**

CAUSES OF VISUAL IMPAIRMENTS

A wide variety of conditions can cause serious visual impairments in children from birth to age 5. Common disorders—for example, **hyperopia** (farsightedness) and **myopia** (nearsightedness)—are almost always correctable with glasses.

The potential causes of visual impairment in children range from hereditary conditions to infectious diseases, to cancer, to injuries, to various environmental conditions. The actual cause of the disorder is not of primary interest to the teacher, who must deal with the functional consequences of the disorders—those functional consequences would seem to be similar from one condition to another. So whether the cause was an infection or a hereditary condition, a similar problem of limited vision is faced by the teacher. Knowing the actual diagnosis may be useful in long-term team planning for the student but not in the actual instruction that takes place (Bishop, 1986).

The widely scattered prevalence of these conditions makes it difficult to assign percentages to particular causes, but some of them are reasonably well known as major causes. One of the most common infectious diseases is rubella (German measles), contracted by the mother during pregnancy. Rubella can cause serious birth defects, mental retardation, and hearing loss in addition to visual problems, but improved control measures and education have combined to reduce the percentage of children blinded by this and other infectious diseases.

Another major cause of visual impairment is **retinopathy of prematurity** (formerly called *retrolental fibroplasia*). This disorder was widely believed to be caused by the overadministration of oxygen to premature infants in an attempt to save the life of the child threatened by other conditions. We now are not so sure that the simple answer of too much oxygen is correct. The condition appears more complicated. For example, it seems to be associated with low birth weight as well.

Another cause of visual impairment is **retinoblastoma,** a tumor of the eye that causes blindness. The condition is often found in the first years of life and is progressive, so heroic measures of treatment such as chemotherapy or radiation or surgery are required to treat it.

Because there have been future projections of more children with multiple disabilities, and because some conditions such as AIDS may also result in visual problems in children, there is a likelihood of more children with visual problems to be educated, with their condition complicated by a variety of other problems as well.

Characteristics of Children with Visual Impairments

One of the most serious obstacles to understanding children with visual impairment is the limited amount of scholarly work being done on the topic. Warren (1994) has done an admirable job of pulling together what is available, but on many significant topics information is scanty and dated. Warren is particularly concerned that parents do not misunderstand the general findings: Children with visual impairments tend to develop at a slower pace than children without disabilities; there is a wide variation in the development of children with visual impairments; and with a rich physical environment and with encouragement to take reasonable risks, parents can increase the adaptive skills of their children.

INTELLECTUAL DEVELOPMENT

In the 1940s and 1950s, educators generally believed that the intelligence of children with visual impairments was not seriously affected by their condition, except for their ability to use certain visual concepts (colors and three-dimensional space, for example). The thinking then was that intelligence unfolds on a genetically determined schedule and is affected by only the most severe environmental trauma. Samuel Hayes (1941) modified the Stanford-Binet for children with visual impairments. His examination of more than two thousand youngsters revealed overall average IQ scores.

Today, we hold a different view of intelligence. We recognize that what we measure as intelligence in school-age children has been notably affected by their cumulative experiences in the early years of development. Lack of vision, then, is both a primary impairment and a condition that can hamper cognitive development because it limits the integrating experiences and the understanding of those

Visual impairment can hamper cognitive development.

experiences that the visual sense brings naturally to sighted children (Kephart, Kephart, & Schwartz, 1974; Tillman & Osborne, 1969). These limitations are especially notable if the children do not receive early intervention in the preschool years.

One of the newest attempts to measure the intelligence of children with visual impairment—the Intelligence Test for Visually Impaired Children (ITVIC)—is based on Warren's (1994) primary factors. The designers of this test identified four measurable areas: orientation, reasoning, spatial perception, and verbal ability; verbal ability and reasoning are closely tied to school achievement (Dekker, Drenth, & Zool, 1991). The ITVIC is one of the few tests specifically designed for such children (as opposed to being adapted from tests designed for sighted children, such as the Hayes-Binet).

A new test of intelligence, the ITVIC, has much promise for children with visual impairment.

LANGUAGE DEVELOPMENT

Sighted children acquire language by listening, reading, and watching movements and facial expressions. They express themselves first through babbling and later by imitating their parents and siblings. Children with visual impairments acquire language in much the same way, but their language concepts are not helped by reading or visual input. A sighted child develops the concept of a ball by seeing different balls; a child with blindness develops the same concept through tactile manipulation of different balls. Both are able to understand the word *ball*, and both are able to identify a ball.

A series of investigations into the language development of children with visual impairments yielded the following conclusions. Visual impairment does not interfere with everyday language usage or communication abilities. The language of children with visual impairments seems like that of their sighted peers (Civelli, 1983; Matsuda, 1984). However, the children with visual impairments had less understanding of words as vehicles, or as standing for, concrete experiences, and they were slower than sighted children to form hypotheses about word meaning. Children with severe visual impairment appeared to be restricted to word meanings from their own personal experience, whereas vision allowed children to broaden and generalize the meanings of words (Anderson, Dunlea, & Kekelis, 1984; Dunlea, 1989).

Visual impairment limits children's conceptual understanding and generalizations in language and vocabulary.

Warren (1994), in a review of the literature on the language of those with visual impairments, arrived at these conclusions:

> It is clear from the literature that the vocabulary of children with visual impairments is heavily grounded in their own perceptual experience and is not simply a parroting of sighted vocabulary. . . . This underscores the importance of the parents' role in ensuring not only that the child's perceptual experience is adequately rich, but also that it is embedded in a context of shared communication. (p. 326)

SENSORY COMPENSATION AND PERCEPTION

Vision is a continuous source of information. We depend on vision to orient ourselves, to identify people and objects, and to regulate our motor and social behavior. People without sight have to rely on other senses for information and for all the other tasks that vision performs. How this is accomplished has been the focus of much speculation and research.

The false doctrine of **sensory compensation** holds that if one sense, such as vision, is deficient other senses are automatically strengthened, in part because of their greater use. Although this may be true in certain cases, research does not show that the hearing or touch sensitivity of children with profound visual handicaps is superior to that of sighted children. For example, Gottesman (1971) tested children ages 2 to 8 who were blind and who were sighted on their ability to identify by touch such things as a key, a comb, a pair of scissors, and geometric forms (triangle, cross). He found no difference between the groups.

PERSONAL AND SOCIAL ADJUSTMENT

No personal or social problems *inevitably* follow from being visually impaired. However, the restricted mobility and consequent limited experiences of children who are visually impaired appear to cause, in some children, a state of passivity and dependency.

The increasing interest in the social adjustment of students with visual impairments resulted in a study of the lifestyles of blind, low-vision, and sighted adolescents (Sacks, Wolffe, & Tierney, 1998). Using a device called a time diary, in which the students identified their primary and secondary activities in 1-hour blocks of time over a 24-hour period, the investigators found that students with visual impairments spent more time on the telephone, engaged in more sedentary activities, spent more time alone, and were bound to their homes by their inability to travel independently.

The students with visual impairments who were chosen for this study had no other impairments and were close to grade level in performance. One could anticipate that children with multiple impairments would fare even worse in the social domain than did these students.

There is a need for programs that prepare students with visual impairments for adult life.

What this study seems to indicate is a need for continued implementation of programs designed to prepare students with visual impairments for adult life. That would mean curricula that focus on career development and social skill competencies. Of course, the study also underscores the importance of mobility training as a key component to social contact for these students.

The teacher of the visually impaired must deal with many realistic issues, for example, spatial perception and communication. It is understandable that the teacher might overlook an issue that turns out to be one of the most important—how the child feels about his or her situation. Recently, there has been an attempt to focus on the child's feelings and to make them a significant part of the instructional program. The child who is deeply depressed and feeling helpless is not a good candidate for braille, print reading, or anything else (Tuttle & Tuttle, 1996). For example, a child who is trying to deny the reality of blindness may resist special learning devices like viewers or magnifying glasses since they symbolize the disability.

There comes to the child with a disability (and to all of us, for that matter) the realization that some things will never be possible (I will never see the stars; I will never know what my mother looks like or when she smiles at me). The reaction to such a realization almost certainly will be disappointment and despair.

For example, the child who is being introduced to braille has to cope with another sensation:

> Reluctantly I began examining my [braille] chart again, not pacified but accepting the inevitable, and the inevitable was bittersweet. I had believed that by going to school I would be able to read the printed page. Though I was only five, I knew now that this would never happen. (Brown, 1958, pp. 18–19)

Several principles have formed the basis of a strategy to help the child go beyond these feelings of self-pity and despair and create a climate of self-expression and self-esteem.

Successful coping includes the following:

- The emphasis is on what a person can do.
- The areas of life in which the person can participate are seen as worthwhile.
- The person is perceived as playing an active role in molding his or her life constructively.
- The accomplishments of the person are appreciated in terms of their benefits to the person and others and not primarily depreciated because they fall short of some irrelevant standard.
- The negative aspects of the person's life, such as the pain that is suffered or difficulties that exist, are felt to be manageable.
- Managing difficulties, in one sense, means overcoming them or ameliorating them through the application of medical procedures, the use of prostheses and other aids, the learning of new skills, and environmental accommodations (social, legal, economic, and so on).
- Managing difficulties also means living on satisfactory terms with one's limitations. (Tuttle & Tuttle, 1996, p. 169)

The role of the teacher in the development of personal and social adjustment is critically important. Martin and Hoben (1977) offered the thoughts of some students with visual impairments about how they had been treated in school:

- Teachers should learn what "legally blind" really means. Lots of legally blind kids can do all sorts of things.
- If a teacher treats me different, the other kids think I'm a teacher's pet.
- I don't want to see an "A" on my report card when I know I earned a "C."
- It's more fun, more challenge when you have to compete. You don't feel like you're an outsider.
- I appreciate the opportunity to get a better position in the classroom, but when the teacher asks me about it in front of the class it makes me feel like an idiot. I would tell teachers: if you want to tell me something that will help, don't make me feel like an idiot doing it. (p. 19)

Many sighted people who have not worked with children who are visually impaired tend to have low expectations of those children's abilities.

Loosely translated, those students were saying, "Don't treat me like I'm helpless. Don't do me any special favors. Let me do it on my own." Many people who have not had experience with persons with disabilities react to them by lowering their expectations. But those students didn't want this kind of favor.

Self-esteem and self-acceptance in children with visual impairments are nurtured by positive interactions with sighted people. (© *Ellen Senisi/The Image Works*)

Great interest has been shown in the self-esteem of students with visual disabilities. However, self-esteem appears to be the by-product of good performance on tasks deemed socially valuable (for example, effective mobility around class and school). Good academic and social behavior will result in good self-esteem rather than the other way around.

After surveying the literature on the self-concepts of children who are blind, Warren (1994) stated that the studies found no overall differences. He noted, however, that "to the extent that people expect of the child that he will not differ from a sighted child, the tendency for the blind child's self-concept to be different from that of the sighted child will be decreased" (p. 232). There would seem to be nothing about visual impairment that increases the likelihood of behavior problems in this group. The sense of self for such youngsters seems similar to that of youngsters from the average community (Warren, 1994, p. 280).

What happens to children with visual impairments over time? Does the lack of experience with the world around them cause developmental problems in motor and social domains? These questions have been difficult to answer because the relative infrequency of such children made it hard to bring together sufficient children to conduct a convincing study.

Recently, however, a prospective national study of children with visual impairments was combined with agency data from a southern state to create a sample of 186 children (ages 1–7) who had developmental curves that could answer these questions (Hatton, Bailey, Burchinal, & Ferrell, 1997). The majority of these children had visual impairments that stemmed from retinopathy of prematurity ($n = 41$), optic nerve hypoplasia ($n = 35$), cortical visual impairment ($n = 19$), and albinism ($n = 14$). Forty percent of the sample also had a co-occurring condition of mental retardation or developmental disabilities.

The results clearly indicated delays in motor and social domains, with less delay in communications. The development of those with the worst vision (worse than 20/800) was clearly different from those with the most vision (20/70 to 20/200). The children with the additional condition of mental retardation and developmental disabilities were significantly slower than those who did not have that additional condition.

Such results are a clear message of the importance of beginning specific developmental experiences to the child with visual impairment during the preschool age range. The negative results of the failure to take early actions are cumulative and sure to affect school performance.

Developmental Profiles

People with normal sight wonder from time to time what it would be like to be blind. It's obvious that adapting to sensory loss has implications that are profoundly personal and social as well as educational. A comprehensive special education program must involve all areas of development and adjustment. We introduce developmental profiles here of two visually impaired youngsters to highlight some of the problems children with visual handicaps have in adapting to their disability. Figure 10.2 shows the patterns of development of Renaldo and Susan. Renaldo has a severe visual disability; Susan, a profound visual disability. Both are being educated in public schools where special provisions, personnel, and equipment are available.

Renaldo is a tall, slim 11-year-old who has a severe visual impairment for which maximum correction has been obtained with the aid of thick glasses. He can read print material and, in the early grades, was able to make a reasonable academic adjustment. As the profile in Figure 10.2 shows, Renaldo scored slightly above average in intelligence as measured by an adaptation of the Stanford-Binet and is currently doing average work as measured by achievement tests administered with no time limits. Yet this profile, though favorable, tends to mask the academic problems Renaldo is likely to encounter. He will be required to use higher thought processes as he progresses through the educational system, and he is already beginning to experience the shift from concrete arithmetic to the more difficult (for him) abstractions of algebra and spatial concepts of geometry.

Renaldo spends most of his time in school with a regular sixth-grade class but leaves the program for about an hour a day to work with a specially trained resource teacher. Only three or four other youngsters are in the resource room with Renaldo, so the teacher can give him a good deal of tutoring in the academic areas in which he needs help.

Of more concern is how Renaldo feels about himself. His visual handicap is serious enough that he is sometimes unsure whether he belongs to the sighted community or to the blind community. He feels deeply about his awkwardness and inability to perform in athletics—an important dimension in the life of an 11-year-old—but he does not discuss this with his schoolmates.

Figure 10.2

Profiles of Two Children with Different Degrees of Visual Impairment

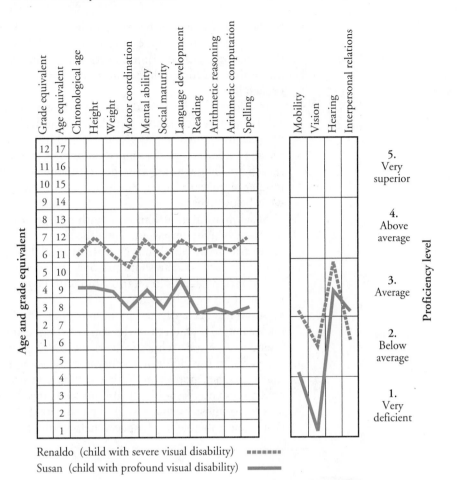

Renaldo (child with severe visual disability) ▪▪▪▪▪▪▪▪

Susan (child with profound visual disability) ——————

Renaldo also has some interpersonal problems. He reacts with a sharp tongue and a quick temper to any slights or negative comments, real or imagined, about his impairment. Consequently, many of the other youngsters ignore or avoid him except when class participation requires interaction. Above all, Renaldo is beginning to wonder about his future: What is he going to do with his life when he grows up? How can he be independent? How will he establish friendships with girls? This is a topic of great importance to his older brother, Brian, who is in high school and whose life seems to revolve around girls. Brian's behavior is a source of amusement to Renaldo now, but in a few years he will have to face social relationship problems more seriously.

Susan's profile is also shown in Figure 10.2. She is an average-looking 9-year-old who has been blind since birth. Like many children who are blind, she has limited light perception that helps her move around, but she cannot read print. She has mastered the Grade 2 braille system, which uses contractions, letter combinations, and shortened forms of words to save time and space in reading. In some respects, Susan is making a better adjustment than Renaldo, despite her more severe handicap. She has a warm, understanding mother who has given her strong emotional support and a professional father who provides a comfortable income for the family. Her mother has tried to be a companion for Susan and has read to her extensively from the time Susan was 3 or 4 years of age. She has helped Susan through some difficult times, particularly when Susan was having trouble mastering braille. Susan's father is more distant; he doesn't seem to know how to approach her.

In addition to her visual handicap, Susan shows some signs of mild neurological damage, which tends to make her physically awkward, but this condition is not serious enough to classify her as multiply disabled. As the developmental profile shows, Susan's performance on tests of mental ability and her development in speech and language are average, testimony perhaps to the intensive work with her mother in the early years. But in arithmetic and spelling, her performance is somewhat below average.

Susan lives in an urban area with a large population where a number of children are visually impaired. The school system buses these children from around the district to a school that provides a special program for them. Susan is well accepted by her classmates and has one or two close sighted friends. She has not yet had to face problems in relationship with boys or to deal with the often cruel behavior of young adolescents.

Susan has been affected in an important way by the educational trend of placing exceptional children in the least restrictive environment. She does not have to attend a large state school for persons with blindness far from her home and family, as did many children a generation or so ago. Sometime in the next three or four years, her mother and father will have to decide whether they want her to attend a residential school that provides advanced curriculum and educational facilities for youngsters with visual impairments. But for now, they are happy that she is at home and able to get special help within the local school system.

Early Intervention

A child's experiences during the period from birth to age 5 are critical to subsequent development. It is especially important that the systematic education of visually impaired children begin as early as possible. Sighted children absorb a tremendous amount of information and experience from their environment in the ordinary course of events. Parents and teachers must specially design parallel experiences for children who are visually impaired (see Chapter 3 for more information).

The characteristics we observe in a 10-year-old who has visual impairment are often a blend of the primary problem (loss of vision) and a number of secondary problems that have developed because the child has missed certain sequential experiences. For example, many youngsters with a visual disability are passive. Passivity is not a natural or inevitable by-product of low vision; it is present because the child does not have a well-established motivation to move.

For the sighted child, the environment is filled with visual stimulation: toys, bottles, people, color, and shapes. The child has a natural impulse to move toward these elements. The child with a severe visual disability isn't aware of these elements unless someone points them out. For a child who is blind, the bottle appears magically. The child is not motivated to go after it; in fact, the child does not even realize that he or she can do something—be active—to get the bottle.

When adapting instruction to the educational needs of children who are visually impaired, teachers should emphasize concreteness, unifying experiences, and learning by doing. *(© Steve Goldberg/ Monkmeyer Press Photo Service)*

 *It is important to let children take control of a task once they demonstrate an ability to do so.*

An easily understood concept for the sighted child is **object permanence.** By the age of 6 or 7 months, sighted children realize that even when objects disappear from their visual field (mother left the room; the ball rolled under the couch), they still exist. This knowledge makes the world more orderly and predictable. And it makes sense to go after objects even if they are not in the line of sight. Object constancy is a more difficult concept for children with visual disabilities to understand. They need deliberate instruction and an organized environment before they can understand the concept and begin to act on it.

Although it's important to help visually impaired youngsters learn tasks, it's also important to let them take over when they are able. Ferrell (1986) described a technique called **fading,** or gradually cutting back help as a child becomes competent at a task. She showed how the process works with the task of eating:

1. Begin by placing your hand completely around the child's hand as the child grasps the spoon. Move the child through the scooping and eating motions.

2. As the child gains control, continue the scooping and eating motions with your hand on the child's wrist.

3. Gradually move your hand from the wrist to the arm, and then to the elbow.

4. Eventually, just touch the arm to remind the child what he or she is supposed to do.

By teaching young children with visual disabilities to do things for themselves, we give these children some of the important experiences that sighted children get naturally.

It is important for parents and teachers to give the child with visual disabilities the opportunity to indicate what he or she wants and not to anticipate the child's needs. "By doing so, they eliminate the child's choice and control of the situation and they foster his dependence. Independence training begins in infancy, not at age 2, 6, or when college is imminent" (Ferrell, 1986, p. 130).

So much of what is important for young children to learn is learned naturally through the visual sense (Piaget & Inhelder, 1969). For youngsters with impairments, that same learning must come through careful planning and instruction. Parents and teachers must work together to see that these children have important experiences and the independence to learn from them.

The importance of starting education early for children with visual impairments was pointed to in a study of thirteen children with visual impairments who were 40 months of age (Hughes, Dote-Kwan, & Dolendo, 1998). The study looked at the play behavior of these children in a special play setting. The results agreed with earlier studies in that the children with visual impairments were significantly delayed in their play skills, particularly symbolic play. Because the children were functioning at expected developmental levels in other domains, such as receptive language, the study underlined the importance of helping these children to develop and facilitate their play behavior. This is particularly important considering the heavy emphasis on play in the usual inclusive preschool settings.

The Individuals with Disabilities Education Act (IDEA), which mandates services for infants and toddlers with disabilities (see Chapter 2), provides for earlier identification and earlier professional services for children with vision problems. Such early intervention programs should reduce the number of secondary problems shown by children who did not have the advantages of earlier services. The work cited in Chapter 3 on early intervention provides additional evidence on the usefulness of early attention.

Educators have also become increasingly sensitive to the importance of the early emotional life of children who are blind. Barraga (1983) provided a representative point of view: "With the visually impaired infant, body play must replace eye play to communicate maternal concerns and love—the facilitators of developing a self-concept. More than the usual amount of time should be spent cuddling, holding, touching, stroking and moving the baby" (p. 31).

Children with visual impairments may exhibit delays in their play skills.

Identification

Most children with severe and profound visual disabilities are identified by parents and physicians long before they enter school. The most common exceptions are children with multiple disabilities. It is possible for another condition—for example, cerebral palsy or mental retardation—to mask a visual impairment. The key to identification is a comprehensive examination. Many of these components do not require formal testing, just the observations of those around the child. For example, the family can be very helpful in determining whether a child has mastered functional living skills. And a classroom teacher is a good source of information about a child's social and emotional development.

Most states require preschool vision screening, which identifies children with moderate vision problems. Throughout this textbook, we discuss the importance of early experiences in cognitive development. Obviously, early identification allows us to broaden those experiences for the child with a visual disability through maximum correction and preschool programs.

Mild, correctable visual impairments often go undiagnosed until a child enters elementary school. School systems use different methods to detect visual impairments in children. Some refer children with suspected problems directly to an ophthalmologist or an optometrist. Others routinely screen youngsters to determine whether they have vision difficulties, and they refer those who do not pass that screening for more comprehensive assessment.

The standard school screening instrument is the Snellen chart, which has rows of letters in gradually smaller sizes that children read at a distance of 20 feet. A variation that is useful for screening young children and people who do not know letter names consists of capital *E*s pointing in different directions. The individual is asked to indicate the direction in which the arms of the *E* are pointing. Scores are based on how accurately the subject identifies the letters (or directions of the *E*s) using one eye at a time. A reading of 20/20 is normal.

The National Society for the Prevention of Blindness is the oldest voluntary health agency involved in preventing blindness. For preschoolers and school-age children, it has developed a number of screening tests that use the Snellen chart or modifications of it. For infants, evaluation is based on observation of how the eyes are used. For 3- to 5-year-olds, both observation and the Snellen *E* chart are used. The consensus is that early diagnosis and treatment can prevent visual impairments in some children.

Figure 10.3 provides examples of some near-acuity cards provided by the Lighthouse for the Blind. These lists would seem to have considerable advantage over the typical Snellen chart for low-vision children. It becomes important to know what the students can read at near point, and the gradations of print here can give some understanding of the student's limits in responding to print.

More extensive tests use elaborate equipment (such as the Keystone Telebinocular and the Bausch & Lomb Orthorater) to measure vision at far and near points and to test muscle balance, fusion, usable vision, and other characteristics. The Titmus Vision Tester (manufactured by Titmus, P.O. Box 191, Petersburg, VA 23804) is the most widely used test of visual acuity and is used to screen vision in preschool children, school-age children, and adults. Most people who have taken a driver's license test have been screened for vision problems by the Titmus.

Once a vision problem is discovered, the extent of the problem can be identified by using the Program to Develop Efficiency in Visual Functioning (Barraga, 1983). This scale assesses the level of visual functioning by presenting a series of increasingly smaller words, sentences, and pictures. The purpose of the test is to determine the extent to which a child is able to use his or her vision even though that vision is impaired.

Just as the pediatrician is the first line for identifying children with disabilities in preschool years, so the teacher is the prime source of identification of mild disabilities in school-age youngsters. Efforts have been made to sensitize classroom teachers to identify exceptional children.

"Blind Student Leaps Barriers"

Sure but sightless, Timothy Cordes arrived on the campus of the University of Notre Dame four years ago, an 18-year-old freshman from Eldridge, Iowa, who wanted to enroll in the biochemistry program.

Faculty members tried, politely, to dissuade him. Just how, they wondered aloud, could a blind student keep up with the rigorous courses and demanding laboratory work of biochemistry?

Mr. Cordes graduated Sunday from Notre Dame with a degree in biochemistry and a 3.991 grade-point average on a four-point scale. . . . His German shepherd, Electra, led him to the lectern to deliver the valedictory speech as his classmates rose, applauded and yelled his name affectionately.

Mr. Cordes starts medical school in two months, the second blind person ever admitted to a U.S. medical school. He does not plan to practice medicine, preferring research. "I've just always loved science," he said. . . .

Armed with Electra, a high-powered personal computer and a quick wit, Mr. Cordes received the top grade, A, in all his classes save for an A-minus in a Spanish class. Two weeks ago, he earned a black belt in the martial arts tae kwon do and jujitsu.

"He is really a remarkable young man," said Paul Helquist, a Notre Dame biochemistry professor. Mr. Helquist had doubts at first but ultimately recommended Mr. Cordes for medical school. "He is by far the most brilliant student I've ever come across in my 24 years of teaching.". . .

"I don't see myself as some sort of 'Profiles in Courage' story," [Mr. Cordes] said. "If people are inspired by what I've done, that's great, but the truth is that I did it all for me. It was just hard work. It's like getting the black belt. It's not like I just took one long lesson. It was showing up every day and sweating and learning and practicing."

His sophomore-year roommate, Patrick Murowsky, said: "The thing about Tim is that he's fearless and he just seems to have this faith. Once we were late for a football game and we had to run to the stadium. He had no qualms about running at top speed while I yelled 'jump,' or I would yell 'duck' and he would duck. And we made it. He is simply amazing to be around sometimes."

Mr. Cordes has Leber's disease, a genetic condition that gradually diminished his vision until he was blind at age 14.

When doctors at the University of Iowa first diagnosed the disease when he was age 2, "it was the saddest moment of my life," his mother, Therese, said. She said the doctors told her, "He won't be able to do this, and don't expect him to be able to do this."

"So I went home," she said, "and just ignored everything they said.". . .

The study of biochemistry relies heavily on graphics and diagrams to illustrate complicated molecular structures. Mr. Cordes compensated for his inability to see by asking other students to describe the visual aids or by using his computer to re-create the images in three-dimensional forms on a special screen he could touch. . . .

"Tim has always exceeded people's expectations of him," said Therese Cordes, who, with her husband, Tom, watched him graduate. "He really does inspire me."

What Is the Context?

Timothy Cordes graduated from the University of Notre Dame. His next accomplishment was being only the second blind person ever admitted to a U.S. medical school. Tim Cordes asserts there is no mystery to his achievement—he just worked hard. As a child, Tim and his family were told there would be many limitations to what he could do, predictions they ignored. In school, Tim asked other students to describe the visual aids presented in class, or he used a special computer screen that allowed him to touch three-dimensional images.

Pivotal Issues for Teachers

What are some of the ways you can encourage students with visual impairment in your classroom? How can you instill in them the confidence that people with visual impairments can achieve their dreams to attend college?

Educational Adaptations

Children with Visual Impairments

Formal efforts in the United States to educate children with visual handicaps began in Boston in 1829 with the establishment of the residential school now called the Perkins School for the Blind. Not until 1900 was the first public school class for children who were blind organized, in Chicago. Some thirteen years later, another class for children with severe visual impairments was established.

Prior to the twentieth century, no distinctions were made between children with low vision and children who were functionally blind. During the last few decades, a rapid growth in public school programs for children with low vision has been stimulated by the Education for all Handicapped Children Act (PL 94-142). Currently, there are thirty-five teacher preparation programs and fourteen orientation and mobility (O&M) programs based in universities preparing professionals to work with children with low vision (Goodrich & Sowell, 1996).

The history of the education of children with multiple handicaps that included visual disabilities is that they often were refused education in schools for the blind and were placed in settings that focused on their other disabilities while often ignoring the visual problems. As Hatlin (1998) pointed out, it is no longer possible for educators of the visually impaired students to ignore multiply impaired children.

> Today, these previously underserved students constitute the majority of students who have visual impairments. Reported increases in the percentage of students who have visual impairments with other disabilities are dramatic. Since the mid-1980s estimates regarding the prevalence of these children have risen from 50% to as high as 75% of the total number of children with visual impairment. (p. xv)

Figure 10.3

Near-Acuity Cards from Lighthouse for the Blind

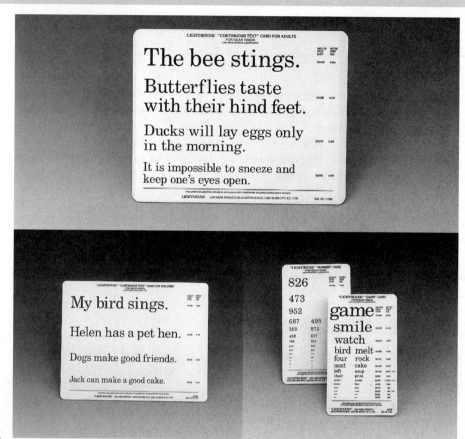

Source: M. Wilkinson (1996). "Clinical Low Vision Services," in A. Corn & A. Koenig (Eds.), *Foundations of Low Vision: Clinical and Functional Perspectives,* p. 158. New York: American Foundation for the Blind. © Lighthouse International.

Children with visual impairments need teachers to give them concrete experiences and to explain the relationships among those experiences.

Adaptations in both materials and equipment are needed to fully utilize the visually handicapped person's senses of hearing, touch, smell, residual vision, and even taste. Lowenfeld (1973) proposed three general principles that are important for adapting instruction to the educational needs of children who are visually impaired:

1. *Concreteness.* Children with severe and profound visual disabilities learn primarily through hearing and touch. To understand the surrounding world, these children must work with concrete objects they can feel and manipulate. Through tactile observation of real objects in natural settings (or models of dangerous objects), students with visual handicaps come to understand shape, size, weight, hardness, texture, pliability, and temperature.

2. *Unifying experiences.* Visual experience tends to unify knowledge. A child who goes into a grocery store sees not only shelves and objects but also the relationships of shelves and objects in space. Children with visual impairments cannot understand these relationships unless teachers allow them the *experience* of the grocery store. The teacher must bring the "whole" into

perspective, not only by giving students concrete experiences—in a post office, on a farm—but also by explaining relationships.

Left on their own, children with severe and profound visual disabilities live a relatively restricted life. To expand their horizons, to enable them to develop imagery, and to orient them to a wider environment, it is necessary to develop experiences by systematic stimulation: Lead children through space to help them understand large areas; expose them to different sizes, shapes, textures, and relationships to help them generalize the common qualities of different objects and understand the differences. Their verbalization of similarities and differences stimulates mental development.

3. *Learning by doing.* To learn about the environment, these children have to be motivated to explore that environment. A blind infant does not reach out for an object unless that object attracts the child through other senses (touch, smell, hearing). Stimulate the child to reach and to make contact by introducing motivating toys or games (rattles, objects with interesting textures).

Though decades old, these basic principles have proved to be sound practice to the present day.

Children with visual disabilities have the ability to listen, relate, and remember, skills that must be developed to the fullest. These children have to learn to use time efficiently because the process of acquiring information or performing a task can be cumbersome and time consuming. For the teacher, that means organizing material, giving specific directions, providing firsthand experiences, and using sound principles of learning.

The term *assessment* describes a process that must occur before a student with a suspected disability receives special educational services. Four specific steps are taken in assessments: screening, eligibility, instructional planning, and progress evaluation (Lewis & Russo, 1998).

Routine vision screenings are administered to many students before they enter school. While severe visual impairments are readily apparent without formal screening, some milder problems might escape notice. Students with other disabilities such as mental retardation might have visual problems that could go undetected without screening. Screening merely identifies students with possible developmental problems. A medical diagnosis of blindness is often sufficient to demonstrate the need for special educational services, but sometimes a functional visual evaluation may be necessary to determine the degree of usable vision. These results can do much to shape the approach taken by special education teachers.

To design an instructional plan one must first find out what the student's current level of achievement is, what his/her potential is, and other information about learning style and responsiveness to various forms of instruction. A comprehensive assessment would contain information about the child's skills (see Turnbull, Turnbull, Shank, & Leal, 1995):

- Concept development and academic skills
- Communication skills
- Social and emotional skills

- Sensory motor skills
- Daily living skills
- Orientation and mobility skills
- Career and vocational skills

In addition to a variety of formal tests (for example, the Test of Visual-Motor Perceptual Skills, which provides information on how the student's brain processes visual imagery) designed to capture the above skill areas, assessment is made from observations and criterion reference tests. For example, if you want to know if the student can borrow in subtraction, you give him or her some additional problems and watch what the student does (Lewis & Russo, 1998; Silberman & Brown, 1998).

All this information is drawn together with input from the parents into an IEP meeting, in which the basic goals and objectives of the program for the student are determined, together with the strategies that will be used to reach those goals.

Finally, there is the question of whether the student is progressing toward these goals in a satisfactory manner. If a student is not progressing satisfactorily, re-adjustments in the IEP and the instructional program are called for.

If a student is not progressing toward the IEP goals, the IEP can be revised.

ADAPTING THE LEARNING ENVIRONMENT

The goal of moving students with visual impairments into the regular classroom or as close as possible (least restrictive environment) is proceeding, as Figure 10.4 indicates. Almost half of the students with visual impairments are found in the regular classroom, and another 21 percent are in a resource room program, which means they spend the majority of their time in the regular classroom. Only 10 percent of these children can now be found in a residential school, and they probably have a variety of disabilities requiring very specialized care.

As is true of children with other kinds of exceptionality, the various learning environments provided for children with visual impairments represent a continuum of care. The goal of full inclusion or integration is modified by the particular needs of the individual child and, sometimes, by the availability of services.

Inclusion

Inclusion has a major impact on young children with visual impairments, raising the question of how thoroughly such children should be integrated into normal preschool settings. There are serious arguments within the profession about the merits of integration compared with the merits of specially trained personnel and special equipment that can be found in a residential or day school for the visually impaired. Lowenfeld (1982), one of the respected voices in the field, stated, "I believe uncompromisingly that integration of the blind into society is on all age levels in their and in society's best interest" (p. 69). But that view is not shared equally by others.

Erwin (1993) laid out a series of guidelines for the effective integration of young children with visual impairment. Not surprisingly, merely placing the child within a normal preschool setting, without careful planning and without

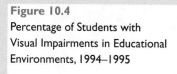

Figure 10.4

Percentage of Students with
Visual Impairments in Educational
Environments, 1994–1995

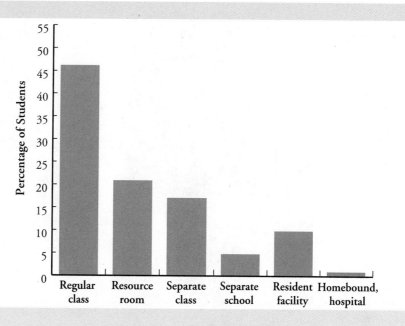

Source: U.S. Department of Education
(1997). *Nineteenth Annual Report to Congress on the Implementation of
the Individuals with Disability Education Act.*
Washington, DC: U.S. Department of
Education.

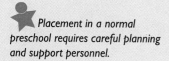

*Placement in a normal
preschool requires careful planning
and support personnel.*

support personnel, will not produce good results. An important aspect of the
integrative approach that Erwin describes is a partnership and teamwork between the classroom teacher and the visual consultant teacher; otherwise, the
visually impaired child may be socially isolated in integrated settings, particularly when the only focus in such a setting is academic (Kekelis & Sachs,
1988).

The curriculum framework for the preschool that focuses on cognitive development, language development, self-help, refining gross motor skills, and so on
seems to fit the child with visual impairments as well as it fits other children.
The preschool setting needs to be accepting of the philosophy of family involvement in the program as part of the total effort for all children in that setting.
Finally, Erwin (1993) calls for research on the dynamics of blind children and
their integration into various social groups beyond the immediate family,
whether those groups include primarily blind children or primarily sighted
children.

Social Aspects of Inclusion. One of the most significant dimensions of the educational programs for children with visual difficulties should be the social needs of
the children. Such needs are shortchanged in mainstream settings if the general education teacher knows little about the special needs of visually impaired children.
Merely placing children with special needs in a classroom with other children does
not guarantee good social interaction. And the same is certainly true for visually
impaired children (Sacks, 1992). Some organized efforts to improve social skills
are required, because visually impaired children are rejected by classmates more
often than are other children (Jones & Chiba, 1985).

Training packages have been designed to help visually impaired children with
their posture, facial expressions, assertiveness, and speech (Kekelis, 1992). In one
instance, attempts were made to bolster the social skills of these children by means

For some children who are visually impaired, the least restrictive environment is a mainstreamed regular classroom; other children need some form of special resource room program. (© Steve Goldberg/ Monkmeyer Press Photo Service)

of teacher instruction and peer prompting. The training consisted of modeling, using prompts, discussing the need for social behaviors, and role playing. The peer-mediated training turned out to produce more improvement than did the teacher instruction, and the social behavior that the children learned was maintained over time.

Sacks and Kekelis (1992) made some suggestions for regular education teachers and teachers of visually impaired students:

- Identify classmates whom the visually impaired student prefers.
- Encourage the visually impaired student to express positive feelings toward his or her classmates.
- Encourage the visually impaired student to choose a partner for play or academic tasks.
- Encourage the visually impaired student to help his or her sighted peers.
- Facilitate discussions about friendship with the visually impaired student to help him or her become more aware of the feelings of others.

Sacks and Kekelis (1992) pointed out that recess and lunchtime offer not merely breaks in the routine but opportunities for students to practice social skills and interactions.

The teacher may ask himself or herself a number of questions:

- Does the visually impaired student play with and talk to peers as much as his or her classmates?
- Do students talk with their visually impaired classmates in the classroom, play with them on the playground, and invite them to after-school and weekend activities?

- Does the visually impaired child show affection and display preferences for classmates?
- Do I observe interactions during recess and, when necessary, intervene so that the visually impaired child is not isolated on the playground? (Kekelis & Sacks, 1988)

A negative answer to any of these questions calls for constructive action by the special teacher working with the regular classroom teacher. One cannot count on a favorable social adaptation without some help and assistance from the teachers involved.

Although the field of educating children with visual disabilities was one of the first to mainstream, opinions differ about the usefulness of the integration approach as it is now being conducted. For example, educators disagree about whether the child with visual disabilities is harmed by being labeled as a student with special problems. Instead, the treatment program, for many professionals, includes the student's acceptance of his or her visual impairment as part of his or her identity (Harrell & Curry, 1987). Also, placing all services in a noncategorical program with children with other handicaps may result in children with visual disabilities not receiving the special services (such as braille and mobility) that they need to perform well in the educational setting. Hatlin and Curry (1987, p. 7) asked, "Can 'generalists' in special education teach blind children to prepare lunch—let alone fulfill the children's basic instructional needs?"

The necessity for ongoing teamwork between professionals is clear. Teamwork is a prerequisite for a successful educational plan for the student with visual impairment. One problem that such students need to overcome is the tendency to lapse into passivity because they lack the skill to assert themselves in a socially acceptable way. The sample assertive statements listed in Table 10.2 can help students develop effective relationships with others. A clumsy statement can complicate social relationships considerably.

Collaborating with the Education Team: The Itinerant Teacher. The move toward mainstreaming has made the role of the itinerant teacher very important for children with visual disabilities. This teacher travels from school to school providing special materials, consultation with school personnel, and individualized instruction. An unsolved problem is how to provide within the framework of the ordinary school the specialized training that children with visual impairments need. It is clear from Figure 10.4 that the vast majority of children with visual disabilities are being educated in regular classrooms.

The itinerant teacher ensures that instructional materials can be used easily by children with visual impairments.

Bishop (1986) questioned groups of general education and special teachers, principals, parents, and students about the factors necessary for successful inclusion. The most important school factors are:

- An accepting and flexible regular classroom teacher
- Peer acceptance and interaction
- Available support personnel
- Adequate supplies and equipment (such as braille books)

The successful integration of the exceptional child does not happen by chance or accident. It requires a well-thought-out plan and capable people applying themselves

TABLE 10.2   Teaching Assertive Behavior

The Situation	Assertive Statement
You want to ask for time or distance.	"I need to think about that one for a while."
You need to get a commitment from someone.	"When can you give me a firm answer?"
You want to make sure the receiver is getting your message.	"I want to make clear the point that _____."
You want to make sure you are getting the message.	"I'm confused; tell me again."
You want to share a positive feeling.	"I really like the way you _____."
You are feeling upset.	"I get embarrassed when _____."

Additional support may be needed if the visually impaired child's first language is not English.

to the task; otherwise, the possibility for social isolation of the child is great. An additional complicating factor is cultural differences between the child with visual difficulties and the school. A child who is blind and from a Hispanic background has numerous challenges to overcome as well as, possibly, a language barrier and a set of family values differing from the values taught at school (Correa, 1987).

Wherever the child with visual impairments is placed, ideally one professional—often the classroom teacher or the teacher with special skills in instructing students with visual impairments—should take the role of **service coordinator.** This individual brings together all the information that relates to the child (the comprehensive assessment, for example) and leads a team of professionals who, with the parents, develop an IEP for the student. The creation of a working team made up of persons of different backgrounds and skills is of paramount importance if an IEP is to be written and executed.

Itinerant teachers are especially important for general education teachers, most of whom have had limited experience in meeting the special needs of children who are visually impaired. Itinerant or resource room teachers can help classroom teachers understand the problems these children face.

For example, the classroom teacher of a boy with a severe visual disability was upset because he wanted to sit near the closed-circuit television monitor and because he tended to hold books close to his eyes. The teacher was afraid he would damage his vision. The expert advice of a resource room teacher dispelled that misconception. Another classroom teacher believed that a very bright light should always be available for children with visual disabilities. In fact, dim light does not harm the eyes and may be more comfortable for students with cataracts, albinism, and certain other conditions.

Dim light may be more comfortable for students with low vision.

Individualized Education Program

The IEP for children with visual disabilities should include a variety of goals—some focusing on the effective use of the learning environment, some on instructional content, and some on skills that the student will need to perform effectively in the mainstream. It will likely take a team of professionals to implement the goals.

As Sacks and Silberman (1998) pointed out, one of the consequences of the diversity of children with visual and other disabilities is that the teacher becomes a team member rather than teaching in isolation.

> They are working as members of a team that includes professionals in specializations such as visual impairment, severe disabilities, deafblindness, early childhood, learning disabilities, general education and occupational and physical therapies and also includes the families of these children and youth. (p. xix)

Some sample IEP goals for such a child are shown in Table 10.3. Note that Jerry has both academic and social goals in his IEP, reflecting the comprehensive goals of the program. The regular classroom teacher may need some outside help from an itinerant teacher to carry out these objectives successfully.

Special Schools

Before the emphasis since the early 1980s on the least restrictive environment and the inclusive classroom, the education of children with visual impairments was often conducted in large residential state schools. With the rapidly growing trend for such students to be educated in the local schools, the question of what happens to the residential school and its often elaborate facilities arose.

Erin (1993) pointed out that the children attending residential schools may have additional disabilities and that the schools have been redesigned to provide an effective environment for such children. Also, these schools provide outreach services, offering information, assessment, and technical assistance to students who are visually impaired and to their teachers in the public schools. Erin proposed a future in which such schools could play three distinct roles:

- *Resource centers for students with visual impairments.* These facilities would function as state or regional sites to distribute materials and provide technical assistance and outreach services to neighborhood schools. They would also participate in professional preparation activities.

- *Life skills centers for students with severe disabilities.* These centers would specialize in assisting students with severe and multiple disabilities, with an emphasis on those with visual impairments.

- *Magnet schools for students with visual impairments.* These schools would provide direct instruction for the academic learner with a visual impairment. Short-term placements that would be arranged by contract with individual school districts and that would address functional needs would be common.

In short, residential schools would address diverse needs as they play a role in the future education of children with visual impairments.

TABLE 10.3   Sample IEP Goals and Objectives

Long-Term Goals	Short-Term Objectives
Jerry will use special aids and materials in order to perform at grade level in reading and mathematics.	1. Jerry will demonstrate effective use of various tools of magnification. 2. Jerry will demonstrate effective keyboarding skills that allow him to do word processing. 3. Jerry will score within one grade level of the class norm in academic achievement tests.
Jerry will establish effective social relationships with some of the nondisabled members of the class.	1. Jerry will join and participate in one of the clubs or organizations in the school that stress social interactions. 2. Jerry will receive a number of votes by other students to work on class projects with them. 3. In class parties, Jerry will join in the activities and interact with other class members.

One argument for the continuation of special schools for children with visual impairments comes from parents. A survey of 985 parents of students in schools for the visually impaired reported widespread satisfaction with how the school was operating (AER, 1995). The parents stated clearly that they felt that a range of options should be available to educate children with visual impairments and that the needs of one child are very different from the needs of another child even though both have visual impairments. Over 70 percent of the parents responding to the survey reported that their local school system did not have specialized personnel or equipment.

Parents also mentioned the loss of the opportunity for social integration with children without disabilities. Some, however, downplayed the importance of such social integration. A few quotations give the gist of their argument:

1. "At the school for the blind there is an opportunity to be 'typical' with peers, of not always being different—the chance to be average instead of being behind peers or 'remarkable.'"

2. "Being able to be with peers 'like yourself' and not having to feel 'you're the only one different' is important."

3. "My daughter is able to interact with peers like herself—not singled out as unusual or disabled. This is a more natural learning environment—she is not distracted or teased for her disability." (AER, 1995, p. 46)

The survey report strongly recommended that the continuum of services remain intact and be strengthened.

Another reason for placing a child with visual impairment in a special school is to receive a curriculum that cannot be provided in the general education classroom. The Texas School for the Blind and Visually Impaired, for example, is implementing a career education model that begins in the elementary school and continues through secondary school and beyond. At the elementary school level, the emphasis is on career awareness. Students may interview persons about their jobs and what they do to function in those jobs (Lock, 1995). At the middle school level, the emphasis is on career investigation. Students take a course in Introduction to Work and assess their own abilities, aptitudes, and interests. At the secondary school level, students focus on career preparation and career specialization, and the academic subjects are tailored to those objectives.

Obviously, such a curriculum would not be appropriate for students without disabilities in the public school, but it is beneficial for students with visual disabilities. For children with visual disabilities who attend public schools during the school year, the Texas School for the Blind and Visually Impaired also provides summer programs with an emphasis on career education.

ADAPTING CURRICULUM

Most of the instructional material presented to children with visual disabilities is similar or identical to the material presented to sighted children, particularly when they spend the majority of their time in the regular classroom. However, some modifications should be made to address specific areas of adaptive difficulty.

Literacy

An important thing to realize in the increasing trend to include children with visual problems in the general education classroom is that they cannot just be placed there and forgotten. Special adaptations of the environment and the instruction are called for, as are specially trained personnel to help the student.

For example, a common practice in regular elementary classrooms is *round robin reading,* or having each student read to the class in turn. Such a practice can be discouraging for children with visual problems because it highlights their reading problems and their need to use magnification tools.

Koenig and Rex (1996) suggest targeted practice in reading fluency so that a student with visual impairment becomes comfortable with the use of the optical tools and also comfortable reading in front of others. Other devices, such as *echo reading* (teacher and student reading together) and *choral reading* (small groups of readers read aloud at the same time), can bring more confidence to the child with visual problems.

The writing skills of students with visual impairments can be helped by the use of bold-lined paper, felt-tipped pens, and mounted magnifiers. While manuscript and cursive writing are always desirable and need to be practiced, it would seem that keyboarding skills are equally called for in this era of the computer. Computers can be equipped with screen enlargement programs and synthetic speech output to allow students to use all aspects of the writing process: prewriting, drafting, revising, editing, and publishing.

Mathematics

Another example of how specific content can be designed to help children with a profound visual disability master concepts was provided by Huff and Franks (1973) for teaching fractions. It is easy enough to understand fractions with a visual demonstration. But students who cannot see must acquire that understanding through the sense of touch. Huff and Franks demonstrated that blind children in kindergarten through third grade can master fractions by working with three-dimensional circles of wood and placing them in a form board nest that can include fractional parts to make up a full circle. Once they have placed a whole circle, the children can learn to assemble blocks representing a third of a circle and put them together in the nest to form the whole. This kind of tactile experience helps children who are blind not only master the idea of fractional parts but discriminate among the relative sizes of various fractional parts (for example, halves versus quarters).

In the middle grades (fourth through eighth or ninth grade), students who are visually impaired work with supplementary materials to help themselves absorb the information that sighted children learn. They use talking books and recorded lessons, and they do remedial work when necessary.

A standard tool for learning mathematics is the abacus, used in many Asian countries to instruct all children. The Cranmer Abacus, a special version of the device, is a substantial help to persons who are visually impaired. The beads in the Cranmer Abacus do not move as rapidly as the beads in the usual abacus and thus can be read more easily by touch. Also, the rods are spaced farther apart for more convenient finger access to the beads. This is another example of the adaptation of devices to meet the special needs of children with visual impairments.

ADAPTING TEACHING STRATEGIES

Educators are increasingly recognizing that students who are blind require a modified curriculum, not just an adapted standard curriculum. Hatlen and Curry (1987) identified three areas of special instruction:

- Concepts and skills that require more practice by those with visual handicaps (for example, teaching the concept *square* in a variety of settings, sizes, and functions)
- Concepts and skills that are specific to the needs of those with visual handicaps (for example, reading by listening, a "gestalt" [overall understanding] for serial learning and self-advocacy)
- Concepts that sighted children learn through incidental visual observation (for example, walking down the street, using public transportation)

The movement toward integrated education in the least restrictive environment has left many youngsters who are visually disabled with little explicit training in communication skills and the activities of daily living. Because they lack visual cues, youngsters with severe and profound visual disabilities often have trouble starting conversations, maintaining the interest of their conversation partners, and

Because they lack visual cues, children with visual impairments often have difficulty starting, maintaining, and not interrupting conversations.

learning not to interrupt. Residential school programs taught not only communication skills but also personal hygiene, grooming, how to dress oneself, how to eat, and cooperative living.

All those skills are important to the child's later adaptation. They should be taught in a carefully controlled and emotionally safe learning situation. Because many classroom teachers have neither the training nor the time to teach them, educators may have to fall back on some form of team teaching or even separated programs to tackle the job (Hatlin & Curry, 1987).

One of the problems faced by teachers and administrators is whether the child is a candidate as a print reader or should be taught how to read braille. Such a decision has long-term implications for the student, because it will send him or her down a path of *print reading* or make the focus *braille reading*. Table 10.4 lists distinguishing characteristics that will help educators decide which path is appropriate for a given youngster.

For instance, Doris is a 7-year-old with serious visual problems. Her vision has been assessed at 20/200, but she has shown an ability to deal with print reading, even though slowly. She seems eager to learn to read print and has a stable eye condition (that is, her vision will not deteriorate) and no additional disabilities. In these circumstances, she would be chosen for a program that stresses print reading and that uses all the technology available to help Doris become a print reader.

If Doris had had an unstable eye condition or was strongly frustrated by trying to read print and had good tactile skills, the decision might well have been to introduce her to braille reading. There are no set rules for such decisions—each one has to be made taking into account the individual characteristics of the child.

Communication Skills

Using Braille. People with profound visual disabilities must develop a series of special communication skills. For children who are blind, using braille is a key skill for communicating with the sighted world.

Braille is a system of touch reading developed in 1829 by Louis Braille, a Frenchman who was blind. The system uses embossed characters in different combinations of six dots arranged in a cell two dots wide and three dots high (see Figure 10.5). The symbols are embossed on heavy paper from left to right, and users usually read with both hands, one leading, the other following. Advanced readers may use the second hand to orient themselves to the next line while reading the line above, and they may read as much as one-third of the lower line with the second hand. Punctuation, music, and mathematical and scientific notations are based on the same system. Standard English braille was accepted in 1932 as the system for general use, although many other communication systems have been tried. It has been developed on several levels of difficulty.

Even the most efficient braille reader has an average reading rate about two or three times slower than that of the average print reader. Thus, we can understand why students who are blind fall progressively farther and farther behind sighted students.

━━ TABLE 10.4 Characteristics of Candidates for Print Reading and Braille Reading Programs	
Characteristics of a Likely Print Reader	**Characteristics of a Likely Braille Reader**
■ Uses vision efficiently to complete tasks at near distances	■ Shows a preference for exploring the environment tactilely
■ Shows interest in pictures and demonstrates the ability to identify pictures or elements within pictures	■ Uses the tactile sense efficiently to identify small objects
■ Identifies his or her name in print or understands that print has meaning	■ Identifies his or her name in braille or understands that braille has meaning
■ Uses print to perform other prerequisite reading skills	■ Uses braille to acquire other prerequisite reading skills
■ Has a stable eye condition	■ Has an unstable eye condition or a poor prognosis for retaining the current level of vision in the near future
■ Has an intact central visual field	■ Has a reduced or nonfunctional central field to the extent that print reading is expected to be inefficient
■ Shows steady progress in learning to use his or her vision as necessary to ensure efficient print reading	■ Shows steady progress in developing the tactile skills necessary for efficient braille reading
■ Is free of additional disabilities that would interfere with progress in a developmental reading program in print	■ Is free of additional disabilities that would interfere with progress in a developmental reading program in braille

Source: Adapted from A. J. Koenig and M. C. Holbrook (1995). *Learning Media Assessment of Students with Visual Impairments: A Resource Guide for Teachers.* Austin: Texas School for the Blind and Visually Impaired. Reprinted by permission.

Braille Literacy. One of the concerns of teachers for children with visual impairments is that within the framework of the inclusive or mainstreamed class these children will not get sufficient instruction in the special communication skills they need. This feeling is so strong that it has spawned a movement to pass legislation requiring all children with visual impairments to be taught braille or at least be reviewed for the possibility of learning braille (Spungin, 1989).

The recent amendments (PL 105-17) to IDEA (1997) require that the IEP include "in the case of a child who is blind or visually impaired, provision of in-

Figure 10.5
Braille Alphabet and Numerals

The six dots of the braille cell are arranged and
numbered thus: 1 ●● 4
2 ●● 5
3 ●● 6

The capital sign, dot 6, placed before a letter makes it a capital. The number sign, dots 3, 4, 5, 6, placed before a character makes it a figure and not a letter.

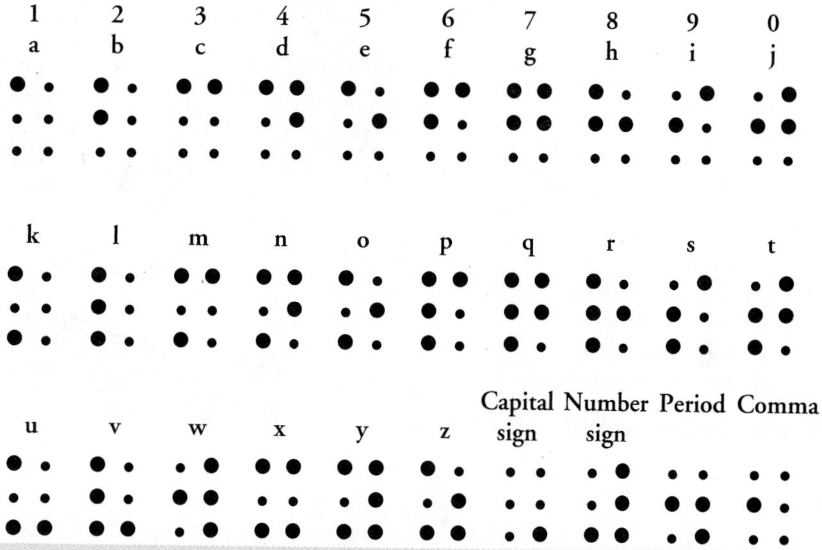

1 2 3 4 5 6 7 8 9 0
a b c d e f g h i j
k l m n o p q r s t
u v w x y z
Capital sign
Number sign
Period
Comma

Source: Division for the Blind and Physically Handicapped, Library of Congress, Washington, DC 20542.

Recent IDEA provisions include braille instruction for students with visual impairments.

struction in Braille and the use of Braille unless the IEP team determines that instruction in Braille or the use of Braille is not appropriate for the child." The IEP also is expected to consider whether the child requires assistive technology devices or services. The lawmakers added "orientation and mobility services" to the list of approved related services. Such language is supposed to ensure that the child with visual impairments will receive in public schools special services to meet their learning needs.

In many communities, an unchanging number of itinerant teachers manage a growing caseload of children. These teachers have less and less time to teach braille or to translate print to braille for their students. Teachers in some communities have only three hours a week on average to provide direct services to children with visual impairments, and many teachers have even less time. Under such circumstances it is understandable why these children are not able to read rapidly or efficiently (Ferrell & Suvak, 1995). When highly specialized instruction is needed so a youngster can learn other material—whether the child has auditory problems and is trying to learn total communication or has visual problems and is trying to learn braille—it becomes very important for the school to provide sufficient time and practice so the children master these crucial skills at a functional level.

One of the most significant decisions for a student is whether to learn print or braille. It's important to meet with the family to discuss this decision.

As noted, one of the most significant decisions to be made about a student with visual impairment is the primary reading method: print or braille? The decision is often made by a committee of people who bring together all the

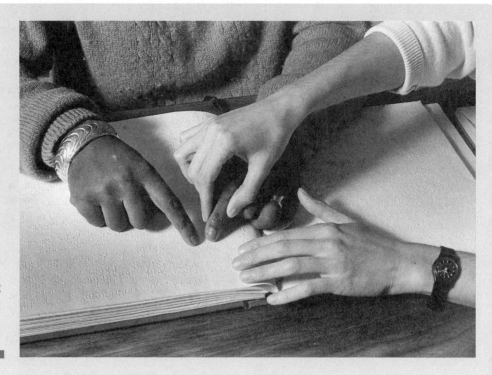

For children who are blind, learning to use braille is a key skill for communicating with the sighted world. *(© Jerry Speier/Design Conceptions)*

information known about the child. The decision is based on a number of factors. The child in question may have some residual distance vision but no near vision and thus could be instructed in braille. For some parents, however, accepting the notion that their child who has limited vision will be instructed in braille, which they consider to be a symbol of total blindness, is not easy. Extensive discussion with the family before instituting the program will be called for (Holbrook & Koenig, 1992).

Some students can be instructed in both print and braille. They learn readiness skills and word identification strategies in a style of parallel instruction, and the decision about which channel to emphasize is postponed until the teacher and the school gain experience with the child's learning style.

The learning experience approach to reading offers many advantages. It uses students' actual experiences as the basis for reading instruction and is a highly motivating approach for a student. But adaptations have to be made for children with visual handicaps. For example, the class visits a local fire station. Afterward, the student with visual impairment dictates a story about the experience, and the teacher writes down exactly what the student says, using a braillewriter or a special slate and stylus. The student and the teacher then read the story together. They can continue to discuss and elaborate on the story, and the teacher can develop reading strategy lessons using the story as a base—for example, thinking about the firefighters' various activities at the firehouse and when fighting a fire.

Braille writing is another part of the curriculum for children with profound visual handicaps. It is taught after the child learns braille reading. People can use various devices for writing the symbols. The easiest and fastest is the braille type-

Braille writing can be taught after the child learns braille reading.

writer, or braillewriter. It has six keys corresponding to the six dots of the braille cell. A proficient user can type 40 to 60 words a minute. Braille can also be written by hand, by means of a special slate and stylus.

Listening. Sykes (1984) defined *listening* as "the ability to hear, understand, interpret, and critically evaluate what one hears" (p. 99). Listening is the foundation of all language arts. It is an especially important skill for those with visual disabilities because they receive much of the information they process through listening (to talking books, tapes, verbal intercourse) and because of the importance of listening to the perception of obstacles.

Environment Skills

Mastering the Environment. Mastering the environment is especially important to children who are blind, for their physical and social independence. The ease with which they move about, find objects and places, and orient themselves to new physical and social situations is crucial in determining their role in peer relationships, the types of vocations and avocations open to them as adults, and their own estimation of themselves.

How do we help children who are blind master the environment? We have to teach them, from a very early age, not to be afraid of new experiences or injury. Sighted children skin their knees, bump their shins, fall from trees, and step in holes. Children who are blind must have the same chance if they are going to learn to control themselves and the environment. This means encouraging risk taking.

Children with visual impairment should be taught to feel the difference in the weight of their forks when they have successfully cornered a few peas and when they haven't. They also should learn a system of marking and organizing clothes for both efficiency and good grooming.

Models—of the classroom, the playground, the child's neighborhood—can help children who are visually impaired understand the relationship of one place or size to another. Models are not a substitute for experience. But they are an extension of experience and a means of drawing perceptual relationships between areas too large to be included at one time in direct experience.

Table 10.5 lists a number of home and community experiences that are within the easy reach of most children with visual disabilities. The child can even compile such a list. As the child begins to extend his or her repertoire, the list will grow longer and longer so that there is an impressive set of skills and knowledge that have been mastered.

Involve parents by asking them to provide a model of the child's classroom so the child can learn the relationship of one place to another.

Orientation and Mobility. The greatest limitations imposed by blindness are the problems of becoming oriented to one's environment and immobility. The situations that force dependence and can cause the greatest personality and social problems for individuals who have visual impairments usually involve mobility. Adults use tools for improving mobility such as long canes, guide dogs, and sighted guides. But children also must learn to move about their environment

TABLE 10.5	Home and Community: Some Early Experiences for Young Children

Home Experiences	Community Experiences
■ Helping prepare a snack or bake cookies	■ Playing at the city park with siblings and friends
■ Picking up the morning newspaper	■ Splashing in the wading pool at a public swimming pool
■ Helping stack dishes in the dishwasher	■ Exploring the grocery store and stores at a mall
■ Helping rake leaves or plant flowers	■ Visiting a farm with animals and machinery
■ Picking up clothes or toys	■ Eating at a fast-food restaurant and at a more formal restaurant
■ Playing with siblings or friends in the backyard	■ Visiting a petting zoo
■ Calling grandmother and grandfather on the telephone	■ Visiting public places like the post office, fire station, and library

Source: A. J. Koenig (1996). "Growing into Literacy," in M. Cay Holbrook (Ed.), *Children with Visual Impairments: A Parent's Guide*. Bethesda, MD: Woodbine House. Reprinted with permission.

independently and safely, so orientation and mobility have become part of the curriculum in all programs for children with visual impairments.

Simply defined, **orientation and mobility (O&M)** involves an understanding of one's location in a given environment (orientation) coupled with the ability to physically move through that environment safely and independently (mobility) (Cioffi, 1995). It is not uncommon for young people to have one of these skills in greater amount than the other, so attention has to be focused on one of them. The goal of any mobility program is to bring the individual to his or her highest desired level of safe, independent travel. Students with visual disabilities become independent when they can move about in the environment to meet their own needs. These skills are central to a strong curriculum that stresses independence.

The adult adjustment of persons with visual impairments relies heavily on the person being mobile. A key element of special education for such children has been O&M services. Much of the O&M training involves teaching visual skills that can be used. One of these visual skills is *scanning*, which is the use of head and eye movements to search for and localize a target. Horizontal scanning can

The goal of an O&M program is to develop a child's mobility skills to the safest, most independent level possible.

The general education teacher can help by identifying landmarks and clues in the classroom, for example, attaching braille markers to important areas in the room.

It is important for the schools to provide time and practice for children to learn braille. *(© Steve Goldberg/Monkmeyer Press)*

pick up vertical targets such as poles that hold street signs, and vertical scanning helps locate the street sign itself.

Another visual skill is *tracing,* visually following single or multiple stationary lines to help maintain a line of direction. Hedgelines, overhead fluorescent lights, and contrasting baseboards can serve as tracing cues. Also important for effective mobility is *tracking,* visually following a moving target, whether a car or a pedestrian (Smith & Geruschat, 1996).

Although much of this training is a matter of supervised practice, there are some optical devices that can help. Using a telescopic device to read street signs or magnification at near point for maps, timetables, and price tags can enhance mobility efficiency.

As in other skills, the earlier such training is instituted the better, with preschool ages being none too early to begin (Smith & O'Donnell, 1991).

The role of the O&M specialist has many dimensions to it. He or she can contribute as a member of the educational team, provide developmentally appropriate goals for the educational plan, develop and implement educational activities for working with the child and family, analyze the child's travel environments for safety factors and possible modifications, and train other educational service providers in O&M principles (Anthony, Fazzi, Lampert, & Pogrund, 1992).

Because learning mobility with a degree of personal independence is one of the most desirable educational goals, special teachers provide O&M instruction to teach the child to use sensory information to establish and maintain his or her position in the environment and move safely, efficiently, and gracefully (Hill, 1992). The skill areas that are covered in such instruction include the following:

- Ability to identify and make use of landmarks and clues
- Knowledge and use of compass directions
- Knowledge and use of indoor and city number systems
- Ability to align the body to objects and with sounds for the purpose of maintaining a straight line of travel
- Use of systematic search patterns to explore novel objects and environments
- Recovery skills
- Knowledge of where, when, and how to solicit aid (Hill, 1992, pp. 25–26)

Mobility training is a complex task requiring considerable skill, and not all teachers of visually impaired persons have had the special training that qualifies them to give O&M instruction.

A major focus in mobility training is learning how to avoid obstacles. Many people who are blind are able to avoid obstacles very well. They make turns in hallways. They stop before they run into a door. How do they do it? Do they sense a change of air pressure on their faces? Do they use residual light and dark vision? Do they use their sense of hearing? Some fifty years ago, in a classic study, Cotzin and Dallenbach (1950) carried out a series of experiments to find the answer.

Cotzin and Dallenbach asked people with blindness to walk down a path and stop when they sensed an obstacle. Then the researchers began to systematically eliminate various possibilities. They put a velvet hood over the face to eliminate cues from air pressure; they used blindfolds to rule out residual vision; they plugged the ears to eliminate hearing—each in turn. Out of these experiments came a single definitive answer: The subjects' judgment suffered only when their ears were blocked. Clearly, they were using sound to detect barriers in their path, much as bats do. The knowledge that hearing is an essential element in obstacle perception has led educators to focus on enhancing (in natural and artificial ways) the use of hearing to increase mobility.

Despite a variety of experiments with more sophisticated devices to aid in travel, the long white cane, so long recognized as a symbol of the individual with visual impairments, continues to be the instrument of choice, even to its use with preschoolers (Pogrund, Fazzi, & Lampert, 1992). There seems to be a consensus among active O&M practitioners that the cane has numerous advantages over alternatives, even though there is little firm research evidence to support that posi-

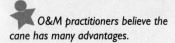
O&M practitioners believe the cane has many advantages.

tion (Leong, 1996). It certainly extends the mobility of young children during a period when exploration and orientation to objects in the environment are very important.

Personal mobility and independence have particular importance for adolescents who are ready to break away from family restraints and protection. The ability to control oneself and one's environment is essential to becoming independent and gaining the respect of peers. The schools are using physical education programs to sharpen the orientation and mobility skills of visually impaired youngsters. Barraga and Erin (1992) suggested that "for children who are blind or who have low vision, movement may be the most accurate replacement for vision in clarifying information about the world" (p. 45).

In most cases, we increase the mobility of individuals who are visually impaired by teaching them ways to get around or to use available tools. But there is another way to ease the restrictions on those who are blind. Society has a responsibility to remove obstacles wherever possible. That responsibility became law in 1991 with the passage of the Americans with Disabilities Act, which directs businesses and public officials to remove barriers for persons with disabilities (see Chapter 2). Removing barriers includes attaching braille symbols to elevators, widening aisles for wheelchair access, and making public telephones accessible.

Map and Chart Reading.   An important curriculum adaptation for children with visual impairments is models or tactile maps representing spatial relationships that students can master through their sense of touch. Berla (1981) discovered that students who are visually impaired, in particular, younger pupils, can improve their ability to read maps if they are specifically taught systematic techniques for exploring maps. Teachers should not expect students to discover complex search techniques themselves. Just as sighted children need help in learning problem-solving techniques, children with visual impairments need instruction in specific search skills.

Special maps alone are not enough. Students must first understand what the maps represent. A map of one's neighborhood can be an important part of the O&M curriculum.

Skills in the Learning Environment

The itinerant or resource teacher in the public school must often instruct students and classroom teachers on some of the special skills that the child with visual disabilities should master. Some of these skills are important keys to the child's effectively mastering the learning environment (Torres & Corn, 1990):

- *Fire drills.* The child with visual disabilities needs to be instructed to take hold of the nearest moving child or adult and quickly follow the others. No particular child should be assigned to the task of aiding the child because he or she might be absent or away when needed.
- *Field trips.* Giving prior notice to the place where these children will be visiting is important. The person in charge (such as the museum director) might be able to make adaptations that will aid the child with vision problems.

- *Auditorium.* The child should be allowed to sit close to the stage to get the maximum amount of information from the experience.

- *Lunchroom.* Some type of orientation is needed so the child with visual disabilities learns where the essential things are. The cafeteria staff can be alerted to help the student with food choice, and peers can help with finding a seat.

Some daily living skills are noted in Figure 10.6. Thinking of a plate as the face of a clock facilitates finding food on a plate. Other useful adaptations of daily activities are the different ways of folding one-, five-, and ten-dollar bills and special arrangements of clothes in a closet. Such simple steps can make the daily life of the child with visual impairments easier. The things that sighted children learn as a matter of easy experience have to be planned. But, with such planning, the student with visual disabilities can perform effectively and truly become a member of the group.

Figure 10.7 shows a page from a story designed to help sighted persons interact with a blind child without feeling strange or not knowing what to do. The theme is that, with only occasional help, the blind person can do many things that the sighted person can do. Helping the sighted person feel at ease is one step toward the integration of students with visual impairments into the general classroom.

Additional Skills Training

Some additional skills can help the child with visual disabilities respond more effectively to the educational program. The itinerant teacher can be of great help to the regular classroom teacher, who might not be familiar with how to teach such skills.

Skills should include keyboarding and daily living skills such as cooking, shopping, and orientation.

- *Keyboarding.* Students can learn keyboarding and word-processing skills for neater written assignments. Personal computers can be modified so there is both braille and large-print output.

- *Daily living.* The child with visual impairment may need direct instruction to acquire skills that come more easily to sighted students, such as good grooming, cooking, and using a grocery store. The teacher should be able to assist the child in learning these skills.

In addition to the skills just noted, areas such as enhancing visual skills by the proper lighting and positioning of materials plus supplementary instruction in topics such as sex education, social skills, and the use of technology are often a part of the special education curriculum.

TECHNOLOGY

Assistive Technology

Children may be reluctant to use machines that can assist persons who are visually impaired.

Often, the biggest stumbling block to using assistive technology is the children's reluctance. Many youngsters are self-conscious about devices that make them look "strange" or "weird." To overcome this self-consciousness, it's important to intro-

How do people with visual impairments pay for things when they can't see their money?

Coins are easy to recognize by feeling them. Dimes are small and slim with ridges around the edges; pennies are small with smooth edges; nickels are bigger and thick; quarters have ridges and are bigger but thinner than nickels.

People who are visually impaired use this trick to recognize dollar bills: In their wallet, one-dollar bills are left unfolded; five-dollar bills are folded in half the short way; and ten-dollar bills are folded in half the long way.

How do children who are visually impaired find their toys and clothes?

Children with visual impairments have to be very neat. They have to put their things in the same place every day in order to find them.

To pick out what to wear in the morning, children who are visually impaired can feel the texture of their clothes. They know jeans feel different from wool pants. Or they may remember in what order their clothes are hung in the closet.

To decide what top matches what bottom, aluminum clothing tags can be sewn in each piece of clothing. On the tags, braille markings indicate the color. Children with visual impairments must learn what colors go together.

How do children with visual impairments find the food on their plate?

To find the food on their plate, imagine the plate is a clock. They are told at what time the food is placed.

On this plate, the hamburger is at 12 o'clock, the salad is at 3 o'clock and the french fries are at 8 o'clock.

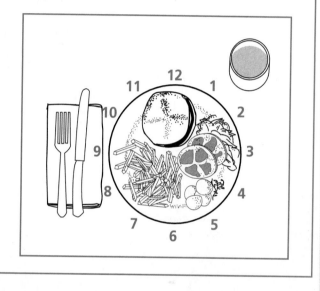

Figure 10.6   Life Skills Training for Children with Visual Impairments

Source: Adapted from R. Tannebaum (1988). *A Different Way of Seeing.* New York: American Foundation for the Blind. Reprinted with permission from the American Foundation for the Blind, 11 Penn Plaza, Suite 300, New York, NY 10001. Copyright © 1984.

duce these tools in a positive way (by playing games, for example) when the children are young.

Technology has given us the capability to translate printed language into spoken language and braille. It also allows us to move easily from one form of communication to another, such as transferring from braille to written English and back again. Obviously, this technology has enormous potential for students with visual impairments and for their teachers:

> Teachers can type a lesson or test and then, using the appropriate hardware or software, convert the material to large print, braille, regular print, or speech, depending upon the needs of the student. The student, on the other hand, could do homework or tests in braille and convert it to print for the teacher. (Todd, 1986, p. 292)

For Listening.   **Synthetic speech** is the production of sound—of phonemes into words—by means of a computer. The process allows us to convert written words

Figure 10.7
My Friend Jodi Is Blind

Jodi said, "You never walked with a blind person before, did you?" She held on to my elbow and asked me to walk one step ahead of her so she could follow. She said I should tell her when we got near steps, doors or holes in the ground.

Once I learned how, it was easy for us to get around together. Jodi said, "Now we are next to the cafeteria." I asked her how she knew that. She said, "Silly, my nose knows."

Source: N. Schwartz (1987). *My Friend Jodi Is Blind*, p. 5. New York: The Lighthouse. Illustration by Peter Vey. Copyright © 1987 by The Lighthouse Inc., New York.

into speech so that those with severe and profound visual handicaps can listen to books, newspapers, and even typed letters and manuscripts.

The increasing popularity of talking books—books on tape—is a boon for those with visual disabilities. In addition to commercially made tapes, the Talking Book program produces books on tape and makes them available at no charge to children and adults who are visually impaired.

The Speech Plus Talking Calculator is a hand-held calculator that announces (using a twenty-four-word vocabulary) each entry and the result of each operation. It is a relatively inexpensive device.

For Reading and Writing.   The rapidly growing use of the computer in the public schools has created yet another dilemma for children with visual impairments. Since many of these youngsters will be in inclusive settings (the general education classroom), how can they stop from falling farther and farther behind their classmates who find it easy to use this new tool? One way to help children with visual impairments is to pay attention to **access technology,** adaptations to a computer's normal operations that allow a student with disabilities to use and benefit from the computer's operations (Taylor & Murphy-Head, 1996). Examples of such adaptations are listed in Table 10.6. In short, a

Access technology refers to adaptation of a regular computer for the student with visual disabilities.

TABLE 10.6 Examples of Access Technology	
Problem	**Access Solution**
The student cannot see the screen.	Use a standard desktop publishing program with a wide variety of fonts and type sizes.
The student cannot hear feedback.	Use plug-in amplified speakers or headphones.
The student has trouble shifting between the screen and the keyboard or desktop.	Position the keyboard on a slant board directly below the monitor.
The student is too heavy-handed, causing the keystrokes to repeat.	Use an alternative keyboard that generally allows the student to control the repeat rate.

variety of steps can be taken to make sure the child with visual disabilities can participate with their classmates in the use of the computer as a key learning tool.

When optical devices are not sufficient, a closed-circuit television (CCTV) system can provide electronic magnification. A video camera directed at an object or symbol projects the image onto a television monitor. CCTVs are costly, but for appropriate users they can be a highly effective means of enlarging and viewing information (Ward, 1996).

At the Massachusetts Institute of Technology, a computer automation has been developed that translates ink print into Grade 2 braille. The procedure is being used at the American Printing House for the Blind. An expansion of the computer braille translator, the MIT Braille Emboss, is used with a telewriter. When teachers of blind persons want braille output for new materials, they request it by telephone from a computer center, and it is returned in braille by means of a teletypewriter. Currently braille translations are made by microcomputers that are usually available in schools for the blind.

Although in the future even more exotic technology may provide help for students with visual impairments, a number of devices are available now. Portable computer devices allow students to take notes and do assignments without the need for a computer in each classroom. Both print and braille copies can be printed from these devices. With additions, they allow the student to listen to synthesized speech. Portable talking dictionaries are within financial reach and a welcome addition, because a braille dictionary can cost over $1,000. It would be good to get these devices in the hands of as many students as possible, because they will allow much more effective use of students' time than was previously possible.

TRANSITION

From School to Work

The transition from school to work is an extremely important aspect of the total educational program. Although there have been attempts to use sheltered workshops, where students produce goods in a protected setting that is publicly subsidized, the newer emphasis is on placement in real job settings whenever possible (Sacks & Bullis, 1988). The secondary school program then becomes a part-time academic and part-time workplace program to give the student a chance to experience employment while still in a supervised setting. The academic program focuses on functional reading and other skills that can enhance the student's chance of success in the workplace.

John, a teenager with a visual disability, was exposed to several different jobs and learned a series of generic work skills (such as greeting and conversation skills). This type of experience should serve John in good stead in whatever occupation he finally decides to enter.

CASE STUDY: JOHN

John, age 17, has been visually handicapped since birth. Congenital cataracts, which were removed at age 2, left him with light perception in his left eye and usable residual vision in the right eye. John is able to read standard print with a hand-held magnifier or specially prescribed lenses, but his reading rate is slow and extremely labored. John has received the services of a teacher of visually handicapped students throughout his school years, first in an elementary resource room and later from itinerant teachers. John has been mainstreamed into regular education classes since the third grade, even though his skill levels range from fourth grade in math comprehension to eighth grade in spelling. His reading comprehension, organization, and note-taking skills are particularly weak and require constant support, yet his educational program has continued to emphasize academic pursuits.

Although John attends his neighborhood high school, he has few friends. He spends much of his leisure time alone and finds interaction with peers difficult and sometimes rather awkward. Encouraged by his VH [vocational high school] teacher, John has begun to participate in the drama club. He is quite verbal and enjoys acting a variety of roles; however, he is easily intimidated when questioned about his visual impairment or difficulty with reading. At home, John is responsible for his personal needs, but does not consistently perform other job tasks around the house. He has repeatedly volunteered to help mow the lawn or prepare meals, but his parents are hesitant to allow him to perform such jobs because of his limited vision. Although John's parents recognize the importance of allowing him to become more independent, they are fearful of his safety and have not allowed him to travel by himself throughout the community or spend his own money as readily as his siblings or same-aged peers.

At a recent IEP meeting, John's VH teacher, along with other team members (orientation and mobility specialist, vocational coordinator, vocational rehabilitation counselor, school psychologist, John, and his parents) discussed future educational and vocational goals for him. As they spoke, it was apparent that John's parents perceived his academic performance much differently from other team members. His parents believed that John was functioning at or above grade level on most academic tasks and felt that he would be able to attend college. Conversely, team members did not recognize John's desire to develop more independent living and travel skills, as well as wanting to secure a job for himself. When questioned about job preference, John seemed interested in working at a radio station or developing his acting skills. At the suggestion of the vocational coordinator, John was asked to participate in a series of community vocational experiences, where he would be able to explore and to learn about a variety of jobs through hands-on experience. Reluctantly, John's parents allowed him to do so.

Instead of full participation in a regular education setting, John now spent half of his school day in a community classroom at a real job site. Assisted by a vocational special education teacher and his VH teacher, John gained exposure to landscape gardening, sorting and packaging, and basic office skills. Each experience lasted approximately three months. In addition, he developed a set of generic work behaviors and social skills (basic greetings and conversational skills through role plays and modeling) that transferred to other settings. In the community classroom environment, time was also spent developing functional math and reading skills that included money management, time management, and completion of job applications. John was expected to travel to work independently in the morning, and back to his local high school in the afternoon. As a result of this initial vocational experience, John's educational program has shifted from a purely academic focus to one that is more functionally based. He will continue to participate in the community classroom program during his final year of high school, while working with his special education teachers and vocational counselors to secure employment after high school. (Kekelis & Sacks, 1988)

PROGRAM EVALUATION

Despite vigorous arguments about which setting is best for children with visual impairments, little evidence is available to support the various points of view. Does the child with visual disabilities profit from being integrated into a regular school program?

Some agree with Harrell and Curry (1987):

> There is no evidence that the provision of educational services to visually impaired students in regular classrooms and integrated settings is of greater benefit to the pupil than are more intensive segregated programs that offer carefully planned opportunities for successful interactions with nonhandicapped peers. (p. 372)

Falvey (1988), however, pointed out that if a great deal of money is spent on residential school programs, little is left for strengthening the delivery of services in local schools. Also, although residential schools allow children with visual disabilities to form friendships, these friendships inevitably are limited to others with visual disabilities. But the low incidence of children with visual disabilities means that many local schools will have few such children, so necessary, intensive special education in areas such as personal hygiene, grooming, eating, and cooperative living—to say nothing of mobility training—may be difficult to obtain in general education classrooms.

A NATIONAL AGENDA

Table 10.7 provides a roster of national agenda items for children with visual impairments. The items include students' and parents' rights, appropriate and timely service, and appropriate case loads and personnel preparation programs. This list presents the professional expectations of what should be happening if good educational practice for children with visual impairments is to be observed. For those programs that are not meeting these needs, it is a wake-up call that they are falling short of appropriate norms for good practice. The list itself can be a checklist for parents and others who want to make sure good practice is being adhered to.

TABLE 10.7   National Agenda Goal Statement for Children with Visual Impairments

1. Students and their families will be referred to an appropriate education program within 30 days of identification of a suspected visual impairment.

2. Policies and procedures will be implemented to ensure the right of all parents to full participation and equal partnership in the education process.

3. Universities, with a minimum of one full-time faculty member in the area of visual impairment, will prepare a sufficient number of educators of students with visual impairments to meet personnel needs throughout the country.

4. Service providers will determine caseloads based on the needs of students and will require ongoing professional development for all teachers and orientation and mobility instructors.

5. Local education programs will ensure that all students have access to a full array of placement options.

6. Assessment of students will be conducted, in collaboration with parents, by personnel having expertise in the education of students with visual impairments.

7. Access to developmental and educational services will include an assurance that instructional materials are available to students in the appropriate media and at the same time as their sighted peers.

8. Educational and developmental goals, including instruction, will reflect the assessed needs of each student in all areas of academic and disability-specific core curricula.

Source: *National Agenda for the Education of Children and Youth with Visual Disabilities Including Those with Multiple Disabilities* by A. L. Corn, P. Hatlen, K. M. Hubener, F. Ryan, and M. Siller. © 1996. Reprinted with permission from the American Foundation for the Blind.

Family and Lifespan Issues

In the preceding chapters, we have been concerned with what happens to exceptional children after they leave school and try to make their way in the world. After all, educational programs are supposed to prepare students for life in the community. We have the same concerns for children with visual impairments.

There is a limited supply of evidence available on this topic, but one longitudinal study (Freeman, Goetz, Richards, & Groenveld, 1991) provided a fifteen-year follow-up study of sixty-nine legally blind persons who were 10 years old at the time of the original investigation. The follow-up data were collected through structured interviews conducted by the first two authors of the study.

The importance of multiple disabilities becomes clear in the results. Of the forty participants in the study whose only disability was visual, 71 percent received a normal psychiatric diagnosis, and 44 percent were in open employment. However, of the twenty-nine participants with other disabilities, only 24 percent received a normal psychiatric diagnosis, and only 17 percent were employed.

In education, 20 percent completed secondary school and went no further. Nineteen percent attended a university, and 6 percent graduated. Twenty percent did not complete secondary school, and another 17 percent were always in special classes. Freeman et al. felt that many of these subjects could have been employed, though they were not. Among those with partial sight, there was a strong tendency to try to "pass" as normal, to avoid the presumed stigma of blindness.

Freeman et al. felt that study of the resilience of some children needs to be pursued further—that is, students who appear to persevere against odds to reach a good adaptation. We know little about this topic and thus are unable to provide guidance about how to achieve the state of resilience. Certainly, there is sufficient evidence of good adult adjustment, given the right set of conditions and past experience.

A Final Word

We need to remember that comparisons of children with visual impairments and sighted children reveal only what *is,* rather than what could be with a more comprehensive intervention program. As Warren reminds us, "In virtually every area of development there are visually impaired children whose developmental progress is at least at the norm for, and at the high end of the distribution for, sighted children" (1994, p. 334). In this area, as in others, individual differences should be used to guide educational strategies, not some general average that may not be applicable to a particular child.

Summary of Major Ideas

1. Children with visual impairments are classified in several ways. Educational classifications rest on the special adaptations necessary to help these children learn.

2. A moderate visual disability can be almost entirely corrected with visual aids. Aids are not as effective for a child with a severe visual disability, but the child can use residual vision to learn. A child with a profound visual disability cannot use vision as a learning tool.

3. The way we interpret the outside world is a function of our brain, experience, and eyes. A visual impairment can hamper the individual's understanding of the world, but such understanding can be enhanced through extending the experiential world of the child with vision impairment.

4. Hereditary factors are a major cause of visual disabilities in young children. Other major causes are infectious diseases, injuries, and poisonings. Many of these children have multiple disabilities, not just visual impairments.

5. Today most educators agree that the cumulative experiences of children as they develop affect intelligence. Youngsters with visual impairments lack the integrating experiences that come naturally to sighted children. The challenge for educators is to compensate for this through special instructional programs.

6. One of the byproducts of restricted mobility and limited experience can be a passive orientation to life. Teachers play a critical role in helping students with visual impairments be active and independent.

7. A growing number of children with visual impairments are being included in public school programs.

8. The educational program for students with visual disabilities should emphasize concrete learning, unifying experiences, and learning by doing, or directly teaching things that children with vision learn independently.

9. It is important for parents and teachers to help children with visual disabilities develop their skills. It is equally important to let these children do things for themselves and to experience as much as possible the things that sighted children experience.

10. The development of programs that will deliver services to children with developmental problems from birth on promises valuable early assistance to children with visual impairments and their families.

11. The many needs of students with visual impairments demand a continuum of special services, from preschool programs to special schools.

12. The trend toward inclusion of children with visual disabilities has left many such youngsters without the special skills training they need to live independently.

13. Braille reading is slower than regular reading, which can affect the academic performance of students with profound visual impairments.

14. Orientation and mobility training are critically important parts of the curriculum for children with visual disabilities. Such services should be available in the public schools.

15. Technology is improving the means of communication for those with visual disabilities. It has also broadened their occupational choices. Keyboarding and word processing are particularly useful skills, and access technology is equally important in today's schools.

Unresolved Issues

1. *Multiple disabilities.* The growing number of children who have two or more handicaps presents a serious issue for the schools. Some youngsters with visual impairments are either mentally retarded or deaf, or they have special learning or motor problems as well. We have to adapt educational programs to accommodate children with multiple disabilities, an adjustment that complicates an already serious challenge.

2. *Making technology accessible.* Technology is wonderful—when it is usable. The widespread distribution of technological developments for those with visual disabilities has been impeded by the cost and size of equipment. In the same way, we have to increase accessibility to the computers and word processors that are transforming the academic and work worlds of those with visual disabilities.

3. *Reform.* The new educational reform movement, which emphasizes the inclusion of students at all levels of ability and performance, places a special responsibility on general and special education teachers to operate as a team to provide services for children with visual disabilities.

Key Terms

access technology p. 428
accommodation p. 391
braille p. 417
ciliary muscles p. 391
convergence p. 392
cornea p. 391
extrinsic muscles p. 392
fading p. 401
hyperopia p. 392
iris p. 391
lens p. 391
moderate visual disability p. 390

myopia p. 392
object permanence p. 401
orientation and mobility (O&M) p. 422
profound visual disability p. 390
pupil p. 391
retina p. 391
retinoblastoma p. 393
retinopathy of prematurity p. 393
sensory compensation p. 395
service coordinator p. 412
severe visual disability p. 390
synthetic speech p. 427

Questions for Thought

1. Differentiate among moderate, severe, and profound visual impairments. p. 390

2. Why is lack of vision both a primary disability and a condition that can hamper cognitive development?   pp. 393–394

3. How does a visual impairment impede the development of language?   p. 394

4. What effect do restricted mobility and consequent limited experiences have on the personal and social adjustment of children with visual disabilities? pp. 395–398

5. When and how should preschoolers be screened for vision problems? pp. 402–403

6. Briefly describe Lowenfeld's three general principles for adapting instruction to the educational needs of children who are visually impaired (concreteness, unifying experiences, and learning by doing).　pp. 407–408

7. What are the key components of an effective program to integrate students with visual disabilities into general education classes?　pp. 408–411

8. How are maps and models used to help children with visual impairments master their environment?　pp. 421, 425

9. List three devices that expand the communication capabilities of those with visual disabilities and three that can improve their mobility.　pp. 417–425

Resources for Further Study

REFERENCES OF SPECIAL INTEREST

Barraga, N., & Erin, J. (1992). *Visual handicaps and learning.* (3rd ed.). Austin, TX: PRO-ED.

> A comprehensive, readable introduction to the problems of schoolchildren who have visual disabilities, this book provides good discussions of the impact of visual impairment on children, ways to conduct comprehensive assessments of individual children, and the nature of differential programming.

Corn, A., & Koenig, A. (Eds.) (1996). *Foundations of low vision: Clinical and functional perspectives.* New York: American Foundation for the Blind.

> This book of eighteen chapters and many different contributors focuses on what low vision really means to the person who lives with it. It stresses the psychological and social implications of low vision and provides up-to-date information on mobility training and the instruction of children with low vision in academic programs.

Olmstead, J. (1991). *Itinerant teaching: Tricks of the trade for teachers of blind and visually impaired students.* New York: American Foundation for the Blind.

> This book is a detailed account of the role played by the itinerant teacher who serves in a supporting role to other teachers providing services to children with visual disabilities. It includes tips to improve integration for these children and shows how to organize services and consultation and how to help with the development of the individualized education program. It is a practical and informative publication.

Sacks, S., Kekelis, L., & Gaylord-Ross, R. (1992). *The development of social skills by blind and visually impaired students.* New York: American Foundation for the Blind.

> The eventual success or failure of an adult with visual impairment will rest in no small measure on the person's ability to form reasonable social relationships with other persons. This book provides an explanation of why it is so difficult for children with visual impairments to form effective social relationships and suggests useful intervention strategies. The authors demonstrate why the teaching of social skills is an integral part of the curriculum for visually impaired students.

Sacks, S., & Silberman, R. (Eds.) (1996). *Educating children with visual impairments with other disabilities.* Baltimore: Paul H. Brookes.

> This is an important book because over half of the current population of children with visual impairments also have other disabilities that complicate their educational pro-

gram. This book, which includes chapters on learning disabilities, orthopedic disabilities, neurological disabilities, and emotional and behavioral problems, discusses how additional disabilities complicate the education of children with visual impairments and what can be done.

Warren, D. (1994). *Blindness and children: An individual differences approach.* New York: Cambridge University Press.

In this excellent review of what we know from research and scholarly review on the education of children with visual impairments, Warren reviews three major areas: the child's interaction with the physical world, the acquisition of cognitive skills, and adaptation to the social world. A separate section surveys what longitudinal studies have told us. The reference section is a valuable source for those seeking to understand these students.

JOURNALS

Exceptional Children
The Council for Exceptional
Children (CEC)
1920 Association Dr.
Reston, VA 20191-1589
TTY: 703-264-9446
E-mail: **cecpubs@cec.sped.org**
http://www.cec.sped.org

Journal of Applied Behavior Analysis
Mary Louise Wright
Department of Human Development
University of Kansas
Lawrence, KS 66045-2133
E-mail: **jabamlw@idir.net**
http://www.envmed.rochester.edu/
wwwrap/behavior/jaba/jabahome.htm

Journal of Special Education Technology
Peabody College, Box 328
Vanderbilt University
Nashville, TN 37203
http://peabody. vanderbilt.edu/peabody

*Journal of Visual Impairment
and Blindness*
(formerly *New Outlook for
the Blind*)
The Sheridan Press
c/o American Foundation
for the Blind
P.O. Box 465
Hanover, PA 17331

800-635-7181
E-mail: **pubsvc@tsp.sheridan.com**

*Journal of the Association for Persons with
Severe Handicaps*
TASH (The Association for the
Severely Handicapped)
29 W. Susquehanna Ave., Suite 210
Baltimore, MD 21204
E-mail: **info@tash.org**

Teaching Exceptional Children
The Council for Exceptional
Children (CEC)
1920 Association Dr.
Reston, VA 20191-1589
TTY: 703-264-9446
E-mail: **cecpubs@cec.sped.org**

RE: view (formerly *Education of the
Visually Handicapped*)
Heldref Publications
4000 Albemarle St., NW
Washington, DC 20016
http://www.heldref.org

PROFESSIONAL ORGANIZATIONS

American Foundation for the Blind
11 Penn Plaza, Suite 300
New York, NY 10001
Toll-free hotline: 800-AFBLIND
(800-232-5463)
http://www.afb.org/afb

Division for the Visually Handicapped
c/o Council for Exceptional Children
1920 Association Dr.
Reston, VA 22091-1589
http://www.cec.sped.org

National Association for Parents of the
Visually Impaired, Inc.
P.O. Box 317
Watertown, MA 02272
(800) 562-6265
http://www.

National Association for
Visually Handicapped
22 West 21st St., 6th Floor
New York, NY 10010
http://www.navh.org

II

Children with Multiple and Severe Disabilities

FOCUSING questions

Why is it necessary to determine the degree of functioning for each disability of a person with multiple and severe disabilities?

Why is independence training stressed in today's classrooms?

Why are age-appropriate and functional activities so important for students with severe disabilities?

Why is the curriculum for persons with multiple and severe disabilities often a variation of the regular curriculum?

Children with disabilities do not always fit neatly into well-defined categories. There are individual differences among children with hearing, visual, cognitive, and emotional impairments. We also find children who have more than one impairment and children who are severely disabled. These youngsters are even more heterogeneous than other children with special needs.

This chapter focuses on children with disabilities that we have discussed in other chapters of this book. But the children who are the subject of this chapter have multiple disabilities, and the disabilities are so severe that the child needs some type of support for the rest of his or her life. Such support might include a driver for transportation, a companion to provide assistance in feeding or toileting, or a job coach working in the community.

Understand that not all individuals who have multiple disabilities are mentally retarded. Persons with multiple disabilities vary widely in cognitive abilities. Some have profound mental retardation and will need continuous caregiving to meet their needs. Young men and women with Ushers syndrome are deafblind but have normal cognitive abilities. A cognitively gifted child who is spastic may not be able to control muscle movements and may need a sophisticated voice output communication system so that he or she can express his or her thoughts. This individual may need assistance in controlling his body movements to be able to type to express his thoughts.

Andrew Rothstein, a person with extensive experience in working with persons with physical disabilities and low-incidence disabilities, has suggested the classification shown in Table 11.1 for the purpose of educating persons with multiple and severe disabilities.

If they are provided with early intervention and appropriate education and therapies, individuals in the first group—those with mild physical and high cognitive abilities—are able to attain full educational experiences, including college and independent living and working experiences. Individuals in the second group—those with severe physical disabilities but high cognitive abilities—need extensive therapies and probably prostheses in the form of wheelchairs, crutches,

TABLE 11.1 Examples of Multiple and Severe Disabilities

Physical Disability	Intellectual Capacity	
	High	**Low**
Low	1. Example: High cognitive functioning and mild cerebral palsy.	3. Example: Low cognitive functioning and mild cerebral palsy.
High	2. Example: Severe cerebral palsy and high functional cognitive abilities.	4. Example: Severe cognitive dysfunction and severe cerebral palsy.

or leg braces, and they may not be able to control their motor movements. To communicate, these children need augmented and alternative communication devices (computers, videodiscs, and other devices). They are capable of completing their education and living independent lives with some support.

Individuals in the third group—those with mild physical disabilities and low cognitive abilities—require some physical therapies, but the degree of their retardation may limit their work experiences to activities supervised by a job coach. Those in the fourth group have such severe and multiple disabilities, including retardation, that they may never acquire a sign or vocal language, but they can learn to make requests and indicate refusal through gestures, facial expressions, body movements, tangible symbol systems, and other augmentative or alternative forms of communication (Dunst & Lowe, 1986; Gothelf, Crimmins, Mercer, & Finnochiaro, 1994). These persons require early and continuous intervention to enable them to live as fully as possible.

 ## A Note About Terminology

In the field of multiple and severe disabilities, major advances have been made in recent years. Specialists in this field hold different opinions about the language to use to describe the individuals they serve. Clearly, throughout this book we favor terminology that reflects a humanistic, "people-first" approach to writing about persons with disabilities—using, for example, the term *individual with cerebral palsy* rather than *cerebral palsy child.*

The professionals in the field of multiple and severe disabilities have been leaders in the efforts to make regular schools accessible and welcoming to students with multiple and severe disabilities. They perceive not only benefits to nondisabled students but enormous value in providing opportunities for disabled students to interact, to establish friendships, and to be exposed to a diverse cultural population comprising individuals from different social, economic, and cultural groups (Falvey, 1995; Meyer, Park, Grenot-Scheyer, Schwartz, & Harry, 1998). They believe that these positive lifestyle changes will develop not only social skills but academic ones as well, which will aid persons with disabilities in their employment and living settings (Smith & Nelson, 1997).

One further issue: Although the words *train* and *teach* are synonyms, *teach* is more widely preferred because it refers to any act of communication that imparts knowledge or skills. *Train* implies a concentration on particular skills intended to prepare a person for a desired role. There is a movement in the field of multiple disabilities to use only the word *teach,* because some individuals in the field consider the word *train* demeaning.

 ## Definition

Children with multiple and severe disabilities possess such a diverse combination of characteristics that it is difficult to give a succinct statement that includes them all. Probably the most useful definition is the one adopted by the organization most concerned with this group of people and their families: The Association for

Because children with severe disabilities have physical, cognitive, or emotional problems of an intense nature, they almost always require services beyond those traditionally offered by general and special education programs. (© J. Berndt/Stock Boston)

Many children with severe disabilities have normal intelligence or are gifted.

Persons with Severe Handicaps (TASH). The definition accepted by TASH is as follows:

> Persons with severe handicaps include individuals of all ages who require extensive ongoing support in more than one life activity in order to participate in integrated community settings and to enjoy a quality of life that is available to citizens with fewer or no disabilities. Support may be required for life activities such as mobility, communication, self-care, and learning as necessary for independent living, employment, and self-sufficiency. (Original by Bureau for the Education of the Handicapped, April 1985; revised and adopted by TASH, December 1985, and revised November 1986; see Meyer, Peck, & Brown, 1991, p. 19)

The Association for Persons with Severe Handicaps recently changed its name to Association for Persons with Severe Disabilities. The name change indicates the changes in terminology occurring in the field and the movement toward the use of nondiscriminatory language. The term *disability* refers to the state of the individual—that is, persons with vision, hearing, or other impairments. The term *handicapped* refers to environmental conditions that restrict a person with disabilities, such as lack of ramps or elevators for persons who use wheelchairs for mobility. This chapter is concerned with persons who have *multiple and severe disabilities*.

Any definition of individuals with multiple or severe disabilities must be broad, because it would include a very heterogeneous population, for example, persons with autism, psychiatric disorders, deafblindness, and combinations of health, motor, or cognitive impairments (Bigge, 1991; Fewell & Cone, 1983). Children who are severely retarded generally have other disabilities and are considered to be multiply disabled. However, not all children with multiple disabilities, or even with one severe disability, are mentally retarded. The motion picture *My Left Foot* tells the story of Christy Brown, who is a severely spastic man with cerebral palsy but without mental retardation. Brown learned to type with one toe and wrote several books (Brown, 1982). It took a long time for those in Brown's environment to realize that he did not have multiple disabilities but one severe disability that almost completely disrupted his functioning. Fortunately, he received specialized assistance that allowed him to express his intelligence.

Generally, children with multiple disabilities have sensory deficits, motor disabilities, health or neurological disorders, or genetic inheritances that interfere with the normal progression of development of cognitive, social, and physical skills.

Prevalence of Multiple and Severe Disabilities

Where one disability is present, an additional disability may also be present (Shea, 1983). Teachers usually do not have many of these children in general education classes. They may encounter one or two children with physical disabilities or speech or language problems or perhaps a child who is gifted and who has visual and hearing losses. It is generally thought that most of these children require so much specialized intervention that often they are educated either in special education classes in regular schools with a great deal of professional support from an interdisciplinary team or in special schools. Students with severe and multiple disabilities are generally placed in regular school buildings, but their instruction is spread across general education classes, resource rooms, and separate classes (U.S. Department of Education, 1996). Resource rooms are widely used to serve students with multiple and severe disabilities. Brown and Lehr (1996) note an increase in educating these students in inclusive settings, following the trend of educating more students with disabilities in general education classes.

Meyer (1991) suggested that students who have multiple disabilities account for only one-half of 1 percent of the total special education population. In 1983, the *Federal Register* reported that 67,539 individuals were receiving special education. Of that group, only 0.07 percent were considered to have multiple and severe disabilities (Evans, 1991).

Baldwin (1997) reported that there are 11,053 persons who are deafblind throughout the nation. He suspected that, because of underreporting, a more realistic total is between 7,657 and 12,274. Baldwin also reported that 2 out of every 1,000 individuals receiving special education have more than one disability.

Causes of Multiple and Severe Disabilities

A discussion of causes of multiple and severe disabilities could go on at great length, because many conditions cause these problems, although many of these problems are rare. For example, as of the early 1990s, only five children had ever been diagnosed with Leigh disease, which causes widespread damage to the central nervous system, particularly to the brainstem (Behrman, Vaughn, & Nelson, 1987). Most low-incidence disorders—there are more than a thousand (Kopp, 1983)—are not highlighted in this text.

A number of things can cause multiple and severe disabilities: genes passed to the child by one or both parents; a negative influence during pregnancy, such as the mother's use of alcohol or other harmful drugs; or events that occur during birth, such as breech birth (emerging feet first) or anoxia (lack of oxygen during birth). After birth, accidents or child abuse can cause multiple and severe disabilities (Cohen & Warren, 1987). Whatever the cause of the disabilities, keep in mind the following realities about learners with severe and multiple disabilities:

- Learning is not only possible but probable.
- There are more similarities with their peers without disabilities than there are differences (Falvey & Grenot-Scheyer, 1995, p. 131).

Characteristics of Children with Multiple and Severe Disabilities

In this section, we discuss some of the major categories in which the largest numbers of children with multiple and severe disabilities are found, including autism, deafblindness, behavior disturbance, hearing impairment, and mental retardation.

AUTISM, PERVASIVE DEVELOPMENTAL DISORDERS (PDD), AND PERVASIVE DEVELOPMENTAL DISORDERS NOT OTHERWISE SPECIFIED (PDDNOS)

Autism, **pervasive developmental disorders (PDD)**, and **pervasive developmental disorders not otherwise specified (PPDNOS)** are large heterogeneous categories of developmental disabilities that are difficult to pinpoint because their origins are unknown. The disorders in these categories are neurological disorders that lead to deficits in the child's ability to communicate, understand language, play, develop social skills, and relate to others (NICHCY, 1997). The Individuals with Disabilities Education Act (IDEA) defines **autism** as

> a developmental disability significantly affecting verbal and non-verbal communication and social interaction usually evident before age 3, that adversely affects a child's educational performance. Other characteristics often associated with autism are engagement in repetitive activities and stereotyped movement, resistance to environmental change or change in daily routines, and unusual sensory experiences. (NICHCY, 1997, p. 1)

The term *PDD* is used to group an array of disorders that have similar characteristics: impairment in social skills, imaginative activities, and verbal and nonverbal skills; a limited number of interests; and behaviors that tend to be repetitive (Tsai, 1998). However, PDD have now been grouped into five separate categories, one of which is autism. These categories have some impairments in common, but persons in one category may have some skills that those in the other categories do not possess. It should be kept in mind that diagnosticians may classify any one of these disorders as autism. Thus a teacher (or parent) may be confronted with a child classified as autistic who really belongs in one of the other categories, where outcome expectations may differ and appropriate teaching strategies may vary.

This issue is further confused by the fact that autism is a heterogeneous category, as is the broad category of PDD, particularly PDDNOS. Autism was a rather small disability category; now it is one of the most common within the category of developmental disorders (Cohen, 1998). Discussion of the five categories of PDD follow: autism, Rhett disorder, childhood disintegrative disorder, Asperger's disorder, and autism and PDDNOS.

Because these disorders tend to run in families, a genetic defect is suspected. Autism is more common among boys, while Rhett disorder is more common among girls. Children with autism appear to be developing normally until around 2 years of age. These disorders are very troubling to parents, who tend to seek a cure or a miracle to transform their once developing child back to age-appropriate developmental functioning (Cohen, 1998). As Cohen notes, there is almost a sense of desperation among parents trying an array of approaches that may work for some children but rarely for many and never for all.

Autism

There are major disagreements in the field about the cause of autism. At one time, most professionals believed autism was caused by the mother's coolness and by emotional problems in the home. But few accept those theories today. Schopler and Bristol (1980) provided what is still an accurate summary of what we know about the causes of autism:

- For individual children, the specific causes are usually unknown.
- There is probably no single underlying cause to account for autism; instead, there are probably multiple causes.
- Most likely the primary causes involve some form of brain abnormality or biochemical imbalance that impairs perception and understanding.

Based on their work with people with autism, Johnson and Koegel (1982) found that some individuals with the disorder

Autism is one of the least understood disabilities.

- Are unable to relate to others
- Have impaired or delayed speech and language and often repeat phrases (echolalia)
- Show sensory disabilities and often are overresponsive or underresponsive to light, noise, touch, or pain
- Exhibit either inappropriate behavior (serious, prolonged temper tantrums) or flat affect
- Engage in repetitive self-stimulatory behaviors that can interfere notably with learning
- Fail to develop normal, appropriate play behaviors
- Exhibit obsessive ritualistic behaviors that make these individuals extremely resistant to change

Some individuals who are classified as autistic have high cognitive abilities that are undermined by their other behaviors and lack of language (Atwood, 1993). Several adults with autism have written books about their lives and how they perceive their problem (Williams, 1992). Williams writes that "none of us fit the stereotype" and suggests that persons who are classified as autistic have more personal, social, and written language skills than they have functional verbal skills (p. 196).

Rhett Disorder

The infant with Rhett disorder is apparently normal at birth and in development through the first months of life. Then there is a deceleration in head growth, a loss of hand skills, and the development of repetitive hand movements. In addition, there is a loss in social engagement (eye contact), poorly coordinated body movements, and impaired language development (Cohen, 1998; American Psychiatric Association, 1994; NICHCY, 1998).

Childhood Disintegrative Disorder

Persons with childhood disintegrative disorder possess normal development in at least the first two years of life but then experience a decline before they are 10 years old. The skills that were developed are lost in major areas of functioning (Cohen, 1998; NICHCY, 1998).

Asperger's Disorder

Persons with Asperger's disorder have normal cognitive and language development. The disorder is primarily noted in the child's lack of interaction with peers, the lack of use of nonverbal behaviors such as eye contact, and a general lack of interest (NICHCY, 1998). Cohen (1998) suggests that persons with Asperger's disorder are often considered eccentric and lacking in common sense.

Autism and PDDNOS

There is a fine line of difference between a diagnosis of autism and one of PDDNOS (NICHCY, 1998). Tsai (1998) notes that confusion in diagnosis may stem from the fact that a person with PDDNOS displays some, but not all, of the behaviors and features common to autism. In a sense, autism and PDDNOS can be viewed as a continuum of disorders, with autism the more severe and children with PDDNOS possessing few or several of the symptoms (Mauk, Reber, & Batshaw, 1997). For example, a child who has been diagnosed as having PDDNOS may use speech appropriately but have difficulty in interacting with others. PDDNOS children, in contrast to those with autism, may do well on manipulative and visual skills tests and may show special aptitude in music, mathematics, or reading.

TREATMENT PROGRAMS

Lovaas's Young Autism Program

In an interesting book, a mother noted that her normally developing children "became" autistic between 18 and 22 months of age, displaying many of the behaviors associated with autism (Maurice, 1993). After many diagnoses and reviews by specialized personnel, she adopted Lovaas's (1981) Applied Behavior Approach and with the assistance of trained personnel was able to return her children to normal development by ages 4 to 5.

Lovaas's (1981) program is an applied behavioral program initiated as soon as the child is identified; appropriate diagnostic tools are administered by a professional trained in the Lovaas method. It is intensive, one-on-one in-home training for 40 hours a week. A child who begins to demonstrate that he or she is learning and has some communication ability may, with the home therapist, attend an early childhood program for a short period of time (30 minutes per day) (Cohen, 1998). The

Some children with autism can attain normal cognitive functioning by age 7.

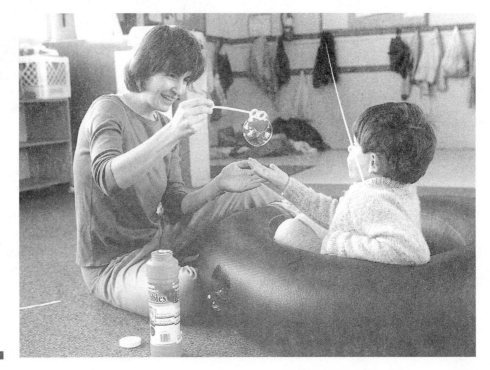

Autistic children are often withdrawn and unresponsive, but teachers and parents can reach them through a structured early educational program focusing on applied behavioral analysis and reinforcement in both school and home settings. (© Elizabeth Crews)

child must also have markedly reduced any self-injurious or aggressive behavior. If the child is successful in the early childhood program, the experience is extended for longer periods, although the child is still accompanied by the home therapist.

Cohen (1998) estimated that the process may take several years. It is a very expensive program, and few families can afford the cost of $20,000 to $60,000 per year (Batshaw, 1997). A major problem is that the early childhood teacher must be trained in the Lovaas method, must understand the principles of prompting, fading, and reinforcing desired behaviors, and must be able to administer the program in a one-on-one situation (Lovaas, 1993).

Lovaas's program is one of the few that have demonstrated successful gains, with 50 percent of his study population maintained to age 13 (Lovaas & Buch, 1997). The results are currently being replicated in other centers. For an overview of basic behavioral principles, see Parrish (1997).

TEACCH

The TEACCH program also uses behavioral principles but is more comprehensive in its educational approach (TEACCH loosely stands for Treatment and Education of Autistic and Related Communication Handicapped Children). It includes classroom teaching, training parents as co-therapists, and a range of related services (Schopler & Mesihov, 1997). The goal of the TEACCH program is to increase the child's level of functioning and not necessarily to "cure" the child. The educational classroom is based on known characteristics of autistic children, who are visual rather than hearing learners and prefer alternative modes of communication, such as signs or pictures, rather than the written word (Cohen, 1998). The data suggest that children in the program improve their IQ scores and functional work skills (Cohen, 1998; Lord & Schopler, 1994).

Other Programs

Autism Research Center is an offshoot of the Lovaas program (Koegel & Koegel, 1995). The Koegel program emphasizes the child's motivation, that is, what he or she shows an interest in within an atmosphere of play. The program uses natural reinforcers related to the activity. For example, a child may look at the water fountain and be offered a drink. Learning to communicate and interact are key goals of the program (Cohen, 1998).

LEAP (for Learning Experiences, an Alternative Program for Preschoolers and Parents) is unique in that it was designed to integrate students with autism with regularly developing children. The program emphasizes language, social skills, and adaptive behavior. It uses a variety of strategies, and parent training is integral (Strain, Kohler, & Goldstein, 1996).

Other techniques include auditory integration training (Rimland & Edelson, 1994a, 1994b) and facilitative communication (Biklin & Cardinal, 1997). Each technique has reported some success with a small number of children with autism. Facilitative communication has been the subject of strong controversy (see JASH, Fall 1994).

DEAFBLIND IMPAIRMENT

IDEA (PL 101-476) defines children who are deafblind functionally as

> having circulatory and visual impairments, the combination of which creates such severe communication and other developmental and learning needs that they cannot be appropriately educated in special education programs solely for children and youth with hearing impairments, visual impairments or severe disabilities, without supplementary assistance to address the educational needs due to these dual concurrent disabilities. (PL 101-476, 20 U.S.C. Chapter 33, Section 1422 [2]; see Everson, 1995, p. 6)

The Helen Keller National Center defines **deafblind** more specifically as someone

> (1) with central vision acuity of 20/200 or worse in the better eye with corrective lenses and/or a visual field of 20 degrees or less in the better eye . . . or with a progressive visual loss . . . ; (2) who has either a chronic hearing impairment so severe that most speech cannot be understood . . . ; (3) and for whom the combination of impairments . . . causes extreme difficulty in daily life activities. (Everson, 1995)

The Education Program

When one of the two major systems that bring information to the child is impaired, the special education program emphasizes the unimpaired sense. For the child who is hearing impaired, the visual channel is used to establish a communication system based on signing, finger spelling, picture communication systems, and lip reading. For the child who is visually handicapped, the program uses auditory and tactile aids to help compensate for the visual-channel problem.

In the education of children and adolescents who are deafblind, the focus has changed from multistate centers to allowing states to develop their own programs. The states are now responsible for both the education of youngsters with deafblindness impairments and the transition of young adults (ages 21 and older) "from education to employment," including "vocational, independent living, and

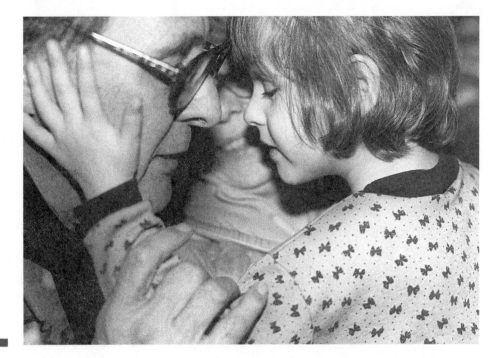

The key to development is the transaction between the child and caregiver. *(© Mimi Forsyth/ Monkmeyer Press Photo Service)*

other post-secondary services" (U.S. Department of Education, 1985, pp. 2–3). These programs have brought comprehensive diagnostic processes and facilities and qualified personnel in contact with children and adolescents who are deaf and blind.

Early Intervention

Concern for the infant who is deafblind begins with the family. A major disruption has occurred in the life of this child. It should be met by the family, who will help establish realistic goals for the child and initiate special instructional techniques consistently (Huebner, Prickett, Welch, & Joffee, 1995; Murphy, 1983, p. 21). Visual evaluation and intervention are critical for infants who are deafblind for two main reasons: Efficient vision use is important for learning, and visual functioning can be improved (Michael & Paul, 1995, p. 201).

An infant who is deafblind needs to realize that he or she has needs.

The first step with any individual, particularly one who is multiply disabled, is to help that person maintain sufficiently focused attention to realize the following: (1) he or she exists; (2) others exist; (3) he or she has needs; (4) these needs can be met; (5) some of the needs will be met by himself or herself; and (6) some, if not most, of these needs will be met by others (Murphy & Byrne, 1983, p. 355). This is the genetic sequence of the development of the self (Schore, 1994). Many infants who possess deafblind impairments can go beyond point 6 and, as they develop, begin to meet many, if not most, of their own needs.

The key to all development is to begin joint attention, that is, transaction between the caregiver (usually the mother) and the infant (Donnellan, Mirenda, Mesaros, & Fassbinder, 1984, p. 34). With the infant who is deafblind, this joint attention begins through touch. As communication develops through touch, it is augmented by any residual hearing or vision through the use of hearing aids and glasses or the more recently developed sonic directional devices that give the infant vibrational feedback about the location of objects (Bower, 1989).

Without intervention, infants who are deafblind focus on their own bodies and show little interest in object use. They do little exploration of the environment and resist new stimuli, becoming prone to self-stimulation (Downing, 1995; Taylor, 1988).

In addition, changes occur as the brain matures, and a child without the ability to see or hear is deprived of normal sensory stimulation that facilitates normal development. Without early intervention to offset these lacks, the changes in the brain are degenerative and abnormal (Murphy & Byrne, 1983; Sameroff & Haith, 1996). Thus, immediate programming is needed for these children as soon as their condition is diagnosed.

One early intervention approach that has been particularly successful with children who are deafblind is the Van Dijk method. The Van Dijk method is a movement-based approach that considers the sensorimotor experiences to be the foundation of all learning (Writer, 1987, p. 191). The aim is to enhance the quality of the child's interaction with people and objects. Van Dijk proposed that through body contact with others, children who are deafblind learn that they are separate persons and that other people are present in the environment. In addition, Van Dijk suggested that children with disabilities need to learn that their movements can affect others, a process he calls *resonance* (Van Dijk, 1986).

Table 11.2 presents guidelines for vocational training. IDEA mandates transitional services, goals, and objectives for the IEP of students who are deafblind. These IEPs should be outcome-oriented process objectives that promote movement from school to postschool activities (Everson, 1995).

BEHAVIOR DISTURBANCE AND HEARING IMPAIRMENT

A child with both a hearing loss and behavioral difficulties may have developed the behavioral problems because of the lack of environmental input resulting from the sensory disability.

Nothing inherent in a hearing deficit should create additional social or psychological problems (Schlesinger, 1983, p. 83). Most of the social and psychological problems found in persons with hearing deficits are secondary outgrowths of their lack of hearing in a speech-dominated world. Fredericks and Baldwin (1987) cautioned against diagnosing a person as having more than one disability because an individual may have only one disability with secondary characteristics growing out of the lack of environmental input from the sensory disability.

Unfortunately, many children with hearing impairments have behavior problems. Many researchers believe that the secondary problem can be avoided if intervention is begun early and the strengths of the child are reinforced (Mencher & Gerber, 1983). Children who are deafblind and whose parents are deaf tend to have fewer problems than children who are deaf and whose parents have normal hearing (Moores, 1996).

Teaching early communication skills to children who are deaf enhances cognitive, language, and social development and is a major step in preventing behavior problems.

Part of the problem for children with hearing losses is that so much of what they cannot hear they can feel vibrationally or see in shadow movements in the environment around them. This causes them to become confused and frustrated and to act out in consequence. Teaching caregivers to look at and explain by gesture, signing, or pointing to the event for the hearing-impaired child can keep some of the challenging behaviors from occurring. The aim of many intervention programs is to teach signing at an early age, so the child who is deaf can communicate with others and therefore not be isolated.

━━○ **TABLE 11.2 Jobsite Training Guidelines for Individuals Who Are Deafblind**

1. Always orient the worker to the setting, materials, and activities.
2. Ensure optimal positioning for efficient use of residual auditory and visual skills.
3. Always use task analyses to test and teach specific and related job skills.
4. Although it is always most desirable to have a worker respond to naturally occurring stimuli, for most individuals who are deafblind and have multiple impairments, it may be more efficient to provide a planned system of prompts and cues.
5. Selection of prompts and cues should consider types of visual and hearing losses, amount and extent of residual hearing and/or vision, age of onset of sensory losses, communication systems, and related disabilities (if any).
6. Prompts and cues include visual or tactual signed instruction, tactual cues, enhanced visual and/or auditory cues, model prompts, physical prompts, large print or braille cues, enlarged photographs, low-vision aids, hearing aids, assistive listening devices, and other assistive technology.
7. Prompts and cues should be defined as permanent or temporary. All temporary cues and prompts should be faded along with the job coach or other employment personnel. Before presenting a temporary cue or prompt, know how you are going to fade it! Before presenting a permanent cue or prompt, ensure that it is site and age appropriate.
8. Choose an instructional format that includes a system of least-to-most intrusive prompts and/or time delay combined with whole task instruction, backward chaining, or forward chaining.
9. For individuals who have significant visual impairments or are blind but have some residual hearing, combine auditory prompts with tactual cues and prompts.
10. For individuals who have profound hearing losses or are deaf but have some residual vision, combine signed instruction with model prompts, enlarged visual cues, and physical prompts.
11. For individuals who are profoundly deaf and legally blind, combine tactual instruction and cues with physical (hand-over-hand) prompts.

Source: J. Everson (1995). (Ed.), *Supporting Young Children Who Are Deaf-Blind in Their Communities: A Transition Planning Guide for Service Providers, Families, and Friends* (p. 167, Table 7.2). Baltimore: Paul H. Brookes. Reprinted with permission.

MENTAL RETARDATION WITH ANOTHER DISABILITY

A child who has a hearing loss may be classified as mentally retarded because of a lack of appropriate teaching, not a lack of intelligence.

A major problem for children who are mentally retarded is the slowness with which they learn or retain what they have learned. When this slowness is combined with other problems, the difficulty of teaching these children is compounded. Many special educators are concerned with the excessive use of the term *dual diagnosis* to classify individuals, particularly those with mental retardation. The term *dual diagnosis* is limited to the combination of mental retardation and behavioral and psychiatric dysfunction (Dykens & Kasari, 1997). In Prader-Willi syndrome, there appears to be a higher frequency of both behaviors than there is in Down syndrome or nonspecific retardation. Thus, assuming that challenging behaviors are a necessary part of retardation is faulty reasoning.

Some children do have more than one disability; an individual with a hearing loss may also possess mental retardation. However, a careful and appropriate assessment of a child with a hearing loss may reveal that the child's poor performance is due to the hearing loss and not to poor cognitive functioning. In other words, the second disability is an outgrowth of the first disability. The child's low score on a standardized test may reflect that he or she is not able to accurately hear spoken language, or that the child uses a sign language but the test was administered orally.

Persons with limited cognitive abilities also tend to be very rule oriented and rigid, applying a rule to all situations rather than being flexible. For example, a person with mental retardation who learns to open a door by pushing it may push all doors, even those that need to be pulled or to have a knob turned.

A teacher may believe that a person with mental retardation who is not following directions in the classroom is actively resisting the teacher's effort or is emotionally disturbed to the point of being unable to relate to reality. The teacher should investigate, however, whether the child is depressed because of his or her inability to understand instruction. The teacher can ask the parents if the child has poor sleep habits, has a poor appetite, and is generally sad and listless. If so, the child may need to be treated for depression and receive training in social skills to help solve what must be terrible emotional feelings beyond the cognitive understanding of a person with mental retardation (Evans, 1991). The sections that follow discuss the importance of teaching self-determination skills to assist in the reduction of depressed states (Wehmeyer, Agran, & Hughes, 1998).

Teaching strategies that take advantage of the person's rule orientation by teaching rules can be very effective.

MENTAL RETARDATION AND CEREBRAL PALSY

People tend to assume that children with cerebral palsy are mentally retarded, and a relationship does exist between the two conditions. Whatever genetic or environmental insult damages the motor control centers of the central nervous system sufficiently to cause **cerebral palsy** can cause enough damage to the cerebral cortex to create retardation. But the relationship is not universal. Dorman and Pellegrino (1998) report that only 25 to 30 percent of children with cerebral palsy have lower IQ scores than typically developing children.

It is hard to justify a diagnosis of mental retardation in youngsters with cerebral palsy if we are using intelligence tests that are normed on children with adequate speech, language, and motor abilities. Many children with cerebral palsy have expressive problems in both speech and psychomotor areas. Their test results, then, are not necessarily valid. All we can conclude is that when these children are tested with instruments normed on other populations, about half of them show IQ scores below 70 or 80. However, IQ tests have serious limitations in terms of evaluating children with multiple disabilities.

Standardized intelligence testing often does not take into account a child's disability.

Often the poor speech and spastic movements of children with cerebral palsy give the layperson and the professional the impression that these individuals are mentally retarded. Actually, there is little relationship between the degree of physical impairment and intelligence in children with cerebral palsy. A child who is severely spastic may be intellectually gifted; another with mild physical involvement may be severely retarded.

Although IQ tests—the most common instruments used to determine retardation—are inappropriate for those with disabilities in speech and motor areas, the subtest scores on an IQ test can reveal more about a child's strengths than the total or derived score reveals. Thus, we find these subtest scores helpful when we must design an individualized teaching strategy to capitalize on those strengths (Boothroyd, 1983, p. 146). Keep in mind that most of the current remedial efforts in special education focus on the children's strengths, not their weaknesses.

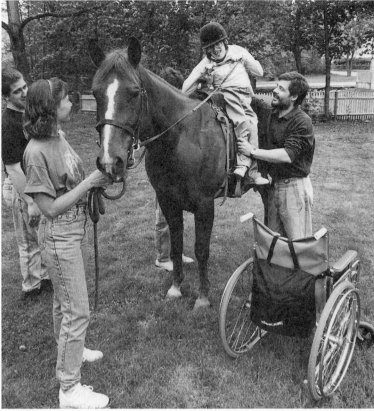

Parents and therapists need to teach children with severe disabilities to turn outward from their internal world to the outer world of the environment and other people for stimulation. *(© Jerry Howard/ Positive Images)*

To assess adequately whether retardation exists, we need to be sure that whatever test of intelligence yields information on how to provide an intervention design will lead to an outcome better than the outcome of an intervention design constructed solely on the basis of observation (Evans, 1991, p. 40). IDEA suggests that assessments be "timely, comprehensive, and multidisciplinary" (Section 1435) and by the year 2000 include participation of children and youth with disabilities in state and district assessment programs (NICHCY, 1998).

Early Intervention

 Parents and teachers need to teach these children how to transact with the world.

A critical need of children with multiple and severe disabilities is early intervention, so the parents can provide appropriate and consistent care. Parents and therapists need to help children with severe disabilities recognize that they are persons in an environment and that they can influence the environment. The adults need to teach these children to turn outward from their internal world to the external world of the environment and other people for stimulation. If they do not, these children tend to respond to internal rather than external stimuli and use their genetic capacity for curiosity to explore by manipulating their internal world through body movements. As Murphy (1983) wrote, once children fail to turn outward to the environment, it is almost impossible to get them to respond to the world around them. In addition, the child who responds to his or her internal world is likely to develop self-stimulating behaviors, some of which, such as head banging and eye poking, can be physically, psychologically, and socially damaging to the child and hard to eliminate.

An excellent example of this pattern is described in the work of Fraiberg (1977), who found that infants who are blind and were institutionalized appeared to be mentally retarded and developed problematic self-stimulating behaviors. On the other hand, children who are blind and were reared in regular homes and received ample physical stimulation did not develop these behaviors, and most were cognitively normal. Teaching **self-determination skills** to these children has several advantages. It promotes autonomous behavior, develops independence in making choices in leisure and recreational times, and cultivates important safety skills and the ability to make choices effectively (Wehmeyer, Agran, & Hughes, 1998).

Considerable evaluation is required to determine the nature of the impairment and the kind of intervention needed to help the child function as effectively as possible. These evaluations have to be conducted periodically by an interdisciplinary team to determine if progress is being made and what changes, if any, are needed in the intervention process. Table 11.3 shows the types of professionals included on an interdisciplinary team and the services they provide (Rainforth, York, & MacDonald, 1992).

After evaluation, a decision is made about what type of classroom is most appropriate for the child. Some children with multiple and severe disabilities will be placed in regular settings. For example, in 1994, 9.1 percent of children with multiple disabilities were served in the general education classroom, 19.8 percent in resource rooms, 44 percent in separate classrooms, 22 percent in separate schools, 3 percent in residential facilities, and 2 percent at home. Recently, there has been a movement to have these students served for all or part of their education in regular schools (U.S. Department of Education, 1997). Schools hire personnel especially prepared to work with and teach these individuals. Most of the specialized classrooms are located in regular schools. There are advocates who insist that all children, regardless of the severity of their disability, be included with their agemates in neighborhood schools (Falvey, 1995; Stainback & Stainback, 1996). Many in the field disagree (Kauffman & Hallahan, 1994). The major dispute between those advocating full inclusion and those who do not concerns children with low intellectual capacity and high physical disability (see number 4 in Table 11.1). These issues were discussed in detail in Chapter 2.

A major question to be considered when planning intervention is how do multiple and severe disabilities influence each other and shape the individual's experience of the environment. For example, if a child is disabled both cognitively and physically, his or her academic accomplishments will be less than those of one who is mildly retarded and physically disabled. Multiple disabilities are not simple additions of disabilities. They interact with each other and confound the individual's condition (Mencher & Gerber, 1983).

As Mencher and Gerber (1983) suggested, helping to improve the functioning of an individual with a disability begins with identifying and developing the child's assets. Because 93.8 percent of the deafblind population have some residual vision or hearing (Baldwin, 1997), the residuals need to be identified and enhanced to improve the child's functioning. By encouraging the child's assets, the instructional staff hopes to avoid the development of negative challenging behaviors, such as self-stimulation, self-injury, tantrums, and aggression.

For a child with both deafness and blindness, the therapist needs not only to determine if there is residual hearing or vision but also to determine how the child responds to sensory stimulation (including touch and smell) and what kinds of therapy are needed. The next step is to recommend potential management procedures to

Coping skills need to be reinforced as they emerge.

TABLE 11.3   Professional Members of an Interdisciplinary Team

Audiologist: To provide and coordinate services to children with auditory handicaps, including detecting the problem and managing any existing communication handicaps.

Early Childhood Special Educator: To ensure that environments for handicapped infants and preschoolers facilitate children's development of social, motor, communication, self-help, cognitive, and behavioral skills and enhance children's self-concept, sense of competence and control, and independence.

Physician: To assist families in promoting optimal health, growth, and development for their infants and young children by providing health services.

Nurse: To diagnose and treat actual and potential human responses to illness; for disabled infants and preschoolers, this means (1) promoting the highest health and developmental status possible and (2) helping families cope with changes in their lives resulting from the child's disabilities.

Nutritionist: To maximize the health and nutritional status of infants and preschoolers through developmentally appropriate nutrition services within family and community environments.

Occupational Therapist: To promote children's independence, mastery, and sense of self-worth in their physical, emotional, and psychosocial development. Purposeful activity is used to expand the child's functional abilities, such as self-help skills; adaptive behavior and play skills; and sensory, motor, and postural development. These services are designed to help families and other caregivers improve children's functioning in their environment.

Ophthalmologist: To determine the extent of the child's visual capacity.

Physical Therapist: To enhance the sensory motor development, neurobehavioral organization, and cardiopulmonary status of disabled or at-risk infants and preschool children within a family and community context.

Psychologist: To derive a comprehensive picture of child and family functioning and to identify, implement, or evaluate psychological interventions.

Social Worker: To improve the quality of life for infants and toddlers and their families who are served by PL 99-457 through the provision of social work services.

Speech-Language Pathologist: To promote children's communications skills in the context of social interactions with peers and family members, in school, and in the community.

Source: From L. Rossetti (1990). *Infant-Toddler Assessment.* Boston: Little, Brown. Adapted from the Carolina Institute for Research on Infant Personal Preparation (1988). *Proceedings of a Working Conference.* Unpublished manuscript, revised.

Two or more appropriate members of an interdisciplinary team are needed for an accurate assessment.

the parents and teachers who work with them to obtain needed resources, such as a hearing aid, special glasses, or a comprehensive intervention program. A comprehensive system in the community can greatly assist families by providing easy access to needed services (Harbin & West, 1998). The parents also need to be made aware of the supports available in the community (Everson, Burwell, & Killan, 1995).

Consider these five axioms when providing service for the severely disabled:

- Young children with severe disabilities have a right to services that improve their quality of life and maximize their developmental potential.
- Early childhood services for children with severe disabilities are effective in improving the quality of life and maximizing developmental potential.

■ Intervention services that begin earlier in the child's life will be more effective than services that begin later.

■ Early childhood services that involve families are more effective than those that do not (Westlake & Kaiser, 1991, p. 432).

■ Including children with disabilities in regular classrooms increases their social skills and interpersonal relationships (Helmstetter, Peck, & Giangreco, 1994).

A comprehensive system in the community can greatly assist families by providing easy access to needed services.

The aim of special education is to support individuals with disabilities so they can become as independent as possible in the activities of daily life and work and develop the social skills expected by society. For most children with multiple disabilities, achieving those goals requires a long and specialized process, but much has been accomplished in recent years.

Identification of Children with Multiple and Severe Disabilities

Most children with multiple and severe disabilities are identified at birth through simple screening techniques. The Apgar scoring system (Apgar & Beck, 1973), described in Chapter 3, is administered at one minute and five minutes after birth. It assesses the child's motor functioning, skin color, heart rate, respiration, and general appearance. The Brazelton Neonatal Behavioral Assessment Scale (Brazelton, 1973) may also be administered to assess the same areas.

Some vision defects such as cataracts are easy to spot. Most hearing defects are difficult to identify and may not be detected until the child is 2 or 3 months of age. Most physical defects can be diagnosed early by observing the infant's lack of normal reflex and body movement. Some physical disabilities may not be diagnosed until late in the first year of life, and autism may not be evident until the second year of life or, in some children with disabilities, not until adolescence.

Infants who are premature or of low birth weight (usually both) may have experienced lack of oxygen during the birth process (anoxia), usually as a result of the umbilical cord's being wrapped around the neck or of being breech born (delivery feet first). Such children are monitored carefully, because these types of birth are often associated with disabilities.

Other defects such as some types of spina bifida (see Chapter 12; Batshaw, 1997; Williamson, 1987) can easily be identified from obvious physical deformities. In some types of spina bifida, an opening is present on the spinal cord, and children who are affected may have enlarged heads from excess spinal fluid in the brain cavity (hydrocephalus). These children have surgery shortly after birth to drain the excess fluid from the brain because if the condition is allowed to continue, it will cause retardation. The process of draining is called *shunting*.

Children with Down syndrome can also be identified, from their flat facial profile and upwardly slanted eyes, as well as from their low Apgar scores (Batshaw & Perret, 1992). Children with Down syndrome may require immediate medical supervision for survival.

Individuals with spina bifida and Down syndrome can suffer from multiple disabilities and must be examined carefully at birth to determine their immediate needs. Children in both groups, however, vary across a wide range of cognitive functioning and will need intensive intervention to help them achieve their highest potential.

Educational Adaptations

Children with Multiple and Severe Disabilities

Over the years, a philosophy of teaching students with multiple and severe disabilities has been evolving from research, experience, and common sense. Today the objective is to teach functional, age-appropriate skills in integrated school and nonschool settings and to base teaching on ongoing, systematic evaluation of the student's progress. The approach has become more age oriented; hence, it is more developmentally oriented. Recall that age appropriateness is defined by what the average individual without disabilities can do at a given age.

Keep in mind that many children with multiple and severe disabilities are cognitively normal; they are capable of mastering the regular curriculum when they receive the necessary supports (augmentative communication devices, motorized wheelchairs, low-vision aids). Here, however, *we focus on students who cannot follow the regular school curriculum and who have not mastered the self-help skills that lead to independence.*

Boothroyd (1983) suggested that the type of intervention chosen for the child after evaluation may be one of the following:

- *Corrective:* Try to minimize the loss through medical procedures.

- *Preventive:* Attempt to prevent the occurrence of secondary disabilities.

- *Circumvention:* Enrich the environment to provide alternative stimulation for what the child cannot receive (for example, touch for sight).

- *Compensatory:* Provide prostheses such as hearing aids and other types of technical assistance to help the child gain access to the environment.

- *Remedial:* Fill in the gaps in development through frequent evaluations to determine what may have been missed in training and education.

ADAPTING THE LEARNING ENVIRONMENT

In the past, many children with multiple and severe disabilities were excluded from public schools because they did not fit into ongoing special education programs or because they were not toilet trained. Many of these youngsters were assigned to a residential institution for the more severe of their disabilities. For example, a child who was both mentally retarded and hearing impaired might have been placed in a residential institution serving people with mental retardation or mental illness; often the institution had neither the facilities nor the personnel to provide education for someone with a hearing loss.

Provisions for children with disabilities are different today because of parent involvement and the efforts of the Association for Persons with Severe Disabilities, the Council for Exceptional Children, the National Association for Retarded Citizens, the American Association on Mental Retardation, and other advocacy groups. The Civil Rights Act and the Education for All Handicapped Children Act of 1975 (Public Law 94-142) made it mandatory for public schools to educate all children.

According to Turnbull and Turnbull (1991), legislation and court decisions have guaranteed children with disabilities

- A free public education

- An objective evaluation of their strengths and weaknesses

- Appropriate and individualized education programs

Students with multiple and severe disabilities can participate at least partially in most school and non-school activities, increasing their confidence and their peers' perceptions of them as valuable, productive members of society. (© Gale Zucker)

⭐ *Students who are severely disabled should participate in regular classroom activities for at least part of the day.*

- Education within the least restrictive environment
- The right to procedural due process so they can challenge the actions of state and local educational authorities

The procedural safeguards included in IDEA 1997 are extensive. They include parents' rights to timely resolution of complaints, to confidentiality, whether to accept services, to examine records, and to receive written notices in their native language of all their rights (U.S. Department of Education, 1997). In addition, the parents, guardians, or surrogates of each child have the right to share with educators in making decisions that affect the child's education.

These laws and court decisions also have mandated the development of community programs for many children who previously were institutionalized. Brown, Nietupski, and Hamre-Nietupski (1976) advocated very early that "severely handicapped students should be placed in self-contained classes in public schools. . . . They have a right to be visible functioning citizens integrated into the everyday life of complex public communities" (p. 3). This thinking has been expanded to the idea of placing these students in a regular classroom for at least part of the day. In planning for children with multiple disabilities, Baumgart et al. (1982) suggest the following:

- Partial participation in chronological age-appropriate environments and activities is educationally more advantageous than exclusion from such environments and activities.

- Students with multiple and severe disabilities, regardless of their degree of dependence or level of functioning, should be allowed to participate at least partially in a wide range of school and nonschool environments and activities.

- The kinds and degrees of partial participation in school and nonschool environments and activities should be increased through direct and systematic instruction.

- Partial participation in school and nonschool environments and activities should result in a student being perceived by others as a more valuable, contributing, striving, and productive member of society.

- Systematic, coordinated, and longitudinal efforts must be initiated at a young age to prepare for at least partial participation in as many environments and activities with nondisabled chronological age-appropriate peers and other persons as possible. (Baumgart et al., 1982, p. 19)

Inclusion: Integrated Settings

Youngsters with severe and multiple disabilities should be taught in a variety of integrated environments, both in and out of school. An integrated setting is any setting where persons without disabilities and persons with disabilities are both present. These students have difficulty generalizing skills and applying skills they have learned in one setting to another. Mary, a 16-year-old with severe disabilities, has just completed the bed-making program at school. But she cannot make her bed at home or at her grandmother's house because she is not able to generalize the skills across different environments, from school to home and to her grandmother's house.

There are many ways to help youngsters generalize skills. One is to teach the skill in the environment in which the person will use it. This kind of real-world training requires multiple integrated educational settings, both at school and in the community. This training is not classroom based; it is community based. If we want to teach shopping skills, we do not use a pretend store in the classroom. Instead, we go out into the community to grocery stores, department stores, and specialty shops.

Today, a growing body of literature supports the concept of integrating these students in public schools and community settings:

- Positive changes have been reported in the attitudes of nondisabled individuals toward their peers with severe disabilities at various age levels (Grenot-Scheyer, 1994; Voeltz, 1980).

- Integration has led to improvements in the social and communication skills of children with severe disabilities (Jenkins, Speltz, & Odom, 1985; Newton, Horner, Ard, LeBaron, & Sapperton, 1994).

- Integration has improved interaction between students with severe disabilities and their nondisabled agemates (Roberts, Burchinal, & Bailey, 1994).

- Integration facilitates adjustment to community settings as adults (Hasazi, Gordon, & Roe, 1985; Helmstetter, Peck, & Giangreco, 1994).

One of the major findings about including persons with multiple and severe disabilities in general education classrooms is that the participation increases their

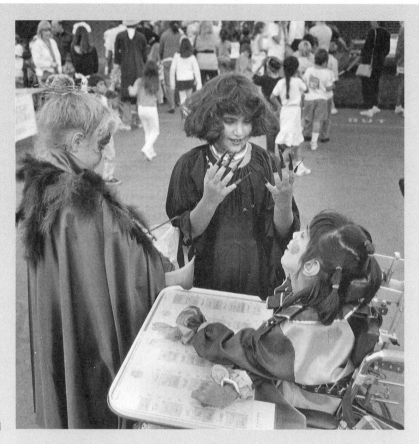

To maximize the integration opportunities for students with severe disabilities, teachers should limit the ratio of disabled to nondisabled students in any setting and use students without disabilities as peer tutors. (© Spencer Grant/Monkmeyer Press Photo Service)

Interacting with students who have severe disabilities teaches tolerance to students who are not disabled.

social and interpersonal skills. They display increased responsiveness to others, increased reciprocal interactions, and increased displays of affect toward others (Grenot-Scheyer, 1994). In addition, the inclusion of those with multiple and severe disabilities in general education classrooms has an impact on their peers who do not have disabilities. The latter show increased tolerance for others, increased tolerance for diversity, and growth in their own personal development (Helmstetter, Peck, & Giangreco, 1994).

Whatever the age of the students or the severity of their disabilities, integration provides them with a curriculum that is the most functional and age appropriate possible. Guiltinan (1986) suggested several ways for teachers and administrators to make inclusion work.

MAKING INCLUSION WORK

- Limit the ratio of disabled to nondisabled students in any setting.
- Highlight your student's strengths. If the student has well-developed gross motor skills but weak fine motor skills, integrate her or him into sports rather than art.
- Provide "extra help" at first to start the process.
- Encourage students with disabilities to dress like their peers. Send home dress tips to parents.

■ Use students without disabilities to be peer tutors and friends to the student with disabilities.

■ Be positive when talking to other teachers or students about the student with disabilities.

■ Arrange the classroom schedule to maximize integration opportunities. (adapted from Guiltinan, 1986, pp. 4–5)

ADAPTING CURRICULUM

Data Collecting

The ongoing collection of data about a student's responses is the core of an educational program.

Collecting data is an everyday activity for most people. We collect data about the weather to help us choose our clothes and plan for the weekend; we often compare prices before we make a purchase; gauges and dials give us the data we need to keep our cars in good running condition. Without data, decisions are based on guesses and intuition. It is not surprising, then, that we need information to make intelligent programming decisions for children with disabilities. Wolery, Bailey, and Sugai (1988) suggested several reasons why data collection is necessary:

■ To pinpoint students' status

■ To monitor progress and determine the program's effectiveness

■ To provide feedback to students and parents

■ To document efforts and demonstrate accountability

Teachers of students with multiple and severe disabilities collect data on all kinds of things: the number of steps a student making a sandwich completes correctly, the length of time it takes a student to complete a vocational assembly task (such as packaging drill bits), the percentage of community information signs a student reads correctly, the amount of time a student spends on off-task behaviors. This kind of information enables teachers and other service providers to plan programs that meet a student's needs and to make decisions about the student's educational progress.

The teacher takes the individual through as many stages as possible by

■ Conditionally reinforcing simple responses related to causality, such as picking up a toy or touching someone to signal a need

■ Interactional coaching, turn taking, imitation of facial expressions, gestures, and sound

■ Individual teaching at the time of engaging in functional activities

The communication skills taught to persons with multiple and severe disabilities are functional in that they are relevant to the individual's survival and independent functioning in the community as appropriately (societally determined) as possible (Bradley, Ashbaugh, & Blaney, 1994; Goetz, Guess, & Campbell, 1987).

Fuchs and Deno (1994) suggested that measurement of students' status and progress must

■ Be repeated on material of comparable difficulty (to curriculum taught) over time

- Incorporate valid indicators of the critical outcomes of instruction
- Rely on a data base that permits quantitative and qualitative descriptions of students' performance to assist teachers in adjusting and enhancing their instruction

Functional Age-Appropriate Skills

Teaching functional skills that students will use in daily living is an important part of the curriculum.

The skills taught to students with severe disabilities must be both functional and age appropriate. Functional skills can be used immediately by the student, are necessary in everyday settings, and increase to some extent the student's independence. Folding a sheet of paper in half is not a functional skill; folding clothes is (Brown & Lehr, 1989; Snell, 1993).

Age-appropriate skills are appropriate to the student's chronological age, not mental age. A 16-year-old boy who is severely disabled is not taught how to solve a four-piece jigsaw puzzle of a dog, although it may correspond to his mental age. Instead, the focus is on activities the boy can carry out to some degree as his nondisabled agemates do—for example, eating in a restaurant, using a neighborhood health club, or operating a television set or personal stereo. If the skills are not age appropriate, they are not likely to be functional. Moreover, age-appropriate skills give students with severe disabilities a measure of social acceptance.

Clearly, some youngsters with severe disabilities cannot do many tasks that their nondisabled agemates can do. Nevertheless, most of them can at least take part in certain activities. Partial participation enables students with disabilities to interact with their nondisabled agemates as much as possible (Falvey, 1995; Sailor, 1991).

The standard practice is to teach each step. Take, for example, buying a hamburger: You open the door, stand in line, ask for what you want, pay for it, accept any change, wait until it is served, move from the order line to the reception area, receive the food, take it to the accepted place for eating, and clean up afterward. Some students with autism and others with severe physical disabilities may be apraxic—that is, they cannot realize what to do when confronted with a situation such as opening a door and will stand in front of the door in confusion. Thus, teaching how to open different types of doors becomes the first step. After each step is mastered, the individual who has multiple and severe disabilities must be taught that the same (or very similar) procedures apply at the pizza parlor, the ice cream store, and so on. Preparation may begin in the classroom, but it also must be taught in the actual community for **generalization** and maintenance to take place (Lehr & Brown, 1996). Rewarding and reinforcing each successfully completed step are very important.

Generalization of Skills.   The major problem for the teacher or facilitator of individuals with multiple and severe disabilities is to teach the individual that what he or she has learned can be applied in other settings. Traditionally, skills were taught in the classroom and were not transferred to or used in other settings by these individuals.

To understand the importance of this concept, consider a practical example. Most of us have forgotten how we learned to go to a store or to a fast-food restaurant to buy something. We learned it at some time, however, probably through guided instructions from our parents or by imitating them. Children with multiple and severe disabilities must be taught each step that is necessary to complete what to us might seem to be a simple task. They also must learn that they can apply these steps in other settings. It is not an easy process but one that requires persistence, repetition, and a variety of settings in which to use the skills.

Assessment of Skills.   Federal regulations about assessing or evaluating the skills of individuals with multiple and severe disabilities are quite clear: The evaluation must be appropriate to the needs of the individual, his or her family, and the recommended potential early intervention program. The regulations are also concerned with cultural and language issues. Any evaluation must be based on the reality of the family's culture and the individual's experience. Most normed tests assume uniform cultural experiences; thus, they are obviously biased against individuals whose life experiences vary from those of the dominant middle class.

Good assessment is the foundation of good instruction. Knowing what a person can do and what he or she needs to learn how to do provides the initial step for instruction. A basic tenet of professional education has been to plan instruction at the level of a child's functioning and then take him or her to the next step. In other words, needs are focused on strengths. Authentic assessments comprise a variety of tasks in which the person generates a response in a real-life situation, rather than choosing a response on a piece of paper (Gage & Falvey, 1995).

Although commercial assessment devices are available, they sometimes fail to meet the individual needs of students with multiple and severe disabilities. Norm-referenced tests are not very helpful for classroom teachers. IQ scores and developmental-age quotients do not give us specific information about what students can and cannot do. **Criterion-referenced tests**—tests that compare students' levels of functioning to a standard of mastery—are more useful. Because children with multiple and severe disabilities are a heterogeneous group, commercial assessment devices must be adjusted to each child's age and type of disabilities, to the teacher's qualifications, and to the characteristics and demands of the school, the community, and the student's home environment.

The constraints of many published assessment instruments have led many teachers to develop their own. Brown, Nietupski, & Hamre-Nietupski (1976) outlined a process called *ecological inventory* that teachers can use to develop and individualize functional curriculum for their students. The process consists of six phases.

1. Delineate the four curriculum domains: domestic skills, vocational skills, leisure and recreational skills, and community living skills.

2. Identify those environments in the community that require the use of these skills.

3. Identify the smaller environments (subenvironments) in which students with multiple and severe disabilities function or might function.

4. Make an inventory of the age-appropriate and age-related activities that occur in the subenvironments (activities related to the bathroom, for example, include toileting and cleaning the sink).

5. Identify the skills that must be taught to perform the tasks.

6. Use special teaching procedures to instruct students with multiple and severe disabilities in the performance of the identified skill in a natural environment.

The assessment of a student's skill must take place in the setting where the student will use the skill.

Figure 11.1 shows part of an ecological inventory for an adolescent with a severe disability. The domain here is community living skills. One of the environments (a current environment) is the doctor's office. Subenvironments are all the settings in which the student must be able to function to get to the doctor's office and be examined. The focus here is on the examination room and the activity of removing one's clothes. The skills are the tasks that a person must carry out to remove his or her clothes.

Preparing an ecological inventory is time-consuming, but the information it provides is extremely valuable. The inventory can be used to assess a student's current level of functioning and to plan the educational agenda (skills that must be taught and the order in which to teach them). An ecological inventory, then, can be the basis of the individualized education program. Furthermore, because the curriculum is specific to a certain youngster, it is likely to be the most functional, most appropriate curriculum possible.

ADAPTING TEACHING STRATEGIES

Teaching and Assessing

Intervention begins with diagnosis, frequently at birth.

There are two approaches to teaching children with multiple and severe disabilities. One recognizes that development starts before birth, that it continues rapidly in the first year, and that the individual is more flexible and more easily influenced by environmental input during the early years. The other, newer approach uses knowledge of genetically determined development to decide what the child will need to know to function in a specific environment and what skills the child already possesses. The teacher then develops strategies to teach the child specific activities that will lead to mastery of a set of functional skills that support independence.

To understand these approaches, it is necessary to understand some of the basics of normal (ordinary) development.

One of the great achievements in human beings is the ability to communicate by using symbols, usually words or signs. A symbol is something that stands for something else—a person, event, attitude, feeling, concept. It usually refers directly to the thing signified; for example, "Mama" is mother, usually a specific mother. A gesture is not a symbol unless it is part of a system, such as sign language, in which specific gestures always mean the same thing. Gestures that are not part of a sign language system usually have a variety of meanings. For example, the gesture of pointing can mean "See the dog," "Bring me a toy," or "I want to go outside."

It has been discovered that a symbol system grows out of genetically programmed prelinguistic behaviors such as cries, grunts, the social smile, eye contact, and interaction with another followed by babbling; finally, around 12 months of age, a child's oral sounds become words (Bates, 1979; Dromi, 1992). After 12 months of age, the average child proceeds rapidly from one word to the mastery of thousands by age 5, using them in a variety of ways to express logical communications and cognitive functioning.

Both speech and gestures can be part of a communication system. Persons who are most severely cognitively disabled, however, may never learn either speech or a

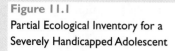

Figure 11.1

Partial Ecological Inventory for a Severely Handicapped Adolescent

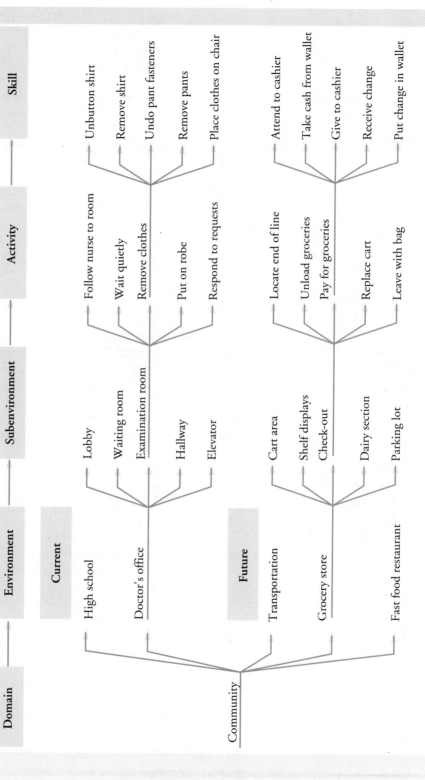

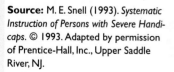

Some type of communication system needs to be taught to children who otherwise would have difficulty communicating.

gestural system and have to rely on nonlinguistic systems to communicate their wants and needs (Sternberg, 1991).

At the beginning of the education process, an early intervention teacher does not know how far the individual with multiple disabilities will develop. The prelinguistic system usually begins at birth and definitely begins by 2 months of age for the individual with severe retardation. Therefore, education must begin early to identify the prelinguistic vocalizations and gestures so they can be developed into a communication system and ideally a symbol system consisting of signs or words.

A major problem with children with multiple and severe disabilities is that they tend to lack the natural, genetically programmed inquisitiveness, curiosity, and desire to manipulate objects that come automatically to the average, nondisabled child. The facilitator (teacher or family member) must encourage children with multiple and severe disabilities to learn that they can use their genetically programmed prelinguistic skills and sounds to communicate—that is, they can use a gesture to show, to request, to accept, or to refuse. These simple sensorimotor patterns can help the individual move from internal worlds to the external world (Dunst & Lowe, 1986). Developing these genetically programmed gestures into a communication system enables the individual with severe and profound disabilities to relate to people in his or her environment.

The techniques of teaching persons with multiple and severe disabilities to use these genetically programmed sensorimotor patterns is called augmented or alternative communication (Beukelman & Mirenda, 1992; Flippo, Inge, & Barais, 1995; Meyer, Peck, & Brown, 1991; Miller, 1993). It is hoped that such teaching will move the child from the genetic reflex state of movements, signals, and gestures to pictures and signs and then to symbols, verbal speech, or sign language.

Preschool

Most young children with multiple and severe disabilities attend special preschools for half a day or a full day. Mastery of communication skills is usually the major aim of the curriculum. The ability it teaches to recognize the self as a person is also included (recall our discussion of Murphy and Byrne's [1983] six-step developmental sequence earlier in this chapter). The curriculum does not teach isolated skills; it teaches activities and routines that combine functional communication with physical and social needs. In addition, specialized personnel, such as physical, speech, and occupational therapists, will assist by providing appropriate therapies.

A major goal of the preschool is to move the children forward so they will begin to act on the environment by manipulating objects, making requests to satisfy their needs, and exercising their natural curiosity—in other words, learning how to learn. The skills should relate to communication, mobility, social skills, and self-management. The best generalization and maintenance occurs when the skill

- Has immediate utility to the individual
- Produces something the student wants
- Was acquired in the social context where it will be used

- Is appropriate for the student's level of development
- Is practical and useful
- Is adaptable (Goetz, Guess, & Campbell, 1987)

Those characteristics are the guidelines for the development of any skill, from drinking from a cup or eating an apple to working in a fast-food restaurant.

In addition to overcoming the child's disabilities, the teacher or facilitator must overcome two other obstacles: (1) Caregivers usually are less flexible and less permissive than teachers in encouraging creative activity, and they are more intrusive in their interactions with children with multiple and severe disabilities. They tend to do things for the children, such as putting on their coats, instead of teaching them how to do things. This is a less-than-ideal learning strategy (Linden, Kankkunen, & Tjellstrom, 1985). (2) The child with multiple disabilities is usually less inquisitive, more withdrawn, less active, and less fun than a child without disabilities, and engages in little play with objects. The teacher has to help families learn new strategies and also help the child overcome his or her lack of involvement with the environment. The teacher does so by teaching family members the meaning of their child's gestures and how to be more interactive with their child.

Primary and Secondary School

In elementary school, individuals with multiple and severe disabilities and those with severe retardation are likely to have similar curricula, which are continuations of efforts to teach functional skills that lead to clear communication and independence. If the child is moderately retarded, more complex skills can be taught—skills that are useful, practical, survival oriented, and socially appropriate.

Major efforts are being made to teach these children self-determination skills and to help them become more involved in their own decision making (Wehmeyer, Agran, & Hughes, 1998). Self-determination skills include the expression of rights (the ability to say no, ask for favors, and make requests) and the ability to express positive and negative feelings. Some students will have to express their feelings nonverbally or with the help of augmentative or alternative communication systems.

Teachers can directly introduce the skill, discuss it, identify steps, model the skill, rehearse or role-play, and assist the student in generalizing the skills. Table 11.4 lists social skill training instructional steps in assertiveness.

An example of a curriculum for all ages is the Syracuse Community Referenced Curriculum Guide (Ford et al., 1989). The curriculum stresses five areas of school concern: (1) self-management; (2) home living, including eating, food preparation, hygiene, and toileting; (3) vocational jobs at all levels, from cleaning blackboards to working at a fast-food chain or motel; (4) recreational leisure with family and friends, fitness, and travel; and (5) general community functioning, including shopping, eating out, and using community services.

A guide for planning inclusive education, *Choosing Options and Accommodation for Children (COACH)*, emphasizes collaborative teamwork with the family as the cornerstone of educational planning (Giangreco, Cloninger, & Iverson, 1998). The manual includes clear statements of goals, activities, and sample

TABLE 11.4   Skills Needed for Assertiveness

Skill Area	Discrete Skills
Expression of rights	Identifies and articulates rights
	Identifies and articulates associated responsibilities
	Discriminates conflicts between rights of individual(s) and groups
	Identifies and articulates personal beliefs and values
	Identifies and articulates differences among assertive, nonassertive, and aggressive behaviors
	Discriminates among statements of wants, needs, opinion, and fact
	Understands inherent risk factor in assertion
Verbal assertion skills	Expresses rights statement in brief, concise, and direct manner
	Communicates rights statement in first person
	Discriminates between and employs refusals and behavior-change requests
	Communicates opinions and beliefs appropriately
	Employs appropriate tone of voice
	Uses intonation and timing effectively
	Responds appropriately to aggression and persists in assertion
Nonverbal assertion skills	Uses and understands body language
	Uses gestures and facial expressions appropriately
	Makes eye contact appropriately
	Uses appropriate posture and body positioning
Expression of elaborations	Communicates understanding of others' feelings, opinions, or experiences
	Employs negotiation, compromise, and persuasion skills
	Modulates voice characteristics to match elaboration
Conversation skills	Practices active listening skills

Source: From M. L. Wehmeyer, M. Agran, & C. Hughes (1998). *Teaching Self-Determination to Students with Disabilities: Basic Skills for Successful Transition* (p. 222). Baltimore: Paul H. Brookes. Reprinted with permission.

forms, including forms for interviews, assessments, and IEPs, and community and school worksheets.

The key elements of the curriculum are to develop throughout elementary, middle, and high school individualized programs that lead to successful transition into the community and adult lifestyles. A teacher trained in alternative instructional strategies is necessary to accomplish these goals.

Communication boards and other augmentative systems have been developed to help the nonvocal student add to and supplement available speech. (© Spencer Grant/The Picture Cube)

Teaching Strategies for Nonvocal Students

Many children with severe physical and cognitive disabilities have major communication impairments. They often are unable to use speech functionally. This inability to communicate is one of the most formidable obstacles that children with multiple and severe disabilities face. It prevents them from interacting successfully with their environments and impedes their ability to learn from interactive experiences, things that nondisabled children do readily.

Augmentative and alternative communication devices have been developed to help students who are nonvocal communicate. A simple device is the *communication board*, a piece of cardboard or other stable material on which pictures, words, or symbols can be written or attached. Computer screens also can serve as communication devices. These devices are designed not to replace speech but to add to and supplement available speech. With these devices the student can indicate needs, preferences, and responses by pointing to items (direct selection). The student may also look in the direction of an item (scanning), and the teacher recognizes the student's response (Beukelman & Mirenda, 1994).

Technology for Nonvocal Students

Computers with speech synthesizers produce messages and written text. Custom-made keyboards, touch screens, and the mouse provide students with access to a wide array of curriculum.

Technological advances have increased the sophistication of augmentative devices. There are wall charts that are battery operated, voice synthesizers in several different languages, and a wide range of devices for computer access. Beukeleman and Mirenda (1994) mention that a compact disc containing over sixteen thousand product descriptions can be obtained from Trace Research and Development Center, S-151 Waisman Center, 1500 Highland Avenue, Madison, WI 53705.

TECHNOLOGY

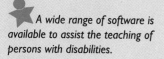

A wide range of software is available to assist the teaching of persons with disabilities.

A national commitment to support and encourage the development of computer technology for use by and with persons with disabilities is contained in IDEA as amended in 1997. The act encourages widespread use of computer technology with persons with disabilities for education, measurement, vocational training, and transition to the world of work (Greenwood, 1994).

Instructional Technology

Computers are becoming standard equipment in classes for children with disabilities. Curriculum software—programs too numerous to mention—is being developed continuously. There are programs designed specifically for individuals with learning, hearing, vision, motor, and cognitive disabilities (see Council for Exceptional Children, 1994).

Assistive Technology

Some children may need to use head pointers to type. Some can use a single finger to call up software (the curriculum) to read, and they can respond to it with single-finger pressure. Notebook computers, which are the size of a textbook and weigh from seven to eight pounds, are very useful for children with disabilities who possess a communication system (Cary & Sale, 1994).

TRANSITION

From Home and School to Community and Work

The recent emphasis on transitional programming from high school to work and many plans for supportive employment (Bellamy, Rhodes, Mank, & Albin, 1988) have opened new vistas for persons with multiple and severe disabilities. Persons with multiple and severe disabilities can be empowered to make decisions about their own preferences for work, living arrangements, and leisure activities (Brown & Gothelf, 1996; Brown & Lehr, 1996; Demchak, 1994; Gothelf, Crimmins, Mercer, & Finocchiaro, 1994). Wehmeyer, Agran, and Hughes (1998) suggest that for assertive training for transition, the teacher should include a series of basic elements and activities, which are listed in Table 11.5. Such empowerment suggests moving toward supportive apartments, homeownership, and cooperative and shared living space (Brown & Gothelf, 1996). The group home may not be the ideal housing model. Some articles indicate a shift from program-centered to person-centered decision making. An important aspect of this perspective is the belief that person-centered programs will improve the mental and physical health of persons with severe disabilities (Bradley, Ashbaugh, & Blaney, 1994; Newton, Horner, Ard, LeBaron, & Sapperton, 1994).

Transition programs from school to adult life aim for lifestyles for those with multiple and severe disabilities that develop their valued participation in the world of work with its routines, its monetary benefits, and its social relationships that

TABLE 11.5	Empirically Validated Transition Support Strategies	
Support Strategy	**Definition**	**Example**
Teach social skills	Teach student social behaviors that facilitate interactions with significant others in a manner considered socially appropriate.	A student initiates conversation with peers without disabilities while at lunch or between classes.
Teach self-management and independence	Teach student self-management skills to enable him or her to perform expected behaviors more independently.	Using pictures of household tasks while cleaning her home, a young woman looks at a picture, performs the task, records completion of the task, and moves on to the next task.
Identify independence objectives	Survey student's environments (e.g., home, community, school, work) through observation and by interviewing student and significant others to identify areas in which performance is not consistent with expectations.	In a restaurant in which a student works, ask the supervisor to identify specific tasks that the student is not performing consistently when serving food.
Assess social acceptance	Assess student's acceptance of everyday performance via evaluations completed by student's teachers, employers, and others and by comparing student's performance to that of peers.	A student compares her evaluation of her attendance at school with her teacher's evaluation.
Identify co-worker, peer, and family support	Identify individuals who may provide supports for a student at home, school, work, or in the community.	Co-workers are identified who may assist a new employee in learning required job skills and who may interact socially with the employee during breaks or lunch.
Identify student's preferences and choices	Identify student's expectations and preferences with respect to daily living and support choice making by observations and interviews with student and other stakeholders; in addition, assess student's choice-making and decisionmaking skills.	Observe a graduating senior's participation in his or her chosen recreation activity during free time over a 2-week period.
Monitor social acceptance across time	Establish a continuous schedule by which student, teachers, employers, co-workers, and significant others evaluate acceptance of student's performance; use evaluations to identify and discuss discrepancies between observed and expected performance.	A schedule is established in which an employee's job supervisor completes evaluation of employee's social behavior on a weekly basis. Supervisor discusses each evaluation with the employee, including areas that differ from the supervisor's expectations.
Identify environmental support	Identify naturally occurring cues in the student's workplace and other environments that will support him or her in initiating and completing expected and desired behavior.	A man employed in housekeeping in a motel learns to empty wastebaskets when they are overflowing with trash.

(continued)

	TABLE 11.5　Empirically Validated Transition Support Strategies (continued)	
Support Strategy	**Definition**	**Example**
Match support to student's needs	Match existing support identified to those areas in which student needs support.	An employee fails to take breaks or return back to his or her work station on time. The employee is taught to go on break when co-workers leave their job stations and return to work when co-workers do.
Teach choice making and decision making	Teach the student skills that are necessary to make choices and decisions and to express preferences, and provide opportunities to exercise choice.	A high school sophomore chooses to work in a child care center rather than a fast-food restaurant.

Source: M. L. Wehmeyer, M. Agran, & C. Hughes (1998). *Teaching Self-Determination to Students with Disabilities: Basic Skills for Successful Transition* (pp. 64–65). Baltimore: Paul H. Brookes. Reprinted with permission.

A transition coordinator assists in the transition from school to work.

build the self-confidence and self-efficacy of the individual (O'Neill, Gothelf, Cohen, Lehman, & Woolf, 1991). To aid in transition, it is useful to interview the family (IDEA 1997 mandates involvement of the family) to ascertain their hopes and expectations for their child and to secure information about family support and transportation. The process should begin as early as when the child is 12 years of age. A family vocational interview form can be obtained from Margaret D. Hutchins, Illinois State University Campus, Box 5910, Normal, IL 61761.

Also included in IDEA 1997 is the concept of involving the student in making decisions about his or her future. The focus should be not only on limitations but also on recognition of the individual's skills and areas in which he or she can act independently. This includes becoming as autonomous as possible in all environments, self-regulation, self-evaluation, self-confidence, and ways to reach desired goals (Wehmeyer, Agran, & Hughes, 1998). To be able to accomplish this participation, the individual needs to be taught to move from high school vocational skills development to the community setting in which the work is to take place. This requires a *transition coordinator,* who plans for and assists in the transition (Bellamy, Rhodes, Mank, & Albin, 1988; Falvey, Coot, Bishop, & Grenot-Scheyer, 1989; O'Neill, Gothelf, Cohen, Lehman, & Woolf, 1991).

Competitive paid employment at or above the minimum wage is still infrequent for persons with multiple and severe disabilities who may need ongoing support to perform in a work setting. Supportive employment is subsidized with government funds to encourage the employment of individuals with multiple and severe disabilities. It is conducted in a variety of settings (for example, fast-food restaurants, supermarkets, parks, and libraries) with additional support provided to include supervision and skills development for the individual.

The goal is to hold a paying job successfully (functional competence) and to live one's own life. Ideally, to support these goals, working side by side with those with multiple and severe disabilities, the nondisabled will perceive them as valued members of society (O'Neill et al., 1991). Public acceptance should lead to acceptance of these persons taking part in leisure activities, developing relationships with nondisabled persons, and pursuing interests of their own (O'Neill et al., 1991).

The goal of the transition coordinator is to find age-appropriate settings in the community, prepare the person in that setting, and teach the individual how to function in that setting in accordance with the expectations of nondisabled persons (Falvey, 1989; Kregel, 1994).

An individual transition plan (ITP) is now being developed for each individual in these programs. The ITP requires a great deal of information from the school, the individual, the parents, and the community. Questions to be answered include the following:

- What will the student need to learn before leaving school?
- Where will the person live as an adult?
- What activities will replace school for recreation?
- How will this individual support himself or herself?
- What will he or she do in leisure time?
- How will this person travel using community transportation?
- How will he or she gain access to medical care?
- What will be the relationship with his or her family? (adapted from O'Neill et al., 1991)

Persons with multiple and severe disabilities differ from one another. They have similar but different needs. No one set of treatments can cover everyone adequately. It is clear that the coordinator must have the skill to develop a plan for each person. The teacher or coordinator will need to collect information on the individual's past to find the most suitable community site, to conduct a task analysis of what will be required at that work site, and then to initiate a prescriptive program to meet these demands. To encourage persistence in work habits, the coordinator will try to match the individual to certain activities on the basis of the person's preferences.

Family and Lifespan Issues

Attempts to normalize the lifestyles of children with multiple and severe disabilities would be largely a waste of time if we did not provide for the normalization of the lifestyles of adults in the community. Over the past twenty-five years, substantial efforts have been made to create community living and vocational arrangements to provide for adults who have returned to the community from institutions and to prevent the institutionalization of youngsters who have been living in the community.

LIVING ARRANGEMENTS

The number of programs for community living has been growing since 1961, when President John F. Kennedy established the Presidential Committee on Mental Retardation (Rusch, Chadsey-Rusch, & Lagomarcino, 1985). Today, these programs include living facilities, vocational and rehabilitation workshops, and recreational services. Coordinated team planning in the community is considered the appropriate manner to support people with disabilities so they can live independently in their community (Bradley, Ashbaugh, & Blaney, 1994).

Major efforts are being made to enable persons with severe and profound disabilities to live and work as independently as they are able (Brown & Gothelf, 1996). The emerging trend emphasizes the involvement of the person with a disability and his or her family in decision making about work, leisure, and living arrangements (Bradley, Ashbaugh, & Blaney, 1994; IDEA, 1997).

VOCATIONAL OPPORTUNITIES

Another step in the integration of adults with multiple and severe disabilities is providing appropriate vocational opportunities. Various options exist, among them day treatment and day habilitation programs, sheltered workshops, and supportive competitive employment. Table 11.6 lists other services that are available.

Day Treatment Programs

The day treatment program is the most restrictive setting for adults with multiple and severe disabilities. These programs are

> designed to provide therapeutic activities for disabled workers whose physical or mental impairment is so severe as to make their productive capacity inconsequential. Therapeutic activities include custodial activities (such as activities that focus on teaching basic living skills) and any purposeful activity so long as work or production is not the main purpose. (U.S. Department of Labor as cited in Bellamy, Rhodes, Bourbeau, & Mank, 1986, p. 260)

The purpose of these centers is to teach necessary life skills. Rather than providing vocational opportunities, the day treatment center provides continuing education.

Day Habilitation Programs

Day habilitation programs are funded by the individual states. They are based in classrooms, but much of the experience provided takes place in the community. Transportation is furnished by the program.

Sheltered Workshops

The **sheltered workshop** provides vocational services to adults with disabilities (Bellamy et al, 1986). The U.S. Department of Labor defines a sheltered workshop as

> a charitable organization or institution conducted not-for-profit, but for the purpose of carrying out a recognized rehabilitation program for handicapped workers, and/or providing such individuals with remunerative employment or other occupational rehabilitating activity of an educational or therapeutic nature. (cited in Bellamy et al., 1986, p. 260)

Although the goal of sheltered workshops is to prepare individuals with multiple and severe disabilities to obtain and maintain competitive employment, placement out of the segregated work environment rarely occurs (Bellamy et al.).

	TABLE 11.6 Vocational Rehabilitation Services
Service	**Description of Service**
Evaluation	To determine a person's interests, capabilities, aptitudes, and limitations, and the range of services needed to prepare the individual for employment
Counseling and guidance	To help the person aim for a job in keeping with his or her interests, capabilities, aptitudes, and limitations
Medical and hospital care	To attend, if needed, to mental or physical problems that are obstacles to job preparation
Job training	To provide training that fits the person's needs and that leads to a definite work goal; can include personal adjustment training, prevocational training, vocational training, on-the-job training, and training in a sheltered workshop
Maintenance payments	To cover increases in a person's basic living expenses because of participation in vocational rehabilitation
Transportation	To support and maximize the benefits of other services being received
Services to family members	To help the person achieve the maximum benefit from other services being provided
Interpreter services	To assist persons with hearing impairments
Reader services	To assist the person with visual impairments, including note-taking services and orientation and mobility services
Aids and devices	To provide the person with needed aids and devices, such as telecommunication devices, sensory aids, artificial limbs, braces, and wheelchairs
Tools and equipment	To provide the person with tools and equipment needed to perform the job
Recruitment and training services	To provide new work opportunities in public service employment
Job placement	To help the person find a job, taking into consideration the person's abilities and training; includes placement into supported employment
Job follow-up	To help the person make whatever adjustments are needed to succeed at the job into which he or she has been placed
Occupational licenses or permits	To provide the person with the occupational licenses or permits that the law requires a person have before entering an occupation
Other	To provide other services that an individual may need to become employable

Source: L. Kupper (Ed.) (1991). "Options After High School for Youth with Disabilities." *NICHCY Transition Summary*, no. 7, p. 8. Available from the National Information Center for Children and Youth with Disabilities, P.O. Box 1492, Washington, DC 20013.

"The Miracles of Brea"

Our second child, Brea, was born three years ago with a muscle weakness. She had a club foot, a dislocated hip and some joint stiffness. She has a tracheostomy due to chronic respiratory problems and is fed via G-button because of swallowing difficulties. At night while Brea sleeps, we put her on a CPAP (continuous positive airway pressure) machine to put positive pressure into her lungs.

Brea says a few words and seems to understand almost everything. She can sit up when put in a sitting position, plays with her toys and loves books. She can scoot backwards on her bottom a little bit, but tires easily. That is the extent of her mobility. We are waiting for the insurance company to approve a wheelchair but for now we carry her everywhere. Brea is absolutely beautiful. She is happy and cheerful when healthy and entertained. She tends to get bored and irritable in the evening and it can be frustrating finally getting her to sleep. (She is very normal that way!)

Busy Days

My husband, Gil, and I work full time—he is in land surveying and I am a first-grade teacher. For the last three years, Brea has had a nurse who arrives when I go to work and leaves when I get home. In addition to the normal household and family chores waiting for me when I get home, there are breathing treatments, lung suctioning, chest therapy and blended food therapy. There is always physical therapy to be done, not to mention cuddling and playing with Brea as well as our five-year-old, Ross, and our dog, Willie. Then, of course, there is bath time, dinner time and book time before bed. Often during the winter months, Brea has pneumonia and has to be rushed to the hospital or is at home connected to oxygen tanks with an IV in her arm. Needless to say, our stress level is high!

Making Changes and Coping

Gil and I have always been outdoors people—on the go, travelling a lot. It has been hard to lose that freedom. We like to do things as a family but sometimes Brea is just not well enough to participate. When she is well enough to join us, we choose our activities carefully because she cannot stay in one position for too long and she needs breathing treatments every four to six hours.

We try to choose things to do together that will not add to our stress. We avoid large, quiet groups and indoor restaurants. We boat, bicycle and go to the beach, zoo or the homes of close friends. We have taken vacations with Brea and all of her medical equipment. It is tiring but worth it just to have a change of scenery. Sometimes we leave Brea with her grandmother and go on day trips with Ross. We are very fortunate to have my mom so close.

It is very hard to successfully deal with the stress and heartbreak of having a child like Brea. You have to be "thick-skinned" (not my strong point) and you have to be able to "transcend" the pain (I tend to be earth-bound!). Taking Brea anywhere can be very painful for me, especially when I notice people's reactions to her or watch other little girls. But, not taking her places is equally painful because she is my child and she should be there with me. I am constantly having to push aside negative and painful feelings, focusing instead on the sweetness of Brea, who she is and all the love we share. I am not denying my feelings or pain, but I do not waste too much energy on them.

Gil and I used to say maybe things will get easier. We finally realized that they probably won't.

We just have to be happy with our lives now. I want to be happy and I want my family to be happy. This is a terrible blow but our lives will go on and I want them to go on happily.

Some days I have a bad attitude. I am embarrassed by my inability to handle things gracefully. On some of those days, I just go ahead and be a grump or feel sorry for myself and Brea all day. (I apologize to people later if necessary!) I cry, rant and rave—whatever I need to do. And then I feel better.

I take long runs four or five times a week. I go to church and have met a lot of supportive and inspiring people there. I read whenever I have time. I eat well, take vitamins and buy myself something nice whenever I can afford it! None of this takes away the pain but it helps me to deal with it.

Brea will have hip surgery this summer and will be in a body cast for eight weeks. In the fall she will be attending a preschool program for children with disabilities, which will be at my school for the first time ever. We are hoping that she will be healthy enough to attend on a regular basis.

Different Kinds of Miracles

Ever since Brea was born, I have been hoping to write a miracle story—the kind where the child beats all the odds, surprises all the doctors and lives a normal life. Although that miracle has not taken place, I can see other miracles at work here—the miracle of Brea who is happy and loving in spite of all her hardships. The miracle of my husband and I—basically immature and unprepared for this crisis—handling it (sometimes ineptly and other times well). And the miracle of my little boy, Ross—happy, healthy and telling his playmate on the way home from school, "Wait till you see my sister!"

Source: "The Miracles of Brea" by Chelle Howatt, *Exceptional Parent* (April–May 1993), pp. 22–23. Reprinted with the expressed consent and approval of *Exceptional Parent*, a monthly magazine for parents and families of children with disabilities and special health-care needs. Subscription cost is $36 per year for 12 issues; call 1-877-372-7368. Offices are at 555 Kinderkamack Rd., Oradell, NJ 07649.

What Is the Context?

A mother explains the many difficulties and hidden rewards of having a child with multiple disabilities. Despite having to modify family activities to accommodate Brea's needs, the family remains active outdoors. The mother relies on emotional support from the family and community and has developed several ways to relieve the everyday stress of caring for Brea. The family's goal is to continue their lives with as much normalcy and happiness as possible.

Pivotal Issues for Teachers

How has the family's attitude helped Brea develop? How has the family adapted its activities to accommodate Brea's disabilities? What kinds of support does the family need from the community and from social programs?

Supportive Competitive Employment

Day treatment centers and sheltered workshops violate many of the philosophical tenets of inclusion, supportive employment, and paid employment. The settings are segregated, and they do not fall within the boundaries of normalization, least restrictive environment, or partial participation. These shortcomings have increased the popularity of **supportive competitive employment** training programs. These programs are attractive because both the individual and the public benefit (Bellamy et al., 1986).

Hill and Wehman (1983) presented an analysis of workshop versus competitive employment costs over a four-year period. They followed ninety adults labeled as having moderate or severe disabilities and measured many different variables, including the number of months each person worked, the number of staff hours needed at each workplace, the income earned, and the cost of operation. After four years, the competitive employment program had saved the public $100,000.

Data that encourage supportive competitive employment and discourage sheltered workshop employment are growing. But determining how to deliver the most effective and efficient vocational opportunities to people with multiple and severe disabilities remains an unsolved problem. Rusch, Chadsey-Rusch, and Johnson (1992, p. 146) described supportive employment approaches.

APPROACHES TO SUPPORTIVE EMPLOYMENT

- *Individual placement model:* The individual is hired by an employer, and a job coach assists the employee, gradually decreasing the amount of support until the employee is able to perform the task without assistance.
- *Clustered placement model:* A group of six to eight individuals working for a company receives continuous guidance and supervision from a job coach employed by the company.
- *Mobile work crew:* A group works out of a van at several locations in the community under the supervision of a job coach, who provides continuous guidance and direction.

One can see in those models the movement from independence to continuous supervision. The models allow many individuals with multiple and severe disabilities the opportunity to engage in meaningful work instead of spending their lives isolated within their homes. Currently, fewer than 30 percent of the population with multiple and severe disabilities are employed in some capacity, but it is hoped that this percentage can be greatly increased in the future.

Szymanski (1994) suggested that lifespan considerations for transition should include interventions that

- Are designed to be maximally under the control of the individual rather than others
- Are designed to facilitate independence or interdependence and autonomy
- Use the least intrusive means that are effective
- Use the most natural interventions for the particular work environment (pp. 406–407)

Fewer than 30 percent of people with multiple and severe disabilities are employed.

The Rehabilitation Research and Training Center at Virginia Commonwealth University is a valuable resource for technical assistance and information on supportive employment. (See the listing under "Professional Organizations," at the end of this chapter.) The goal of the center is to "improve supportive employment outcomes for individuals with the most severe disabilities."

Never underestimate the impact on a family of having a child with severe and multiple disabilities. Some families suffer grief and mourn because they do not have their ideal child. Others show amazing strength in coping with the emotional, physical, and economic demands placed on them.

Some families face the lifelong challenge of providing assistance to a child with sensory impairments who is in a wheelchair. Consider the needs of a child who uses a wheelchair. One wheelchair will not serve for a lifetime. The child will require larger prostheses as he or she ages. Leg braces will need to be lengthened; wheelchairs will need to be larger; glasses and hearing aids will need to be replaced. From the outset, the family needs expert diagnosis and treatment plans.

The environmental issues for families that we discussed in Chapter 2 are relevant here. Having a child with severe and multiple disabilities causes added stress. It modifies the family's concept of itself and creates lifetime demands that can be anticipated from infancy. Consider a child with a speech deficit or a child with Down syndrome. For the former, there is a possibility of complete remediation, and the latter may attain nearly normal cognitive functioning, independent living, and supportive employment. Such accomplishments are difficult to predict for children with multiple and severe disabilities.

Through intervention, questions will focus on how far the child can progress. Is the child likely to be able to master sign language, control a motorized wheelchair, or use a word processor or a communication board? Some children will be able, and some will not. Those who are can move on to independent living and supportive employment. The others may be their family's responsibility for life. Family resources will be siphoned into child care, equipment, and therapies. The needs of the child with multiple and severe disabilities will absorb large amounts of time that otherwise would be spent in husband-wife interactions or family-peer interactions. Brothers and sisters will be involved in caring for their disabled sibling and lose some of their playtime or peer-interaction time.

These families need expert counseling and a case coordinator who is fully aware of community resources and services. Counseling can assist family members in working through their grief and accepting their child's disabilities. Even so, the child may never have the status of other children in the family.

If the family is headed by a single parent, multiple supports will be needed. In many cases, the single caregiver may have to seek public assistance to survive economically and provide the therapies and education the child requires. A working parent (usually the mother) may have to give up her career (see Chapter 3). In a two-parent family, if it is an economic necessity for both parents to work, the loss of income will worsen their problems. As we have seen in cases of children with autism, the family may not be able to afford the preferred treatment.

Active and passive rejection of a child may be a serious issue that needs to be addressed. An additional problem is that so much is unknown about some of these disabilities, such as autism. The family may spend enormous amounts of time seeking an accurate diagnosis and placement for the child.

Finding a baby sitter or respite services to allow the family to have some respite or leisure time is a significant problem. Autistic children may be very rejecting of strangers. A child who is physically disabled and sensory impaired may need feeding and toileting assistance beyond what a baby sitter is willing to provide. Parents who need and seek respite care may require the services of a trained specialist for their child with behavior disorders and sensory impairments.

In essence, a family's needs and problems are intensified by a child with multiple and severe disabilities.

Summary of Major Ideas

1. Not all persons with multiple and severe disabilities are mentally retarded, and many can achieve an adult status of independent living and competitive work.

2. Some individuals with multiple and severe disabilities possess some degree of mental retardation. These individuals may need supportive employment and supervised living arrangements as adults.

3. The Association for Persons with Severe Handicaps (TASH) definition of multiple and severe disabilities includes persons of all ages who need extensive, ongoing support in more than one life activity.

4. The current effort in the field of multiple and severe disabilities is to begin intervention as soon after birth as the disability has been diagnosed and to provide appropriate treatment, prostheses, family support, and education to assist the individual to develop to his or her full potential.

5. The current practice in the field of multiple and severe disabilities is to teach the person to perform functional activities in settings in which he or she will use these skills.

6. Communication grows out of nonsymbolic cries, grunts, and gestures. The individual can be taught to use these sounds and gestures to make requests, indicate refusals, and communicate wants and needs. Some individuals will never reach the symbolic stage of communication by using sign language or words.

7. The major focus of all work with individuals with multiple and severe disabilities is to help them acquire, insofar as possible, the skills that their nondisabled peers of the same age possess.

8. Major curricula are available for most forms of multiple and severe disabilities.

9. Educating individuals with multiple and severe disabilities and assisting them in the development of life adjustment skills is a lifelong process for both the individuals and their families.

10. The best hope for facilitating the normalization and development of persons with multiple and severe disabilities lies with family members and the professionals who work with these persons.

11. Both the individual and the family need to be involved in all decisions regarding the student.

Unresolved Issues

1. *Community acceptance.* The special education profession has made significant advances in providing curriculum and teaching and intervention strategies, but not all workplaces or communities are prepared to accept individuals with multiple and severe disabilities. Supportive employment is an attempt to open up workplaces to persons with multiple and severe disabilities. The goal of providing a variety of meaningful work and vocational opportunities that will benefit both individuals with multiple and severe disabilities and their employers has not been fully achieved.

2. *Cost of intervention and support.* The costs of intervention and life support are high. Persons with multiple and severe disabilities need specialized training from numerous professionals as well as specialized teaching tools and prostheses. They may require lifetime support. Funds for these services are not always readily available.

3. *Inclusion and its issues.* Not all special educators believe in inclusion, which aims to place all youngsters with disabilities in regular schools and enables them to spend some time in the general education classroom. Stainback and Stainback (1989) argued for a merger of general education and special education. They and many other proponents of inclusion wish to see all children with disabilities in regular schools and classrooms. However, as Semmel, Abernathy, Butera, and Lesar (1991) wrote, "Both the regular and special education teachers are not generally dissatisfied with the *current* special education system" (p. 19). Other dissenters feel general education teachers and administrators have not been involved with special educators in planning inclusion and attempting to implement it (Kauffman and Hallahan, 1995). Still other special educators question the political motivation that initiated the inclusion movement (Kaufman, 1989). The debate will continue over whether the general education classroom is the least restrictive environment for all students with disabilities. The arguments pro and con were nicely summarized by Thousands and Villa (1991), Jenkins and Pious (1991), and Halpern (1991–1992).

Key Terms

autism p. 444
cerebral palsy p. 452
criterion-referenced tests p. 463
deafblind p. 448
generalization p. 462
pervasive developmental disorders (DDD) p. 444

pervasive developmental disorders not otherwise specified (PDDNOS) p. 444
self-determination skills p. 454
sheltered workshop p. 474
supportive competitive employment p. 478

Questions for Thought

1. What are some of the categories of multiple and severe disabilities? pp. 444–453

2. What are the basic characteristics of children with PDD and autism? pp. 444–446

3. Why is early intervention particularly important for children with multiple and severe disabilities?   pp. 453–456

4. What are the five possible types of intervention, according to Boothroyd? p. 457

5. How can children be taught to generalize skills within an integrated environment?   p. 459

6. How can the integration of students with and without disabilities be made to work?   pp. 460–461

7. Why is it important to teach age-appropriate skills?   p. 462

8. What are the guidelines for the development of skills relating to communication, mobility, social skills, and self-management?   pp. 467–468

9. What special means of communication have been developed to help nonvocal students?   p. 469

10. What are the advantages and disadvantages of each of the following vocational arrangements for adults with multiple and severe handicaps: day treatment programs, day habilitation, sheltered workshops, and supportive competitive employment?   pp. 474, 478

◗▬▬ *Resources for Further Study*

REFERENCES OF SPECIAL INTEREST

Bradley, V., Ashbaugh, J., & Blaney, B. (1994). *Creating individual supports for people with disabilities.* Baltimore: Paul H. Brookes.

 This guide helps individuals change community- and state-based agencies to organizations that become community supports for individuals with disabilities.

Ford, A., Schnorr, R., Meyer, L., Davern, L., Black, J., & Dempsey, P. (1989). *The Syracuse community-referenced curriculum guide for students with moderate and severe disabilities.* Baltimore: Paul H. Brookes.

 This is a collection of curriculum suggestions from preschool and elementary, middle, and high school students concerning transition into the community and community living suggestions.

Gerry, M. H., & McWhorter, C. M. (1991). "A comprehensive analysis of federal statutes and programs for persons with severe disabilities." In L. H. Meyer, C. Peck, & L. Brown (Eds.), *Critical issues in the lives of people with severe disabilities,* pp. 521–525. Baltimore: Paul H. Brookes.

 This chapter provides a current review of the varied federal statutes regarding persons with severe and multiple disabilities. It also describes some current operating programs.

Giangreco, M., Cloninger, C., & Iverson, V. (1994). *Choosing options and accommodations for children.* Baltimore: Paul H. Brookes.

 This is a manual of assessment and planning suggestions for the inclusion of students with disabilities into general education classrooms.

Lehr, D. H., & Brown, F. (1989). *Persons with profound disabilities.* Baltimore: Paul H. Brookes.

Twenty leaders in the field discuss in twelve chapters issues of teaching, policy, integration, research, and suggestions for practice. This book presents current thinking on persons with multiple and severe disabilities.

Meyer, L. H., Peck, C. A., & Brown, L. (1991). *Critical issues in the lives of people with severe disabilities*. Baltimore: Paul H. Brookes.

This book presents statements by The Association for Persons with Severe Disabilities containing TASH resolutions, the reasons behind their thinking, anecdotes, serious reviews of all research issues, and suggestions on how to organize the classroom and teach. It is highly recommended for anyone who works with individuals with multiple and severe disabilities or for anyone who wishes to know more about this topic and related issues.

Wehmeyer, M. L., Agran, M., & Hughes, C. (1998). *Teaching self-determination skills to students with disabilities*. Baltimore: Paul H. Brookes.

A broad compendium of ideas and techniques for teaching independence skills to students. The acquisition of these skills will contribute greatly to students' transition.

JOURNALS

Journal of the Association for Persons with Severe Handicaps (JASH)
11201 Greenwood Ave. North
Seattle, WA 98133

Journal of Visual Impairments and Blindness
The Sheraton Press
450 Fame Ave.
Hanover, PA 17331

PROFESSIONAL ORGANIZATIONS

The Association for Persons with
Severe Disabilities (TASH)
29 West Susquehanna Ave., Suite 210
Baltimore, MD 21204
http://www.tash.org

The Autism Society
7910 Woodmount Ave., Suite 650
Bethesda, MD 20814
http://www.autism.org

National Clearinghouse on Children
Who Are Deafblind
Teaching Research
345 N. Monmouth Ave.
Monmouth, OR 27361
http://www.tr.wosshe.edu/dblink

National Information Center for
Children and Youth with
Disabilities (NICHCY)
P.O. Box 1492
Washington, DC 20013-1492
http://www.nichcy.org

Rehabilitation Research and
Training Center
Virginia Commonwealth University
1314 West Main St.
P.O. Box 842011
Richmond, VA 23284-2011
http://www.vcu.edu/rrtcweb

12

Children with Physical Disabilities and Health Impairments

FOCUSING questions

Is every physical disability or health condition a disabling condition?

How does the age at which a child becomes physically disabled affect the child's adjustment to the condition?

What unique problems are faced by children with disabilities that are caused by accident or illness (disease)?

Why is it important for the general classroom teacher to discuss a student's condition openly with the student's classmates?

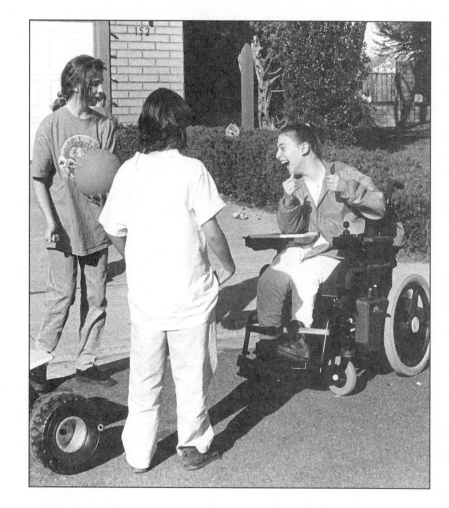

nfants and young children without disabilities acquire cognitive, language, and social competence by interacting with their physical and social environments (Bower, 1989). They interact by using coordinated motor patterns that are genetically programmed to appear early in life and to assist them in learning what they need to know to adapt to their homes and environments (Bower).

This chapter is concerned with infants and children whose physical disabilities or health impairments interfere with their ability to interact with people and objects in their environment to the extent that they are not able to reach the normal milestones of development that their agemates reach easily. Some of the issues we discuss here you have encountered in other chapters, such as Chapter 11 on children with multiple and severe disabilities. However, only 20 percent of the children with chronic illnesses or physical disabilities have impairments that are classified as severe and profound (Lehr & Noonan, 1989). Because of medical intervention and technology, many of these children are living normal, healthy lives and can function in regular environments. Until now, this has been a relatively small and diverse group. The situation may change, however, as technology helps to save the lives of very small premature infants (below 4 pounds) and as the increase in severe child abuse causes the population of children with physical disabilities to grow.

A child's physical interaction with the environment is a major source of learning.

Definitions

The population of children with physical disabilities is heterogeneous. It includes youngsters with many different conditions. Most of these conditions are unrelated, but for convenience, researchers often group them into two categories: physical disabilities and health impairments. A **physical disability** is a condition that interferes with a child's ability to use his or her body. Many, but not all, physical disabilities are *orthopedic impairments*—a term that generally refers to conditions of the muscular or skeletal system and sometimes to physically disabling conditions of the nervous system. A condition that requires ongoing medical attention is a **health impairment.**

According to the Individuals with Disabilities Education Act (IDEA), a person is disabled if he or she has a mental or physical impairment that substantially limits participation in one or more life activities. When a child's conditions—whether medical or physical—interfere with his or her ability to take part in routine school or home activities, the child has a physical disability. By this definition, a student with an artificial arm who takes part in all school activities, including physical education, is not physically disabled. But when a physical condition leaves a student unable to hold a pencil, walk from class to class, or use conventional toilets—when it interferes with the student's participation in routine school activities—the child is physically disabled. This does not mean that the child cannot learn. But it does place a special responsibility on teachers and therapists to adapt materials and equipment to meet the student's needs and help the student learn to use these adaptations and develop a strong self-concept.

Health impairments—for example, asthma, cystic fibrosis, heart defects, cancer, diabetes, and hemophilia—usually do not interfere with the child's ability to participate in regular classroom activities and do not require curricular adaptations. But

Early intervention with a child who has physical disabilities and health impairments can minimize the severity of certain conditions and help the child participate in his or her environment, which in turn helps the child acquire the skills necessary for success in school.
(© Michael D. Sullivan/Texas Stock)

these conditions can require medication or special medical treatment and can restrict physical activities and diet. Teachers should familiarize themselves with the student's medical history, first-aid procedures, and any restrictions recommended by the child's physician.

 ## *Prevalence of Physical Disabilities and Health Impairments*

How many children have physical disabilities? The question is difficult to answer because of the way physical disabilities are defined and the way they are reported. Although we could determine the incidence of conditions that can result in physical disabilities, these figures would greatly overestimate the number of children whose participation in routine activities is actually limited by those conditions. The U.S. Department of Education (1996) estimated that about 0.5 percent of all school-age children have physical or health disabilities. This figure includes severely and profoundly disabled children as well as children with milder physical disabilities and health impairments described in this chapter.

For example, about 2 million persons in the United States have epilepsy (NICHCY, 1997). There are approximately 125,000 new cases each year, about 50 percent of which are children and adolescents (NICHCY). Medication can control seizures completely in most of the people with the disorder and reduce the number of seizures in most others. With regular medication, then, most children with epilepsy can participate in the same activities as their friends and classmates. Less than half of the total number of children with epilepsy are considered physically disabled.

This example applies to most other categories of physical and health disorders. Most of these children function well in regular classes, if the classrooms are accessible for wheelchairs or crutches or the support that persons with health impairments need is available (such as people who know how to clean and regulate oxygen tubes and other lifesaving devices).

Local variations in the classification of disabilities further complicate the process of determining the prevalence of physical disabilities among schoolchildren. For example, one state may classify a large number of students as "other health impaired," and another state may classify similar students as "learning disabled." Or one state may classify students as "multihandicapped," and another may classify similar students according to the primary disabling conditions, such as "orthopedically impaired" (U.S. Department of Education, 1996).

Finally, at the national level there is no specific educational category for children with physical disabilities. Table 12.1 lists the number and percentage of children receiving special education and related services during the 1994–1995 school year who were classified as "orthopedically impaired" and "other health impaired." Taken together, the figures probably provide the best estimate of the number of school-age children with physical disabilities. Current figures reveal that only about 3.5 percent of all the children receiving special education and related services (or 0.27 percent of the entire school population) are physically disabled (U.S. Department of Education, 1996).

The low incidence of youngsters with physical disabilities limits the exposure of educators to their special needs. In the course of their careers, special education teachers might work with only a few students with physical disabilities, and these students' disabilities might be very different. Most of these children attend schools in which there is a staff of support personnel (occupational therapists, physical therapists, physicians, nurses, special educators). If a public school does not have the necessary support staff, it may contract for services in special schools.

Causes of Physical Disabilities and Health Impairments

The cause of a disabling condition and the age at which the child acquires it determine how the child will face it.

Physically disabling conditions and health impairments can be either congenital or acquired. The cause of a condition and the age at which the condition develops influence the kinds of problems that children with physical disabilities and health impairments face as well as the implications for their teachers.

CONGENITAL DISABILITIES

Children with congenital conditions are born with physical disabilities or develop them soon after birth. These children do not have the same developmental experiences that other children do. The extent of the differences depends on the type and severity of the condition. At one extreme, some youngsters never sit or walk. At the other extreme, some children with congenital conditions grow up and adapt with the help of prostheses or technical devices. Modern technology has provided devices and aids, such as head pointers and communication boards, to help these children attain normal growth and development while they try to compensate for their disability (Schreiner, Donar, & Kettrick, 1987).

TABLE 12.1 The Disability of Students Receiving Special Education in School Year 1994–1995		
Disability	Total	Percentage
Orthopedic impairments	60,604	1.2
Other health impairments	105,509	2.2
Traumatic brain injury	7,188	0.1

Source: U.S. Department of Education (1996). *18th Annual Report to Congress on the Implementation of IDEA.* Section 618.

ACQUIRED DISABILITIES

Some children progress through normal developmental sequences and experiences and then develop or acquire—through injury or disease—a physically disabling condition. Some of these children are not able to use their preinjury experiences during rehabilitation. For example, a child with a traumatic brain injury may not be able to roll over, sit, or stand up, but remembers how to do it and tries to imitate the process. Most children with physical disabilities stemming from injuries are motivated to regain or replace their former abilities. When a child loses an ability, however, he or she usually goes through a period of mourning. The ability to adjust to a physical disability caused by injury depends on many factors, including the reactions of others, the importance of the lost abilities to the child's lifestyle, and the child's previously established style of coping (Heinemann & Shontz, 1984).

 Not all physical disabilities are genetic. Some are acquired during the prenatal period and others at or after birth.

Classification and Characteristics

Children with specific physical and health conditions are classified as physically (or orthopedically) disabled or as health impaired. This section provides an overview of the characteristics of children with common physical disabilities and health impairments.

CHILDREN WITH PHYSICAL DISABILITIES

Children with physical disabilities have many different types of conditions. Although there are important differences among these conditions, there are also similarities. Most affect one system of the body in particular: the **neurological system** (the brain, spinal cord, and nerves) or the **musculoskeletal system** (the muscles, bones, and joints).

Clearly, the severity of the disability is a critical variable to consider when determining the amount of help and the kinds of adaptation a student needs. All children with physical disabilities have some limitations in their motor skills. For some, these limitations are severe: They cannot walk or sit independently or use their hands. Their dependence on others for getting around, for eating, and even for toileting can both frustrate and embarrass them. And conditions that affect appearance can increase these youngsters' social discomfort.

Neurological Conditions

The neurological system (often referred to as the *central nervous system*) is made up of the brain, the spinal cord, and a network of nerves that reach all parts of the body. The spinal cord and nerves carry messages between the brain and the rest of the body. Among its other functions, the brain controls muscle movement, and receptors in the muscles and joints send sensory feedback about speed, direction of movement, and body position to the brain.

With a neurological condition like cerebral palsy, the brain either sends the wrong instructions or interprets feedback incorrectly. In both cases, the result is poorly coordinated movement. With a spinal cord injury or deformity, pathways between the brain and the muscles are interrupted, so messages are transmitted but never received. The result is muscle paralysis and loss of sensation beyond the point where the spinal cord (or nerve) is damaged. Children with these neurological conditions have motor skill deficits that can range from mild incoordination to paralysis from the neck down. The most severely involved children are totally dependent on other people or sophisticated equipment to carry out academic and self-care tasks.

Teachers can help students who have neurological conditions by adapting the learning environment to their needs. But because neurological conditions often affect the brain, teachers must first determine which behaviors the child can and cannot control and whether problems reflect a physical or socio-emotional disability. They also have a responsibility to any exceptional child to create a supportive atmosphere that fosters the child's acceptance by providing classmates with information about the student's condition.

Cerebral Palsy.   **Cerebral palsy** refers to a disorder of movement caused by damage to the motor control centers of the brain (Figure 12.1) (Batshaw, 1997; Dorman and Pellegrino, 1998). *Cerebral* refers to the brain and *palsy* to disorders of movement (NICHCY, 1987). The damage that results in cerebral palsy can occur before birth, during the birth process, or after birth from an accident or injury (a blow to the head, lack of oxygen). The condition affects muscle tone (the degree of tension in the muscles), interferes with voluntary movement and full control of the muscles, and delays gross and fine motor development.

In **spastic (pyramidal) cerebral palsy,** muscle tone is abnormally high (hypertonia) and increases during activity. Muscles and joints are tight or stiff, and movements are limited to affected areas of the body (see Figure 12.1). Some children are *hemiplegic:* Just one side of the body (either left arm and left leg or right arm and right leg) is affected. Others are *diplegic:* Their whole body is involved, but their legs are more severely involved than their arms. Still others are *quadriplegic:* Involvement is equally distributed throughout the body.

With *spastic quadriplegia,* all four limbs are spastic. The whole torso is involved as well as the mouth, tongue, or pharynx, and other disorders, such as visual and hearing impairment, almost always exist. The child has difficulty controlling movements (Batshaw, 1997).

In *dyskinetic cerebral palsy,* tonal abnormalities involve the whole body. The individual's muscle tone is changing constantly, often rigid while he or she is awake and decreased when asleep (Pellegrino, 1997).

All children with cerebral palsy have problems with posture and movement.

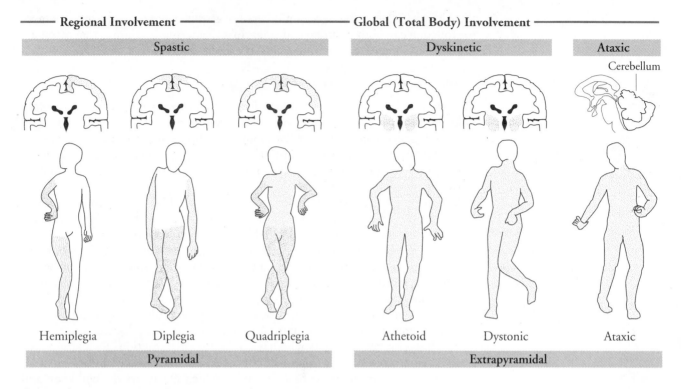

Figure 12.1   Regions of the Brain Affected by Various Forms of Cerebral Palsy
(The darker the shading, the more severe the involvement)
Source: J. P. Dorman & L. Pellegrino (1998). *Caring for Children with Cerebral Palsy: A Team Approach* (p. 12). Baltimore: Paul H. Brookes. Reprinted by permission of the author.

Ataxic cerebral palsy is a condition in which voluntary movement involving balance is abnormal. These persons have difficulty controlling their hands and arms, and their gait is unsteady.

Children can have one or a combination of these types of cerebral palsy. The form and degree of physical involvement varies from child to child. In addition, the affected areas of the body also vary. A child with *mixed type cerebral palsy* has severe problems with balance and coordination, which affect ambulation.

Additional problems that can be associated with cerebral palsy include learning disabilities, mental retardation, seizures, speech impairments, eating problems, sensory impairments, and joint and bone deformities such as spinal curvatures and contractures (permanently fixed, tight muscles and joints). Scissor or toe walking is common among children with cerebral palsy who are able to walk.

Approximately 40 percent of children with cerebral palsy have normal intelligence; the remainder have mild to severe retardation (Batshaw, 1997). Those classified as hemiplegic, the most common form of cerebral palsy, are most likely to have normal intelligence (Batshaw, 1997). The probability of normal intelligence decreases and the probability of secondary problems increases with the severity of the condition. But most children with cerebral palsy are not severely involved and do not have all or even some of the associated problems. This is an extremely heterogeneous group of children. Each child has unique abilities and needs. Technological advances in recent years have greatly improved the long-term well-being of these children (NICHCY, 1989). They are more like their classmates who do not have a disability than they are different.

Epilepsy. Epilepsy is a disorder that occurs when the brain cells are not working properly (March of Dimes, 1989). It is often called a seizure disorder. Epilepsy can occur in one hemisphere of the brain (*partial seizure*) or in both (*generalized seizure*). Some children may experience both types, and this condition is called *mixed seizure disorder.* Generalized seizures include the following types:

Mild or severe seizures can occur in epilepsy.

- *Toxic-clonic seizures.* This is the most common type of seizure and involves major firing of neurons in both hemispheres of the brain. The child generally loses consciousness and falls to the floor. The clonic phase of the seizure is characterized by jerking of the body, sweating, and incontinence (Brown, 1997).

- *Absence seizures.* During this seizure, the child has a blank expression, perhaps blinking before becoming unconscious, is unaware of the surroundings, and cannot be awakened. There may also be jerking of the arms. Afterward, the child is not aware of having had the seizure, which lasts less than ten seconds (Brown, 1997).

- *Atypical absence seizures.* The onset of this type of seizure is more gradual than that of the absence type, but it lasts longer and creates greater confusion. It is more serious because a child who has atypical absence seizures is likely to have other types of seizures as well (Brown, 1997).

- *Myclonic and atonic seizures.* Myclonic seizures start with abrupt jerking of the muscles; in infancy they are called *infantile spasms.* Atonic seizures are the opposite of myclonic ones. They are characterized by a sudden loss of muscle tone, falling, and loss of consciousness (Brown, 1997).

Partial seizures are limited to one hemisphere of the brain. When the individual loses consciousness, they are called *complex partial seizures.* When consciousness is not lost, they are called *simple partial seizures* (Batshaw & Perret, 1992).

Fortunately, once epilepsy is diagnosed, medication can completely control it in 70 to 90 percent of cases. Surgery is often recommended for those who do not respond to medication (Freeman & Vining, 1990). Epilepsy does not interfere with performance in school. Most individuals with epilepsy have normal intelligence (Brown, 1997) There are 2 million children and adolescents with epilepsy in the United States (NICHCY, 1997).

Tourette Syndrome. Tourette syndrome should not be confused with epilepsy, although it is generally classified as a seizure disorder (Batshaw & Perret, 1992). This syndrome consists of multiple motor, facial, and vocal tics, which vary in intensity. Sometimes the child can control them. They appear to intensify when the child is tired, excited, or anxious (Batshaw & Perret, 1992).

Neural Tube Defects. The most common type of neural tube defects (defects of the backbone and spinal cord) are *spina bifida, encephalocele,* and *anencephaly* (March of Dimes, 1997).

The most common form of spina bifida is *spina bifida occulta,* which is a small defect or gap on the backbone. The spinal cord and nerves usually are normal (March of Dimes, 1997). Another form of spina bifida is *meningocele,* which involves a cyst or lump that can be removed surgically; and the person can then

"Living a Lesson in Friendship"

Jake Geller will leave his Medway home this morning in a lift-equipped van that will take him and his parents to Phoenix, where he will be a freshman at Arizona State University.

The trip will be one of the longest and most difficult of his life. Geller, 19, has muscular dystrophy, which makes any type of travel an elaborate effort.

But after Geller's parents drop him off on Aug. 17, he will not be alone. His lifelong friend, Jack Buchholz, will be his roommate and serve as his personal care attendant.

While many people have been amazed by Buchholz's dedication to his friend, Buchholz himself is unfazed.

"It's not that big a deal," he insisted. "Waking up a half hour earlier in the morning is not that difficult."

Buchholz will get Geller, who uses a wheelchair, out of bed every morning, dress him, and help him shave and shower. At night, he will undress him, help him with such routine bathroom chores as brushing his teeth, and put him into bed.

Buchholz knows the routine by heart: for the past three summers, he and Geller have been roommates at the Computer-Ed High Tech Camp at Lasell College in Newton. During those summers, Buchholz has learned what is required of him as a personal care attendant, including being woken up in the middle of the night by Geller when he is uncomfortable.

"Sometimes I get pretty mad when he does that," Buchholz said. "But I always apologize in the morning."

The two make an unusual pair. Geller, 19, is interested in theater, computers, and broadcasting. He was editor of his high school yearbook and a student council member.

Buchholz, 18, was captain of the soccer and track teams at Hopkinton High School. He also was on the swimming team and hockey team.

The two have been good friends since they were in kindergarten, and they say their decision to attend the same college is based more on their strong friendship than Geller's need for assistance. . . .

"I wasn't going to go [someplace] just because Jack was, but it certainly does help," Geller said.

Arizona State is one of the most accessible American universities for people with disabilities, Geller says. Plus, it has a broadcast journalism program, which he will join. For Buchholz, Arizona State has the advantage of being in a good climate and near his relatives in Chandler, Ariz. . . .

Buchholz goes to the plays Geller is in, while Geller goes to Buchholz's soccer games. When they get together to watch a video, they often end up talking through the whole movie. And they have been attending the computer camp since 1991 — for the first few years as campers, and more recently as counselors.

Geller was diagnosed with Duchenne muscular dystrophy when he was 3. It is the most common form of muscular dystrophy in children, and it is progressive. Most of those who have it die in their 20s or 30s from respiratory problems, though new treatments offer some hope for longer survival, said Marcia Randall, the program services coordinator for the Muscular Dystrophy Association of Boston.

Geller's mind is fixed on his future in broadcast journalism; at Medway High School, he was technical director and a reporter for the school's cable-access channel.

Geller says he is grateful to Buchholz for the sacrifices he has made, and Geller hopes to hire a personal care attendant in the next few months to help him at school and take the burden off his friend.

But don't expect them to be spending any less time together.

"As a pair, they're inseparable," said George Murphy, the director of the computer camp where the two have spent the last few summers. "Their personalities mesh together so well that they're a great team. I think of them as a pair of superheroes, each with his own strength."

Source: S. Kiehl (1998). "Living a Lesson in Friendship." *Boston Globe*, August 12. Reprinted courtesy of The Boston Globe.

What Is the Context?

The article discusses Jake Geller's transition as he moves across the country to attend college. He plans to study broadcast journalism. His longtime friend will be his roommate and aide. Geller's interests include theater, computers, and broadcasting.

Pivotal Issues for Teachers

How should schools ensure access to students with physical disabilities? What kinds of help do you think Geller needs each day?

---

develop normally. A more severe form of spina bifida is *myelomeningocele,* in which nerve roots are involved and spinal fluid may leak out of the cord. Surgery is necessary to close the back, and varying degrees of leg paralysis and bladder and bowel problems remain (March of Dimes, 1997).

Encephalocele is a major malformation of the brain resulting in severe retardation. *Anencehaly* is an opening in the brain that usually results in spontaneous abortion or infant death (Brown, 1997).

The cause of spina bifida is considered unknown; however, if women who have given birth to a child with spina bifida or myelomeningocele are given folic acid (a type of vitamin B) before a subsequent pregnancy, they tend not to have another child with neural tube defects (Brown, 1997). The U.S. Public Health Service recommends that women of childbearing age take 0.4 milligrams of folic acid a day as a preventive measure, because spina bifida occurs in the first 26 to 28 days of pregnancy, usually before a woman is aware of her condition (March of Dimes, 1997).

Folic acid taken by the mother before pregnancy tends to reduce the chances of spina bifida in the child.

The location and extent of injury to the spinal cord determine the degree of physical involvement and loss of function. Injuries to the upper segments of the spinal cord can leave the individual quadriplegic, with no function in the trunk, arms, or legs. Injuries to lower levels of the spinal cord result in varying degrees of paralysis in the legs (paraplegia). Fortunately, about 80 percent of persons with spina bifida have injury in the lower back, and most can walk with aids (March of Dimes, 1997).

Secondary or medical problems associated with myelomeningocele and spinal cord injury, as with cerebral palsy, include loss of bladder and bowel control (requiring catheterization or surgical intervention) and joint and bone deformities (spinal curvatures and contractures). In addition, children with myelomeningocele typically are hydrocephalic (hydrocephalus is the buildup of cerebrospinal fluid in the skull). A shunt is surgically inserted to drain excess fluid from the brain (Figure 12.2).

Figure 12.2
Ventriculoperitoneal Shunt

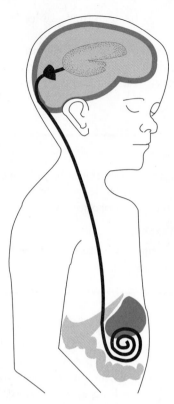

Source: G. Williamson (1987). *Children with Spina Bifida: Early Intervention and Preschool Programming*, p. 83, Figure 4.1. Baltimore: Paul H. Brookes. Copyright © 1987. Used by permission of Paul H. Brookes Publishing.

About 75 percent of children with myelomeningocele have low average intelligence. However, the population is very heterogeneous, and numerous disabilities are related to this disorder. The degree of physical involvement determines the extent to which mobility and performance of daily activities are affected (March of Dimes, 1997).

Spinal cord injuries are caused by car, motorcycle, in-line skating, and diving accidents and by disease. Adolescents older than age 15 and young adults are at the greatest risk for spinal cord injuries because of their active lifestyles and tendency to take risks (Gilgoff, 1983).

Musculoskeletal Conditions

The musculoskeletal system includes the muscles and their supporting framework, the skeleton. Conditions that affect the musculoskeletal system can result in progressive muscle weakness (muscular dystrophy), inflammation of the joints (arthritis), or loss of various parts of the body (amputation). Severe burns can lead to amputation, damage to muscles, or scars that impede movement. Severe scoliosis (curvature of the spine) can limit movement of the trunk, can cause back pain, and eventually may compress the lungs, heart, and other internal organs.

Most children with musculoskeletal conditions have normal intelligence.

Most children with musculoskeletal conditions have normal intellectual abilities (Batshaw & Perret, 1992). They do not necessarily encounter academic difficulties, but their physical limitations and social and emotional adjustment can create educational problems.

Teachers can help students with musculoskeletal conditions by making adjustments for pain or poor endurance and encouraging as much physical activity as

Musculoskeletal conditions affect the muscles and the skeleton. They often severely limit a child's motor skills and can increase the child's social discomfort but usually do not impair intellectual and academic abilities. (© Alan Carey/ The Image Works)

possible. They can arrange for a splint to hold a pencil or spoon or for a different faucet handle for a bathroom sink. They can be sensitive to the child's need for help with toileting and make arrangements for someone to respond quickly and competently. And they can encourage classmates to volunteer to help the child with difficult activities.

Muscular Dystrophy. Muscular dystrophy is a disease of the muscles that affects movement. The most common form, Duchenne, is a genetic disorder that occurs primarily but not exclusively in boys (Dorman & Batshaw, 1997). The disease appears at about 2 to 5 years, and by age 12 the child may not be able to walk. The disease gradually weakens the heart and diaphragm, leading to death. Other forms of muscle disorder, such as congenital myopathies, occur less frequently.

Arthritis. **Arthritis** is a group of disorders that involve the joints. Symptoms include swollen and stiff joints, fever, and pain in the joints during acute flare-ups. Prolonged inflammation can lead to joint deformities, which eventually can affect mobility. Students may require frequent medication or miss school if surgery is needed. There are three forms of juvenile rheumatoid arthritis, and a multidisciplinary team is required to evaluate, identify, and recommend appropriate therapies, medications, exercises, and educational adaptations (Bigge, 1991).

Marfan Syndrome. Marfan syndrome is a genetic disorder that produces poorly developed muscles and a curved spine. Individuals with Marfan syndrome may have long, thin limbs, prominent shoulder blades, spinal curvature (scoliosis), and flat feet or long fingers and thumbs. This syndrome affects about twenty thousand persons a year. The heart and blood vessels are usually affected. The greatest danger is damage to the aorta, which can lead to heart failure. Children with Marfan syndrome need to avoid heavy exercise and lifting heavy objects (March of Dimes, 1993).

Achondroplasia.   Achondroplasia is a genetic disorder that affects 1 in 20,000 births. Children with this disorder usually develop a normal torso but have a straight upper back and a curved lower back (swayback). These children are at risk of sudden death during sleep from compression of the spinal cord interfering with their breathing. The disability may be lessened through the use of back braces or by surgery (March of Dimes, 1997).

Polio.   Polio was a common disease before the development of vaccines that offset the responsible virus. The virus could invade the brain and cause mild to severe paralysis of the body. There were also milder cases of partial paralysis. The virus is still present, and every child needs to be immunized for protection against this disease (March of Dimes, 1997).

Post Polio Muscle Atrophy.   Post polio muscle atrophy appears in some individuals who had polio early in life. Muscles that were previously damaged weaken, and in some persons muscles that were not previously affected weaken as well (March of Dimes, 1997).

Clubfoot.   Clubfoot is a major orthopedic problem affecting about nine thousand infants each year. The term is used to describe various ankle or foot deformities: twisting inward (*equinovarus*), the most severe form; sharply angled at the heel (*calcaneo valgus*), the most common type; or the front part of the foot turning inward (*metatarsus adductus*). These conditions can be treated with physical therapy, and a cast on the foot can solve the problem in most instances. In severe cases, surgery is necessary. With early treatment, most children can wear regular shoes and take part in all school activities (Dorman & Batshaw, 1997; March of Dimes, 1997).

Cleft Lip and Cleft Palate.   Cleft lip and cleft palate are openings in the lip or roof of the mouth, respectively, that fail to close before birth. The cause is unknown. Most cleft problems can be repaired through surgery (March of Dimes, 1997; see also Chapter 8).

CHILDREN WITH HEALTH IMPAIRMENTS

Youngsters with health impairments require ongoing medical attention. Like physical disabilities, health impairments stem from a wide variety of conditions.

Metabolic Disorders

There are many metabolis disorders; refer to Meyer (1997) for a more complete listing. School personnel may encounter a child with *osteogenesis imperfecta*, or brittle bone disease, which results in multiple fractures and may be misinterpreted as child abuse. These children usually have normal intelligence, but care must be taken in physical activities to prevent fractures (Bigge, 1991).

Cardiopulmonary Conditions

The **cardiopulmonary system** includes the heart, blood, and lungs. When a health problem affects the cardiopulmonary system, a child may have problems in breathing (for example, asthma, cystic fibrosis), or the heart may not pump blood properly (heart defects). Some children with these conditions cannot run, climb stairs, or even walk from one part of the school to another. Although it is possible to limit strenuous exercise for these children, simply sitting in school all day takes more energy than some of them can produce. Their inability to take part in normal activities with their agemates can create social problems for these youngsters. Adding to these problems is the high susceptibility of these children to illness. Frequent absences put them at an academic disadvantage in spite of their normal intelligence.

Suggested classroom modifications are listed in Table 12.2. Suggestions for individual children may vary even within a syndrome. Individualized health-care plans should be mandatory. In all cases, the teacher should be given complete information about each child's condition, as well as instructions for appropriate therapies and assistive technologies.

Teachers can help students with cardiopulmonary conditions by scheduling important activities when the child has the most energy.

Teachers can help a student with a cardiopulmonary condition by adapting instruction and the learning environment to the child's needs. For example, they can schedule the most important learning activities during the child's period of greatest energy, allow the child to rest at certain intervals, give the child extra time to complete assignments, arrange for locker space close to the classroom, or provide alternatives (and academic waivers) for physical education classes that exceed the child's capabilities.

Asthma.   **Asthma** is a condition affecting an individual's breathing. It usually has three features: Lungs are swollen, breathing is difficult, and the airways react negatively to a variety of environmental conditions (such as dust, smoke, cold air, and exercise). Asthma may also cause acute constriction of the bronchial tubes (Batshaw & Perret, 1992).

In children, the condition varies from mild to severe. Asthma usually does not pose a major problem for the teachers of children with this condition. Nevertheless, all teachers need to know how to deal with the frequent absences of children with severe asthma and what symptoms indicate that a child is having a severe attack. Teachers who have a child with asthma in their classes need a doctor's suggested plan of medication, a list of symptoms that indicate daily or emergency medical attention, and some indication of the degree to which the child can safely exercise and participate in classroom activities.

Health conditions often result in absences, forcing teachers to adjust their instructional plans.

Asthma in a child can pose a serious problem for the parents. They need accurate diagnosis and treatment plans from appropriate medical personnel. Medication may be necessary throughout an individual's life, and those who are seriously affected are likely to require emergency treatment from time to time.

Cystic Fibrosis.   Cystic fibrosis is the most frequently occurring lethal genetic disease in the United States (*Science*, 1990). Children affected with this disorder have severe respiratory and digestive problems. Recently, geneticists have identified the gene accounting for 70 percent of the cases (*Science*). Currently, an experiment is being conducted to determine if the problem can be avoided by supplying normal genes to a child afflicted with this disease. Techniques for screening prospective parents for the lethal gene are being developed (*Science*). It is hoped that in the future, gene treatment can control both cystic fibrosis and muscular dystrophy.

Acquired Immunodeficiency Syndrome

Acquired immunodeficiency syndrome (AIDS) is a breakdown of the body's immune system caused by the **human immunodeficiency virus (HIV)**. Ninety percent of AIDS cases in children are the result of the virus being transmitted from the infected mother during pregnancy, the birth process, or breast feeding (Rutstein,

TABLE 12.2   Potential Classroom Modifications and Teacher Skill Requirements

Chronic Condition	Potential Modifications	Skills Required
Asthma	Avoidance of allergens; participation in physical activity; administration of medication as needed	CPR; recognition of signs and symptoms of respiratory distress and of medication side effects
Congenital heart disease	Participation in physical activity; administration of medication as needed; diet or fluids	CPR; recognition of the signs and symptoms of heart failure and of medication side effects
Diabetes	Diet; bathroom frequency; availability of snacks and source of sugar; balance of exercise and food	Recognition of signs and symptoms of hypoglycemia (rapid onset) and of hyperglycemia (slow onset)
Leukemia	Participation in physical activity; exposure to communicable diseases	Recognition of signs and symptoms of infection and of bleeding
Seizure disorder	Participation in physical activity; environment; administration of medication as needed	Seizure management; recognition of signs and symptoms of distress during and after seizure and of medication side effects
Spina bifida	Participation in physical activity; environment to accommodate mobility and movement; fluids; pressure relief	Recognition of signs and symptoms of shunt blockage, of urinary infections, and of skin breakdowns; use of equipment and mobility devices
Sickle cell anemia	Participation in physical activity; fluids	Recognition of signs and symptoms of impending crisis
Juvenile rheumatoid arthritis	Participation in physical activity; environment (stairs); administration of medication as needed; frequency of movement; classroom activities (writing, carrying books)	Recognition of signs and symptoms of increased inflammation and of broken bones
Hemophilia	Physical activity	Recognition of signs and symptoms of bleeds; management of bleeding (cuts and scrapes)
Cystic fibrosis	Physical activity; administration of medication as needed; diet	Recognition of signs and symptoms of respiratory distress and of medication side effects
Kidney disease	Physical activity; diet and fluids; bathroom privileges; medication administration	Recognition of signs and symptoms of fluid retention and of medication side effects

Source: Adapted from J. L. Bigge (1992). *Teaching Individuals with Physical and Multiple Disabilities* (3rd ed.), p. 52. New York: Merrill.

Conlon, & Batshaw, 1997). About one-third acquire the virus during pregnancy and most of the others during the birth process. A child may also become infected through a transfusion of contaminated blood.

Among adults, the disease is transmitted through sexual contact, by using contaminated needles to administer drugs intravenously, or through transfusions of infected blood. Adolescents exposed to any of these are as much at risk of contracting the disease as adults.

The outlook for children with AIDS is grim: severe developmental delays, brain damage, and early death. In 1993, 15,000 infants were born HIV infected; approximately 6,000 developed AIDS, and nearly 3,000 died. AIDS is a serious concern in our society, and communities are still formulating policies on how to work with infants and children who have the infection (including how those children are to be educated).

Professionals must respond to each child individually to best care for his or her health needs and to maximize his or her competencies. Infants need careful diagnosis, and individualized family service plans (IFSPs) must be developed to ensure adequate medical and educational services (Crocker, 1989).

Cooley's Anemia and Sickle Cell Anemia

Cooley's anemia is a blood cell disease of genetic origin; it is most frequently found in persons living in the Mediterranean area or among those of Mediterranean stock. The child appears healthy at birth but soon becomes listless, has a poor appetite, and contracts frequent infections. Cooley's anemia is treated with frequent blood transfusions. At this time, there is no known cure.

Sickle cell anemia is an inherited blood disease most commonly found among African Americans and Hispanics of Caribbean ancestry. Oxygen-carrying red blood cells usually are round, but in children with sickle cell anemia they are crescent or sickle shaped. The sickle cells are not as flexible as the round cells and can be trapped in body organs. When the red blood cells are trapped, oxygen is not carried through the body, and the resulting shortage of oxygen can leave the child highly vulnerable to infection. Currently, massive doses of penicillin are administered to children with sickle cell anemia to prevent the development of infections. The penicillin dosage continues throughout early childhood until the individual's immune system can fight the infections (summarized from March of Dimes, 1997).

Substance Abuse

It is estimated that in 1990, 4.8 million women of childbearing age used illicit drugs (Shriver & Piersal, 1994). This figure does not include the women who used legal drugs such as alcohol and tobacco—30.5 million women consumed alcohol, and 17.4 million used nicotine (Shriver & Piersal).

The media overemphasize the effects of maternal drug use in children born to these women, but some serious disabilities can occur. For example, although research has *not* demonstrated negative effects from prenatal exposure to heroin or marijuana, negative effects have been found in children whose mothers used cocaine or alcohol during pregnancy. The effect of alcohol on the fetus is the most thoroughly researched aspect of prenatal exposure to drugs.

Alcohol.   The most adverse effects have been observed in the children of mothers who consumed alcohol heavily (more than 8 ounces per day) while they were pregnant. This consumption results in **fetal alcohol syndrome** (FAS) or a milder form, *fetal alcohol effects* (FAE). Many children with FAS have low birth weight and severe feeding problems. The most severe cases of FAS result in facial abnormalities, mental retardation, and challenging behaviors. Those with FAE will have milder forms of intellectual and behavioral impairments, and they usually do not have facial abnormalities (Batshaw & Conlon, 1997). Both FAS and FAE can present a variety of learning problems and difficulties with social interaction. Children with this condition have disorders in three categories: growth deficiencies,

In 1993, 15,000 infants were born with HIV.

Some disorders from fetal alcohol syndrome are not diagnosed until childhood or adolescence.

facial malformations, and central nervous system effects in the form of mental retardation and challenging behaviors. These disorders are generally diagnosed in childhood and adolescence. Facial and physical abnormalities may require medical treatment (Batshaw & Perret, 1997; Shriver & Piersal, 1994). Generally, children exposed to alcohol (less than 8 ounces per day) have lower birth weight, decreased height, and smaller heads. There appears to be a relationship between an expectant mother's binge drinking (five or more drinks per day) and her child's lower cognitive functioning.

Cocaine.   An expectant mother's use of cocaine has been associated with her child's lower birth weight, shorter body length, and smaller head circumference. The newborn infant exposed to cocaine may show irritability, restlessness, poor feeding, and sleep problems (Batshaw & Conlon, 1997). Some studies have found cognitive deficits, challenging behaviors, and lower achievement; however, the results are not the same for all cocaine-exposed children. Cohen and Erwin (1994) found that only one-fourth of their sample of children exposed to cocaine prenatally exhibited problem-causing behavioral characteristics in the classroom. Moreover, half of the sample hardly resembled the cultural stereotype of the drug-exposed child at all (p. 248).

In summary, Shriver and Piersal's (1994) statement merits attention:

> Knowledge that a child has been exposed to drugs prenatally will not automatically qualify the child for early special education, *nor should it.* For example, information that children exposed in utero to crack cocaine will automatically have some type of learning disability, or that children exposed to alcohol will automatically be developmentally delayed, is unsubstantiated by current research. (p. 176, emphasis added; see also Hansen & Ulrey, 1992)

Heroin.   The most common effects for infants whose mothers use heroin are low birth weight and preterm delivery (Lockhart, 1996). The infant may have severe withdrawal symptoms, increased blood pressure, and potential nutritional problems. Another issue is that heroin is frequently mixed ("cut") with other substances that can be harmful to the fetus. For example, if the mother's heroin is cut with quinine, serious malformations can occur in the infant, such as deafness (Lockhart).

Marijuana.   Mothers who use marijuana may have smaller babies in terms of total weight, arm mass, and overall decreased body size (Lockhart, 1996). These infants may be highly irritable and exhibit increased sensitivity to noises in the environment.

Other Health-Related Conditions

Other health-related conditions include chronic and sometimes life-threatening diseases such as cancer (leukemia, malignant tumors), diabetes, and hemophilia. Children with these conditions may require extensive medical treatment or periodic hospitalization. When working with a student who has a serious health disorder, teachers should obtain current information about the child's condition so needed changes can be made in expectations and school activities. Also, teachers should be sensitive to the social and emotional status of the child, keep activities as normal as possible, and provide support. Children with diabetes or hemophilia may require regular medication or other medical treatment. Teachers working with these children should be knowledgeable about medical procedures needed at

Teachers should keep activities as normal as possible and provide support.

Chronic diseases involving long-term medical treatments usually mean that a student will miss school, sometimes for prolonged periods, and that the individual may experience pain and fatigue, which can interfere with learning. *(©Audrey Gottlieb/Monkmeyer Press Photo Service)*

school, limitations on activities, and emergency procedures that may be necessary if problems arise (see Table 12.2).

TECHNOLOGY-DEPENDENT HEALTH CONDITIONS

Children who depend on technological devices to survive are increasingly included in regular and special education classes (Levine, 1996). Most of these children have chronic health or physical disabilities and will require technological assistance for long periods of their lives, although some outgrow the conditions in early childhood and do not require continued mechanical aids for survival.

Technology-dependent children are encouraged to live normal lives, and most of them can acquire academic, social, and language skills at an age-appropriate time. In 1984, the Supreme Court ruled that technology-dependent children have a right to live at home (instead of in a hospital or nursing facility) and to attend school and have nursing procedures provided for them.

A Home-Care Success Story

By the end of his first day of life, Alex Hughes had been placed on a respirator and transferred from a community hospital to a neonatal intensive care unit (NICU).

He had severe hyaline membrane disease, bronchopulmonary dysplasia, and multiple complications. Within days, Alex was baptized and given last rites.

With intensive care, though, his condition gradually improved. At 9 months he was transferred to Children's Memorial Hospital in Chicago, where he underwent a tracheostomy. At 15 months, the treatment team found a ventilator setting on which Alex was stable, and a joint decision was made to send him home. The alternative was two or three more years of high-tech hospital care. His mother, Ann Hughes, had been living at the hospital and at a nearby Ronald McDonald House; meanwhile, she was eight months pregnant with her second child. Alex's father, Steve, was making regular visits from home, forty miles away.

"We had been thoroughly trained in using the ventilator, but all of a sudden the equipment looked very scary," Ann recalls. They maintained the ventilator, ordered supplies, changed the tracheostomy tube three times a week, and measured oxygen saturation with a pulse oximeter.

They worked closely with nurses and therapists and consulted by telephone with doctors at Children's Memorial and with their own pediatricians, who took responsibility for Alex's general care and reviewed the need for physical, speech, and occupational therapy. "Our pediatricians listened to us and believed what we had to say," Steve says. "They trusted our judgment and our ability to assess Alex's condition."

Alex was gradually weaned from the ventilator and from the need for in-house nursing care. He is now off the ventilator entirely, and the tracheostomy has been closed. At 4½ years of age, he is doing well physically but is still not talking and tends to be withdrawn. He is attending a school for physically and developmentally handicapped youngsters.

"Everything we went through has been worth every second just to have him home," his mother says. "His improvement has been extraordinary." Sister Katie, 2½, is developmentally close to Alex and is his best friend. "She's a good influence," says Ann. "She's better than a therapist" (Goldberg, 1991, pp. 26–32).

In the following sections, we discuss some of the devices that educators may encounter.

Tube Feeding

Some infants are born with or develop problems that prevent them from being able to eat. These children may have poorly developed sucking and swallowing reflexes; the sucking reflex is necessary to pull food into the mouth to be swallowed (Batshaw, 1997; Krajicek, Steinke, Hertzdeng, Anastasiow, & Skandel, 1991). They may also have abnormal muscle tone in the lips or tongue, which makes eating difficult or causes vomiting, or they may have a malformed breathing tube and esophagus, which allow food to enter the lungs.

When a child cannot receive enough nutrients through mouth feeding, a tube is inserted into the stomach, and food is fed directly into it. This is called *gastrostomy feeding* (Eicher, 1997; Haynie, Porter, & Palfrey, 1989). As an alternative, the tube may be passed through the nose (nasogastric tube). The nasogastric technique cannot be used for longer than a few months, because the esophagus becomes irritated. Gastrostomy is usually the preferred treatment (Batshaw, 1997). Figure 12.3 illustrates gastrostomy and nasogastric tube feedings. There are several types of tubes; a physician or specialist determines the best type for the child. Children who require tube feeding can live regular lives and engage in normal play and learning activities.

Tube feeding allows children with severe eating problems to live regular lives.

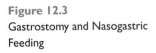

Figure 12.3
Gastrostomy and Nasogastric
Feeding

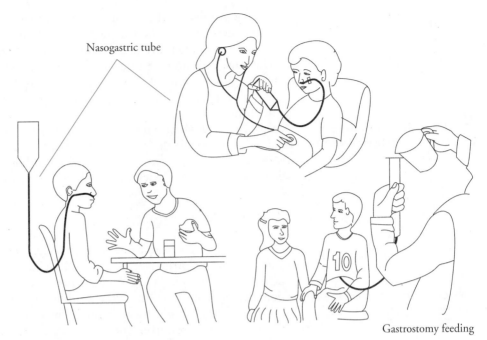

Nasogastric tube

Gastrostomy feeding

Parents and teachers need to learn how to manage the feeding and handle the equipment associated with it. In addition, careful monitoring is necessary to ensure that the child is receiving adequate nutrition.

Intravenous Feeding

In some children, intravenous feeding is administered through a large, deep vein in the neck or chest. Children usually require this procedure if they need long-term care, such as chemotherapy or antibiotic therapy, or if the bowels are incapable of absorbing adequate nutrients (Levy & O'Rourke, 1997).

Catheterization and Colostomy

Catheterization and colostomy are used to remove wastes from the bladder and bowels when the nerves that normally stimulate their removal fail to function properly or a physical disability has damaged the signal area in the bladder or bowels. A child can be taught to insert a tube to remove the urine (catheterization). Colostomy is a surgical procedure in which a doctor inserts a tube that allows waste from the bowels to be collected in a bag attached to the child's abdomen. The child can be taught to empty the pouch that contains the waste. Of course, when the child is an infant, the parents or caretakers have to learn to perform these procedures. These children usually possess normal intelligence and can take part in school activities.

Oxygen-Dependent Children

Premature infants frequently suffer from severe respiratory distress. The therapy of providing oxygen to premature and low-birth-weight infants can cause a thickening and drying of the lung tissue (bronchopulmonary dysplasia), further complicating the problem and prolonging oxygen therapy (Krajicek et al., 1997). Children with cystic fibrosis (a dysfunction of mucous production), severe asthma, and some diseases of the heart also require oxygen therapy.

The most common method of treatment is providing oxygen through a nasal cannula. Other means of delivering oxygen are a nasal mask or, if the nasal passage is blocked, a tracheostomy (a tube inserted into the windpipe through a surgical opening).

Car seats and wheelchairs equipped with respirators and other oxygen-supplying equipment are available. They allow the infant and young child to be transported more easily from home to school or for out-of-home experiences. Parents and personnel who care for or teach these children need specialized training.

Oxygen-dependent children require personnel trained in the proper use of their equipment.

CHILD ABUSE

Children who suffer from child abuse may acquire disabilities that are not caused by any genetic or birth disorder. Child abuse has become a leading cause of injury and death for children in the United States, outpacing the leader of the past, childhood accidents. Because they exhibit all the symptoms and disabilities of children with genetic or birth disorders, many of these children are misclassified by health-care workers. For example, Cohen and Warren (1987) found that about one-third of the children in a center for cerebral palsy were victims of child abuse and may or may not have had cerebral palsy before the abuse.

Child abuse is a major cause of some children's disabilities.

There is an epidemic of child abuse in the United States. There has been an increase of a million cases of reported child abuse since 1980, bringing the total to 2 million cases reported in 1987 (Zirpoli, 1990). Zirpoli writes that some professionals believe that the actual number of cases is at least twice the number reported (p. 6). Many abused children are placed in special education classes because their symptoms and needs are the same as those of children with genetic disabilities.

TRAUMATIC BRAIN INJURY AND ACCIDENTS

Accidents that involve the head are usually referred to as *traumatic brain injuries* (TBI). The results of these injuries may resemble spina bifida, cerebral palsy, or other physical disabilities. TBI can result in cognitive, social, and language defects as well. Public Law 101-476 includes TBI as a separate disability category (NICHCY, 1997). It is a leading cause of death and disability in children in the United States. The current professional orientation is to attempt to distinguish these children from those with genetic dysfunctions. Although the two groups appear similar, treatment may reverse some of the disorders caused by TBI, whereas genetic disabilities such as paralysis are not able to be reversed. For example, Kevin Murphy, who was completely paralyzed in an automobile accident, had a full recovery and today is a leader in the field of special education, specializing in the severely and profoundly disabled.

Other accidents may lead to broken bones, the loss of limbs, or incurable paralysis. Car seats for children have greatly reduced the number of fatal and damaging injuries to infants and preschoolers. Although there has been concern recently about air bag safety, seat belts and air bags have further reduced the number of deaths and serious injuries resulting from car accidents.

Traumatic brain injuries can result in cognitive, social, and language defects that treatment sometimes reverses. (© *Spencer Grant/The Picture Cube*)

 Developmental Profiles

Paolo and Margaritte are two children with physical disabilities. Their developmental profiles in Figure 12.4 show that they are like their classmates in many ways but very different in others.

Paolo was born with cerebral palsy, a condition that affects his nervous system and makes it hard for him to coordinate his muscles. Although he has average intelligence, he has never learned to sit by himself or walk. He cannot control the movements of his face and arms. When he tries to speak, he makes grunts and groans instead of words.

For many years, Paolo's doctors and school personnel thought he was mentally retarded. When Paolo was 8, he learned to use an electronic communicating system. He has not stopped "talking" since. He now uses a Touch Talker that is programmed with the alphabet and about a hundred words and phrases. By touching squares on the keyboard, Paolo can construct sentences and "speak," using the device's voice synthesizer. Paolo's communication system is mounted on his wheelchair, so he is never at a loss for words.

Now 15, Paolo attends a regular tenth-grade class at a public high school. His schedule includes weekly occupational and physical therapy classes, which focus on the skills required for using the school bathrooms. These skills include maneuvering the electric wheelchair in and out of the bathroom, transferring to the toilet, and adjusting clothing. In other respects, Paolo is fairly independent. He has several pieces of specially designed equipment, and his therapists are continually looking for new devices to improve his communication and self-care abilities.

After Paolo was introduced to electronic communication systems, he developed a strong interest in computers, a subject he hopes to study in college. His parents

Figure 12.4

Profiles of Two Children with Physical Disabilities

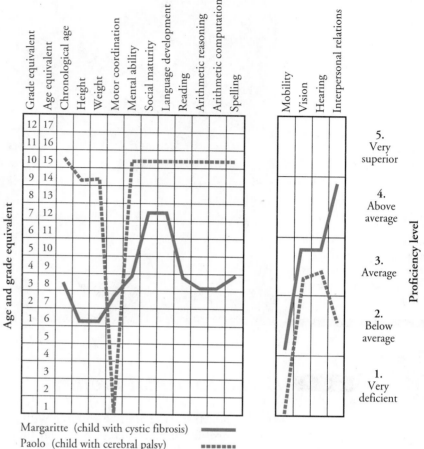

Margaritte (child with cystic fibrosis)

Paolo (child with cerebral palsy)

and sister are excited about his wanting to go to college and, as usual, will do what they can to help him achieve this goal. They have always been his greatest supporters and have helped him develop an optimistic outlook on life.

Paolo sometimes regrets that he has cerebral palsy. Although he has a couple of close friends, he believes that his appearance, his bulky equipment, and his inability to speak have limited his social relationships. His friends agree that he has a wonderful personality but that it does take a while to get to know him. Paolo looks forward to having girlfriends, getting married, and eventually having a family. He knows he will run into problems but feels confident about overcoming them.

Margaritte is 8 years old. She has cystic fibrosis, a disease that affects many organs in the body, especially the lungs. The disease has left her pale, thin, and short for her age. Her breathing problems have caused her chest to become barrel shaped, which is typical for children with cystic fibrosis. Margaritte has had frequent bouts with pneumonia since she was 3 months old. She is a regular patient at the local hospital, where she has become a favorite with the nurses.

Margaritte is in the third grade. She is a good student, but frequent absences have made it hard for her to keep up. Even when her health is better, she has trouble breathing and wheezes and coughs all day long at school. She is usually tired by lunchtime, so she has a regular appointment with the school nurse. The nurse "claps" Margaritte's chest to loosen the secretions in her lungs, letting her breathe more easily for a while. During lunch and recess, she rests, reads, or works on assignments she has missed. She would like to play with her friends, but their activity exhausts her. She chooses to save her energy for the afternoon.

Margaritte knows that cystic fibrosis is a progressive disease and that she may not live to adulthood. Her teacher has explained the condition to Margaritte's classmates and has always tried to answer their questions honestly. Whenever Margaritte is sick, the class sends letters to her. This gives the students another chance to ask the teacher questions or express their concerns, and it reminds Margaritte that they are her friends and are looking forward to her return.

EARLY INTERVENTION

Early intervention with children who have physical disabilities and health impairments is critical. The expression *early intervention* takes on two meanings in the context of children with physical disabilities and health impairments: It means (1) identifying a disorder at birth and in infancy and (2) identifying an acquired health disorder as soon as it is apparent, which may be in infancy, in early childhood, or later in life.

Early intervention means starting therapy or treatment immediately following diagnosis.

In some children, physical disabilities can be corrected with early medical treatment. In other children, early intervention can minimize the severity of certain physical disabilities and health conditions or prevent the development of additional disabling or medical conditions. For example, children with cerebral palsy who receive physical and occupational therapy may have fewer joint contractures or deformities that could decrease function in later years. In addition, correct physical management procedures, adaptations, and devices, if implemented by teachers, families, and others, can help the child participate in daily activities at home, at school, and in the community and acquire needed motor and self-care skills to increase independence in preparation for public school placement. The early development of adequate skills also gives children a foundation for increasing interactions in their environments and helps them acquire the cognitive, language, and social skills that are necessary for success in school.

Identification of Children with Physical Disabilities and Health Impairments

The identification of children with physical disabilities and health impairments is primarily the responsibility of physicians: pediatricians; neurologists, who specialize in conditions and diseases of the brain, spinal cord, and nervous system; and orthopedists and orthopedic surgeons, who are concerned with muscle function and conditions of the joints and bones. Other specialists involved in identification include physical and occupational therapists.

The identification process involves a medical evaluation, which includes a medical and developmental history (illnesses, medical history of family members, problems during pregnancy and labor, developmental progress), a physical examination, and laboratory tests or other special procedures needed for accurate diagnosis. Comprehensive assessment of a child's performance is an ongoing process mandated by PL 101-476. It provides information to the teacher, therapist, and family concerning what the child can do, what the child does not know now, and what the child needs to learn for the future (Carpignano & Bigge, 1991).

Educational Adaptations

*Children
with Physical
Disabilities
and Health
Impairments*

ADAPTING THE LEARNING ENVIRONMENT

The academic curriculum and academic skills do not necessarily present problems to children with physical disabilities. Children who miss school frequently or for long periods because of illness or surgery, however, may require special attention to catch up. Some children with health problems are unable to last a full day in school, so the teacher must teach the essentials over a shorter period of time or arrange for some home instruction.

Instructional adaptations may be necessary for children with physical disabilities to participate fully and benefit from classroom instruction. Teachers can adapt existing instructional materials, modify skill sequences or performance requirements, or use adaptive and assistive devices. And they should work cooperatively with physical and occupational therapists when they have students with physical disabilities. Therapeutic techniques must be integrated into daily programs.

Not all children need the same number or types of adaptations. The necessary adaptations depend on the child's physical capabilities and individual needs. Related services play an important role in four areas of concern: communication, interaction with instructional materials, physical education, and emergency and medical procedures.

Inclusion

The needs of students with physical disabilities are met in a variety of learning environments. At one time, educators believed that the social, educational, and medical needs of these students could best be met by placing them in classes for the orthopedically impaired or in schools for the physically disabled. As public understanding and acceptance of people with physical disabilities increased, so did support for the concept of inclusion. Placement in integrated environments better prepares students to become well-adjusted, contributing members of society.

In keeping with these goals, IDEA encourages schools to educate students in the least restrictive environment and to offer the services necessary for students to succeed in that environment. Although changes in reporting methods make it difficult to compare past and current figures, the U.S. Department of Education (1997) reported that more than 92 percent of students with physical disabilities are being educated in public school environments and that the number of students with physical disabilities in public schools is increasing. Delaware educates 90 percent of these children in general education classes; Vermont 97 percent. Most states use the general education classroom, resource room, and separate class (U.S. Department of Education).

Individualization requires that the learning environments discussed in Chapter 2 be available to students with physical disabilities. This means students are in general education classrooms, resource rooms, special classes, special schools, perhaps at home or in hospitals—according to their needs.

Students with physical disabilities who have no other learning impairments can achieve their greatest potential in the regular classroom. Here these children have the same learning opportunities and expectations as their peers. If children with physical disabilities are going to learn to live in integrated environments as adults, they must attend regular schools and classes to the greatest extent possible

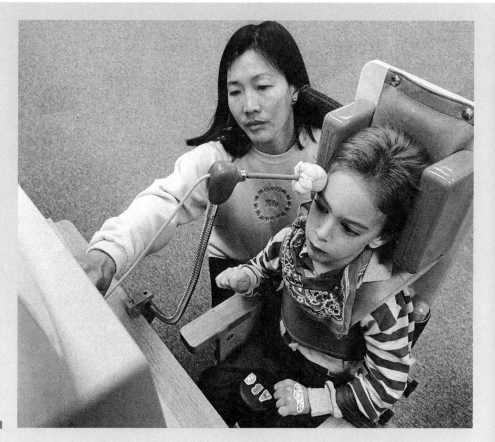

Students with physical disabilities may need to master augmented and alternative forms of communication to complete their schoolwork. (© Bob Daemmrich/Stock Boston)

(Brown & Gothelf, 1996). Adjustments, like providing additional space to maneuver a wheelchair, extra time to change classes, or access to an elevator or a computer terminal, are often the key to enabling a child to participate in a challenging curriculum and in meaningful social interaction.

Some students may need tutoring by a resource room teacher to catch up with the class after a long absence. Others may go to adapted physical education or physical therapy while classmates go to physical education. These services are most effective as integral supports to general education rather than as separate entities. Some students, however, require such extensive adaptation that their needs can be met only in a separate class.

For students without learning impairments, placement in a special class should be temporary, and instruction should be geared toward reducing barriers that prevent participation in regular classes. For example, school personnel determined that Paolo had normal intelligence but could not communicate his needs or complete academic tasks because of severe cerebral palsy. It took approximately two years of intensive training to teach Paolo to use an electronic communication system and to bring him up to grade level in essential reading, spelling, and math skills. During that time, he was assigned to a special class; it was understood, however, that the assignment was temporary. The goal of Paolo's educational program was to integrate him in the regular classroom. His special education teacher arranged for him to visit general education classes during a variety of activities

Students with physical disabilities but no specific learning impairment require adjustments—space to maneuver a wheelchair, time to change classes, or access to an elevator or computer terminal—before they can successfully participate in the regular school setting. (© Richard Howard/Black Star)

Some schools use closed-circuit television and computers to stay in contact with students who need to be at home.

and to have lunch with children his age. When Paolo was finally placed in the regular classroom, he knew his classmates and was prepared to enter the general education curriculum. Also, his classroom teacher understood his needs, and the special education teacher and related services continued to be resources.

Children who are recovering from an acute illness, a serious accident, or surgery may have to continue their school program at home or in the hospital. In some cases, children's hospitals run their own schools. In others, an itinerant teacher maintains contact between homebound or hospitalized students and their regular teachers. Schools also have begun to use closed-circuit television and computers connected via telephone lines to maintain contact with homebound students.

Collaboration: The Role of Related Services.   Occupational and physical therapists recently have started working in educational settings, and school nurses are expanding their traditional roles. These professionals support the efforts of teachers in three primary ways:

- They provide direct services to students.
- They develop IEPs and specific programs in cooperation with the classroom teacher.
- They prepare the classroom teacher to carry out or follow through on specific interventions.

For example, Bridgit, a child with myelomeningocele, goes to physical therapy three times a week to work on increasing her walking speed and endurance. The occupational therapist is teaching her to manage her clothing more independently.

The therapists report Bridgit's achievements to her teacher and have helped the teacher incorporate their methods into Bridgit's routine trips to the bathroom. As a result, Bridgit practices her walking and dressing skills daily. Although she continues to need help going to the bathroom, trained aides are available to assist her.

Some teachers may be trained to provide direct services generally associated with another discipline. For example, a teacher might teach a child to use a wheelchair. The nurse or therapist assesses the child's needs, determines the proper method of intervention, and then, with the educational team, decides who should carry out the intervention. The decision is based on several factors.

Members of the interdisciplinary team must assist the teacher in the day-to-day work with children who have health impairments and physical disabilities.

DECIDING WHO PROVIDES SERVICES

- Who can perform the function legally?
- Who has the expertise now?
- Who else could learn the necessary skills?
- Who is consistently available to teach the task?
- When and where does it makes sense to teach the task?
- How quickly will the child learn to perform the task?

If the classroom teacher is selected to carry out tasks outside his or her expertise, a nurse or therapist provides the teacher with training and ongoing consultation to ensure that the student's needs are being met. Usually, an interdisciplinary support team is needed to provide the range of necessary services.

Just as it may not be appropriate for a teacher to carry out certain related services, it may not be appropriate to carry out all therapy or medical programs in a school setting. Related services as defined in IDEA include developmental, corrective, and other supportive services, such as speech pathology and audiology, psychological services, physical and occupational therapy, recreation, counseling, and transportation (IDEA, PL 105-17, 1997). The courts have ruled that a health service such as clean intermittent catheterization must be provided in school when without it the student would be unable to receive an education in the least restrictive environment. Similarly, a child with cerebral palsy might need occupational therapy to achieve educational goals. In contrast, a child recovering from a broken leg would not be eligible to receive physical therapy in school because the child could remain in the least restrictive environment and make satisfactory educational progress without those services. Medical services that are not educationally relevant, then, remain the legal and financial responsibility of parents and health-care providers.

Assistive technology service, including training professional personnel, was added to IDEA in 1996.

Collaboration: Emergency and Medical Procedures. Teachers, therapists, and other school personnel who work with children who have physical disabilities or health conditions should know about the nature of the child's condition, restrictions on activities, medications, and emergency procedures. School districts should have a policy for handling medical procedures and emergencies. The policy should indicate what to do in case of seizures, severe falls or blows to the head, severe bleeding, fainting, choking, and other emergencies. Teachers should have the policy in writing and should know whom to notify first in case of emergency, how to notify them, how to have the rest of the class supervised during the emergency, and how to intervene during the emergency (Bigge, 1991). In addition, written records should be maintained, recording the administration of medications and instances of seizures, accidents, or injuries.

Instructional Materials and Classroom Equipment

Many students with physical disabilities have difficulty using common instructional materials and classroom equipment. They can't hold a book or turn pages. They can't use the classroom tape recorder, film projector, or slide projector. Following are suggestions for adaptations:

- Book stands can help students hold a book.
- Elastic or rubber bands and larger paper clips can be used to secure the pages of an open book.
- An easy page-turning device is a rubber thimble attached to the end of a pencil.
- Electric page turners can hold the child's book and turn the pages automatically when the child activates a switch.
- Tape recorders can be adapted by placing cardboard over all buttons except the play and stop buttons, to prevent accidental activation.
- Tape recorder buttons can be extended by attaching pieces of wood or plastic to them, enabling students to use the machine independently (Bigge, 1991).
- Carousel slide projectors can be adapted to allow operation with a single switch so the student can activate the projector (Goossens & Crain, 1985).
- Tape recorders can be turned on and off by means of a single switch (Burkhart, 1986; Levin & Scherfenberg, 1987).

Increasingly, computers and computer programs are accessible with a mouse replacing the keyboard. The pace of technological evolution is so rapid that we cannot predict what will be available when you, the readers, begin to teach. More and more interactive materials are becoming available on a daily basis. Inquiries to information networks such as those described in Chapter 11 will be essential for teachers to keep current.

Accessibility of Facilities

Section 504 of the Rehabilitation Act of 1973 laid the groundwork for moving students with physical disabilities to less restrictive environments by requiring that public buildings be accessible to all people. School buildings built after the passage of this legislation should be accessible. Older buildings, however, may require renovations. Minimal renovations might include adding ramps at entrances. Extensive renovations might include installing an elevator in a two-story building and renovating the restrooms in addition to adding ramps. The American National Standards Institute (1980) developed accessibility standards for new facilities;

these guidelines also can be used to determine if facilities are accessible for students with impaired mobility.

MAKING FACILITIES ACCESSIBLE

- Walkways should be at least 36 inches wide and have a continuous surface that is not interrupted by steps or abrupt changes of more than one-half inch.

- Ramps should be at least 36 inches wide. Indoor and outdoor ramps should have a slope of not more than 1 foot for every 12 feet and 1 foot for every 20 feet, respectively.

- Entrances and doorways should be 32 inches wide to allow for easy passage of a wheelchair. The threshold should be beveled and have a maximum edge height of three-quarters of an inch.

- An accessible restroom should be available for both males and females on all floors. Stalls should be 60 inches wide and 60 inches deep and have stall doors that swing out to easily accommodate a wheelchair and allow for transfers to and from the toilet. Grab bars should be mounted on each side of the stall. Toilet seats should be 17 to 19 inches from the floor. Sinks should be no more than 34 inches from the floor. The clearance underneath a sink should be at least 29 inches, so a wheelchair can fit. Mirrors, shelves, and towel dispensers should be no more than 40 inches from the floor.

ADAPTING CURRICULUM

The unique needs of children with physical disabilities demand expansion of the traditional school curriculum into three areas: motor skills and mobility, self-care skills, and social and emotional adjustment.

Skill Development

Motor Skills and Mobility.   Motor skills and mobility constitute a critical area of skill development for children with physical disabilities. These skills are necessary to maintain upright postures (sit, stand), perform functional movements (reach, grasp), and move around in the environment. The programming priorities for motor skill development should include developing functional movements and postures that are needed to perform classroom and school activities (Smith and Krajicek's 1991 video illustrates appropriate positioning techniques):

- Development of head control and trunk control to maintain an upright sitting posture to perform needed activities throughout the school day (attending and listening, writing, using a computer or communication device, eating)

- Development of arm movements and fine motor skills for performance of needed activities throughout the school day (holding a pencil and paper to write, holding a book and turning pages, using keyboards or switches to access a computer or communication device)

- Development of standing and balance for assisted ambulation (using braces and crutches)
- Development of skills needed to maneuver a wheelchair in the classroom and throughout the school environment (using arms to propel, learning to use an electric wheelchair with a joystick or other control, turning corners and entering doorways, negotiating ramps and curbs, crossing streets)

Physical and occupational therapists assume the primary responsibility for setting goals in motor development and mobility. They must work closely with teachers, other professionals, and parents, however, for the child to meet these goals. Teachers should become familiar with the basic working components of mobility equipment (wheelchairs, braces, crutches, walkers) and report needed repairs or adjustments to the child's therapist. Therapists should provide teachers and others with information related to the child's physical condition, limitations, and abilities.

Classroom teachers and others may be required to learn special techniques to help children perform motor tasks during the school day. These techniques can include physical management procedures and the use of adaptive positioning equipment. Positioning, handling, lifting, and transfer techniques are physical management procedures that teachers and others use to do the following: (1) help the student maintain good body alignment in a variety of positions (postures) and perform functional movements and skills in the context of daily activities, (2) prevent the development of secondary contractures and deformities, and (3) increase the benefits of therapy by implementing intervention programs throughout the day (Rainforth & York, 1987).

A child with spastic cerebral palsy who constantly leans sideways in the wheelchair will have tremendous difficulty reaching the keyboard on the computer and striking the correct keys or using the mouse. With help from a physical therapist or occupational therapist, the teacher can learn to position the student in the wheelchair, use a slant board to move the keyboard closer to the child, and relax the child's arms and bring them forward to rest on the keyboard.

Adaptive positioning equipment may be needed in the classroom to promote good body alignment in sitting, standing, and other positions. This equipment works as an adjunct to therapy and helps the child carry out necessary activities in the classroom. Teachers work cooperatively with therapists in using positioning equipment and selecting a position that matches the practical and movement demands of classroom activities (Rainforth & York, 1987).

Lifting and transfer techniques are used to help the child move from one position to another, for example, from the wheelchair to the toilet or into positioning equipment. To prevent injury to the teachers or the child, a therapist must train the teachers before they attempt to move the child. Many children can learn to help in this process or to move themselves independently if they have the ability to stand and adequate arm strength.

Self-Care Skills. Being able to take care of themselves is another critical area for children with physical disabilities. Self-determination and independence training are very important for these children as well. (See Chapter 11 for a full discussion of these issues.) Self-care skills include eating, toileting, dressing, bathing, and grooming. Students with severe physical involvement may require physical assistance in eating or may have to be fed. Some children need assistive devices or physical help to perform many of these tasks, for example, utensils with built-up or larger handles, special plates and cups, or nonskid mats to stabilize the child's plate.

Skills to be developed in toileting include performing transfers from the wheelchair to the toilet or assisting others in accomplishing transfers. Children who lack sitting stability and trunk control need an adapted toilet seat that provides a more stable sitting surface or back supports with straps to help them maintain an upright position. Hand-held utensils and other aids can make toileting more convenient for the student.

Students who have health conditions that require medication on a routine basis (injections for diabetes) or a periodic basis (inhalants for asthma) should be taught as early as possible to administer the medication themselves. Teachers or school nurses must monitor the process closely, however, because they ultimately are responsible for seeing that the correct procedures are followed and that appropriate legal permission from parents, guardian, or physicians is secured before any medication is administered.

Social and Emotional Adjustment.   Children with physical disabilities sometimes feel powerless. Christie knows that she has leukemia and that she will probably live only a few more months. She is frequently absent from school. She misses her friends when she is away from school, but when she returns, she no longer feels a part of the group. Besides being sick, she is lonely and is keeping to herself more and more. Josh faces an entirely different problem. He is recovering from a traumatic brain injury that has left him confined to a wheelchair. He is no longer able to do many things for himself, and he has discovered that temper tantrums are an effective way to get people to respond to his needs immediately. It seems that the more people try to help Josh, the more aggressive he becomes.

Although withdrawal and aggression are normal stages in the process, children like Christie and Josh need support and help in accepting and adjusting to their disabling conditions. Christie's and Josh's behavior patterns are similar to those of children who face continuing academic or environmental problems: They have lost control over certain aspects of their lives.

Harvey and Greenway (1984) found that children with physical disabilities have "a lower sense of self-worth, greater anxiety, and a less integrated view of self" than do children without handicaps (p. 280). Orr (1989), however, found children with physical disabilities in several settings who had positive self-concepts. Research shows that people are more likely to accept their physical disability when the environment is supportive (Heinemann & Shontz, 1984), when they achieve some sense of control over their disability, and when they begin to demonstrate new competence. In addition to using the methods described in Chapter 11, teachers can enhance the social and emotional adjustment of children with physical disabilities in several ways.

A major goal of education is to assist children with physical disabilities to achieve and maintain a positive self-concept.

ADAPTING TEACHING STRATEGIES

Increasing the Understanding of the Disabling Condition

The teacher of a student with a physical disability should learn as much as possible about the condition—its cause, treatments, prognosis, and educational implications. Then, in cooperation with the child's parents, the teacher should help the child and other students understand relevant aspects of the condition. One of the major functions of organizations like the Epilepsy Foundation of America, the American Cancer Society, the March of Dimes Birth Defects Foundation, and United Cerebral Palsy is to provide information to the public. Many of these organizations offer teaching kits or help in developing educational workshops to increase children's and adults' understanding of a particular condition. Commercial materials are also available to help children learn about a variety of disabilities.

When teaching children about disabling conditions, help them understand that a physical disability is an individual difference, not something to fear, ridicule, or be ashamed of:

- Honestly answer questions about a condition.

- Acknowledge and respect the way children (and adults) feel without condoning maladaptive behaviors (teasing, name calling).

- Discuss the incidents that can occur at school—an epileptic seizure, an insulin reaction—and ask students to decide how they could help or how they should behave during such an incident.

Emphasizing the Quality of Life

Teachers can help students adjust to physical disabilities by helping them see their disabilities as just one aspect of their lives and of themselves. One elementary school approached this situation by offering a group counseling session, an hour each week, for children with physical disabilities (Williams & Baeker, 1983). One goal of the group was to develop a support system; another was to recognize individual limitations and strengths. Within the regular classroom a teacher might have students list what they like or admire about each of their classmates. This kind of exercise often gets surprising results, and it is a good starting point for illustrating that children have different assets. Although children with physical disabilities must be allowed to talk about their limitations, they also should be encouraged to inventory their abilities, including the ability to help others. A physical disability cannot be ignored, but these children can learn to focus on the more positive aspects of their lives. For a child like Christie, who faces a terminal illness, the process can be difficult. Her teachers must first overcome their own feelings about death, especially the death of a child.

Finally, teachers can improve the quality of life for a child like Christie by helping classmates show their interest and concern. When Christie is absent, her teacher has the other students send her letters, keeping her informed of the latest activities and reminding her that she is missed. When Christie returns to school,

Focus on positive characteristics by asking students to list what they like or admire about their classmates.

the teacher carefully avoids overprotecting and favoring the child and keeps her involved in as many activities as her condition allows.

Increasing the Sense of Control

Although Josh and Christie cannot control their physical disabilities, they can control many other aspects of their lives. It is revealing to have children with physical disabilities list the aspects of their lives that they believe they cannot control. Josh knew he could no longer move independently, and he thought he was powerless. School personnel worked with Josh and his family to show the child that his temper tantrums were in fact one way to control people and events. They also helped Josh understand how he could achieve the same results in a more constructive way. Josh learned that his family and classmates were happy to help him when necessary and were interested in socializing with him when he took a more positive approach. He found that people understood his frustration and could help him find ways to express that frustration without damaging his relationships with others. Although he still has a severe physical disability, Josh now believes that he can control many aspects of his life.

Physical Education

Before physical education or planned-play programs begin, the teacher should obtain from the child's physician information related to physical limitations, precautions, and restrictions on physical activities. School personnel should be aware of medical and emergency procedures related to the child's condition. Special adaptations may be needed in physical education programs or for playground activities to accommodate children with physical disabilities or health conditions. Classroom teachers should work closely with physical education teachers to design programs for children with physical disabilities or to include these children in games and playground activities.

Special equipment is available to help students. For example, a lowered basketball hoop can be used for wheelchair basketball, and a bowling ball ramp allows students in wheelchairs to bowl with their classmates. In many cases, all that's needed is a change in rules or procedures. For instance, a child in a wheelchair can play softball or baseball by batting and then having another child run the bases. The child with the disability can coach the runner to either run or stay on base. Students with physical disabilities should participate as fully as possible in physical education, recreational, and play activities. These students can play a major role in helping teachers and school personnel come up with ways to adapt activities for them.

TECHNOLOGY

Assistive Communication

Students with physical disabilities who cannot acquire understandable speech or legible writing skills must be provided with augmented and alternative communication systems (Johnson, Baumgart, & Helmstetter, 1996). Some children with cerebral palsy, for example, have severe involvement of the oral muscles used in speech and limited fine motor abilities that hamper their writing skills. Muscular dystrophy or arthritis can leave children so weak that they tire easily when writing. Teachers and parents should work closely with speech therapists in selecting, designing, and implementing augmented and alternative communication devices for children with physical disabilities.

Speech: Boards and Electronic Devices.   The most common augmented and alternative methods for speech are communication boards and electronic devices with synthesized speech output. Most children use the board or electronic device by pointing with a finger or fist to a word or symbol. Children who are not able to point accurately use a hand-held pointer, a head-mounted wand, or a mouthstick. Youngsters with limited use of their hands may use their eyes instead, visually focusing on the intended word or letter.

A single switch may be necessary for students who have limited or no use of their hands. The type of switch depends on the child's movement abilities. Numerous commercial switches are available, and many can be made at home. A switch is used with devices that light each possible selection on the board by rows, then columns. When the correct row is lit and the child presses the switch a second time, the correct sentence, phrase, word, or letter is "spoken." Although this method is slower than accessing the device by pointing or use of a keyboard, it does accommodate students with severe physical involvement. Many electronic communication devices can be connected to a computer for word processing or computer-assisted instruction.

Supplemental boards or overlays for electronic devices may be needed for academic content areas. For example, a mathematics board contains numbers, mathematics symbols, and words related to current classroom instruction. Other subject boards reflect the content and vocabulary of the specific academic subject (science, social studies, history). These boards should be revised or replaced as classroom content changes throughout the school year.

The provision of augmented and alternative communication devices for students with unintelligible speech is critical (Beukelman & Mirenda, 1992; Flippo, Inge, & Barcus, 1995). Many of these students may be denied placement in a less restrictive environment (resource room or general education classroom) because of their lack of spoken language. Professionals should work cooperatively with speech therapists, parents, and others to select an appropriate device, teach the student how to use it, and help others communicate with the student. (More specific information on the selection, design, and use of communication boards and other electronic devices is found in Chapters 8 and 11.)

Writing: Aids and Systems.   A variety of aids and augmented and alternative systems are available for written communication. Students with physical disabilities that cause muscle weakness, involuntary movements, and poor coordination of the fingers and hands may require a writing aid or an alternative system to complete written assignments in school and at home in a neat and timely manner.

Students with physical disabilities should participate as fully as possible in physical education, recreational, and play activities.
(© Bob Daemmrich/Stock Boston)

ADAPTATIONS FOR WRITING

- Hand splints to aid in grasping a crayon or pencil
- Special pencil holders
- Slant board to support forearms
- Clipboard, heavy weight, or masking tape to secure paper while writing
- Wide-lined paper (Bigge, 1991)

Technological advances greatly facilitate learning for children with physical disabilities.

Computers as Writing Aids.　Computers are another alternative means for written communication. Word-processing software can be used to complete written assignments and makes the computer more efficient than a typewriter. Keyguards are available for most types of computer keyboard. For students who cannot use a standard keyboard because they lack fine motor skills, other methods may be needed. For the student with limited fine motor skills, expanded keyboards with large keys are easier to use. A student with muscular dystrophy, however, might use a miniature keyboard because he or she lacks the range of motion in the arms required to use a standard keyboard, yet has good finger movement within a limited range. Alternative keyboards are placed directly on the student's lap, desk, or lap

A critical area of skill development for children with physical disabilities is motor skills and mobility, which are necessary to maintain upright postures, perform functional movements, and move around in the environment. *(© Jerry Speier/ Design Conceptions)*

tray for easy access. Most interactive computer programs will have an arrow appearing on the screen. This arrow, called a cursor, can be controlled by a device called a mouse, which is attached to the computer. For example, Manuel, a wheelchair-bound student with advanced muscular dystrophy, has very little strength. However, he can control the mouse with two fingers. With the mouse, he can move the cursor on the screen and interact with the computer program, which gives him access to a world of knowledge and games. In this manner, students with severe physical involvement need not be able to use the keyboard. They can use the mouse, which requires far less effort.

TRANSITION

For all individuals with disabilities, the transition from school to work and independent living presents a range of challenges, such as obtaining a driver to take them to and from work, remodeling an apartment so that all appliances can be reached from a wheelchair, or having a live-in aide with special knowledge of how to deal with various kinds of equipment.

The National Center for Children and Youth with Disabilities (NICHCY, 1991) has prepared a Transition Summary for parents, teachers, and individuals to assist individuals with disabilities in moving into work and independent living. The center indicates that research has demonstrated an enormous qualitative difference in the lives of people with disabilities because of recent legislation leading to changes to assist these individuals throughout the transition process. Postsecondary programs, on-the-job education, internships and apprenticeships, adult education, trade school, and technical schools as well as college and career education are all available with some support (NICHCY, pp. 15–19).

Family and Lifespan Issues

LENGTH OF LIFE

Children with health impairments like diabetes, cystic fibrosis, AIDS, and cancer face shortened lives. These conditions follow different courses, however, which can present children with tremendous uncertainties. For youngsters with diabetes, even strict compliance with prescribed medication and diet does not guarantee good health or a normal lifespan, and violations often do not have immediate serious effects. Children with cystic fibrosis face a prognosis that is more certain but also more pessimistic: Few survive into adulthood, although recent treatments are increasing the lifespan of some individuals (*Science,* 1990). Children with advanced cancers face death daily.

Nevertheless, most children want to live as normally as possible. When a child with a terminal illness attempts to participate fully in life's activities, we may consider the child valiant. For a child with a condition like diabetes, which has a less certain course, efforts to live normally—eating the same foods as friends and family, strenuous exercise—may violate prescribed care. We may think this child is unaccepting, ambivalent, or noncompliant, but he or she may be experiencing a daily conflict between health needs and happiness. When we recognize the conflict, we can offer more effective support and accommodation (Bradley, Ashbaugh, & Blaney, 1994).

As a child with a terminal illness or progressive condition approaches the point where death becomes a certainty, he or she may face tremendous fear and grief, as may family members, classmates, and school personnel. Teachers must confront their own feelings about death and dying before they can offer support to children and their families.

Dealing with terminal illness and death is a major issue for the child, the caregivers, and all members of the interdisciplinary team.

DISCRIMINATION

People with physical handicaps face intentional and unintentional discrimination from other people and from the "system." Fear, ignorance, lack of experience, and inflexibility are the most common causes of discrimination. It is difficult to reconcile the fact that individuals limited by physical handicaps must also deal with limitations unnecessarily imposed on them by others.

Section 504 of the Rehabilitation Act of 1973 prohibits employers from discriminating against people with handicaps who are otherwise qualified for employment. The act further requires that all agencies receiving federal funds must make their programs and buildings accessible to those with handicaps.

The Americans with Disabilities Act (ADA) (1990) went into effect in 1991. It mandated the removal of many of the obstacles that individuals with disabilities face and an end to intentional or unintentional discrimination. The legislation requires employers to make reasonable efforts to hire people with disabilities. Although it has substantially reduced some types of barriers, violations and other types of discrimination persist. Public information and advocacy are still necessary to increase acceptance and access for people with physical disabilities.

Summary of Major Ideas

1. A physical disability is a condition that interferes with a child's ability to use his or her body; a health impairment is a condition that requires ongoing medical attention.

2. A physical disability or health impairment is not a handicap unless it limits the individual's participation in routine activities.

3. The cause of the disability or disorder has a large impact on the problems that children with physical disabilities face. Those with congenital conditions tend to make necessary adaptations to those conditions. Children whose disabilities are caused by injury generally go through a period of mourning before they finally accept and adjust to their conditions. Children whose conditions are caused by disease have the same adjustment problems as other physically disabled youngsters but also face uncertainty and the academic pressure that stems from frequent absence.

4. It is difficult to determine the prevalence of children with physical disability because of the way physical disabilities are defined and reported. Estimates place the proportion of children receiving special education services because of physical disability at 2.5 percent of all students enrolled in special education programs, or at 0.27 percent of the general school population.

5. Children with neurological conditions suffer from motor disabilities ranging from mild incoordination to total paralysis, and intellectual deficiencies sometimes complicate their development. Children with musculoskeletal conditions have motor skill deficits that in severe cases prevent walking or even sitting up. Children with cardiopulmonary conditions have breathing or heart problems that limit their participation in physical activities. Children with chronic life-threatening health conditions may require extensive medical treatment or hospitalization in acute stages.

6. Children with physical disabilities, like other exceptional children, should be taught in the least restrictive environment. For most of these children, this means the general education classroom with extra attention in the resource room if needed. Special classes are a means of bringing children with normal intelligence up to grade level and equivalent capabilities and integrating them as quickly as possible into general education classrooms. Homebound or hospital services are essential to the educational program of some children, if only temporarily.

7. Teachers can help students with physical disabilities by adapting the learning environment to individual needs. For example, by widening the aisles in the classroom to accommodate a wheelchair, the teacher can reduce the impact of the disability on the student.

8. The implementation of the educational program for children with physical disabilities often involves physical therapists, school nurses, and occupational therapists. These specialists and others (speech therapists, parents) should work in close cooperation with the classroom teacher to reinforce skill learning.

9. Content and instructional adaptations for children with physical disabilities and health impairments may be needed in the areas of communication, use of instructional materials and classroom equipment, physical education, and emergency and medical procedures. The degree of adaptation varies from child to child.

10. Curricular changes for children with physical disabilities who have normal intelligence focus on motor skills and mobility, self-care skills, and social and emotional adjustment.

11. Teachers can facilitate the social and emotional adjustment of their students in several ways: by increasing students' understanding of the condition, by emphasizing the quality of life, and by increasing feelings of self-control.

Unresolved Issues

1. *Participation in the mainstream (inclusion).* Professionals and laypeople continue to disagree about the extent to which children with physical disabilities can or should be mainstreamed. Much of the controversy stems from misconceptions and different experiences. In fact, there is no single "right" method. Decisions must be made case by case, based on individual needs, not on a diagnosis or disability. We cannot assume that certain children do not fit or cannot benefit from inclusion until they prove otherwise.

2. *Educational teamwork.* Students with physical disabilities often require an educational team consisting of members from diverse backgrounds. Professionals from traditional medical disciplines may have trouble adjusting to work in educational settings. Different terminology, methods, and philosophies further challenge the planning and implementation of coordinated educational programs. Unfortunately, some training programs do not prepare teachers and other personnel to be effective team members. Individual school programs should work toward developing models of team service delivery that address the educational needs of individual students.

3. *Technology.* More than any group of exceptional children, students with physical handicaps use adaptive equipment and assistive devices. These devices include specially designed spoons, customized electric wheelchairs, and electronic communication systems. For many people, adaptive equipment means the difference between dependence and independence. With technological advances have come new and better adaptations, but at a cost. School systems, insurance companies, and public assistance programs disagree about who should bear the cost of expensive equipment.

Key Terms

acquired immunodeficiency syndrome (AIDS) p. 497
arthritis p. 495
asthma p. 497
cardiopulmonary system p. 496
cerebral palsy p. 489
epilepsy p. 490
fetal alcohol syndrome (FAS) p. 499

health impairment p. 485
human immunodeficiency virus (HIV) p. 497
musculoskeletal system p. 488
neurological system p. 488
physical disability p. 485
spastic (pyramidal) cerebral palsy p. 489

Questions for Thought

1. What is the difference between a physical impairment and a disability? Provide examples of physical impairments that may not be disabilities. p. 485

2. Why are accurate prevalence figures for children with physical disabilities difficult to obtain?   pp. 486–487

3. What are several practical things that teachers can do to help children with physical disabilities caused by disease?   p. 489

4. What problems do children whose conditions are caused by disease or terminal illness face? p. 489

5. To what extent is a child's intelligence affected by spina bifida? p. 492

6. What role do related services play in the educational program for students with physical disabilities? p. 510

7. What four types of motor skill development are necessary to master the functional movements and postures needed to perform classroom and school activities? pp. 513–514

8. Name two of the stages through which children with physical disabilities and other health impairments pass. Explain the passage through them. p. 515

9. Under what conditions are people most likely to accept their physical disabilities? p. 515

10. How do communication boards work? p. 518

Resources for Further Study

REFERENCES OF SPECIAL INTEREST

Batshaw, M., & Perret, Y. (1992). *Children with handicaps: A medical primer* (3rd ed.). Baltimore: Paul H. Brookes.

> The third edition of this exemplary text explains how genetic abnormalities, problems during pregnancy and early infancy, and nutritional deficiencies can cause disabilities. It also describes how these problems affect the nervous and musculoskeletal systems and, in turn, child development. A few physically disabling conditions also are discussed.

Bigge, J. (1991). *Teaching individuals with physical and multiple disabilities* (3rd ed.). Columbus, OH: Charles E. Merrill.

> Bigge presents a detailed examination of problems that students with physical disabilities encounter and important components of education for these students. Chapters focus on assessment, methods of instruction, and components of the curriculum. Throughout the book are many examples of adaptations that minimize the impact of physical disabilities and help students benefit from the educational program.

Dorman, J. P., & Pellegrino, L. (1998). *Caring for children with cerebral palsy.* Baltimore: Paul H. Brookes.

A comprehensive text emphasizing an interdisciplinary team approach to assessment, management, treatment, and total functioning of persons with cerebral palsy and their families.

Krajicek, M., Steinke, T., Hertzden, D., Anastasiow, N., & Skandel, S. (1997). *Handbook for the care of infants and toddlers with disabilities and chronic conditions.* Austin, TX: PRO-ED.

This manual is designed to assist day-care and home-care workers in integrating children with physical disabilities and health problems into general education classes.

March of Dimes (1992–1993). Public health information sheets: *Clubfoot; Cleft lip and cleft palate; Polio; Post polio muscle atrophy; Spina bifida; Marfan syndrome; Thalassemia.* (Available from March of Dimes, Community Service Department, 1275 Mamaroneck Avenue, White Plains, NY 10605.)

Orelove, F., & Sobsey, D. (1991). *Educating children with multiple disabilities: A transdisciplinary approach* (2nd ed.). Baltimore: Paul H. Brookes.

This book includes chapters on team programming, motor development and cerebral palsy, handling and positioning, medical concerns, developing instructional adaptations, specific skill areas (self-care, communication), and working with families.

Rowley-Kelley, F. L., & Reigel, D. H. (1993). *Teaching students with spina bifida.* Baltimore: Paul H. Brookes. Also, Rosenthal, R., Dukes, B., Cosgrove, S., Rowley-Kelley, F. L., & Simpson, G. (1993). *Teaching students with spina bifida* (video). Baltimore: Paul H. Brookes.

This book and the video can be ordered as a set. The two together provide a comprehensive set of techniques, strategies, and information about positioning for those who work with students with spina bifida.

Schleichkorn, J. (1983). *Coping with cerebral palsy: Answers to questions parents often ask.* Austin, TX: PRO-ED.

This book offers easy-to-understand information on cerebral palsy and its medical, educational, and psychological impacts on children. One chapter deals with special issues, including financial assistance, respite care, access to special equipment, sex education, and marriage.

Umbreit, J. (Ed.). (1988). *Physical disabilities and health impairments: An introduction.* Columbus, OH: Charles E. Merrill.

Information on the cause, treatment, prognosis, and educational implications of numerous disabling conditions is included in chapters written in lay terms by physicians who specialize in treating particular conditions.

Williamson, G. (1989). *Children with spina bifida.* Baltimore: Paul H. Brookes.

This is a complete and thorough discussion of all forms of spina bifida. A particular strength of this book is its examples of treatment and curriculum.

JOURNALS

Journal of Applied Behavior Analysis
University of Kansas
Lawrence, KS 66044

Journal of the Association for Persons with Severe Handicaps (JASH)
(formerly *AAESPH Review*)
11201 Greenwood Ave. North
Seattle, WA 98133

*Physical and Occupational Therapy
in Pediatrics*
The Haworth Press Inc.
10 Alice St.
Binghamton, NY 13904-1580

Physical Therapy
American Physical Therapy Association
1111 N. Fairfax St.
Alexandria, VA 22314-1488

PROFESSIONAL ORGANIZATIONS

Brain Injury Association, Inc.
(formerly National Head Injury
Foundation)
1776 Massachusetts Avenue, NW
Suite 100
Washington, DC 20036
http://www.biausa.org

Epilepsy Foundation of America (EFA)
4351 Garden City Dr., Suite 406
Landover, MD 20785
http://www.efa.org

March of Dimes Birth Defects Foundation
P.O. Box 1657
Wilkes-Barre, PA 18703
http://www.modimes.org

National Center for Children and
Youth with Disabilities (NICHCY)
P.O. Box 1492
Washington, DC 20013-1492
http://www.peds.umn.educ/
Centers/ihd

United Cerebral Palsy Association, Inc.
1660 L Street, NW, Suite 700
Washington, DC 20036
http://www.ucpa.org

Afterword

 ## *New Millennium, New Opportunities*

What lies ahead for exceptional children? The new millennium can signify a new beginning, the opportunity to try new ideas. But there is truth in the old adage, "You can't know where you are going if you don't know where you have been."

The forces that shaped the educational enterprise in the twentieth century surely will appear in some form in the twenty-first century as well, and we need to be aware of those forces as we look toward the future. As the philosopher Santayana pointed out, "Those who are ignorant of history will be forced to relive it."

New opportunities will be brought about, in part, by the exploding technological revolution. Access to information, which used to be the exclusive possession of educators, is now available to anyone who can use a computer. Also, increased public awareness of the importance of education in the postindustrial world—in the information age—should result in increased understanding and support for the needs of education.

We end this text with some thoughts about the changes that will likely take place in educating exceptional children in the immediate future and what lies ahead for education in general.

 ## *Issues Affecting General Education*

At the beginning of the new century, forces outside of education will predominate in creating changes in education or at least in demanding the attention of educators. Following are eight issues that we see as strong influences on the educational system.

1. *Poverty and children.* We in the United States have lived through periods of prosperity that are unparalleled in the world. Yet we still face the uncomfortable statistic that one in every five children in this country will exist in conditions of poverty sometime before their seventeenth birthday. One cause behind that statistic is the growing number of one-parent families. Schools will have to develop better and more comprehensive strategies for educating these children. Surely there will be greater collaboration between the disciplines of health, social work, and education. This collaboration is already happening, but we know that poverty is associated with a number

of children whom we call "exceptional." Unless we can find some answers to the problems of poverty in our society, we can anticipate larger numbers of exceptional children with special needs and we will expect the schools to provide an appropriate education for them.

At this writing, it is still unclear what the ultimate effect of such social programs as welfare reform will mean to the development of young children. Will limited health care or inferior child care in their early years create additional burdens for the educational system to bear when the children of families receiving public assistance reach school age? Will we be spending more time interacting with families rather than individual children? If we believe the ecological model detailed in this text, that would seem to be a likely event with all its implications for modification of teacher training and service delivery.

2. *Changing family patterns.* Not very long ago, the predominant family pattern was the father as the breadwinner and the mother as the primary caregiver. Mothers who stayed at home raising children were more easily able to communicate with the school about the education of the children in the family.

That pattern has been largely replaced by the two-parent working family or the one-parent working family, and the schools will have to adapt to this new pattern. One adaptation may well be a longer school day, already in place in many school systems. This new pattern also means that the family has less time to spend with their children and less time to consult with the schools about their children's education. Educators of exceptional children emphasize the importance of the family in the upbringing of exceptional children. So how is the interrelationship between professionals and families to take place?

3. *Cultural diversity.* The latter part of the twentieth century has seen a major increase in children from diverse cultural backgrounds who have come to school with a variety of behavioral patterns and, in some cases, values different from those of mainstream American culture. The educational enterprise has had to take into account these differences while still making clear the expectations of American society for an educated citizen. Students with special needs have a particularly difficult time reconciling cultural differences and, at the same time, trying to become educated in the face of their special needs.

4. *Exploding technology.* The rapid emergence of new tools of communication between teacher and student and between student and student has often amazed educators, who wonder what the next technical marvel will be. Many students now have independent access to huge bodies of information beyond the school. Entire encyclopedias can now be placed on a single CD. This will surely change the role of the teacher in the new century from being a provider of knowledge to being more of a mentor to aid students in finding and processing information more effectively and evaluating the quality of the information already available to them.

5. *Medical advances.* The future changes in special education will depend on many changes in the broader society. Some trends can be noted today, while others await unpredictable future events. We have already seen increases in the births of children with multiple disabilities occurring, ironically, because of advances in medical knowledge and skills. Young children who previously

would have died survive but cannot be saved from the damage to their neural systems. There may be serious problems in helping such children reach a level of self-sufficiency. At the same time, advances in gene therapy may contribute to a decline in some physical disabilities and health impairments.

6. *Transition to work: employability.* As American society enters more deeply into the information age, will this have a negative impact on the employability of exceptional children? The bar likely will be raised on how much education will be required to maintain self-sufficiency. It is tempting to be depressed by such trends because we see the negative numbers rising. What we do not see is the creative efforts of future generations to more adequately cope with such problems. In each generation, scientists, educators, and citizens rise to the challenge and propose new ways of accomplishing old goals, and there is no reason to believe that this will not happen again.

7. *Diversions.* More than ever before, students have a multitude of diversions from their studies. There is not only television but a multitude of entertainment possibilities resulting from the same technology that promises so much access to important information. How do we wean students (and adults) from computer and TV games to more serious knowledge and information sources?

8. *Education standards.* As the recognition of the importance of education grows, some societal concerns are being played out in the development of more stringent standards in content fields. Historians, scientists, and mathematicians all vie with one another by putting forth high academic standards that they expect students to meet. There is much talk of not allowing students to progress to the next level until they have demonstrated mastery of a preceding set of standards. Some content specialists do not think of exceptional children when they draft these standards or of the consequences of these policies on students with special needs. We must remind them that simple policies designed to solve complex problems usually end up in serious trouble.

We aspire to create an educational environment that will support excellence for all, which does not mean, of course, the same educational setting or content for all. Unfortunately for us, our educational enterprise does not have the luxury of attacking the issues listed here one at a time. It has to respond to all of them simultaneously, recognizing that they interact in complex ways.

Exceptional Children in the Twenty-First Century

While the forces listed here—and many others that we are not yet wise enough to recognize—will affect all students, there are other issues of special concern to children with special needs.

1. *The inclusion philosophy.* The last decade of the twentieth century has shown a strong shift to educating children with special needs in the general education classroom, but will that remain the pattern in the new century? Indeed, what will the "regular" classroom look like? Perhaps more important, what will be the education that these exceptional children will receive? And will it be similar at the elementary, middle, and secondary school levels?

2. *Early childhood.* As one educator recently mentioned, early childhood education is getting earlier and earlier. The trend is clear. Already legislation has committed us to provide services to infants and toddlers with disabilities and their families. This means we have to rethink what we mean by an "appropriate education for children with special needs" and how we collaborate with professionals from the health and social service areas. This is a true frontier, one that requires hardy pioneers and adaptive professionals to chart the way. General education teachers will need significant preparation to work successfully with the exceptional students in their classrooms. Every member of the education team will need to share talents and knowledge to help exceptional children achieve their goals for the future. And most likely, a continuum of services will include the general education classroom and a variety of services beyond the classroom to meet the needs of exceptional children and their families.

3. *Who will deliver special services?* The assumption used to be that the special education teacher would teach a small group of children with special needs, and the preparation of special teachers reflected that assumption. But now that the special educator is a consultant or a team member, working closely with the general education teacher, shouldn't personnel preparation reflect that changing model? Will sufficient special teachers be available, or will we have to think more seriously of preparing aides and other support personnel to make up the difference?

4. *What are our goals for children with disabilities?* One of our current goals for many exceptional children is for them to live independently as adults, which means they have a job and are able to support themselves without the tangible help of the larger community. Is that goal still viable in the information age, or must we encourage these students to consider group living or supportive industries as service delivery programs? Should we tie our school curriculum more closely to the job market that is out there in the new century rather than to a past job market that is dwindling before our eyes? How will we define success in the future?

5. *What are our goals for gifted students?* The current trend in the public schools is for gifted students to be incorporated in the general education classroom. At the same time, we are spending generous sums of money on graduate and professional schools because we realize the enormous need for a well-educated citizenry. Recognition of the special educational needs of our brightest students seems incomplete now but surely will be more evident to the next generations. Past attempts to help the brightest students have yielded benefits to all of education in terms of more understanding of how to instruct students in problem solving and problem finding, of creative performance, and so on. Indeed, creative solutions to the problems noted in this afterword will come in large measure from the fertile minds of children whom we now call "gifted." It is in the best interests of all society to see to it that talent is discovered, nurtured, and encouraged to the maximum extent possible.

6. *Technology.* In the past, students with special needs often led the educational enterprise in the creative use of technology. Special educators, having had to find a way around communication barriers and perceptual problems, introduced many technical innovations to general education. With the advent of the Internet and the computer as significant players, we have to re-

double our efforts to make sure that exceptional children have access to the same sources of information that general education students have. Although there has been significant advancement in assistive and educational technology, more will be needed.

7. *Decisions, decisions, decisions.* All these issues have a number of options or potential courses of action attached to them. One thing seems sure: The status quo is not a serious option. Things are going to change whether we want them to or not. The only question is will we, as educators, be creating the change or just desperately reacting to the ideas that noneducators present to policy makers?

   Policy has been defined as the rules and standards by which we allocate scarce resources to almost unlimited needs. If that is so, what factors will help us make hard decisions or select among options?

Criteria for Decision Making

1. *Cost.* Decisions are rarely reached without calculating the cost. Educating children with special needs has always cost more than educating students in general education. We have to calculate whether the more costly solution is also the most effective solution, and whether the public will be willing to pay the bill.

2. *Effectiveness.* If we are asking the public to bear additional expense, we need to be able to convince them that our programs and services are worth it. That means we need to show the effectiveness of our programs in some easily demonstrable way. The new generation of professionals will surely be spending more time on accountability than we have done in the past.

3. *Personnel Needs.* Personnel needs will be even more complex than in the past. This is particularly true in the field of early childhood education, since services to young children with disabilities (from birth on) will be added to existing responsibilities. Who will be these early childhood interventionists? Where will they come from? Who will prepare them for their new tasks?

4. *Values.* Much of what we do depends on the value orientation we have as a society. Will we hold to the recognition of every person as valuable and to be cherished, or will persons be accepted only if they clearly make some form of tangible contribution to society? Should we go to the additional trouble it will take to help all individuals learn all they are capable of learning? Each generation has to decide that anew—it does not profit us to be complacent about such fundamental issues.

The answer to these issues may well be designed or discovered by some of the readers of this textbook. There is a new recognition and a readiness to accept options other than the status quo when those options are well grounded in research and demonstrated practice and pay attention to the criteria noted here. It is not true that all the interesting explorations and discoveries have been made by past generations. Further discovery of the potential of the human mind and the organization of more viable educational and social models lie in front of us.

Glossary

Academic achievement learning disabilities Problems with academic subjects that are due to underlying disorders in information processing.

Access technology Equipment, such as a computer mouse, that allows a student to use a computer program or that adapts the computer for a person with disabilities.

Accommodation Changes in the shape of the lens of the eye in order to focus on objects closer than 20 feet.

Acoupedic method See *auditory method.*

Acoustic method See *auditory method.*

Acquired immunodeficiency syndrome (AIDS) A breakdown of the body's immune system, allowing the body to become vulnerable to a host of fatal infections that it normally is able to ward off.

Adaptive behavior The effectiveness or degree with which individuals meet the standards of personal independence and social responsibility expected for their age and cultural group.

Alpha-fetoprotein test A blood test given to pregnant women to detect fetal disabilities.

American Sign Language (ASL) A manual language used by many people with hearing impairments that meets the universal linguistic standards of spoken English.

Amniocentesis A procedure for analyzing the amniotic fluid (a watery liquid in which the embryo is suspended) to discover genetic defects in the unborn child.

Anxiety-withdrawal A pattern of deviant behavior in which children are shy, timid, reclusive, sensitive, submissive, overdependent, and easily depressed.

Apgar test A screening test administered to an infant at one minute and five minutes after birth.

Aphasia The loss of the ability to speak as a result of brain injury or trauma.

Applied behavioral analysis (ABA) A learning approach that is based on individual analyses of a student's functioning and relies on the learning of behaviors to remediate learning problems.

Aptitude-achievement discrepancy A discrepancy between a student's ability (measured on intelligence tests) and academic achievement; a factor in the diagnosis of learning disabilities.

Arthritis Inflammation of the joints that causes them to swell and stiffen.

Articulation The movement of the mouth and tongue that shapes sound into speech.

Articulation error Mispronunciation such as *ring* for *king.*

Assessment A process for identifying a child's strengths and weaknesses; it involves five steps: screening, di-

agnosis, classification, placement, and monitoring or discharge.

Assistive technology Tools that enhance the functioning of persons with disabilities.

Asthma A condition affecting a person's breathing.

At-risk infant An infant who has a greater chance of displaying developmental delays or cognitive or motor deficits due to a variety of factors.

Attention deficit disorder (ADD) A conduct disorder that leaves children unable to pay attention or work at a task; impulsiveness is another characteristic of the disorder. Often found in combination with hyperactivity (attention deficit hyperactivity disorder [ADHD]).

Attention-deficit hyperactivity disorder (ADHD) A disorder that causes children to have difficulty settling down to do a particular task, especially desk work.

Audiogram A graphic record of hearing acuity at selected intensities throughout the normal range of audibility, recorded from a pure-tone audiometer, which creates sounds of preset frequency or intensity.

Audiometer An instrument for testing hearing acuity.

Audition Thought transformed into words and received by a listener through hearing.

Auditory global method See *auditory method.*

Auditory method A method of teaching deaf students that involves auditory training and makes extensive use of sound amplification to develop listening and speech skills. Also called *acoupedic method, acoustic method, auditory global method, aural method,* and *unisensory method.*

Augmented communication Methods of communicating that are based on symbols or gestures rather than speech.

Aural method See *auditory method.*

Authentic assessment Measuring a child's ability by means of an in-class assignment.

Autism A neurological disorder leading to deficits in functioning, particularly in communication and social skills.

Behavior disorder A serious emotional disturbance.

Behavior modification Techniques designed to change behaviors and to increase the use of socially constructive behaviors.

Blindness See *profound visual disability.*

Bone-conductor test A measure of a person's ability to hear sounds by recording the sounds received in the brain.

Braille A system using embossed characters in different combinations of six dots arranged in a cell that allows people with profound visual impairments to read by touch as well as to write by using special aids.

Brainstorming   A technique in which a group of people discuss a particular problem, trying to come up with as many solutions as possible; often used with gifted children.

Cardiopulmonary system   The heart, blood, and lungs.

Central hearing loss   Hearing loss that results from damage to sound-processing areas in the brain.

Central processing   Classification of a stimulus through the use of memory, reasoning, and evaluation; the second step in the information-processing model.

Cerebral palsy   A condition caused by damage to the motor control centers of the brain before birth, during the birth process, or after birth.

Choreoathetoid cerebral palsy   A type of cerebral palsy in which changes in muscle tone cause uncoordinated, jerky movement.

Chorionic villus biopsy   A test used to detect disabilities in a fetus during the first trimester.

Ciliary muscles   Muscles that control changes in the shape of the lens so the eye can focus on objects at varying distances.

Circle of friends   A social contact technique that brings together disabled and nondisabled children to discuss their likes and dislikes under the leadership of a facilitator.

Class action suit   Legal action that applies to the individual who brings the particular case to court and to all members of the class to which that individual belongs.

Classification   The organization of information.

Cleft palate   Failure of the bone and tissue of the palate (roof of the mouth) to fuse during early prenatal development; often associated with cleft lip.

Cognition   The process of knowing and thinking.

Cognitive behavior modification   A variation of behavior modification that focuses on the conscious feelings and attitudes of the individual.

Cognitive intervention strategy   A strategy that focuses on the cognitive processes of learning to help remediate learning disabilities.

Cognitive strategies   See *executive function.*

Combined method   See *total communication method.*

Communication   The exchange of thoughts, information, feelings, or ideas.

Communication board   Chart containing symbols, letters, or words that nonspeaking students can point to in order to communicate their thoughts and needs.

Communication disorder   An impairment in articulation, fluency, voice, or language.

Conduct disorder   A pattern of deviant behavior in which children defy authority; are hostile toward authority figures; are cruel, malicious, and assaultive; and have few guilt feelings. This group includes children who are hyperactive, restless, and hyperkinetic.

Conductive hearing loss   A condition that reduces the intensity of the sound vibrations reaching the auditory nerve and inner ear.

Congenital   Present in an individual at birth.

Content acceleration   Curriculum modification that moves students through the traditional curriculum at a fast pace.

Content enrichment   Curriculum modification that expands the material for study, giving students the opportunity for a greater appreciation of a topic.

Content novelty   Curriculum modification that introduces material that normally would not appear in the general curriculum, to help students who are gifted master important ideas.

Content sophistication   Curriculum modification that challenges students who are gifted to use higher levels of thinking to understand ideas that average students of the same age find difficult or impossible to understand.

Contingent social reinforcement   A behavior modification technique using a token system to teach appropriate social behavior.

Continuum of services   A range of personnel to provide needed specialized services such as speech, physical, or occupational therapy.

Convergence   Change in the extrinsic muscles of the eye.

Cooperative learning   A set of instructional strategies that emphasize the use of groups for teaching students techniques of problem solving and working constructively with others.

Cornea   The transparent anterior portion of the tough outer coat of the eyeball.

Creativity   Mental process by which an individual creates new ideas and products or recombines existing ideas and products in a fashion that is novel to him or her.

Criterion-referenced tests   A test designed to measure a child's development in terms of absolute levels of mastery, as opposed to the child's status relative to other children.

Cued commands   A method of teaching children how to interact with their environment and the people around them.

Culture   The attitudes, values, customs, and language that form an identifiable pattern or heritage.

Cumulative disorders   Elements that gradually lower the functional intelligence of children and increase their adaptive problems.

Curriculum compacting   Content modification that allows students who are gifted to move ahead. It consists of three steps: finding out what the students know, arranging to teach the remaining concepts or skills, and providing a different set of experiences to enrich or advance the students.

Deaf   Having such severe hearing disorders (usually congenital) that understanding speech through the ear alone, with or without the use of a hearing aid, is impossible.

Deafblind   A person who possesses both a severe hearing loss and a severe loss of vision.

Decibels (dB)   A measurement of the relative intensity of sound.

Deinstitutionalization   Releasing as many exceptional children and adults as possible from the confinement of residential institutions into their local communities.

Developmental disabilities   Mental retardation and related conditions (e.g., cerebral palsy, epilepsy) that create a substantial delay in the child's development and require intervention from many professional disciplines.

Developmental learning disabilities   Problems in processing information—attention problems, memory problems, disorders in thinking and using language. Also called *neuropsychological learning disabilities.*

Developmental scales   Instruments used to compare an infant's physical, emotional, and intellectual skills to other same-age children's development.

Developmental screening   A brief assessment of a child's developmental progress to determine if the child is at risk or is delayed.

Developmental therapy   An intervention strategy for children with behavior disorders that emphasizes the sequential learning of social behaviors and communication and academic skills.

Developmentally appropriate practices   Early childhood curriculum practices that match the level of development of the child and presented in ways children learn (e.g., play).

Diagnostic achievement tests   Tests that help determine the process a student is using to solve a problem or decode a reading passage.

Diagnostic prescriptive model   A teaching approach using cognitive strategy instruction to address learning problems.

Dialect   A regional variation in pronunciation or language use.

Differential diagnosis   Pinpointing atypical behavior, explaining it, and distinguishing it from similar problems of other children with disabilities.

Differential reinforcement   A behavior modification technique that provides rewards if the student can increase the time between displays of unacceptable behavior.

Diplegic   Involvement of the entire body, especially the legs, in a physical condition.

Divergent thinking   The ability to produce many different answers to a question.

Down syndrome   A chromosomal abnormality that leads to mild or moderate mental retardation and, at times, a variety of hearing, skeletal, and heart problems.

Due process   A set of legal procedures designed to ensure that an individual's constitutional rights are protected.

Dyscalculia   The inability to perform mathematical functions.

Dyslexia   A severe reading disability involving difficulties in understanding the relationship between sounds and letters.

Dyslexic   Affected by dyslexia.

Dysphonia   A disorder in voice quality.

Early childhood intervention   Systematic efforts designed to prevent deficits or to improve an existing disability in children between birth and age 5.

Ecological inventory   A process that teachers can use to develop and individualize functional curriculum for their students.

Ecological model   A view of exceptionality that examines the individual in complex interaction with environmental forces and believes that exceptionalities should be remediated by modifying elements in the environment to allow more constructive interactions between the individual and the environment.

Educational assessment   The systematic gathering of educationally relevant information to make legal and instructional decisions about the provision of special services.

Environmental modification   A strategy creating an environment in which the child can succeed.

Environmental risks   Factors in the life of the child from conception that can interfere with normal development or cause a disability.

Epilepsy   A group of diseases of the nervous system marked primarily by seizures.

Exceptional child   A child who differs from the norm in mental characteristics, sensory abilities, communication abilities, social behavior, or physical characteristics to the extent that special education services are required for the child to develop to maximum capacity.

Executive function   The hypothesized decision-making element that controls reception, central processing, and expression.

Expression   The choice of a single response from a group of possible responses; the third step in information processing.

Extrinsic motivation   Motivating students to complete a task by promising a reward.

Extrinsic muscles   Muscles that control the movement of the eyeball in the socket.

Facilitative communication   Method of communicating in which an instructor holds the arms and wrists of a student to help him or her overcome tremors and communicate.

Fading   Gradually cutting back on help as a child becomes competent at a task.

Family-focused approach   Helping parents become more autonomous and less dependent on professionals.

Family harmony   The perception that each partner in a marriage is taking his or her part in an acceptable manner.

Family life cycle   The stages—couple, childbearing and preschool, school age, adolescence, launching, postparental, aging—through which the family moves.

Feedback   The result of a response to a stimulus.

Fetal alcohol syndrome   Defects in a child as a result of the mother's heavy use of alcohol during her pregnancy.

Finger spelling   Spelling in the air or in the palm of another person by using a manual alphabet.

Flexible pacing   Allowing students to move through the school subjects or program at their own pace.

Fluency   The flow of speech.

Fragile X syndrome   A restriction at the end of the X chromosome that may result in mental retardation or learning disabilities.

Frequency   The number of vibrations (or cycles) per second of a given sound wave.

Functional assessment   A step-by-step assessment of the student's behavior to better understand the intent of the behavior.

Generalization   The ability to apply a skill learned in one situation to a new one.

Genetic counseling   A source of information for parents about the likelihood of their having a child with genetically based disabilities.

Gifted   Term used to describe persons with intellectual gifts.

Grouping   Bringing together students of similar abilities or levels of achievement for instruction.

Hard of hearing   A person with a hearing loss and some residual hearing.

Head Start   A federally funded educational preschool program for children living in poverty.

Health impairment   A condition that requires ongoing medical attention.

Hearing impairment   Any hearing loss, from mild to severe.

Helping teacher   A direct-service special teacher who works in the classroom with the regular teacher to provide support, encouragement, and therapeutic tutoring.

Hemiplegic   Involvement of one side of the body in a physical condition.

Hidden talent   A talent, such as musical, that has not been identified by the home or school and that may not be developed or expressed.

Human immunodeficiency virus (HIV)   A virus that breaks down the body's immune system, causing AIDS.

Hyperactivity   Excessive movement or motor restlessness, generally accompanied by impulsiveness and inattention.

Hyperbilirubinemia   Incompatibility in the Rh factor of the mother's and fetus's blood that can lead to hearing loss.

Hyperopia   Farsightedness.

Idea Part C   The Individuals with Disabilities Act, Part C; the section of the act that deals with infants and toddlers.

Immaturity   A pattern of deviant behavior in which children are inattentive, sluggish, uninterested in school, lazy, preoccupied, and reticent.

Incidence   The number of new cases occurring in a population during a specific interval of time.

Inclusion   The process of bringing children with exceptionalities into the regular classroom.

Independence training   A curriculum that teaches persons with disabilities the skills so they can live independently.

Individualized education program (IEP)   A program written for every student receiving special education; it describes the child's current performance and goals for the school year, the particular special education services to be delivered, and the procedures by which outcomes are to be evaluated.

Individualized family services plan (IFSP)   An intervention program for young children and their families that identifies their needs and sets forth a program to meet those needs.

Inert knowledge   Knowledge stored in memory but not linked to other knowledge.

Instructional technology   The computer and tools that support the use of the computer.

Integrated classroom   A classroom administered jointly by general and special education teachers. Usually one-third of the class is made up of youngsters with mild handicaps.

Intensity   The relative loudness of a sound.

Interactive approach   An approach to treating language disorders that uses the natural inclination of the child to talk about what he or she is doing to improve his or her language use.

Inter-individual difference   A substantial difference among people along key dimensions of development.

Intra-individual difference   A major variation in the abilities or development of a single child.

Intrinsic motivation   Motivation that is internal to the student; self-motivation.

Invulnerability   The concept used to explain how some at-risk children are able to develop without disabilities.

Iris   The colored muscular partition in the eye that expands and contracts to regulate the amount of light admitted through the pupil.

Itinerant teacher   A teacher who serves several schools, visiting exceptional children and their classroom teachers at regular intervals or whenever necessary.

Karyotyping   A process by which a picture of chromosomal patterns is prepared to identify chromosomal abnormality.

Knowledge structure   A bank of interrelated information in long-term memory that helps us recognize and recall patterns to use in solving problems.

Language   An organized system of symbols used to express and receive meaning.

Language disorder   The impairment or deviant development of comprehension or use (or both) of a spoken, written, or other symbol system.

Learned helplessness   The belief that nothing one does can prevent negative things from happening.

Learning disability   A disorder that manifests itself in a discrepancy between ability and academic achievement. Learning disabilities do not stem from mental retardation, sensory impairments, emotional problems, or lack of opportunity to learn.

Least restrictive environment   The educational setting in which a child with special needs can learn that is as close as possible to the general education classroom.

Lens   The elastic biconvex body that focuses light on the retina of the eye.

Life space interview   A careful interview with a student directly after a crisis situation or event, in which the student discusses the event with the teacher and generates alternative solutions to the problem.

Low vision   See *severe visual disability.*

Manual method   A method of communicating with persons with severe hearing impairments by using gestural signs.

Medical model   A view of exceptionality that implies a physical condition or disease within the patient.

Memory disorder   The inability to remember what has been seen, heard, or experienced.

Meningitis   An infection of the membranes covering the brain and spinal cord that can cause hearing loss.

Mental retardation   A combination of subnormal intelligence and deficits in adaptive behavior, manifested during the developmental period.

Metacognition   The ability to think about one's own thinking and monitor its effectiveness.

Mixed hearing loss   A condition involving problems in the outer ear as well as in the middle or inner ear.

Mnemonic   A rhyme or made-up system that helps students remember facts or concepts.

Modeling   Imitating the behavior of others.

Moderate visual disability   A visual impairment that can be almost entirely corrected with the help of visual aids.

Morphology   The structure of words and the way affixes change meaning or add information.

Multidisciplinary team   A group of professionals who work with children with disabilities to help them achieve their full potential.

Multisensory approach   A method for remediating reading disabilities that uses the child's hearing, vision, and motor skills.

Muscular dystrophy   A musculoskeletal disease that leads to the progressive deterioration of skeletal muscles.

Musculoskeletal system   The muscles, bones, and joints of the body.

Myelomeningocele   The protrusion from the spinal cord of a sac of fluids containing portions of the spinal cord itself.

Myopia   Nearsightedness.

Neurological system   The brain, spinal cord, and nerves.

Neuropsychological learning disabilities   See *developmental learning disabilities.*

Nondiscriminatory evaluation   A full individual examination appropriate to a student's cultural and linguistic background.

Normalization   The creation of a learning and social environment as normal as possible for the exceptional person.

Norm-referenced achievement   See *standard achievement tests.*

Object permanence   The understanding that objects that are not in the visual field still exist.

Operant conditioning   A technique of behavior modification that works by controlling the stimulus that follows a response.

Oral-aural method   An approach to teaching deaf students that uses residual hearing through amplified sound, speech reading, and speech to develop communication skills.

Orientation & mobility (O&M) training   Teaching a person with visual loss or with blindness how to move through space.

Otitis media   An infection of the middle ear that can cause hearing impairment.

Parent empowerment   The expectation that parents will play a major role in decisions about their child's care.

Parental participation   The inclusion of parents in the development of their child's individualized education program and their right to access their child's educational records.

PDDNOS   Pervasive developmental disabilities not otherwise specified.

Perceptual-motor disabilities   Difficulty in understanding or responding to the meaning of pictures or numbers.

Performance assessment   A measure of the application of knowledge.

Phenylketonuria (PKU)   A single-gene defect that can produce severe retardation because of the body's inability to break down phenylalanine, which when accumulated at high levels in the brain results in severe damage; can be controlled by a diet restricting phenylalanine.

Phonation   The production of sound by the vibration of the vocal cords.

Phoneme   A sound; the smallest unit of speech.

Phonological error   Mispronunciation of speech sounds.

Phonology   The sound system of a language; the way sounds are combined into meaningful sequences.

Physical disability   A condition that interferes with the individual's ability to use his or her body.

Positive reinforcement   The application of a positive stimulus immediately following a response.

Postlinguistic deafness   The loss of hearing after spontaneous speech and language have developed.

Pragmatics   The understanding of how language is used in communication in particular settings.

Preacademic instruction   Instruction in the developmental skills that prepare children for reading, writing, and arithmetic.

Prelinguistic deafness   The loss of hearing before speech and language have developed; referred to as *deafness.*

Prenatal care Monitoring of a pregnancy by the mother and her physician.

Prereferral services Services to help children at risk for disabling conditions to adapt to the regular classroom before they are singled out for special services.

Prevalence The number of people in a given category in a population group during a specified period of time.

Problem-based learning A problem that encourages the student to define the issue, organize the components, and then solve the problem.

Problem finding The ability to review an area of study and to perceive those elements worthy of further analysis and study.

Problem solving The ability to reach an appropriate answer by organizing and processing available information in a systematic way.

Profound visual disability A vision impairment that prohibits the use of vision as an educational tool; in legal terms, *blindness*.

Punishment The application of actions to reduce undesirable behavior.

Pupil The central opening of the eye through which light enters.

Pure-tone test Sounds produced mechanically to various levels of decibels to determine a person's range of hearing.

Reasoning The ability to generate new information through the internal processing of available information.

Reception The visual or auditory perception of a stimulus; the second step in information processing.

Reciprocal teaching A technique in which small groups of students and teachers take turns leading a discussion.

Residential school A public or private institution for children with disabling conditions.

Resonation The process that gives the voice its special characteristics.

Resource room An instructional setting to which an exceptional child comes for specific periods of time, usually on a regularly scheduled basis.

Respiration Breathing; the process that generates the energy that produces sound.

Respite care The services of a trained individual to relieve the primary caregiver of a child with disabilities on a short-term basis.

Retina The light-sensitive innermost layer of tissue at the back of the eyeball.

Retinoblastoma A tumor of the eye that causes blindness.

Retinopathy of prematurity A disease of the retina in which a mass of scar tissue forms in back of the lens of the eye. Both eyes are usually affected, and it occurs chiefly in infants born prematurely who receive excessive oxygen.

Rh incompatibility The condition that can develop when a mother who is Rh negative carries an Rh-positive child; the mother's antibodies can cause deafness and other serious consequences for the fetus unless the condition is identified and treated.

Rochester method A method of teaching deaf students that combines the oral method and finger spelling.

Rubella German measles, which in the first three months of pregnancy can cause visual impairment, hearing impairment, mental retardation, and birth defects in the fetus.

Scaffolding A strategy in which a teacher models the expected behavior and guides the learning of the student.

Self-contained special class A separate class in which a special education teacher assumes primary responsibility for the education program of students with disabilities.

Self-determination skills A curriculum that teaches a student with disabilities how to make individual decisions and personal choices.

Self-evaluation A technique for behavior change that asks the student to compare his or her behavior to some criterion and make a judgment about the quality of the behavior being exhibited.

Self-instruction A technique for behavior change in which students talk to themselves, encouraging themselves with verbal prompts to persist in solving an academic or social problem.

Self-monitoring A technique for behavior change that requires students to determine whether a target behavior has occurred and then record its occurrence.

Self-reinforcement A technique for behavior change in which students reward themselves with a token or tally after meeting some performance standard.

Semantics The component of language that governs meanings of words and word combinations.

Sensorineural hearing loss A defect of the inner ear or the auditory nerve in transmitting impulses to the brain.

Sensory compensation The theory that if one sense avenue is deficient, other senses are automatically strengthened.

Service coordinator An individual who gathers all the information that relates to a child with a disability and heads up the team that prepares the child's individualized education program.

Severe visual disability A vision impairment that is only partially corrected by visual aids but allows the child to use vision as a channel for learning; in legal terms, *low vision*.

Sheltered workshop A not-for-profit facility providing vocational services to adults with disabilities.

Simultaneous method See *total communication method*.

Snellen chart A chart consisting of rows of letters in graduated sizes that is used to determine visual acuity. A variation used with younger children and people who do not know the letter names consists of capital *E*s pointing in different directions.

Social language learning An approach to treating language disorders that uses speech and language in a functional way to satisfy needs.

Social learning approach   A system designed to develop critical thinking and independent action by students with mild retardation.

Socialized aggression   A pattern of deviant behavior displayed by children who are hostile and aggressive and have few guilt feelings but who are socialized within their group, usually a gang.

Sonography   The use of sound waves to take a picture of a fetus in its mother's uterus.

Spastic (pyramidal) cerebral palsy   A form of cerebral palsy marked by tight muscles and stiff movements.

Special class   A class held for children who need more special instruction than the resource room can give them.

Special courses   Curriculum designed to meet students' diverse achievements and aptitudes.

Special education   The educational help devised for children who differ significantly from the norm.

Special Olympics   A program that allows children with disabilities to participate in competitions in a variety of physical events and games.

Special school   A day school, organized within a school system, for a group of children with specific exceptionalities.

Speech   The systematic oral production of words of a given language.

Speech disorder   A disorder of articulation (how words are pronounced), voice (how words are vocalized), or fluency (the flow of speech).

Speech-language pathologist   A trained professional who provides supervision and administration, diagnosis, consultation, and direct services for individuals who have communication disorders.

Speech reading   Lip reading; the visual interpretation of spoken communication.

Spina bifida   The separation of a portion of the spinal cord.

Standard achievement tests   Tests that measure the student's level of achievement compared with the achievement of students of similar age or grade. Also called *norm-referenced tests*.

Student acceleration   Passing students through the educational system as quickly as possible.

Stuttering   A disorder of fluency.

Syntax   The way in which words are organized in sentences.

Synthetic speech   The production of sound—of phonemes into words—by means of a computer.

Target behaviors   In behavior modification, the characteristics we want to change or enhance.

Task analysis   A method that breaks down complex tasks into simpler component parts, teaches each of the components separately, then teaches them together; a procedure under which a child receives positive reinforcement for each step or part of the total task as it is completed.

Task training   A remediation strategy that emphasizes the sequencing and simplification of the task to be learned, using task analysis and teaching one skill at a time.

Teacher-consultant   A specially trained consultant who provides differentiated instruction for gifted students in the general education classroom.

Teratogen   A substance ingested by the mother that can damage the growth and development of the fetus.

Time-out   The physical removal of a child from a reinforcing situation for a period of time, usually immediately following an unwanted response.

TORCHS   An acronym given to a cluster of infections that can result in hearing loss and other disabilities: *toxoplasmosis*, *rubella*, *cytomegalovirus*, *herpes simplex virus*, and syphilis.

Total communication method   A method of teaching deaf students that combines finger spelling, signs, speech reading, speech, and auditory amplification. Also called *combined method* and *simultaneous method*.

Transient adaptation problem   A behavior problem that is temporary, for example, one that occurs due to a family problem that is later resolved.

Transition services   Programs that help exceptional students move from school to the world of work and community.

TTY, TDD, TT   Alternative names for a telephone that produces written text.

Ultimate functioning   The degree to which people with severe disabilities are able to take a productive part in a variety of community situations appropriate to their chronological age.

Underachievement   A student's achievement below what would be expected from intelligence data and not due to a disability.

Unisensory method   See *auditory method*.

Verbal language   A spoken language; a language based on speech sounds.

Vicarious learning   Learning that occurs to someone who observes how others' behaviors are reinforced; the learner is not an active participant in the event.

Visual acuity   The ability to see details clearly or identify forms at a specified distance.

Voice   The production of sound in the larynx and the selective transmission and modification of that sound through resonance and loudness.

Voice disorder   A variation from accepted norms in voice quality, pitch, or loudness.

Zero reject principle   The principle that all children with disabilities must be provided a free and appropriate public education and that local school systems cannot decide not to provide needed services.

References

Adelman, H., & Taylor, L. (1991). Issues and problems related to the assessment of learning disabilities. In H. L. Swanson (Ed.), *Handbook on the assessment of learning disabilities* (pp. 21–44). Austin, TX: PRO-ED.

Affleck, G., Tennen, H., & Rowe, J. (1991). *Infants in crisis: How parents cope with newborn intensive care and its aftermath*. New York: Springer-Verlag.

Affleck, J., Madge, S., Adams, A., & Lowenbrau, L. (1988). Integrated classroom versus resource model. *Exceptional Children, 54*, 339–348.

Allen-Hagen, B. (1991). Public juvenile facilities, 1989: Children in custody. *Juvenile Justice Bulletin*, 1–10.

Als, H. (1997). Earliest intervention for preterm infants in the newborn intensive care unit. In M. Guralnick (Ed.), *The effectiveness of early intervention* (pp. 47–76). Baltimore: Paul H. Brookes.

American Disabilities Act of 1990 (PL 101–336). Office of Special Education and Rehabilitation Service. U.S. Department of Education, Room 3132, Switzer Bldg., Washington, DC.

American Psychiatric Association. (1994). *Diagnostic and statistical manual of mental disorders* (4th ed.). Washington, DC: American Psychiatric Association.

American Speech-Language-Hearing Association. (1991). Committee on prevention of speech, language, and hearing problems. *ASHA, 33*(9), Supple. 6.

Amistad: Stories of Hispanic children with disabilities. (1997). Lawrence, KS: Beach Center on Families and Disabilities.

Anastasiow, N. J. (1982). *The adolescent parent*. Baltimore: Paul H. Brookes.

Anastasiow, N. J. (1986). *Development and disability*. Baltimore: Paul H. Brookes.

Anastasiow, N. J. (1996). Psycho-biological theory of affect and self development. In S. Harel & J. Shonkoff (Eds.), *Early childhood intervention* (pp. 111–112). Jerusalem, Israel: JDC-Brookdale Institute.

Anastasiow, N. J., Frankenberg, W., & Fandall, A. (1982). *Identifying the developmentally delayed child*. Baltimore: University Park Press.

Anastasiow, N. J., Hanes, M., & Hanes, M. (1982). *Language patterns in poverty children*. Austin, TX: PRO-ED.

Anastasiow, N. J., & Nucci, C. (1994). Social, historical and theoretical foundations of early childhood special education and early intervention. In P. Safford (Ed.), *Early childhood special education: Vol. 5. Yearbook in early childhood education* (pp. 7–25). New York: Teachers College Press.

Andrews, J. F., & Jodron, J. (1998). Multimedia stories for deaf children. *Teaching exceptional children, 3*(5), 28–33.

Anita, S. (1982). Social interaction of partially mainstreamed hearing impaired children. *American Annals of the Deaf, 127*, 18–25.

Anthony, T., Fazzi, D., Lampert, J., & Pogrund, R. (1992). Movement focus: Orientation and mobility for young blind and visually impaired children. In R. Pogrund, D. Fazzi, & J. Lampert (Eds.), *Early focus: Working with young blind and visually impaired children and their families*. New York: American Foundation for the Blind.

Apgar, V., & Beck, J. (1973). *Is my baby all right?* New York: Trident Press.

Atkinson, J. (1993). The Cambridge assessment and screening of vision in high risk infants and young children. In N. Anastasiow & S. Harel (Eds.), *The at-risk infant* (pp. 33–46). Baltimore: Paul H. Brookes.

Atwood, A. (1993, July). Movement disorders and autism acquired in review of communication abound. *American Journal of Mental Retardation, 99*(4), 450–451.

Badian, N. A. (1983). Dyscalculia and nonverbal disorders of learning. In H. R. Mykelbust (Ed.), *Progress in learning disabilities* (Vol. 5, pp. 235–264). New York: Grune & Stratton.

Badian, N. (1988). The prediction of good and poor reading before kindergarten entry: A nine-year follow-up. *Journal of Learning Disabilities, 21*, 98–103, 123.

Bailey, D. B., Buysee, V., Edmondson, R., & Smith, T. M. (1994). Building family-centered practices in early intervention: A team-based model for change. *Infants and Young Children, 5*(1), 73–82.

Bailey, D. E., Simeonsson, R. J., Winton, P. J., Huntington, G. S., Comfort, M., Isbell, P., O'Donnell, K. J., & Helm, J. M. (1986). Family-focused intervention: A functional model for planning, implementing, and evaluating family services in early intervention. *Journal of the Division of Early Childhood, 11*(1), 156–170.

Baker, J. M., & Zigmond, N. (1995). The meaning and practice of inclusion for students with learning disabilities. *Journal of Special Education, 29*(2), 163–180.

Baker, L., & Brown, A. L. (1984). Metacognitive skills in reading. In P. D. Pearson (Ed.), *Handbook of reading research* (pp. 353–394). New York: Longman.

Baldwin, A. (1987). Undiscovered diamonds. *Journal for the Education of the Gifted, 10*(4), 271–286.

Baldwin, V. (1991). Understanding the deaf-blind population census. *Traces*. Traces Project, Teaching Research Division, Western Oregon State College, Monmouth, OR 97361.

Baldwin, V. (1997). *Annual census report.* Monmouth, OR: National Technical Assistance Consortium, Teaching Research Division.

Bandura, A. (1989). Human agency in social cognitive theory. *American Psychologist, 44,* 1175–1184.

Barr, D. (1990). A solution in search of a problem: The role of technology in educational reform. *Journal for the Education of the Gifted, 14,* 79–95.

Barraga, N. (1983). *Visual handicaps and learning* (rev. ed.). Austin, TX.: Exceptional Resources.

Barraga, N. C. (1982). *Visual handicaps and learning* (2nd ed.). Austin, TX: Pro-Ed.

Bates, E. (1979). On the evolution and development of symbols. In E. Bates (Ed.), *The emergence of symbols: Cognition and communication in infancy* (pp. 1–32). New York: Academic Press.

Batshaw, M. L. (Ed.). (1997). *Children with disabilities: A medical primer* (3rd ed.). Baltimore: Paul H. Brookes.

Batshaw, M. L., & Perret, Y. M. (1988). *Children with handicaps: A medical primer* (2nd ed.). Baltimore: Paul H. Brookes.

Batshaw, M., & Perret, Y. (1992). *Children with handicaps: A medical primer* (3rd ed.). Baltimore: Paul H. Brookes.

Batshaw, M. L., & Rose, N. (1997). Birth defects, prenatal diagnosis and fetal therapy. In M. L. Batshaw (Ed.), *Children with disabilities* (pp. 35–52). Baltimore: Paul H. Brookes.

Baum, S., Renzulli, J., & Hebert. (1995). Reversing underachievement: Creative productivity as a systematic intervention. *Gifted Child Quarterly, 39*(4), 224–235.

Baumeister, A., & Woodley-Zanthos, P. (1996). Prevention: Biological factors. In J. Jacobson & J. Mulick (Eds.), *Manual of diagnostic and professional practice in mental retardation* (pp. 229–242). Washington, DC: American Psychological Association.

Baumgart, D., Brown, L., Pumpian, I., Nisbet, J., Ford, A., Sweet, M., Messina, R., & Schroeder, L. (1982). Principle of partial participation and individualized programs for severely handicapped students. *Journal of the Association for Persons with Severe Handicaps, 7*(2), 17–26.

Bayley, N. (1993). *Bayley scales of infant development* (2nd ed.). San Antonio: Psychological Corporation.

Beckwith, L. (1988). Intervention with disadvantaged parents of sick preterm infants. *Psychiatry, 5*(1), 242–249.

Behrman, M. (1984). *Handbook of microcomputers in special education.* San Diego: College Hill Press.

Behrman, R., Vaughn, V., & Nelson, W. (1987). *Nelson textbook of pediatrics.* Philadelphia: Saunders.

Bellamy, G., Rhodes, L., Mank, D., & Albin, J. (1988). *Supportive employment.* Baltimore: Paul H. Brookes.

Bellinger, D., Levitan, A., Waternaux, C., Needleman, H., & Rabinowitz, M. (1987). Longitudinal analysis of prenatal and postnatal lead exposure and early cognition. *New England Journal of Medicine, 316,* 1037–1043.

Bellugi, U. (1988). Language development. *The Mind (vol. 7).* New York: WNET, Educational Broadcasting.

Bellugi, U., & Studdert-Kennedy, A. (Eds.). (1984). *Signed and spoken language.* Deerfield Beach, FL: Verlag Chemie.

Berger, N. (1978). Why can't John read? Perhaps he's not a good listener. *Journal of Learning Disabilities, 11,* 633–635.

Berla, E. (1981). Tactile scanning and memory for a spatial display by blind students. *Journal of Special Education, 15,* 341–350.

Berliner, D. C. (1992). Redesigning classroom activities for the future. *Educational Technology, 32*(10), 7–13.

Bernal, E. (1979). The education of the culturally different gifted. In A. Passow (Ed.), *The gifted and the talented: Their education and development* (Seventy-eighth Yearbook of the National Society for the Study of Education, Part 1). Chicago: University of Chicago Press.

Best, S., Carpignano, J., Sirvis, B., & Bigge, J. (1991). Psychosocial aspects of physical disability. In J. Bigge (Ed.), *Teaching individuals with physical and multiple handicaps* (3rd ed., pp. 102–131). New York: Merrill.

Beukelman, D., & Mirenda, P. (1992). *Augmentative and alternative communication.* Baltimore: Paul H. Brookes.

Biklen, D., & Cardinal, D.H. (Eds.). (1997). *Contested words, contested science.* New York. Teachers College Press.

Bigge, J. (1991a). Instructional adaptations. In J. Bigge (Ed.), *Teaching individuals with physical and multiple disabilities* (3rd ed., pp. 233–256). Columbus, OH: Charles E. Merrill.

Bigge, J. (1991b). *Teaching individuals with physical and multiple disabilities.* New York: Merrill.

Bishop, V. (1986, November). Identifying the components of success in mainstreaming. *Journal of Visual Impairment and Blindness,* pp. 939–946.

Blackman, J. A. (1983). *Medical aspects of developmental disabilities in children, birth to three.* Iowa City: The University of Iowa, Division of Developmental Disabilities.

Blackorby, J., & Wagner, M. (1996, March–April). Longitudinal outcomes of youth with disabilities. *Exceptional Children, 62*(5), 399–413.

Blakeslee, S. (1991, September 15). Study ties dyslexia to brain flow affecting vision and other senses. *New York Times,* pp. 1, 10.

Blance, G., Stedal, K., & Smith, V. (1994, Winter). Stuttering: The role of the classroom teacher. *Teaching Exceptional Children, 26*(2), 10–12.

Bloodstein, O. (1995). *A handbook on stuttering* (5th ed.). San Diego: Singular.

Bloom, B. (1978). New views of the learner: Implications for instruction and curriculum. *Educational Leadership, 35,* 563–575.

Bloom, L. (1991). *Language development from two to three.* New York: Cambridge University Press.

Boone, D., & McFarlane, S. (1988). *The voice and voice therapy*. Englewood Cliffs, NJ: Prentice-Hall.

Boothroyd, A. (1983). Assessment and intervention from a development point of view. In G. Mencher & S. Gerber (Eds.), *The multiply handicapped hearing impaired child*. New York: Grune & Stratton.

Boothroyd, A. (1988). *Hearing impairments in children*. Washington, DC: Alexander Graham Bell Association for the Deaf.

Borkowski, J., & Day, J. (1987). *Cognition in special children: Comparative approaches to retardation, learning disabilities and giftedness*. Norwood, NJ: Ablex.

Botuck, S., & Winsberg, B. (1991). Effects of respite on mothers of school-age and adult children with severe disabilities. *Mental Retardation, 29*(1), 43–47.

Bower, T. G. R. (1989). *The rational infant*. New York: W. H. Freeman.

Bradley, R. H., & Caldwell, B.W. (1984). 174 children. In A. Gottfried (Ed.), *Home environment and early cognitive development* (pp. 5-54). New York: Academic Press.

Bradley, V., Ashbaugh, J., & Blaney, B. (1994). *Creating individual supports for people with developmental disabilities*. Baltimore: Paul H. Brookes.

Bransford, J., Sherwood, R., Vye, N., & Rieser, J. (1986). Teaching thinking and problem solving. *American Psychologist, 41*(10), 1078–1089.

Brazelton, T. (1973). *Neonatal behavioral assessment scale*. Philadelphia: Lippincott.

Bredekamp, S. (1987). *Developmentally appropriate practices in early childhood programs serving children from birth through to age eight*. Washington, DC: National Association for the Education of Young Children.

Breske, S. (1994). Coping vulnerability in children with disabilities. *Teaching Exceptional Children, 27*(1).

Bricker, D. (1993, Spring). A rose by any name. Or is it? *Journal of Early Intervention, 17*(2), 89–96.

Bricker, D., & Cripes, J. (1992). *An activity based approach to early intervention*. Baltimore: Paul H. Brookes.

Bristol, M. (1987). Mothers of children with autism or communication disorders: Successful adaptation and the double ABCX model. *Journal of Autism and Developmental Disorders, 17*, 469–486.

Bristol, M., & Gallagher, J. (1986). Research on fathers of young handicapped children: Evolution, review, and some future directions. In J. Gallagher & P. Vietze (Eds.), *Families of handicapped persons* (pp. 81–100). Baltimore: Paul H. Brookes.

Bristol, M. G., Gallagher, J., & Schopler, E. (1988). Mothers and fathers of young developmentally disabled and nondisabled boys: Adaptation and spousal support. *Developmental Psychology, 24*(3), 441–451.

Bronfenbrenner, U. (1979). Content of child rearing: Problems and prospects. *American Psychologist, 34*, 844–850.

Bronfenbrenner, U. (1989). Ecological systems theory. *Annals of Child Development, 6*, 187–249.

Brown, C. (1982). *My left foot*. London: Pan.

Brown, E. (1958). *Corridors of light*. Yellow Springs, OH: Antioch.

Brown, F., & Gothelf, C. (1996). Self determination for all individuals. In D. Lehr and F. Brown (Eds.), *People with disabilities who challenge the system*. Baltimore: Paul H. Brookes.

Brown F., & Lehr, D. (1989). *Persons with profound disabilities*. Baltimore: Paul H. Brookes.

Brown, F., & Lehr, D. H. (1996). Making activities meaningful for students with severe multiple disabilities. *Teaching Exceptional Children, 25*(4), 12–16.

Brown, L. (1997). Seizure disorders. In M. L. Batshaw (Ed.), *Children with disabilities* (pp. 553–594). Baltimore: Paul H. Brookes.

Brown, L., Nietupski, J., & Hamre-Nietupski, S. (1996). Criterion of ultimate functioning. In M. Thomas (Ed.), *Hey, don't forget about me* (pp. 14–21). Reston, VA: Council for Exceptional Children.

Brown, L., Schwarz, P., Udvari-Solner, A., Kampschooer, E., Jolenson, F., Jorgensen, J., & Greenewald, L. (1991). How much time should students with severe intellectual disabilities spend in regular education classrooms and elsewhere? *Journal for the Association of the Severely Handicapped, 16*(1), 39–47.

Brown, R. (1958). *Words and things*. New York: Free Press.

Bruder, M., & Chandler, L. (1996). *Transition*. In S. Odom & M. McLean (Eds.), *Early intervention/early childhood special education*. Austin, TX: PRO-ED.

Bruininks, R., Thurlow, M., & Gilman, C. (1987). Adaptive behavior and mental retardation. *Journal of Special Education, 21*(1), 69–88.

Burkhart, L. (1986). *More homemade battery devices for severely handicapped children with suggested activities*. College Park, MD: Author.

Butler-Por, N. (1987). *Underachievers in school: Issues and intervention*. New York: Wiley.

Cairns, R. B. (1983). The emergence of developmental psychology. In W. Kessen (Ed.), *Handbook of child psychology: Vol. 1* (4th ed.), pp. 41–102. New York: Wiley.

Calderon, R., & Greenberg, M. (1997). The effectiveness of early intervention for deaf children and children with hearing loss. In M. Guralnick (Ed.), *The effectiveness of early intervention* (pp. 455–482). Baltimore: Paul H. Brookes.

Calvert, D., & Silverman, S. (1983). *Speech and deafness* (2nd ed.). Washington, DC: Alexander Graham Bell Association for the Deaf.

Camarata, S. (1995). A rationale for naturalistic speech intelligibility intervention. In M. Fay, J. Windsor, & S. Warren (Eds.), *Language intervention: Preschool through elementary years* (pp. 63–84). Baltimore: Paul H. Brookes.

Cameron, R., & Greenberg, M. (1997). The effectiveness of early intervention for deaf children and children with hearing loss. In M. Guralnick, *The effectiveness of early intervention* (pp. 455–482). Baltimore: Paul H. Brookes.

Cantwell, D. (1982). Childhood depression: A review of current research. In B. Lahey & A. Kazdin (Eds.), *Advances in clinical child psychology* (Vol. 5). New York: Plenum Press.

Capute, A., & Accardo, P. (Eds.). (1996). *Developmental disabilities in infancy and childhood, Vols. 1 & 2* (2nd ed.). Baltimore: Paul H. Brookes.

Carney, A., & Moellar, M. (1998, February). Treatment efficacy: Hearing loss in children. *Journal of Speech Language Hearing Research, 6*(41), 561–584.

Carpignano, J., & Bigge, J. (1991). Assessment. In J. Bigge (Ed.), *Teaching individuals with physical and multiple disabilities* (3rd ed., pp. 230–236). New York: Merrill.

Cary, D., & Sale, P. (1994, Fall). Notebook computers increase communication. *Teaching Exceptional Children, 27*(1), 62–69.

Castro, G. (1987). Plasticity and the handicapped child: A review of efficacy research. In J. Gallagher & C. Ramey (Eds.), *The malleability of children* (pp. 103–114). Baltimore: Paul H. Brookes.

Center on Human Development and Disabilities (CHDD) (1997). Study to measure differences in brain structure caused by prenatal alcohol exposure. *Language problems in children and adolescents with FAS.* Seattle: University of Washington Health Science Center.

Chalfant, J. (1985). Identifying learning disabled students: A summary of the national task force report. *Learning Disabilities Focus, 1*, 9–20.

Chalfant, J. (1989). Learning disabilities: Public issues and promising approaches. *American Psychologist, 44*(2), 392–398.

Chalfant, J., & Pysh, M. (1989). Teacher assistance teams: Five descriptive studies on 96. *Remedial and Special Education (RASE), 10*(6), 49–58.

Chambers, J., Parrish, T., Lieberman, J., & Wolman, J. (1998). *What are we spending on special education in the US?*

Chandler, K., Chapman, C., Rand, M., & Taylor, B. (1998). Students' reports of school crime: 1989 and 1995. *1989 and 1995 School Crime Supplement to the National Crime Victimization Survey.* TAG Report (Numerical data; Research/technical report).

Chase, W. G., & Chi, H. T. (1981). Cognitive skills: Implications for spatial skills and large scale environments. In J. Harvey (Ed.), *Cognition, social behavior, and environment.* Hillsdale, NJ: Erlbaum.

Chi, M. (1978). Knowledge structures and memory development. In R. Siegler (Ed.), *Children's thinking: What develops?* (2nd ed., pp. 73–96). Hillsdale, NJ: Erlbaum.

Chomsky, N. (1988). *Language and problems of knowledge.* Cambridge: MIT Press.

Cioffi, J. (1995). Orientation and mobility issues and support strategies for young adults who are deaf-blind. In J. Everson (Ed.), *Supporting young adults who are deaf-blind in their communities.* Baltimore: Paul H. Brookes.

Civelli, E. (1983). Verbalism in young children. *Journal of Visual Impairment and Blindness, 77*(3), 61–63.

Clark, D. B. (1988). *Dyslexia: Theory and practice of remedial instruction.* Parkton, MD: York Press.

Clymer, E. W., & McKee, B. G. (1997). The promise of the World Wide Web and other telecommunication technology within deaf education. *American Annals of the Deaf, 42*(2), 104–106.

Cohen, D. J., Paul, R., & Volkmar, F. (1987). Issues in classification of pervasive developmental disorders. In D. J. Cohen, A. M. Donnellan, & R. Paul (Eds.), *Handbook on autism and pervasive developmental disorders* (p. xvi). Silver Spring, MD: V. H. Winston & Sons.

Cohen, S. (1998). *Targeting autism.* Berkeley: University of California Press.

Cohen, S., & Erwin, E. (1994). Characteristics of children with prenatal drug exposure being served in special education programs in New York City. *Topics in Early Childhood Education, 14*(2), 232–253.

Cohen, S., & Warren, K. (1987). Preliminary survey of family abuse of children served by United Cerebral Palsy centers. *Developmental Medicine and Child Neurology, 29*, 12–18.

Cole, K. (1995). Curriculum model and language facilitation in the pre-school years. In M. Fey & J. Reiche (Eds.), *Communication intervention for school-age children* (pp. 39–60). Baltimore: Paul H. Brookes.

Coleman, L. (1985). *Schooling the gifted.* Menlo Park, CA: Addison-Wesley.

Coleman, M. R., & Gallagher, J. J. (1992). *State policies for identification of nontraditional gifted students.* Chapel Hill: University of North Carolina, Gifted Education Policy Studies Program.

Collins, B., Gast, D., Ault, M., & Wolery, M. (1991). Small group instruction: Guidelines for teachers of students with moderate to severe handicaps. *Education and Training in Mental Retardation, 26*, 18–32.

Compton, C., & Brandt, F. (n.d.). *Assistive listening devices.* Washington, DC: National Information Center on Deafness.

Conference of Executives of American Schools for the Deaf. (1976). *American Annals of the Deaf, 121*, 4.

Correa, V. (1987, June). Working with Hispanic parents of visually impaired children: Cultural implications. *Journal of Visual Impairment and Blindness*, 260–264.

Council for Exceptional Children (1994, October–November). *Exceptional Children, 61*(2, Special Issue).

Council for Exceptional Children (1997). Reading difficulties versus disabilities. *Today 4*(5), pp. 1, 9, 13.

Cramer, J., & Oshima, T. (1992). Do gifted females attribute their math performance differently than other students? *Journal for the Education of the Gifted, 16*(1), 18–35.

Cramer, R. (1991). The education of gifted children in the United States: A Delphi study. *Gifted Child Quarterly, 35* (2), 84–91.

Cramer, S., & Ellis, W. (1996). *Learning disabilities.* Baltimore: Paul H. Brookes.

Crocker, A. C. (Ed.). (1989). Developmental disabilities and HIV infection. *Mental Retardation, 27*(4, Special Issue).

Crocker, A., & Nelson, R. (1983). Mental retardation. In M. Levine, W. Carey, A. Crocker, & R. Gross (Eds.), *Developmental-behavioral pediatrics* (pp. 756–769). Philadelphia: Saunders.

Crockett, J., & Kauffman, J. (1998). Classrooms for students with learning disabilities. In B. Wong (Ed.), *Learning about learning disabilities* (2nd ed., pp. 489–525). Orlando, FL: Academic Press.

Crockett, J., & Kauffman, J. (1999). *The least restrictive environment: Origins and interpretations.* Mahwah, NJ: Erlbaum.

Cromer, R. (1978). The basis of childhood dysphasia: A linguistic approach. In D. Wyke (Ed.), *Developmental dysphasia.* New York: Wiley.

Cross, T. (1997). Psychological and social aspects of educating gifted students. *Peabody Journal of Education, 72,* 3–4, 180–200.

Cruickshank, W., Bentzen, F., Ratzeburg, F., & Tannhauser, M. (1961). *A teaching method for brain-injured and hyperactive children.* Syracuse, NY: Syracuse University Press.

Culatta, R., & Goldberg, S. A. (1995). *Stuttering therapy: An integrative approach to theory and practice.* Needham, MA: Allyn & Bacon.

Cummins, J. (1986). Psychological assessment of minority students: Out of content, out of focus, out of control? In A. Willig & H. Greenberg (Eds.), *Bilingualism and learning disabilities: Policy and practice for teachers and administrators.* New York: American Library.

Current plight of borderline students: Where do they belong? *Education and Training in Mental Retardation and Developmental Disabilities, 33*(2), 83–94.

Curtis, S., & Tallal, P. (1991). On the nature of impairment in language in children. In J. Miller (Ed.), *New directions in research on child language disorders* (pp. 189–210). Boston: College-Hill Press.

Davis, D. (1988). Nutrition in the prevention and reversal of mental retardation. In F. Menolascino & J. Stark (Eds.), *Preventive and curative intervention in mental retardation* (pp. 177–222). Baltimore: Paul H. Brookes.

De Weerd, J. (1974). Federal programs for the handicapped. *Exceptional Children, 40*(6), 441.

DeFries, J. C., & Alarcon, M. (1996). Genetics of specific reading disability. *Mental Retardation & Developmental Research Review, 2,* 39–47.

deGrott, M. (1965). *Thought and choice in chess.* The Hague: Mouton.

Delwein, P., Fewell, R., & Pruess, J. (1985). The efficacy of intervention at outreach sites of the program for children with Down syndrome and other developmental delays. *Topics in Early Childhood Special Education, 5*(2), 78–87.

Demchak, M. (1994, Fall). Helping individuals with severe disabilities find leisure activities. *Teaching Exceptional Children, 27*(1), 48–53.

Denckla, M. (1994). Measurement of executive function. In G. Lyon (Ed.), *Frames of reference for the assessment of learning disabilities* (pp. 117–142). Baltimore: Paul H. Brookes.

Deno, L. (1985). Curriculum-based measurement. *Exceptional Children, 52*(2), 219–232.

Deshler, D., Ellis, E., & Lenz, S. (1996). *Teaching adolescents with learning disabilities: Strategies and methods* (2nd ed.). Denver: Love.

Devenow, P., & Rickey, M. (1998). Hypertext reading tool at the fingertips. *Perspectives, 16*(3), 14–15.

Dickens, M., & Cornell, D. (1993). Parent influences on the mathematics of self concept of high ability adolescent girls. *Journal for Education of the Gifted, 17*(1), 53–73.

Dickman, G. E. (1996). Learning disabilities and behavior. In S. C. Cramer & W. Ellis (Eds.), *Learning disabilities* (pp. 215–228). Baltimore: Paul H. Brookes.

Donnellan, A. M., Mirenda, P. L., Mesaros, R. A., & Fassbinder, L. (1984). Analyzing the communicative function of aberrant behaviors. *Journal of the Association for Persons with Severe Handicaps, 9,* 201–212.

Dore, J. (1986). The development of conversational competence. In R. L. Schiefelbusch (Ed.), *Language competence, assessment and intervention* (pp. 85–96). Boston: Little, Brown.

Dorman, J., & Batshaw, M. L. (1997). Muscles, bones and nerves. In M. L. Batshaw (Ed.), *Children with disabilities* (pp. 315–322). Baltimore: Paul H. Brookes.

Dorman, J., & Pellegrino, L. (1998). *Caring for children with cerebral palsy.* Baltimore: Paul H. Brookes.

Downing, J. (1995). Instructional strategies for learners with dual sensory impairments in integrated settings. In K. Huebner, J. Prickett, T. Welch, & E. Jaffee (Eds.), *Hand in hand* (pp. 141–148). New York: AFT Press.

Drasgow, E. (1998, Spring). American sign language as a pathway to linguistic competence. *Exceptional Children, 64*(3), 329–342.

Dromi, E. (1993). The development of prelinguistic communication: Implications for language evaluation. In N. J. Anastasiow & S. Harel (Eds.), *The at-risk infant* (pp. 19–26). Baltimore: Paul H. Brookes.

Dunst, C. J. (1996). Early intervention in the USA. In M. Branbring, A. Beelman, & H. Rauh (Eds.), *Intervention in early childhood* (pp. 157–180). New York: Aldine de Gruyter.

Dunst, C. J., & Lowe, L. W. (1986). From reflex to symbol: Describing, explaining, and fostering communication competence. *Augmentative and Alternative Communication, 2,* 11–18.

Dunst, C., & Trivette, C. (in press). Early intervention with young at-risk children and their families. In R. Ammerman, & M. Herser (Eds.), *Handbook of prevention and treatment with children and adolescents: Intervention in the real world.* New York: Wiley.

Dykens, E., & Leckman, J. (1990). Developmental issues in fragile X syndrome. In R. Hodapp, J. Burock, & E. Zigler (Eds.), *Issues in the developmental approach to mental retardation* (pp. 226–245). New York: Cambridge University Press.

Dykens, E. M., & Kasari, C. (1997, November). Maladaptive behavior in children with Prader-Willi syndrome, Down syndrome, and nonspecific mental retardation. *American Journal of Mental Retardation, 102*(3), 228–237.

Edgar, E. (1987). Secondary programs in special education: Are many of them justified? *Exceptional Children, 53*(6), 555–561.

Edgar, E. (1998). Where does weather come from? A response to "Behaviorial disorders: A postmodern perspective." *Behavioral Disorders, 23*(3), 160–165.

Edgerton, R. (1988). Perspectives on the prevention of mild mental retardation. In F. Menolascino & J. Stark (Eds.), *Preventive and curative intervention in mental retardation* (pp. 325–342). Baltimore: Paul H. Brookes.

Eicher, P. (1997). Feeding. In M. L. Batshaw (Ed.), *Children with disabilities* (pp. 621–641). Baltimore: Paul H. Brookes.

Elder, G., Jr. (1998). The life course in developmental theory. *Child Development, 69*(1), 1–12.

Elmquest, D., Morgan, D., & Bolds, P. (1992). Substance use among adolescents with disabilities. *International Journal of the Addictions, 27,* 1475–1483.

English, R. (1995). *Educational audiology across the lifespan.* Baltimore: Paul H. Brookes.

Epstein, C. (1988). New approach to the study of Down syndrome. In F. Menolascino & J. Stark (Eds.), *Preventive and curative intervention in mental retardation* (pp. 35–60). Baltimore: Paul H. Brookes.

Erikson, J. (1989). *The Connecticut infant and toddler assessment system (IDA).* New Haven: Yale University Institute for Child Study.

Erin, E. (1993). Social participation of young children with visual impairments in specialized and integrated environments. *Journal of Visual Impairment and Blindness, 87,* 138–142.

Etscheidt, S., & Bartlett, L. (1999). The IDEA amendments: A four-step approach for determining supplemental aids and services. *Exceptional Children, 65* (2), 163–174.

Evans, D. (1996). Policy issues for inclusive schools: Toward a unified educational system. In J. Paul et al. (Eds.), *Special education practice: Applying the knowledge, affirming the values, and creating the future.* Pacific Grove, CA: Brooks/Cole Publishers.

Evans, I. M. (1991). Testing and diagnosis: A review and evaluation. In L. H. Meyer, C. Peck, & L. Brown (Eds.), *Critical issues in the lives of people with severe disabilities* (pp. 25–44). Baltimore: Paul H. Brookes.

Everson, J. (Ed.). (1995). *Supporting young adults who are deaf-blind in their communities.* Baltimore: Paul H. Brookes.

Everson, J., Burwell, J., & Killan, S. (1995). Working and contributing to one's community. In J. Everson (Ed.), *Supporting young adults who are deaf-blind in their communities* (pp. 131–158). Baltimore: Paul H. Brookes.

Falvey, M. (1988, September). Letters to the editor. *Journal of Visual Impairment and Blindness,* 3–4.

Falvey, M. (1989). *Community-based curriculum* (2nd ed.). Baltimore: Paul H. Brookes.

Falvey, M. A. (Ed.). (1995). *Inclusive and heterogeneous schooling.* Baltimore: Paul H. Brookes.

Falvey, M. A., Coot, J., Bishop, K. D., & Grenot-Scheyer, M. (1989). Educational and curricular adaptations. In S. Stainback, W. Stainback, & M. Forest (Eds.), *Educating all students in the mainstream of regular education.* Baltimore: Paul H. Brookes.

Falvey, M., & Grenot-Scheyer, M. (1995). Instructional strategies. In M. Falvey, *Inclusive and heterogeneous schooling.* Baltimore: Paul H. Brookes.

Farber, B. (1986). Historical context of research on families with mentally retarded members. In J. Gallagher & P. Vietze (Eds.), *Families of handicapped persons* (pp. 3–24). Baltimore: Paul H. Brookes.

Farran, D. (in press). Another decade of intervention for children who are low income or disabled. In J. Shonkoff & M. Meisels (Eds.), *Handbook of early intervention.* Cambridge, England: Cambridge University Press.

Farwell, R. (1976). Speech reading: A research review. *American Annals of the Deaf, 121,* 19–30.

Federal Register. (1977). Nondiscrimination on basis of handicap. Washington, DC, May 4, pp. 22, 676–22, 702.

Feldman, D. (1984). A follow-up of subjects scoring above 180 IQ in Terman's Genetic Studies of Genius. *Exceptional Children, 50,* 518–523.

Fernald, G. (1943). *Remedial techniques in basic school subjects.* New York: McGraw-Hill.

Ferrell, K. (1986). Infancy and early childhood. In G. Scholl (Ed.), *Foundations of education for blind and visually handicapped children and youth.* New York: American Foundation for the Blind.

Fewell, D., & Cone, J. (1983). Identification and placement of severely handicapped children. In M. Snell (Ed.), *Systematic instruction of the moderately and severely handicapped* (2nd ed.). Columbus, OH: Charles E. Merrill.

Fewell, R., & Rich, J. (1983). *Learning through play.* Austin, TX: DLM Teaching Resources.

Fey, M., Catts, H., & Larrivee, L. (1995). Preparing preschoolers for the academic and social challenges of school. In M. Fey, J. Windsor, & S. Warren (Eds.), *Language intervention: Preschool through elementary years* (pp. 3–58). Baltimore: Paul H. Brookes.

Fey, M., Cleave, P., & Long, S. (1997, February). Two models of grammar facilitation in children with language impairments. *Journal of Speech & Hearing Research, 40*(5), 5–19.

Fey, M., Windsor, J., & Warren, S. (Eds.). (1995). *Language intervention: Preschool through elementary years.* Baltimore: Paul H. Brookes.

Field, T. (1984). Affective and interactive disturbances in infants. In J. D. Osofsky (Ed.), *Handbook of infant development* (pp. 972–1005). New York: Wiley.

Field, T. (1989). Interaction coaching for high risk infants and their parents. *Prevention in Human Services, 1,* 8–54.

Flavall, J. H. (1995). Young children's understanding of thinking and consciousness: Current directions. *Science, 2,* 40–43.

Fleishner, J. (1994). Diagnosing and assessment of mathematics learning disabilities. In G. Lyon (Ed.), *Frames of reference for the assessment of children with learning disabilities* (pp. 444–458). Baltimore: Paul H. Brookes.

Fletcher, J., & Forman, B. (1994). Issues in definitions and measurement of learning disabilities. In G. Lyon (Ed.), *Frames of reference for the assessment of children with learning disabilities* (pp. 185–202). Baltimore: Paul H. Brookes.

Flippo, K., & Brown, J. (Eds.). (1995). *Assistive technology.* Baltimore: Paul H. Brookes.

Ford, A., Schnorr, R., Meyer, L., Davern, L., Black, J., & Dempsey, P. (1989). *Syracuse community referenced curriculum guide.* Baltimore: Paul H. Brookes.

Ford, D., Harris, J., & Schuerger, J. (1993). Racial identity development among gifted black students: Counseling issues and concerns. *Journal of Counseling and Development, 71,* 409–417.

Forness, S. (1992). Broadening the cultural-organizational perspective in exclusion of youth with social maladjustment. *Remedial and Special Education, 13*(1), 55–59.

Forness, S., & Kavale, K. (1984). Education of the mentally retarded: A note on policy. *Education and Training of the Mentally Retarded, 19*(4), 239–245.

Forness, S., & Kavale, K. (1988). Psychopharmacologic treatment: A note on classroom effects. *Journal of Learning Disabilities, 32,* 48–55.

Fowler, A. (1998). Language in mental retardation: Associations with and dissociations from general cognition. In J. Burack, R. Hodapp, & E. Zigler (Eds.), *Handbook of mental retardation and development* (pp. 290–333). New York: Cambridge University Press.

Fox, L., Hanline, M., Vail, C., & Galant, K. (1994). Developmentally appropriate practices: Applications for young children with disabilities. *Journal of Early Intervention, 18*(3), 243–257.

Fraiberg, S. (1977). *Insights from the blind: Comparative studies of blind and sighted infants.* New York: Basic Books.

Frasier, M. (1987). The identification of gifted black students: Developing new perspectives. *Journal for the Education of the Gifted, 10*(3), 155–190.

Frasier, M. (1991). Disadvantaged and culturally diverse gifted students. *Journal for the Education of the Gifted, 14*(4), 234–245.

Fredericks, B., & Baldwin, V. (1987). Individuals with sensory impairments: Who are they? How are they educated? In L. Goetz, D. Guess, & K. Stremmel Campbell (Eds.), *Innovative program design for individuals with dual sensory impairments* (pp. 3–14). Baltimore: Paul H. Brookes.

Freeman, J. M., & Vining, E. (1990). Is surgery the answer for childhood epilepsy? *Contemporary Pediatrics, 5*(109), 88–95.

Freeman, R., Goetz, E., Richards, D., & Groenveld, M. (1991). Defiers of negative prediction. A 14-year follow-up study of legally blind children. *Journal of Visual Impairment and Blindness, 85,* 365–370.

Frostig, M., Lefever, W., & Whittesey, J. (1964). *Developmental test of visual perception.* Palo Alto, CA: Consulting Psychological Press.

Fuchs, D., & Fuchs, L. (1994). Inclusive schools movement and the radicalization of special education reform. *Exceptional Children, 60*(4), 294–309.

Fuchs, L., & Deno, E. (1992). Effects of curriculum within curriculum-based measurement. *Exceptional Children, 58,* 232–243.

Fuchs, L., & Deno, S. (1994, September). Must instructionally useful performance assessment be based in the curriculum? *Exceptional Children, 6*(1), 15–24.

Fuchs, L., & Fuchs, D. (1997). Performance assessment using complex tasks: Implications for children with high-incidence disabilities. Unpublished paper, Vanderbilt University.

Fuchs, L., Fuchs, D., Hamlett, C., Phillips, N., & Bentz, J. (1994). Classroom curriculum-based assessment. *Exceptional Children, 60*(6), 518–537.

Fuchs, S., Fuchs, D., Hamlett, N., Phillips, N., & Korn, K. (1995, August). General educator's specialized adaptation for students with learning disabilities. *Exceptional Children, 61*(5), 440–459.

Furuno, S. F., O'Reilly, K. A., Inatsuka, T., Hosaka, C. N., & Falb, B. Z. (1993). *Helping babies learn: Developmental profile and activities for infants and toddlers.* Tucson, AZ: Communication Skill Builders, The Psychological Corporation.

Gadov, K. (1986). *Children on medications: 1 & 2.* San Diego: College-Hill Press.

Gage, N., & Berliner, D. (1988). *Educational psychology* (4th ed.). Boston: Houghton Mifflin.

Gage, S., & Falvey, M. (1995). Strategies to develop appropriate curricula and educational programs. In M. Falvey, *Inclusive and heterogeneous schooling.* Baltimore: Paul H. Brookes.

Gagne, R. (1985). *Conditions of learning*. New York: Holt, Rinehart & Winston.

Gallagher, D. (1998). The scientific knowledge base of special education: Do we know what we think we know? *Exceptional Children, 64*(4), 493–502.

Gallagher, J. J. (1985). *Teaching the gifted child* (3rd ed.). Boston: Allyn & Bacon.

Gallagher, J. (1989). The family as a focus for intervention. In S. Meisels & J. Shonkoff (Eds.), *Handbook of early intervention*. Boston: Houghton Mifflin.

Gallagher, J. (1991a). Educational reform, values and gifted students. *Gifted Child Quarterly, 35*(1), 12–19.

Gallagher, J. (1991b). Issues in gifted education. In N. Colangelo & G. David (Eds.), *Handbook of gifted education*. Boston: Allyn & Bacon.

Gallagher, J. (1991c). Longitudinal interventions: Virtues and limitations. *American Behavior Scientist, 34*(4), 431–439.

Gallagher, J. (1993). An intersection of public policy and social science: Gifted students and education in mathematics and science. In L. Penner, G. Batsche, H. Knoff, & D. Nelson (Eds.), *The challenge in mathematics and science education: Psychology's reponses*. Washington, DC: American Psychological Association.

Gallagher, J. (1997). We make a difference: No Nobel prizes though. *Journal of Early Intervention, 21,* 88–91.

Gallagher, J. (1998). Planning for young children with disabilities and their families: The evidence from IFSP/IEPs. Frank Porter Graham Center, University of North Carolina at Chapel Hill, Chapel Hill, NC.

Gallagher, J. (Ed.) (1974). *Windows on Russia*. Washington, DC: U.S. Government Printing Office.

Gallagher, J., & Bristol, M. (1988). Families of young handicapped children. In M. Wang, M. Reynolds, & H. Walberg (Eds.), *Handbook of special education: Research and practice: Vol. 3. Low incidence conditions*. Oxford, England: Pergamon Press.

Gallagher, J., & Coleman, M. (1994). Cooperative learning and gifted students: Five case studies. *Cooperative Learning, 14*(4), 21–26.

Gallagher, J., Cross, A., & Scharfman, W. (1981). Parental adaptation to a young handicapped child: The father's role. *Journal for the Division of Early Childhood 3,* 3–14.

Gallagher, J., & Desimone, L. (1995). Lessons learned from implementation of the IEP: Applications to the IFSP. *Topics in Early Childhood Special Education, 15*(3), 353–378.

Gallagher, J., & Gallagher, S. (1994). *Teaching the gifted child* (4th ed.). Boston: Allyn & Bacon.

Gallagher, J., Harbin, G., Eckland, J., & Clifford, R. (1994). State diversity and policy implementation. In L. Johnson, R. J. Gallagher, M. L. LaMontagne (Eds.), *Meeting early intervention challenges*. Baltimore: Paul H. Brookes.

Gallagher, S. (1992). *Assessment in the science classroom*. Williamsburg, VA: Center for Gifted Education, College of William & Mary.

Gallaudet Research Institute. (1997). *Annual survey of deaf and hard of hearing children and youth: 1995–1996 school year*. Washington, DC: Gallaudet University.

Gallimore, R., Bernheimer, L., & Weisner, T. (1999). Family life is more than managing crisis: Broadening the agenda of research on families adapting to childhood disability. In R. Gallimore, L. Bernheimer, D. MacMillan, D. Speece, & S. Vaughn (Eds.), *Developmental perspectives on high incidence handicapping conditions papers in honor of Barbara Keogh*. Mahwah, NJ: Erlbaum.

Gannon, J. (1981). *Deaf heritage: A narrative history of deaf America*. Silver Spring, MD: National Association of the Deaf.

Gardner, H. (1985). *Frames of mind: The theory of multiple intelligence*. New York: Basic Books.

Gardner, H. (1993). *Multiple intelligences: The theory in practice*. New York: Basic Books.

Gardner, J. (1978). *Morale*. New York: Norton.

Gardner, J., & Bates, P. (1991). Attitudes and attributions on use of microcomputers in school by students who are mentally handicapped. *Education and Training in Mental Retardation, 26,* 98–107.

Garnett, K. (1989, Winter). Math learning disabilities. *The Forum,* 11–14.

Garnett, K. (1996). *Thinking about inclusion and learning disabilities: A teacher's guide*. Reston, VA: Council for Exceptional Children.

Garnett, K., & Lackaye, T. (1993). *Modifying and adapting materials for students with disabilities in mainstreamed classrooms*. New York: Department of Special Education, Hunter College.

Garrett, M. (1996). The structure of language processes: Neurological evidence. In M. Gazzaniga (Ed.), *Cognitive neuroscience* (pp. 881–899). Cambridge, MA: The MIT Press.

Garwood, G., & Sheehan, R. (1989). *Designing a comprehensive early childhood system*. Austin, TX: PRO-ED.

Genaux, M., Morgan, D., & Friedman, S. (1995). Substance use and its prevention: A survey of classroom practices. *Behavior Disorders, 20*(4), 279–289.

George, P. (1988). Tracking and ability grouping: Which way for the middle school? *Middle School Journal, 20,* 21–28.

George, P., & Scheft, T. (1998). Children's thoughts about the future: Comparing gifted and nongifted students after 20 years. *Journal for the Education of the Gifted, 21*(2), 224–239.

Gershon, E., Hamovit, J., & Guroff, J. (1983). A family study of schizoaffective, bipolar I, bipolar II, unipolar, and normal control probands. *Archives of General Psychiatry, 39,* 1157–1167.

Getman, G. (1965). The visuo-motor complex in the acquisition of learning skills. In B. Straub & J. Hellmuth (Eds.), *Learning disorders* (Vol. 1). Seattle: Special Child Publications.

Getzels, J. (1978). Paradigm and practice: On the impact of basic research in education. In P. Suppes, *Impact of re-*

search in education. Washington, DC: Natural Academy of Education.

Giangreco, M., Cloninger, C., & Iverson, V. (1998). *Choosing outcomes and accommodations for children (COACH).* Baltimore: Paul H. Brookes.

Gilgoff, I. (1983). Spinal cord injury. In J. Umbreit (Ed.), *Physical disabilities and health impairments: An introduction* (pp. 132–146). Columbus, OH: Charles E. Merrill.

Gillingham, A., & Stillman, S. (1960). *Remedial training for children with specific disabilities in reading, writing, and penmanship.* Cambridge: Educational Publishing Service.

Gleason, B. (Ed.). (1993). *The development of language* (3rd ed.). New York: Macmillan.

Glick, M. (1998). A developmental approach to psychopathology in people with mild mental retardation. In J. Burack, R. Hodapp, & E. Zigler (Eds.), *Handbook of mental retardation and development* (pp. 563–582). New York: Cambridge University Press.

Goetz, L., Guess, D., & Campbell, K. (1987). *Innovative programs for individuals with dual sensory impairments.* New York: Grune & Stratton.

Goldberg, A. (1991). Children on ventilators: Breathing easier at home. *Contemporary Pediatrics, 7,* 59–79.

Goldin-Meadow, S. (1998). The resilience of language in humans. In C. Snowden & M. Hanberger (Eds.), *Social influence on vocal development* (pp. 293–311). New York: Cambridge University Press.

Goleman, D. (1995). *Emotional intelligence.* New York: Bantam Books.

Good, T. (1987). Teacher expectations. In D. Berliner & B. Rosenshine (Eds.), *Talks to teachers.* New York: Random House.

Goodlad, J. (1985). The great American schooling experiment. *Phi Delta Kappan, 67*(4), 266–271.

Goodrich, G., & Sowell, V. (1996). Low vision: A history in progress. In A. Corn & A. Koenig (Eds.), *Foundations of low vision: Clinical and functional perspective* (pp. 397–414). New York: American Foundation for the Blind.

Goossens, C., & Crain, S. (1985). Augmentative communication: Intervention resource. Birmingham, AL: Sparks Center for Developmental and Learning Disabilities, University of Alabama.

Gothelf, C. (1991). Personal communication.

Gothelf, C., Crimmins, D., Mercer, C., & Finocchiaro, P. (1994, Fall). Teaching choice-making skills to students who are deaf-blind. *Teaching Exceptional Children, 26*(1), 13–15.

Gottesman, M. (1971, June). A comparative study of Piaget's developmental schema of sighted children with that of a group of blind children. *Child Development,* 573–580.

Gottfried, A. (Ed.). (1984). *Home environment and cognitive development.* New York: Academic Press.

Gottlieb, G. (1997). *Synthesizing nature-nurture: Prenatal roots of instinctive behavior.* Mahwah, NJ: Erlbaum.

Gottlieb, J., Alter, M., & Gottlieb, B. W. (1991). Mainstreaming mentally retarded children. In J. Matson & J. Mulick (Eds.), *Handbook of mental retardation* (2nd ed., pp. 63–73). New York: Pergamon Press.

Gottlieb, J., Alter, M., Gottlieb, B., & Wisner, J. (1994). Special education in urban America: It's not justifiable for many. *Journal of Special Education, 27,* 453–465.

Graham, E. M., and Morgan, M. A. (1997). Growth before birth. In M. L. Batshaw (Ed.), *Children with disabilities* (pp. 53–70). Baltimore: Paul H. Brookes.

Gray, D. B., & Kavanaugh, J. H. (1985). *Biobehavioral measures of learning disabilities.* Parkton, MD: York Press.

Greenspan, S., Switzky, H., & Granfield, J. (1996). Everyday intelligence and adaptive behavior: A theoretical framework. In J. Jacobson & J. Mulick (Eds.), *Manual of diagnostic and professional practice in mental retardation* (pp. 127–136). Washington, DC: American Psychological Association.

Greenwood, C. (1994). Advances in technology-based assessment within special education. *Exceptional Children, 61*(2), 102–104.

Grenot-Scheyer, M. (1994, Winter). The nature of interactions between students with severe disabilities and their friends and acquaintances without disabilities. *The Journal of the Association for Persons with Severe Handicaps, 19*(3).

Greschwind, N. (1985). The biology of dyslexia. In D. B. Gray & J. F. Kavanaugh (Eds.), *Biobehavioral measures of dyslexia* (pp. 1–120). Parkton, MD: York Press.

Gresham, F. (1981). Social skills training with handicapped children: A review. *Review of Educational Research, 51*(1), 139–176.

Gresham, F. (1998). Social skills training: Should we raze, remodel or rebuild? *Behavior Disorders, 24*(1), 19–25.

Grisso, T. (1996). Introduction: An interdisciplinary approach to understanding aggressive behavior in children. In C. F. Ferris & T. Grisso (Eds.), *Understanding aggressive behavior in children.* New York: Annals of the New York Academy of Sciences, Volume 794, p. 6.

Guetzloe, E. (1988). Suicide and depression: Special education's responsibility. *Teaching Exceptional Children, 20*(4), 24–28.

Guiltinan, S. (1986, Fall). How to . . . tips on integration. *SPLASH Flash,* 4–5. (Printed by the Office of Education for Exceptional Children, Kentucky Department of Education.)

Gullo, D. (1992). *Developmentally appropriate teaching in early childhood.* Washington, DC: National Educational Association of America.

Guralnick, M. (Ed.). (1997). *The effectiveness of early intervention.* Baltimore: Paul H. Brookes.

Guralnick, M. (1998, June). Effectiveness of early intervention: A developmental perspective. *American Journal of Mental Retardation, 102*(4), 319–345.

Guralnick, M., & Bricker, D. (1987). The effectiveness of early intervention for children with cognitive and general developmental delays. In M. Guralnick & F. C. Bennett (Eds.), *The effectiveness of early intervention for at-risk*

and handicapped children (pp. 115–168). New York: Academic Press.

Guskey, T., Passaro, P., & Wheeler, W. (1997). Mastery learning in the regular classroom: Help for at risk students with learning disabilities. In *Educating exceptional children* (9th ed., pp. 42–45). Guilford, CT: Dushkin Publications.

Gutman, B. (1996, October–November). The validity of categorical learning disabilities services: The consumer's view. *Exceptional Children, 62*(2), 111–124.

Hagerman, R., Schreiner, R., Kemper, M., Wittenberger, M., Zahn, B., & Habicht, K. (1989). Longitudinal IQ changes in fragile X males. *American Journal of Medical Genetics, 33,* 513–518.

Hallenbeck, B., & Kauffman, J. (1995). How does observational learning affect the behavior of students with emotional or behavioral disorders: A review of research. *The Journal of Special Education, 29*(1), 45–71.

Halpern, A. (1991–1992, December–January). Transition: Old wine in new bottles. *Exceptional Children, 58*(3), 202–212.

Hammill, D., Brown, V., Larsen, S., & Weiderholt, L. (1987). *Test of adolescent language—2.* Austin, TX: PRO-ED.

Hansen, R., & Ulrey, G. (1993). Knowns and unknowns in the outcomes of drug-dependent women. In N. J. Anastasiow and S. Harel (Eds.), *The at-risk infant* (pp. 115–126). Baltimore: Paul H. Brookes.

Harbin, G. (1993). Family issues of children with disabilities. In N. J. Anastasiow and S. Harel (Eds.), *The at-risk infant* (pp. 101–114). Baltimore: Paul H. Brookes.

Harbin, G., & West, T. (1998). *Early intervention service delivery models and their impact on children.* Available from Frank Porter Graham Child Development Center, CB #8040, University of North Carolina, Chapel Hill, NC.

Harms, T., & Clifford, R. (1994). *Early childhood environmental rating scale.* New York: Teachers College Press.

Harrell, R., & Curry, S. (1987). Services to blind and visually impaired children and adults: Who is responsible? *Journal of Visual Impairment and Blindness,* pp. 368–376.

Harry, B. (1992). *Cultural diversity, families, and the special education system.* New York: Teachers College Press.

Harry, B. (1994). *Applications and misapplications of ecological principles in working with families from diverse cultural backgrounds.* Vision 2000 Conference, Tampa, FL.

Harry, B. (1997, Winter). Leaning forward or bending over backwards: Cultural reciprocity in working with families. *Journal of Early Intervention, 21*(1), 62–72.

Hart, B., & Riley, T. (1995). *Meaningful differences in the everyday experiences of young children.* Baltimore: Paul H. Brookes.

Harvey, D., & Greenway, A. (1984). The self-concept of physically handicapped children and their non-handicapped siblings: An empirical investigation. *Journal of Child Psychology and Psychiatry, 25,* 273–284.

Hasazi, S., Gordon, L., & Roe, C. (1985). Factors associated with the employment status of handicapped youth exiting high school from 1979 to 1983. *Exceptional Children, 51,* 455–465.

Hasselbring, T. (1996). Florida's future in special education: Applications of technology. In J. Paul et al. (Eds.), *Special education practice: Applying the knowledge, affirming the values, and creating the future.* Pacific Grove, CA: Brooks/Cole Publishers.

Hatlin, P. (1998). Foreword. In S. Sacks & R. Silberman (Eds.), *Educating students who have visual impairments with other disabilities* (pp. xv–xvi). Baltimore: Paul H. Brookes.

Hatlin, P., & Curry, S. (1987). In support of specialized programs for blind and visually impaired children: The impact of vision loss on learning. *Journal of Visual Impairment and Blindness, 81,* 7–13.

Hatton, D., Bailey, D., Burchinal, M., & Ferrell, K. (1997). Developmental growth curves of preschool children with vision impairments. *Child Development, 68*(5), 788–806.

Hawley, R. (1987). School children and drugs: The fancy that has not passed. *Phi Delta Kappa, 68,* K1–K8.

Hayden, A. H., & Haring, N. G. (1977). The acceleration and maintenance of developmental gain in Down's syndrome school-age children. In P. Mittler (Ed.), *Research to practice in mental retardation: Care and intervention* (pp. 129–142). Baltimore: University Park Press.

Hayes, S. (1941). *Contributions to a psychology of blindness.* New York: American Foundation for the Blind.

Haynie, M., Porter, S., & Palfrey, J. (1989). *Children assisted by medical technology in educational settings: Guidelines for care.* Boston: Project School Care, Children's Hospital.

Hechtman, L., & Weiss, G. (1985). Long-term outcome of hyperactive children. In S. Chess & A. Thomas (Eds.), *Annual progress in child psychiatry and child development—1984.* New York: Brunner/Mazel.

Heinemann, A., & Shontz, F. (1984). Adjustment following disability: Representative case studies. *Rehabilitation Counseling Bulletin, 28*(1), 3–14.

Heinicke, C. (1993). Factors affecting the efficacy of early family intervention. In N. J. Anastasiow and S. Harel (Eds.), *The at-risk infant* (pp. 91–100). Baltimore: Paul H. Brookes.

Heller, K., Holtzman, W., & Messick, S. (Eds.). (1982). *Placing children in special education: A strategy for equity.* Washington, DC: National Academy Press.

Helmstetter, E., Peck, C., & Giangreco, M. (1994, Winter). Outcomes of interaction with peers of moderate and severe disabilities: A statewide survey of high school students. *The Journal of the Association for Persons with Severe Handicaps, 19*(4), 260–276.

Henderson, L., & Meisels, S. (1994). Parental involvement in the developmental screening of their young children. *Journal of Early Intervention, 18*(2), 141–154.

Hill, E. (1992). Instruction in orientation and mobility skills for students with visual handicaps. *Division for the Visually Handicapped Quarterly, 37*(2), 25–26.

Hill, N., & Wehman, P. (1983). Cost-benefit analysis of placing moderately and severely handicapped individuals into competitive employment. *Journal of the Association for Persons with Severe Handicaps, 8,* 30–38.

Hill, R. (1959). Generic features of families under stress. *Social Casework, 49,* 139–150.

Hobbs, N. (1970). Project Re-Ed: New ways of helping emotionally disturbed children. In Joint Commission on Mental Health of Children, *Crisis in child mental health: Challenge for the 1970's.* New York: Harper & Row.

Hobbs, N. (1979). *Helping disturbed children: Psychological and ecological strategies: II. Project Re-Ed, twenty years later.* Nashville: Vanderbilt University, Center for the Study of Families and Children.

Hodapp, R., Burack, J., & Zigler, E. (1990). *Issues in the developmental approach to mental retardation.* New York: Cambridge University Press.

Holbrook, M., & Koenig, A. (1992). Teaching Braille reading to students with low vision. *Journal of Visual Impairment and Blindness, 86,* 44–48.

Holden-Pitt, R., & Diaz, J. (1998, April). Thirty years of the annual survey of deaf and hard of hearing children and youth. *American Annals of the Deaf, 143*(2), 72–76.

Hollingworth, L. S. (1942). *Children above 180 I.Q. Stanford-Binet: Origin and development.* New York: World Book Company.

Horowitz, F., & Haritos, C. (1998). The organism and the environment: Implications for understanding mental retardation. In J. Burack, R. Hodapp, & E. Zigler (Eds.), *Handbook of mental retardation and development* (pp. 20–40). New York: Cambridge University Press.

Huebner, K., Prickett, J., Welch, T., & Jaffee E. (Eds.). (1995). *Hand in hand* (Vol. 1). New York: AFB Press.

Huff, R., & Franks, F. (1973). Educational materials development in primary mathematics: Fractional parts of wholes. *Education of the Visually Handicapped, 5,* 46–54.

Hughes, C., Ruhl, K., & Misra, A. (1989). Self-management with behaviorally disordered students in school settings: A promise unfulfilled. *Behavioral Disorders, 14*(4), 250–262.

Hughes, M., Dote-Kwan, J., & Dolendo, J. (1998). A close look at the cognitive play of preschoolers with visual impairments in the home. *Exceptional Children, 64*(4), 451–462.

Humphries, T., Paden, C., & O'Rourke, T. (1980). *A basic course in American sign language.* Silver Spring, MD: T. J. Publishers.

Hunt, J. (1961). *Intelligence and experience.* New York: Ronald Press.

Huston, A. (1994). Children in poverty: Designing research to affect policy. *Social Policy Report, 8*(2), 1012.

Hutchinson, T. A. (1995, Winter). IDEA and the Provence profile-efficient early assessment. *ECO Letter, 4*(1), 11–13.

Huttenlocher, P. (1988). Developmental neurobiology: Current and future challenges. In F. Menolascino & J. Stark (Eds.), *Preventative and curative intervention in mental retardation* (pp. 101–111). Baltimore: Paul H. Brookes.

Hynd, G. (1992). Neurological aspects of dyslexia. *Journal of Learning Disabilities, 25,* 100–113.

Individuals with Disabilities Act (IDEA) of 1997, PL 105–17. U.S. Department of Education, Washington, DC.

Infant Health and Development Project. (1990). Enhancing the outcome of low-birth-weight premature infants. *Journal of the American Medical Association, 263*(22), 3035–3042.

Interagency Committee. (1990). *Learning disabilities: A report to Congress.* Washington, DC: U.S. Government Printing Office.

Jamieson, J. (1994). Teaching as transaction: Vygotskian perspective on deafness and mother-child interaction. *Exceptional Children, 60*(5), 434–449.

Jamieson, J. (1995, Spring). Interaction between mothers and children who are deaf. *Journal of Early Intervention, 19*(2), 108–117.

Jenkins, J., & Pious, C. (1991, May). Full inclusion and the REI: A reply to Thousands and Villa. *Exceptional Children, 57*(6), 561–562.

Jenkins, J., Speltz, M., & Odom, S. (1985). Integrating normal and handicapped preschoolers: Effects on child development and social interaction. *Exceptional Children, 52*(1), 7–17.

Johnson, D. (1988). Review of research in specific writing and mathematical disorders. In J. F. Kavanaugh & T. J. Truss (Eds.), *Learning disabilities: Proceedings of the national conference* (pp. 79–180). Parkton, MD: York Press.

Johnson, D., & Johnson, R. (1986). *Cooperation and competition: Theory and research.* Edna, MN: Interaction Book Company.

Johnson, D., Johnson, R., & Holubec, E. (1988). *Cooperation in the classroom* (rev. ed.). Edina, MN: Interaction Book Company.

Johnson, D., Johnson, R., & Holubec, E. (1990). *Circles of learning: Cooperation in the classroom.* Edina, MN: Interaction Book Co.

Johnson, H. C. (1989). Behavior disorders. In F. J. Turner (Ed.), *Child psychopathology: A social work perspective* (pp. 73–140). New York: Free Press.

Johnson, J., Baumgart, D., & Helmsteller, E. (1996). *Augmenting basic communication skills in natural context.* Baltimore: Paul H. Brookes.

Johnson, J., & Koegel, R. L. (1982). Behavior assessment and curriculum development. In R. L. Koegal, A. Rincover & A. L. Egel (Eds.), *Educating and understanding autistic children* (pp. 1–32). San Diego: College-Hill Press.

Johnson, L., Gallagher, R., LaMontagne, M., Jordan, J., Gallagher, J., Hutinger, P., & Karnes, M. (1994). *Meeting early intervention changes.* Baltimore: Paul H. Brookes.

Johnson-Martin, N., Attermeier, S., & Hacker, B. (1990). *Carolina curriculum for preschoolers with special needs.* Baltimore: Paul H. Brookes.

Johnson-Martin, N., Jens, K., & Attermeir, S. (1991). *Carolina curriculum for infants and toddlers with special needs.* (2nd ed.). Baltimore: Paul H. Brookes.

Journal of the Association for Persons with Severe Handicaps (JASH). (1994). Vol. 19 (whole).

Jusczyk, E. W. (1997). *The discovery of spoken language.* Cambridge: MIT Press.

Kagan, S. L. (1994). Readying schools for young children. *Phi Delta Kappan,* 226–233.

Kaiser, A., & Gray, D. (1993). *Enhancing children's research foundation for intervention: Vol. 2. Communication and language series.* Baltimore: Paul H. Brookes.

Kasari, C., & Bauminger, N. (1998). Social and emotional development in children with mental retardation. In J. Burack, R. Hodapp, & E. Zigler (Eds.), *Handbook of mental retardation and development* (pp. 411–433). New York: Cambridge University Press.

Katsiyannis, A., & Maag, J. (1998). Disciplining students with disabilities: Issues and considerations for implementing IDEA 1997. *Behavior Disorders, 23*(4), 276–289.

Kauffman, J. (1986). Growing out of adolescence: Reflections on change in special education for the behaviorally disordered. *Behavioral Disorders, 12,* 290–296.

Kauffman, J. (1989). The regular education initiative as Reagan-Bush education policy: A trickle-down theory of education of the hard to teach. *Journal of Special Education, 23,* 256–278.

Kauffman, J. (1994). One size does not fit all. *Beyond Behavior, 5*(3), 13–14.

Kauffman, J., & Hallahan, D. (1995). *The illusion of full inclusion.* Austin, TX: PRO-ED.

Kauffman, J., & Hallahan, D. (1997). A diversity of restrictive environments. In J. W. Lloyd, E. Kameeui, & D. Chard (Eds.), *Issues in educating students with disabilities* (pp. 324–342). Mahwah, NJ: Erlbaum.

Kauffman, J., & Hallahan, D. P. (Eds.). *Handbook of special education.* Englewood Cliffs, NJ: Prentice-Hall.

Kauffman, J., Lloyd, Baker, & Riedel. (1995). Inclusion of all students with emotional or behavioral disorders? Let's think again. *Phi Delta Kappan 76* (7), 542–546.

Kaufmann, F. (1981). The 1964–68 presidential scholars: A follow-up study. *Exceptional Children, 48,* 164–169.

Kavale, K., & Forness, S. (1997). Defining learning disabilities. In J. W. Lloyd, E. Kameeui, & D. Chard (Eds.), *Issues in educating students with disabilities* (pp. 3–26). Mahwah, NJ: Erlbaum.

Kavale, K., Forness, S., & Bender, M. (Eds.). (1988). *Handbook of learning disabilities: Vol. 1. Dimensions and diagnoses; Vol. 2. Methods and intervention; Vol. 3. Programs and practices.* Boston: College-Hill/Little, Brown.

Kekelis, L., & Sacks, S. (1988). Mainstreaming visually impaired children into regular education programs: The effects of visual impairment on children's interactions with peers. In S. Z. Sacks, L. S. Kekelis, & R. J. Gaylord-Ross

(Eds.), *The development of social skills by visually impaired children* (pp. 1–42). San Francisco: San Francisco State University.

Kekelis, L., & Sacks, S. (1992). The effects of visual impairment on children's social interactions in regular education programs. In S. Sacks, L. Kekelis, & R. Gaylord-Ross (Eds.), *The development of social skills by blind and visually impaired students* (pp. 59–82). New York: American Foundation for the Blind.

Kelly, L. (1995, February). Processing bottom-up and top-down information by skilled and average deaf readers and implications for whole language learning. *Exceptional Children, 61*(4), 315–334.

Keogh, B. (1996). Strategies for implementing policy. In S. Cramer & W. Ellis, *Learning disabilities.* Baltimore: Paul H. Brookes.

Kephart, J., Kephart, C., & Schwarz, G. (1974). A journey into the world of the blind child. *Exceptional Children, 40,* 33–37, 421–429.

Kephart, N. (1964, December). Perceptual-motor aspects of learning disabilities. *Exceptional Children, 31,* 201–206.

Kerr, M. & Nelson, C. (1998). *Strategies for managing behavior problems in the classroom* (3rd ed.). Upper Saddle River, NJ: Merrill.

Kettman, J., Klinger, R., Vaughn, S., Schuman, J., Cohen, P., & Forgan, J. (1998, March/April). Inclusion or pull-out: Which do students prefer? *Journal of Learning Disabilities, 31*(2), 148–151.

Kirk, S. (1950). A project for pre-school mentally handicapped children. *American Journal of Mental Deficiency, 55,* 305–310.

Kirk, S., Kirk, W., & Minskoff, E. (1985). *The Phonic Remedial Reading Program.* San Rafael, CA: Academic Therapy Publications.

Kirk, S. A. (1963). Behavioral diagnosis and remediation of learning disabilities. *Proceedings of the Conference on the Explorations into the Problems of the Perceptually Handicapped Child.* Evanston, IL: Fund for the Perceptually Handicapped Child.

Kirk, S. A., & Kirk, W. D. (1971). *Psycholinguistic learning disabilities* (rev. ed.). Urbana: University of Illinois Press.

Kitano, M. (1992). A multicultural education perspective on serving the culturally diverse gifted. *Journal for the Education of the Gifted.*

Kline, F. M., Deshler, D. D., & Schumaker, J. B. (1991). *Implementing learning strategies instruction in class settings, a research perspective: Barriers to strategy instruction.* Mimeo, University of Kansas Institute for Research in Learning Disabilities.

Knitzer, J., Steinberg, Z., & Fleisch, B. (1990). *At the schoolhouse door.* New York: Bank Street College.

Knowlton, E. (1998). Considerations in the design of personalized curricular supports for students with developmental disabilities. *Education and Training in Mental Retardation and Developmental Disabilities, 33*(2), 95–107.

Koegel, R. L., & Koegel, L. C. (Eds.). (1995). *Teaching children with autism*. Baltimore: Paul H. Brookes.

Koenig, A., & Rex, E. (1996). Instruction of literacy skills to children and youths with low vision. In A. Corn & A. Koenig (Eds.), *Foundations of low vision: Clinical and functional perspective* (pp. 280–305). New York: American Foundation for the Blind.

Koester, L. S., Karkowski, A., & Traci, M. (1998). How do deaf and hearing mothers regain eye contact when their infants look away? *American Annals of the Deaf, 143*(1), 5–13.

Kolb, B. (1995). *Brain plasticity and behavior*. Mahwah, NJ: Erlbaum.

Kolloff, P. (1997). Special residential high schools. In N. Colangelo & G. Davis (Eds.), *Handbook of gifted education* (2nd ed.). Boston: Allyn & Bacon, 198–206.

Kolstoe, O. (1976). *Teaching educable mentally retarded children* (2nd ed.). New York: Holt, Rinehart & Winston.

Kolvin, I., Miller, F. J. W., Scott, D. M., Gazonts, S. K. M., & Fleeting, M. (1990). *Continuities of deprivation? The Newcastle 1000 family study*. Adershot, England: Arcburn Gover.

Koorland, M. A. (1986). Applied behavior analysis and the correction of learning disabilities. In J. K. Torgesen & B. Y. L. Wong (Eds.), *Psychological and educational perspectives on learning disabilities* (pp. 297–326). San Diego: Academic Press.

Kopp, C. (1983). Risk factors in development. In M. M. Haith & J. J. Campos (Eds.), *Handbook of child psychology* (Vol. 2, pp. 1081–1188). New York: Wiley.

Korinek, L., & Polloway, E. (1993). Social skills: Review and implications for instruction for students with mild mental retardation. *Advances in Mental Retardation and Developmental Disabilities, 5*, 71–92.

Krajicek, M. (1991). *Handbook for the care of infants and toddlers with disabilities and chronic conditions*. Lawrence, KS: Learner Managed Designs.

Krajicek, M., Steinke, T., Hertzdeng, D., Anastasiow, N., & Skandel, S. (Eds.). (1990). *Instructor's guide for the handbook for the care of infants and toddlers with disabilities and chronic conditions*. Austin, TX: PRO-ED.

Krajicek, M., Steinke, T., Hertzdeng, D., Anastasiow, N., & Skandel, S. (Eds.). (1997). *Handbook for the care of infants and toddlers with disabilities and chronic conditions*. Austin, TX: PRO-ED.

Kregel, J. (1994, Fall). *Natural support and the job coach: An unnecessary dichotomy*. Richmond: Virginia Commonwealth University, Rehabilitation and Research Training Center.

Krupski, A. (1986). Attentional problems in youngsters with learning disabilities. In J. K. Torgesen & B. Y. L. Wong (Eds.), *Psychological and educational perspectives on learning disabilities* (pp. 161–192). San Diego: Academic Press.

Kulik, J., & Kulik, C. (1997). Ability grouping. In N. Colangelo & G. Davis (Eds.), *Handbook of gifted education* (2nd ed., pp. 230–242). Boston: Allyn & Bacon.

Lackaye, T. (1997). General education teachers' willingness to use and current use of academic interventions for students with learning disabilities. Unpublished dissertation. New York: Columbia University.

Lamb, M. (1986). *The role of the father in child development* (3rd ed.). New York: Wiley.

Lambert, N., & Windmiller, M. (1981). *AAMD Adaptive Behavior Scale* (School ed.). Monterey, CA: McGraw-Hill.

Lane, H., Hoffmeister, R., & Bahan, B. (1996). *A journey into the deaf-world*. San Diego: Dawn Sign Press.

LaSasso, C. J., & Mobley, R. T. (1996). National survey of reading instruction for deaf and hard of hearing students in the U.S. *The Volta Review, 95*(1), 31–58.

Lehr, D., & Brown, F. (1996). *People with disabilities who challenge the system*. Baltimore: Paul H. Brookes.

Lehr, D., & Noonan, M. (1989). Issues in the education of students with complex health care needs. In D. Ellis (Ed.), *Sensory impairments in mentally handicapped persons* (pp. 139–160). San Diego: College-Hill Press.

Lejeune, J., Gautier, M., & Turpin, R. (1959). Etudes des chromosomes somatiques de neuf enfants. *C. R. Academie Sic., 248*, 1721–1722.

Leland, H. (1991). Adaptive behavior scales. In J. Matson & J. Mulick (Eds.), *Handbook of mental retardation* (2nd ed.). New York: Pergamon Press.

Lenz, B., Ellis, E. S., & Scanlon, D. (1996). *Teaching learning strategies to adolescents and adults with learning disabilities*. Austin, TX: PRO-ED.

Leonard, L. (1998). *Children with specific language impairments*.

Leonard, L. B. (1993). Intervention approaches for young children with communication disorders. In N. J. Anastasiow & S. Harel (Eds.), *The at-risk infant*. Baltimore: Paul H. Brookes.

Leone, P., Greenburg, J., Trickett, E., & Spero, E. (1989). A study of the use of cigarettes, alcohol and marijuana by students identified as "seriously emotionally disturbed." *Counterpoint, 9*(3), 6–7.

Leong, C. (1995). Effects of on-line reading and simultaneous DEC talk aiding in helping below-average and poor readers comprehend and summarize text. *Learning Disability Quarterly, 18*(2), 101–116.

Lerner, J. (1997). *Learning disabilities* (6th ed.). Boston: Houghton Mifflin.

Lerner, R. M. (1986). *The nature of human plasticity*. New York: Cambridge University Press.

Leske, M. (1981). Prevalence estimates of communicative disorders in the U.S. Language, hearing, and vestibular disorders. *ASHA*, 229–237.

Levin, J., & Scherfenberg, L. (1987). *Selection and use of simple technology in home, school work, and community settings*. Minneapolis: Abelnet.

Levine, J. (1996, Spring). Including children dependent on ventilators in schools. *Teaching Exceptional Children,* 28(3), 25–29.

Levy, S., & O'Rourke, M. (1997). Technological assistance. In M. L. Batshaw (Ed.), *Children with disabilities* (pp. 687–708). Baltimore: Paul H. Brookes.

Lewis, T., Chard, D., & Scott, T. (1994). Full inclusion and the education of children and youth with emotional and behavioral disorders. *Behavior Disorders,* 19(4), 277–293.

Lewis, T., & Russo, R. (1998). Educational assessment for students who have visual impairments with other disabilities. In S. Sacks & R. Silberman (Eds.), *Educating students who have visual impairments with other disabilities* (pp. 39–72). Baltimore: Paul H. Brookes.

Liberman, I. Y., & Liberman, A. M. (1990). Whole language versus code emphasis. *Annals of dyslexia, 40,* 51–75.

Liberman, I., & Shankweiler, D. (1985). Phonology and the problem of learning to read and write. *Remedial Special Education,* 6, 8–17.

Lillo-Martin, D. (1997). In support of the language acquisition device. In Marschark, M., Simple, P., Lillo-Martin, D., Campbell R., & Everhart, V. (Eds.), *Relations of language and thought.* New York: Oxford University Press.

Linden, G., Kankkunen, A., & Tjellstrom, A. (1985). Multi-handicaps and ear formation in hearing impaired children. In G. Mencher & S. Gerber (Eds.), *The multiply handicapped hearing impaired child* (pp. 67–82). New York: Grune & Stratton.

Linder, T. (1993). *Transdisciplinary play-based assessment and intervention.* Baltimore: Paul H. Brookes.

Locke, J. (1993). *The child's path to spoken language.* Cambridge, MA: The MIT Press.

Lockhart, P. C. (1996). Infants of substance-abusing mothers. In A. Capute & P. Accardo (Eds.), *Developmental disabilities in infancy and childhood* (pp. 215–229). Baltimore: Paul H. Brookes.

Loeben, R. (1997). Key issues in the development of aggression and violence from childhood to early adolescence. *Annual Review of Psychology, 48,* 371–410.

Lombardino L., Riccio, C., Hynd, G., & Pinheiro, S. (1997, August). Linguistic deficits in children with reading difficulties. *American Journal of Speech-Language Pathology,* 6(3), 71–78.

Lord, C., & Schopler, E. (1994). TEECH Services for preschool children. In S. L. Harris & S. S. Handleman (Eds.), *Preschool programs for young children* (pp. 87–106). Austin, TX: PRO-ED.

Lovaas, O. (1981). *Teaching developmentally disabled children: The ME books.* Austin, TX: PRO-ED.

Lovaas, O. J. (1993). The development of a treatment project for developmentally disabled and autistic children. *Journal of Applied Behavior Analyses, 26*(4), 617–630.

Lovaas, O., & Buch, G. (1997). Intensive behavioral intervention with young children with autism. In N. Singh, *Prevention and treatment of severe behavior problems.* Pacific Grove, CA: Brooks/Cole Publishers.

Loveland, K., & Tunali-Kotoski, B. (1998). Development of adaptive behavior in persons with mental retardation. In J. Burack, R. Hodapp, & E. Zigler (Eds.), *Handbook of mental retardation and development* (pp. 521–541). New York: Cambridge University Press.

Lowenfeld, B. (1982). In search of better ways. *Education of the Visually Handicapped,* 14(3), 69–77.

Lowenfeld, B. (Ed.). (1973). *The visually handicapped child in school.* New York: Day.

LPR. (1997). *Laws affecting children with special needs, individuals with disabilities act.* Available from LPR, 747 Dresher Road, P.O. Box 980, Horsham, PA 19044-0980.

Luckasson, R., Coulter, D., Polloway, E., Reiss, S., Schaleck, R., Snell, M., Spitalnek, D., & Stark, J. (1992). *Mental retardation: Definition, classification and systems of supports.* Washington, DC: American Association on Mental Retardation.

Luetke-Stahlman, B. (1994). Procedures for socially integrating preschoolers who are hearing, deaf, and hard-of-hearing. *Topics in Early Childhood Special Education,* 14(4), 472–487.

Lyon, G. (Ed.). (1994). *Frames of reference for the assessment of learning disabilities.* Baltimore: Paul H. Brookes.

Lyon, G. R. (1995). Toward a definition of dyslexia. *Annals of Dyslexia, XLV,* 3–27.

Lyon, G.R. (1996). The state of research. In S. Cramer & W. Ellis (Eds.), *Learning disabilities* (pp. 3–64). Baltimore: Paul H. Brookes.

Lytle, R., & Rovins, N. (1997, April). Reforming deaf education. *American Annals of the Deaf,* 142(1), 7–15.

Maag, J., & Howell, K. (1992). Special education and the exclusion of youth with social maladjustments: A cultural-organizational perspective. *Remedial and Special Education, 13*(1), 47–54.

MacDonald, J., & Gillette, Y. (1986). Communicating with persons with severe handicaps: Role of parents and professionals. *Journal of the Association for Persons with Severe Handicaps,* 11(4), 255–265.

MacMillan, D., Siperstein, G., & Gresham, F. (1996). A challenge to the viability of mild mental retardation as a diagnostic category. *Exceptional Children,* 62(4), 356–372.

MacMillan, D., & Speece, D. (in press). Utility of current diagnostic categories for research and practice. In R. Gallmore, D. MacMillan, D. Spence, & S. Vaughn (Eds.), *Development perspectives on children with high incidence disabilities.* Mahwah, NJ: Erlbaum.

Mahaffey, K., Annest, J., Roberts, J., & Murphy, R. (1982). National estimate of blood lead levels: United States, 1976–1980. *New England Journal of Medicine, 307,* 573–579.

Mahshie, J. (1998). Balloons, penguins and visual displays. *Perspectives,* 16(4), 20–24.

Malian, I., & Love, L. (1998). Leaving high school: An ongoing transition study. *Teaching Exceptional Children, 30*(3), 4–10.

Mann, V. A., & Liberman, A. M. (1984). Phonological awareness and verbal short-term memory. *Journal of Learning Disabilities, 17,* 592–599.

March of Dimes (1993). Public health information sheets: "Clubfoot"; "Cleft lip and cleft palate"; "Polio"; "Post polio muscle astrophy"; "Spina bifida"; "Marfan syndrome"; "Achondroplasia"; "Sickle cell anemia"; "Thalassemia." (Available from March of Dimes, Community Service Department, 1275 Mamaroneck Ave., White Plains, NY, 10605.)

March of Dimes Defects Foundation. (1990). *Genetics Counseling.* (Available from March of Dimes Defects Foundation, 1275 Mamaroneck Avenue, White Plains, NY 10605.

March of Dimes Defects Foundation. (1997). *Polio, club foot, cleft palate, cerebral palsy, Marfan syndrome, Cooley syndrome, sickle cell anemia, acondroplasia, thalassemia.* Available from March of Dimes, Community Service Department, 1275 Mamaroneck Avenue, White Plains, NY 10605.

Marfo, K., Dedrick, C., & Barbour, N. (1998). Mother-child interactions and the development of children with mental retardation. In J. Burack, R. Hodapp, & E. Zigler (Eds.), *Handbook of mental retardation and development* (pp. 637–668). New York: Cambridge University Press.

Marschark, M. (1993). *Psychological development of deaf children.* New York: Oxford University Press.

Marschark, M., & Harris, M. (1996). Success or failure in learning to read. In J. Oakhill & C. Cornoldi (Eds.), *Reading comprehension difficulties* (pp. 279–300). Hillsdale, NJ: Erlbaum.

Marschark, M., Simple, P., Lillo-Martin, D., & Everhart, U. (1997). *Language and thought: The view from sign language and deaf children.* New York: Oxford University Press.

Marston, D. (1996). A comparison of inclusion only, pullout only and combined service models for students with mild disabilities. *Journal of Special Education, 30,* 121–132.

Martin, G., & Hoben, M. (1977). *Supporting visually impaired students in the mainstream.* Reston, VA: Council for Exceptional Children.

Masataka, N. (1996). Perceptions of motherese in a signed language by six-month-old deaf infants. *Developmental Psychology, 32,* 874–879.

Mastropieri, M., Jenne, T., & Scruggs, T. (1988). A level system for managing problem behaviors in a high school resource program. *Behavioral Disorders, 13*(3), 202–208.

Matsuda, M. (1984). A comparative analysis of blind and sighted children's communication skills. *Journal of Visual Impairment and Blindness, 78*(1), 1–4.

Mattison, R., Spitznagel, E., and Felix, B. (1998). Enrollment predictors of the special education outcome for students with SED. *Behavior Disorders, 23*(4), 243–256.

Mauk, G., & White, K. (1995, Winter). Giving children a sound beginning: The promise of universal hearing screening. *Volta Review, 97*(1), 5–32.

Mauk, J., Reber, M., & Batshaw, M. (1997). Autism and other pervasive developmental disorders. In M. L. Batshaw, *Children with disabilities.* Baltimore: Paul H. Brookes.

Maurice, C. (1993). *Let me hear your voice.* New York: Fawcett Columbine.

McAnally, P., Rose, S., & Quigley, C. (1987). *Language learning practices with deaf children.* Boston: Little, Brown.

McCall, R. (1987). Developmental function, individual differences and the plasticity of intelligence. In J. Gallagher & C. Ramey (Eds.), *The malleability of children* (pp. 25–36). Baltimore: Paul H. Brookes.

McCarthy, M. (1994). Inclusion and the law: Recent judicial decisions. *Phi Delta Kappa Research Bulletin*, No. 13.

McCathren, R., Yoder, P., & Warren, S. (1995). The role of directives in early language intervention, *Journal of Early Intervention, 19*(2), 91–101.

McClearn, G. (1993). Behavioral genetics: The last century and the next. In R. Plomin & G. McClearn (Eds.), *Nature, nurture & psychology.* Washington, DC: American Psychological Association, 27–51.

McCubbin, H., & Patterson, J. (1983). The family stress process: The double ABCX model of adjustment and adaptation. *Marriage and Family Review, 6,* 7–37.

McCune-Nicolich, L. (1986). Play-language relationships: Implications for a theory of symbolic development. In A. Gottfried & C. Brown (Eds.), *Play interactions.* Lexington, MA: Lexington Books.

McDonnell, L., McLaughlin, M. & Morrison, P. (Eds.). (1997). *Educating one and all: Students with disabilities and standards-based reform.* Washington, DC: National Academy Press.

McLean, L., & Cripe, J. (1997). The effectiveness of early intervention for children with communication disorders. In M. Guralnick (Ed.), *The effectiveness of early intervention* (pp. 349–428). Baltimore: Paul H. Brookes.

McLeskey, J., Lancaster, & Grizzle. (1995). Learning disabilities and grade retention: A review of issues with recommendations for practice. *Learning Disabilities Research and Practice, 10*(2), 120–128.

McLoughlin, J., & Lewis, R. (1991). *Assessing special students: Strategies and procedures* (3rd ed.). Columbus, OH: Charles E. Merrill.

McNulty, B., Soper, E., & Smith, D. (1984). *Effectiveness of early childhood special education of handicapped children.* Denver: Colorado State Department of Education.

McReynolds, L. (1986). Functional articulation disorders. In G. Shames & E. Wiig (Eds.), *Human communication disorders: An introduction* (2nd ed.). Columbus, OH: Charles E. Merrill.

Meadow, K. (1980). *Deafness and children.* Berkeley: University of California Press.

Meese, R. (1997). Adapting textbooks for children with learning disabilities in mainstreamed classrooms. In *Educating exceptional children* (9th ed., pp. 39–41). Guilford, CT: Dushkin Publications.

Meisels, S. (1987, January). Uses and abuses of developmental screening and school readiness testing. *Young Children,* 4–9.

Meisels, S., Jablon, J., Marsden, D., Dichtelmiller, M., & Dorfman, A. (1994). *The work sampling system* (2nd ed.). Ann Arbor, MI: Rebus Planning Associates.

Meisels, S., Marsden, D., Wiske, M., & Henderson, L. (1997). *The early screening inventory* (rev. ed.). Ann Arbor: University of Michigan.

Meisels, S. J. & Provence, S. (1989). *Screening and assessment: Guidelines for identifying young disabled and developmentally vulnerable children and their families.* Arlington, VA: Zero to Three/National Center Clinical Infant Program.

Meisels, S., & Shonkoff, J. (Eds.). (1990). *Handbook of early intervention.* New York: Cambridge University Press.

Mencher, G., & Gerber, S. (1983). *The multiply handicapped hearing-impaired child.* New York: Grune & Stratton.

Menolascino, F. J., Levitas, A., & Greiner, C. (1986). The nature and type of mental illness in the mentally retarded. *Psychopharmacology Bulletin, 22,* 1060–1071.

Mercer, C. (1992). *Students with learning disabilities* (4th ed.). Columbus, OH: Charles E. Merrill.

Metz, I. (1991). Albuquerque, New Mexico. In M. Anderson & P. Goldberg (Eds.), *Cultural competence in screening and assessment* (pp. 8–10). National Early Childhood Technical Assistance System. Pacer Center, 4826 Chicago Avenue South, Minneapolis, MN 55417-1095.

Meyer, G. (1997). Syndromes of inborn errors of metabolism. In M. L. Batshaw (Ed.), *Children with disabilities.* Baltimore: Paul H. Brookes.

Meyer, L. H., Park, H. S., Grenot-Scheyer, M., Schwartz, I. S., & Harry, B. (1998). *Making friends: The influence of culture and development.* Baltimore: Paul H. Brookes.

Meyer, L. H., Peck, C. A., & Brown, L. (1991). *Critical issues in the lives of people with severe disabilities.* Baltimore: Paul H. Brookes.

Michael, M., & Paul, P. (1995). Early intervention with deaf-blindness. In S. Huebner, J. Prickett, T. Welch, & E. Jaffee (Eds.). *Hand in hand* (pp. 130–140). New York: AFT Press.

Miller, J. (1993). Augmentative and alternative communication. In M. Snell (Ed.), *Instruction of students with severe disabilities* (pp. 319–338). New York: Merrill.

Miller, J., & Paul, R. (1995). *The clinical assessment of language comprehension.* Baltimore: Paul H. Brookes.

Minnes, P. (1998). Mental retardation: The impact upon the family. In J. Burack, R. Hodapp, & E. Zigler (Eds.), *Handbook of mental retardation and development* (pp. 693–712). New York: Cambridge University Press.

Moats, L. G. (1994). Assessment of spelling in learning disabilities. In G. Lyon, *Frames of reference for the assessment of learning disabilities.* Baltimore: Paul H. Brookes.

Money, J. (1977). The syndrome of abuse dwarfism (psychosocial dwarfism). *American Journals of Diseases of Children, 131,* 508–513.

Montour, K. (1977). William James Sidis, the broken twig. *American Psychologist, 32,* 265–279.

Moores, D. (1989). *Educating the deaf* (3rd ed.). Boston: Houghton Mifflin.

Moores, D. (1996). *Educating the deaf: Psychology, principles, and practices* (4th ed.). Boston: Houghton Mifflin.

Moores, D., Kluwin, T., & Mertens, D. (1985). *High school program for the deaf in metropolitan areas* (Research Monograph No. 3). Washington, DC: Gallaudet Research Institute.

Morse, W. (1976). The helping teacher/crisis teacher concept. *Focus on Exceptional Children, 8,* 1–11.

Murphy, K. (1983). The educator-therapist with deaf, multiply disabled children: Some essential criteria. In G. Mencher & S. Gerber (Eds.), *The multiply handicapped hearing-impaired child* (pp. 13–16). New York: Grune & Stratton.

Murphy, K., & Byrne, D. (1983). Selection of optimal modalities as avenues of learning in deaf, blind, multiply disabled children. In G. Mencher & S. Gerber (Eds.), *The multiply handicapped hearing-impaired child* (pp. 335–396). New York: Grune & Stratton.

Myklebust, H. (1965). *Development of disorders in written language, 7.* New York: Grune & Stratton.

Naglai, A. (1991). Manhattan, New York. In M. Anderson & P. Goldberg (Eds.), *Cultural competence in screening and assessment* (pp. 14–15). Pacer Center, 4826 Chicago Avenue South, Minneapolis, MN 55417-1095.

Nakamura, K. (1997). *The deaf resource library* (on-line). Available http://pantheon.yaleeduc/~Nakamura/deaf/

National agenda for the education of children and youth with visual disabilities including those with multiple disabilities (1996). New York: American Foundation for the Blind.

National Council on Educational Standards and Testing. (1992). *Raising standards for American education: A report to Congress, the Secretary of Education, the National Education Goals Panel and the American people.* Washington, DC: Author.

National Information Center on Children and Youth with Disabilities. (1997). *Autism/PDD, cerebral palsy, epilepsy, learning disabilities, traumatic brain injury.* Available from NICHCY, P. O. Box 1492, Washington, DC.

National Information Center on Children and Youth with Disabilities (NICHCY). (March 1997). *Learning Disabilities.* (Fact Sheet N. 7). Washington, DC: N. Amos.

National Information Center on Children and Youth with Disabilities. (1998). *IDEA 1998.* Available from NICHCY, P. O. Box 1492, Washington, DC.

National Information Center on Deafness (1989). *Deafness: A factsheet.* NICD, Gallaudet University, 800 Florida Ave., N.E., Washington, DC 20002-3695.

National Information Center on Deafness. (1994). *What are TTY's, TT's, and TDD's?* Washington, DC: Author.

National Information Center on Deafness (NICD). (1997a). *Assistive listening devices: A consumer-oriented summary.* Washington, DC: Gallaudet University.

National Information Center on Deafness. (1997b). *Deafness: A fact sheet.* Silver Spring, MD: Author.

Neel, R., Meadows, N., Levine, P., & Edgar, E. (1988). What happens after special education: A statewide follow-up study of secondary students who have behavioral disorders. *Behavioral Disorders, 13*(3), 209–216.

Neidecker, E. (1987). *School programs in speech and language: Organization and management* (2nd ed.). Englewood Cliffs, NJ: Prentice-Hall.

Nelson, C., & Pearson, C. (1991). *Integrating services for children and youth with emotional and behavior disorders.* Reston, VA: Council for Exceptional Children.

Nelson, J., Crabtree, M., Marchand-Martella, N., & Martella, R. (1998). Teaching good behavior in the whole school. *Teaching Exceptional Children, 30*(4), 4–9.

Nelson, K., Camarata, S., Welsh, J., Butskovsky, L., & Camarata, M. (1996, August). Effects of imitative and conversational recasting treatment on the acquisition of grammar in children with specific language impairment and younger language-normal children. *Journal of Speech and Hearing Research, 39*(4), 850–859.

Newton, J., Horner, R., Ard, W., LeBaron, N., & Sapperton, G. (1994). Social aspects and social relationship of individuals with disability. *Mental Retardation, 32*(5), 393–402.

Northern, J., & Downs, M. (1978). *Hearing in children* (2nd ed.). Baltimore: Williams & Wilkins.

Norvick, R. (1993). Activity based intervention and developmentally appropriate practice: Points of convergence. *Topics in Early Childhood Special Education, 3*(4), 403–417.

Oakes, J. (1985). *Keeping track.* New Haven, CT: Yale University Press.

Odom, S., & McLean, M. (1996). *Early intervention/early childhood special education.* Austin, TX: PRO-ED.

Ogura, T. (1991). A longitudinal study of the relationship between early language development and play development. *Journal of Child Language, 18,* 273–294.

O'Hara, D., & Levy, J. (1987). Family intervention. In K. Kavale, S. Forness, & M. Bender (Eds.), *Handbook of learning disabilities* (pp. 215–235). Boston: College-Hill/Little, Brown.

Oller, D. K. (1985). Infant vocalizations. In S. Harel & N. J. Anastasiow (Eds.), *The at-risk infant* (pp. 323–332). Baltimore: Paul H. Brookes.

Olswang, L. B., Rodriguez, B., & Timler, G. (1998, February). Recommending intervention for toddlers with specific language learning difficulties. *American Journal of Speech-Language Pathology, 7*(1), 23–32.

Olszewski, P., Kulieke, M., & Buescher, T. (1987). The influence of the family environment on the development of talent: A literature review. *Journal for the Education of the Gifted, 11*(1), 6–28.

O'Neil, J., Gothelf, C., Cohen, S., Lehman, L., & Woolf, S. (1991). *A curricular approach to support the transition to adulthood of adolescents with visual or dual sensory impairments and cognitive disabilities.* Albany: New York State Education Department, Office of Special Education and Rehabilitation Services.

Onslow, M., Costa L., Andrews, C., Harrison, E., & Packman, A. (1996, August). Speech outcomes of a prolonged speech treatment for stuttering. *Journal of Speech and Hearing Research, 39*(4), 734–749.

Orr, D. (1989). *Measurement of self-concept among disabled children.* Unpublished doctoral dissertation, Harvard University, Cambridge, MA.

Orton, S. T. (1937). *Reading, writing, and speech problems in children.* New York: Norton.

Osborn, A. (1957). *Creative imagination* (3rd ed.). New York: Scribner's.

Pappas, D. (1985). *Diagnosis and treatment of hearing impairment in children.* San Diego: College-Hill.

Parasnis, I. (Ed.). (1997). *Cultural and language diversity and the deaf experience.* New York: Cambridge University Press.

Parette, H. (1991). The importance of technology in the education and training of persons with mental retardation. *Education and Training in Mental Retardation, 26,* 165–178.

Parke, B. N. (1989). *Gifted students in regular classrooms.* Boston: Allyn & Bacon.

Parmer, R., Cawlet, H., & Frazota, R. (1996). Word problem-solving by students with and without mild disabilities. *Exceptional Children, 62*(5), 415–429.

Parnes, S., Noller, R., & Biondi, A. (1977). *Guide to creative action.* New York: Scribner's.

Parrish, J. M. (1997). Behavior management. In M. L. Batshaw (Ed.), *Children with disabilities* (4th ed., pp. 657–708). Baltimore: Paul H. Brookes.

Patterson, G. (1980). *Mothers: The unacknowledged victims* (Monographs of the Society for Research in Child Development, No. 45, Serial No. 186). Chicago: University of Chicago Press.

Patton, J. R. (1986). *Transition: Curricular implications.* Honolulu: Project Ho-ko-ko, University of Hawaii.

Paul, J., & Epanchin, B. (Eds.). (1986). *Emotional disturbance in children* (3rd ed.). Columbus, OH: Merrill.

Paul, J., & Epanchin, B. (Eds.). (1991). *Emotional disturbance in children* (4th ed.). Columbus, OH: Charles E. Merrill.

Paul, P., & Quigley, S. (1994). *Education and deafness.* White Plains, NY: Longman.

Paul, R. (1996a, February). Clinical implications of natural history of slow expressive language development. *American Journal of Speech-Language Pathology, 5,* 5–12.

Paul, R. (1996b). *Language disorders from infancy through adolescence.* St. Louis: Mosby Year Book.

Paul, R. (1996c, Spring). First-second language English literacy. *Volta Review, 98*(2), 5–16.

Pavenstedt, E. (1967). *The drifters: Children from disorganized families.* Boston: Little, Brown.

Pear, R. (1992, January 19). The hard thing about cutting infant mortality is educating mothers. *New York Times,* p. E5.

Pellegrino, L. (1997). Cerebral palsy. In M. L. Batshaw (Ed.), *Children with disabilities* (pp. 499–528). Baltimore: Paul H. Brookes.

Pennington, B. (1991). *Diagnosing learning disorders.* New York: Guilford Press.

Pennington, B. (1997). *Towards an integrated understanding of dyslexia.* Department of Psychology, Denver University, Denver, CO.

Perkins, D. (1995). *Outsmarting IQ: The emerging science of learnable intelligence.* New York: Free Press.

Perkins, D., & Salomon, G. (1989). Are cognitive skills context bound? *Educational Researcher, 18*(1), 16–25.

Perrone, P. (1997). Gifted individuals' career development. In N. Colangelo & G. Davis (Eds.), *Handbook of gifted education* (2nd ed., pp. 398–407). Boston: Allyn & Bacon.

Peterson, N. (1987). Parenting the young handicapped and at-risk child. In N. Peterson (Ed.), *Early intervention for handicapped and at-risk children: An introduction to early childhood special education* (pp. 409–446). Denver, CO: Love.

Petitto, L., & Marentette, P. (1991, March). Babbling in the manual mode: Evidence for the ontogeny of language. *Science, 251,* 1493–1495.

Piaget, J., & Inhelder, B. (1969). *The psychology of the child.* New York: Basic Books.

Pinker, S. (1991). Rules of language. *Science, 253,* 530–535.

Plomin, R., & McClearn, G. (Eds.). (1993). *Nature, nurture and psychology.* Washington, DC: American Psychological Association.

Plomin, R., & Petrill, S. (1997). Genetics and intelligence: What's new? *Intelligence, 24*(1), 53–77.

Plomin, R., DeFries, J., & McClearn, G. (1980). *Behavioral genetics: A primer.* San Francisco: Freeman.

Plomin, R., DeFries, J., Smith, J., & Roderique, T. (1991). Issues in program design for elementary students with mild retardation: Emphasis on curriculum development. *Education and Training in Mental Retardation, 26,* 142–150.

Pogrund, R., Fazzi, D., & Lampert, J. (Eds.). (1992). *Early focus: Working with young blind and visually impaired children and their families.* New York: American Foundation for the Blind.

Powell, T., & Gallagher, P. (1993). *Brothers and sisters* (2nd ed.). Baltimore: Paul H. Brookes.

Premack, D. (1959). Toward empirical behavior laws: I. Positive reinforcement. *Psychological Review, 66,* 291–333.

Pressley, M. et al. (1990). *Cognitive strategy instructor.* Cambridge, MA: Brookline Press.

Pressley, M., Brown, R., El-Dinary, P. B., & Afflerbach, P. (1995). The comprehension instruction that students need. *Learning Disabilities Research and Practice, 10*(4), 215–224.

Pueschel, S. (1991). Ethical considerations related to prenatal diagnosis of fetuses with Down syndrome. *Mental Retardation, 29*(4), 185–190.

Pueschel, S., Scola, P., Weidenman, L., & Bernier, J. (Eds.). (1995). *The special child* (2nd ed.). Baltimore: Paul H. Brookes.

Pugash, M., & Johnson, L. (1995). Unlocking expertise among classroom teachers through structured dialogue: Extending research on peer collaboration. *Exceptional Children, 62*(2), 101–110.

Quay, H., & Werry, J. (Eds.). (1986). *Psychopathological disorders of childhood* (3rd ed.). New York: Wiley.

Quigley, S., Jenne, W., & Phillips, S. (1968). *Deaf students in colleges and universities.* Washington, DC: Alexander Graham Bell Association.

Rainforth, B., & York, J. (1987). Handling and positioning. In F. Orelove & D. Sobsey (Eds.), *Educating children with multiple handicaps: A transdisciplinary approach* (pp. 67–104). Baltimore: Paul H. Brookes.

Rainforth, B., York, J., & MacDonald, C. (1992). *Collaborative teams for students with severe disabilities.* Baltimore: Paul H. Brookes.

Ramos-Ford, H., & Gardner, H. (1997). Giftedness from a multiple intelligences perspective. In N. Colangelo & G. David (Eds.), *Handbook of gifted education.* Boston: Allyn & Bacon.

Ramsey, E., & Walker, H. (1988). Family management correlates of antisocial behavior among middle school boys. *Behavioral Disorders, 13*(3), 187–201.

Rand, D., & Gibbs, L. (1989). A model program for gifted girls in science. *Journal for the Education of the Gifted, 12*(2), 142–155.

Redl, F. (1959). *Mental hygiene and teaching.* New York: Harcourt Brace Jovanovich.

Reis, S., & Callahan, C. (1989). Gifted females: They've come a long way, or have they? *Journal for the Education of the Gifted, 12*(2), 99–117.

Renzulli, J., Smith, L., & Reis, S. (1982). Curriculum compacting: An essential strategy for working with gifted students. *Elementary School Journal, 82,* 185–194.

Rimland, B., & Edelson, S. (1994a). Auditory integration training and autism. San Diego: Autism Research Institute. Also *Autism Research Review, 8*(2).

Rimland, B., & Edelson, S. (1994b). The effect of auditory integration training on autism. *American Journal of Speech and Language Pathology, 3*(2), 16–24.

Rittenhouse, R. (1985). *TTY language in deaf adolescents: A research report.* Normal: Illinois State University.

Rivers, K., Lombardino, L., & Thompson, C. (1996, February). Effects of phonological decoding training on children's word recognition. *American Journal of Speech-Language Pathology, 5*(1).

Roberts, J., Burchinal, M., & Bailey, D. (1994). Communication among preschoolers with and without disabilities in same-age and mixed-age classes. *American Journal of Mental Retardation, 99*(3), 231–249.

Robertson, C., & Whytte, L. (1983). Prospective identificction of infants with hearing loss and multiple handicaps. In G. Mencher & S. Gerber (Eds.), *The multiply handicapped hearing-impaired child* (pp. 27–54). New York: Grune & Stratton.

Robins, L. (1966). *Deviant children grow up.* Baltimore: Williams & Wilkins.

Rogoff, B., & Chavajay, P. (1995). What's become of research on the cultural basis of cognitive development? *American Psychologist, 50*(10), 859–877.

Roizen, N. J. (1997). Down syndrome. In M. L. Batshaw (Ed.), *Children with disabilities* (pp. 361–376). Baltimore: Paul H. Brookes.

Rondal, J. (1995). *Exceptional language development in Down syndrome.* New York: Cambridge University Press.

Roseberry-McKibbin, C. (1997). Distinguishing language disorders in linguistically and culturally diverse students. *Educating exceptional children* (9th ed., pp. 109–112). Guilford, CT: Dushkin Publications.

Ross, P. (Ed.). (1993). *National excellence.* Washington, DC: U.S. Department of Education.

Rossetti, L. (1986). *High-risk infants.* Boston: College Hill/Little, Brown.

Rossitti, L. (1990). *Infant-toddler assessment.* Austin, TX: PRO-ED.

Rourke, B. P. (1994). Neuropsychological assessment of children with learning disabilities. In G. Lyon (Ed.), *Frames of reference for the assessment of learning disabilities* (pp. 475–514). Baltimore: Paul H. Brookes.

Rourke, B. P. (Ed.). (1991). *Neuropsychological validation of learning disability subtypes.* New York: Guilford Press.

Rourke, P. (Ed.). (1995). *Syndrome of non-verbal learning disabilities.* New York: Guilford.

Rusch, F., Chadsey-Rusch, J., & Lagomarcino, T. (1987). Preparing students for employment. In M. Snell (Ed.), *Systematic instruction of persons with severe handicaps* (3rd ed., pp. 471–490). Columbus, OH: Charles E. Merrill.

Rutstein, R., Conlon, C., & Batshaw, M. L. (1997). HIV and AIDS. In M. L. Batshaw (Ed.), *Children with disabilities* (pp. 163–181). Baltimore: Paul H. Brookes.

Rutter, M. (1988). Epidemiological approaches to developmental psychology. *Archives of General Psychology, 45,* 486–495.

Sabatino, D., Miller, P., & Schmidt, C. (1981). Can intelligence be altered through cognitive training? *Journal of Special Education, 15,* 125–144.

Sacks, S. (1992). The social development of visually impaired children: A theoretical perspective. In S. Sacks, L. Kekelis, & R. Gaylord-Ross (Eds.), *The development of social skills by blind and visually impaired students* (pp. 3–12). New York: American Foundation for the Blind.

Sacks, S., & Silberman, R. (1998). *Educating students who have visual impairments with other disabilities.* Baltimore: Paul H. Brookes.

Sacks, S., Wolffe, K., & Tieney, D. (1998). Lifestyles of students with visual impairments: Preliminary studies of social networks. *Exceptional Children, 64*(4), 463–478.

Safford, P., Sargent, M., & Cook, C. (Eds.). (1994). Instructional models in early childhood special education: Origins, issues and trends. In P. Safford (Ed.), *Early childhood special education* (pp. 96–117). New York: Teachers College Press.

Sailor, W. (1991). Teaching. In L. H. Meyer, C. Peck, & L. Brown (Eds.), *Critical issues in the lives of persons with severe disabilities.* Baltimore: Paul H. Brookes.

Sale, P., & Carey, D. (1995). The sociometric status of students with disabilities in a full inclusion school. *Exceptional Children, 62*(1), 6–19.

Salvia, J., & Ysseldyke, J. (1988). *Assessment in special and remedial education.* Boston: Houghton Mifflin.

Sameroff, A. (1990). Neo-environmental perspectives on developmental theory. In R. Hodapp, J. Burack, & E. Zigler (Eds.), *Issues in the developmental approach to mental retardation.* New York: Cambridge University Press.

Sameroff, A., & Haith, M. (Eds.). (1996). *The five to seven shift.* Chicago: University of Chicago Press.

Sattler, J. (1988). *Assessment of children* (3rd ed.). San Diego: Sattler.

Satz, P., & Morris, R. (1981). Learning disability subtypes: A review. In F. J. Pirozzolo & M. C. Wittock (Eds.), *Neuropsychological and cognitive processes in reading* (pp. 109–141). New York: Academic Press.

Sawyer, R. (1988). In defense of academic rigor. *Journal of the Education of the Gifted, 11,* 5–19.

Scarr, S. (1982). Development is internally guided, not determined. *Contemporary Psychology, 27,* 852–853.

Schachter, M., & Demerath, R. (1996). Neuropsychology and mental retardation. In J. Jacobson & J. Mulick (Eds.), *Manual of diagnostic and professional practice in mental retardation* (pp. 165–178). Washington, DC: American Psychological Association.

Schery, T., & O'Connor, L. (1995). Computers as a context for language intervention. In M. Rey, J. Windson, & S. Warren (Eds.), *Language intervention.* Baltimore: Paul H. Brookes.

Schiefelbusch, R. L., Sullivan, J.W., & Ganz, V. K. (1980). Assessing children who are at risk. In S. Harel (Ed.), *The at-risk infant* (pp. 277–284). Amsterdam: Excerpta Medica.

Schill, W. (1988). *Five transition policy studies including pertinent literate synthesis: Transition research on problems of handicapped youth*. Seattle: University of Washington School of Education.

Schlesinger, H. (1983). Early intervention: The prevention of multiple handicaps. In G. Mencher & S. Gerber (Eds.), *The multiply handicapped hearing-impaired child* (pp. 83–116). New York: Grune & Stratton.

Schloss, P. (1983). Classroom-based intervention for students exhibiting depressive reactions. *Behavioral Disorders, 8*, 231–236.

Schopler, E., & Bristol, M. (1980). *Autistic children in public school* (ERIC Exceptional Children Education Report, Division TEACCH). Chapel Hill, NC: University of North Carolina.

Schopler, E., & Mesihov, G. (1997). *Learning and cognition in autism*. New York: Plenum.

Schore, A. (1994). *Affect regulation and the origin of the self*. Hillsdale, NJ: Erlbaum.

Schreiner, M., Donar, M., & Kettrick, R. (1987). Pediatric mechanical ventilation. *Pediatric Clinics of North America, 34*(1), 47–60.

Schuman, J., Vaughn, S., Haager, D., McDowell, J., Rothstein, L., & Saumell, L. (1995). General education teacher planning: What can students with learning disabilities expect? *Exceptional Children, 61*(4), 335–352.

Schweinhart, L., & Weikart, D. (1998, March). Why curriculum matters in early childhood research. *Educational Leadership, 57*–60.

Scola, P. (1991). Infections. In J. Matson & J. Mulick (Eds.), *Handbook of mental retardation* (2nd ed.). New York: Pergamon Press.

Scott, K., & Carran, D. (1987). The epidemiology and prevention of mental retardation. *American Psychologist, 42*(8), 801–804.

Seligman, M., & Peterson, C. (1986). A learned helplessness perspective on childhood depression. In M. Rutter, C. Izard, & P. Read (Eds.), *Depression in young people: Developmental and clinical perspectives*. New York: Guilford.

Semmel, N., Abernathy, T., Butera, G., & Lesar, S. (1991, September). Teacher perceptions of the regular education initiative. *Exceptional Children, 58*(1), 9–24.

Serna, L., & Patton, J. (1989). Science. In G. Robinson, J. Patton, E. Polloway, & L. Sargent (Eds.), *Best practices in mild mental retardation* (pp. 197–199). Reston, VA: Council for Exceptional Children.

Shames, G., & Rubin, H. (1986). *Stuttering then and now*. Columbus, OH: Charles E. Merrill.

Shantz, M., & Ebeling, K. (1991). Patterns of language related behaviors: Evidence for self-help in acquiring grammar. *Journal of Child Language, 18*, 295–313.

Shea, R. (1983). Habilitation facilities at the Glenrose School Hospital. In G. Mencher & S. Gerber (Eds.), *The multiply handicapped hearing-impaired child* (pp. 45–50). New York: Grune & Stratton.

Shearn, J., & Todd, S. (1997, August). Parental work: An account of the day to day activities of parents of adults with learning disabilities. *Journal of Intellectual Disability Research, 41*(Pt. 4), 285–301.

Shneidman, E. (1987). *Definition of suicide*. New York: Wiley.

Shonkoff, J. P., & Hauser-Cram, P. (1988). Early intervention for disabled infants and their families. *Pediatrics, 80*, 650–658.

Shore, B., Cornell, D., Robinson, A., & Ward, V. (1991). *Recommended practices in gifted education: A critical analysis*. New York: Teachers College Press.

Short, E. J., & Ryan, E. B. (1984). Metacognitive differences between skilled and less skilled readers: Remediating deficits through story grammar and attribution training. *Journal of Educational Psychology, 76*(7), 225–235.

Shriberg, L., & Kwiatowski, J. (1988). A follow-up study of children with phonological disorders of unknown origin. *Journal of Speech and Hearing Disorders, 53*(2), 144–145.

Shriver, M., & Piersal, W. (1994, Summer). The long-term effects of intrauterine drug exposure: Review of recent research and implications for early childhood special education. *Topics in Early Childhood Special Education, 14*(2), 161–183.

Siegler, R. (Ed.). (1986). *Children's thinking: What develops?* Englewood Cliffs, NJ: Prentice-Hall.

Silver, L. B. (1990). Attention-deficit hyperactivity disorder: Is it a learning disability? *Journal of Learning Disabilities, 23*, 394–397.

Silverman, L. (1997). Family counseling with the gifted. In N. Colangelo & G. Davis (Eds.), *Handbook of gifted education* (2nd ed., pp. 382–397). Boston: Allyn & Bacon.

Silverman, L. (Ed.). (1993). *Counseling the gifted and talented*. Denver, CO: Love.

Simmons, W., & Resnick, L. (1993). Assessment as the catalyst of school reform. *Educational Leadership, 50*(5), 11–15.

Simon, H. (1979). Information processing models of cognition. *Annual Review of Psychology, 30*, 363–396.

Simonoff, E., Bolton, P., & Rutter, M. (1998). Genetic perspectives on mental retardation. In J. Burack, R. Hodapp, & E. Zigler (Eds.), *Handbook of mental retardation and development* (pp. 41–79). New York: Cambridge University Press.

Sizer, T. (1985). *Horace's compromise: The dilemma of the American high school*. Boston: Houghton Mifflin.

Skeels, H. M. (1966). Adult status of children with contrasting early life experiences. *Monographs of the Society for Research in Child Development, 31*(3), no. 105.

Skilberg, L., Aram, D., & Kwiatkowski, J. (1997). Developmental apraxia of speech I–III. *American Journal of Speech-Language Pathology, 4*, 273–357.

Skinner, B. (1953). *Science and human behavior.* New York: Free Press.

Slavin, R. (1988). Synthesis of research on grouping in elementary and secondary schools. *Educational Leadership, 46*(1), 67–77.

Slavin, R. (1991). Are cooperative learning and "untracking" harmful to the gifted? *Educational Leadership, 48*(6), 68–71.

Smith, A., & Geruschat, D. (1996). Orientation and mobility for children and youth with low vision. In A. Corn & A. Koenig (Eds.), *Foundations of low vision: Clinical and functional perspective* (pp. 306–321). New York: American Foundation for the Blind.

Smith, A., & Krajicek, M. (1991). The following videocassettes are available: *Home gastronomy care for infants and young children; Clean intermittent catheterization; Nutrition for infants with special needs; Communication for preverbal infants and young children; Home oxygen for infants and young children; Positioning for infants and young children with motor problems; Infection control in child care settings; Feeding infants and young children with special needs; Home tracheostomy care for infants and young children.* Lawrence, KS: Learner Managed Designs.

Smith, A., & O'Donnell, L. (1991). *Beyond arms reach: Enhancing distance vision.* Philadelphia: Pennsylvania College of Optometry Press.

Smith, D., & Nelson, J. (1997). Goal setting, self-monitoring, and self-evaluation for students with disabilities. In M. Agran (Ed.), *Student-directed learning* (pp. 80–110). Pacific Grove, CA: Brookes/Cole.

Smith, J. (1998). Histories of special education. *Remedial and Special Education, 19*(4), 196–200.

Snell, M. (1988). Curriculum and methodology for individuals with severe disabilities. *Education and Training in Mental Retardation, 23*(4), 302–314.

Snell, M. E. (Ed.). (1993). *Systematic instruction of persons with severe handicaps.* Columbus, OH: Prentice-Hall.

Snowling, M. J., & Perrin, D. (1988). Cognitive processes in written language dysfunction. In R. L. Schiefelbusch & L. Lloyd (Eds.), *Language perspectives* (pp. 147–185). Austin, TX: PRO-ED.

Snowman, J. (1991, Fall). Memory and problem solving: The overlooked partnership. *Educational Forum,* 9–11.

Solnit, G., Taylor, M., & Bednarczyk, A. (1992). *Access for all: Integrating deaf, hard of hearing and hearing students.* Washington, DC: Gallaudet University Press.

Stainback, S., & Stainback, W. (1988). *Understanding and conducting qualitative research.* Reston, VA: Council for Exceptional Children.

Stainback, S., & Stainback, W. (1989). No more teachers of students with severe handicaps. *TASH Newsletter, 19*(9).

Stainback, S., & Stainback, W. (1992). *Curriculum considerations on inclusive classrooms: Facilitating learning for all students.* Baltimore: Paul H. Brookes.

Stainback, S., & Stainback, W. (1996). *Inclusion: A guide to educators.* Baltimore: Paul H. Brookes.

Stanovich, K. (1986). Cognitive processes and the reading problems of learning disabled children. In J. K. Torgesen & B. Y. L. Wong (Eds.), *Psychological and educational perspectives on learning disabilities* (pp. 85–131). San Diego: Academic Press.

Steinberg, A., & Knightly, C. (1997). Hearing: Sounds and silences. In M. L. Batshaw (Ed.), *Children with disabilities* (pp. 241–274). Baltimore: Paul H. Brookes.

Stephens, T., Blackhurst, A., & Magliocca, L. (1982). *Teaching mainstreamed students.* New York: Wiley.

Stepien, W., Gallagher, J., & Workman. (1993). Problem-based learning for traditional and interdisciplinary classrooms. *Journal for the Education of the Gifted, 16*(4), 338–357.

Sternberg, L. (Ed.). (1991). *Functional communication.* New York: Springer-Verlag.

Stevenson, H., Chen, C., & Lee, S. (1994). Motivation and achievement of gifted children in east Asia and the United States. *Journal for the Education of the Gifted, 16*(3), 223–250.

Stone, C., & Conca, L. (1993). The origin of strategy deficits in children with learning disabilities. In L. J. Meltzer (Ed.). *Strategy assessment and instruction for students with learning disabilities* (pp. 23–60). Austin, TX: PRO-ED.

Strain, P., Kohler, F. W., & Goldstein, H. (1996). Learning experiences: An alternate program. In E. D. Hibbs & P. S. Jensen (Eds.), *Child and adolescent disorders* (pp. 573–587). Washington, DC: American Psychological Association.

Stromswald, K. (1996). The cognitive and aural base of language acquisition. In M. S. Gazzanica (Ed.), *Cognitive neuroscience* (pp. 855–870). Cambridge: MIT Press.

Sturomski, N. (1997, July). Inventions for students with learning disabilities. *NICHCY News Digest, 25,* 2–18.

Subotnik, R., Kassan, L., Summers, E., & Wasser, A. (1993). *Genius revisited: High IQ children grow up.* Norwood, NJ: Ablex.

Swank, L. (1997, November). Linguistic influence in the emergence of written word decoding in first grade. *American Journal of Speech-Language Pathology, 6*(4), 62–66.

Swanson, L. (1987). Verbal decoding effects on visual short-term memory of learning disabled and normal readers. *Journal of Educational Psychology, 70,* 539–544.

Sykes, K. (1984). *The curriculum for children with visual handicaps.* Unpublished manuscript, University of Arizona, Tucson.

Szymanski, P. (1994). Transition: Life-span considerations for empowerment. *Exceptional Children, 60*(5), 402–410.

Tager-Flushberg, H. & Sullivan, K. (1998). Early language development in children with mental retardation. In J. Burack, R. Hodapp, & E. Zigler (Eds.), *Handbook of mental*

retardation and development (pp. 208–239). New York: Cambridge University Press.

Tallal, P., Miller, J., Badi, G., Wang, X., Nagarajon, S., Schreiner, C., Jenken, W., & Merzenich, M. (1996, December). Language comprehension in language-learning impaired children improved with acoustically modified speech. *Science, 271,* 81–84.

Tallal, P., Miller, S., & Fitch, R. (1993). Neurological bases of speech: A case for the preeminence of temporal processing. *Annals of New York Academy of Science, 682,* 27–47.

Tallal, P., Ross, R., & Curtis, D. (1985). Familial aggregation in specific language impairments. *Journal of Speech and Hearing Disorders, 54,* 167–173.

Taylor, R. (1988). Assessment policies and procedures. In L. Sternberg (Ed.), *Educating students with severe or profound handicaps* (pp. 103–118). Austin, TX: PRO-ED.

Taylor, R. & Murphy-Head, M. (1996). Access technology with computers for students who have visual impairments with other disabilities. In S. Sacks & R. Silberman (Eds.), *Educating students who have visual impairments with other disabilities* (pp. 469–496). Baltimore: Paul H. Brookes.

Terman, L., & Oden, M. (1947). *The gifted child grows up: Twenty-five-year follow-up of a superior group (Vol. 4).* Stanford, CA: Stanford University Press.

Thousands, J., & Villa, P. (1991). A futuristic view of REI: A response to Jenkins, Pious, and Jewell. *Exceptional Children, 57*(6), 556–560.

Tillman, M., & Osborne, R. (1969). The performance of blind and sighted children on the Wechsler Intelligence Scale for children: Interaction effects. *Education of the Visually Handicapped, 1,* 1–4.

Tindal, G., & Marston, D. (1986). Approaches to assessment. In J. K. Torgesen & B. Y. L. Wong (Eds.), *Psychological and educational perspectives on learning disabilities* (pp. 54–84). San Diego: Academic Press.

Todd, J. (1986). Resources, media, and technology. In G. Scholl (Ed.), *Foundations of education for blind and visually handicapped children and youth.* New York: American Foundation for the Blind.

Tomblin, J. B., Record, N., Buchwater, P., Zhang, X., Smith, E., & O'Brien M. (1997, December). Prevalence of specific language impairment in kindergarten children. *Journal of Speech and Hearing Research, 40,* 1245–1260.

Torgesen, J. (1988). Problems in the study of learning disabilities. In M. Hetherington & J. Hagen (Eds.), *Review of research in child development* (Vol. 5, pp. 162–184). Chicago: University of Chicago Press.

Torgesen, J. (1994). Issues in the assessment of executive function. In G. Lyon (Ed.), *Frames of reference for the assessment of learning disabilities* (pp. 475–514). Baltimore: Paul H. Brookes.

Torgesen, J., & Licht, B. (1983). The learning disabled child as an inactive learner. In J. McKinney & L. Feagens (Eds.),

Topics in learning disabilities (Vol. 1, pp. 100–130). Norwood, NJ: Ablex.

Torgesen, J. K., & Wong, B. Y. L. (1986). *Psychological and educational perspectives on learning disabilities.* San Diego: Academic Press.

Torres, I., & Corn, A. (1990). *When you have a visually handicapped child in your classroom: Suggestions for teachers.* New York: American Foundation for the Blind.

Tralli, R. (1996). The Strategies Intervention Model: A model for supported inclusion at the secondary level. *Remedial and Special Education, 17*(4), 204–216.

Trieber, F. A., & Lahey, B. R. (1983). Toward a behavioral model of academic remediation with learning disabled children. *Journal of Learning Disabilities, 16,* 11–116.

Trybus, R. (1985). *Today's hearing impaired children and youth: A demographic and academic profile.* Washington, DC: Gallaudet Research Institute.

Tsai, L. (1998). *Pervasive developmental disorders.* NICHCY Briefing Paper FS20, National Information Center for Children and Youth with Disabilities, Washington, DC.

Turnbull, A. T., & Turnbull, H. R. (1989). *Parents speak out* (3rd ed.). Columbus, OH: Charles E. Merrill.

Turnbull, A., & Turnbull, H. R. (1991). Family assessment and family empowerment. In L. Meyer, C. Peck, & L. Brown (Eds.), *Critical issues in the lives of people with severe disabilities* (pp. 485–488). Baltimore: Paul H. Brookes.

Turnbull, A., & Turnbull, H. R. (1997). *Families, professionals, and exceptionality: A special partnership* (3rd ed.). Upper Saddle River, NJ: Merrill.

Turnbull, A., Turnbull, H., Shank, M., & Leal, D. (1995). *Exceptional lives: Special education in today's schools.* Upper Saddle River, NJ: Prentice-Hall.

Tuttle, D., & Tuttle, N. (1996). *Self-esteem and adjusting with blindness* (2nd ed.). Springfield, IL: Charles C. Thomas.

Upsur, C. (1990). Early intervention as preventive intervention. In S. Meisels & J. Shonkoff (Eds.), *Handbook of early childhood intervention* (pp. 633–650). New York: Cambridge University Press.

U.S. Department of Education. (1985, September 3). *New services for deaf-blind children program (SEP memorandum).* Washington, DC: U.S. Government Printing Office.

U.S. Department of Education. (1988). *Tenth annual report to Congress on the implementation of the Education of the Handicapped Act.* Washington, DC: Author.

U.S. Department of Education. (1996). *16th annual report to Congress on the implementation of Public Law 94-142.* Washington, DC: Government Printing Office.

U.S. Department of Education. (1997). *18th annual report to Congress on the implementation of Public Law 94-142: The Education of All Handicapped Children Act.* Washington, DC: U.S. Government Printing Office.

Vaillant, G., & Milofsky, M. (1980). Natural history of male psychological health: IX. Empirical evidence for Erikson's model of the life-cycle. *American Journal of Psychiatry, 137*(11), 1348–1359.

Valletutti, P. J. (1987). Social problems. In K. Kavale, S. Forness, & M. Bender (Eds.), *Handbook of learning disabilities: Vol. 1. Dimensions and diagnoses* (pp. 211–226). Boston: College-Hill/Little, Brown.

Van Dijk, J. (1986). An educational curriculum for deaf-blind multiply handicapped persons. In D. Ellis (Ed.), *Sensory impairments in mentally retarded people* (pp. 375–382). San Diego: College-Hill Press.

Van Tassel-Baska, J. (1998). *Excellence in educating gifted and talented learners* (3rd ed.). Denver: Love Publishing.

Vanderwood, M., McGrew, K., & Ysseldyke, J. (1998). Why we can't say much about students with disabilities during education reform. *Exceptional Children, 64*(3), 359–370.

Vaugh, S., McIntosh, R., & Spencer-Rowe, J. (1991). Peer rejection is a stubborn thing: Increasing peer acceptance of rejected students with learning disabilities. *Learning Disabilities and Practice, 6*, 83–98.

Vellutino, F. (1987, March). Dyslexia. *Scientific American, 256, 3.*

Verstegen, D. (1998, February). Landmark court decisions challenge state special education funding. *CSEF Brief, 9.*

Villa, R., & Thousand, J. (1988). Enhancing success in heterogeneous classrooms and schools. *Teacher Education and Special Education, 11*(4), 144–154.

Voeller, K. S. (1994). Techniques for measuring social competence in children. In G. Lyon, *Frames of reference for the assessment of learning disabilities.* Baltimore: Paul H. Brookes.

Voeltz, L. (1980). Children's attitudes toward handicapped peers. *American Journal of Mental Deficiency, 84*, 455–464.

Wagner, M. (1995). Outcomes for youth with serious emotional disturbance in secondary school and early adulthood. *The Future of Children, 5*, 90–112.

Wagner, M., Newman, L., D'Amico, R., Jay, E., Buter-Nalin, P., Marker, C., & Cox, R. (1991). *Youth with disabilities: How are they doing?* Menlo Park, CA: SRI International.

Walker, H., Forness, S., Kauffman, J., Epstein, M., Gresham, F., Nelson, C., & Straw, P. (1998). Macro-social validation: Referencing outcomes in behavioral disorders to societal issues and problems. *Behavior Disorders, 24,*(1), 7–18.

Warren, D. (1994). *Blindness and children: An individual differences approach.* New York: Cambridge University Press.

Warren, F. (1985). Call them liars who would say all is well. In H. Turnbull & A. Turnbull (Eds.), *Parents speak out: Then and now.* Columbus, OH: Merrill.

Warren, S. F., & Kaiser A. P. (1988). Research in early childhood language intervention. In S. L. Odom & M. B. Karnes (Eds.), *Research in early childhood special education* (pp. 89–108). Baltimore: Paul H. Brookes.

Washington, V., & Gallagher, J. J. (1986). Family roles, preschool handicapped children and social policy. In J. J. Gallagher & P. M. Vietze (Eds.), *Families of handicapped persons: Research, programs, and policy issues.* Baltimore: Paul H. Brookes.

Waxman, R., Spencer, P., & Poisson, S. (1996, Fall). Interactions between mothers and deaf and hearing children. *Journal of Early Intervention, 20*(4), 341–355.

Webber, J. (1992). A cultural-organizational perspective on special education and the exclusion of youth with social maladjustment. *Remedial and Special Education, 13*(1), 60–62.

Wehby, J., Symons F., & Cunale, J. (1998). Teaching practices in classrooms for students with emotional and behavior disorder: Discrepancies between recommendations and observations. *Behavior Disorders, 24*(1), 19–25.

Wehmeyer, M., Agran, M., & Hughes, C. (1998). *Teaching self determination to students with disabilities.* Baltimore: Paul H. Brookes.

Werner, E. E. (2000). Individual differences needs: A thirty-year study of resilient high-risk infants. *Zero to Three, 8*, 1–5.

Werner, E. E., & Smith, R. S. (1992). *Overcoming the odds.* Ithaca, NY: Cornell University Press.

Westlake, C. P., & Kaiser, A. (1991). Early childhood services for children with severe disabilities: Research, values, policies and practice. In L. Meyer, C. Peck, & L. Brown (Eds.), *Critical issues in the lives of people with severe disabilities* (pp. 429–458). Baltimore: Paul H. Brookes.

Wheeler, D., Jacobsen, J., Paglieri, R., & Schwartz, A. (1993). An experimental assessment of facilitative communication. *Mental Retardation, 31*, 49–60.

Whitehouse, D. (1987). Medical services. In M. Esterson & L. Bluth (Eds.), *Related services for handicapped children* (pp. 41–52). San Diego: College-Hill Press.

Whitmore, J. (1980a). *Giftedness, conflict, and underachievement.* Boston: Allyn & Bacon.

Whitmore, J. R. (1980b). The etiology of underachievement in highly gifted young children. *Journal for the Education of the Gifted, 3*(1), 38–51.

Wiggins, G. (1991, February). Standards not standardization: Evoking quality student work. *Educational Leadership,* 18–25.

Wilcox, S. (1994). Struggling for a voice. In V. John-Steiner, C. Panofsky, & L. W. Smith (Eds.), *Sociocultural approaches to language and literacy* (pp. 109–138). New York: Cambridge University Press.

Wilkinson, M. (1996). Clinical low vision services. In A. Corn & A. Koenig (Eds.), *Foundations of low vision: Clinical and functional perspectives.* New York: American Foundation for the Blind.

Will, M. C. (1986). Educating children with learning problems: A shared responsibility. *Exceptional Children, 52,* 411–415.

Williams, K., & Baeker, M. (1983). Use of small groups with chronically ill children. *Journal of School Health, 53,* 205–208.

Williamson, G. (1987). *Children with spina bifida.* Baltimore: Paul H. Brookes.

Wilson, V., Little, J., Coleman, M., & Gallagher, J. (1998). Distance learning: One school's experience on the information highway. *Journal of Secondary Gifted Education, 9* (2), 89–100.

Wilson, W. (1994). University of Washington Child Development and Mental Retardation Center. Newsletter. Seattle, Washington.

Wolery, M. (1992). Preschoolers with learning disabilities. *Topics in Early Childhood Special Education, 12*(2).

Wolery, M., Bailey, D., & Sugai, G. (1988). *Effective teaching: Principles and procedures of applied behavior analysis with exceptional children.* Boston: Allyn & Bacon.

Wolf, M. (1981). Talent search and development in the visual and performing arts. In I. Sato (Ed.), *Balancing the scale of the disadvantaged gifted* (pp. 103–116). Los Angeles: National/State Leadership Training Institute on the Gifted and Talented.

Wong, B. (1986). Problems at issue of identification of learning disabled. In J. K. Torgesen & B. Y. L. Wong (Eds.), *Psychological and educational perspectives on learning disabilities* (pp. 3–22). San Diego: Academic Press.

Wong, D. (1998). Suit says welfare slights the disabled. *Boston Globe,* August 12, B1, B6.

Wood, F. (1982). Defining disturbing, disordered, and disturbed behavior. In F. Wood & K. Laken (Eds.), *Disturbing, disoriented, or disturbed?* Reston, VA: Council for Exceptional Children.

Wood, F., & Smith, C. (1985). Assessment of emotionally disturbed/behaviorally disordered students. *Diagnostique, 10,* 40–51.

Wood, L., Rankin, J., & Beukelman, D. (1997, August). Word prompt programs: Current uses and possibilities. *American Journal of Speech-Language Pathology, 6*(3), 57–65.

Wood, M. (1998). Whose job is it anyway? Educational roles in inclusion. *Exceptional Children, 64*(2), 181–195.

Wood, M., Combs, C., Gunn, A., & Weller, D. (1986). *Developmental therapy in the classroom.* Austin, TX: PRO-ED.

Writer, J. (1987). A movement-based approach to the education of students who are sensory impaired/multihandicapped. In L. Goetz, D. Guess, & K. Stremel-Campbell (Eds.), *Innovative program design for individuals with dual sensory impairments* (pp. 191–224). Baltimore: Paul H. Brookes.

Yairi, E., Ambrose, N., & Cox, N. (1996, August). Genetics of stuttering: A cultural review. *Journal of Speech and Hearing Research, 39,* 771–784.

Yell, M. L. (1989). *Honig v. Doe:* The suspension and expulsion of handicapped students. *Exceptional Children, 56,* 60–69.

Yule, W., Rutter, M., Berger, M., & Thompson, J. (1974). Over and underachievement in reading. *British Journal of Educational Psychology, 44,* 1–12.

Zeitlin, S., & Williamson, G. (1994). *Coping in young children.* Baltimore: Paul H. Brookes.

Zigler, E., & Black, K. (1989). America's family support movement: Strengths and limitations. *American Journal of Orthopsychiatry, 5*(1), 6–19.

Zigmond, N. (1997). Educating students with disabilities. In J. W. Lloyd, E. Kameeui, & D. Chard (Eds.), *Issues in educating students with disabilities* (pp. 377–390). Mahwah, NJ: Erlbaum.

Zigmond, N., & Baker, J. (1990). Mainstream experiences for learning disabled students. *Exceptional Children, 57,* 176–185.

Zigmond, N., Jenkins, J., Fuchs, L., Deno, S., Fuchs, D., Baker, J., Jenkins, L., & Contino, J. (1995). *Phi Delta Kappan,* 531–540.

Zill, N., & Nord, C. (1993). *Running in place.* Washington, DC: Child Trends Inc.

Zippirch, M. (1995, January). Teaching web making as a guided planning tool to improve student narrative writing. *Remedial and Special Education, 16*(1), 3–15.

Zirpoli, T. (1990). Physical abuse: Are children with disabilities at greater risk? *Intervention in School and Clinic, 26*(1), 6–12.

Name/Source Index

Abernathy, T., 481
Abrams, 370
Abroms, 172
Accardo, P., 87
Adams, A., 239
Adelman, H., 225, 257
AER, 414
Affleck, J., 101, 102, 109, 110, 239
Agran, M., 104, 299, 452, 454, 467, 468*f*,
    470, 472, 472*f*, 483
Alarcón, M., 227
Albin, J., 470, 472
Allen-Hagen, B., 285
Allman, T., 113
Als, H., 100
Alter, M., 204, 222
Ambrose, N., 317
American Foundation for the Blind, 432*f*
American National Standards Institute,
    512–13
American Psychiatric Association, 446
American Speech-Language-Hearing Associ-
    ation, 387
Ad Hoc Committee on Service Delivery in
    the Schools, 312
Anastasiow, N. J., 84, 90, 92, 94, 104, 324,
    502, 525
Anderson, 394
Andrews, C., 317
Andrews, J. F., 381
Anita, S., 358
Annest, J., 175
Anthony, T., 424
Apgar, V., 456
Arcus, 264
Ard, W., 459, 470
Armstrong, N., 380
ASHA, 316, 365
Ashbaugh, J., 216, 461, 470, 474, 482, 521
Association for Persons with Severe Handi-
    caps, The (TASH), 441–42
Atkinson, J., 227
Attermeier, S., 105, 113
Ault, M., 204

Badian, N. A., 236
Baeker, M., 516
Bahan, B., 371, 374
Bailey, D. B., 11, 12, 265, 397, 459, 461
Baker, J., 60, 240
Baker, L., 248
Baldwin, A., 139

Baldwin, V., 443, 450, 454
Balla, D., 186
Bandura, A., 197, 205, 296
Barais, 466
Barcus, J., 518
Barnett, 251
Barr, D., 45
Barraga, N., 391*f*, 402, 403, 425, 436
Barrows, 155
Bates, E., 464
Bates, P., 206
Batshaw, M. L., 89, 90, 91, 92, 93, 94,
    351–52, 353, 387, 446, 447, 456, 489,
    490, 492, 494, 495, 496, 497–98, 499,
    500, 502, 524
Baum, S., 137
Baumeister, A., 174, 178
Baumeister, S., 178
Baumgart, D., 458, 459, 517
Bauminger, N., 180
Bayley, N., 95
Beck, J., 456
Beckman, P., 109
Beckwith, L., 101, 102
Bednarczyk, A., 357, 370
Behrman, R., 443
Belanich, J., 380
Bellamy, G., 470, 472, 474, 478
Bellinger, D., 175
Bellugi, U., 230, 310, 354, 376
Bender, M., 222, 225, 252, 257
Bennett, 172
Bentz, J., 235
Berger, M., 239
Berger, N., 228
Berla, E., 425
Berliner, D. C., 55, 68, 266
Bernal, E., 139
Bernheimer, L., 210
Bernier, J., 176, 270
Beukelman, D., 334, 336, 337*f*, 466, 469,
    518
Bigge, J. L., 442, 495, 496, 498*f*, 507, 512,
    519, 524
Biklin, D., 80, 448
Biondi, A., 153
Bishop, K. D., 472
Bishop, V., 392, 411
Black, J., 482
Black, K., 11
Blackhurst, A., 363
Blackman, J. L., 92

Blackman, L., 189*f*, 216
Blackorby, J., 46, 206, 208, 241
Blakeslee, S., 227
Blance, G., 332
Blaney, B., 216, 461, 470, 474, 482, 521
Bloodstein, O., 342
Bloom, B., 121–22
Bloom, L., 247, 309, 314, 316, 331, 343,
    356
Boathouse, 63
Bocian, K., 187
Bolds, P., 268
Bolton, P., 173, 265
Boone, D., 318
Boone, R., 250, 251*f*
Boothroyd, A., 351, 452, 457
Borkowski, J., 178
Botuck, S., 210
Bourbeau, 474
Bower, T. G. R., 308, 313, 315, 334, 450,
    485
Bradley, R. H., 98
Bradley, V., 216, 461, 470, 474, 482, 521
Brandt, F., 380
Bransford, J., 154
Brazelton, T., 456
Bredekamp, S., 103
Breske, S., 253
Bricker, D., 88, 95, 96, 103
Bristol, M., 13, 14, 15, 210, 212, 445
Bronfenbrenner, U., 8, 267
Brookfield-Norman, 194
Brooks, 178, 203
Brothers, S., 338
Brown, A. L., 248
Brown, E., 396
Brown, F., 462, 470, 474, 482, 509
Brown, L., 65, 442, 458, 463, 466, 482,
    490, 492, 493
Brown, R., 315
Brown, V., 52
Browning, K., 95
Bruder, M., 337
Bruininks, R., 169
Buch, G., 447
Buescher, T., 26
Bullis, 430
Bullock, L., 304
Burack, J., 169, 216
Burchinal, M., 397, 459
Burkhart, L., 512
Burns, 203, 250

Burskovsky, L., 319
Burwell, J., 451*f*, 455*f*
Butera, G., 481
Butler-Nalu, P., 209*f*
Butler-Por, N., 137
Buysee, V., 11
Byrne, D., 449, 450, 466

Cairns, R. B., 84
Calderon, R., 355
Caldwell, B. W., 98
Callahan, C., 134, 140*f*
Calvert, D., 376
Camarata, M., 319
Camarata, S., 319, 328, 331
Campbell, K., 461, 467
Canle, J., 290
Cantwell, D., 263
Capute, A., 87
Cardinal, D. H., 448
Carey, D., 197
Carpignano, J., 507
Carr, T., 380
Carran, D., 181, 184*f*
Carstensen, 272
Cary, D., 470
Castro, G., 205
Catts, H., 328
Chadsey-Rusch, J., 473, 478
Chalfant, J., 41, 47, 48, 185, 287
Chambers, J., 40
Chambers, V., 129
Chandler, K., 267
Chandler, L., 337
Chapman, C., 267
Chard, D., 287
Chase, W. G., 154
Chavajay, P., 24
Chen, C., 116
Chess, S., 266
Chi, H. T., 154
Chi, M., 154
Chiba, 409
Chomsky, N., 313–14, 356
Cicchetti, 186
Cioffi, J., 422
Civelli, E., 394
Clarilo, 251
Clark, D. B., 132, 229–30, 239, 245, 257
Cleave, P., 332
Clifford, R., 86, 100
Cloninger, C., 467, 482
Clymer, E. W., 381
Code of Federal Regulations, 261
Cohen, L., 53*f*
Cohen, S., 91, 444, 445, 446, 447, 472, 500, 503
Colangelo, N., 163
Cole, K., 329

Coleman, L., 126
Coleman, M. R., 126, 138, 141, 159
Colenbrander, A., 391*f*
Collins, B., 204
Columbo, 248
Combs, C., 269
Compton, C., 380
Conca, L., 233
Cone, J., 442
Conference of Executives of American Schools for the Deaf, 377
Conlon, 497–98, 499, 500
Cook, C., 84
Coons, P., 232
Coot, J., 472
Corn, A., 406*f*, 425, 436
Cornell, D., 134, 147, 164
Correa, V., 412
Cosgrove, S., 525
Costa, L., 317
Cotzin, M., 424
Coulder, D., 167*f*, 168*f*
Council for Exceptional Children (CEC), 96, 223, 237, 470
Cox, N., 317
Cox, R., 209*f*
Crabtree, M., 262, 282
Crain, S., 512
Cramer, J., 133
Cramer, S., 222, 223, 229, 237, 245
Crimmins, D., 470
Cripe, J., 88, 334, 340
Cripes, J., 103
Crocker, A. C., 183, 499
Crockett, J., 240, 241
Cromer, R., 179, 308–309
Cross, A., 109, 212
Cross, T., 126
Cruickshank, W., 227
Csikszentmihalyi, M., 157, 158
Culattla, R., 340
Cummins, J., 26
Curry, S., 411, 416, 417, 431
Curtis, D., 312, 319
Curtis, S., 224, 227, 228, 229, 319
Cuthbertson, D., 39

D'Amico, R., 209*f*
Dallenbach, K., 424
Davern, L., 482
Davis, D., 175
Davis, G., 163
Day, J., 178
De Weerd, J., 86
DeFries, J. C., 171, 227
deGrott, M., 154
Dekker, R., 394
Delcourt, M., 147, 148*f*
Delwein, P., 204

Demchak, M., 470
Demerath, R., 172
Dempsey, P., 482
Denckla, M., 233
Denhoff, E., 300
Deno, E., 186, 461
Deno, L., 235
Derosier, 268
Deshler, D. D., 229, 230, 245, 246, 248
Desimone, L., 57
Diagnostic and Statistical Manual of Mental Disorders (DSM IV), 269
Diaz, J., 352
Dichtelmiller, M., 235
Dickens, M., 134
Dickman, G. E., 230
Division for the Blind and Physically Handicapped, Library of Congress, 419*f*
Dolendo, M., 402
Dolnic, E., 353
Donar, M., 487
Donnellan, A. M., 449
Dore, J., 318
Dorfman, A., 235
Dorman, J. P., 452, 489, 493*f*, 495, 496, 524
Dote-Kwan, J., 402
Downing, J., 263, 284, 450
Downs, M., 379
Drenth, P., 394
Drew, C., 196*f*
Dromi, E., 237, 307, 317, 321, 464
Dukes, B., 525
Dunlea, A., 394
Dunst, C. J., 30, 84
Dweck, C., 205
Dykens, E. M., 170, 451

Earls, 267
Ebelin, K., 313, 356
Eckland, J., 86
Edelson, S., 448
Edgar, E., 46, 180, 299
Edgerton, R., 208
Edmondson, R., 11
Eicher, P., 502
Ellis, E., 225, 229, 230, 245, 246
Ellis, W., 222, 223, 229, 237, 245
Elmquist, D., 268
English, K., 326, 353, 364, 380, 387
Epanchin, B., 279
Epstein, C., 172
ERIC Digest, 65*f*
Erikson, J., 99
Erin, E., 413, 425
Erin, J., 436
Erwin, E., 91, 408, 409, 500
Evans, D., 80, 443, 452, 453
Everhart, U., 88
Everson, J., 448, 450, 451*f*, 455*f*

Falant, K., 104
Falb, B. Z., 105, 113
Falvey, M. A., 431, 444, 454, 462, 463, 472, 473
Fandall, A., 94
Farber, B., 13, 210
Farran, D., 88
Farwell, R., 385
Fassbinder, L., 449
Fazzi, D., 424
Fazzi, P., 424
Federal Register, 220, 443
Feldman, D., 122, 135, 300
Ferguson, D., 80
Fernald, G., 219
Ferrell, K., 397, 401, 402, 419
Feuerstein, R., 203
Fewell, D., 442
Fewell, R., 102, 204
Fey, M., 328, 329, 331, 332, 340, 343
Field, T., 100, 330
Finocchiaro. P., 470
Fitch, R., 227, 228, 229
Flavall, J. H., 233
Fleeting, M., 88
Fleisch, B., 287, 304
Fleishner, J., 230
Fletcher, J., 230, 236
Flippo K., 466, 518
Ford, A., 80, 467, 482
Ford, D., 139
Forest, M., 60, 190, 198
Forgnone, 180
Forman, B., 230, 236
Forness, S. R., 4, 186, 222, 223, 225, 229, 252, 257, 283, 297
Fowler, A., 179
Fox, L., 104
Fraiberg, S., 454
Frankenburg, W., 94
Franks, F., 416
Frase, 116
Frasier, M., 121, 139
Fredericks, B., 450
Freeman, J. M., 492
Freeman, R., 433
French, B., 262
Friedman, S., 268
Friedrith, B., 352
Frostig, M., 219, 227
Fuchs, D., 60, 235, 240
Fuchs, L., 60, 186, 235, 461
Fuchs, S., 240
Furuno, S. F., 105, 113
Gable, R., 304
Gadov, K., 229
Gage, N., 55
Gage, S., 463
Gagne, R., 247

Galaburda, A., 317
Gallagher, J., 13, 14, 15, 20, 26, 27, 57, 70, 86, 89, 109, 126, 130, 131*f*, 138, 142*f*, 148, 149*f*, 153, 155, 156–57, 159, 163, 210, 212, 377
Gallagher, P., 20, 21, 30
Gallagher, S., 20, 27, 130, 131*f*, 148, 149*f*, 156*f*, 163
Gallaudet Research Institute, 374
Gallimore, R., 210
Gamble, 20
Gannon, J., 373
Ganz, V. K., 321
Gardner, H., 52, 118, 119, 119*f*, 157
Gardner, J., 150, 206
Garnett, K., 240, 253, 257
Garrett, M., 314
Gartner, A., 19*f*
Garwood, G., 89
Gast, D., 204
Gautier, M., 172
Gaylord-Ross, R., 436
Gazonts, S. K. M., 88
Genaux, M., 268
George, P., 126, 141, 147
Gerber, S., 450, 454
Gerry, M. H., 482
Gershon, E., 263
Geruschat, D., 423
Getman, G., 219, 227
Getzels, J., 118
Giangreco, M., 456, 459, 460, 467, 482
Gibbs, L., 134, 135*f*
Gibney, C., 279, 281*f*
Gillette, Y., 380
Gillingham, A., 219, 227
Gilman, C., 169
Glaser, 119
Gleason, B., 316
Goetz, E., 433
Goetz, L., 461, 467
Goldberg, A., 502
Goldberg, S. A., 340
Goldstein, H., 448
Goldin-Meadow, S., 88, 356
Goleman, D., 158
Gonzales, 116
Good, T., 26
Goodlad, J., 58, 80
Goodrich, G., 407
Goossens, C., 512
Gordon, L., 459
Gordon, N., 30
Gothelf, C., 352, 470, 472, 474, 509
Gottesman, M., 395
Gottfried, A., 99
Gottlieb, B. W., 204, 222
Gottlieb, G., 9, 30
Gottlieb, J., 204, 222

Graham, E. M., 89
Gray, D. B., 230, 331, 343
Greenberg, J., 268
Greenberg, M., 355
Greenway, A., 515
Greenwood, C., 470
Grenot-Scheyer, M., 444, 459, 460, 472
Greschwind, N., 226
Gresham, F., 171, 187, 201, 297–98
Griesler, 268
Grigg, N. C., 465*f*
Grisso, T., 265
Grizzle, 69
Groenveld, M., 433
Guess, D., 461, 467
Guetzloe, E., 272
Guiltinan, S., 460, 461
Gullo, D., 103
Gunn, A., 269
Guralnick, M., 84, 87, 88, 95, 96, 103
Guroff, J., 263
Guskey, T., 247
Guterman, 240

Hacker, B., 105
Hagerman, R., 173
Haith, M., 450
Halenbeck, B., 295, 296, 297
Hallahan, B., 229
Hallahan, D., 454, 481
Halpern, A., 481
Hamby, D., 30
Hamlett, C., 235
Hamlett, N., 240
Hammill, D., 52
Hamovit, J., 263
Hamre-Nietupski, S., 458, 463
Hanes, M., 324
Hanline, M., 104
Hansen, R., 91, 175, 500
Harbin, G., 86, 253, 455*f*
Hardiman, M., 196*f*
Haring, N. G., 95
Haritos, C., 184
Harms, T., 100
Harrell, R., 411, 431
Harris, J., 139
Harris, M., 354
Harrison, E., 317
Harry, B., 24, 25, 30, 262, 304
Hart, B., 319
Harvey, D., 515
Hasazi, S., 459
Hassan, M. W., 107
Hasselbring, T., 44, 45*f*
Hatlin, P., 407, 416, 417
Hatton, D., 397
Hauser-Cram, P., 88, 101
Hawley, R., 265

Hayden, A. H., 95
Hayes, Samuel, 393
Haynie, M., 502
Haywood, 203
Hechtman, L., 300
Heinemann, A., 488, 515
Heinicke, C., 108, 255
Heller, K., 26
Helmstetter, E., 456, 459, 460, 517
Henderson, L., 95
Henker, 283
Herbért, 137
Hertzden, D., 104, 112, 502, 525
Hickson, L., 189f, 216
Higgins, K., 250, 251f
Hill, E., 424
Hill, N., 478
Hinshaw, 283
Hobbs, N., 280, 297
Hoben, M., 396
Hocutt, A., 4
Hodapp, R., 169, 216
Hoffman, M., 203
Hoffmeister, R., 371, 374
Hoffner, G., 278
Holbrook, M. C., 418f, 420
Holden-Pitt, R., 352
Hollinger, 133
Hollingworth, L., 123
Holtzman, W., 26
Holubec, E., 66, 67
Horner, R., 459, 470
Horowitz, F., 184
Hosaka, C. M., 105, 113
Houghton, J., 380
Howar, C., 477
Howell, K., 261, 262
Huebner, K., 449
Huff, R., 416
Hughes, C., 104, 292, 402, 452, 454, 467, 468f, 470, 472, 472f, 483
Humphries, R., 378f
Hunt, J., 85
Hutchinson, T. A., 99
Huttenlocher, P., 176
Hynd, G., 223

IDEA, 41, 511
Idstein, P., 61f
Illback, R., 304
Inatsuka, T. T., 105, 113
Infant Health and Development Project, 101
Inge, K. 466, 518
Inhelder, B., 402
Interagency Committee, 223, 228
Iverson, V., 467, 482

Jablon, J., 235
Jamieson, J., 369, 382
Janko, S., 62

JASH, 448
Jay, E., 209f
Jenkins, J., 459, 481
Jenne, T., 279
Jenne, W., 381
Jens, K. G., 105, 113
Jeter, J., 404
Jodron, J., 381
Joffee, E., 449
Johnson, D., 191, 203
Johnson, H. C., 285
Johnson, J., 66, 67, 445, 517
Johnson, L., 49
Johnson, R., 66, 67, 191, 203
Johnson-Martin, N., 105, 113
Jones, 409
Jusczyk, E. W., 308, 309

Kagan, S. L., 203, 264
Kaiser, A., 331, 343, 456
Kaiser, A. P., 331
Kankkunen, A., 365, 467
Kaplan, 312
Karkowski, A., 369
Kasari, C., 180, 451
Kassan, L., 123–25
Kauffman, J., 60, 240, 241, 266, 283, 287, 295, 296, 297, 304, 454, 481
Kavale, K. A., 186, 222, 223, 225, 229, 252, 257, 297
Kavanaugh, J. H., 230
Kekelis, L., 394, 409, 410, 411, 431, 436
Kelly, L., 372
Keogh, B., 189f, 240
Kephart, C., 394
Kephart, J., 227, 394
Kerr, M., 286, 289, 293, 294
Kettman, J., 240
Kettrick, R., 487
Kiehl, S., 492
Killan, S., 451f, 455f
Kirk, S. A., 85, 219
Kirk, W., 219
Kitano, M., 139
Kline, F. M., 248
Kluwin, T., 370
Knightly, C., 346, 348f, 349, 352, 365
Knitzer, J., 262, 287, 304
Koegel, L. C., 448
Koegel, R. L., 445, 448
Koenig, A., 406f, 415, 418f, 420, 436
Koenig, J., 422f
Koester, L. S., 369
Kohler, F. W., 448
Kolb, B., 87
Kolloff, P., 126, 146
Kolstoe, O., 198
Kolvin, I., 88, 89
Koorland, M. A., 243, 244
Kopp, C., 89, 443

Korinek, L., 179, 180
Korn, K., 240
Krajicek, M., 104, 112, 502, 503, 513, 525
Kregel, J., 473
Krupski, A., 228
Kulieke, M., 26
Kulik, C., 146
Kulik, J., 146
Kupersmidt, 268
Kupper, L., 475f
Kwiatowski, J., 340

Lackaye, T., 239, 240, 245, 257
Lagomarcino, T., 473
Lahey, B. R., 243
Lahey, M., 343
Lamb, M., 15
Lambert, N., 186
Lambros, K., 187
Lampert, J., 424
Lancaster, 69
Lane, H., 371, 374
Larrivee, L., 328
Larsen, S., 52
LaSasso, C. J., 370
Le Couteur, 265
Leal, D., 405
LeBaron, N., 459, 470
Leckman, J., 170
Lee, S., 116
Lefever, W., 219
Leggett, 205
Lehman, L., 472
Lehr, D. H., 443, 462, 470, 482, 485
Lejeune, J., 172
Leland, H., 186
Lenz, B., 225
Lenz, S., 229, 230, 245, 246
Leonard, L., 314, 319, 321, 328, 332
Leone, P., 268
Leong, C., 425
Lerner, J. L., 102, 229, 239, 248, 250
Lesar, S., 30, 481
Levin, J., 512
Levine, J., 501
Levine, P., 299
Leviton, A., 175
Levy, J., 253, 254f, 255
Levy, S., 503
Lewis, R., 49
Lewis, T., 287, 405, 406
Liberman, A. M., 228, 229, 249
Liberman, I. Y., 229, 249
Licht, B., 228
Lieberman, J., 40
Lillo-Martin, D., 88, 354, 355
Linden, G., 365, 467
Linder, T., 102, 104, 105

Lipsky, D. K., 19*f*
Little, J., 159
Llinas, R., 317
Lloyd, 60
Locke, J., 179, 415
Lockhart, P. C., 500
Logan, D., 196*f*
Lombardino, L., 332
Long, S., 288, 332
Lord, C., 447
Lovaas, O., 446, 447
Love, L., 46–47
Loveland, K., 172
Lovitt, T., 80
Lowenbrau, L., 239
Lowenfeld, B., 407
Luckasson, R., 167*f*, 168*f*, 169
Luetke-Stahlman, B., 357
Lusthaus, E., 190
Lylte, R., 369
Lyon, G. R., 219, 223, 225, 227, 229, 235, 237, 249, 258

Maag, J., 261, 262
MacDonald, C., 454
MacDonald, J., 380
MacMillan, D., 4, 171, 187, 222
Madje, S., 239
Magliocca, L., 363
Mahaffey, K., 175
Mahshie, J., 380
Maker, C., 139, 147
Malian, L., 46–47
Mank, D., 470, 472, 474
Mann, V. A., 228, 249
March of Dimes, 92, 490, 492, 493, 494, 496, 499, 525
Marchand-Martella, N., 262, 282
Marder, C., 209*f*
Marentette, P., 355
Marschark, M, 88, 365
Marsden, D., 235
Marsden, J., 95
Martella, R., 262, 282
Martin, G., 299, 396
Masataka, N., 369
Mascia, J., 380
Mastropieri, M., 279
Mathus, 297
Matsuda, M., 394
Mauk, G., 355, 365
Mauk, J., 446
Maurice, C., 446
McBride, 180
McCall, R., 20
McCarthy, M., 75
McCathren, R., 328
McClead, 175
McClearn, G., 121, 170, 171, 264
McCune-Nicolich, L., 328

McDonnell, L., 69, 80, 194
McFarlane, S., 318
McGrew, K., 194
McHale, 20
McIntire, J., 140*f*
McIntosh, R., 224
McKee, B. G., 381
McKinney, J., 4
McLaughlin, M., 69, 80, 194
McLean, L., 88, 334, 340
McLean, M. E., 99, 103, 113
McLeskey, J., 69
McLoughlin, J., 49
McNulty, B., 88
McWhorter, C. M., 482
Meadow, K., 357
Meadow, N., 299
Meadows-Orlan, K. P., 387
Meese, R., 241
Meisels, S. J., 84, 88, 95, 235
Mencher, G., 450, 454
Menke, 175
Mercer, C., 229, 230, 249, 470
Mertens, D., 370
Mesaros, R. A., 449
Mesihov, G., 447
Messick, S., 26
Metz, I., 325
Meyer, G., 443, 496
Meyer, L. H., 442, 466, 482
Michael, M., 449
Miles, 263, 284
Miller, F. J. W., 88
Miller, J., 318, 466
Miller, P., 201
Miller, S., 227, 228, 229
Milofsky, M., 89
Mirenda, P. L., 334, 449, 466, 469, 518
Misra, A., 292
Mithaug, 299
Moats, L. G., 230
Mobley, R. T., 370
Moffitt, 267, 268
Money, J., 90
Montague, 4
Montessori, M., 185
Montour, K., 136
Moores, D., 102, 318, 346, 350, 355, 359, 370, 371, 372, 374, 376, 377, 381, 382, 450
Morelock, 122
Morgan, D., 268
Morgan, M. A., 89
Morris, R., 227
Morris, S., 127
Morrison, P., 69, 80, 194
Morrison, R., 224
Morse, W., 286
Murphy, K., 88, 449, 450, 453, 466

Murphy, R., 175
Murphy-Head, M., 428
Myklebust, H., 219

Naglai, A., 325
Nakamura, K., 380
National Council on Educational Standards and Testing, 68
National Information Center for Children and Youth with Disabilities (NICHCY), 84, 86, 220, 248, 349, 444, 446, 453, 486, 490, 492, 504, 520
National Information Center on Deafness (NICD), 347, 348, 349, 350, 352, 356, 359, 360, 377, 381, 382
National Joint Committee for Learning Disabilities, 220–21
Needleman, H., 175
Neel, R., 299
Neidecker, E., 323, 326, 334, 343
Nelson, C., 263, 264*f*, 286, 289, 293, 294, 304
Nelson, J., 262, 282
Nelson, K., 319
Nelson, R., 183
Nelson, W., 443
Newman, L., 209*f*
Newton, J., 459, 470
NICD. *See* National Information Center on Deafness (NICD)
NICHCY. *See* National Information Center for Children and Youth with Disabilities (NICHCY)
Nietupski, J., 458, 463
Noller, R., 153
Noonan, M., 485
Nord, C., 15
Northern, J., 379
Novich, R., 104
Nucci, C., 84

O'Brien, 60, 198
O'Connor, L., 329, 336
O'Donnell, L., 424
O'Hara, D., 253, 254*f*, 255
O'Neill, J., 263, 267, 472, 473
O'Reilly, K. S., 105, 113
O'Rouke, T. J., 378*f*
O'Rourke, M., 503
Oakes, J., 66
Oden, M., 136
Odom, S. L., 99, 103, 113, 459
Ogura, T., 328
Oller, D. K., 321
Olmstead, J., 436
Olszewski, P., 26
Onslow, M., 317
Orelove, F., 525
Ormsbee, 263, 284
Orr, D., 515

Orton, S. T., 219
Osborn, A., 158
Osborne, R., 394
Oshima, T., 133

Packman, A., 317
Padden, C., 378f
Palfrey, J., 502
Palinscar, 200
Palsha, 12
Pappas, D., 353
Parasnis, I., 345, 374
Parette, H., 206
Parke, B. N., 131, 147
Parnes, S., 153
Parrish, J. M., 447
Parrish, T., 40
Passaro, P., 247
Paterson, 267
Patterson, G., 269
Patton, J. R., 193, 199f, 206, 207f
Paul, J., 80, 279
Paul, P., 346, 348f, 349, 354, 356, 365,
   372, 373, 374, 377, 379, 387, 449
Paul, R., 316, 318, 319, 325, 343, 370
Payette, 251
Pear, R., 92
Pearpoint, J., 60
Pearson, C., 263, 264f
Peck, C. A., 442, 456, 459, 460, 466,
   482
Pellegrino, L., 452, 489, 493f, 524
Pennington, B., 226, 230
Perkins, D., 44, 118, 163
Perret, Y. M., 89, 90, 91, 93, 94,
   351–52, 353, 387, 456, 492, 494,
   497, 500, 524
Perrin, D., 223
Peterson, C., 272
Peterson, N., 13
Petito, L., 355
Petrill, S., 8
Phillips, N., 235, 240
Phillips, S., 381
Piaget, J., 402
Pierpoint, J., 198
Pierseal, W., 499, 500
Pinker, S., 309, 310, 313, 356
Pious, C., 481
Plomin, R., 8, 121, 170, 171, 264
Pogrund, R., 424
Poisson, S., 369
Polloway, E., 167f, 168f, 179, 180,
   199f, 207f
Porter, A., 62
Porter, S., 502
Powell, T., 20, 21, 30
Premack, D., 200
Pressley, M., 241, 245, 246f, 258
Prickett, J., 449

Provence, S., 95
Pruess, J., 204
Pueschel, S., 172, 176, 270
Pugash, M., 49
Pysh, M., 47, 287

Quay, H., 269, 272, 304
Quigley, S., 346, 348f, 349, 354, 356, 363,
   365, 372, 373, 374, 377, 379, 381, 387
Quinn, 297

Rabinowitz, M., 119, 175
Rainforth, B., 454, 514
Ramos-Ford, H., 120f
Ramsey, E., 263, 266
Rand, D., 134, 135f
Rand, M., 267
Rand, Y., 203
Rankin, J., 336, 337f
Reber, M., 446
Redl, F., 288
Reigel, D. H., 525
Reis, E., 189f, 216
Reis, S., 134, 147–48
Renzulli, J., 123, 137, 147–48, 152
Resnick, L., 68
Rex, E., 415
Rhodes, L., 470, 472, 474
Rice, M., 343
Rich, J., 102
Richards, D., 433
Riedel, 60
Rieser, J., 154
Rimland, B., 448
Risley, T., 319
Rittenhouse, R., 380
Rivers, K., 332
Roberts, J., 175, 459
Robertson, C., 354
Robins, L., 263, 267
Robinson, A., 147, 164
Robinson, G., 199f, 207f
Roe, C., 250, 459
Rogers, 74
Rogoff, B., 24
Roizen, N. J., 347f
Romera, V., 140f
Rondal, J., 3, 179, 217
Rose, N., 92, 93
Roseberry-McKibbin, C., 324
Rosenthal, R., 525
Ross, P., 116, 163
Ross, R., 319
Rosselli, H., 80
Rossetti, L., 89, 455f
Rourke, B. P., 223, 225, 227, 228, 229,
   230, 233
Rovins, N., 369
Rowe, J., 101, 109
Rowley-Kelley, F. L., 525

Rozian, N. J., 350
Rubin, H., 340
Rueda, 262
Ruhl, K., 292
Rusch, F., 473, 478
Russ, S., 167f, 168f
Russo, R., 405, 406
Rutherford, 297
Rutter, M., 30, 89, 173, 239, 263, 265
Ryan, E. B., 248

Sabatino, D., 201
Sacks, S., 392f, 395, 409, 410, 411, 413,
   430, 431, 436
Safford, P., 84
Sailor, W., 462
Sale, P., 197, 470
Salganik, 116
Salomon, G., 44
Salvia, J., 186
Sameroff, A., 170, 176–77, 450
Sapperton, G., 459, 470
Sargent, L., 199f, 207f
Sargent, M., 84
Satz, P., 224, 227
Scanlon, D., 225
Scarr, S., 110
Schachter, M., 172
Schalock, R., 167f, 168f
Scharfman, W., 212
Scheft, T., 126
Scherfenberg, L., 512
Schery, T., 329, 336
Schiefelbusch, R. L., 321
Schill, W., 46
Schleichkorn, J., 525
Schlesinger, H., 450
Schloss, P., 272
Schmidt, C., 201
Schnorr, R., 482
Scholl, G., 391f
Schopler, E., 13, 15, 210, 212, 445, 447
Schore, A., 87, 449
Schreiner, M., 487
Schuerger, J., 139
Schultz, 203
Schumaker, J. B., 248
Schuman, J., 240
Schumm, J. S., 243f
Schwartz, G., 394
Schwartz, N., 428f
Schweinhart, L., 104
Science, 497, 521
Scola, P., 176, 270
Scott, D. M., 88
Scott, K., 181, 184f
Scott, T., 287
Scruggs, T., 279
Seligman, M., 272
Semmel, N., 481

Serna, L., 206, 207f
Shames, G., 340
Shank, M., 405
Shankweiler, D., 229, 249
Shatz, M., 313, 356
Shea, R., 443
Shearn, J., 253
Sheehan, R., 89
Sher, B., 156f
Sherwood, R., 154
Shinn, M., 49, 263
Shneidman, E., 273
Shonkoff, J. P., 84, 88, 101
Shontz, F., 488, 515
Shore, B., 147, 148f, 164
Short, E. J., 248
Shriberg, L., 340
Shriver, M., 499, 500
Siegler, R., 118
Silberg, 265
Silberman, R., 392f, 406, 413, 436
Silva, 267
Silver, L. B., 228
Silverman, L. B., 123–24, 136
Silverman, S., 376
Simeonsson, R., 12, 30, 216
Simmons, W., 68
Simon, H., 118
Simonoff, E., 173, 265
Simple, P., 88
Simpson, G., 263, 284, 525
Siperstein, 171
Sizer, T., 58
Skandel, S., 104, 112, 502, 525
Skeels, H. M., 84
Skinner, B. F., 201, 243
Skodak, 84
Slavin, R., 67, 141, 203
Smith, A., 423, 424, 513
Smith, C., 275
Smith, D., 88
Smith, J., 34
Smith, L., 147–48
Smith, R. S., 88, 89, 91, 110
Smith, S., 251f
Smith, T. M., 11
Smith, V., 332
Snell, M. E., 63, 167f, 168f, 195, 462,
    465f
Snidman, 264
Snowling, M. J., 223
Snowman, J., 247
Sobsey, D., 525
Solnit, G., 357, 370
Soper, E., 88
Southern, 160
Sowell, V., 407
Sparrow, 186
Speece, D., 222
Speltz, M., 459

Spencer, P., 369
Spencer-Rowe, J., 224
Spenciner, L., 53f
Spero, E., 268
Spitalnik, D., 167f, 168f
Spungin, S., 418
Stainback, S., 60, 80, 188, 189f, 191, 216,
    239, 295, 454, 481
Stainback, W., 60, 80, 188, 189f, 191, 216,
    239, 295, 454, 481
Stanley, 133, 151
Stanovich, K., 219
Stark, I., 167f, 168f
Starko, A., 157, 164
Starnes, C., 30
Stedal, K., 332
Steinberg, A., 346, 348f, 349, 352, 365
Steinberg, C., 262
Steinberg, Z., 287, 304
Steinke, T., 104, 112, 502, 525
Stepien, W., 155, 156f
Sternberg, L., 118, 178, 466
Stevenson, H., 116
Stieber, 267
Stillman, S., 219, 227
Stone, C., 233
Stouthamer-Loeber, 268
Strain, P., 448
Stromswald, K., 308
Strully, 197
Studdert-Kennedy, A., 354, 376
Sturomski, N., 225, 245, 246
Subotnik, R., 123–25
Sugai, G., 461
Sullivan, J. W., 321
Sullivan, K., 179
Summers, E., 123–25
Suvak, 419
Swank, L., 333
Swanson, L., 227
Switzky, 203
Sykes, K., 421
Symons, F., 290
Szymanski, P., 478

Tager-Flushberg, H., 179
Takahira, 116
Tallal, P., 224, 227, 228, 229, 312, 317,
    319, 333
Tannebaum, R., 427f
Taylor, B., 267
Taylor, L., 225, 257
Taylor, M., 357, 370
Taylor, R., 59f, 81, 110, 428, 450
Tennen, H., 101, 109
Terharr-Younkers, 126
Terman, L., 123, 124, 135, 136
Thomas, A., 266
Thompson, C., 332
Thompson, J., 239

Thousands, J., 198, 481
Thurlow, M., 169
Tierney, D., 395
Tillman, M., 394
Tjellstrom, A., 365, 467
Todd, J., 427
Todd, S., 253
Torgesen, J. K., 219, 228, 233
Torres, I., 425
Traci, M., 369
Tralli, R., 240, 241, 248
Tricket, E., 268
Trieber, F. A., 243
Trivette, C., 30
Trybus, R., 371
Tsai, L., 444, 446
Tunali-Kotoski, B., 172
Turkington, C., 174f
Turnbull, A. P., 19f, 26, 31, 97, 108, 109,
    210, 212, 217, 405, 457
Turnbull, H. R., 26, 31, 97, 108, 109, 210,
    212, 217, 405, 457
Turpin, R., 172
Turstein, 497–98
Tuttle, D., 395, 396
Tuttle, N., 395, 396

U.S. Department of Education, 5f, 6f, 67f,
    86, 222, 239, 310, 327, 345, 349, 379,
    409f, 443, 449, 454, 458, 486, 487,
    488f, 508
U.S. Department of Labor, 474
U.S. House of Representatives, 72
Ulrey, G., 91, 500
Umbreit, J., 525

Vail, C., 104
Vaillant, G., 89
Valletutti, P. J., 224
Van Dijk, J., 450
Van Tassel-Baska, J., 134, 164
Vanderwood, M., 194
Vaugh, S., 224
Vaughn, S., 243f
Vaughn, V., 443
Vellutino, F., 228
Verstegen, D., 76
Vey, P., 428f
Villa, P., 481
Villa, R., 198
Vining, E., 492
Voeller, K. S., 233
Voeltz, L., 459
Von Euler, C., 317
Vye, N., 154

Wagner, M., 46, 180, 206, 208, 209f, 241,
    299
Walker, H., 263, 266, 267, 284, 300
Wallace, I., 322f

Wallace, J., 322f
Ward, M., 429
Ward, V., 147, 164
Warren, D., 22, 393, 394, 397, 433, 437
Warren, K., 444, 503
Warren, S., 328, 329, 331, 340, 343
Wasser, A., 123–25
Waternaux, C., 175
Watkins, R., 343
Waxman, R., 369
Webber, J., 262
Wechsler, D., 166
Wehby, J., 290
Wehman, P., 478
Wehmeyer, M. L., 104, 452, 454, 467, 468f, 470, 472, 472f, 483
Weidenman, L., 176, 270
Weiderholt, L., 52
Weikart, D., 104
Weisner, T., 210
Weiss, G., 300
Welch, T., 449
Weller, D., 269
Welsh, J., 319
Werner, E. E., 3, 88, 89, 91, 110
Werry, J., 269
West, T., 455f

Westlake, C. P., 456
Whalen, 283
Wheeler, W., 247
White, 123, 267
White, K., 355, 365
Whitehead, 44
Whitmore, J. R., 136–37, 140
Whittesey, J., 219
Whyte, L., 354
Wiggins, G., 70
Wilkinson, M., 406f
Will, G. F., 183
Will, M. C., 41
Williams, K., 445, 516
Williamson, G., 104, 456, 494f, 525
Wilson, V., 159
Windmiller, M., 186
Windsor, J., 329, 331, 340, 343
Winsberg, B., 210
Wishner, J., 222
Wiske, M., 95
Wolery, M., 194, 204, 225, 236, 461
Wolf, M., 138
Wolffe, K., 395
Wolman, J., 40
Wong, B. Y. L., 219, 258
Wong, D., 248, 252

Wong, Y. L., 219
Wood, F., 260, 275, 279, 281f, 288, 291f
Wood, L., 336, 337f
Wood, M., 63, 64f, 240, 269
Woodley-Zanthos, P., 174
Woolf, S., 472
Workman, D., 155, 156f
Writer, J., 450

Yairi, E., 317
Yell, M. L., 74, 76
Yoder, P., 328
York, J., 454, 514
Ysseldyke, J., 49, 186, 194
Yule, W., 239

Zeisloft, B., 113
Zeitlin, S., 104
Zigler, E., 8, 11, 169, 216
Zigmond, N., 240, 241
Zill, N., 15
Zimmerman, 132
Zipprich, M., 230
Zirpoli, T., 90, 504
Zool, J., 394

Subject Index

AAMR. *See* American Association on Mental Retardation (AAMR)

abacus, 416

ability grouping. *See* grouping

absence seizures, 490

academic achievement
 by gifted female students, 125
 inter-individual differences in, 52
 learning disabilities and, 220, 239–40
 parental encouragement of, 372–73
 of students with hearing impairments, 345, 370–72
 time on task and, 266–67
 U.S. *vs.* other countries, 116–17
 visual impairments and, 404

academic achievement learning disabilities, 225, 226*f*, 229–33

academic aptitude, 50

academic skills, differential instruction for students with mental retardation, 194–95

academic standards movement
 exceptional children and, 69
 inclusion movement and, 68–69, 78

acceleration
 content, 148, 149*f*
 course, 144*f*
 grade, 144*f*, 160
 student, 159–60
 of students with hearing impairments, 372

acceptance finding, 154

accessibility of facilities, 512–13

access technology, for students with visual impairments, 428–29, 435

accidents. *See also* injuries
 disabilities caused by, 504

accommodation (eye), 391

accountability, 70, 142

achievement tests
 diagnostic, 52, 235
 identification of gifted students through, 132
 standard (norm-referenced), 52

achondroplasia, 496

acoupedic communication method, 376

acoustic communication method, 376

acquired disabilities, 488

acquired immunodeficiency syndrome (AIDS), 497–99
 mental retardation and, 176

action plans, making (MAP), for students with mental retardation, 198

adaptive behavior, mental retardation and, 167–69, 186

Adaptive Behavior Inventory for Children (ABIC), 186

Adaptive Behavior Scale, American Association on Mental Deficiency (AAMD), 54, 186

adaptive skills
 for students with visual impairments, 416–26
 transient problems, 275

ADHD. *See* attention-deficit hyperactivity disorder (ADHD)

adjustment. *See also* personal adjustment; social adjustment
 to community, 39–40

adolescents
 peer group influence and, 22–23
 spinal cord injuries, 494

adoption, of children with disabilities, 84–85

adults. *See also* transition
 with deafblindness, 451*f*
 with emotional problems, 299–301
 with hearing impairments, 384–85
 with learning disabilities, 241, 252–53
 with mental retardation, 198–200, 208–209, 214–15
 with multiple and severe disabilities, 470, 472–73, 478–79, 481
 with multiple and severe injuries, 474, 475*f*, 478
 sheltered workshops for, 208, 430, 474, 478
 with visual impairments, 430

advanced classes, 141, 145*f*, 146, 151

advocacy, by parents, 19–20, 39

African-American students
 gifted, 128–30
 in programs for students with mental retardation, 26
 self-identity of, 139

age-appropriate skills, for children with multiple and severe disabilities, 462–64

age-inappropriate behavior, 260, 261*f*

aggressive behavior. *See also* emotional problems
 causes of, 269, 270*f*
 intervention for, 302
 peer groups and, 267
 in students with physical disabilities and health impairments, 515

agraphia, 230

alcohol abuse, 499–500
 at-risk infants and, 91
 behavior problems and, 268
 emotional problems and, 265
 fetal alcohol syndrome, 174–75

alphabetic principle, 370

alpha-fetoprotein test, 92–93

America 2000 (Goals 2000), 66, 67*f*, 78

American Association on Mental Deficiency (AAMD), 54, 186

American Association on Mental Retardation (AAMR), 166, 169, 457

American Asylum for the Education and Instruction of the Deaf, 34

American Printing House for the Blind, 429

American Psychiatric Association, 4

American School for the Deaf, 34

American Sign Language (ASL), 333–34, 355, 376–77. *See also* sign language
 as a language minority, 374

American Speech-Language-Hearing Association, 309

Americans with Disabilities Act (ADA) (PL 101-336), 99, 345, 425
 discrimination against people with disabilities and, 521

amniocentesis, 93, 172

amputation, 494

anarthria, 329*f*

anemia, 499

anencephaly, 492

Angelou, Maya, 128

anoxia, 88, 456

antisocial behavior, 269

anxiety-withdrawal, 271–73

Apgar, Virginia, 94

Apgar test, 94, 456

aphasia, 329*f*

applied behavioral analysis (ABA), students with learning disabilities and, 243–45, 247

Applied Behavior Approach, for autism, 446

apraxia, 329*f*, 462

aptitude-achievement discrepancy, 220

arithmetic manipulatives, 250

arrest rates, for youth with disabilities, 207

arthritis, 494, 495, 518

articulation, 318
 defined, 307
 hearing impairments and, 363
 intervention for, 337

articulation disorders
 defined, 311*f*
 primary, 339
 therapy for, 328

articulation errors, 316

articulation-phonology disorders, 316–17
 defined, 330*f*
 developmental profiles, 319–20

ASHA, 335

Asperger's disorder, 446

asphyxia, hearing loss and, 353

assertiveness skills, 412*f*, 468*f*

assessment, 40–41, 49
 authentic, 69, 70
 culture and, 26, 54–55

defined, 49
for early intervention, 104–105
informal, 51*f*
of learning disorders, 234–35
of mental retardation, 166
of multiple and severe disabilities, 454,
463–64
play as, 105
process, 49
role of, 50–55
tools, 69–70
of visual impairments, 405–406
assimilation approach, for culturally diverse
students, 139
assistive communication, for students with
physical disabilities and health impairments, 517–20
assistive listening devices (ALDs), 380
assistive technology
defined, 46, 47*f*, 77
IDEA requirements, 511
of students with hearing impairments,
379–81
for students with multiple and severe disabilities, 470
tools for, 47*f*
visual impairments, 426–29, 435
Association for Children with Learning
Disabilities, 20
Association for Persons with Severe Handicaps, The (TASH), 63, 441–42, 442,
457, 480
asthma, 497, 498*f*
ataxic cerebral palsy, 490, 493*f*
athetoid cerebral palsy, 493*f*
atonic seizures, 490
at-risk infants. *See also* infants; low-birth-
weight infants; premature infants
conditions related to, 89–91
environmental causes, 90–91
factors affecting, 111–12
genetic disorders and, 89
hospital intervention strategies for,
100–101
pregnancy and birth effects, 89
prevention, 91–93
attentional disorders
diagnosis of, 238
early intervention for, 238
learning disabilities and, 228–29
attention-deficit hyperactivity disorder
(ADHD), 28. *See also* attentional disorders; hyperactivity
characteristics of, 4–5, 270
computers and, 298
intervention techniques, 271
learning disabilities and, 228–29
treatment for, 270–71, 283
atypical absence seizures, 490
audiograms, 350*f*, 351*f*, 364
audiologists, 98*f*, 364, 455*f*
audiometers, 348
audiometry, 364–65
behavioral observation, 364–65
play, 365
pure-tone, 364

audition, 307
auditory brainstem response (ABR), 365, 366
auditory communication method, 375–76
auditory global communication method, 376
auditory processing
developmental delays in language and, 319
learning disabilities and, 227
preschool, 248
augmented and alternative communication
systems, 312*f*, 333–34
for students with multiple and severe
disabilities, 464, 469*f*
for students with physical disabilities and
health impairments, 517–18
aural communication method, 375
authentic assessment, 69, 70
authentic evaluation, of multiple and severe
disabilities, 463
autism, 444–48, 479
causes of, 445
characteristics, 170, 445, 447*f*
communication disorders and, 313*f*, 330*f*
fragile X syndrome and, 174
heredity and, 265
pervasive developmental disorders not
otherwise specified (PDDNOS) and,
446
prevalence of, 4
treatment programs, 446–48
Autism Research Center, 448

babbling, language development and,
314–15, 355–56
Baldwin, James, 129
barriers, removal of, for students with visual
impairments, 425
basal readers, 249
Bayley Scales, 95
behavior
desirable, supporting, 291*f*
inclusion and, 61
behavioral differences, 3
behavioral observation audiometry, 364–65
behavior change, 278–83, 290, 291*f*
behaviorism, 243–45
behavior modification
objections to, 279
for students with communication disorders, 331
for students with emotional problems,
278–79
for students with mental retardation,
200–201
behavior problems
biological risk factors, 263–66
causes of, 302
child dangerousness, 264*f*
child risk factors, 264*f*
controlling, 291*f*
defined, 260, 301
employment and, 299–301
factors affecting, 263–68
family risk factors, 264*f*, 265–66
hearing impairments and, 450
immediate crisis, 284
modeling acceptable behavior for, 295–97

placement, 302
school risk factors, 266
skill mastery techniques and, 290–98
social risk factors, 266–68
substance abuse and, 268
teacher response to, 290
transient adaptation problems and, 275
underlying dynamics, 284
Bell, Alexander Graham, 373
bilingual students, 75
assessment of communication disorders
in, 325
students with hearing impairments as,
377–78
bilirubin, 94
Binet, Alfred, 166
Binet-Simon Tests of Intelligence, 123
biological factors. *See* genetics
birth defects, alpha-fetoprotein test and,
92
birthing process. *See also* pregnancy
abnormal, 88, 89–90
breech birth, 88, 456
bladder disabilities, 503
blindness. *See also* deafblindness; visual
impairments
achievement and, 404
defined, 390
denial of, 395
inclusion issues, 36–39
light perception, 399
social development and, 37, 38
special schools, 34
Blissymbols, 338–39
bodily-kinesthetic intelligence, 120*f*
bone-conductor test, 365
borderline mental retardation, 187
boredom, of gifted students, 147
bottom-up approach, for reading instruction, 249
bowel disabilities, 503
braille, 396, 417–21, 427
Braille, Louis, 417
braille markers, 422
braille translators, 429
braillewriters, 37, 420–21
brain
damage to, learning disabilities and, 219,
227
development of, infections and, 176
traumatic brain injuries (TBI), 504, 505*f*,
515
brainstorming, 156
Brazelton Neonatal Behavioral Assessment
Scale, 456
breech birth, 88, 456
brittle bone disease, 496
bronchopulmonary dysplasia, 503
Brown, Christy, 443
Brown v. *Board of Education*, 75
Buchholz, Jack, 490–91
Burchenal, Joan, 231–32
Burchenal, Joseph, 231–32
Bureau for the Education of the Handicapped, 86
burns, 494

cadmium, mental retardation and, 175
cancer, 500
cannonball theory of gifted students, 136
Captioned Films for the Deaf, 360
cardiopulmonary conditions, 496–97, 522
career development counseling, for girls, 134
career education, for students with mild mental retardation, 193
caregivers
  loss of, 91
  motherese spoken by, 314
  responsiveness to child by, 315f
Carolina Curriculum, 105
case manager/advocate system, 40
case managers, 285
catheterization, 503
Center for Special Education Finance, 42
Center for Talented Youth, Johns Hopkins University, 133
central auditory processing disorders (CAPDs), 312f
central hearing losses, 348
central nervous system, 489
  learning disabilities and, 221
cerebral palsy, 489–90, 493f
  augmented and alternative communication for, 518
  breech birth and, 88
  child abuse-related, 503–504
  child-family interactions and, 12
  communication disorders and, 312, 313f, 330f, 338–39
  daily care, 13
  developmental profile, 505–506
  early-intervention centers for, 106–107
  gifted students with, 140–41
  inclusion issues, 509–10
  mental retardation and, 452–53
  occupational and physical therapy, 511
  problems associated with, 490
  programs for children with, 84
Chall, Jean, 231
challenging behaviors, 87–88
chart reading, for students with visual impairments, 425
child abuse, 90, 266, 496, 503–504
child-family interaction, 12–15
childhood disintegrative disorder, 446
child-rearing practices, as early intervention, 88
Choosing Options and Accommodation for Children (COACH), 467–68
choral reading, 415
chorionic villus biopsy, 93
chromosomal abnormalities, 171–74
chronic diseases, 501f, 522
ciliary muscles, 391
circles of friends, 63
  for students with mental retardation, 190, 191, 198
circumvention intervention, 457
Civil Rights Act, 457
class action suits, 75
classification, in assessment process, 49
classification skills, mental retardation and, 177–78

classroom
  acceptance of students with mental retardation into, 191
  adaptations for students with learning disabilities for, 241–42f
  discipline, inclusion and, 61
  equipment for students with physical disabilities and health impairments, 512
  gifted students and, 131
  morale, of students with hearing impairments, 379
cleft lip, 496
cleft palate, 496
  articulation-phonology disorders and, 317
  communication disorders and, 330f
  hearing disorders and, 350
closed captioning, 360, 366
closed-circuit television (CCTV), 429
clubfoot, 496
cluster grouping, 144f, 147
cluster placement model, 478
COACH (Choosing Options and Accommodation for Children), 467–68
cocaine, 91, 500
cochlea, 346
cochlear implants, 365, 384
cognitive abilities, 177–78, 179, 248
cognitive modeling, 202f
cognitive strategies
  for gifted students, 119, 150–58, 161
  learning disorders and, 233
  for students with emotional problems, 292–93
  for students with hearing impairments, 372
  for students with learning disabilities, 247–48
collaborative services
  for students with emotional problems, 284–86
  for students with learning disabilities, 240
  for students with physical disabilities and health impairments, 510–12
college, for students with disabilities, 253, 490
colostomy, 503
combined communication method, of students with hearing impairments, 377
communication
  augmented and alternative, 464, 469f, 517–18
  defined, 307, 340
  developmental delays in, 319
  electronic systems, 505
  innate need, 356
  method for students with hearing impairments, 375–77
  nonverbal, 307
  process of, 307–308
  skills required for, 307
  strategies for behavior disorders, 291f
  verbal, 307
communication boards, 469, 469f, 518
communication developments, 334

communication deviations, 334
communication differences, 3, 312f. See also dialects
communication disorders. See also language disorders; speech disorders
  articulation-phonology disorders, 316–17
  assessment of, 321–22
  classification of, 316–18
  consultative services for, 326
  curriculum adaptations for, 334
  defined, 308–309, 311f, 334
  developmental profiles, 319–20
  early intervention for, 88, 321–22, 341
  evaluation and diagnosis, 323–24
  family and lifespan issues, 339–40
  family patterns of, 312, 319
  focused stimulation for, 332
  hearing loss and, 357–60
  identifying, 321, 323
  inclusion issues, 326
  individual vs. group therapy for, 341
  instructional technology for, 335–37
  intensive-cycle scheduling for, 326
  interactive approaches for, 331
  intervention for, 331–32
  itinerant services for, 326
  linguistic diversity and, 324–25
  multicultural language issues, 341
  phonological training for, 332–33
  prevalence of, 310–12
  screening for, 323
  self-esteem and, 332
  teaching strategy adaptations, 326–34
  technological aids for, 335, 338–39
  types of, 311–12f
  unresolved issues, 341
communication skills
  adaptive behavior scales, 186
  differential instruction for students with mental retardation, 194, 195, 196f
  preschool, 248
  for students with mental retardation, 168f
  for students with multiple and severe disabilities, 461–62, 464, 466
  for students with visual impairments, 417–21
community
  adjustment to, 39–40
  experiences for students with visual impairments, 421, 422f
  influence of, 22
  programs for previously institutionalized children, 458
  re-education programs and, 281
community living skills. See also daily living skills; home living skills
  for people with multiple and severe disabilities, 464, 473–74
  for students with mental retardation, 198, 199f
  in students with mental retardation, 168f
compensatory intervention, 457
competence, in re-education programs, 280

complex partial seizures, 492
comprehensive services, 44
computation skills, for students with mental retardation, 199*f*
computers. *See also* assistive technology; instructional technology; technology
advantages of, 46, 47*f*, 78
for gifted students, 159
in special education, 46–47
for students with learning disabilities, 251–52
for students with visual impairments, 415
as writing aids, 519–20
Computer Users in Speech and Hearing (CUSH), 335
concentration, flow and, 158–59
concreteness, visual impairments and, 407
conditionally branched interactions, 47
conduct disorders, 269–71, 301. *See also* behavior problems
conductive hearing losses, 346–47, 352*f*, 381
congenital disabilities, 487
congenital heart disease, 498*f*
congenital myopathies, 495
Connecticut Infant and Toddler Assessment procedure (IDA), 95
consonant sounds, hearing impairments and, 363
consultative service, for students with communication disorders, 326
consumer economics training, for students with mental retardation, 198, 199*f*
content acceleration, 148, 149*f*
content enrichment, 148–49, 150
content instruction, learning disabilities and, 248–51
content novelty, 149*f*, 150
content sophistication, 149*f*, 149
context, 5–10. *See also* environment; families
defined, 5–10
ecological approach, 7–8
of family, 12
giftedness and, 121–22
types of, 6–7
contingent social reinforcement, 201
continuous progress, 144*f*
continuum of placement options, 41
continuum of services, 35, 60
contracts
student contingency, for emotional problems, 293
student-teacher, for behavior problems, 297
between teachers and gifted underachievers, 137
control, sense of
in mothers, 109
in students with physical disabilities and health impairments, 515, 517
conversational skills, 468*f*
Cooley's anemia, 92, 499
cooperative learning, 66–67
defined, 66
gifted students and, 141, 142

projects, 65*f*
for students with learning disabilities, 247
for students with mental retardation, 203–204, 205
teams, 66
cooperative parent programs, 372
coping
ability, assessment of, 54
by parents of children with multiple and severe disabilities, 476–77
strategies for gifted students with disabilities, 141
Cordes, Timothy, 404–405
corrective intervention, 457
Corsiglia, Joan, 231–32
Council for Exceptional Children, 457
Council for Learning Disabilities, 239
counseling
career development, for girls, 134
for families, 479
genetic, 91–92, 183
re-education programs, 281
course acceleration, 144*f*. *See also* acceleration
court actions, 74–77
Cramer Abacus, 416
creative problem solving, 153–54
creativity
defined, 154
factors affecting, 154
in gifted students, 118, 154–56, 161
in students with multiple and severe disabilities, 467
Crick, Francis, 171, 182
criterion-referenced tests, 463
cross-age grouping, 144*f*
cues, for students with deafblindness, 451*f*
culture
assessment and, 26, 54–55
communication disorders and, 324–25, 341
deaf community as, 360–61, 374
defined, 23
diagnosis and, 75
diversity of, 24–26
early intervention programs and, 109
emotional problems and, 262, 267–68, 275
family adjustments and, 25–26
identification of gifted students and, 138–40
influence of, 23–24
intelligence tests and, 52
of poverty, 214
special education and, 77
curriculum adaptations, 65*f*
for early intervention, 104–105
for gifted and talented students, 45, 147
options, 43*f*
for students with communication disorders, 334
for students with emotional problems, 289–90
for students with hearing impairments, 371–72
for students with learning disabilities, 240

for students with mental retardation, 45, 192–200
for students with multiple and severe disabilities, 461–64
for students with physical disabilities and health impairments, 513–15
for students with visual impairments, 415–16
Curriculum-Based Measurement, 186–87, 235
curriculum compacting, 147–48
curriculum reform, gifted student programs, 141
cystic fibrosis, 497, 498*f*, 503
developmental profile, 506–507
lifespan issues, 521
cytomegalovirus (CMV), hearing loss and, 352, 353

daily care
for families of children with mental retardation, 210–212
parental response to, 13
daily living skills. *See also* community living skills; home living skills; living arrangements
adaptive behavior scales, 186
instruction for students with visual impairments, 426, 427
in students with mental retardation, 168*f*
Davis, Bernice, 17
Davis, Deidre, 16–17
Davis, Hilton, 17
day care, 104, 111
day programs, for people with multiple and severe injuries, 474
deaf and hard of hearing students. *See* hearing impairments
deafblindness, 448–50
assessment, 449
defined, 448
early intervention, 449–50
education program, 448–49
evaluation, 454–55
jobsite training, 451*f*
prevalence of, 443
deaf community, 345, 360–61, 374
deafness. *See also* deafblindness; hearing impairments
defined, 311*f*, 346
postlinguistic, 346
prelinguistic, 346, 381, 383
research and training funding, 71
death, symbolic, 12–13
decibels (dB), 346
decision making, by people with multiple and severe disabilities, 472
deinstitutionalization, 35, 458
Delaware County Parents Involved Network (PIN), 277
delinquency
arrest rates for youth with disabilities, 207
causes of, 267–68
emotional disturbance and, 261
demonstrations, for students with learning disabilities, 244

depression, in children with mental retardation, 452
detachment disorder, 277
Detosta, Geraldine, 366
developmental appropriate practice (DAP), 103–104
developmental delays
    in communication, 319
    environment and, 6–7
    of organically injured *vs.* familial retarded groups, 170
    preventing, 87–88
    special education, 204
developmental disabilities. *See also* mental retardation
    adaptive behavior, 167–69
    biological factors affecting, 171–76
    characteristics of children with, 177–80
    curriculum adaptations, 192–200
    defined, 166
    developmental profiles, 180–81
    educational reform and, 193–94
    environmental factors affecting, 176–77
    family and lifespan issues, 209–13
    instructional technology, 206
    learning environment adaptations, 185–92
    levels of, 169–71
    teaching strategies, 200–206
    transition, 206–209
developmental learning disabilities, 225–29
developmental profiles, 56–57
    communication disorders, 319–20
    defined, 9–10
    emotional problems, 273–75
    gifted students, 127, 130–31
    hearing impairments, 361–62
    learning disorders, 233–34
    mental retardation, 180–81
    physical disabilities and health impairments, 505–507
    visual impairments, 398–400
developmental scales, 87, 105
developmental screening, 94–95
Developmental Sequence Performance Inventory (DSPI), 204
deviant behaviors. *See also* emotional problems
    heredity and, 264
Dexedrine, 229, 270
diabetes, 498f, 500
    fetal damage and, 89
    hearing disorders and, 351
    lifespan issues, 521
diagnosis
    of attentional disorders, 238
    of communication disorders, 323–24
    cultural background and, 75
    defined, 49
    differential, of learning disorders, 235
    of Down syndrome, 172
    dual, 451
    of dyslexia, 230
    educational, of learning disorders, 235
    of learning disabilities, 235, 255
    of mental retardation, 186

diagnostic achievement tests, 50
    advantages and disadvantages of, 51f
    defined, 52
diagnostic evaluation, 56
diagnostic prescriptive model, for students with learning disabilities, 245–46
dialects, 312f, 334–35. *See also* communication differences
diet
    at-risk infants and, 90
    lead poisoning and, 175–76
    phenylketonuria and, 173
differences. *See also* culture; diversity; inter-individual differences; intra-individual differences
    behavioral, 3
    classroom and, 49–50
    communication, 3, 312f
    intellectual, 3
    learning disabilities and, 223
    peer rejection and, 27
    physical, 3
    sensory, 3
    types of, 3
differential diagnosis, of learning disorders, 235
differential instruction, for students with mental retardation, 194–200
differential reinforcement, for students with mental retardation, 201
diplegic cerebral palsy, 489, 493f
directed teaching approach, to teaching reading, 249
direct instruction, for students with learning disabilities, 244
directional microphones, for hearing aids, 379
directives, following, for students with communication disorders, 328
direct-service helping teachers, for students with emotional problems, 285–86
disabilities. *See also* specific conditions
    attitudes toward, 34
    categories of, 3
    detecting in infants, 93–95
    early treatment of, 93–94
    giftedness and, 140–41
    parental response to, 12–13
    teaching children about, 516
    transition issues, 110
discrimination, 521
disruptive behavior
    teacher response to, 290
    think-time strategy for, 282–83
distance learning, for gifted students, 159
distancing, learning disabilities and, 141
distortion errors, in language, 317
divergent thinking, 157
diversity. *See also* culture; differences
    of culture, 24–26
    of families, 14, 25–26
    of gifted students, 138–40
    linguistic, 324–25
Dix, Dorothea, 34
Dove, Rita, 129

Down syndrome, 451. *See also* mental retardation
    causes of, 172
    characteristics of children with, 170, 182–83
    defined, 83, 182
    developmental profile, 181
    diagnosis of, 172
    early intervention programs, 88, 95–96
    hearing disorders and, 350
    identification of, 456
    language development and, 179
    learning disabilities and, 222
    plastic surgery for, 174f
    prenatal tests for, 92, 93
    social development and, 180
    special education, 204
dramatization, for students with mental retardation, 195
drill and practice, for students with mental retardation, 206, 207f
drug abuse. *See also* substance abuse
    behavior problems and, 268
    emotional problems and, 265
    mental retardation and, 174
    physical disabilities and health impairments and, 499, 500
    in school, 267
drug therapy, for students with emotional problems, 283, 302
dual-career families, 15
dual diagnosis, 451
dual enrollment in high school and college, 144f, 151
Duane, Drake D., 231
Duchenne muscular dystrophy, 490, 495
due process, 73
dysarthria, 329f
dyscalcula, 230
dyskinetic cerebral palsy, 489, 493f
dyslexia, 229–30, 231–32
    diagnosis of, 230
    prevalence of, 231
    reading approach for, 250
Dyslexia Neuroanatomical Laboratory (Orton Society), 232
dysphonia, 318, 329f
dystonic cerebral palsy, 493f

ear
    bones, 346
    hearing loss and, 346–48
    middle-ear infections, 321, 353
    structure of, 346–48, 349f
eardrum, 347
early childhood intervention centers, 102–104
Early Childhood Special Education Assistance Act, 86
early childhood special educators, 98f, 455f
early college admission, 151
early intervention, 83–110
    assessment for, 104–105
    curriculum for, 104–105
    defined, 84
    for Down syndrome, 83

education programs, 102–107
effectiveness of, 88–89, 110
family issues, 108–10
goals of, 84, 95
in the home, 101–102
legislative support for, 85–86
origins of, 84–85
purpose of, 87
settings and strategies, 100–102
staff turnover, 111–12
for students with communication disorders, 321–22, 341
for students with deafblindness, 449–50
for students with hearing impairments, 383
for students with learning disabilities, 235–38
for students with mental retardation, 83, 184, 214
for students with multiple and severe disabilities, 453–56, 464
for students with physical disabilities and health impairments, 486f, 507
for students with visual impairments, 400–402
early-intervention centers, for children with cerebral palsy, 106–107
early school admission, 144f, 151
Early Screening Inventory, 95
ECHO, 38
echolalia, 445
echo reading, for students with visual impairments, 415
ecological inventory, for students with multiple and severe disabilities, 463–64, 465f
ecological model of exceptionality, 8, 28
ecological strategies, 7–8
defined, 280
for students with emotional problems, 280–83
ecology, 5–10. See also context; environment; families
Edelman, Marian Wright, 129
educational adaptations
for gifted students, 143–60
special education, 42–48
for students with communication disorders, 326–27
for students with hearing impairments, 368–79
for students with learning disabilities, 239–43
for students with mental retardation, 185–206
for students with multiple and severe disabilities, 457–70
for students with physical disabilities and health impairments, 508–20
for students with visual impairments, 407–16
Educational Center for the Arts, 139
educational diagnosis of learning disorders, 235
educational reform
gifted student programs and, 141–42

mental retardation and, 193–94
visual impairments and, 435
educational restructuring. See restructuring
Education for All Handicapped Children Act of 1975 (PL 94-142), 57, 71–73, 349, 364, 457
definition of learning disabilities under, 220
identification and assessment requirements under, 234
individualized education programs, 188
multidisciplinary approach, 284
Education of All Handicapped Children Act Amendments (PL 99-457), 73–74
Part H, 86, 96, 99
education teams. See multidisciplinary teams; teams; team teaching
effective education programs, for gifted students, 147
elaborations, expression of, 468f
electronic hearing aids, 384
emergency procedures, for students with physical disabilities and health impairments, 511–12
emotional adjustment, of students with physical disabilities and health impairments, 515
emotional intelligence, 158
emotional problems. See also behavior problems
anxiety-withdrawal, 271–73
biological risk factors, 263–66
blaming children with, 260
causes of, 263–68, 302
characteristics of, 268–73
child dangerousness, 264f
child risk factors, 264f
classification of, 268–73
computer learning approaches for, 298
conduct disorders, 269–71
cultural differences and, 262, 267–68, 275
curriculum adaptations for, 289–90
daily care issues, 13
defined, 260–63, 301
developmental profiles, 273–75
drug therapy for, 302
family and lifespan issues, 298–301
family risk factors, 264f, 266
of gifted underachievers, 137
identification, 275
immediate crisis, 284
inclusion issues, 286–88, 301–302
individualized education programs (IEPs), 289
intervention strategies, 278–83
learning environment and, 262, 284–98
mental retardation and, 179–80
multidisciplinary teams for, 284–86, 302
overexcitability in gifted students, 125
placement, 275–76, 302
school failure and, 263
school risk factors, 266–67
school's ability to provide support for, 287
serious emotional disturbances, 261–62
social risk factors, 267–68

substance abuse and, 265, 268
teaching strategies for, 290–98
transient adaptation problems and, 275
underlying dynamics, 284
employment. See also vocational opportunities
of adults with deafblindness, 451f
of adults with emotional problems, 299–301
of adults with hearing impairments, 384–85
of adults with learning disabilities, 241, 252–53
of adults with mental retardation, 208–209, 214–15
of adults with multiple and severe disabilities, 470, 472–73
changing job market, 214–15
supportive, for adults with multiple and severe disabilities, 470, 472
empowerment
of parents, 108
of people with multiple and severe disabilities, 470
encephalitis, 176
encephalocele, 492
Engleman, Judy, 211
enrichment triad experiences, for gifted students, 151, 152f
environment, 32–77. See also context; learning environment; least restrictive environment
at-risk infants and, 90–91
developmental delays and, 6–7
emotional problems and, 264–65, 266–68
giftedness and, 121–22
heredity and, 8–9, 264–65
mental retardation and, 176–77
modification of, for students with emotional problems, 280–83
skills instruction for students with visual impairments, 421–25
epilepsy, 490, 492
prevalence of, 486, 492
error analysis, 54f
escape/avoidance, 141
evaluation. See assessment
excellence movement, 141, 142
exceptional children. See also specific conditions
categories of, 3–5, 28
context of, 5–10
defined, 2–3
educators' perception of, 6
identification of, 28–29
prevalence of, 4
Exceptional Parent, 211, 477
executive function
defined, 119, 178
diagnostic prescriptive model and, 245
learning disabilities and, 233
mental retardation and, 178–79
expectations
gifted students and, 128–29
of and for girls, 134, 161

Express III, 338–39
expression of elaborations, 468f
expression of rights, 468f
expressive language, 52
extensive support, for students with mental retardation, 169
extrinsic motivation, 203
extrinsic muscles (eye), 392
eye
    structure of, 392f
    visual interpretation process, 390–92

facilitators, for students with mental retardation, 190–91
facility accessibility, 512–13
fact-oriented instruction, 44
faded, overt self-guidance, 202f
fading
    for students with mental retardation, 202–203
    for students with visual impairments, 401
familial mental retardation, 8
familial retarded group, 169–70
families. See also fathers; mothers; parents
    child-family interaction, 12–15
    of children with communication disorders, 339–40
    of children with emotional problems, 266, 267–68
    of children with hearing impairments, 382–83
    of children with learning disabilities, 253–55
    of children with mental retardation, 209–12
    of children with multiple and severe disabilities, 472, 473–80
    of children with visual impairments, 433
    counseling for, 479
    current approach to participation by, 19f
    diversity of, 14, 24–26
    early intervention and, 101–102
    importance of, 29
    individualized family services plans (IFSPs), 97–101
    influence of, 10–12
    IQ and, 122
    parent empowerment, 15, 18
    parents as advocates, 19–20
    parents as collaborators, 18, 19f
    relationships with professionals, 15, 18
    resilience of, 215
    responsibilities of, 13–15
    roles in, 15, 18–22
    siblings, 20–22
    stress in, 90, 109–10, 111, 253–54
    of students with mental retardation, 209–12
    traditional participation by, 19f
    violence in, emotional problems and, 266
    working mothers, 15
family-focused approach, 11–12, 108
farsightedness, 392
FAS. See fetal alcohol syndrome (FAS)
fathers. See also families; parents
    aggressive behavior and, 269

changing roles of, 15
of children with mental retardation, 212
loss of, 91
responsibilities of, 14–15
feedback, for students with learning disabilities, 244
Fefferman, Charles, 135–36
Fernald State School for the Mentally Retarded, 34
fetal alcohol effects (FAE), 175, 499
fetal alcohol syndrome (FAS), 91, 174–75, 499
field trips, for students with visual impairments, 425
figurative language, teaching to students with hearing impairments, 373
financial formulas, 76
fine motor skills, 248
finger spelling, 355, 375, 377
    alphabet, 378f
fire drills, instruction for students with visual impairments, 425
flexible pacing, 143–45
fluency disorders, 317
    defined, 311f, 330f
    intervention for, 331–32
FM hearing aids, 366
focused stimulation, 332
following directives, 328
foster homes, 84–85
fragile X syndrome, 170, 174
Freeman, Martha, 231, 232
friends, circles of, 63, 190, 191, 198
friendships, 63
full inclusion, 16, 17, 60, 61, 78. See also inclusion
full-time special classes, for gifted students, 145f
functional assessment, for students with emotional problems, 279–80
functionalism, for students with communication disorders, 331
functional skills
    academic, 168f
    age-appropriate, for children with multiple and severe disabilities, 462–64
funding
    court cases affecting, 76
    for research and training, 71
    pooling requirements, 74
    for services for children with disabilities, 29, 71–72

Galaburda, Albert, 232
Gallaudet, Thomas Hopkins, 373
Gallaudet University, 372, 376, 382
Galton, Francis, 121
gastrostomy tube feeding, 502, 504f
Geller, Jake, 490–91
gender. See also girls
    intellectual performance and, 133–35
general-education classroom
    conditions for integration of students with disabilities into, 65f

role of, 64f
social relationships in, 63
students with mental retardation in, 188–90
general-education teachers, inclusion and, 60–61, 63
generalization of skills, 459, 462–63
    social, 293
genetic counseling
    at-risk infants and, 91–92
    defined, 91–92
    mental retardation and, 183
genetic disorders, 171, 497
    at-risk infants and, 89
    deafness, 349, 350–51
    preventing, 91–92
genetics
    autism and, 265
    communication disorders and, 312, 319
    deviant behaviors and, 264
    emotional problems and, 263–66
    environment and, 8–9, 264–65
    giftedness and, 8, 121–22
    hearing impairments and, 349, 350–51
    intelligence and, 8
    learning disabilities and, 226–27
    mental illness and, 8
    mental retardation and, 89, 171–74
geniuses, 135–36
German measles. See rubella (German measles)
gestural language, 345, 464
    intelligence tests and, 354–55
gifted and talented students
    achievement tests and, 70
    boredom of, 125–26
    challenges of, 125–27
    choosing among multiple talents, 125, 126
    cognitive strategies for, 150–58
    culturally diverse, 138–40
    curriculum adaptations for, 43, 147
    defined, 117
    developmental profiles, 9, 10f, 127, 130–31
    with disabilities, 140–41
    educational adaptations for, 143–60
    encouraging creativity in, 154–58
    expectations of, 128–29
    factors affecting, 121–22
    federal legislation, 74
    female, 124–25, 133–35
    heredity and, 8, 121–22
    heterogeneous grouping and, 67
    identification of, 131–33, 138–39
    inclusion and, 147
    instructional technology for, 158
    with learning disabilities, 141
    learning environment adaptations for, 143–46
    lifespan issues, 160–61
    with multiple and severe disabilities, 440
    in other countries, 117
    parents of, 27, 28
    peer group adjustment, 125–26
    personality characteristics, 125–27

programs for, 141–42, 148f, 149
social adjustment of, 126–27, 130, 160
special courses for, 147
students of extraordinary ability, 135–36
studies of, 122–25
transition of, 160
underachievers, 136–38
unresolved issues, 162
Gifted Child Center, 125
giftedness, defined, 117–18, 161
girls
  expectations of and for, 134, 161
  gifted, 124–25, 133–35
  mathematics achievement by, 133–34
  role models for, 134, 135
  science achievement by, 135
  self-confidence of, 134, 135
goals
  of early intervention, 84, 95
  for inclusion, 508
  in individualized education program
    (IEP), 59f, 180, 188
  national education, 66, 78
  social competence, 180
  for students with mental retardation,
    192–93
  for students with mild mental retarda-
    tion, 192–93
Goals 2000, 66, 67f, 78
government, training for students with
  mental retardation, 198, 199f
grammar
  American Sign Language and English
    differences, 376–77
  prelinguistic hearing loss and, 356
"Grandma's law," 200
graphemes, teaching to students with hearing impairments, 370
gross motor skills, 248
group achievement tests, identification of
  gifted students through, 132
Group for the Advancement of Psychiatry
  (GAP), Psychopathological Disorders
  in Children classification system,
  269
grouping
  cluster, for gifted students, 144f, 147
  cross-age, 144f
  gifted students and, 67, 141, 144f,
    145–46, 161
  heterogeneous, 66, 67, 141
  in-class flexible, for gifted students,
    144f
  multi-age, for gifted students, 144f
  subject, for gifted students, 144f
group instruction
  for students with learning disabilities,
    240
  for students with mental retardation, 204
group intelligence tests, identification of
  gifted students through, 132
guilt, of nondisabled siblings, 21–22

Handicapped Children Early Intervention
  Program (HCEEP), 86
handicaps, defined, 522

hard of hearing. *See also* hearing
  impairments
  defined, 311f
  developmental profile, 361–62
HCEEP (Handicapped Children Early Intervention Program), 86
Head Start, 8, 62, 85, 111–12
health and safety skills, in students with
  mental retardation, 168f, 198, 199f
health impairments. *See also* physical disabilities and health impairments
  AIDS and HIV, 497–99
  asthma, 497
  cardiopulmonary conditions, 496–97
  Cooley's anemia, 92, 499
  cystic fibrosis, 497
  defined, 485–86
  early intervention programs and, 104
  metabolic disorders, 496
  other health-related conditions, 500–501
  prevalence of, 4, 6f
  requirements of, 485–86
  sickle cell anemia, 499
  substance abuse, 499–500
health services, 511
hearing. *See also* ear
  threshold levels, 348f
hearing aids, 312, 366, 368, 379–80, 384
Hearing Disability Association of America,
  239
hearing impairments. *See also* deafblindness
  academic achievement and, 345, 370–72
  age of onset of, 346
  behavior problems and, 450
  causes of, 349–54, 352f, 381
  central hearing losses, 348
  characteristics of children with, 354–55,
    363–64
  cocaine and, 500
  communication disorders and, 330
  communication methods, 375–77
  conductive hearing losses, 346–47, 352f,
    381
  curriculum adaptations for, 371–72
  defined, 346
  developmental delays and, 87
  developmental profiles, 361–62
  early intervention for, 88, 383
  educational adaptations for, 368–79
  education approaches, 448
  employment issues, 384–85
  environmental causes of, 349, 351–54
  family and lifespan issues, 382–83
  general education teachers and, 363–64
  genetic causes of, 349, 350–51
  identification of, 362–64, 456
  inclusion issues, 370–71
  interpreters, 359–60
  language development and, 355–57
  mixed hearing losses, 348
  parent involvement and, 368–70
  postlinguistic deafness, 346
  postsecondary programs, 381–82, 384
  prelinguistic deafness, 346, 381, 383
  prevalence of, 6f, 349
  research and training funding, 71

school's role in identification of, 362–63
sensorineural hearing losses, 348, 352f,
  383
social and personal adjustment and,
  357–61, 366–67, 369f
special schools, 34
special services, 360
speech disorders and, 308
teaching strategies, 373–74, 379
testing methods, 364–65
transition and, 381–82
types of, 346–48, 383
unresolved issues, 385–86
hearing loss. *See also* hearing impairments
  defined, 345
heart defects, 496
heavy metals, 175–76
Heinicke, Samuel, 373
Helen Keller National Center for Technical
  Assistance, 345, 448
helping teachers, for students with emotional problems, 285–86
hemiplegic cerebral palsy, 489, 490, 493f
hemophilia, 498f, 500
heredity. *See* genetics
heroin, 91, 500
herpes simplex virus, hearing loss and, 353
heterogeneous grouping, 66, 67. *See also*
  grouping
  gifted student programs and, 141
high academic standards, 68, 193–94
high-cost teacher behavior, for students with
  emotional problems, 290–91
high-incidence disabilities, 4, 5f
high-IQ students, 122
Hispanic students
  gifted, 130
  in programs for learning disabilities, 26
Holcomb, Bob, 373
home environment
  early intervention programs, 101–102
  experiences for students with visual im-
    pairments, 421, 422f
  supportiveness of, Down syndrome and,
    95–96
home health care, 501–502
home living skills. *See also* community living skills; daily living skills; living
  arrangements
  responsibilities for students with mental
    retardation, 207
  in students with mental retardation, 168f
Home Observation Measure of the Environment (HOME) scale, 98
home visitors, for early intervention
  programs, 101–102
homophones, speech reading and, 375
honors courses, for gifted students, 141,
  145f, 146
hospitals, intervention strategies in,
  100–101
Hotel Express III, 338–39
Howe, Samuel Gridley, 34
human immunodeficiency virus (HIV),
  497–99
  mental retardation and, 176

Hunter College, elementary school for gifted students, 124
hydrocephalus, 106, 456, 493
hyperactivity. *See also* attentional disorders; attention-deficit hyperactivity disorder (ADHD)
  computers and, 298
  employment issues, 300
  learning disabilities and, 228–29
  lifespan issues, 300–301
hyperbilirubinemia, 350
hypermedia, 206
hypernasality, 317, 318
hyperopia, 392
hyponasality, 318

IDA. *See* Connecticut Infant and Toddler Assessment procedure (IDA)
IDEA. *See* Individuals with Disabilities Education Act (IDEA) (PL 101-476)
idea finding, 153
identification
  of gifted students, 131–33, 138–39
  of students with learning disabilities, 220
  of students with learning disorders, 234–35
  of students with mental retardation, 170–71, 213
  of students with multiple and severe disabilities, 456
  of students with physical disabilities and health impairments, 507
  of students with visual impairments, 402–403
idioms, teaching to students with hearing impairments, 373
idiot savant children, 3
IEPs. *See* individualized education programs (IEPs)
IFSPs. *See* individualized family services plans (IFSPs)
Illinois Math and Science Academy, 146
immigrant children, thinking processes of, 24
inborn errors of metabolism, 172
incidental teaching, 331
inclusion. *See also* full inclusion
  academic standards *vs.*, 68–69, 78
  amount of time in general-education classroom, 64–65
  balancing with least restrictive environment, 78
  classroom discipline and, 61
  core beliefs of, 60
  court cases, 75–76
  defined, 35, 58–59
  emotional problems and, 301–302
  general-education teachers and, 60–61, 63
  gifted students and, 147
  limitations of, 61
  movement, 42, 58–60, 68–69, 78
  socialization and, 197–98, 409–11
  special education *vs.*, 59–60

for students with communication disorders, 326
for students with disabilities, 62, 111
for students with emotional problems, 286–88
for students with learning disabilities, 239–40, 241, 242–43*f*
for students with mental retardation, 187–88, 189, 197–98
for students with multiple and severe disabilities, 36–39, 459–61, 481
for students with physical disabilities and health impairments, 508–12, 523
for students with visual impairments, 408–12
support for, 64
supportive, 241, 242–43*f*
independent living, 46–47
  for students with mental retardation, 208
  for students with visual impairments, 401–402
individual differences. *See* differences; inter-individual differences; intra-individual differences
individualized education programs (IEPs), 37, 56–58
  for braille instruction, 418–19
  defined, 56, 57, 72, 77–78
  environment and, 7
  example, 189*f*
  goals and objectives in, 59*f*, 188
  positive and negative effects, 57
  social competence goals in, 180
  student participation in developing, 292
  for students with communication disorders, 324
  for students with emotional problems, 276, 289
  for students with hearing impairments, 371
  for students with mental retardation, 188, 198
  for students with visual impairments, 406, 413, 414*f*
individualized family services plans (IFSPs), 96–101, 108
  assessment for, 98–99
  for communicative disorders, 323
  defined, 73, 96
  development of, 99–100
  focus on family in, 97
  legal requirements for, 96
  multidisciplinary team for, 97–100
individual placement model, 478
Individuals with Disabilities Education Act (IDEA) (PL 101-476), 43, 73–74, 86, 108, 261, 345, 349, 485
  amendments, 39, 86, 187, 418–19
  autism defined in, 444
  braille provisions, 418–19
  collaborative services requirements, 511
  deafblindness defined in, 448
  emotional problems defined in, 261–62
  family involvement in transition of people with multiple and severe disabilities, 472

identification and assessment requirements under, 234
inclusion goals, 508
intelligence testing, 453
learning disabilities defined in, 220
Part C, 86, 96, 100
provisions for children with visual impairments, 402
individual transition plans (ITPs), 473
induction loop devices, 380
infantile spasms, 490
infants. *See also* at-risk infants; low-birth-weight infants; premature infants
  detecting disabilities in, 93–95
  development of, 87
  with Down syndrome, stimulation of, 182
  evaluating hearing loss in, 365
  hearing impaired, 88, 368–70
  language development, 314–15
  premature, 100–101
infant-teacher ratios, in day care and early childhood centers, 104
infections, mental retardation and, 176
inferences, teaching to students with hearing impairments, 373
informal assessments, 50
  advantages and disadvantages of, 51*f*
information processing, mental retardation and, 177–79
information subtest (Wechsler Preschool and Primary Scale of Intelligence), 236
infrared devices, for students with hearing impairments, 380
injuries
  multiple and severe injuries, 473–74, 475*f*, 478
  spinal cord, 489, 494
  traumatic brain injuries (TBI), 488*f*, 504, 505*f*, 515
institutionalization
  community programs following, 458
  costs of, 285
  court cases affecting, 75
  for students with mental retardation, 83
instructional coaches, teachers as, 159
instructional planning, 49
instructional technology
  defined, 44, 77
  for gifted students, 158
  for students with communication disorders, 335–37
  for students with hearing impairments, 381
  for students with learning disabilities, 251–52
  for students with mental retardation, 206
  for students with multiple and severe disabilities, 470
  tools for, 45*f*
integrated settings, for children with multiple and severe disabilities, 459–61
integration facilitators, for students with mental retardation, 198
intellectual development
  mental retardation and, 186

preschool and, 85
visual impairments and, 393–94
intellectual differences, 3
intelligence
cerebral palsy and, 490
components of intellectual competence,
118–19
emotional, 158
epilepsy and, 492
gender and, 133–35
influence of heredity and environment
on, 8
multidimensional, 52
multiple, 59, 119–21
multiple and severe disabilities and, 440f
myelomeningocele and, 494
subnormality, mental retardation and,
166–67, 169
visual impairments and, 434
intelligence quotient (IQ)
family and, 122
of gifted students, 123
scores, 52
tests for students with multiple disabilities, 452–53
verbal *vs.* performance, 167
very high, 135–36
Intelligence Test for Visually Impaired Children (ITVIC), 394
intelligence tests, 117–18
cultural differences and, 52
development of, 123
diagnosis of mental retardation through,
186
hearing impairments and, 354–55
identifying intellectual subnormality
through, 166–67
as predictors of academic performance,
51–52
for students with multiple disabilities,
452–53
intensive-cycle scheduling, for students
with communication disorders, 326
interactive approaches
for students with communication
disorders, 331
for teaching reading, 249
interdisciplinary teams. *See* multidisciplinary teams
inter-individual differences
defined, 9, 28, 50
developmental profiles and, 10
special education and, 42
intermittent support, for students with
mental retardation, 169
international baccalaureate courses, 145f
Internet access, for students with hearing
impairments, 381
Internet-Expanded Writing Process, 250,
251f
interpersonal intelligence, 120f
interpersonal relations
in students with visual impairments,
399
training for students with mental retardation, 199f

interpreters, for students with hearing impairments, 359–60, 379
intervention
for students with communication disorders, 331–32
for students with emotional problems,
278–83
types of, 457
interviews, 50, 51f
intra-individual differences
defined, 9, 28
developmental profiles and, 10
hearing impairments, 361
learning disabilities and, 223
special education and, 42
intrapersonal intelligence, 120f
intravenous feeding, 503
intrinsic motivation, 203
invulnerability, 91
IQ. *See* intelligence quotient (IQ)
Itard, Jean, 185
itinerant teaching
for students with communication
disorders, 326
for students with visual impairments,
411–12
ITPs. *See* individual transition plans
(ITPs)

Javits, Jacob, 74
Javits Act (PL 100-297), 74
Jemison, Mae C., 129
Johns Hopkins University, Center for Talented Youth, 133
joint attention, for students with deafblindness, 449
Jordan, Vernon, 129
joy, re-education programs and, 281
junior high school, restructuring, 66
just manageable difficulties (JMD),
297
juvenile rheumatoid arthritis, 498f

karyotyping, 172
Kauai Longitudinal Study, 88, 91
Kendall Demonstration Elementary School,
382
Kennedy, Geri, 36
Kennedy, John F., 71, 212, 473
keyboarding instruction, for students with
visual impairments, 426
kidney disease, 498f
knowledge structure, 154–55
Kozlik, Ted, 38

language
defined, 308
elements of, 309–10
language acquisition
mental retardation and, 179
rates, 319
visual impairments and, 394
language development, 313–16
assessment of, 52–53
characteristics of, 314
sequence of, 314–16

stimulating in students with hearing impairments, 385
of students with hearing impairments,
355–57
visual impairment and, 394
language disorders, 229. *See also* communication disorders; speech disorders
articulation-phonology disorders,
316–17, 319–20, 330f
causes of, 318
defined, 308–309, 311f
early intervention for, 237
prevalence of, 341
language experience approach, to teaching
reading, 249–50
language skills instruction
for students with mental retardation,
177, 179, 194, 195, 196f, 199f
for students with visual impairments, 415
Latino students
gifted, 130
in programs for learning disabilities, 26
law, training for students with mental retardation, 198, 199f
lead poisoning, 92, 184
mental retardation and, 175–76
LEAP program, 448
learned helplessness
anxiety-withdrawal and, 273
defined, 273
learning disabilities and, 141
by students with mental retardation, 205
learning
by doing, for students with visual impairments, 408, 421
knowledge structure and, 152–53
perceptual systems and, 226
problem-based, 153–54
learning disabilities, 218–55
achievement and, 225, 226f, 229–33,
239–40
appropriate placements, 256
assessment, 234–35
causes of, 219, 223–24, 236–37, 255, 256
characteristics of children with, 224, 236
classification of, 225–33
classroom adaptations for, 241–42f
cognitive instruction for, 247–48
collaborative team models for, 240
communication disorders and, 313f
cooperative learning for, 247
culture and, 26
curriculum adaptations for, 240
defined, 219, 220–22, 256
developmental profile, 233–34
diagnosis of, 235, 255
diagnostic prescriptive model, 245–46
differential diagnosis of, 235
dyslexia, 229–30, 231–32
early intervention for, 235–38, 256
educational adaptations for, 239–43
educational diagnosis of, 235
family issues, 253–55
fragile X syndrome and, 174
generalized, 171
genetic causes, 226–27

gifted students with, 141
historical overview, 219
identification of, 220, 234–35
inclusion issues, 239–40
instructional technology for, 251–52
language and reading disorders, 229
learning environment adaptations for, 239–40
lifespan issues, 253–55
mastery learning for, 247
mathematics disorders, 230–31
mnemonic devices for, 247
multiple sensory techniques, 239
neuropsychological/developmental, 220, 221, 225–29
preschool curriculum, 248
prevalence of, 4, 222–23
range of services for, 256
remedial instruction, 239
specific, 171
spelling disorders, 230
strategy intervention model, 246
teaching strategies for, 243–51
textbook adaptations for, 241–42f
transition, 252–53, 256
writing disorders, 230
Learning Disabilities Association of America (LDA), 63–64
learning environment. See also educational adaptations
adaptation of, 42, 43f
adaptations for gifted students, 143–46
adaptations for students with emotional problems, 284–98
adaptations for students with learning disabilities, 239–40
adaptations for students with mental retardation, 185–92
adaptations for students with visual impairments, 408–415
changing, 278
emotional problems and, 262
skills for students with visual impairments, 425–26
learning experience approach, to reading, by students with visual impairments, 420
learning problems, 224. See also learning disabilities
learning strategy programs, 245–46
least restrictive environment, 458
balancing with inclusion, 78
court cases, 75–76
defined, 42–43, 73
for students with emotional problems, 286
for students with mental retardation, 188–89
for students with physical disabilities and health impairments, 508, 512–13, 522
for students with visual impairments, 400, 408, 416
Leber's disease, 404
le'Eprèe, Abbè de, 373
legal blindness, 396
defined, 390
family and lifespan issues, 433

legislation, 70–77, 85–86. See also Education for All Handicapped Children Act of 1975 (PL 94-142); Individuals with Disabilities Education Act (IDEA) (PL 101-476); specific laws
Leigh disease, 443
letter recognition, 229
leukemia, 498f, 515
levels program, for students with emotional problems, 279
lifesaving techniques for at-risk infants, 111
life skills centers, for students with visual impairments, 413
life span interview, for students with emotional problems, 288
lifespan issues
development and transition, 29
for gifted students, 160–62
special education perspective, 39
for students who stutter, 340
for students with communication disorders, 339–40
for students with cystic fibrosis, 521
for students with developmental disabilities, 209–13
for students with diabetes, 521
for students with emotional problems, 298–301
for students with hearing impairments, 382–83
for students with hyperactivity, 300–301
for students with learning disabilities, 253–55
for students with legal blindness, 433
for students with multiple and severe disabilities, 473–80, 479–80
for students with physical disabilities and health impairments, 521
for students with visual impairments, 433
lifting and transfer techniques, 514
Lighthouse for the Blind, 403
lighting, for students with visual impairments, 412
light perception, in children with visual impairments, 399
limited support, for students with mental retardation, 169
linguistic diversity, 324–25
linguistic intelligence, 120f
lip reading, 366, 375
listening
assessment of, 52
assistive technology for, 427–28
defined, 421
for students with visual impairments, 421
literacy skills, for students with hearing impairments, 355
living arrangements
independent living, 39–40, 208, 401–402
for people with multiple and severe injuries, 473–74
living skills. See community living skills; daily living skills; home living skills; independent living

Lo, Andrea, 37
logical-mathematical intelligence, 120f
Lovaas method, for treatment of autism, 446–47
low-birth-weight infants, 111. See also at-risk infants; infants; premature infants
communication disorders in, 330
cytomegalovirus and, 352
hearing loss in, 352, 353–54
multiple and severe disabilities in, 456
low-incidence disabilities, 4, 6f, 443
low vision, 390
lunchroom, orientation to, for students with visual impairments, 426
lunchtime, social skills and, 410

magnet schools
for gifted students, 145f, 146
for students with visual impairments, 413
magnification tools, for students with visual impairments, 415
mainstreaming, 44, 204. See also inclusion
maladaptive behavior. See also behavior problems
cultural values and, 262
modeling acceptable behavior, 295–97
malleability of children, 78
Mann, Horace, 34
manual communication methods, of students with hearing impairments, 375
MAP (making an action plan), for students with mental retardation, 198
map reading, for students with visual impairments, 425
Marfan syndrome, 495
marijuana, 500
Massachusetts Institute of Technology, 429
Massachusetts School for Idiotic and Feeble-minded Youth, 34
mastering the environment, for students with visual impairments, 421
mastery learning
for students with hearing impairments, 379
for students with learning disabilities, 247
mathematics achievement
gender and, 133–34
U.S. student performance, 116
mathematics disorders, 230
mathematics instruction
acceleration in, 159–60
learning disabilities and, 250
for students with learning disabilities, 244–45
for students with mental retardation, 199f
for students with visual impairments, 416
task analysis approach, 194
medical models of exceptionality, 8, 28
medical procedures, for students with physical disabilities and health impairments, 511–12
medical screening at birth, 94
memory
knowledge structure and, 152–53
learning disabilities and, 228
mental retardation and, 178
meningitis, 353

meningocele, 492
mental disturbance, 313f
mental illness, 8, 261
mental retardation. *See also* Down syndrome; mental retardation and developmental disabilities (MR/DD); mild mental
   retardation (MMR); moderate mental retardation; severe mental retardation
   achievement tests and, 70
   adaptive behavior and, 167–69
   biological factors contributing to, 171–74
   borderline, 187
   career education, 193
   causes of, 171–77, 213
   cerebral palsy and, 452–53, 490, 505
   characteristics of children with, 177–80
   chromosomal abnormalities and, 171–74
   communication disorders and, 312, 313f
   curriculum adaptations, 43, 192–200
   defined, 166, 167f, 169, 213
   developmental patterns, 170
   developmental profiles, 10, 180–81
   diagnosis of, 186
   differential instruction, 194–200
   educational adaptations for, 185–206
   educational reform and, 193–94
   emotional problems and, 179–80
   environmental factors and, 176–77
   evaluating, 452–53
   familial, 8
   family support, 209–212
   fetal alcohol syndrome and, 174–75
   general education classrooms, 188–90
   genetic disorders and, 89
   goals for students, 192–93
   heavy metals and, 175–76
   identification of, 170–71, 213
   inclusion issues, 187–88, 189, 197–98
   independent living, 208
   individualized education programs
      (IEPs), 188
   infections and, 176
   institutionalization for, 83
   intellectual subnormality and, 166–67,
      169
   intensity of support for, 169
   language skills and, 177, 179
   lead poisoning and, 92
   learning disabilities and, 222
   learning environment adaptations,
      185–92
   levels of, 169–71
   mild, early intervention programs for, 88
   multiple and severe disabilities and, 440
   multiple risk factors for, 177
   organically injured group, 169–70
   with other disabilities, 451–53
   prenatal nutrition and, 90
   prereferral teams, 185–87
   prevention of, 181, 183–84, 214
   primary prevention of, 181, 183, 184f
   research and training funding, 71
   resource room, 191–92
   right of students to public education,
      74–75
   rule-oriented behavior and, 452

secondary prevention of, 181, 184
   sensory deficits and, 87
   skills mastery, 205–206
   social relationships, 207
   social skills and, 179–80, 196–98
   social supports, 188, 190, 191
   special classes, 192
   special education, 204–205
   Special Olympics, 212–13
   support facilitators, 190–91
   teacher consultants, 190–91
   teaching strategies, 200–206
   tertiary prevention of, 181, 184
   toxic agents causing, 174–76
   transition, 206–208, 208–209
mental retardation and developmental
   disabilities (MR/DD), defined, 166, 169,
   213
metabolism
   disorders, 496
   inborn errors of, 172
metacognition
   diagnostic prescriptive model and, 245
   learning disabilities and, 233
metatarsus adductus, 496
methylphenidate (Ritalin), 283. *See also*
   Ritalin
microcephaly, 93
middle ear infections
   communication disorders and, 321
   hearing loss and, 353
   listening and language strategies and,
      322f
middle schools
   gifted students and, 141, 142
   restructuring and, 66
mild mental retardation (MMR)
   characteristics of children with, 177–79
   defined, 169
   goals for students, 192–93
   identification of, 171
   social learning approach, 197
   vocational training, 198–200
minority groups
   cultural diversity of, 24–26
   deaf community as, 374
minority students
   assessing mental retardation for, 187
   culture-bound assessment measures and,
      54–55
   with disabilities, 16–17
   disproportionate number in special
      education programs, 275
   expectations of, 128–29
   gifted, 74, 138–40
   self-identity of, 139–40
   understanding of own cultural back-
      ground, 139–40
MIT Braille Emboss, 429
mixed hearing losses, 348
mixed seizure disorder, 490
mixed type cerebral palsy, 490
MMR. *See* mild mental retardation (MMR)
mnemonic devices, 247
mobility
   curriculum adaptations for, 513–14

equipment, 479–80, 514
   orientation and mobility (O&M) train-
      ing, 421–25
   skill development, 520f
   training for students with visual impair-
      ments, 421–25
modeling
   acceptable behavior, 295–97
   role models for girls, 134, 135
   social skills, 293
   for students with communication disor-
      ders, 328
   for students with learning disabilities,
      244
Model Secondary School for the Deaf, 382
models (physical), for students with visual
   impairments, 421, 425
moderate hearing impairments, 361–62
moderate mental retardation, 169, 177–79,
   195
moderate visual disabilities, 390, 391f, 434
Montreal Children's Hospital, 300
morphology, 311f, 318
Morrison, Toni, 129
motherese, 314
mothers. *See also* parents
   age at pregnancy, Down syndrome and,
      172
   of children with mental retardation, 212
   loss of, 91
   responsibilities of, 14–15
   sense of control of, 109
   working, 15
motivation
   autism treatment and, 448
   extrinsic, 203
   of gifted female students, 125
   of gifted students, 122
   intrinsic, 203
   of students with hearing impairments,
      366–67
   of students with mental retardation, 203,
      205
   of students with visual impairments, 400
motor skills
   adaptive behavior scales, 186
   curriculum adaptations for, 513–14
   skill development, 520f
motor writing problems, 250
MR/DD. *See* mental retardation and developmental disabilities (MR/DD)
multi-age grouping, for gifted students, 144f
multidisciplinary teams
   collaborative team models, 240
   defined, 97
   educational teamwork, 523
   for individualized family services plans
      (IFSPs), 97–100
   intervention, 18f
   members of, 98f, 455f
   prereferral teams, 185–87, 275
   service coordinators for, 285
   for students with communication disor-
      ders, 321
   for students with emotional problems,
      284–86, 302

for students with learning disabilities, 240
for students with mental retardation, 185–87, 203–204, 275
for students with physical disabilities and health impairments, 511, 523
teacher-assistance teams, 47–48, 77
team-assisted individualization, 203–204
multimedia programs, of students with hearing impairments, 381
multiple and severe disabilities, 3, 487. *See also* physical disabilities and health impairments
categories of, 440–41
causes of, 443–44
characteristics of children with, 444–53
child's sense of control and, 453
communication disorders and, 313f
curriculum adaptation for, 461–64
defined, 442–43
early intervention for, 453–56, 464
education adaptations, 457–70
evaluation of, 463–64
family and lifespan issues, 473–80, 479–80
functional age-appropriate skills for, 462–64
with hearing impairments, 385
identification of children with, 455
inclusion issues, 36–39, 459–61, 481
interaction of, 454
intervention and support costs, 481
low-incidence disorders, 443
mental retardation and, 440, 443
parental response to, 12–13, 479
preschool teaching strategies, 466–67
prevalence of, 4, 6f, 443
primary and secondary school teaching strategies, 467–68
self-determination skills instruction, 467
service axioms, 454–55
supportive employment approaches, 478–79, 481
teaching strategies, 464–69
terminology, 441
unresolved issues, 481
with visual impairments, 402, 407, 433
multiple and severe injuries
living arrangements, 473–74
vocational opportunities, 474, 478
vocational rehabilitation services, 475f
multiple intelligences theory, 52, 119–21
multiple sensory techniques, for students with learning disabilities, 239
Murphy, Kevin, 504
muscular dystrophy, 490–91, 494, 495, 497
augmented and alternative communication, 518
computer use and, 520
Muscular Dystrophy Association, 490
musculoskeletal conditions, 488, 494–96, 522
musical intelligence, 120f
myclonic seizures, 490
myelomeningocele, 492, 493, 494, 510–11
myopia, 392

nasogastric tube feedings, 502, 504f
National Academy of Science, 69
National Assessment of Educational Progress, 117
National Association for Retarded Citizens, 457
National Association for the Education of Young Children (NAEYC), 103
National Association of Retarded Citizens, 20
National Center for Educational Statistics, 267
National Education Association (NEA), 103
national education goals, 66, 78
National Information Center on Deafness (NICD), 345, 356–57, 359, 360, 382
National Joint Committee on Learning Disabilities, 239
National Longitudinal Transitions Study of Special Education Students, 206, 299
National Society for the Prevention of Blindness, 403
National Technical Institute for the Deaf, 381–82
Native American students, 140
native languages, 325
nearsightedness, 392
need-to-know tables, 154, 155f
negative reinforcement, for students with mental retardation, 201
neighborhood, 22
neonatal intensive-care units, 100
neural tube defects, 92, 93, 492–94
neurological conditions, 488, 489–94, 522
neuropsychological/developmental perspective, on learning disabilities, 225
neuropsychological learning disabilities, 220, 221, 225–29
New England Asylum for the Blind (Perkins School), 34
New Jersey Commission for the Blind, 37
NICD. *See* National Information Center on Deafness (NICD)
noise pollution, 353
nondisabled siblings
adjustment of, 28
concerns of, 20–22
nondiscriminatory evaluation, 72
nondisjunction, 172
non-English-speaking children, communication disorders in, 324–25
nonlinear interactions, computers and, 47
nonschooled individuals, thinking processes of, 24
nonverbal communication, 307, 321, 468f
nonvocal students, 469–70
normalization, 35
norm-referenced tests, 50, 51f
North Carolina School of Science and Mathematics, 146, 159
nursery schools, 84
nurses, 98f, 455f
nutrition. *See* diet
nutritionists, 455f
object permanence, understanding of, by children with visual impairments, 401

observation, 50, 51f
occupational knowledge training, for students with mental retardation, 198, 199f
occupational therapists, 98f, 455f
in early intervention programs, 102
for students with physical disabilities and health impairments, 510–11
Office of Special Education and Rehabilitation Services, 86
omission errors, in language, 317
one-on-one instruction, for students with mental retardation, 204
operant conditioning
for students with communication disorders, 331
for students with emotional problems, 278–79, 290
ophthalmologists, 98f, 455f
optical devices, 423
oral-aural communication methods, 375
oralism (speech), 373
organically injured group, mental retardation, 169–70
organizational strategies, diagnostic prescriptive model and, 245
orientation and mobility (O&M) training. *See also* mobility
specialists, 424
for students with visual impairments, 421–25
orphanages, 84–85
orthopedic impairments
defined, 485, 486
percentage of students receiving special education, 488f
prevalence of, 6f
Orton Dyslexia Society, 231–32
osteogenesis imperfecta, 496
other health impairments, 487, 500–501. *See also* physical disabilities and health impairments
percentage of students receiving special education, 488f
otitis media
communication disorders and, 321
hearing loss and, 353
listening and language strategies and, 322f
Outward Bound, 138f
"overexcitabilities," 125
overt external guidance, 202f
overt self-guidance, 202f
oxygen-dependent children, 503

paralysis, polio-related, 496
paraplegia, T-3, 16
parents. *See also* families; fathers; mothers
academic achievement encouraged by, 372–73
advocacy by, 19–20, 39
assistance to, 254f
autism and, 445
of children with hearing impairments, 368–70
of children with mental retardation, 212
of children with multiple and severe disabilities, 476–77

as collaborators, 18, 19f
communication disorders and, 340
deaf, 382–83
empowerment of, 15, 18
expectations of girls, 134
of gifted and talented children, 27, 28
learning disabilities and, 253
as models for children with communication disorders, 328
observations of children by, 18
participation of, 73
reinforcement of learning by, 18
residential schools for students with visual impairments and, 414
response to children with disabilities by, 12–13, 479
stress of, 90, 109–10, 111, 253–54
student contingency contracts and, 293
as teachers, 18
Parents Involved Network (PIN), 277
Parent to Parent program, 209–210, 212
Parks, Ben, 65f
partial seizures, 490, 492
partial sightedness, 390
part-time special classes, 145f
patterns, knowledge structure, 152
PBL. See problem-based learning (PBL)
PDD. See pervasive developmental disorders (PDD)
PDDNOS. See pervasive developmental disorders not otherwise specified (PDDNOS)
peer collaboration, for teachers, 48–49
peer-mediated training, for students with visual impairments, 410
peers
    adjustment of gifted students to, 125–26
    aggressive behavior and, 267
    influence of, 22–23
    as models of acceptable behavior, 295–97
    rejection by, 22–23, 27
    support for students with mental retardation, 197–98
peer tutoring, 65f, 247
penicillin, 499
Pennsylvania Association for Retarded Children (PARC) v. Commonwealth of Pennsylvania, 74–75
perception
    learning and, 226
    visual impairments and, 394–95
perceptual-motor disabilities
    early intervention and, 237–38
    learning disabilities and, 227
performance assessment, 69
performance feedback, for social skills, 293
performance IQ, 167
performing arts talents, 132
Perkins School (New England Asylum for the Blind), 34
personal adjustment. See also social adjustment
    of students with hearing impairments, 357–61
personal care attendants, 490–91
personnel preparation standards and plans, 73
pervasive developmental disorders (PDD), 444, 445

pervasive developmental disorders not otherwise specified (PDDNOS)
    autism and, 446
    defined, 444–45
pervasive support, for students with mental retardation, 169
phenylalanine, 94, 173
phenylketonuria (PKU), 93–94, 173–74
    screening infants for, 184
phonation, 307
phonemes, 249
    articulation-phonology disorders and, 317
    computer presentation of, 333
    teaching to students with hearing impairments, 370
phonological awareness, 332–33
phonological errors, 316
phonological impairments, 249, 333
phonology, 179
    defined, 309, 311f
    dialects and, 334
    learning disabilities and, 229
    training, for students with communication disorders, 332–33
physical differences, 3
physical disabilities and health impairments
    accessibility of facilities for, 512–13
    achondroplasia, 496
    acquired, 488
    arthritis, 495
    assistive communication, 517–20
    asthma, 497, 498f
    causes of, 487–88, 522
    cerebral palsy, 489–90
    classification and characteristics, 488–504
    classroom equipment for, 512
    cleft lip, 496
    cleft palate, 496
    clubfoot, 496
    congenital, 487
    congenital heart disease, 498f
    curriculum adaptations, 513–15
    cystic fibrosis, 498f
    defined, 485–86, 522
    developmental profiles, 505–507
    diabetes, 498f
    discrimination issues, 521
    early intervention for, 486f, 507
    educational adaptations, 508–20
    educational teamwork for, 523
    epilepsy, 490, 492
    hemophilia, 498f
    identification of children with, 507
    inclusion issues, 508–12, 523
    instructional materials for, 512
    juvenile rheumatoid arthritis, 498f
    kidney disease, 498f
    leukemia, 498f
    Marfan syndrome, 495
    muscular dystrophy, 494, 495
    musculoskeletal conditions, 494–96
    neural tube defects, 492–94
    occupational and physical therapy, 510–11

physical education, 517
polio, 496
post polio muscle atrophy, 496
prevalence of, 486–87, 522
programs for, 84
quality of life and, 516–17
schools for students with, 34
seizure disorder, 498f
sickle cell anemia, 498f
skill development and, 513–15
spina bifida, 498f
student's sense of control, 515, 517
teaching children about, 516
teaching strategies, 516–17
technology for, 517–20, 523
Tourette syndrome, 492
transition, 520
unresolved issues, 523
physical education
    for students with physical disabilities and health impairments, 509, 517
    for students with visual impairments, 425
physical therapists, 455f
    in early intervention programs, 102
    for students with physical disabilities and health impairments, 510–11
Pidgin Sign English (PSE), 376, 377
pitch, 318
pitch disorder, 330f
PKU. See phenylketonuria (PKU)
plastic surgery, for Down syndrome, 174f
play
    as assessment, 105
    in early intervention programs, 102
    for students with communication disorders, 327–28
    teaching to disabled children, 104
play audiometry, 365
pluralistic approach, for culturally diverse students, 139
polio, 496
portable computer devices, 429
portable talking dictionaries, 429
positive reinforcement
    for social skills, 297–98
    for students with emotional problems, 278–79
    for students with mental retardation, 201
postlinguistic hearing loss, 346, 361–62
post polio muscle atrophy, 496
postsecondary programs, for students with hearing impairments, 381–82, 384
poverty
    at-risk infants and, 90
    culture of, 214
    gifted students and, 128–29
powerlessness of students with physical disabilities and health impairments, 515
practice and drill,
    for students with communication disorders, 336
Prader-Willi syndrome, 451
pragmatics, 179, 318, 356
    defined, 311f
    dialects and, 334

pregnancy. *See also* birthing process; prenatal care
  alpha-fetoprotein test and, 92–93
  events putting infants at risk, 89–90
  mother's age at, Down syndrome and, 172
  prenatal care, 90, 112
  substance abuse and, 91
  termination of, 172
prelinguistic hearing loss, 383
  defined, 346
  developmental profile, 361–62
  language development and, 356
  postsecondary education and, 381
  social adjustment and, 358
prelinguistic period
  assessment, 237, 321
  language development during, 355–56
Premack's principle, 200
premature infants, 100–101, 111. *See also* at-risk infants; infants; low-birth-weight infants
  communication disorders and, 330
  cytomegalovirus and, 352
  hearing loss in, 352, 353–54
  hospital intervention strategies for, 100
  multiple and severe disabilities in, 456
  physical disabilities and health impairments, 485
  respiratory distress in, 503
prenatal care. *See also* pregnancy
  at-risk infants and, 89, 90, 91, 92–93, 111
  mental retardation and, 183
prereferral system, 48, 287
prereferral teams, 185–87, 275. *See also* multidisciplinary teams
preschool children
  with communication disorders, 321–22
  with learning disabilities, 248
  with mental retardation, 184
  with multiple and severe disabilities, 466–67
  vision screening, 403
preschools, 84, 85
Presidential Committee on Mental Retardation, 473
preventive intervention, 457
prevocations, differential instruction for students with mental retardation, 194, 198–200
primary prevention, of mental retardation, 181, 183, 184*f*, 214
principals, inclusion and, 61
privacy, sexual relationships and, 197
problem-based learning (PBL), 153–54
problem behavior, 260
problem finding, 118, 151
problem-oriented instruction, 44
problem solving, 118
  cognitive strategies, 151–53
  computers for, 206
  ill-structured problems and, 118
  knowledge structure and, 153
  for students with mental retardation, 199*f*, 206, 207*f*
procedural due process, 458
prodigies, 135–36

profound hearing impairments, 362
profound visual disabilities, 434. *See also* blindness
  defined, 390, 391*f*
  developmental profile, 398–400
program evaluation, 49, 431–32
Program to Develop Efficiency in Visual Functioning, 403
Project Re-Ed, 281
prolonged schooling, for gifted students, 160, 162
prompts
  diagnostic prescriptive model and, 245
  for students with deafblindness, 451*f*
psychomotor development, 53
Psychopathological Disorders in Children classification system, 269
psychosocial development, 53–54
Public Law 88-164, 71
Public Law 94-142, 86. *See* Education for All Handicapped Children Act of 1975 (PL 94-142)
Public Law 99-457. *See* Education of All Handicapped Children Act Amendments (PL 99-457)
Public Law 100-297, 74
Public Law 101-476. *See* Individuals with Disabilities Education Act (IDEA) (PL 101-476)
Public Law 102-569. *See* Rehabilitation Act (PL 102-569)
public schools. *See* schools
punctuality, culture and, 55
pupil evaluation, 49
pupil (eye), 391
pure-tone audiometry, 364

quadriplegic cerebral palsy, 489, 493*f*
quality of life, 516–17

race. *See also* minority groups
  prenatal care and, 92
ramps, for accessibility, 513
Randall, Marcia, 490
readiness skills, 194
reading
  aids for students with visual impairments, 428–29
  assessing level, 187
  cognitive strategies for, 248
  functional vocabulary, 196*f*
  learning disabilities and, 226, 227, 229, 236–37
  learning process, 249–50
  task analysis approach, 194, 195
  teaching approaches, 249–50
  teaching to students with hearing impairments, 370, 372, 386
  teaching to students with mental retardation, 195, 199*f*
  teaching to students with visual impairments, 415
  visual processing deficits and, 227
  whole-word method for teaching, 195
reading disorders, 229

real-life assessment, 69
reasoning ability, of gifted students, 119
recasting, for students with communication disorders, 328
receptive language, 52
recess, social skills and, 410
reciprocal teaching, 200
record keeping, computers for, 45
re-education programs, 280–81
referral, 40–41
Registry of Interpreters for the Deaf, Inc., 360
Rehabilitation Act (PL 102-569), 345
  Section 504, building accessibility, 512
  Section 504, discrimination against people with disabilities, 521
Rehabilitation Research and Training Center at Virginia Commonwealth University, 478–79
rehearsal, as memory aid, 178
reinforcement
  contingent social, 201
  differential, 201
  negative, 201
  positive, 201
  for students with hearing impairments, 379
relationship-building skills, 40
remedial instruction, for students with learning disabilities, 239
remedial intervention, 457
Renzulli Enrichment Triad model, 137
residential schools, 34
  for gifted students, 145*f*, 146
  for students with visual impairments, 413–14, 431–32
residual hearing, 368
resonance, 450
resonation, 307
resource centers, for students with visual impairments, 413
resource room, 42, 43, 45*f*, 58
  for students with communication disorders, 327
  for students with emotional problems, 287, 289
  for students with learning disabilities, 241
  for students with mental retardation, 191–92
  for students with multiple and severe disabilities, 443
  for students with physical disabilities and health impairments, 509
respiration, 307
respiratory distress, 503
respite care, 210, 480
restrooms, accessible, 513
restructuring, 58–66, 78
retention, grade, 69
retina, 391
retinopathy of prematurity (retrolental fibroplasia), 393
Rhett disorder, 446
Rh (hyperbilirubinemia), hearing disorders and, 350

RhoGAM, 350
rights, expression of, 468*f*
risk taking
  by adolescents, 494
  encouraging, in students with visual impairments, 421
Ritalin, 228–29, 270
  emotional problems and, 265–66
Rochester method, finger spelling, 377
Rockefeller, Nelson, 241
role models. *See also* modeling
  for girls, 134, 135
role playing
  social skills, 293
  for students with communication disorders, 327–28
Rothstein, Andrew, 440
round robin reading, for students with visual impairments, 415
rubella (German measles)
  fetal damage and, 89
  hearing loss and, 352
  mental retardation and, 176, 183
  visual impairments and, 392–93
rubella vaccine, 176, 352
rule-oriented behavior, 452

scaffolding, for students with mental retardation, 200
scanning, for orientation and mobility training, 422–23
schizophrenia, 261
Scholastic Aptitude Test, 133
School of Nursing, University of Colorado, 104
schools
  educational adaptations, 42–48
  emotional problems and, 266–67
  exceptional students and, 35
  historical perspective, 34
  influence of, 22
  legislation affecting, 70–74
  requirement to educate all children, 457–58
  site-based management, 67–70
  violence, and emotional problems in, 267
science achievement, by girls, 135
scissor walking, 490
scoliosis, 494
screening, 49, 94–95
secondary education, for students with mental retardation, 215
secondary prevention, of mental retardation, 181, 184, 214
secondary problems, early intervention and, 88
Seeing Essential English (*SEE* I), 376, 377
segregation, of special needs students, 60
Seguin, Edward, 185
seizure disorders, 490, 492, 498*f*
SELD (slow expressive language development), 319
self-awareness
  cultural, of teachers, 26
  for students with emotional problems, 292

self-care skills
  curriculum adaptations for, 514–15
  for students with mental retardation, 168*f*
  for students with physical disabilities and health impairments, 514–15
self-confidence
  anxiety-withdrawal and, 273
  of gifted underachievers, 136–37
  of girls, 134, 135
  re-education programs and, 280
  of students with emotional problems, 293
  of students with mental retardation, 205–206
self-control, in students with emotional problems, 292
self-destructive behavior, 280
self-determination skills, in students with multiple and severe disabilities, 454, 467
self-direction skills, in students with mental retardation, 168*f*
self-efficacy, for students with mental retardation, 205
self-esteem
  communication disorders and, 332
  of students with physical disabilities and health impairments, 515
  of students with special needs, 17
  of students with visual impairments, 397
self-evaluation, for students with emotional problems, 292
self-identity, of minority group students, 139–40
self-instruction
  for students with emotional problems, 292
  for students with mental retardation, 202–203
self-management, for students with emotional problems, 292–93
self-monitoring
  diagnostic prescriptive model and, 245
  for students with emotional problems, 292
self-reinforcement, for students with emotional problems, 292
self-stimulation, 87–88
  in children with deafblindness, 450
  in children with multiple and severe disabilities, 453–54
semantics, 179, 318
  defined, 309, 311*f*
  dialects and, 334
sense training, for students with mental retardation, 185
sensorineural hearing losses, 348, 352*f*, 383
sensory compensation and perception, in students with visual impairment, 394–95
sensory deficits, developmental delays and, 87
sensory differences, 3
sentences, early language development, 316
sentences subtest (Wechsler Preschool and Primary Scale of Intelligence), 236
serious emotional disturbance (SED), 261–62, 299
service coordinators
  for multidisciplinary teams, 285
  for students with visual impairments, 412

service integration, 73
severe hearing loss, 362
severe mental retardation
  defined, 169
  phenylketonuria and, 172–73
severe visual disabilities, 434
  defined, 390, 391*f*
  developmental profile, 398–400
sexual relationships, mental retardation and, 197
sheltered workshops
  for people with mental retardation, 208
  for people with multiple and severe injuries, 474, 478
  for people with visual impairments, 430
shoplifting, 281*f*
short-term memory, knowledge structure and, 154
Shriver, Eunice Kennedy, 212
shunts, for hydrocephalus, 456, 493
siblings, nondisabled, 20–22, 28
sickle cell anemia, 92, 498*f*, 499
Sidis, William, 135–36
signaling devices, for students with hearing impairments, 360
Signed English, 334
Signing Exact English (*SEE* II), 376, 377
sign language, 368, 369
  American Sign Language (ASL), 333–34, 355, 374, 376–77
  behavior problems and, 450
  defined, 307
  finger spelling, 355, 375, 377, 378*f*
  interpreters, 359
  for students with hearing impairments, 375, 376–77
simple partial seizures, 492
simulation
  for students with mental retardation, 206, 207*f*
  visual impairments and, 407–408
simultaneous communication method, for students with hearing impairments, 377
Sinclair, Brittany, 366–67
site-based management, 67–70, 142
skills
  assessment, for students with multiple and severe disabilities, 463–64
  curriculum adaptations for students with physical disabilities and health impairments, 513–15
  generalized, 459, 462–63
skills mastery
  defined, 43*f*
  for students with mental retardation, 205–206
  for students with emotional problems, 290–98
SLI (specific language impairment), 319
slow auditory processing, 333
slow expressive language development (SELD), 319
Smith, Jane, 65*f*
smoking. *See* tobacco use
Snellen charts, 403

social adjustment
functional age-appropriate skills and, 462
in general-education classrooms, 63
of gifted students, 126–27, 130, 160
maladjustment, 261
social skills and, 63, 180
of students with cerebral palsy, 506
of students with hearing impairments, 357–61, 366–67, 369f
of students with mental retardation, 207
of students with multiple disabilities, 37, 38
of students with physical disabilities and health impairments, 515
of students with visual impairments, 395–98, 412, 414
social disabilities
communication disorders and, 330f
learning disorders and, 233
social language learning, for students with communication disorders, 331
social learning approach, for students with mental retardation, 197
social learning theory, aggressive behavior and, 269
social reform, emotional problems and, 302–303
social risk factors, emotional problems and, 267–68
social skills
adaptive behavior scales, 186
assessment of, 54
differential instruction for students with mental retardation, 194, 196–98
inclusion and, 409–11
models for, 295–97
positive reinforcement and, 297–98
preschool, 248
in students with emotional problems, 290–97, 293–94
in students with mental retardation, 168f, 169, 179–80, 196–97, 205
in students with visual impairments, 409–11
social supports, for students with mental retardation, 176–77, 188, 190, 191
social workers, 98f, 102, 455f
society. See also environment
influence of, 22
socioeconomic class, vocabulary and, 319
sonography (ultrasound), 93
spastic cerebral palsy, 489, 493f, 514
spatial intelligence, 120f
special classes
for gifted students, 145f, 146–47
for students with mental retardation, 192
special education
court actions affecting, 74–77
defined, 42, 50
educational adaptations for, 42–48
educational restructuring in, 58–66
inclusion vs., 59–60
legislation affecting, 70–74
lifespan perspective, 39
role of, 64f

for students with emotional problems, 275, 276
for students with learning disabilities, 222–23
for students with mental retardation, 204–205
for students with multiple and severe disabilities, 443, 456, 481
teachers, 58
technology in, 46–47
Special Olympics, 212–13
special schools
for gifted students, 145f
for students with hearing impairments, 34
for students with visual impairments, 34, 413–14
specific language impairment (SLI), 319
specific learning disabilities, 171
speech. See also verbal language
assessment of, 52
defined, 307, 308f
of students with hearing impairments, 367
speech disorders. See also communication disorders; language disorders
articulation-phonology disorders, 316–17
defined, 308, 311f
developmental profiles, 319–20
speech-language pathologists, 98f, 455f
choice of therapy by, 326–27
role of, 321, 323, 328–31
speech-language therapists, 310f
in early intervention programs, 102
Speech Plus Talking Calculator, 428
speech reading, 375, 385
speech synthesis, 469
speech therapy software, 37–38
Speech Viewer III, 380
spelling disorders, 230
spelling instruction, 250
Speyer School, 123
spina bifida, 93, 456, 492, 493, 498f
spinal cord deformities, 489
spinal cord injuries, 489, 494
spontaneous abortion, 89
staff-infant ratios, in day care and early childhood centers, 104
staff turnover, in early childhood intervention programs, 111–12
standard achievement tests, 52, 70
Stanford-Binet Intelligence Scale, 123
Stanford-Binet Intelligence Test, 117, 393
stapes, 346
Strategies Intervention Model (SIM), 246
strategy intervention model, for students with learning disabilities, 246
strategy learning, for students with learning disabilities, 241, 245–46
stress
child abuse and, 90
in families of children with mental retardation, 210

learning disabilities and, 253–54
parental, 90, 109–10, 111
student acceleration, 159–60
student contingency contracts, 293
student-teacher contracts, 293, 297
Study of Mathematically Precocious Youth, 133
stuttering, 317, 329f
intervention for, 332, 337
lifespan issues, 340
substance abuse, 499–500. See also drug abuse; tobacco use
at-risk infants and, 91, 112
behavior problems and, 268
emotional problems and, 265
substitution errors in language, 317
sucking, deficient, 321
suicide, 272–73
supportive employment
for adults with learning disabilities, 252–53
for adults with multiple and severe disabilities, 470, 472, 478–79, 481
supportive inclusion, for students with learning disabilities, 241, 242–43f
support resources, for adults with mental retardation, 208
"survival words," 192, 195
swayback, 496
symbolic death, of child, 12–13
symbols, communication through, 464
symptoms, re-education programs and, 281
syntax
American Sign Language and English differences, 376–77
defined, 309, 311f, 318
dialects and, 334
prelinguistic hearing loss and, 356
teaching to students with hearing impairments, 373
synthetic speech, 427–28, 518

tactile experience, 416
tactile maps, 425
talent, 128, 132. See also gifted and talented students
talking books, 428
TASH. See Association for Persons with Severe Handicaps, The (TASH)
task analysis, 194–95
for students with emotional problems, 279
for students with learning disabilities, 243
Tay-Sachs disease, 89, 92, 93
teacher-assistance teams, 48, 77. See also multidisciplinary teams; team teaching
teacher-consultants, 43, 44
for gifted students, 147
for students with mental retardation, 190–91
teacher-counselors, in re-education programs, 281

teachers
cultural self-awareness of, 26
general-education, inclusion and, 60–61, 63
of gifted students, 130–31
high-cost behavior, 290–91
as instructional coaches for distance learners, 159
site-based management and, 67
of students with emotional problems, 290–91
of students with learning disabilities, 254–55
of students with visual impairments, 396
teacher-training programs, for students with hearing impairments, 385
teaching strategies
for students with communication disorders, 326–34
for students with emotional problems, 290–98
for students with hearing impairments, 373–74, 379
for students with learning disabilities, 243–51
for students with mental retardation, 200–206
for students with multiple and severe disabilities, 464–69
for nonvocal students, 469
for students with physical disabilities and health impairments, 516–17
team-assisted individualization, for students with mental retardation, 203–204
teams. *See also* multidisciplinary teams; team teaching
cooperative learning, 66
prereferral, 185–87, 275
for students with hearing impairments, 371
teacher-assistance, 48, 77
team teaching. *See also* multidisciplinary teams; teacher-assistance teams
for students with mental retardation, 191
for students with visual impairments, 409, 411–12, 413
technology
for nonvocal students, 469–70
in special education, 46–47
for students with communication disorders, 335
for students with emotional problems, 298
for students with hearing impairments, 379–81
for students with multiple and severe disabilities, 469–70
for students with physical disabilities and health impairments, 517–20, 523
for students with visual impairments, 426–29, 435
technology-dependent health conditions, 501–503
TEECH program, 447
teenage pregnancy, 90, 112
telecommunication devices for the deaf (TDDs), 381

Telecommunications for the Deaf (TDI), 360
teletypewriter-printer device (TTY), 380–81
teratogens, 174
Terman, Lewis, 117
Terman Longitudinal Study, 124*f*
terminal illness, 515, 517, 521
tertiary prevention, of mental retardation, 181, 184, 214
Test of Adolescent Language-2, 52
Test of Visual-Motor Perceptual Skills, 406
Texas School for the Blind and Visually Impaired, 415
textbooks, for students with learning disabilities, 241–42*f*
therapists
home early intervention programs and, 102
occupational, 98*f*, 102, 455*f*, 510–11
physical, 102, 455*f*, 510–11
speech-language, 102, 310*f*
think-time strategy, 282–83
Third International Mathematics and Science Study (TIMSS), 116
Thomas, Lewis, 232
time diaries, 395
time on task
emotional problems and, 266–67
school success and, 266–67
for students with hearing impairments, 379
time-out
for students with emotional problems, 281–83
for students with mental retardation, 201
TIMSS. *See* Third International Mathematics and Science Study (TIMSS)
Titmus Vision Tester, 403
tobacco use, 499, 500
at-risk infants and, 91
behavior problems and, 268
toe walking, 490
token system, for students with mental retardation, 201
top-down approach, for reading instruction, 249
TORCHS, hearing disorders and, 351
total communication method, 373–74, 377
Touch Talker, 339, 505
Tourette syndrome, 492
toxic agents, mental retardation and, 174–76
toxic-clonic seizures, 490
toxoplasmosis, 351
toys, 102. *See also* play
T-3 paraplegia, 16
Trace Research and Development Center, 469
tracing, 423
tracking, 423
training, defined, 441
transacting, 253
transdisciplinary play-based assessment, 105
transferable knowledge, 46
transient adaptation problems, 275
transition
of gifted students, 160

of students with communication disorders, 337
of students with disabilities, 110
of students with emotional problems, 299
of students with hearing impairments, 381–82
of students with learning disabilities, 252–53, 256
of students with mental retardation, 206–208
of students with multiple and severe disabilities, 470–73
of students with physical disabilities and health impairments, 520
of students with visual impairments, 430–31
transition coordinators, for people with multiple and severe disabilities, 472
transition services, 39–40, 74
translocation, 172
trauma anxiety, 277
traumatic brain injuries (TBI), 504, 505*f*
percentage of students receiving special education, 488*f*
powerlessness and, 515
treatment combinations, for students with emotional problems, 283
trust, in re-education programs, 280
TTY, 380–81
tube feeding, 502–503
Turner syndrome, 89
tutorials, for students with mental retardation, 207*f*
tutoring
peer, 65*f*, 247
for students with hearing impairments, 372
for students with learning disabilities, 241
twin births, neural tube defect and, 93
twin studies, of emotional problems, 263

UCLA Family Development Service Intervention Roles Profile, 108
ultrasound, 93
underachievers, 136–38, 162
unifying experiences, 407
unisensory communication method, 376
United Cerebral Palsy Association, 20, 100
unstable eye conditions, 417
urban students, gifted, 128–29, 138–40
U.S. Department of Education, Captioning and Adaptations Branch, 360
U.S. Department of Labor, 474
U.S. Vocational and Rehabilitation Department, 252
Usher's syndrome, 440

values, peer groups and, 267
values education, in gifted student programs, 150
Van Dijk method, 450
verbal IQ, 167
verbal language, 309–10. *See also* speech
very high IQ students, 135–36

Vineland Adaptive Behavior Scales, 55*f*, 58, 186
Vineland Social Maturity Scales, 54
violence, 266, 267
vision. *See also* eye
    defined, 390
    preschool skills, 248
    screening, 403, 405–406
    visual interpretation process, 390–92
visual acuity tests, 390, 403
visual arts talents, 132
visual consultant teachers, 409
visual impairments. *See also* blindness; deaf-blindness; legal blindness
    achievement and, 404
    adaptive skills, 416–26
    assessment, 405–406
    assistive technology, 426–29, 435
    braille use, 417–21
    causes of, 392–93, 434
    characteristics of children with, 393–98
    communication skills, 417–21
    coping with, 395–96
    curriculum adaptations, 414
    definition of terms, 390
    developmental delays and, 87
    developmental profiles, 398–400
    early intervention for, 400–402
    educational adaptations for, 407–16
    educational reform and, 435
    education approaches, 448
    environmental skills instruction for, 421–25
    eye and, 390–92
    family and lifespan issues, 433
    identification of, 402–403, 456
    inclusion issues, 408–412
    individualized education programs (IEPs), 406, 413, 414*f*
    intellectual development and, 393–94
    language development and, 394
    learning disabilities and, 227
    learning environment adaptations for, 408–415
    listening, 421
    mastering the environment, 421

    mild, correctable, 403
    moderate visual disabilities, 390, 391*f*, 434
    with multiple disabilities, 407, 433
    national agenda, 432
    orientation and mobility training, 421–25
    percentage of students in educational environments, 409*f*
    prevalence of, 6*f*
    profound visual disabilities, 390, 391*f*, 398–400, 434
    program evaluation, 431–32
    secondary problems, 400
    sensory compensation and perception and, 394–95
    severe visual disabilities, 390, 391*f*, 398–400, 434
    social issues, 395–98, 409–11, 414
    special schools, 413–14
    transition, 430–31
    unresolved issues, 435
    unstable eye conditions, 417
vocabulary
    socioeconomic class and, 319
    teaching to students with mental retardation, 195, 196*f*
vocational opportunities. *See also* employment
    for adults with mental retardation, 198–200
    for adults with multiple and severe injuries, 474, 475*f*, 478
    for students with mental retardation, 200
Vocational Rehabilitation departments, state governments, 360
Vogel, Lynn, 65*f*
voice, of students with hearing impairments, 367
voice disorders, 311*f*, 318, 329*f*, 330*f*

walkways, accessible, 513
"water on the brain." *See* hydrocephalus
Watson, James, 171, 182
Wechsler scales, 166–67
    Wechsler Intelligence Scale for Children, 58

Wechsler Intelligence Scale for Children—III, 52, 53*f*
Wechsler Preschool and Primary Scale of Intelligence, 236
wheelchairs, 479–80
whole language instruction, 370
whole-word reading instruction method, 195
Wild Boy of Aveyron, 185
Will, Jon, 182–83
Williams, Carroll, 232
Williams syndrome, 179
Wilson, Woodrow, 241
Winfrey, Oprah, 128
women. *See also* gender; girls; mothers
    gifted student studies of, 124–25
word problems, learning disabilities and, 245
word-prompt programs, 336–37
words
    early language development, 314–15
    recognition of, by students with learning disabilities, 229
    teaching to students with hearing impairments, 373
Work Sampling System, 235
work-study skills, for students with mental retardation, 168*f*, 194, 198–200
work-welfare programs, 252
World Wide Web, 381
wraparound approach, for students with emotional problems, 286
writing aids, 428–29, 518–20
writing disorders, 230
writing instruction
    for students with mental retardation, 199*f*
    for students with visual impairments, 415
    task analysis approach, 194–95
    teaching approaches, 250

zero reject, 72

Educational Adaptations

Children with Learning Disabilities

★ *Children with learning disabilities require an individualized teaching plan.*

A large group of researchers in the field of learning disabilities have been focusing on the academic problems of children with learning disabilities. Their focus: to analyze what the children must learn and to identify the problems they have in mastering the material. Although this trend has many proponents, there are major differences in recommendations about how to adapt the educational process to help each child.

Historically, approaches to remediation of learning disabilities were based on multiple sensory techniques such as teaching children how to read, spell, write, and compute by using pictures, tracing letters in sand, and drill and practice. Many teachers in remedial instruction still use these techniques for children with learning disabilities and children who are developmentally delayed or mentally retarded. As Clark (1988) writes: "Despite the widespread inclusion of multisensory techniques in rem_____ dyslexic students and the almost unanimous conviction amo_____ we have little empirica_____ ucational point of vie_____ learning disabilities is_____ and social problems_____ riculum with strateg_____ strengths to overcom_____ Thompson, 1974).

ADAPTING THE

★ *Depending on the teacher's support system, students with learning disabilities can learn as much in a regular class as they can in a special class.*

Where should stude_____ question is subject t_____ 1995; Stainback &_____ full inclusion of all_____ Chapter 11). Howe_____ Committee on Lea_____ America do not su_____ (Lackaye, 1997). T_____ may profit from th_____ structional enviro_____ the context of a g_____

Whether child_____ classrooms, resou_____ live in. In its *18t*_____ (1997) reported t_____ percent of those_____ the regular educa_____ disabilities in M_____ in Colorado are_____ students with le_____

Issues of Achi

One of the stu_____ ing disabilities_____ disabilities in

Other studies have not supported inclusion. Zigmond and Baker (1990) reported that students with major learning disabilities did not make progress in academic subjects in regular classrooms. In a further study, Zigmond et al. (1995) concluded that the achievement outcomes of 40 percent of the students with learning disabilities did not reflect gains. In fact, the students fell further behind.

One reason for the failure may be that teachers tend to teach the total class but the student with learning disabilities does not profit from group instruction (Fuchs, Fuchs, Hanlett, Phillips, & Korn, 1995). Guterman (1996) found that the consumer—the student with learning disabilities—viewed the classroom as unrealistic. In general, students with learning disabilities believed the regular classroom was better for social reasons but the resource room was better for learning (Kettman et al., 1998). Early childhood and elementary classrooms may be more successful in educating children with learning disabilities, but high school teachers are under greater pressure to cover course content (Schuman et al., 1995), and the culture of the school is content oriented (Tralli et al., 1996). Crockett and Kauffman (1998) and Keogh (1996) recommend tutorials, one-on-one teaching, and specialized instructional arrangements for students with learning disabilities. One model currently regarded as a solution is the collaborative model.

Collaboration and Inclusion

Collaborative team models composed of a regular education teacher and a special educator bring together the former's knowledge of content and grade-level expectations with the latter's expertise in strategies and skills designed for the student with learni_____

Successf_____ regular and_____ velop clea_____ tablished,_____ and proble_____

Garnet_____ material b_____ abilities. T_____ in this tex_____ the studen_____ mic and_____ learning_____ question_____ a student

ADAP

The cur_____ lum. Th_____ tion to_____ their st_____ the sch_____ abiliti

★ *Successful collaboration requires good problem-solving and interpersonal skills and knowledge of the goals and vocabulary of all team members.*

Issues of Achi

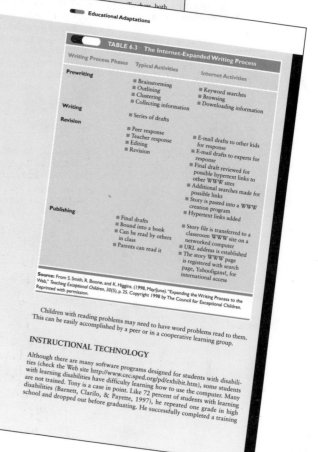

TABLE 6.3   The Internet-Expanded Writing Process

Writing Process Phases	Typical Activities	Internet Activities
Prewriting	■ Brainstorming ■ Outlining ■ Clustering ■ Collecting information	■ Keyword searches ■ Browsing ■ Downloading information
Writing		
Revision	■ Series of drafts	
	■ Peer response ■ Teacher response ■ Editing ■ Revision	■ E-mail drafts to other kids for response ■ E-mail drafts to experts for response ■ Final draft reviewed for possible hypertext links to other WWW sites ■ Additional searches made for possible links ■ Story is pasted into a WWW creation program ■ Hypertext links added
Publishing	■ Final drafts ■ Bound into a book ■ Can be read by others in class ■ Parents can read it	■ Story file is transferred to a classroom WWW site on a networked computer ■ URL address is established ■ The story WWW page is registered with search page, Yahooligans!, for international access

Source: From S. Smith, R. Boone, and K. Higgins. (1998, May/June). "Expanding the Writing Process to the Web," *Teaching Exceptional Children, 30*(5), p. 25. Copyright 1998 by The Council for Exceptional Children. Reprinted with permission.

Children with reading problems may need to have word problems read to them. This can be easily accomplished by a peer or in a cooperative learning group.

INSTRUCTIONAL TECHNOLOGY

Although there are many software programs designed for students with disabilities (check the Web site http://www.cec-sped.org/pd/exhibit.htm), some students with learning disabilities have difficulty learning how to use the computer. Many are not trained. Tony is a case in point. Like 72 percent of students with learning disabilities (Barnett, Clarilo, & Payette, 1997), he repeated one grade in high school and dropped out before graduating. He successfully completed a training

---

Educational Adaptations sections, designed for utility in K–12 classrooms, provide suggestions about how to adapt teaching methods, curriculum, or setting to meet the needs of students with disabilities.